D0204215

Adulthood and Aging

Marion G. Mason
Bloomsburg University of Pennsylvania

Allyn & Bacon
Boston Columbus Indianapolis New York San Francisco Upper Saddle River
Amsterdam Cape Town Dubai London Madrid Milan Munich Paris Montreal Toronto
Delhi Mexico City Sao Paulo Sydney Hong Kong Seoul Singapore Taipei Tokyo

Executive Editor: Jeff Marshall
Editorial Assistant: Courtney Elezovic
Marketing Manager: Nicole Kunzmann
Senior Production Project Manager: Roberta Sherman
Manufacturing Buyer: Debbie Rossi
Cover Administrator: Joel Gendron
Visual Researcher: Martha Shethar
Editorial Production and Composition Service: Laserwords Maine

---

Library of Congress Cataloging-in-Publication Data

Mason, Marion G.
Adulthood and aging / Marion G. Mason. – 1st ed.
p. cm.
Includes bibliographical references and index.
ISBN-13: 978-0-205-43351-3
ISBN-10: 0-205-43351-0
1. Adulthood–Psychological aspects. 2. Aging–Psychological aspects. 3. Adulthood. 4. Aging. I. Title.

BF724.5.M37 2011
155.6–dc22

2010037691

10 9 8 7 6 5 4 3 2 1 EB 14 13 12 11 10

Allyn & Bacon
is an imprint of

www.pearsonhighered.com

ISBN-10: 0-205-43351-0
ISBN-13: 978-0-205-43351-3

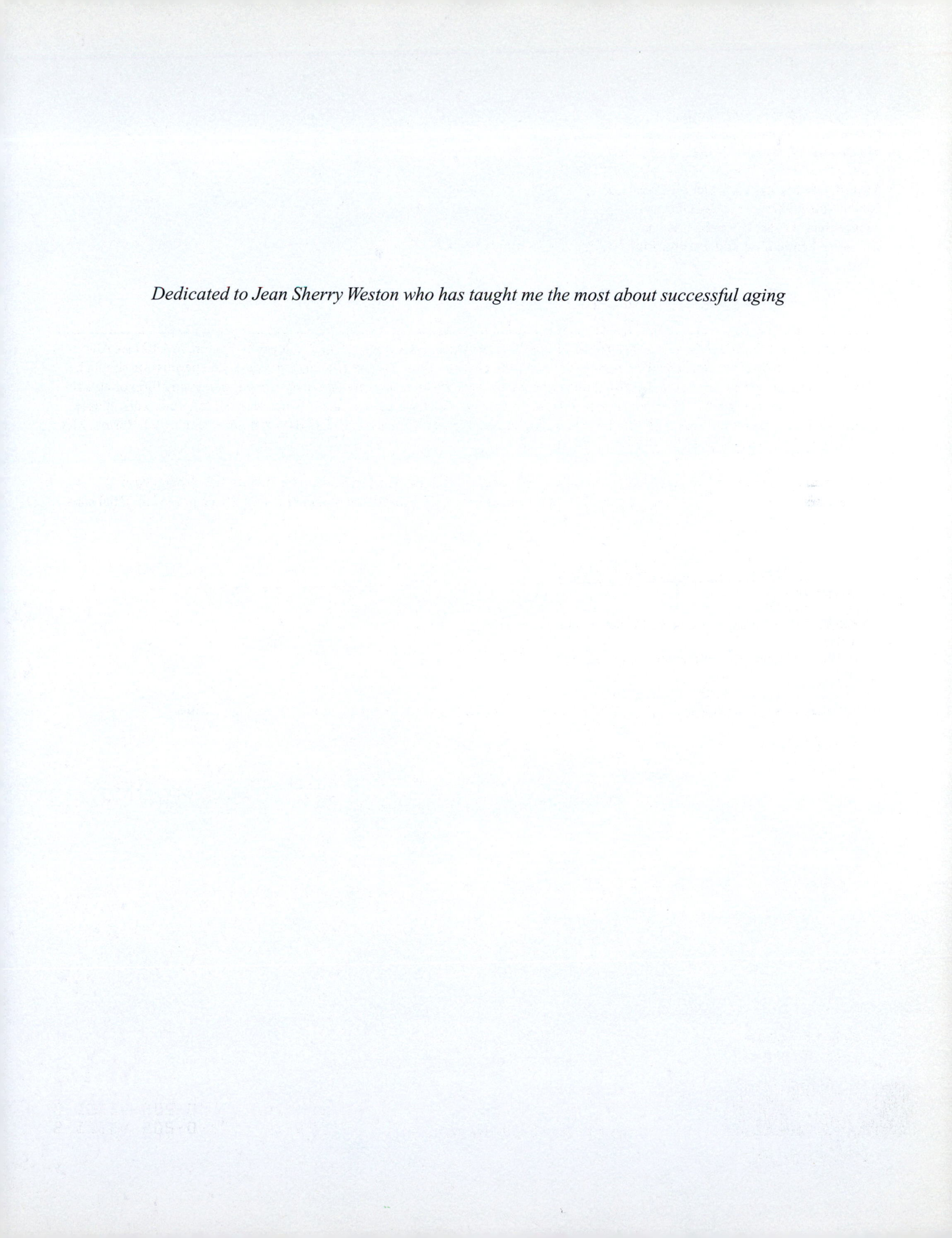

Dedicated to Jean Sherry Weston who has taught me the most about successful aging

CONTENTS

PREFACE

A Fresh Approach to Adult Development and Aging

What an exciting time to explore the field of adult development and aging! So many facets of the aging population, the field of developmental psychology, and the lifestyles and interests of college students are rapidly changing. More than ever there is a need to inform those who will be therapists, health care professionals, social workers, and all others who plan to work with adults in some capacity of the challenges and opportunities that often come our way in adulthood.

Living Long and Aging Well

As the number of adults in their 60s and older grows at dramatic rates this diverse group is teaching all of us that we can influence our quality of life in our older years. Consider that among the 1,500 adults in the New England Centenarian Study (men 100+ and women 102+ years old!) 90% of them were functionally independent until their early 90s (Boston University School of Medicine, 2004, 2007). As more and more of us can point to real-life examples of people we know who serve as role models of successful aging, our larger cultural perspective is shifting from the once strong association between aging and decline to an attitude of hope and optimism. One of the themes running throughout this book is the influence of the choices we make in young and middle adulthood that are likely to shape our quality of life as we age.

Living longer, and thus spending more time in adulthood, allows for a greater distinction and appreciation of the different stages of adulthood. It is stunning to realize that for Americans born in 1900 their life expectancy was 47.3 years while those born in 2000 have a projected life expectancy of 76.9 years (Centers for Disease Control and Prevention, 2007). That is 29.6 years longer than those born 100 years earlier! Now that young adulthood is generally thought to last into our early 40s, and middle adulthood into our mid or late 60s, it is more important than ever to consider the areas of uniqueness, growth, and challenge in each of these important times in life. In this book the reader will find a well-balanced focus on all phases of adulthood.

Expanding the Study of Adult Development

It is clear that the field has benefitted greatly from increased attention given to cross-cultural and multicultural studies, interdisciplinary studies and recent developments in neuroscience.

These themes are launched in the first chapter and carried throughout the book. Developmental psychologists have embraced the wider movement to understand not only large-scale and age/stage-related change but also the ways cultural and individual differences influence those patterns of change. In addition, the field of social gerontology has provided an excellent model for interdisciplinary collaboration in the quest to understand and enhance the late adulthood experience. Finally, for any psychologist interested in age-related change the explosion of new findings in neuroscience, particularly those related to brain imaging, are in some cases enhancing and others changing our cognitive models and approaches to rehabilitation and therapy.

Embracing Positive Psychology

At first glance uninformed college students often jump to conclusions regarding positive psychology, with its emphasis on resilience and subjective well-being, by assuming that the field of adulthood and aging has simply flip-flopped from a view that aging is all "doom and gloom" to the perspective that aging is all "love and laughter." Early and often throughout this book the reader will realize that the central question posed by positive psychology in this context is "How can I do the best I can with what I have to work with?" Adults are continually faced with issues requiring some creative problem solving as they manage their roles, which may include student, employee, spouse, parent, homeowner, community leader, and legal guardian for aging parents—and perhaps all those roles at the same time! The model proposed by Baltes, the selection–optimization–compensation model, is emphasized along with other applications of positive psychology. This foundation also supports the approach taken here that successful aging is not the absence of aging or a naive, artificially optimistic view but rather it is aging well, successfully adapting when needed, and, when the time comes, dying well.

Changing Attitudes of College Students

When I first started teaching Adulthood and Aging many years ago one of my primary challenges to was to convince my traditional age college students that growing old was not a story full of decline and depression. Over the years I've seen several shifts in their attitudes and perspectives. Today traditional-age college students are likely to be in class with "older" students as well as to have frequent contact with older relatives. In the state of Pennsylvania where I teach citizens over 60 can take courses at public universities free of charge, and many in my area take advantage of that offer. Also, I now routinely hear phrases I seldom if ever heard 5 years ago, such as "my grandma sent me email" or "my grandpa texted me," that are indicative of new avenues of intergenerational communication. Being a grandmother myself I can attest to the fact that my grandchildren would much rather text me than talk over the phone.

Not only are college students interacting more with older adults, I have seen an increase in the number of students who are considering working with older adults in their career. As would be expected, college students are concerned about their studies and employment following their undergraduate experience and they are often looking for areas of growth and job opportunities. The sheer size of the aging population has prompted many college students to consider careers that involve working with aging adults. At my university I've seen the psychology and social work majors diversify from the vast majority expressing a desire to work with children and adolescents to a growing number who would like to work with older adults.

Finally, as students interact more with older adults and consider this population as the focus of their career, they are also thinking more of their own aging. In some cases they are watching their parents interact with aging grandparents and wondering what their personal aging experience will be like. I find a growing number of my students want to know how to age well. Through many avenues in university life students are provided useful health information and given important warnings regarding risky behaviors aimed at that early 20s age group. It is a natural extension to ask questions about health issues with aging. As they watch an older relative live with dementia or cancer or recover from a heart attack my students are asking "Will that be me someday?" The book has much to offer the younger college student interested in learning about successful aging and preparing for their own middle and late adulthood experience.

Positive and Topical As We Move Through Adulthood

Writing the first version of a textbook brings the opportunity to bring a new voice to the conversation and to rework the traditional structure of adult development textbooks. The reader will notice a chronological theme to the chapters, integrated research discussions, and opportunities for critical thinking through the text.

Successful Aging Across Adulthood

The Table of Contents provides a good overview of the content and primary themes found in this text.

- Chapter 1, Developmental Psychology Applied to Aging: Introduces the major themes of the multidisciplinary and multifaceted nature of the field, the primary theoretical approaches, and an introduction to the scientific basis of the study
- Chapter 2, Individual and Multicultural Differences: Lays the foundation for the continued discussion of individual and group differences, particularly in the areas of culture, ethnicity, age and ageism, gender, religion, and intraindividual differences
- Chapter 3, Healthy Lifestyles and Successful Aging: Aimed at prevention and physically aging well, this chapter is focused on best practices and common challenges to healthy lifestyles
- Chapter 4, Identity Development and Personality: Emphasizing the growth pattern of continually reshaping our identities across adulthood, this chapter explores themes related to Erikson's developmental view and the influence of personality factors on aging
- Chapter 5, Friendships and Love Relationships: Beginning with friendships, this chapter explores love relationships and lifestyle choices, such as cohabiting and marriage, along with separation and divorce
- Chapter 6, Families, Generations, and Communities: Continuing the themes of the previous chapter, here the discussion shifts to parenting, grandparenting, family role transitions, and living arrangements across adulthood
- Chapter 7, Education, Careers, and Retirement: Emphasizing the changing nature of education and work, this chapter is focused on education, jobs and careers, retirement, and the economic issues surrounding aging
- Chapter 8, Memory and Basic Cognition: Relying on the foundations laid in neuroscience and cognitive psychology, this chapter introduces the topics of brain imaging, memory models, and basic cognitive performance
- Chapter 9, Complex Cognition: Building on the previous chapter, the focus here is on higher-order cognitive processing, including intelligence, creativity, everyday problem solving, and reasoning about moral and ethical dilemmas
- Chapter 10, Typical Physical Aging: The purpose of this chapter is to explore the areas of expected change, distinct from pathological change, by exploring changes in appearance, sensory systems, body systems, and sexuality with age

- Chapter 11, Disease, Illness, and Disorders: Here the discussion shifts to the more common physical illnesses and psychological disorders found among middle age and older adults, while at the same time balancing these trends with group and individual differences
- Chapter 12, Coping and Support in Late Adulthood: Emphasizing coping strategies throughout, this discussion explores adaptive technologies, the importance of social support, and the role of religious and personal outlook in quality of life during late adulthood
- Chapter 13, Dying, Death, and Bereavement: Beginning with end-of-life decisions, this chapter is focused on the transitions required when death is near and when it occurs, not only of the one who is dying but also those experiencing loss and grief
- Chapter 14, Life Satisfaction: The final chapter serves as a gathering place of "lessons learned" by exploring areas of self-concept, wisdom, subjective well-being, and regrets across adulthood

Approachable Yet Challenging Content

This textbook was intentionally written to be engaging and user-friendly to college students and instructors at all levels. The material is presented in a comfortable manner similar to the atmosphere I strive to create in my classroom. The information is given in a way that creates an ebb and flow from theoretical models to research investigations to applied examples.

Research methodology and design are interwoven throughout the text. Each chapter includes a *Research In-Depth* feature that applies an aspect of design, methodology, or statistical analysis to a topic discussed in the chapter. In addition, a *Research Appendix* is included to tie concepts together in the order typically found in a journal article. The Appendix offers readers without a research methodology background a guide to follow when reading standard research journal articles. This also offers instructors options in terms of covering research design as it comes in the chapters or in a concentrated way using the Appendix.

Saturated throughout the text are margin notes prompting students to consider common adult dilemmas such as balancing work and family demands or determining the point at which an older relative is not safe to live independently. In some cases these items prompt readers to consider the point of view of an employer or to take a societal or global view of an issue. These critical-thinking prompts, titled *Your Thoughts?,* will draw students' attention to key points in the reading. They may also be used for classroom lecture discussion-starters as well as topics for discussion boards, reaction papers, and small group discussions. Many of these prompts encourage the readers to form positions on common but difficult dilemmas and reflect on competing value systems.

Pedagogical Features for the Classroom and Outside Assignments

Many of the features distributed throughout the text can be expanded or adapted to serve as class activities and discussion points. As this book was taking shape with each round of reviews and revisions it was gratifying to learn that reviewers valued the pedagogical features of this text as much as I do. Each chapter includes the following features:

- Common Sense: Myth or Reality? This feature presents a series of true–false items that may be answered on the spot and checked at the back of the chapter or, as each item gives the section and page number where the answer is found, readers may scan the text for the answers and more information. The purpose of this feature is to prime students' thinking for the upcoming topics as well as to highlight the notion that common cultural assumptions may not be accurate. These items are also suitable to be used as exam and quiz items.

- Before We Get Started . . . : Exercises designed to encourage preliminary consideration of material found in the upcoming sections and how it may apply to the readers' lives. These exercises prompt students to apply upcoming information to themselves, not only offering opportunities for self-reflection but also the chance to notice individual differences and areas where their personal experiences or outlook differs from what is typical. This feature can be used as a discussion-starter in the classroom or as an outside project. These are particularly suited for surveying friends and family and reporting back to the class.
- Your Thoughts?: Each chapter is enhanced with numerous margin notes encouraging the reader to interact with material by applying it, such as considering how an employer might benefit from certain information, and through prompts that explore difficult cultural and societal questions, such as issues surrounding driving privileges for older adults and physician-assisted death. These items are designed for self-reflection and application of the material. Often I will start class with one of these prompts at the beginning of my lecture presentation and return to it after we have discussed the topic.
- Engaging Vignettes: Sprinkled throughout the chapters are hypothetical scenarios designed to illustrate the ways various research findings, theories, and models may be applied to common adulthood issues and problems. The goal of these vignettes is to allow students to consider the ways research findings and theoretical models might function in real life. These vignettes were created from compilations of numerous stories offered by students and acquaintances across my teaching career.
- Research In-Depth: Included in each chapter, this feature applies a facet of design, methodology, or statistical analysis to a topic discussed in the chapter. By using a topic directly from the chapter students are given an opportunity to learn of the "behind the scenes" research methodology and design that is so often glossed over with statements beginning with "Researchers have found . . . " Attention was also given in these features to the sometimes difficult decisions researchers must make regarding budgets, time, locating participants, and choosing instruments. It is important for students to understand how those necessary decisions made in the design are directly tied to the interpretation of the findings.
- On the Leading Edge: Each chapter has two featured inserts describing recent research and applications that are influencing adult development in interesting ways, such as the use of lifelong education in the prison system and the use of Internet-based software for grief therapy. These features bring research to real life by exploring innovative and clever applications of research findings and available technologies.
- Tables, Figures, and Summaries: Along with useful descriptive and summary tables and figures, each section is followed with a bullet-point summary of the key points. I find that students occasionally need guidance in locating the most important points in the reading or in organizing a lengthy discussion in a concise way. These features are designed to provide that guidance for the readers.
- Chapter Summaries, Comprehension Questions, and Key Terms: Each chapter ends with a bullet-point summary of the chapter, comprehension questions, and a list of key terms for vocabulary review. These features provide students with ideal "quiz yourself" materials. Instructors will find that the chapter summary items easily translate into true–false items on exams while the comprehension questions may be used as short-answer items. The vocabulary may be useful to students in terms of material for flash cards while instructors may use them for fill-in-the-blank items on exams.

- Suggested Readings and Websites: An average of four readings and four websites are provided for each chapter. Designed to provide more information for interested students, these features are also useful to instructors as additional reading and the basis for reaction papers or student presentations. Some instructors may find these readings helpful as extra-credit or substitute assignments.

Acknowledgments

This book began in the late 1990s as an idea that slowly turned into a proposal based on the encouragement of the publisher's representative for Allyn and Bacon at the time, Jenn Shufran. Much has happened between those days of brainstorming ideas and the production of this book as it is now. Without the leadership of many people at Pearson Education, including the early direction given by Karon Bowers and Susan Hartman, this book would have never materialized! Without my editors, beginning with Stephen Frail and finishing with Jeff Marshall, I would have been lost in the forest, or the trees, or both! Their expertise, constructive critique of chapter drafts, and continual encouragement were essential to the success of this text. In addition to giving spot-on advice and holding my work to a high standard, Stephen and Jeff have been the best colleagues to work with. Thanks guys!

In addition to the contribution of my editors, the invaluable feedback from several reviewers guided and informed every chapter. In the busy world of academics it is difficult to make time for our own tasks rather less the work of others. I want to especially thank the following people for giving their time and energy to reading chapters and offering constructive feedback: Brian Carpenter, Washington University; Michael Cheang, University of Hawaii at Manoa; Lisa Fozio-Thielk, Waubonsee Community College; Celia Wolk Gershenson, University of Minnesota TC; Adam Hill, Sonoma State University; Marcia Hostetter, Salem State College; Cynthia Legin-Bucell, Edinboro University of PA; Milene Morfei, Wells College; Joan Share, Georgia State University; and Merry Sleigh, Winthrop University.

Many people have directly contributed to the ideas, tone, and examples in this text. My students in Lifespan Psychology and Adulthood and Aging at Bloomsburg University of Pennsylvania across nearly two decades have served as the primary motivation for this text. Their questions, family stories, and personal desire to age well have fueled my passion for this area of developmental psychology. Numerous colleagues have also provided inspiration and critical resources. I specifically want to thank Drs. Jim Dalton, Eileen Astor-Stetson, Richard Larcom, and Winona Cochran for their continuing support of this project. I also want to thank Sherry and Ivan Rasmussen who provided a great deal of encouragement and a wonderful sanctuary for my writing each summer.

There is another group of people whose presence is saturated throughout this text. Known as the *Tuesday Night Dinner Club*, they have provided a steady stream of information, examples, motivation, and support during the writing of this book. This group gathers around the table of the woman to whom this book is dedicated for a gourmet meal and conversation several times a month. Ranging in age from 50s to 80s, and varying in health status and personal background, this group has taught me the most about the real joys and struggles of aging. Although the group has changed over the years as people have entered and left for various reasons, there is a stable core who have become like family to me. I cannot say *thank you* enough to Jean Sherry Weston, Gunilla Bjerkman Geise, and Sam Geise for their inspiration and support. I am also immensely grateful for the presence of others who frequent Jean's table, including Nancy Phelps, Charlie Phelps, Susan Robishaw, Harriet Bresenhan, Tom Bresenhan, Lenore Askew, and Gail Broome.

I have also learned a great deal about aging and gained much information and inspiration from watching the older generations in my own family. Even though my parents died when I was young, the separate journeys of Floyd and Gladys Ewton through the dying process certainly continue to influence the way I approach both living and dying. I have watched over the years as my husband's mother, Gertrude Mason, has coped with vascular dementia, and how various family members, particularly my sister-in-law Grace Smith and stepdaughter Tana Conley, have sacrificed tremendous amounts of time and energy to care for her. Their love and generosity are exemplary.

As anyone who has taken on a project of this size knows, it can only be accomplished with the support of those closest to you. I am most grateful to my husband, J. Stan Mason, for his continued support not only of this project but of my passion for my students and my work. He is my love and companion on this journey of aging—a part of everything I do. As we approach our 20th wedding anniversary I can say without a doubt that our relationship provides the foundation and strength I need to manage the otherwise chaotic lifestyle I lead. Truly I am blessed!

CHAPTER

1 Developmental Psychology Applied to Aging

These are exciting days for the field of adult development and aging, a relatively new and rapidly growing area of study in psychology. Like so many disciplines, recent advances in technology have added to our understanding of the aging process. Developments in the areas of medical imaging, for example, have provided vast amounts of data on changes within brain structures that may affect numerous aspects of psychological functioning. These techniques offer a new window for watching a brain at work as well as allowing researchers to compare brain functioning in the same organism in various circumstances and across time.

Also, increases in computing power have allowed scientists to test complex statistical models of psychological constructs. Rather than waiting for special cases to occur, or when blocked by the limits of ethical research, scholars can manipulate mathematical models in order to test their research questions. For example, rather than waiting for brain deterioration to occur in an individual or damaging a healthy adult human brain to test a prediction (which is obviously the unethical and unreasonable option!), a statistical model may give insight into the processes involved in cognitive decline.

COMMON SENSE
Myth or Reality?

Mark each of the following items with either an M, if you think it is a myth, or an R, if you think the statement reflects reality. By paying close attention you can find all the answers in this chapter. If needed, the answers are also given at the end of the chapter.

1. _____ The life expectancy for Americans born in 1900 was less than 50 years old.
2. _____ In 2005 the U.S. Census Bureau found that nearly 25% of all Americans age 65 years and older were living below the poverty line.
3. _____ Based on U.S. Census Bureau data, it is projected that there will be over 20 million Americans age 85 and older by the year 2050.
4. _____ When considering research on young, middle, and late adulthood, most of the emphasis is on middle-aged adults.
5. _____ To say that someone is "immature for her age" is to say that her social age is very young.
6. _____ The dominant view of adult development is that it occurs in stages.
7. _____ Most researchers studying the biological foundations of aging are searching for the one major gene that controls the aging process.
8. _____ One of the major theoretical approaches to adult development, connectionist approaches, emphasizes mathematical modeling of human thinking processes.
9. _____ Federal guidelines for research involving human beings allow for researchers to deceive participants by not revealing the real purpose of a study.

Researchers have also benefited from the increasing numbers of older adults, which means increasing numbers of potential participants for their studies. As more and more adults reach their 80s, 90s, and beyond, psychologists and other social scientists have the opportunity to observe individuals over long periods of time as they move through young, middle, and late adulthood. As older adults increase in numbers they also garner greater societal awareness, publicity, and political power, which often leads to increased funding for research and program development. All of these factors are contributing to the growth of the study of adult development and aging, and more importantly, to the betterment of the lives of individuals of all ages.

Before We Get Started . . .

These sections, appearing at the beginning of each chapter, are designed to encourage you to directly engage the concepts discussed in the following pages. For this exercise we start with the following scenario:

A mother and her 6-year-old daughter are working on a sewing project together. The mother reminds her daughter that her birthday is coming soon, and they need to finalize the list of who should be invited to the celebration. There are limits to how many people her daughter can invite, so decisions must be made. As might be expected, her daughter wants to invite some people that the mother would rather not invite.

Consider these questions:

- What advice would you give the mother in terms of how to handle this disagreement?
- What additional information would you like to know about this situation?
- What fields of study would you turn to for more insight into this situation?

As you read through this chapter you will have a chance to think more about this scenario and your initial responses to it.

Why Study Adult Development and Aging?

Some readers have picked up this book because they are interested in the topics, while others are likely to get this book because it is required reading for a course in adult development and aging for their college major, general education requirements, or professional certification. Although reading the book in order to get a high grade in a course or gain ***continuing education units (CEUs)*** is not a bad reason for learning about adult development and aging, there may be a more convincing reason: *The quality of your future is at stake*. No matter how old you are or what your life circumstances are, you are aging. Whether you are in the traditional college age range or older, there is information in this book you can use to move closer to successful, optimal aging. Making thoughtful and deliberate lifestyle choices now can greatly improve your quality of life in the future. This text is designed to inspire readers to take a long-term perspective on their lives. Becoming and remaining mindful of long-term goals can strengthen your motivation to act and think in ways that will improve physical and mental development (Hall & Fong, 2003). Assuming we all live a long life, who wouldn't want to age as successfully or as optimally as possible?

An Aging Population

Beyond a personal desire to age well, another impetus for the study of adult development and aging is the personal and societal effects resulting from the rapidly growing population of older adults. Historically speaking, it is a new and fairly recent situation to have such a large percentage of older adults in society. For Americans born in 1900 their life expectancy was 47.3 years, whereas for those born in 1950 the life expectancy was 68.2 years. Those born in 2000 have a projected life expectancy of 76.9 years (Centers for Disease Control and Prevention [CDC], 2007a), a stunning 29.6 years longer than those born 100 years earlier.

Your Thoughts?

What aspects of American society would you predict have changed the most as the life expectancy has increased over the last 100 years?

Your Thoughts?

What changes in American society would you anticipate between 2020 and 2030 based on these projections?

To illustrate how dramatic this shift in population is let us consider how the numbers of adults living to age 65 has changed. Researchers estimate that about half of all the people who have ever lived to be 65 years old or older are still alive today (Ng, Loong, Liu, & Weatherall, 2000). In the early 1900s less than 5% of Americans lived to age 65 or older, whereas in 1995 the percentage had risen to 80% (Langer & Moldoveanu, 2000). Figure 1.1 shows the increase in the numbers of adults over age 65 in the 20th century and the projected increases in the near future. Whereas in 1950 there were 12.3 million Americans age 65 and older, that number climbed to 35 million in 2000 and is projected to rise to 86.7 million in 2050. A similar trend in population increases can be charted for Americans 85 years old and older, with just over one-half million in 1950, 4.2 million in 2000, and a projected 20.9 million in 2050. The largest projected increases come in the years 2020–2030, when the number of Americans age 65 years and older jumps from 54.6 million to 71.5 million, and in the years 2030–2040, when the number of Americans 85 years old rises from 9.6 million to 15.4 million (Federal Interagency Forum, 2006). When considering characteristics of these older adults, the U.S. Census Bureau (2008a) found that of the 35 million Americans 65 years old or older in 2006, 56.6% were married. In 2005, the U.S. Census Bureau (2006b) found that 14.5% were still employed, and 9.8% were living below the poverty line.

As the population around the world continues to rise, several countries are experiencing the "graying" of their citizens. It is estimated that the world population will rise in number from 6.1 billion in 2000 to 7.2 billion in 2015 (National Intelligence Council, 2000). In the United States the population is projected to increase from just under 300 million (296,639,000) in 2005 to over 400 million (419,854,000) residents by 2050 (U.S. Census Bureau, 2006b). In high-income developed countries, such as the United States, those in the European Union, and Japan, the increased life expectancies and falling fertility rates will add momentum to the already apparent shift toward an older population. This change in age distribution presents many challenges, particularly in terms of economic stability and health care needs. It is likely that

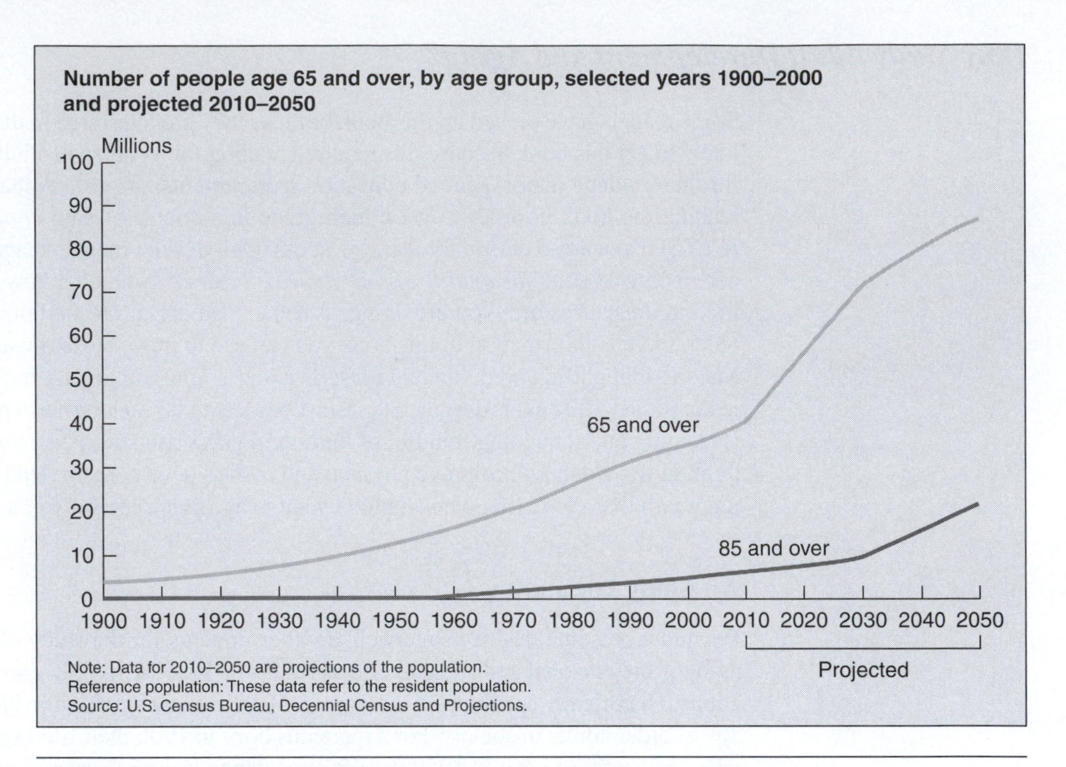

FIGURE 1.1 ***Predictions Based on U.S. Census Bureau Data***

Federal Interagency Forum on Aging-Related Statistics. (2006, May). *Older Americans Update 2006: Key Indicators of Well-Being*. Federal Interagency Forum on Aging-Related Statistics. Washington, DC: U.S. Government Printing Office.

governments will encourage later retirement ages and greater participation in the workforce by women and migrant workers in order to maintain a sustainable worker-to-retiree ratio, which will ease some of the strain on the economic and health systems supporting older adults (National Intelligence Council, 2000).

The shift toward an aging population has gained the attention of the American government as it braces for these significant changes. In 1986 the ***Federal Interagency Forum on Aging-Related Statistics*** (2006) was established with the goal of bringing data on aging together in documents that could be shared with anyone interested, including educators, researchers, and policymakers. The three primary agencies involved, the National Institute on Aging, National Center for Health Statistics, and Census Bureau, along with other agencies are listed in Table 1.1 with their Internet addresses.

Their pooled data, once compiled and collated, reflects five key areas in the study of adulthood and aging:

- Population, including racial and ethnic composition and living arrangements
- Economics, including income, poverty, and participation in the workforce
- Health status, including cognitive function and disability
- Health risks and behaviors, including physical activity, obesity, and smoking
- Health care, including services, expenditures, and facilities

This joint effort is reflective of the demand for current data documenting trends in aging in order to facilitate research and planning. This list also highlights the need for interdisciplinary approaches to the study of adult development and aging.

TABLE 1.1 ***American Agencies in the Federal Interagency Forum on Aging-Related Statistics***

Agency	Website
Administration on Aging	http://www.aoa.gov/
Agency for Healthcare Research and Quality	http://www.ahrq.gov/
Bureau of Labor Statistics	http://stats.bls.gov/
Census Bureau	http://www.census.gov/
Center for Medicare & Medicaid Services	http://www.cms.hhs.gov/
Department of Veterans Affairs	http://www.va.gov/
Employee Benefits Security Administration	http://www.va.gov/
Environmental Protection Agency	http://www.epa.gov/
National Center for Health Statistics	http://www.cdc.gov/nchs/
National Institute on Aging	http://www.nih.gov/nia
Office of the Assistant Secretary for Planning & Evaluation, Health & Human Services	http://aspe.hhs.gov/_/index.cfm
Office of Management & Budget	http://www.whitehouse.gov/OMB/index.html
Social Security Administration	http://www.ssa.gov/
Substance Abuse & Mental Health Services Administration	http://www.samhsa.gov/

From AgingStats.gov, Federal Interagency Forum on Aging-Related Statistics http://www.agingstats.gov

Challenging Issues

The rapidly increasing number of adults in their 60s and beyond brings with it the demand for information from those trying to meet current needs and prepare for the future. Such dramatic changes in age distribution will continue to affect many industries, such as health care, insurance, housing, and transportation. Business developers are working to provide the products and services older adults need or desire. Educational institutions are targeting older populations for programs that provide mental and physical stimulation as well as increase quality of life and personal independence. Governments are working to meet the needs of older adults who need special assistance, while creating educational programs designed to help adults age as successfully as possible. As the field of adult development and aging strives to meet the growing demand for information it is also facing some old and new challenges.

Your Thoughts?

What topics or areas of study can you think of that are unique to childhood or adolescence and irrelevant to adulthood?

In terms of the academic study of adult development and aging, there are theoretical issues that must be considered. One such challenge involves accepting and utilizing the multidisciplinary nature of the study of adulthood. What exactly falls under the heading of *adult development*? Actually, a better question might be, "What does *not* fall in the heading of *adult development*? Is there any aspect of an adult's life that does not develop or change with time? Even with a multidisciplinary approach that is likely to include psychology, sociology, anthropology, political science, history, communication studies, and medical science, there are some preexisting boundaries. In some cases specific aspects of adulthood may lack research due to inadequate technology or data collection methods. In other cases topics traditionally addressed by particular disciplines may be emphasized, leaving others somewhat neglected. For examples, readers of this and other psychology-based books focused on adulthood and aging will soon realize that some topics have received an enormous amount of research coverage, such as divorce and coping strategies in late adulthood, while others have received much less attention, such as the effects of parenting on adults and stages of career development.

Another challenge is to balance an emphasis on later years in adulthood with a need to understand *all* of adulthood. As the demand for more information about older adults increases,

> **Your Thoughts?**
>
> What factors might influence or direct researchers to do more work in some areas and not others?

> **Your Thoughts?**
>
> Do you think it is more important to focus on late adulthood or to give equal focus to young, middle, and late adulthood? Give reasons to support your response.

so too do streams of research funding. Currently, the study of adulthood and aging is "age heavy" in that there is much more emphasis given to individuals in late adulthood than to young and middle-aged adults. This trend is evident in this and other books on adult development. There is a growing awareness that young and middle adulthood can be viewed as a preparatory time for old age, and that the lifestyle choices made during those years will directly affect individuals' quality of life and need for assistance later. While useful, I believe it is unfortunate if this is our only interest in young and middle adulthood. Often significant, life-changing events and steps in personal development take place during those years between adolescence and retirement. Those periods of life deserve equal understanding and appreciation.

A third challenge comes in finding the balance between highlighting the things younger, middle-aged, and older adults have in common and bringing to light the diversity in adult populations. By focusing on averages and general trends we lose sensitivity to the different ways aging is experienced by specific groups, such as women and men or Hispanic Americans and Asian Americans. The current trend in research and in textbooks is to highlight these group differences (Birren & Schroots, 2001). Yet, while these group and individual differences are important to our understanding of aging, by emphasizing differences there is a danger of losing the sense of identity and political power that comes from large groups of people expressing the same needs and desires (Settersten, 2006). For example, it is important to acknowledge that older adults tend to choose to have fewer, yet more intimate, emotionally close friends (Riediger, Li, & Lindenberger, 2006) while also realizing that women tend to have more intimate friendships than men do, and people in lower socioeconomic levels tend to have fewer friends and rely more on family members to fill these friendship roles (Antonucci, 2001).

Research issues provide yet more challenges. For example, researchers wrestle with their desire for the "perfect" study while acknowledging they must design studies with realistic limitations in mind. Researchers seldom have all the supplies, equipment, lab space, available transportation, time, personnel, funding, and access to participants they would prefer. For example, those who are interested in the ways work-related stresses affect household-related stresses may choose to give employees of a particular company a questionnaire asking about their stresses at home and at work. This standard data collection procedure does not take into account many individual differences, such as the differences in stresses experienced uniquely by women and men, parents and nonparents, those early in their careers and those with many years invested in their careers, and stresses that may be unique to particular industries or even specific work environments (such as one hospital as compared to another). Researchers must put limitations on data collection or else the process would take longer than their lifetime, cost more money than their funding sources can provide, and create huge databases that are difficult to analyze comprehensively. Unfortunately, the often unavoidable research limitations may create an incomplete understanding of the topics under investigation.

Section Summary

- Many societies in high-income, developed countries are experiencing the "graying" of their populations.
- American society is projected to change dramatically through the first half of the 21st century in terms of aging and the many effects the large, older adult population will have on the culture, social services, and health care industry.
- Challenging issues in the study of adult development and aging include working with disciplines other than one's own, balancing the emphasis on young, middle, and late adulthood, highlighting both group trends based on age and individual differences, and dealing with the limited resources available for research.

A Psychological Approach to Adult Development and Aging

There are many approaches to the study and understanding of adult development and aging. While it is essential to be mindful of these many perspectives, the focus for this and the following chapters is primarily a psychological one. ***Psychology*** is often described as the scientific study of mental and behavioral processes. There are many ways to partition various facets of psychology, such as by an emphasis on theory, research, or practice. The study of adult development and aging certainly draws from and contributes to all three. Another method is to partition by field, such as experimental, social, or clinical psychology. In this case the focus of this text is primarily ***developmental psychology***, the study of the ways individuals change as they age. The study of human lifespan development is typically divided by age ranges, such as childhood or young adulthood, and topic, such as emotional, personality, cognitive, social, and physical development. The study of ***adult development and aging***, based on these descriptions, can be defined as a part of developmental psychology emphasizing the study of the normal or typical ways mental and behavioral processes change with age beyond adolescence.

Your Thoughts?

What factors might lead to the misunderstanding that psychology is focused only on mental disorders and therapy?

A Multidisciplinary and Multifaceted Endeavor

If you didn't take time to look at the *Before We Get Started* section at the beginning of the chapter please take a few minutes to look at it now. The point of the exercise was to raise awareness of the many ways various disciplines might approach a study of parent–child interactions. The advice that you would give the mother in this situation would be reflective of many personal attributes including your past experiences, preferences in parenting styles, and cultural awareness. Keeping in mind that there are similarities across the disciplines

Developmental psychology focuses on change over time, such as predicting just how closely this grandfather's son and grandson will be like him when they reach his age.

as well as a great deal of variation within each discipline, consider the following differences in emphasis:

- Psychology: What individual characteristics do mother and daughter possess that might influence the mother's reaction?
- Sociology: What societal factors, such as the economic resources and social status of this family, might influence the mother's reaction?
- Anthropology: What is the cultural heritage and background of this family and how might that influence parenting styles and the mother's reaction?

One example of how these disciplines work together and inform each other can be found in the work of Melanie Domenech Rodriguez and her colleagues (Rodriguez, Donovick, & Crowley, 2009) in the area of parenting styles. They began with the classic and foundational research of Diana Baumrind, who found four parenting styles based on parents' levels of responsiveness and demandingness. Parents high in both were labeled *authoritative* while those low in both were labeled *neglectful*. Those high in responsiveness but low in demandingness were labeled *permissive*, while the opposite configuration was labeled *authoritarian*. Rodriguez and her colleagues noted that research focused specifically on Latino parenting styles was sparse, and what was available was somewhat contradictory. Also, pulling from research in sociology, anthropology, and other fields, they suspected that Latino parenting styles may be different in some ways from Baumrind's findings, which were based on the majority, mainstream culture in the United States in the 1960s.

When applying Baumrind's techniques to a group of Spanish-speaking Latino families in which at least one parent was a first-generation immigrant, Rodriguez and her colleagues (2009) found both similarities and differences. Similar to the example in the *Before We Get Started* exercise, a parent and child would be observed while engaging in a cooperation task and a problem-solving task. One key difference from Baumrind's work is an additional dimension to responsiveness and demandingness, that of autonomy granting. They found that Latino parents tended to be *protective*, the label given to parents who were low in autonomy granting. These findings are important not only for understanding of parenting but also for the continued reminder of the need to consider adult development from many perspectives and through the eyes of many disciplines.

Your Thoughts?

What technological changes since the 1960s might increase the likelihood that researchers will include multicultural perspectives in their work?

Like many of the social sciences, there is great variation within the field of psychology itself, each division with its own approach to adult development and aging. Psychology is generally partitioned into work that is theoretical, methodological, empirical (Salthouse, 2006), and applied. All four aspects are important, and each informs the others. Theories, such as Baumrind's parenting styles, inform psychologists of the most important items to study or pay attention to in a research or therapeutic setting, and how those items might be related to other aspects of life. Throughout this text the reader will find many theories, some broadly covering large spans of years and others covering very specific aspects of development. The methodological experts inform the theoreticians and researchers, whether they are working in a laboratory or a clinic, of how best to collect data, analyze it, and interpret it. It is the scientific basis of these methodologies that often sets psychology apart from other disciplines outside of the social sciences that explore human thoughts and behaviors, such as literature or philosophy. Empirical researchers, such as Rodriguez, Donovick, and Crowley (2009), conduct studies and supply data that inform the theorists, methodologists, and practitioners. Rodriguez and her colleagues were careful in following Baumrind's data collection techniques as well as adding their own refinements. And finally, the clinical psychologists and other practitioners who apply scientific findings to real-life situations can inform the others of how well the theories, methodologies, or

Your Thoughts?

Is it important for therapists to understand the scientific foundation of psychology? Why, why not, or under what circumstances?

ON THE LEADING EDGE
Psychology and Hurricane Katrina

Hurricane Katrina, a category 5 storm, devastated much of the coastline in Louisiana and neighboring states in August 2005. The ripple effects of the storm continue to make an impact on the Gulf Coast as many areas have not yet rebuilt or rebounded from the disaster. In retrospect, many professionals, including psychologists, have asked what they may be able to do better when the next crisis of this scale occurs (Gheytanchi et al., 2007).

For many years mental health professionals used a model called the Critical Incident Stress Debriefing (CISD). Generally, this involves a group debriefing within 3 days of the disaster. As data is gathered on this style of response it appears that the treatment is not as effective as was hoped. The current strategies involve a focus on functional recovery, offering support to individuals by encouraging productive coping and problem-solving skills.

Gheytanchi and her colleagues (2007), associated with the National Center on the Psychology of Terrorism, are calling on psychologists of all backgrounds to get involved to address some of the failures of the Hurricane Katrina response. What might cognitive psychologists have to contribute regarding better and more productive communication methods? What might industrial/organizational psychologists have to offer regarding the interaction between military officials, law enforcement, and local citizens? How might those who study personality and those who develop psychological tests (psychometrics) develop screening instruments to use when placing individuals in leadership and management positions? Gheytanchi and her colleagues (2007) also call upon those who study dying, death, and bereavement to get involved. With any disaster there is likely to be death and grieving on a massive scale. With Hurricane Katrina there were numerous bodies in various stages of decay all around. What can be done to ease the traumatizing effects of such situations for local citizens?

The American Psychological Association and other organizations serving mental health professionals along with groups of research psychologists are working hard to answer some of these probing questions and put new practices in place. As the devastation of the oil spill in the Gulf of Mexico that started on April 18, 2010 becomes apparent psychologists will likely have opportunities to try new methods of immediate- and long-term trauma care. Although it may seem like psychology is all about less-exciting laboratory research, the truth is that such data collection will inform those working in the "real world," making a difference in people's lives.

findings facilitate understanding and progress with clients. The authors end their published article with information useful to social workers, teachers, and others who might be working with first-generation Latino families.

The Developmental Psychological Perspective

In its early years developmental psychology was primarily the study of child development. The prevailing attitude was that most, if not all, of the interesting and influential developmental processes occurred in childhood, thus adulthood was simply the unfolding results of earlier lifestyle choices and events. Both Freud's stages of psychosexual development and Piaget's stages of cognitive development, as examples, reach their completion in adolescence (Birren & Schroots, 2001). Despite some early work done by influential psychologists, little interest in adulthood was generated. G. Stanley Hall, an organizer and first president of the American Psychological Association, published a book, *Senescence: The Last Half of Life*, in 1922. During the 1920s and 1930s a group of prestigious scholars at Stanford University conducted the Stanford Later Maturity Study. Yet, the general lack of interest in aging, along with the American focus on the Great Depression and World War II, left the field of developmental psychology primarily one of child development.

The situation began to change after World War II when numerous factors emerged to encourage the psychological study of adult development and aging. Among the most influential was the increasing numbers of adults living into old age. Some of the social sciences, especially sociology, began to explore the implications of a rapidly aging population (Baltes, Staudinger, & Lindenberger, 1999). The social sciences also witnessed the aging of many participants in some long-term studies, providing data on the aging process. The American Psychological Association responded to these new developments by creating the Division on Maturity and Old Age, now called Adult Development and Aging, in the mid-1940s. It was in this milieu that the field of gerontology emerged, bringing a particular emphasis on understanding the precursors across adulthood that led to changes in old age (Baltes, 1987; Baltes et al., 1999). The Gerontological Society of America was founded in 1946 with representation from biology, medicine, and various social sciences, including some psychologists. The Society began publishing the *Journal of Gerontology* that same year. By the 1960s several disciplines had gained appreciation for the study of all of human development (Birren & Schroots, 2001). Governments began to respond to their aging citizenry by forming special agencies and research programs (Baltes, 1987; Birren & Schroots, 2001). The U.S. government established the National Institute on Aging in 1974 and the Federal Interagency Forum on Aging-Related Statistics formed in 1986. The interest in aging was also taking root in the medical community. Along with the increasing numbers of older patients, medical researchers were beginning to make connections between changes in the nervous system and common signs of aging (Birren & Schroots, 2001).

Your Thoughts?

What factors in post–World War II American society might have contributed to a growing interest in the study of aging?

Currently, a great deal of work in psychology, and developmental psychology in particular, is focused on adult development. Once adulthood was recognized as a unique and dynamic period, researchers began to explore new domains such as creativity, wisdom, religion, and spirituality. Energy was devoted to new, age-appropriate mental tests (Birrens & Schroots, 2001), including intelligence tests and those used in clinical settings (Schaie, 2000). Current research in adult development generally falls into four areas based on emphasis. One area investigates *stasis* by searching for and exploring aspects of adult development that remain stable. For example, there is great interest in determining which aspects of personality are stable through adulthood. Another avenue of research is to explore *change* that occurs in distinct age ranges, such as within young (ages 20–45), middle (ages 45–65), or late adulthood (ages 65 and over). Research in this category may, for example, explore the changes experienced by first-time parents that are in their early 20s, and compare that to the experiences of first-time parents in their early 40s. A third category of research is focused on understanding processes of decline. Some of the primary content areas here are particular components of memory, cognitive skills, and physical functioning. The fourth area emphasizes growth-based or positive areas of adult development, such as wisdom, expertise, and spirituality (Commons, 2002). This text includes items from all four of these categories of research.

Your Thoughts?

Which of these areas interest you the most? Why?

Positive and Realistic Approach

At the end of the last century a new movement called ***positive psychology*** took hold within the discipline in general, and within adult development and aging in particular. Positive psychology is often described as a *strengths-based* approach, emphasizing individuals' strengths and resilient qualities that allow for productive coping and personal growth. Within this new movement researchers are primarily focused on life satisfaction, contentment, and well-being (Seligman & Csikszentmihalyi, 2000). Positive psychology has filled a much-needed void in the study of late adulthood. Even though older adults rate themselves as happy as individuals of any other age (Myers, 2005), there is a long-standing perception that old age is filled with doom and gloom (Kite, Stockdale, Whitley, & Johnson, 2005). Psychologists are now considering both what is causing problems in late adulthood, such as disorders and decline, and what is going well, such as healthy self-esteem, high levels of well-being, and spiritual or internal strength. Related to the interest in positive psychology is the movement toward ***optimal aging***. To age successfully is to engage in as many preventive measures as possible while adjusting and coping well with the changes that do occur. The goal of optimal aging, as we will see in Chapter 3, is not to try to look or act like a young adult no matter your age, but rather to be the best you can be, physically and psychologically, in your current situation.

Your Thoughts?

What are some of the problems with trying to look and act like you're 20 years old when you are much older?

ON THE LEADING EDGE
Positive Psychology and Psychotherapy

Seligman, one of the primary promoters of positive psychology, sees this new area as comprising three components: (1) positive emotions that contribute to a pleasant feeling, (2) engagement in important areas of life, and (3) a sense of meaning in life. Recently, his work has grown to include the development of positive psychotherapy. Most traditional methods of therapy involve discussing problems with the goal of easing mental distress. Seligman, Rashid, and Parks (2006) charge that working toward the elimination of symptoms is helpful but less productive than working to enhance clients' positive strengths.

With the hope of moving psychological research and therapy closer to the principles of positive psychology this research group has recently been working on a positive psychotherapy for clients suffering from depression. Those who are depressed are often lacking in positive emotions, personal engagement, and meaning in life. In a radical change in direction, these characteristics, which have most often been viewed as *symptoms* of depression, are conceptualized by this research team as possibly the *cause* of depression.

Seligman and his colleagues have tested several intervention strategies, including training sessions for mental health professionals, group positive psychotherapy exercises, and Web-based activities for clients. Exercises aimed at enhancing positive emotions emphasize optimism, hope, and noticing pleasant experiences in mundane life. Engagement in life is addressed by learning of the client's strengths and interests and then finding programs, classes, community groups, or some other methods of active involvement. Meaningfulness is creating by engaging the client's strengths and interests in ways that benefit others or connect the client to something that is "bigger than one's self." To date the use of positive psychology in the treatment of depression has been successful, proving in many preliminary cases to work better than usual psychotherapy or psychotherapy and medication.

Section Summary

- Developmental psychology can be defined as the scientific study of the ways mental and behavioral processes change within individuals over time.
- The study of adult development and aging is multidisciplinary and multifaceted, reflecting similarities and differences across disciplines as well as among areas of emphasis within disciplines.
- Much of the current emphasis in developmental psychology as it is applied to adulthood and aging is on aspects of adult development that are stable, that change with age, progress in positive and productive ways, and decline with age.

Multiple Dimensions of Age

One of the critical differences between the study of child and adult development is the fact that childhood generally covers about 12 years while adulthood can cover 60 years or more. In an effort to make that long span more manageable, developmental psychologists have a tradition of segmenting adulthood by using one of the easiest factors to identify: age. The most frequently used scheme is to place young adulthood from generally 18 or 20 years old to around 40 or 45 years old, middle adulthood from 40 or 45 years old to about 60 or 65 years old, thus leaving late adulthood to begin around 60 or 65 years old and continue to the end of life. This organizational structure is changing as the number of individuals over age 65 continues to grow. To reflect the diversity within late adulthood, researchers often divide those years into the young-old (60 or 65 years old to 74 years old), the old-old (ages 75 to 84 years old), and the oldest-old group as age 85 and over. These age divisions can serve as efficient labels for loosely grouped age-related roles, stereotypes, and expectations. In contrast to these American labels, some European scholars have referred to adulthood up to pre-retirement as the Second

Your Thoughts?

Can you think of more creative labels for these than young-old, old-old, and oldest-old?

Age, the time of vitality between pre-retirement and the oldest-old as the Third Age, and the end of life as the Fourth Age. The Third Age generally includes people in their 50s, 60s, and 70s (Moen & Spencer, 2006).

Functional Age

Within the study of adult development and aging a greater level of precision than simple age ranges is needed to describe adults at various points in their lives. References to ***chronological age*** can be useful when considering child development, but much less so in adulthood. For example, if you were told only a young child's age in weeks or months, you could make some reasonably accurate predictions about that child's physical and cognitive abilities. For young children developmental milestones are often closely tied to age, such as the age at which we walk, make two-word sentences, write our name, or enter elementary school. ***Normative age-graded influences***, typical events or influences demonstrating a strong relationship to age (Baltes, 1982), are more likely to appear in the early years of the lifespan, such as the typical age for starting elementary school. Many of the developmental milestones associated with adulthood, however, such as age of first or second marriage, becoming a parent, or age at total retirement, can vary greatly. Clearly chronological age is more descriptive for children. The differences between a 3-month-old and a 3-year-old, or between a 3-year-old and a 13-year-old, are enormous. In contrast, the differences between a 43-year-old and a 53-year-old may not be as dramatic or predictable based on age alone.

A more useful concept of age in adulthood is ***functional age***. Rather than simply knowing an adult is 43 years old, we could make better predictions about that person's physical and cognitive abilities if we knew about that person's health, personality, and social interactions. Knowing how an adult functions in various domains provides a more useful physical and psychological profile. One domain or component of functional age is ***biological age***, a comparison of an individual's health, particularly of vital organ systems, to others of similar chronological age. The National Institute on Aging (NIA), for example, prefers to use a biological age composed of many bodily functions including heart functioning and lung capacity rather than chronological age. The NIA refers to these particular functions as ***biomarkers***. Sometimes when we say of someone who is elderly, "He's in great physical shape for his age," we are saying that person is young in terms of biological age as compared to other elderly individuals. When we say of someone in middle age, "I thought she was much older than she is," we may be picking up on cues that indicate a biological age that is strikingly higher than her peers. Another component of functional age is ***psychological age***, comparing one's ability to adjust and cope with changes in the environment to others of similar chronological age. In order to engage in everyday problem solving as well as coping with the major events that come our way, we need to use behavioral, cognitive, and emotional skills. Have you ever thought someone was particularly mature or immature for his or her chronological age? If so, you were assessing psychological age. A third component of functional age is ***social age***, comparing one's social roles and expectations to chronological age and overall functioning. As an example, consider that in American society we tend to think of widowhood as a late-adulthood event. A young woman who becomes a widow prematurely may find that people treat her as if she is older than her chronological age. In this case people would be responding to her social role as a widow rather than her chronological age.

Your Thoughts?

Can you think of some situations in which a focus on maturity is more appropriate than simply chronological age?

Age-Related Influences

In addition to normative age-graded influences, there are two other categories of influence that combine to influence functional age. ***Normative history-graded influences*** are those experienced by a culture or society at a particular point in history that may eventually define

Chronological age can be deceiving when an adult's functional age is that of someone much younger in years.

a generation (Baltes, 1982). One could point to historical examples, such as the influence of the Great Depression and World War II on the thoughts and behaviors of those who lived through them, or to more recent events, such as the availability of personal technologies and the Internet. If you have always had access to a personal computer, cell phone, and the Internet, can you *really* imagine what life was like prior to that? Accepting those technologies as an expected part of everyday life is a critical influence on the thinking, vocabulary, and behaviors of younger generations. I was a junior in college the first time I used a computer, and my first venture on the Internet was several years after becoming a college professor. In talking with my younger college students I find that we view Internet and personal technologies differently. For me they are primarily tools to help me do my work more efficiently and at a higher quality, and to a lesser extent a tool for communication and information gathering. While my younger students acknowledge these uses, they think of these technologies as primarily sources of information, entertainment, and social networking. They meet people, build social communities, play games, and shop online. The impact of readily available technologies will most likely create a ***cohort***, a group of people who have grown up together and have similar normative history-graded experiences. Unlike normative age-graded influences, which are more frequent in childhood, normative history-graded influences are often more influential in adolescence and young adulthood. Although it seems obvious that technology-saturated generations will be qualitatively different from previous ones, it will be many years before we understand the full extent of the influence on technology on younger generations.

RESEARCH IN-DEPTH
Cross-Sectional and Longitudinal Studies

There are numerous design decisions to be made when beginning a scientific study or an ongoing program of research. For those interested in age-related development one of the key choices is whether to use a cross-sectional design, longitudinal design, or some blending of the two. A ***cross-sectional design*** is one in which people of different ages are tested at the same point in time and compared. For example, a cross-sectional design was used by Zucker, Ostrove, and Stewart (2002) to study several variables in women's development, including generativity in middle age. The term ***variable*** refers to any item or factor being studied that can vary, either by person, situation, or both. Generativity, which is discussed in detail in Chapter 4, is the care and concern for other generations, often displayed through mentoring and role modeling. Zucker and her colleagues surveyed a group of young adult women with an average age of 26, a different group of middle-aged women who had an average age of 46, and a third group of older women who had an average age of 66 years old. After comparing the data from the three groups the researchers found that feelings of generativity were stronger in midlife than in young adulthood, and that those feelings tended to plateau in late adulthood.

While these comparisons are interesting and informative, they are made with the underlying assumption that these three groups of women are similar enough to infer that the young adult group will be like the middle-aged group in 20 years, and that both the young adult and middle-aged groups will be like the older adults when they are 66 years old. In some cases these are high-risk assumptions, particularly when cohort differences are involved. What were the older women, now 66 years old on average, taught in their generation about women roles, caregiving, and helping? What were the middle-aged women taught? How was the socialization process, identifying with female gender role expectations, different for those women born 26 years ago versus those born 66 years ago? Accounting for cohort differences is one of the primary challenges in cross-sectional research.

Even though cross-sectional designs are limited in terms of what can be concluded about individual development, they do have some advantages. By surveying all the participants at basically the same time researchers can collect their data very quickly, saving time and often monetary resources as well. Cross-sectional designs can provide indications of what might be a developmental pattern, giving way to new research questions. In order to confirm such developmental trends, and to gain more insight into the potential causes of these tends, it is important to follow the development of the same group of people over time, which is called a ***longitudinal design*** (Hofer & Sliwinski, 2001).

Peterson (2002) explored generativity in middle-aged women by analyzing data collected from a longitudinal study that started with the Radcliffe College graduates of 1964. Over the years these women have been tested many times. The particular items Peterson analyzed came from data collected in 1986 and 1996 from the same women, who were 43 and then 53 at the testing times. His analysis revealed that the test scores of the women at age 43 could predict their scores on several measures of generativity at age 53, particularly the value of caregiving and intergenerational roles (daughter, mother, grandmother) in personal identity. The women who had developed a sense of generativity at age 43 were more invested in their intergenerational roles and spouse/partner roles at age 53. The more generative women were also more likely to care for their immediate community and to feel cared for by others. Without the longitudinal design Peterson could only speculate about growth between ages 43 and 53. By studying the growth of specific women across the 10-year span he can make much stronger statements about developmental paths.

Just as there are shortcomings with cross-sectional design, there are also challenges inherent in longitudinal design. When recruiting participants the researchers are limited to only those who are willing to participate in a multiyear study. Even though all those who begin the study initially agree to participate for the full length of the study, the dropout or attrition rate is always a concern. There are numerous reasons why some participants might withdraw, such as moving to a new location, engaging in a lifestyle that becomes too busy, or losing interest in the study (Hofer & Sliwinski, 2001). In some cases participants may decide after several years that the tasks involved take too much time and energy, or are too hard. It may be that some individuals choose to end participation because they do not want to reveal what has happened in their lives since the last test session, or they may believe that they aren't performing well in the study.

Another concern is the effects of repetitive testing (Hofer & Sliwinski, 2001). Participants who are given the same tests over and over may get better at them with practice, such as improving on repeated intelligence tests, or they may get bored and lose motivation. Also, tests may be updated or revised during the study, making the comparisons more difficult. Finally, a recent review of the literature in aging found that most longitudinal studies lasted for less than a decade, which may not be enough time to truly gauge development trends (Settersten, 2006).

In order to better manage some of these challenges, and gain some of the advantages of cross-sectional research, social scientists are exploring blending both designs so that while longitudinal data is being collected on current participants, new participants are continually brought into the design for both immediate cross-sectional and eventual longitudinal analysis.

> **Your Thoughts?**
>
> What has been one of the most powerful non-normative events in your life so far?

In addition to the influences already discussed, there are those unexpected, personal events that may change our lives in different ways depending on when they occur. These ***non-normative influences*** include chance occurrences, such as winning a large sum of money or surviving a serious car accident. Either of these events may dramatically change people's lives, perhaps in different ways depending on their age. A younger adult will most likely recover from physical injuries sustained in a violent car accident faster and more completely than an older adult with the same injuries. Also considered non-normative influences are more common events that happen in an individual's life at an unusual time. Citing an example from my life, my father died when I was 6 years old. While the unfortunate reality is that all of our parents will die, it isn't normal for this to happen to a child. This non-normative event has been a powerful influence in shaping the person I have become. While there are those sad moments when I wish my father could be with me, such as when I graduated from college, the experience of losing a parent at a young age has given me some wisdom and insight. I believe it taught me early in life to value every day we have with those we love. It also gave me a better sense of perspective and personal priorities in terms of what is a "big deal" in life, and what's not worth getting upset over.

Section Summary

- The ease of categorizing people by age makes it very appealing, and the segmentation of young, middle, and late adulthood is commonplace in American culture.
- When taking a closer look at the ever-changing patterns in society and the many individual differences among adults, it becomes apparent that more precise, descriptive terms are needed.
- Although simple chronological age can easily be determined, other measures such as functional age, composed of biological, psychological, and social age, provides a better view of daily functioning.
- In addition to personal functioning, the detection of normative age-graded, normative history-graded, and non-normative influences also provide a clearer picture of adult functioning than general categorization by chronological age.

Metatheories as Philosophies of Development

Since the middle of the 20th century developmental psychologists have found three metatheories useful in organizing knowledge and designing research. Sometimes referred to as worldviews or metamodels, these metatheories continue to serve as powerful heuristic philosophies of human nature. For example, the mechanistic metatheory highlights environmental or external influences on thoughts and behaviors, whereas the organismic metatheory highlights internal, maturational influences. The contextual metatheory provides a middle ground in emphasizing the continual interaction of both internal and external influences.

Mechanistic Metatheory

The first metatheory we consider, the ***mechanistic metatheory***, employs a machine metaphor (Lerner & Tubman, 1989: McFadden & Gerl, 1990; Webster, 1999). Here the emphasis is on the ways the environment acts on an individual and that individual's behavioral response. The initiator or source of change is external to the individual. From a mechanistic perspective human beings are machine-like in that they are composed of many interacting parts. The goal of research is to figure out what the parts are, how they work, and then how to manipulate them. For example, in the area of cognition a researcher may study the reaction time needed to determine if a word flashed on a computer screen was in a previously learned list. In this scenario research participants would press a computer key to indicate their choice, thus providing a measure of the time between the flashing of the word and the key press, as well as whether the response was correct. This measure of memory can then be represented as a formula or model and modified through training. Indicative of a mechanistic philosophy, this type of study involves ***quantitative design*** in that the items being studied are observable (pressing a computer key) and measurable (reaction time in seconds and number of correct responses). Also indicative of this view, the pattern of development, which in this case is getting better at the memory task, is continuous. Different from stages or leaps in development, a mechanistic metatheory supports the notions that change occurs in smooth, ***continuous*** increases, long-standing plateaus, or decreases in whatever is being measured. Returning to our reaction time example, if we were to graph performance on this memory task from childhood through the end of life we would probably find a steady increase in number of words remembered and a decrease in reaction time until some point in early adulthood, then a general plateau in ability in young and middle adulthood, and finally a decrease in reaction time and a slight decrease in number of words correctly identified in late adulthood. A graph of this data would likely produce a line indicating steady movement or plateau rather than a more jagged or stair-stepped picture. Also consistent with a mechanistic view, researchers may use behavioral analysis methodology to design a conditioning program to enhance performance. By engaging in a practice program (training) and by competing for an incentive, such as desirable prizes for those who remember the most words accurately (reinforcement), it is likely that participants' scores will improve.

Your Thoughts?

Can you think of other human functions that develop in a continuous fashion?

While useful in some areas of development, a mechanistic view is not without critics. Some social scientists find a mechanistic view lacking completeness because it is function-centered and doesn't consider the whole person or the whole context (Baltes et al., 1999). For those who study areas of human development that do not seem to follow a pattern of continuous development, a different approach is needed.

Organismic Metatheory

In contrast to the machine-like view of the mechanistic metatheory, the ***organismic metatheory*** draws upon a biology metaphor to describe human development. This perspective emphasizes individuals' genetically predetermined patterns of development, which are revealed through maturation and influenced by stimulation from the environment. Development is characterized by transitions or cycles of rapid spurts of growth or decline, and stages, periods of stability, or plateau. In contrast to the continuous, quantitative approach of a mechanistic view, an organismic view emphasizes the ***discontinuous***, ***qualitative*** change inherent in stage models (Lerner & Tubman, 1989: McFadden & Gerl, 1990; Webster, 1999). Movement from one stage to the next involves adding to and reworking previous stages to create something more complex and sophisticated (Dawson-Tunik, Commons, Wilson, & Fischer, 2005). Consider, as an example, the stages we move through as our imagination develops. A stable characteristic of most young children is the ability to immerse in their all-encompassing imagination. Often they can't tell the difference between reality and fantasy. As those children move into middle childhood and enter elementary school, they will transition to a new stage in which they can still use their imagination but they have learned when it is appropriate and when it isn't. As concrete thinkers their imaginations tend to be about things they have

Your Thoughts?

What are the advantages of viewing development in terms of stages? What might be some disadvantages?

experienced, seen, or heard. Those same children will transition again into a new stage in high school when they gain skills in abstract and hypothetical thinking. Now, in addition to knowing when to engage their imaginations and when not to, they can integrate abstract and hypothetical thinking in their imaginations, releasing them to use their imaginations with greater complexity and creativity.

Early in developmental psychology's history, when the field was primarily focused on child development, criteria were established for "true" stage theories. In order to qualify, stages must:

- Be qualitatively different from each other
- Be experienced in a standard, sequential manner
- Never be experienced in reverse order or in regression
- Progress toward a final stage or ending point
- Be universally found in all people of all cultures

While these criteria remain important in developmental theory, they are often viewed as too restrictive for adult developmental models (Baltes, 1982). In response to this strict model, stage theories have become the target of many criticisms. It is important to remember that even though stages are usually referred to in a linear, numerical sequence, it is not always the case that a higher stage is necessarily better for a particular individual in a particular circumstance. Another important factor to keep in mind is that movement outside of a given theory of "normal" development doesn't necessarily mean an individual is "abnormal" and in need of correction. While useful in some areas of development, a more complete view of human development may be gained from a blending of stage development models with recognition of the influences of personal circumstances, individual differences, and creative exploration that may not fit well within a stage structure (Courtenay, 1994; Taylor, 1996).

Contextual Metatheory

The third metatheory, the ***contextual metatheory***, has become the dominant philosophy in developmental psychology. It is characterized by emphasizing the bidirectional interaction of both internal and external forces, creating both continuous and discontinuous development. As the field of developmental psychology moved from a child focus to a lifespan focus there grew a dissatisfaction with the perceived need to focus exclusively on either external, environmental forces or internal, maturational unfolding. Researchers found that both the mechanistic and organismic metatheories can be useful and are not necessarily exclusive (Dawson-Tunik et al., 2005). There also grew a need to incorporate the influences of individual differences, areas of diversity, and multiple levels of culture into theories of development (Goodnow, 2002). Rather than searching for continuous growth or decline, or stages leading to a final goal or point in development, the contextual view considers the most probable outcomes or patterns of development, acknowledging the uncertainty of non-normative events and individual differences (Lerner & Tubman, 1989; McFadden & Gerl, 1990; Webster, 1999).

Baltes and his colleagues have led the way in documenting the evolution of lifespan psychology in general, and the study of adult development and aging in particular. Through their work they have found seven core assumptions consistent with the contextual metatheoretical view that influences current lifespan developmental theory. First of all, development is viewed as (1) a lifelong process. All periods in life have an effect and shape the

> **Your Thoughts?**
>
> What psychological or physical gains have you made in the last 10 years? What losses have you experienced?

developmental process. Along with that, each period of life involves simultaneous processes of (2) gains and losses. During every period in life there are areas of growth along with areas of decline. In contrast to the notion that development is linear, unfolding in a predetermined pattern, the current emphasis in lifespan development theory is on the (3) multidirectionality of development. Particular areas of development may simultaneously grow, stabilize, or decline at various rates. Along with that, (4) contextualism is evident through the influences of normative age-graded, normative history-graded, and non-normative influences for individuals, and to a larger extent in society through the assumption of (5) historical embeddedness. Individual development is influenced not only by personal events but also by larger, societal events and movements. Rather than the notion that developmental pathways are set or rigid, current views emphasize the characteristic of (6) plasticity. Most skills and abilities are malleable and can be modified and improved with training at almost any age. This notion of plasticity or flexibility, along with attention given to the ways the aging process is individualized, have been called "the most striking changes" in the study of aging in recent years (Aldwin, Spiro, & Park, 2006). Finally, lifespan developmental theory is part of (7) a multidisciplinary study of development that includes not only other social sciences, such as sociology and political science, but also wider-ranging fields such as medical and biological sciences (Baltes, 1987; Baltes et al., 1999). A more complete understanding of adult development goes beyond psychological considerations to include work in academic areas as well as within major industries, such as health care and education.

Section Summary

- Three popular metatheories have guided much of the research in developmental psychology.
- The mechanistic metatheory emphasizes the role of the environment in initiating change. In this view development is conceptualized as continuous, quantifiable growth, plateau, or decline.
- The organismic metatheory suggests that development occurs in a predetermined way as an individual matures. Here researchers look for periods of stability, called stages, following periods of rapid transition or growth. Development is thought to be discontinuous, occurring in a sequence of qualitatively distinct stages.
- The contextual metatheory blends the other two models by emphasizing both quantitative and qualitative development that is bidirectional between the organism and the environment.
- Current lifespan development theory is consistent with a contextual metatheoretical view in emphasizing a lifelong process involving mutlidirectionality, contextualism, gains and losses, and plasticity.

Theoretical Approaches to Adult Development and Aging

One of the most important functions of a theory is to provide a concise way of understanding and organizing large amounts of data, and by doing so, giving direction to the next steps in research. The three metatheories have given rise to many theories and models of particular aspects of adult development, such as cognitive processing speed or reasoning about moral dilemmas. While the contextual metatheory has become the dominant philosophy, there is no

Your Thoughts?

What would be the advantages and disadvantages to having one unifying theory of adult development?

one particular theory that unifies everything we have learned about the psychology of adult development and aging (Salthouse, 2006). Some feel that such a complete, all-encompassing theory, attempting to account for all the complexities of aging, will never be developed (Settersten, 2006). Lacking a unifying theory, this section introduces four of the most current and frequently utilized theories in the study of adult development and aging. Whereas all four theories consider the interaction of individual and environmental influences, the biological theories of aging and connectionist theories tend to emphasize the internal processes to a greater degree, whereas the sociocultural theories and the selection, optimization, and optimization theory give more attention to environmental influences.

Biological Theories

One of the hallmarks of the field of psychology that separates it from other social sciences is its long-standing emphasis on the biological foundations of thoughts and behaviors. The influence of ***neuropsychology***, sometimes called psychobiology or behavioral neuroscience, is evident in this book and most any treatment of human development. Biological influences on aging are discussed throughout this book, particularly in discussions of successful or optimal aging, normal physical, sensory, and memory changes with age, diseases, and disorders.

Biological theories of aging are generally grouped under two headings: programmed theories and error theories. It is important to note that the various programmed and error theories are not exclusive or in direct competition and may occur simultaneously or sequentially. As technology improves and research methodologies are refined, the trend among gerontologists is to move away from the search for the single "correct" theory and toward a more complex perspective of biological aging (National Institute on Aging [NIA], 2007; Schneider, 1992).

Programmed theories of biological aging propose that a biological timetable controls the aging process. One example, the *programmed longevity theory*, looks for mechanisms that switch certain genes on and off, resulting in deficits associated with aging. While working with animals such as tiny round worms called *nematodes*, scientists have found several genes that may have an effect on aging. It is likely that there are many genes that work together in complex ways to determine the aging process (NIA, 2007). Aging researchers often rely on *quantitative genetic theory*, which focuses on the combined influence of many small genes, and the dynamic nature of genetic influences over time, as do other researchers in the field of behavioral genetics (e.g., Vogler, 2006). Another example of programmed theories, the *endocrine theory*, involves the search for hormonal actions that control the biological clock and speed of the aging process. With age some hormone production decreases, as is evident with testosterone, estrogen, melatonin, and dehydroepiandrosterone (DHEA). While the exact effects of these reductions are not clear, it may be that these processes contribute to the aging process. A third example of programmed theories is the *immunological theory*, highlighting increased vulnerability to infections and diseases through a programmed decline in immune system functions (NIA, 2007). Sometimes called the *immune clock*, our immune system reaches its strongest during adolescence and begins weakening after age 20 (Schneider, 1992). (See Table 1.2 for a list of theories of biological aging.)

Your Thoughts?

How would the study of identical twins shed light on programmed and error theories?

Taking a different approach from the programmed theories, some researchers are looking for *probable* outcomes (Gottlieb, 2001) of the interaction between genetically programmed aging and various environmental influences. The ***error theories of biological aging*** examine these additional, accidental, or external influences on physiological aging. Error theories may also be referred to as damage, random event, stochastic, or variable-rate theories. One example of an error theory, the *wear and tear theory*, proposes that cells and tissues simply wear out over

TABLE 1.2 ***Examples of Biological Theories of Aging***

Programmed Theories	*Error Theories*
1. Programmed Longevity Theory	**1.** Wear and Tear Theory
2. Endocrine Theory	**2.** Rate of Living Theory
3. Immunological Theory	**3.** Crosslinking Theory
	4. Free Radical Theory
	5. Somatic DNA Damage Theory

time. Often referred to as *cell senescence*, researchers have found that cells will, at some point, stop proliferating. While there are many unanswered questions about this process and the role these cells play after they stop dividing, researchers are looking at abnormal gene products and telomere shortening (shortening of the tail of a chromosome) for possible clues. Once large numbers of cells stop proliferating, the effects can be seen in major organ systems and the organism will have a continual series of breakdowns. Another error theory, the *rate of living theory*, highlights the simple yet profound notion that organisms have a finite set of resources and energy, and once those are used up the organism cannot continue to live. One course of action consistent with this theory is to look for ways to slow an organism's metabolism and thus increase its lifespan. Researchers have found that caloric restriction in rats and mice, putting them on a diet that has 30% fewer calories and high nutritional quality, can extend their lifespan up to 40% longer. Caloric restriction has also been shown to slow disease processes. This line of research is currently being extended to primates, and has yet to be proven with humans (NIA, 2007; Schneider, 1992).

Your Thoughts?

What social stigma might you face if you decided to reduce your caloric intake by 30%?

The third example of an error theory is the *crosslinking theory*, focused on the tendency of glucose (blood sugar) molecules to attach themselves to proteins, causing many further changes and reactions. For example, glucose may bond with collagen, causing lungs, arteries, tendons, and other tissues to stiffen. There is some evidence to suggest glucose crosslinking is associated with cataracts, reduced kidney function, Alzheimer's disease, and other age-related neurological disorders. A fourth example, the *free radical theory*, first proposed in the mid-1950s, highlights the accumulated damage caused by oxygen radicals. Oxygen is processed within cells by mitochondria to produce the energy needed for cells to function. However, in this process by-products called "oxygen free radicals" are also produced. Damage occurs when these free radicals steal electrons from other molecules, causing instability and other chain reactions. Researchers at the National Institute on Aging have called oxygen a "primary catalyst" for detrimental aging processes. Free radicals can also be caused by tobacco smoke, sun exposure, and other environmental factors. While we do know that our bodies use antioxidants to counter the effects of free radicals, it remains controversial as to whether antioxidant dietary supplements actually increase longevity (NIA, 2007). The final error theory example discussed here, the *somatic DNA damage theory*, emphasizes cell deterioration and malfunction due to genetic mutations that accumulate with age. DNA damage occurs over time and younger cells are generally equipped to make repairs as needed. With aging, it appears that the repairs become less efficient, possibly causing the breakdown of cells, tissues, and organs (NIA, 2007; Schneider, 1992). Considering the possible simultaneous and sequential occurrences of these mechanisms of aging, it becomes clearer as to why researchers are no longer searching for the one correct theory but rather seek to understand the potential interactions and complexities involved (Schneider, 1992). As technology continues to improve and researchers continue to learn more about these processes it is likely that neuropsychology will continue to be a key area in the study of adult development and aging.

Connectionist Approaches

Whereas biological theories emphasize the role of neuropsychology in the study of aging, ***connectionist approaches to development*** emphasize the role of cognitive psychology. Connectionist models were developed during the years following the ***cognitive revolution*** in psychology, marking the transition from the dominant behavioral or learning-based view of human nature (consistent with a mechanistic metatheoretical view) to a philosophy that embraced the study of cognition (and organismic models) as well as behaviors. The cognitive revolution, which occurred in the late 1950s and early 1960s, was sparked by interest in the development of language, memory, conceptual understanding, and other areas of complex cognitive processing. Simultaneous with this shift in psychological research was the emergence of computer technology. Psychologists quickly adopted the computer science model of information processing as the foundational model of human memory (Mason, 2004). Cognitive psychologists have continued to utilize the latest technologies, such as brain imaging equipment that allows observations of neuronal activity and brain changes with age, sophisticated software for mathematical modeling of cognitive processes, and artificial intelligence software for simulating human learning and development.

Your Thoughts?

Are you more likely to trust data produced from animal research or computer modeling? Give reasons to support your choice.

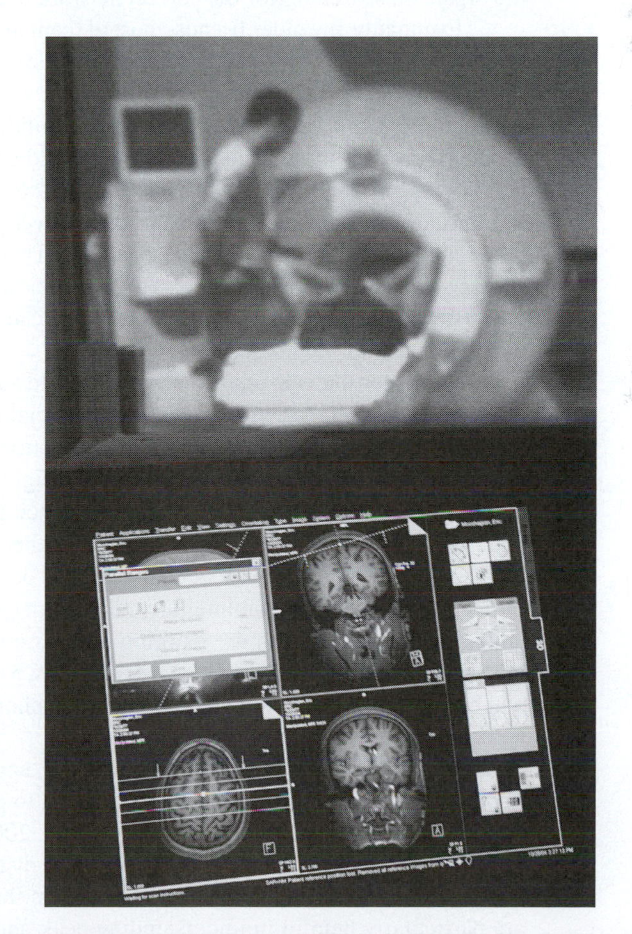

Most prominent in cognitive psychology, connectionist models are used to describe the ways brain cells and neural communication changes with age.

At their core, connectionist theories propose that development involves making associations between basic items or pieces of information, referred to as units, in order to form a network of associations. The process of connecting units is a gradual one requiring repetition, just as learning anything new often involves making many mistakes before good performances or desired outcomes become routine. Over time, distinct networks are formed for certain domains or areas (Munakata & McClelland, 2003). For example, consider the situation many grandparents found themselves in over the last few years as their children and grandchildren introduced computers into their world. I have watched several of my older friends take in units of information, such as the words *mouse*, *click*, and *window*, and connect them to new meanings and to each other in new ways. Before we had computer mice and computer clicks, how many people uttered the phrase "double-click the mouse"? As my friends became more familiar with navigating through computer software it became clear that they had made many connections between numerous units, thus building networks of understanding. Among these networks may be one for sending an e-mail, one for finding the weather forecast, and one for checking the balance in a bank account online. As networks grow in number and complexity, it is important that individuals choose (remember) the appropriate network that will bring about the desired outcome. When I would get a phone call from one of my older friends asking, "How did I send e-mail the last time?" the connectionist model would describe the situation as the organism searching for the correct network to activate.

Eventually, my older friends, most of them in their 70s, developed their networks of understanding enough that they could make reasonable guesses as to how to do things on the computer. These guesses, such as where to put the cursor and click, are weighted by probabilities calculated with data from previous experiences. A very confident guess is heavily weighted, and more likely to be acted upon, whereas a less confident wild guess is lightly weighted. For example, if the cursor changes from an arrow to a hand on the screen my friends have learned to click the mouse to activate a link to another website page. Over time they built a strong mental connection between the units of *hand icon*, *click*, and *link*. That connection has a heavily weighted probability of producing the desired outcome. If, for some strange reason, my friend experienced numerous incidents in which the hand icon didn't indicate a link to a different website page, the weight of that connection would decrease.

When computer science researchers build software programs to imitate human information processing, the *intelligent* aspect of artificial intelligence is that the software modifies its own mathematical equations to adjust connections between units and adjust weights, just as my friends learned to connect and heavily weight the association between the hand icon and clicking. When we say an artificial intelligence program is *learning*, that program is often choosing which network(s) to activate and then creating and adjusting its own weighted connections. If the environment changes, as in our example that the hand icon suddenly didn't indicate a place to click, an intelligent organism (person, animal, or software program) should adjust to the changes. As the learning process continues it will eventually lead to groups of networks and new understandings (Munakata & McClelland, 2003), as would be demonstrated when my friends begin to use computer metaphors in conversation or apply computer-based logic to other areas of life.

Your Thoughts?

What might be the disadvantages or potential drawbacks to the widespread acceptance and popularity of any metaphor for the brain?

Within the study of lifespan psychology, connectionist approaches have been helpful in understanding development that doesn't seem to consistently fit continuous or discontinuous (stage) trajectories (Munakata & McClelland, 2003; Thelen & Bates, 2003). They have also been helpful in understanding developmental disorders and critical periods, which are times of special sensitivity to external influences. In the study of aging, connectionist approaches are particularly helpful in understanding peak performance and decline in various aspects of brain functioning (Munakata & McClelland, 2003), particularly with memory and language processing (Lyddy, Barnes-Holmes, & Hampson, 2001; Thelen & Bates, 2003). Researchers are able imitate human cognition with software using connectionist models, make predictions, and test models in ways that are not physically or ethically possible with humans. For example, Lindfield and Wingfield (1999) collected data from younger and older adults on picture identification when the picture was degraded at various levels. Typically, older adults have more trouble determining the content of a degraded picture than younger adults. The researchers also created a connectionist model of the process with software, entered the data they collected, and showed that slower cognitive processing speed could account for the differences in the picture identification accuracy, and that stress caused by ignoring or inhibiting distracting information did not account for performance differences. In another study, Lyddy et al. (2001) were able to use connectionist modeling to determine which types of training or practice sessions would be best in learning particular language skills. This information could be helpful in understanding what has happened when adults lose some language ability, possibly due to stroke or dementia, and how to design therapies that may alleviate some of the loss. Connectionist approaches continue to dominate much of the research in cognitive processing. They allow researchers to mathematically model and then manipulate computer-simulate brain functions without causing any harm to human beings. These models allow for many of the types of development found in both mechanistic and organismic models, such as continuous and discontinuous growth, as well as interactions with environmental or external influences (Thelen & Bates, 2003), consistent with the contextual metatheory.

Sociocultural Theories

Your Thoughts?

Do you think it is still useful to debate the power of genetically based determinants (nature) and environmental shaping (nurture)? Why, why not, or under what circumstances?

The first two theoretical approaches discussed in this section emphasized personal or internal development while also acknowledging influences in the environment that shape development. Both approaches find their roots in the earlier mechanistic and organismic metatheories, with each emphasizing individual development. As lifespan developmental theory has evolved it now embraces as two of its core assumptions the powerful forces of historical embeddedness and contextualism on development. With that shift came a new interest in theories rooted in the study of external factors, but also acknowledged personal development. ***Sociocultural theories***, as their name implies, emphasize the social, cultural, and societal forces that shape human development. Perhaps the most well-known sociocultural theory, the ***bioecological theory*** developed by Bronfenbrenner, was originally applied to childhood and then later to the entire lifespan.

The main premise of the bioecological theory is that developmental outcomes are the result of multiple interactions between genetically based initial developmental processes and environmental experiences (Bronfenbrenner & Ceci, 1994). In order to understand the ways humans develop and adapt to changing environments, we must consider personal characteristics, the environmental context, the processes unfolding within the person and in the environment, and variability over time (Eamon, 2001). In the bioecological model these interactions are represented in a hierarchical model with the inner layers exerting a more direct impact on the individual as compared to the outer layers. Bronfenbrenner's notion of multiple-person systems and multiple levels of interactions distinguish it from other ecological models (Sontag, 1996).

The first group of interactions surrounding the individual is *microsystems*, the interpersonal relationships and immediate settings that are common to the individual (Bronfenbrenner, 1977). Who are the people you interact with routinely that influence your life? Your relationships with your friends, spouse or partner, roommate, parent, instructor, boss, or even a neighbor may be part of your microsystems. This category also includes the environments in which you usually see these people, such as home, work, or the classroom, and the role you play when interacting with these people in that setting, such as son, spouse, sales clerk, or student.

Your Thoughts?

Can you think of examples of role conflicts that are common among college students? Common among stay-at-home parents? How might the two be different?

The next layer of influence is *mesosystems*, the interactions between personal relationships. In other words, mesosystems are groups of microsystems (Bronfenbrenner, 1977). Have you ever felt tension in one area of your life, such as at work or in the classroom, and then transferred that tension to another area of life, such as inflicting your bad mood on your friends or roommate? Have your roles ever been in conflict? For example, your role as a student may indicate you should be studying for an exam but your role as an employee is challenging that because your supervisor wants you to report to work. These types of situations, in which one relationship is directly affecting another relationship, are occurring in your mesosystems.

The third layer of influence in the bioecological theory is *exosystems.* This layer contains the people, institutions, or policies that have a powerful influence on an individual but generally are removed or distant (Bronfenbrenner, 1977). For example, if you are a public school teacher and your state-level Department of Education decides that changes are needed then you will be forced to adjust to those changes. Perhaps the changes involve taking additional courses or attending training sessions, or something more disruptive such as consolidating schools or changing the academic calendar for year-round classes. In this example you may not have ever met the actual people who made these decisions, nor were you involved directly in the decision-making process. The changes made by this exosystem influence, the state Department of Education, have caused you to change your behaviors. Other exosystem influences may be found in government, health care, and insurance agencies.

The fourth layer is *macrosystems*, containing cultural and societal roles, norms, and expectations that influence development. Bronfenbrenner (1977) views macrosystems as unique from microsystems, mesosystems, or exosystems in that they are less specific to particular relationships or environments. Macrosystems contain unwritten but powerful cultural and societal rules and assumptions, such as how people should dress and act in certain settings. If you are a member of an ethnic or religious culture in which the general expectation is to avoid eating meat or avoid taking in caffeine, that influence is a part of your macrosystem. If you are male and a member of a culture in which men do not wear anything approaching a skirt, such as a kilt, and you show up for work one day in a skirt or kilt, you will likely experience ridicule and punishment for violating that macrosystem expectation.

Another group of influences, again different from microsystems, mesosystems, and exosystems, are those captured in chronosystems. More than change over time in one area of life, *chronosystems* contain the dynamic interactions of the changes with time within the individual, the other systems, and the larger environment (Bronfenbrenner, 1986). To illustrate the chronosystem, imagine a teacher just beginning her career in 1980. Consider what her primary work-related stresses might be and how she might handle them. Consider what she might worry about. For example, she may be very concerned about the impression she is making on the more experienced teachers and as a result analyzes everything they say to her. Now, in your imagination, move her up to the current year. She now has over 25 years of teaching experience and is close to retirement. Chronosystems remind us that she is likely to have different priorities and handle stresses differently than she did in 1980. She is likely to have changed with age, developing a different notion of what is worthy of worry and concern and what isn't. Also, her peers and supervisors have changed, either in their own personal development, or quite literally she has different peers and supervisors. Societal changes and advances in technology have transformed her job into something substantially different from when she started in 1980. Chronosystems provide a way to characterize and account for changes in the personal, interpersonal, social, and cultural influences over time.

Your Thoughts?

In which area have you experienced the most chronosystem change across the last 10 years: personal characteristics, relationships, or culture?

Sociocultural theories, as exemplified by the bioecological model, are consistent with the contextual metatheory in their emphasis on the individual and the environment. Different from the biological theories and connectionist models, these theories are focused more on the social and cultural environments in which the individual is developing. As can be seen in the bioecological model, the primary areas of research are likely to be the interpersonal relationships, relationships among those interpersonal relationships, and various other external forces that affect the developing individual.

Selection, Optimization, and Compensation Theory

The ***selection, optimization, and compensation theory*** of development (SOC) provides a structure around which researchers can organize data about aging and make predictions about future courses of action. Similar to several theories discussed in this section, the SOC theory grew out of a specialized area, in this case resource allocation and coping, to become a more widely applied theory. While all the theories detailed in this section are among the most frequently employed in the study of adult development and aging, the SOC theory continues to gather momentum in the field, perhaps toward a position as the most prominent theory in recent years. It has been even described as a "heuristic tool" or unifying construct that can bring together many areas of knowledge about human development and aging (Riediger et al., 2006). Baltes, well known and respected for his work in lifespan developmental theory, developed the SOC theory as a model of adaptation, describing the ways individuals manage the gains and losses in each phase of life. As we age we seek ways to minimize losses or impairment while maximizing areas of gain and growth, which is the foundation of the SOC model (Baltes et al., 1999; Riediger et al., 2006).

To illustrate the SOC model consider a hypothetical great-grandmother who is widowed and living alone, with a small, fixed income. We'll call her Irene. She is limited in how she can spend her time, energy, and money, and must use the selection function of the SOC theory to choose her priorities and goals. There are many things she would like to do, such as exercise, knit, read, travel, garden, care for great-grandchildren, organize and cook for large family gatherings, and be active in her religious community. Irene knows she cannot possibly do all those things, so she must remain realistic in her choices. She will use the selection component of the SOC approach to problem solving to choose her best options or most important goals (Baltes et al., 1999). She will use a combination of *loss-based selection*, such as accepting the fact that her adult children are busy and have little time to drive her around town, thus putting some constraints on her options, and *elective selection*, determining that spending time with her family is her most important priority. Her focus then becomes searching for ways to contribute to family interaction. When applied to the area of motivation, the selection component of the SOC involves determining one's needs, goals, or priorities (Riediger et al., 2006).

Your Thoughts?

Thinking of all you would like to accomplish in the next 5 years, what two things are the most important?

The optimization and compensation components of the SOC model, when applied to motivation, reflect the choices and behaviors chosen to support the selected goals and to avoid undesired outcomes. Once Irene has selected family interaction as her priority, now she must be proactive in optimizing her resources. For example, if she is presented with a new opportunity, demand, or task, such as a new knitting group in her religious community or a new garden club at the community center, she will evaluate those opportunities in terms of her goals (Riediger et al., 2006). If she determines that these options will take away from her time with her family then she will likely turn them down. On the other hand, if she can get her siblings or grandchildren to go with her to some of the gatherings, then she may choose to get involved.

Your Thoughts?

What choices are you making to optimize the chances that you achieve those goals?

Irene must also compensate for the losses that come with age, such as the loss of her ability to drive her car. Compensation may be in the form of making changes to achieve the desired goals through another route or may require individuals to revise their selected options or goals (Baltes et al., 1999). She may make some changes, such as choosing to attend the religious community of her closest family members so that she can get a ride with them and spend some time with them. She may also make an effort to talk to relatives by phone more often. Optimization and compensation work together to support selected needs and goals (Riediger et al., 2006). Irene may utilize her resources (optimization) by, upon hearing that a family member is getting a new computer, asking for the old one and lessons on how to send e-mail (to compensate for not being able to drive to see relatives). This maintains her goal of staying involved with her family through the computer lessons and her eventual communication through e-mail.

The SOC model is perhaps the most encompassing of the theories explored here. It allows for many individual differences, personal circumstances, and larger environmental influences (Riediger et al., 2006), making it consistent with the contextual metatheory. The options individuals select, and their needs in terms of optimization and compensation, will be influenced by their genetic predispositions as well as their physical and social environmental influences. Baltes (1997) views both the biological potential one has and support from culture-based resources as important in optimizing human development across the lifespan. In their review of the literature for the sixth edition of the *Handbook of the Psychology of Aging*, Riediger and colleagues (2006) suggest that one of the next steps in the use of the SOC should be with connectionist models in order to develop formal, mathematical models of resource allocation and adaptation.

Section Summary

- The biological theories emphasize the ways our genetically initiated developmental processes are shaped by external influences.
- Programmed theories, including the programmed longevity theory, the endocrine theory, and the immunological theory, operate with the basic assumption that a biological timetable controls the aging process.
- Error theories, such as the wear and tear theory, rate of living theory, crosslinking theory, free radical theory, and the somatic DNA damage theory, focus on the ways environmental forces affect the maturation of genetically initiated processes over time.
- The connectionist approaches to human development emphasize the development of cognitive networks that form the foundation of all thought processes. Researchers are able to imitate human cognitive processing with software-based mathematical models, and then manipulate the models in ways that would be impossible or unethical with human participants.
- In contrast to the first two theories, sociocultural theories focus more on the larger external forces that shape behavior, such as societal and cultural expectations.
- The bioecological theory, an example of a sociocultural theory, emphasizes the interaction among relationships and environmental factors, which are categorized into microsystems, mesosystems, exosystems, macrosystems, and chronosystems.
- The selection, optimization, and compensation theory describes the ways individuals manage the gains and losses accompanying each phase of life by selecting the best option from realistic choices, optimizing strengths and resources, and compensating for losses by adjusting strategies or goals.

Scientific Study of Adult Development and Aging

As the field of psychology emerged in the late 1800s it was shaped by its foundational disciplines, primarily physics, medicine, biology, and philosophy. Those disciplines relied heavily on logical, scientifically determined methodologies and interpretations. This tradition continues in psychology today, as can be seen in the ever-growing numbers of research-based articles and books published each year. To understand the latest developments in psychological theory or therapy in the most complete way, one must have a basic understanding of psychological research.

Scientific Approach

One of the defining features of the field of psychology is its reliance on scientifically informed methods of data collection, analysis, and interpretation in order to determine the usefulness and value or "believability" of any statement about human thoughts or behaviors. This reliance on scientific methods and procedures distinguishes psychology from everyday reasoning. At some level all of us must make predictions about our own or someone else's thoughts or behaviors. When we decide to trust someone we are making the prediction that, based on our observations and past experience, this person will be honest and trustworthy. It is likely that across your lifetime you've experienced both the correct prediction, when you thought you could trust someone and you were right, and the wrong prediction, when you trusted someone only to realize later that the person was not trustworthy. It's also likely that you have experienced the same mix of correct and incorrect predictions about yourself. Have you ever had any of these experiences?

Your Thoughts?

What factors might contribute to the observation that some people will follow a superstition even when scientific analysis doesn't support it?

- I thought I had more money in the bank—I haven't spent that much, have I?
- My phone bill shouldn't be this high—I didn't spend that much time on the phone, did I?
- I didn't miss that many typing errors in my paper—did I?
- I can't be gaining weight—I haven't eaten that much, have I?

Psychologists have learned that, while we may think we are fairly good at observing ourselves and others, often our impressions are swayed by personal bias. And, since psychologists are people too, who are just as vulnerable to bias as anyone else, we rely on the methods of science in order to stay as objective in our work as possible.

The goals of accuracy, rigor, and objectivity in collecting and interpreting data are some of the primary motivations for psychologists to use scientific techniques. For example, in order to find out if you had really spent as much money as the bank statement indicates, you need to analyze the data. If you are one who keeps sloppy records or doesn't keep receipts, then your data is incomplete and you cannot determine anything about your transactions. Accuracy in data collection is critical. Perhaps you have the records but you don't know how to figure out the interest, charges, and fees involved in confirming or discounting the bank's assessment of your account. It is important for you and for researchers to know and apply the appropriate formulas and statistical procedures to correctly interpret data. Just like the bank won't change your records because you have a hunch or a feeling that you haven't spent as much money as they say, all those who rely on the outcomes of psychological research shouldn't be comfortable with hunches or guesses either. The conducting of high-quality research requires, at a minimum and as much as possible, accurate data collection, the application of appropriate statistical analysis, strict and rigorous interpretation, and logically sound conclusions.

Ethically Sound Research

High-quality research is also ethically sound research. Important ethical safeguards are not only beneficial to all involved and strongly encouraged by professional associations, they are required by law for any research involving human or animal participants. Once an investigation is thoroughly planned, but before any data is collected, researchers must seek approval from every relevant review board. Any institution through which research is conducted, including universities, medical centers, government agencies, and corporations, should have a group of peers who serve as the ***Institutional Review Board*** (IRB). It is the role of the IRB to protect the researchers, participants, and all institutions involved by ensuring compliance with established federal guidelines. In some cases researchers may need to work with several boards. For example, a university professor who receives a grant from the National Science Foundation (NSF) to study the psychological adjustment of cancer patients in a regional medical center will need approvals from IRBs at the university, NSF, and medical center.

Those who are new to social sciences research procedures may be surprised at the intensity and rigor with which researchers approach ethical guidelines. We have learned from human history that such guidelines are needed. One of the most frequently cited breaches of human trust and judgment in the United States is the Tuskegee Syphilis Study, which began in the early 1930s and continued into the 1970s. Through the Tuskegee Institute in rural Alabama, 399 men who were thought to have late-stage syphilis were prevented from receiving treatment so that scientists could observe the progression of the disease. The men were told they had "bad blood" and were offered free treatment (which was actually no treatment). To make matters even worse, the researchers conducting the study, who worked for the United States Public Health Service, continued to let the men suffer even after it was discovered that penicillin would help and possibly cure the men's disease (Fairchild & Bayer, 1999).

Your Thoughts?

Do you think such a large violation of medical ethics could happen now?

In 1979 the U.S. Department of Health, Education, and Welfare published *The Belmont Report*, designed to provide researchers in biomedical and behavioral areas with ethical guidelines. The guidelines have been expanded to cover a wider variety of types of research and accommodate new technologies. Most of the research discussed in this book involving human participants required compliance with the guidelines set in Code of Federal Regulations, Title 45 Public Welfare, Part 46 Protection of Human Subjects (Office of Human Subjects Research, 2005). These codes define the role of IRBs, establish criteria that all studies should comply with, and give additional guidelines for particular groups of people, some of which are frequently involved in studies of adult development and aging. Called *Special Classes of Subjects* (Office for Human Research Protections, n.d.), these groups include:

- Fetuses and Human In Vitro Fertilization
- Pregnant and Nursing Women
- Children and Minors
- Cognitively Impaired Persons
- Traumatized and Comatose Patients
- Terminally Ill Patients
- Elderly/Aged Persons
- Minorities
- Students, Employees, and Volunteers
- Prisoners
- Participants in International Research Studies

Individuals who serve on IRB committees should be knowledgeable of the federal guidelines and work with researchers in achieving compliance. Research involving animals requires approval from a board similar to the IRB, the ***Institutional Animal Care and Use Committee*** (IACUC). These federally mandated animal-use committees should be established at all research institutions along with IRBs to ensure compliance with Animal Welfare Act guidelines.

Among the important topics covered in the federal guidelines for research with human participants is the requirement of ***informed consent***. Unless special permission is received, any individual who will have the opportunity to participate in a research study should be given enough information prior to the study to decide whether or not to participate. This usually takes the form of a written document to be read and signed by the participant *before* the study is started. This document details what the participants will do in the study, what the benefits of the study are, and how participants' data will be kept confidential. Extra steps are needed when the participants are recruited from the special groups listed above.

While the principle of informed consent is highly valued among researchers, there are some studies in which offering complete information to the participants prior to the study may cause the subjects to alter their responses. Consider, for example, gender bias as a research topic. Do college professors treat male and female students differently? Are employers swayed by gender when hiring? These sorts of questions are difficult to answer. What responses do you think we would get if we simply asked professors or employers if they behave differently toward males or females? It is likely that most people would say they are not gender biased and treat all people the same. It is also likely that if we said to professors or employers, "We are studying gender bias and would like your honest opinion on these questions" that, once

Most research studies begin with participants reading and signing an Informed Consent form.

Your Thoughts?

Would you have a negative reaction to learning that you participated in a study involving deception? Why, why not, or under what circumstances?

attention is drawn to gender, the participants would be extra careful to avoid gender-biased responses. So, how might researchers get a more accurate sample of behavior? One possibility is to ask professors and employers to "evaluate characters' personalities" based on scenarios depicting people in various situations. Professors could be given stories of students' behaviors while working on a group project and employers could be given stories of applicants' behaviors during interviews. By securing IRB approval to use ***deception***, researchers could omit any reference to gender in the informed consent document. Deception, in a research context, occurs when information is withheld and/or participants are given false or misleading information. What the professors and employers would not be told is that some of them would receive certain scenarios with characters with male names, while other participants would receive the exact same scenarios except that the characters had female names. Participants would still be asked to sign typical informed consent documents; however, the documents would indicate that the point of the study was to learn more about professors' or employers' personality evaluations. When deception is used it should always be followed by some form of ***debriefing***. The professors and employers should be told after the study what the real purpose of the study was. Review boards will require researchers to have a plan prior to the study for the debriefing process.

The federal guidelines for protecting human participants and animals in research detail the minimum, foundational guidelines that all researchers must follow. In addition to these guidelines, various professional organizations often have additional criteria they strongly encourage researchers to employ. Any research conducted in the field of psychology should be in compliance with the current edition of the American Psychological Association's (APA) ethics code. The most recent version of the *Ethical Principles of Psychologists and Code of Conduct*, published in 2003, is consistent with federal guidelines wherever they apply, but goes beyond them to give direction in regard to plagiarism, publication credits, sharing data for verification, and the selection of research reviewers. In addition to research guidelines, the APA ethics code also addresses testing and assessment, therapy, education and training, privacy, and other issues involved in providing psychological services.

Deciphering Psychological Research

The majority of Americans will learn of psychological research through the media, relying on reporters and journalists to decipher scientific writings and communicate the latest findings. Students in the study of adult development and aging (or any area of psychology for that matter) need to know how to go beyond quick media presentations to the original scientific works. Several years ago I heard a local news report that gave the impression scientists had discovered that women who give birth at an older age will live longer. I thought it sounded odd that giving birth in her 50s would *cause* a woman to live longer than most other women. I did some background research and found that the story came from a misinterpretation of data collected in the New England Centenarian Study. The ongoing study of men 100 years old and older and women 102 years old and older indicated that women who live such a long time seem to age slower in all respects, including a later age for menopause. The point wasn't that giving birth at a later age *caused* women to live longer, the point was that these women often did give birth at a later age because they had delayed menopause, thus they could (and did) get pregnant at a later age than most women (Boston University School of Medicine, 2007).

Your Thoughts?

Have you ever found an error in a media report?

Often the next step for those who want to go beyond media reports is to turn to articles published in scientific journals. The savvy reader must still beware of the varying levels of quality of journals. Top-tier journals are those with the most rigorous approval process, usually involving review and approval from other scholars, as well as the best reputations and often a long history of publishing high-quality research. Once quality scholarly articles are found, the reader will soon realize that they are organized in generally the same manner:

- Literature Review and Hypotheses
- Research Designs
- Measurements, Methods, and Procedures
- Analyses and Results
- Discussion and Conclusions

That same progression will be followed in the Research Appendix when introducing the basic concepts needed to decipher a journal article. The Appendix includes an overview of basic vocabulary, ways of designing studies, and collecting and analyzing data. Keep in mind that this presentation is far from comprehensive or advanced. Indeed, students in the social sciences often take numerous courses in research design and analysis. Also, research involving computer modeling and highly sophisticated statistical procedures is beyond the scope of this section.

In addition to the concepts presented in the Research Appendix, each chapter contains a Research In-Depth section that introduces an aspect of research through the detailed look at one or more published research studies. Each Research In-Depth section focuses on a study exploring a topic covered in that particular chapter. To get the most from each Research In-Depth section it would be helpful to read the Research Appendix fully before reading through the other chapters in the book, and then refer to it as needed.

Section Summary

- Psychology relies on scientifically informed methods of data collection, analysis, and interpretation in order to provide objectivity in reporting research findings.
- IRB approval of a research study involves taking the appropriate steps to ensure informed consent or proper procedures if deception is used, confidentiality, and participant protections as needed.
- For members of the general public who wish to be as informed as possible, and wish to check popular media reports, the next step in understanding may be to read journal articles.
- The Research Appendix and the Research In-Depth sections of each chapter provide the reader with a basic understanding of the structure of an article, design, data collection, and statistical analysis.

Chapter Summary

The study of adulthood and aging is rapidly growing. New technologies and increased numbers of older adults are among the many forces contributing to the growth of the field. Metatheories have guided researchers as new waves of interest have emerged, moving from a mechanistic to an organismic to a contextual approach. Much of the current work in the field is guided by biological theories, connectionist approaches, sociocultural theories, and the selection, optimization, and compensation theory. Regardless of the approach, psychology is a research-based endeavor, thus it is important to review the key principles of good research, including sound design and ethical compliance. Here are some of the main points from this introductory chapter:

- Societies in high-income, developed countries, including the United States, are experiencing a dramatic increase in the numbers of adults living into their 60s and beyond.
- It is projected that by 2050 the United States will have over 86 million citizens age 65 years and older and over 20 million age 85 years and older.
- The field of adult development and aging is challenged by such issues as balancing emphasis across all of adulthood and limitations in research designs.
- Psychology can be partitioned into subsections of theoretical, methodological, empirical, and applied work.
- The study of aging took hold in many social sciences in the 1940s, developing into an area of study that is both multidisciplinary and multifaceted with specific disciplines.
- Currently, the study of adult development and aging, within the field of developmental psychology, is striving to further the understanding of features that remain stable, those that decline, and those that grow and develop in positive and productive ways with age.
- Acknowledging that in adulthood one's chronological age doesn't provide much information, the use of functional age, consisting of one's biological, psychological, and social ages, is preferred.
- In addition to functional age, it is important to consider the normative age-graded, normative history-graded, and non-normative influences experienced by individual adults.
- The mechanistic metatheory highlights the role of the environment and the individual's response to it, producing a continuous flow of increase, plateau, or decline in various human functions.
- The organismic metatheory highlights the development of internal, predetermined stages that unfold through maturation and stimulation from the environment.
- The contextual metatheory, the dominant theory in lifespan psychology, emphasizes the bidirectional interaction of internal forces, such as genetically predetermined patterns and individual differences, and external forces, such as culture, experience, and other environmental factors.
- Biological theories of aging, consisting of programmed and error theories, emphasize the interaction of genetic influences, maturation, and environmental influences on the aging process.
- Connectionist theories, prominent in cognitive psychology, emphasize the building of networks based on connected units of information.
- Sociocultural theories emphasize the influence of environmental or external forces on development, as illustrated in the components of the bioecological theory, the microsystems, mesosystems, exosystems, macrosystems, and chronosystems.
- The selection, optimization, and compensation theory emphasizes the choices individuals make in their environment by selecting the most important goals or needs, optimizing resources in order to better meet their selected goals, and compensating for losses by either selecting new strategies or selecting adjusted goals.
- Psychology, drawing on its evolution from physics, biology, medicine, and philosophy, uses scientific methods and procedures, appropriate statistical analysis, and logically sound interpretation to try to remain as clear and objective in research as possible.

- In order to receive approval for a study from an IRB, researchers must follow all the federally mandated guidelines, which include informed consent, protection of participants, confidentiality, and the presentation of the case that the potential benefits will outweigh the potential risks involved.
- It is important to be skeptical of media reports of scientific research, and in some cases to go to the articles and books that present the original data.

Key Terms

Continuing education units (CEUs) **(3)**
Federal Interagency Forum on Aging-Related Statistics **(4)**
Psychology **(7)**
Developmental psychology **(7)**
Adult development and aging **(7)**
Positive psychology **(10)**
Optimal aging **(10)**
Chronological age **(12)**
Normative age-graded influences **(12)**
Functional age **(12)**
Biological age **(12)**
Biomarker **(12)**
Psychological age **(12)**
Social age **(12)**
Normative history-graded influences **(12)**
Cohort **(13)**
Cross-sectional design **(14)**
Variable **(14)**
Longitudinal design **(14**
Non-normative influences **(15)**
Mechanistic metatheory **(15)**
Quantitative design **(16)**
Continuous development **(16)**
Organismic metatheory **(16)**
Discontinuous development **(16)**
Qualitative design **(16)**
Contextual metatheory **(17)**
Neuropsychology **(19)**
Programmed theories of biological aging **(19)**
Error theories of biological aging **(19)**
Connectionist approaches to development **(21)**
Cognitive revolution **(21)**
Sociocultural theories of development **(23)**
Bioecological theory **(23)**
Selection, optimization, and compensation theory **(25)**
Institutional Review Board (IRB) **(28)**
Institutional Animal Care and Use Committee (IACUC) **(29)**
Informed consent **(29)**
Deception in research **(30)**
Debriefing **(30)**

Comprehension Questions

1. Give two pieces of data to show that, historically speaking, it is a recent phenomenon to have such a large percentage of older adults in American society.
2. What are two challenging issues faced by those working in the field of adulthood and aging?
3. Give an example illustrating the multidisciplinary aspect of the study of adult development.
4. Describe the history of the study of adult development.
5. What does the term "positive psychology" refer to?
6. Name and explain the three components of functional age.
7. Explain the concepts of normative age-graded, normative history-graded, and non-normative influences, and give an example of each.
8. Compare and contrast the primary characteristics of the mechanistic, organismic, and contextual metatheories.
9. What are the seven core assumptions of lifespan developmental theory?
10. Name and describe one example of a programmed theory and an error theory of biological aging.
11. How is a connectionist model built, and how does this hypothesized human process relate to computer software processing?

12. Name and describe the influences categorized by each of the five components of the bioecological theory of human development.
13. Explain how the use of selection, optimization, and compensation can help individuals fulfill their realistic potential.
14. Describe at least two characteristics of high-quality research based on scientific methods and procedures.
15. What are the primary items an IRB will look for in a research study?
16. Explain the concepts of informed consent and deception as they are used in a research study.

Answers for Common Sense: Myth or Reality?

1. Reality: The life expectancy for Americans born in 1900 was less than 50 years old. (See An Aging Population, page 3.)
2. Myth: In 2005 the U.S. Census Bureau found that nearly 25% of all Americans age 65 years and older were living below the poverty line. (See An Aging Population, page 3.)
3. Reality: Based on U.S. Census Bureau data, it is projected that there will be over 20 million Americans age 85 and older by the year 2050. (See An Aging Population, page 3.)
4. Myth: When considering research on young, middle, and late adulthood, most of the emphasis is on middle-aged adults. (See Challenging Issues, page 6.)
5. Myth: To say that someone is "immature for her age" is to say that her social age is very young. (See Functional Age, page 12.)
6. Myth: The dominant view of adult development is that it occurs in stages. (See Contextual Metatheory, page 17.)
7. Myth: Most researchers studying the biological foundations of aging are searching for the one major gene that controls the aging process. (See Biological Theories, page 19.)
8. Reality: One of the major theoretical approaches to adult development, connectionist approaches, emphasizes mathematical modeling of human thinking processes. (See Connectionist Approaches, page 21.)
9. Reality: Federal guidelines for research involving human beings allow for researchers to deceive participants by not revealing the real purpose of a study. (See Ethically Sound Research, page 30.)

Suggested Readings

Historical View: Psychology As More Than Experimental Science

Cronbach, L. J. (1957). The two disciplines of scientific psychology. *American Psychologist, 12*, 671–684. [1957 APA Presidential Address.] Accessed at *Classics in the History of Psychology* (http://psychclassics.yorku.ca/topic.htm).

Cultural Approaches to Lifespan Development

Trommsdorff, G. (2002). An eco-cultural and interpersonal relations approach to development of the lifespan. In W. J. Lonner, D. L. Dinnel, S. A. Hayes, & D. N. Sattler (Eds.), *Online readings in psychology and culture* (Unit 12, Chapter 1), (http://www.wwu.edu/~culture), Center for Cross-Cultural Research, Western Washington University, Bellingham, WA. Available at http://www.ac.wwu.edu/~culture/Trommsdorff.htm.

Ethical Challenges in the Twenty-First Century

Koocher, G. P. (2007). Twenty-first century ethical challenges for psychology. *American Psychologist, 62*(5), 375–384.

Basic Research Ethics

Prieto, L. R. (2006). Research ethics and the APA Code. From Psi Chi National Honor Society in Psychology, Distinguished Lectures Series. This article can be found at http://www.psichi.org/pubs/articles/article_536.asp.

Suggested Websites

Divisions of the American Psychological Association

To learn more about the special interest areas within APA you can explore the Divisions at http://www.apa.org/about/division.html. Specifically, APA Division 20, Adult Development and Aging, can be found at http://apadiv20.phhp.ufl.edu.

Sections of the American Sociological Association

To further contrast psychology and sociology you can explore the sections of the ASA at http://www.asanet.org/cs/root/leftnav/sections/overview and the section for Aging and the Life-Course at http://www2.asanet.org/sectionaging/.

Links at the Association for Psychological Science

Another extensive list of areas within psychology is provided by the Association for Psychological Science at http://www.psychologicalscience.org/about/links.cfm. You'll find many interesting topics, several that include an interest in adult development and aging.

Ethical Principles and Code of Conduct, American Psychological Association

To learn more about the ethical foundations of psychological research you can browse the Ethical Principles of Psychologists and Code of Conduct at http://www.apa.org/ethics/code.html and the Guidelines for Ethical Conduct in the Care and Use of Animals at http://www.apa.org/science/anguide.html.

CHAPTER

2 Individual and Multicultural Differences

This chapter introduces some of the complexities social scientists encounter when trying to describe large groups of people in general terms. While it is common knowledge that people differ, and sometimes those differences may be used to define a particular subgroup of the population, psychologists have generally been more concerned with broad patterns or similarities in humans rather than more precise differences. In accord with the increased sensitivity to global diversity and the growing minority populations within the United States, social scientists are now fully engaged in cross-cultural, multicultural, and individual-differences research. This can be seen in the growing number of books and journal articles related to individual and multicultural issues and in institutional actions, such as the APA's publication of guidelines for research, training, and therapy with various minority groups.

This chapter is limited in several ways. When considering such a large topic as the many ways human beings might differ and the implications of those differences, there are obviously boundaries limiting the amount of material that can be presented in a few pages. This chapter is designed to introduce and raise awareness of individual and multicultural characteristics, not to fully explore them. The purpose here is not, however, to present diversity issues and then drop these topics for the rest of the book, but rather to present basic information, allowing for diversity issues to be discussed throughout the book. For example, in this chapter we consider gender as a social construct and as a research variable, but we do not consider gender as it relates to all the other chapter topics. Gender, along with the other topic areas discussed here, is discussed many times throughout the book.

A second limitation of the chapter is that while acknowledging that there are many types and layers of individual, cultural, and group characteristics, it is beyond the scope of this chapter to discuss all types of diversity or the various interactions among cultural characteristics.

COMMON SENSE
Myth or Reality?

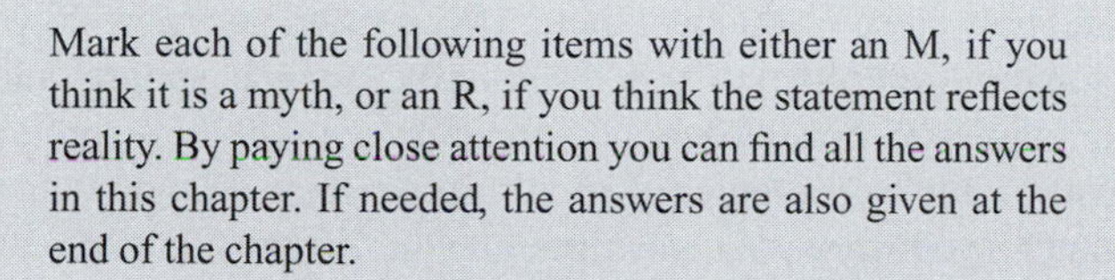

Mark each of the following items with either an M, if you think it is a myth, or an R, if you think the statement reflects reality. By paying close attention you can find all the answers in this chapter. If needed, the answers are also given at the end of the chapter.

1. _____ The study of cross-cultural and multicultural issues has been a priority in psychology since the discipline began.
2. _____ The U.S. Census data from 2005 revealed that approximately 75% of all men ages 65 years and older were married while approximately 45% of all women in that age range were married.
3. _____ Federal agencies estimate that by the year 2050 the Hispanic population will comprise the largest racial minority in the United States.
4. _____ Older adults report higher life satisfaction than young adults.
5. _____ Gender identity is generally formed by about 5 years of age and remains stable throughout adulthood.
6. _____ Researchers have found little differences in the areas of verbal ability and verbal memory in older men and women.
7. _____ When dividing Americans into cultural groups those whose heritage is Chinese, Pakistani, and Hawaiian are usually put together under the label of "Asian Americans."
8. _____ The second half of the last century saw a dramatic increase in the number of participants in non-Christian religions in the United States.
9. _____ Although religions differ in their specifics, they are basically the same in structure, such as having holy writings, worship of one Deity, and engaging in similar lifestyle choices.
10. _____ Humans tend to notice more differences in people in their "in-group" and assume that people in the "out-group" are all quite similar.

For example, when considering racial and ethnic diversity it is easier to categorize Latino Americans as distinct and unique from Caucasian Americans rather than account for individuals with varying degrees of multiracial or multiethnic backgrounds. Though more convenient in research, such reasoning does not consider the differences within cultures. Regardless of these complexities, it is most important that all of us sensitize ourselves to areas of difference.

Before We Get Started . . .

Suppose you and I were introduced for the first time, and I challenged you with this request: "Tell me the 10 most descriptive pieces of information about you that will give me an accurate impression of who you are." What would you say? Take a minute to list 8 or 10 of the most descriptive, characteristic features about yourself. Try not to worry about consistency—you can mix adjectives, roles, titles, whatever seems to stand out. Try not to analyze your responses at this point. Find a convenient place to number from 1 to 10 and list the words that represent your most descriptive characteristics.

Are you finished? Let's compare lists. My list, not in any particular order, would look something like this: wife, psychology professor, short, spiritual, happy, grandmother, workaholic, collects things with crescent moons, American football fan, loves the ocean, and reads a lot. What similarities and differences do you find when comparing our lists?

Trying to understand the influence of culture and individual differences is much like trying to figure out why you picked the items you did. For example, did you put your age on your list? Sometimes age is an important characteristic. I often hear college students planning something big when a friend is turning 21 years old. As another example, I have a friend who just turned 80 years old and is very proud of her age. I would guess that "80 years old" would be on her list. Did you list anything that references your gender? Race or ethnicity? Religion? Political views? Favorite sports team or entertainers? There are many types of characteristics you could have put on your list, such as terms referring to your primary relationships, cultural heritage, physical attributes or health, material items, occupation or college major, career choice, hobbies, and emotional and personality characteristics.

Now consider stereotypes and how closely you meet them. If you listed your age, do you believe you fit the stereotype of someone your age? If you listed a role, such as spouse, adult child, student, basketball player, or employee, how closely do you believe you fit the stereotype of someone in that role? If you listed your race, ethnicity, or cultural heritage, do you believe you fit the stereotype for that group? As you work your way through your list I would guess that there are areas for which you are saying to yourself, "No, I'm not like the typical _____ or the stereotypical _____ at all." Keep in mind that others are saying that too. It's always good to be reminded that even though we have a habit of grouping people, each person in that group has consistent and inconsistent characteristics in terms of the group stereotype, just like you do.

Individual and Group Differences

Your Thoughts?

Do you spend time with people who are culturally different from you?

Psychologists have considered individual characteristics and differences for much longer than sociocultural, multicultural, and cross-cultural differences. Although recent research in aging and individual differences can be found in many distinct areas, such as sleep stages (Bliwise & Bergmann, 1987), leisure skills (Janke, Davey, & Kleiber, 2006), and patterns of disease (Dupre, 2007), a large portion of it is focused on cognitive functioning (Backman et al., 2004) and brain activity (Fabiani, Friedman, & Cheng, 1998), including working memory (Mejia, Pineda, Alvarez, & Ardila, 1998), verbal and spatial memory, and sensorimotor functioning (Shu-Chen, Aggen, Nesselroade, & Baltes, 2001). Interest in cross-cultural and multicultural research within the United States was slow to gain notice and momentum, but once interest developed among psychologists and other researchers in the 1970s and 1980s the field has expanded rapidly. In order to fully understand both the advances and limitations of social science research it is important to continually balance large, broad generalizations of what is typical with the knowledge that there is a great deal of variation and diversity within those generalizations.

Psychological Study of Human Differences

Work began early in psychology's existence in the area of individual differences. The emphasis was on measuring individual traits, such as intelligence, memory, and various personality traits, with much of this early work done in educational, employment, and counseling or therapeutic settings (Dawis, 1992). These early psychologists focused on developing precise testing instruments and corresponding theoretical and mathematical formulae used to quantify various traits. Teachers, employers, and therapists were interested in identifying individuals whose measurements or scores were higher or lower than what was determined to be the average or normal. Over the years the psychological study of measuring individual differences has expanded to form another area of study, ***psychometrics***, and to consider the precursors leading to the development of personal differences as well as related effects (Dawis, 1992).

Psychology as a field of study has been described as "reluctant to recognize culture" (Segall, Lonner, & Berry, 1998) as it relates to other areas of interest. Prior to the middle of the 20th century, roughly the first 80 years of the discipline's existence, psychologists were not active in cross-cultural or multicultural research. Viewing cultural research as the realm of other academic fields, psychologists investigated what they believed to be universal mental and behavioral patterns (Bernal, Trimble, Burlew, & Leong, 2003).

In was in the 1960s that journals publishing specifically cross-cultural psychological research began to appear. The International Association for Cross-Cultural Psychology was formed in 1972, and by 1973 its membership had grown to over 1,000. Since then there has

Your Thoughts?

What might be the advantages of being a member of one of these professional groups?

been a steady increase in activity and interest in cultural psychology (Bernal et al., 2003; Segall et al., 1998). During this time of rapid change numerous groups within professional psychology formed to explore cultural diversity. In 1968 the Association of Black Psychologists organized, with one of its goals to bring more awareness of diversity to the American Psychological Association. Soon after, the Asian American Psychological Association (1972), Society of Indian Psychologists (1975), and the National Hispanic Psychological Association (1979) organized (Suinn, 1999).

It was also in the 1960s and 1970s that American Psychological Association divisions specifically focused on diverse populations began to appear. While researchers could conduct research on culture and difference within their own divisions, such as a member of the Adult Development and Aging division who studies gender differences, the establishment of specific divisions dedicated to the understanding of diverse groups marked a new direction for the APA. In the 1970s the Society for the Psychology of Women (division 35) and the Psychology of Religion (division 36) were established. In the 1980s the Society of the Psychological Study of Lesbian, Gay, and Bisexual Issues (division 44) and the Society for the Psychological Study of Ethnic Minority Issues (division 45) were approved. In the 1990s the APA approved the Society for the Psychological Study of Men and Masculinity (division 51) and International Psychology (division 52) (Street, 1994). Psychologists may have been slow to expand their focus to include sociocultural influences, but once the expansion occurred in the 1960s and 1970s the field has moved rapidly to recognize cultural and individual differences.

Assumptions Regarding *Average* and *Normal*

Prior to addressing issues of individual and group variation directly it is useful to consider some definitions. In fact, much of this chapter is devoted to exploring distinctions and definitions. Most of us use the terms *average* and *normal* frequently and without much thought given to precision definitions or implications. When considering the ways individuals or groups are distinct or unique, it is good to be reminded of our choice of words and the all-too-easy-to-make assumptions that may follow.

The statistical concept of average provides a general summary of a set of numbers. By itself the statistical average does not provide any indication of the variety within a group. For example, the data set of 10, 10, 10, 90, 90, 90 will have the same average as a set with 22, 77, 33, 60, 95, 12 or a set with 50, 50, 50, 50, 50, 50. (The concept of statistical average is also discussed in the Research Appendix.) Suppose you were a teacher and these three data sets represented the quiz scores, on a 100-point scale, of three students. Even though all three have an average of 50, would you approach them in the same way? Probably not. The first student has changed the pattern of failing quizzes (three scores of 10) to excelling on them (three scores of 90). We want to tell that student to keep up the good work! The second student who has highly inconsistent quiz scores may have different issues than the student who consistently scores at 50%. The point of this example is that if all we knew about the three students was their statistical average on quiz scores we would be missing very valuable information, and we may make false assumptions about "students who have a 50% average." As the data sets indicate, these three students appear to be quite unique. Keep in mind whenever you are presented with averages that (1) it is important to know what was used in the calculation, (2) without information on the variety within the group the statistical average gives only a bit of information, and (3) even when using the term in a casual way, such as the "average American," we are similarly missing or ignoring important differences.

The term *normal* is less precise in that it does not have a statistical definition. We often think of normal in personal terms, based on our life experiences. As children *normal* is often characterized by familiar, familial, and local customs. As we get older and our experiences broaden, we learn to appreciate a wide range of accepted thoughts and behaviors as normal within our society. We also realize with age that what is normal is changing. I can remember when it was unusual to see an American male with an earring, and now it is perfectly normal. I can also remember when the general public would make assumptions about people with tattoos, and now they are quite common. (Even I have several!) In addition to developing a sense of normal, we may also develop a sense of *abnormal*. There are any number of professionals, such as medical doctors, psychiatrists, psychologists, professors, law enforcement officials, judges, clergy, or media analysts to name a few, who may label actions *abnormal* and in need of some kind of restraint, correction, therapy, or treatment. It is easy to begin to dichotomize these terms such that thoughts or behaviors are either normal or abnormal, thus when a stranger approaches that person is either normal (and I'm comfortable) or abnormal (and I'm on guard and suspicious). Such a dichotomy dictates that any thoughts or behaviors that are not normal are "sick," "not right," and possibly immoral. This perspective doesn't allow for thoughts or behaviors to simply be *different*. Through sloppy use of these terms it is easy to start to view *normal* as synonymous with conformity to norms and any nonconformity becomes, by default, abnormal.

Your Thoughts?

Are you normal? If not, are you sick and need treatment?

Why is it good to be reminded of the more common conceptions of average and normal? One reason is that, inevitably, you will read something in this or another book about the average adult that doesn't fit you personally. Does that mean you are abnormal and in need of correction or treatment? No. Does that mean the book or the research is in error? No. The average is a statistical term that is calculated from a set of data, which apparently does not describe your personal reality. Statistical average is only a summary of whatever data were used in the calculation.

The second reason these concepts are important is that much of what you will read in this and other psychology books is based on Western, Eurocentric culture (American Psychological

It's good to be reminded that there are many individuals who are not average.

Association [APA], 2003). What you read may or may not feel *normal* to you. Just as there is some truth in the humorous statement that psychology is the "science of white rats and college freshmen," there is also some truth in the accusation that American psychology has been the science of the white, heterosexual, middle-class, Christian lifestyle. Many of the developmental theories that formed the foundation of the study of adult development and aging were based on data from mainstream, white, middle-class males (Sorrell & Montgomery, 2001; Wortley & Amatea, 1982). Does that make them erroneous or false? No, but we have a responsibility to interpret and apply the findings with the limits of the research in mind. As you read through this text you will likely come across some theories that do not fit with your experience. Consider the date of the research and the participants involved. Consider the theorist and that individual's place in history. Psychology as a field is now intensely embracing and exploring individual and multicultural characteristics, but there is much work yet to do in the midst of our rapidly changing culture.

Your Thoughts?

What can psychologists do to change this trend?

Closer Analysis of the Aging Population

Now that we are sensitive to the multiple layers of understanding, considering broad generalizations and the diversity that may be lost in such summaries, let's turn our focus to the aging population. In the previous chapter many figures were given to make the point that the population in the United States is aging. While broad, general summary statistics provide valuable information, as was demonstrated with the concept of average, they can also mask or hide critical points of variation. For example, it is clear that the older population is growing, but what can we learn through further analysis? When the U.S. Census Bureau (2007) compared the rates of growth in various age groups from the year 2000 to 2005 it was discovered that the age range of 55 to 64 years old showed the greatest increase. There were 25% more people in that category in 2005 than in 2000. The second largest increase was in the 85 years old and older category, with 20.2% more people in that range in 2005 than in 2000.

Consider the finding by the U.S. Census Bureau (2008a) that of the 35 million Americans 65 years or older in 2005, 56.6% were married. Do you have any reaction to that data? Are you surprised to find that there were 35 million Americans that old, or that only a little over half were married? A closer look at the data reveals important yet *hidden* information in these figures. Of the 35 million individuals aged 65 and older, approximately 15 million were male and about 20 million were female. If we break down the 56.6% of those who were still married we also find some gender differences. Of the 15 million males 73.3% were married and only 13.1% were widowed. Of the 20 million females 43.8% were married and 42.5% were widowed. (Table 2.1 gives more information.) By exploring the data with gender as the focus it becomes clear that the population 65 years and older in 2006 was predominantly female with many of those women living alone. Nearly 74% of the men had a spouse, thus they were likely

Your Thoughts?

How might this information affect financial planning for men and women?

TABLE 2.1 ***Marriage Statistics for the 35 Million Americans Aged 65 and Older in 2006***

	All Individuals	*Males*	*Females*
Never Married	3.7%	3.8%	3.6%
Married	56.6%	73.3%	43.8%
Widowed	29.9%	13.1%	42.5%
Separated	1.2%	1.3	1.0%
Divorced	8.7%	8.1%	9.1%

Adapted from the U.S. Census Bureau. *Age Data of the United States. The Older Population in the United States: 2006*. Retrieved from http://www.census.gov/population/www/socdemo/age/age_2006.html.

to have an in-house caregiver when needed. Only about 44% of the women had potentially the same situation.

In a different survey the U.S. Census Bureau (2006b) found that 36% of those 65 years and older in 2005 had a high school degree and 18.7% had a bachelor's or advanced degree. Looking beyond those numbers we find that of the males in that category 30.9% were high school graduates and 25.4% had a bachelor's or advanced degree. In contrast, of the females aged 65 years or older, 39.8% were high school graduates (8.9% more than the males) and 13.7% had a bachelor's or advanced degree (11.7% fewer than the males). This may reveal some cohort differences in attitudes toward females and educational attainment and possibly some indication of previous and current earning potential. This gender difference in educational attainment will likely be different in the years to come. The 2005 Census indicated that while only 12.9% of women aged 75 years and older had attained a bachelor's degree or other advanced education, for women ages 25 to 54 years old the percent rose to 30.8. Men in the same categories saw some increase, from 23.3% in the 75 years and older category to 29% in the 25- to 54-year-old group; however, it was not as dramatic as the changes in educational attainment for women.

Just as the breakdown of data by gender exposes hidden information and adds richness to the interpretation, so does the breakdown by racial and ethnic groups. According to the Federal Interagency Forum on Aging-Related Statistics (2006), there are several trends within the American aging population that are worth noting regarding the ethnic and racial composition of Americans aged 65 years and older. As Figure 2.1 indicates, it is estimated that over the 46-year span from 2004 to 2050 the percentage of non-Hispanic white Americans will decrease from 81.9% to 61.3% as the percentage of nonwhites increases. Also of interest is how the balance of ethnic and racial groups will shift. Whereas in 2004 the African American population comprised the largest group, with 8% of the population aged 65 years and older, in 2050 it is estimated that the Hispanic population will comprise the largest racial minority, with 18% of the older population.

Your Thoughts?

What effects do you think these changes will have?

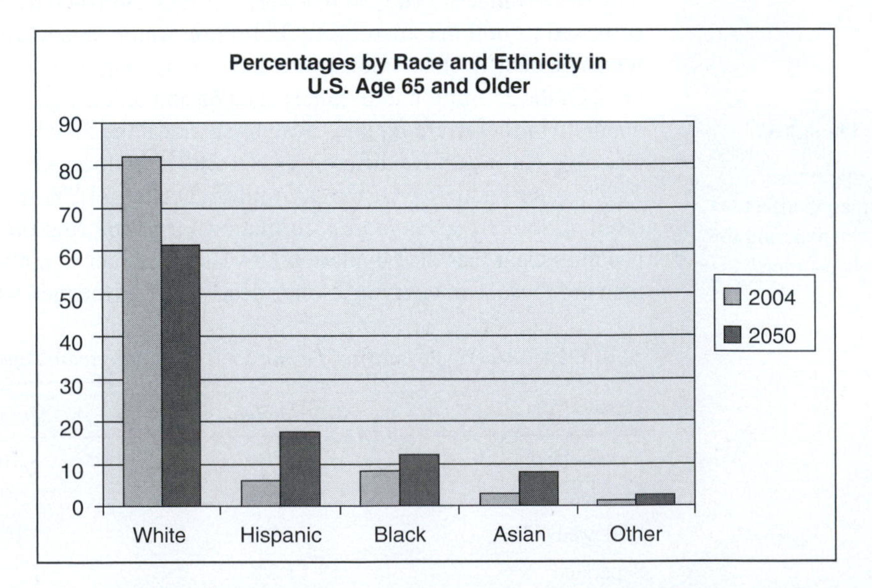

FIGURE 2.1 ***Population Age 65 and Older by Race and Hispanic Origin, 2004 and Projected 2050***

Federal Interagency Forum on Aging-Related Statistics. (2006, May). *Older Americans Update 2006: Key Indicators of Well-Being*. Washington, DC: U.S. Government Printing Office.

Section Summary

- The study of individual differences began in psychology with the aim of applying research in the areas of education, industry, and therapy.
- During the 1970s and 1980s psychologists became quickly and intensely interested in cross-cultural and multicultural research.
- When considering the need to make both broad generalizations of large groups of people and more precise descriptions of individuals and subgroups, it is important to be reminded to watch our assumptions.
- Individuals who are not *normal* or *average* as compared to the people we interact with daily are not *necessarily* abnormal, deviant, and in need of change or therapy.
- It is also important to further analyze data beyond the summary statements of the large group in order to find trends and differences among individuals and subgroups.

Areas of Difference

Recently, there has been more interest among psychologists in individual and cultural differences than at any other point in psychology's history (Sinnott & Shifren, 2001). This section provides an introduction to some areas of individual and multicultural characteristics but certainly not all. The areas of age, gender, race and ethnicity, and socioeconomic status are among the more frequently studied areas, but researchers find that adults show variability in many other areas as well, such as health status, political views, and social preferences (Hinrichsen, 2006). Although these areas will be presented separately it is important to keep in mind that they are not *lived* separately. Some individuals may feel they are in ***double jeopardy*** because they are, for example, elderly and in a cultural minority, or female and poor. Above all, the purpose of this section is to increase sensitivity to areas of difference and the tendency to stereotype. Consider, for example, when I asked you several pages back in a note in the margin to consider the advantages of joining the Association of Black Psychologists, Asian American Psychological Association, Society of Indian Psychologists, or the National Hispanic Psychological Association. Did you assume the question was for a psychologist who shared that cultural background? If so, why?

Your Thoughts?

Can you name some advantages to belonging to one of those professional groups if your heritage was different from the group focus?

Western and Eastern Cultures

Computer technology, the Internet, and the many constant streams of media have provided us with a window on the world unlike any our ancestors experienced. While it is beyond the scope of this text to give appropriate treatment to cross-cultural, multicultural, and individual differences on a global level, it is important to recognize that much of what we read in American social science textbooks reveals what mainstream, white, middle-class Americans feel about themselves and others like them (Liu, Ng, Loong, Gee, & Weatherall, 2003; Sorrell & Montgomery, 2001; Wortley & Amatea, 1982). Before focusing our discussion on primarily data from American participants we first get a glimpse of global differences.

When considering all of humanity from a social science perspective one of the most basic distinctions, or ways of grouping people, is that of Western and Eastern cultures. Basic differences in the ways these two perspectives conceptualize an individual's sense of self, relationships, and place in the world can influence almost every aspect of psychosocial functioning. In Western culture, of which most Americans and Europeans are a part, people tend to think of themselves as independent, self-contained individuals. Eastern cultures, in contrast, are more likely to elevate relationships and interconnectedness more than an individual sense of self (Cohen & Gunz, 2002). This Eastern mindset, often associated with Asian countries, is called ***collectivism***.

When considering self-esteem, for example, those with a Western mindset are more likely to feel good when they can take care of themselves without the help of others. Westerners take pride in their personal strengths. Those in an Eastern culture are more likely to feel good when they think of all the relationships they participate in, gaining satisfaction from their sense of interdependence and mutuality (Kitayama, Markus, Matsumoto, & Norasakkunkit, 1997). Some view the value placed on youth by Western cultures as stemming from the fact that an individual's most independent and self-sufficient years are the youthful ones. An emphasis on interconnectedness would more likely lead to greater attachment to one's intergenerational family, and more positive feelings toward caring for and valuing older adults (Liu et al., 2003).

Your Thoughts?

Do you get more satisfaction from your individual successes or the successes of groups you belong to?

These basic differences in worldview have been found to influence areas of cognitive processing and reasoning as well. For example, when Westerners are presented with apparent contradictions they assume they need to determine which position is correct. When Easterners are presented with contradictions they assume they need to find a compromise, synthesis, or "middle way" (Nisbett & Norenzayan, 2002). Easterners, with a raised awareness of relationships, tend to see more complexity in the world and tend to organize items by their relationships to other items. Westerners tend to organize items by functional rules or categories, highlighting characteristics of the items rather than relationships, leading to less complexity (Nisbett & Norenzayan, 2002). These differences, though they may seem basic, can influence practically all areas of life.

It must be acknowledged that any time vast numbers of human beings are put into two groups and compared, be it younger adults versus older adults, males versus females, or Eastern versus Western culture, such generalizations are filled with oversimplifications and are guilty of ignoring any number of exceptions. Just as it is grossly simplistic to say "all older adults are this way" or "all males are this way," it is equally as simplistic to say that all members of Western culture are one way and all members of Eastern culture are the opposite. Collectivism, for example, is expressed somewhat differently in Chinese cultures than in Japanese cultures (Koltko-Rivera, 2004). Such simplistic thinking can also lead to evaluations, such that one culture is judged to be good or correct, and the other, being the opposite, is bad or wrong.

Age and Ageism

While chronological age is the easiest to measure and to communicate to others, it is not as useful as functional age and its components when describing adults. Others will respond to us not only based on our chronological age but also their assessment of our biological, psychological, and social age. The 60-year-old who has a functional age usually associated with old-old age will be treated differently than the 60-year-old who gives all indications of being in middle adulthood. When the only information available about a person is chronological age it is more likely that stereotyped assumptions will be made about that persons' functional age. A ***meta-analysis*** involving 232 investigations of attitudes toward both young and older adults revealed that when given little or no information other than chronological age younger adults are evaluated more favorably than older adults, particularly in the areas of attractiveness and competence (Kite, Stockdale, Whitley, & Johnson, 2005). The meta-analysis also revealed that when more information about the hypothetical person being evaluated was provided the trend to favor younger adults was much smaller. Information provided about social roles, thoughts, behaviors, and general functioning were often more influential in forming an impression of a particular adult than chronological age.

Your Thoughts?

Regarding the people you spend the most time with, are their ages varied or similar to yours?

RESEARCH IN-DEPTH
Cross-Cultural and Multicultural Research

While the interest in cross-cultural research is a relatively recent addition to the many areas of psychology, the wisdom of other cultures has been recognized and studied for many years. In fact, the wisdom of the East, such as Taoism, Zen, and Buddhism, are sometimes thought of before Western wisdom, such as Greek philosophy. Takahashi and Overton (2002) chose to compare American and Japanese wisdom on the two dimensions of analytical and synthetic reasoning. The analytical part of wisdom, according to this model, involves one's knowledge and level of abstract reasoning. The synthetic reasoning aspect of wisdom focuses on emotions and personal reflection. Before the researchers could collect data, however, they had to work through one of the most difficult parts of cross-cultural research, that being the translation of test items.

To illustrate some of the challenges in translating psychological tests, consider some basic issues in communication. It is important that the test questions are as precise as possible. For example, if I say to you "I bought a dark red shirt," what shade of red do you imagine? Are you thinking of a deep, pure red, or perhaps more burgundy, or maybe a dark brick red? If it was critical that you imagine the color correctly I would need to go to great lengths to describe it. Now consider something abstract, such as trying to distinguish, in a foreign language, the nuanced differences between the terms *happy*, *delighted*, and *satisfied*.

Returning to the matter at hand, when writing questionnaire items for participants of different generations, different backgrounds, or different areas of the United States or other countries, one must understand how words are used in order to write precise questions. When translating questionnaire items into another language researchers need to be as certain as possible that the words they choose for items convey the appropriate meaning.

Takahashi and Overton (2002) wanted to use several measures in their study of American and Japanese wisdom, including an intelligence test that would measure general knowledge base and abstract reasoning, several personality tests to measure reflective understanding, an emotional empathy test, an emotional regulation test, a life satisfaction measure, and a cultural orientation measure. The intelligence test already had a Japanese version, but all the other measures needed to be translated. The first step was to find several volunteers who were fluent in both English and Japanese who also had a background in psychology. Next, one of the volunteers was given the tests to translate into Japanese. The Japanese versions of the tests were then given to another bilingual volunteer to translate back to English. The newly translated English version was then compared to the original English version. All the variations were discussed by the two translators and the researchers. Once those issues were resolved the information was given to a professional translator and another bilingual volunteer to create the final Japanese versions of the tests. While this may seem like a lot of work, when researchers are comparing cultures it is important that the items are understood in the same way by members of both cultures.

The participants in the study were 34 American and 34 Japanese middle-aged adults, with both groups having an average age of approximately 46 years old, and 34 American and 34 Japanese older adults, with an average age of approximately 70 years old. After the data were collected and analyzed, results showed that the older adults in both cultures performed better than the middle-aged adults on four of the five measures of wisdom. When the tasks were analyzed further, the researchers found that the older adults excelled in both the analytical and the synthetic aspects of wisdom.

Takahaski and Overton (2002) found that the American adults performed "significantly better" than the Japanese adults on all the measures of wisdom. The question arises, however, as to whether the Americans performed better because they have more wisdom or because the questionnaire items and answers were based on an American understanding of key words. This highlights the need to have confidence in the translation of psychological instruments when engaging in cross-cultural research. Takahashi and Overton believe the findings may suggest that there are different types of wisdom, and that additional research needs to be done. It may be that the test questions and answers are based on an American concept of wisdom, which may be quite different from a Japanese concept of wisdom. When engaging in cross-cultural or multicultural research it is critical, though difficult, to write questions that allow each culture to express itself while maintaining a sound methodology that allows for comparisons.

Most of the age-based stereotypes Americans hold of older adults are negative (Foos, Clark, & Terrell, 2006; Hess, 2006), including the notion that all older adults are alone, lonely, sick, dependent, depressed, rigid, and unable to cope (Hinrichsen, 2006). ***Stereotypes*** are beliefs or assumptions that a group of people share a set of characteristics, which are often exaggerated and often oversimplified traits. Those holding stereotypes often assume that the target group is uniform, with practically all members holding such traits without exception (Liu et al., 2003; Sinnott & Shifren, 2001). ***Ageism*** is demonstrated by prejudicial, discriminatory behaviors stemming from negative stereotyping based on a person's age, whether young or old. It would be an instance of ageism for an employer to deny a young adult a promotion solely based on the assumption that someone so young would be too immature for the position, just as it would be to deny an older employee a promotion solely based on the assumption that someone so old would not have the energy or mental flexibility to manage the position.

One common example of ageism and its associated detrimental effects is the use of ***elderspeak***. One indicator of the frequently made assumption that someone who looks older is likely to be hearing-impaired and slow in cognitive processing is that we often talk differently to older adults (Kemper & Mitzner, 2001). Called *elderspeak*, people often talk to older adults in the same way they would talk to infants or pets. Elderspeak speech patterns are often slower, more exaggerated, and involve simple grammar and vocabulary. Although it may seem to the speaker that simplifying language is an appropriate or sensitive thing to do, most of the research shows that simple sentences do not improve cognitive performance for older adults and has detrimental social effects. The use of elderspeak reminds older adults of how they are being perceived (their social age). As older adults are spoken to like children, over and over again, it lowers their self-esteem, motivation, and self-efficacy (Hess, 2006). Some older adults are so insulted by elderspeak that they socially withdraw, leading to personal isolation that creates additional problems. Older individuals who feel offended may withdraw from potentially helpful neighbors, relatives, or even medical professionals. Elderspeak is a problem for community-based as well as institutionalized older adults (Hess, 2006; Kemper & Mitzner, 2001). It is important to notice with this example that not all ageism is deliberate or motivated by bad intentions. Some people who engage in elderspeak may sincerely believe they are showing sensitivity and care to older adults. This highlights the need for all of us to become more educated and aware of our own stereotyping, and particularly those going into professions in which they will work with older adults.

Your Thoughts?

Have you personally experienced or witnessed an act of ageism?

Although most of the stereotypes Americans hold of older adults are negative, as demonstrated by the frequent use of elderspeak, there are some positive characterizations of late adulthood. In a survey of 240 participants ranging in age from 18 to 85 years old, Hummert, Garstak, Shaner, & Strahm (1994) found a variety of stereotypes. After grouping the participants by age, a mixture of positive and negative stereotypes of older adults emerged. Older adults were viewed as either:

- Golden Agers
- John Wayne Conservatives
- Perfect Grandparents
- Shrews/Curmudgeons
- Recluses
- Despondent
- Severely Impaired

Hummert and her colleagues also found some differences when sorting the stereotypes by age group. Young adult participants had an additional stereotype, Vulnerable, that the middle-aged and older participants didn't have. Middle-aged participants were unique in adding Liberal Matriarch/Patriarch to their stereotypes of older adults. Older adult participants were distinctive in adding the stereotypes of Small Town Neighbor, Activist, and Elitist to their list of characterizations of their own age group. As demonstrated by creating the longest list of stereotypes, older adult participants held more complex stereotypes of their peers than younger adults did.

Your Thoughts?

Which of these stereotypes, if any, would your older relatives and friends fit in?

The "Golden Agers" stereotype describes those older adults who are adventurous, energetic, healthy, and well traveled.

Clearly the stereotypes are primarily negative, but are the realities of aging also so negative? One of the principles of lifespan developmental theory is the assumption that development is a lifelong process involving gains and losses at all ages (Baltes, 1987; Baltes, Staudinger, & Lindberger, 1999). As the stereotypes of aging reveal, most people are noticing the losses more than the gains. In terms of losses, psychologists have generally focused on changes in physical health, cognitive functioning, and issues related to changing social and work situations. Among the gains studied are the ways individuals learn to regulate their emotions (Consedine, Magal, & Conway, 2004) and maintain composure. Psychologists are also interested in the gains made through life experiences, such as increases in wisdom, maturity (Wentrua & Brandtstadter, 2003), problem-solving ability (Baltes et al., 1999), and life satisfaction. Older adults report higher levels of life satisfaction than young and middle-aged adults. A related concept, subjective well-being, often used as a measure of happiness and contentment, is generally high and remains high during late adulthood (George, 2006). Also on a positive note, the lifespan developmental principle of plasticity reminds all of us that we can improve our level of functioning with effort and practice (Baltes, 1987; Baltes et al., 1999).

Aging, when viewed as a source of diversity, is unique in that all of us who engage in stereotyping will eventually become the stereotyped (Wentura & Brandtstadter, 2003). The American Psychological Association guidelines for therapists working with older adults acknowledge this unique situation by encouraging counselors to be aware of their own issues with personal aging. The *Guidelines for Psychological Practice with Older Adults* details 20 guidelines that fall into 6 basic categories. In addition to (1) awareness of one's personal attitudes toward aging, the *Guidelines* encourage therapists to have (2) general knowledge of diversity and environmental issues, such as circumstances related to gender, sexual orientation, ethnicity, and socioeconomic status; (3) specific knowledge regarding aging-related clinical issues; (4) awareness of the best ways to test and assess the functioning of older adults; (5) awareness of the best types of interventions and therapies; and (6) to engage in continuing education in these areas (APA, 2004b). As American citizens our views, attitudes, and stereotypes of aging may begin to shift as this diverse population of older adults becomes even larger and more varied, American society becomes more informed about the realities of aging beyond simply chronological age, and as *we* become *them* (Hess, 2006).

Gender

Gender is among the most researched and controversial areas of individual differences. It is a convenient research variable due to its generally assumed dichotomous nature; one is either male or female. In this way gender is easily assessed and any data collected can be divided into male and female groups for comparisons. Gender issues are also among the most controversial topics in psychology. Debates continue as to how much of one's sense of gender is biologically determined and how much is socially and culturally shaped. Questions are continually raised about the range and size of gender differences. Are men and women so different in their thoughts and behaviors that we should expect them to have trouble interacting? Or, are women and men actually more alike than different? In this section we explore some of the issues surrounding the psychological study of gender and gender differences. Gender is discussed throughout the text as it relates to the topics in the chapters.

Your Thoughts?

How do the media shape our sense of masculine and feminine characteristics?

There are several ways to approach the concept of gender in research. Generally, when social scientists use the term *sex* they are referring to biological characteristics and processes, whereas use of the broader term ***gender*** refers to one's personal identity and the ways one's sense of gender is reflected socially in attitudes and behaviors (Sinnott & Shifren, 2001). A study of sex differences may place participants in groups based on sex-related hormone levels determined through blood tests, whereas a study of gender may place participants into groups based on how they self-identify as male or female. Some studies will allow for participants to select additional options such as transgendered or "other." Whereas most people think of sex and gender as dichotomous, researchers may place participants in one of numerous levels or categories. For example, researchers may group participants based on high or low levels of estrogen (female hormone) and testosterone (male hormone) as determined by laboratory analysis. A study of gender may, in addition to self-identification, ask participants to rate themselves on how strongly they display certain characteristics, such as nurturing qualities, aggression, intellectual curiosity, or emotional sensitivity as a way to categorize or rank each participant in terms of levels of both traditionally masculine and feminine qualities.

Your Thoughts?

Do you think one's ability to express feelings is more genetically determined or environmentally shaped?

When evaluating gender research it is important to note how sex or gender was measured, the particular aspects of the topic being studied, and if the philosophy or position of the researchers was made clear. Research participants may be asked about their ***gender identity***, which is their sense of being male or female, or their ***gender roles***, which refers to their actual behaviors based on personal and social expectations. Researcher may also be interested in ***gender role stereotypes***, the narrowly defined, oversimplified perceptions of idealized male or female thoughts and behaviors (Sinnott & Shifren, 2001). Consider how differently you would respond to each of these questions:

- Do *you* have difficulty expressing your feelings?
- Do *you* think that difficulty in expressing feelings is typical for men? For women?
- Do *most people* think that difficulty in expressing feelings is typical for women? For men?
- Would a *stereotypical* male have difficulty expressing feelings? Would a *stereotypical* female have difficulty expressing feelings?

The subtle differences in wording in these examples are critical in interpreting participants' responses to such questions. It's also important to note if and where you may have wanted to qualify your response. Did you want to say "it depends"? It is good to be reminded that generalizations regarding large groups of people are always made at the expense of individual differences.

It's also important when evaluating research to note whether the perspective or philosophy of the researchers involved is made known in the article. While it is true that all social scientists should be engaged in objective research, knowing the researchers' perspectives can further inform your understanding to the design of research questions and the interpretation of the findings. For example, knowing that the researcher(s) is particularly sensitive to a type of ***feminism*** can enrich understanding of a study. To be a feminist, whether one's sex or gender is male or female, is to believe that females are worthy of being treated like human beings (as opposed to lesser animals or property). There are many types of feminism, each with its own focus and intensity. There are feminists who focus on the status of women as it is influenced by their social and economic class (socialist feminism), racial or ethnic heritage (racial/ethnic feminism), or biology (essentialist feminism). There are those who are most interested in fairness in employment and legal situations and equal representation in psychological and medical research (liberal feminism) and those who strive to expose deep, widespread, systematic oppression of women (radical feminism) (Rosser & Miller, 2003). While much of the study of gender has focused on women's issues, slowly the field is broadening to include men's issues as well. In the United States college students can find Men's Studies programs along with Women's Studies, as scholars, therapists, and researchers give more attention to men's issues. It may seem at a casual glance that the study of gender differences is simply comparing males and females; however, a closer look reveals just how complex and multifaceted this area of research can be.

Your Thoughts?

How might it benefit a college student to major or minor in Women's or Men's Studies?

Studies exploring gender as it relates to adult development and aging have generally focused in one of three areas (Sinnott & Shifren, 2001). One common focus has been the ways gender identity and gender roles change with age. For example, Kasen, Chen, Sneed, Crawford, and Cohen (2006) observed the changes in gender identity in 758 mothers over a period of 20 years. They found that positive traits associated with both femininity and masculinity increased in the women between the ages of 39 and 59 years old. For women with marital support their feminine traits showed greater increases than unmarried women, while the women with full-time work or high occupational prestige showed greater growth in masculine traits.

Another research focus has been the interaction of gender roles and social/political issues (Sinnott & Shifren, 2001). In the first chapter we became familiar with the terms *age-graded* and *history-graded influences* as those forces experienced primarily because of one's age or one's location in history. A similar term, ***gender-graded influences***, refers to influences experienced primarily because of one's gender. Typical of research on gender-graded influences, Moen and Spencer (2001) found that men are more likely to be in paid work positions throughout adulthood whereas women moved between paid and unpaid work, with the unpaid times usually associated with caregiving for children, grandchildren, and older family members. There are numerous potential consequences to this trend. With a continuous history of work men may be hired ahead of women who have "gaps" in their work history. Women may feel as though they are not as valuable, or their skills are not as valuable, because their caregiving is unpaid work. Also, with more years of employment men are likely to have better retirement incomes.

Your Thoughts?

What other influences or developmental experiences are gender-graded?

The third common area of research in the studies of gender and adult development is focused on comparing the performance of males and females in various areas (Sinnott & Shifren, 2001). One common area of comparison, cognitive abilities, reveals that there is little difference between older males' and females' performances on tests of verbal ability and verbal memory (Parsons, Rizzo, Van Der Zaag, McGee, & Buckwalter, 2005). Another common area of comparison, personality traits, reveals that women tend to be higher in agreeableness

ON THE LEADING EDGE

Women and Divorce in Hong Kong

Winnie Kung of the School of Social Work at the University of Southern California, along with Suet-Lin Hung of the Tsuen Wan Community Center in Hong Kong and Cecilial Chan of the Center for Behavioral Health at the University of Hong Kong, set out to learn more about the effects of divorce on Chinese women. With the tremendous influence of Eastern traditional Chinese culture, Hong Kong has been slow to embrace Western culture and values. Although Chinese women in Hong Kong are seldom placed in arranged marriages, as was the tradition for many years, many of the Eastern traditions remain powerful. Traditional views of marriage as the merging of families and the primacy of family relationships continue to influence societal attitudes. Estimates are that only two or three women per 1,000 in Hong Kong will divorce.

Kung, Hung, and Chan (2004) interviewed 35 recently divorced women to learn more about their struggles. The participants were in their 30s and 40s, and only about half were employed. Regarding education, 43% had grade school education or below, 46% attended high school, and 11% had some college education. Most of the women had been married for over 10 years, and most had full custody of all their children. Only three women lived with members of their extended family, while most lived in single-parent housing. As for their reasons for divorce, 77% of the husbands were having affairs with women, mostly in Mainland China. Other reasons for divorce included physical abuse, the husband's gambling habits, and his lack of parental responsibilities.

Most of the women found that their families were against the divorce. Their own mothers advised them to stay with their husbands for various reasons, such as avoiding the embarrassment to the family or the loss of economic support. As for the husbands' families, many of them knew of the affairs and urged the women to ignore their husbands' behaviors. Following their separation and divorce many of the women were afraid to tell their neighbors and coworkers, often lying to them about why their husbands had disappeared. In addition to dealing with family tensions and negative social interaction, the women also had to deal with the legal system. The participants told the researchers stories of incredibly complex bureaucratic procedures and of mistreatment by lawyers. Of the 35 women interviewed, 24 had given up completely on the legal system to secure alimony or welfare assistance. In a later study Helena Yuen (2010) explored these issues, discovering that little has changed. She found that divorce judgments and related family and financial arrangements are often ignored by officials in both Hong Kong and China.

Based on their research Kung, Hung, and Chan (2004) recognized that the recently divorced women need social support in order to reconsider their status as worthwhile and valuable people. Through opportunities such as empowerment workshops at community centers, the researchers recommended that the women come together, find strength in numbers, and work to challenge and change the system. Follow-up studies will show over time the effects of such an emphasis on women's needs and concerns. In 2006 the official number of spousal abuse reports made to the Social Welfare Department had increased 37% over the previous year (Yuen, 2010), potentially reflecting an increase in the maltreatment of women but also an increase in the number of women willing to report abusive husbands.

and warmth whereas men are stronger in assertiveness and openness to ideas (Costa, Terracciano, & McCrae, 2001).

The study of gender differences remains complex and controversial. There are some psychologists who believe that it is actually detrimental to continue to study gender differences. One issue to contend with is that generally only differences are considered worthy of publishing in journals or noted in the media, while gender similarities are considered boring and unremarkable. The constant stream of media reminders of all the differences makes it easy to assume that there are few if any gender similarities. Some argue that by publishing *all* the gender comparisons in any topic studied, which would include all the occurrences of gender similarities and minor differences along with the dramatic differences, psychologists would have a better understanding of gender comparisons (Eagly, 1995). Others believe that by highlighting gender in every social science study researchers are giving that one variable too much emphasis (Baumeister, 1988).

One of the standard findings in gender studies is that while data analysis shows differences between females and males, analysis also shows a great deal of overlap between the groups and much more variation within each gender group (Sinnott & Shifren, 2001). In other

Your Thoughts?

How closely do you think you fit the common stereotype for your gender group?

words, while we can show statistical differences in extreme behaviors between men and women in some areas, we can also show a great deal of similarities. In addition, we can show that men can vary dramatically when compared to other men, as do women when compared to other women. Some believe that the best course of action to equalize opportunities for the genders is to stop comparing by gender and focus on human variation and individual differences (Baumeister, 1988).

It is doubtful that gender research will fade, partly due to public and academic interest and partly due to the ease in which research participants can be compared by the simple forced-choice item, "Circle one: Male Female." This brief look at the study of gender differences reminds us of just how complex this topic is. We need to examine gender research closely in order to fully understand the aspects of gender being studied, the methods of measures used, and the philosophical perspectives of the researchers involved. This overview of gender studies also reminds us to be careful of stereotyping and assuming that all members of a particular group are the same. Just as people grow more distinct rather than similar with age (Consedine et al., 2004), men and women can vary dramatically from their same-gender peers (Sinnott & Shifren, 2001).

Culture, Ethnicity, and Race in America

Among the first variables we think of when we see the term *multicultural* are racial and ethnic cultures. Early in America's history the mood of the country was one of a "melting pot" where the desire was to blend cultures. People wanted to feel as though they fit in with what they perceived to be American society, customs, and lifestyle (Percil & Torres-Gil, 1991). Many current European Americans, whose families have been in the United States for generations, have blended their cultures to the point that in many cases there are few ethnic or racial cultural distinctions left. Such is not the case with African Americans, Latin Americans, and Asian Americans. It is predicted that by the middle of this century about half of the American population will be able to trace their roots to European counties and the other half will be primarily African American, Latin American, and Asian American in heritage (Angel & Angel, 2006). This shift in the cultural dynamics in the United States has been accompanied by a desire to respect and celebrate cultural uniqueness (Percil & Torres-Gil, 1991). For social scientists this shift has brought a desire to consider cultural development and a new appreciation for just how difficult such an undertaking is.

Based on population estimates, the primary ethnic groups in the United States are Hispanic Americans, African Americans, Asian Americans and Pacific Islanders, and American Indians and Alaska Natives (Bernal et al., 2003). While it is easy to slip into the assumption that the members of each cultural group are similar (Fischer & McWhirter, 2001), it's good to be reminded of the diversity within each group. Hispanic or Latin Americans, one of the fastest growing ethnic minority groups in the United States, may trace their heritage to Mexico, Cuba, Puerto Rico, countries in South and Central America, or Spain (Bernal et al., 2003; Haber, 2005). Individuals from these various regions bring their own political history, religious practices, and customs to the Latin American culture. African Americans, who trace their heritage to various African, Caribbean, and Latin countries, generally do not have the current levels of immigration as those of Latin and Asian ethnic groups nor the linguistic diversity of those groups. There is, however, wide diversity in terms of education, socioeconomic status, and religious beliefs among African Americans in the United States (Haber, 2005). Throughout this text attention is given to multicultural issues, including some of those dealt with by Hispanic and African Americans.

Your Thoughts?

Is your cultural ancestry something you think about often?

There are fewer studies targeting Asian Americans than there are focused on African or Latin Americans. One reason for this may be the tremendous linguistic differences among

Asian Americans (Angel & Angel, 2006). Although there are variations among Hispanic languages the differences are not as dramatic as is found among Asian languages. Designing research questions that translate well across linguistic lines and make sense in multiple cultures is difficult. Asian Americans may have a cultural heritage that includes Chinese, Japanese, Vietnamese, Korean, Cambodian, Hmong, Laotian, Thai, Filipino, Indonesian, Hindi, Asian Indian, Pakistani, Fijian, Samoan, Tongan, or Hawaiian ancestry (Angel & Angel, 2006; Bernal et al., 2003; Haber, 2005). Immigrants bring with them their language, values, and lifestyles. They also bring their political history, which may affect their adaptation to American society. For example, whereas many Chinese Americans have generally chosen to immigrate, many Vietnamese immigrants were likely to have been forced to move from their homeland and native Hawaiians were, for the most part, colonized. Often labeled "Asian and Pacific Islanders," this large and diverse group is also one of the fastest growing minority groups in the United States (Browne & Broderick, 1994).

Certainly, the trend in American society and in the social sciences is to embrace multiculturalism. According to the APA *Guidelines for Multicultural Education* (2003) ***multiculturalism*** is a perspective that recognizes distinct cultures (including religious groups), treating them with equal respect and status. The term ***diversity***, first popular in employment settings, refers to the variations in individuals' cultural backgrounds. ***Culture*** is an enormously broad term including a group's sense of art, science and technology, moral and governance systems, symbols and beliefs, social customs, language and education system, and health care practices. Taking a multicultural approach may involve ***cross-cultural*** perspectives, involving different cultures, or ***transculturation***, emphasizing the merging of once separate or different cultures. For social scientists choosing to include culture as a variable in their studies, defining groups in which to place participants may be difficult. In addition to the vast diversity found within these minority groups, boundaries between groups become even more blurry when the cultures themselves are continually evolving and blending with each new generation. One way to handle the delicate challenge of categorizing participants by culture is to pass the task on to them by asking each participant to state his or her ethnicity or race. ***Ethnicity***, often referring to one's ancestry or common genealogy, is the cultural group one identifies with, accepting its culture and norms. Ethnicity involves one's personal choice whereas ***race*** generally refers to a cultural group one is assigned to, usually based on physical characteristics. The definition of race is quite controversial, with some advocating that race is based in genetic traits common to a certain group of people, whereas others, including the APA (2003), view race as the social category others place an individual in based on that individual's physical appearance. Ethnicity and race may not always coordinate in a predictable way. Consider the following hypothetical scenarios:

Your Thoughts?

How many cultures are represented in your local area?

- A boy of European American racial heritage is raised in a Hispanic neighborhood, accepting the cultural identity of his peers.
- A couple of European American racial heritage adopt a girl from China as an infant, raising her as a "typical American girl."
- A child of an African American mother and European American father is labeled "biracial" and, at different points in her life, identifies more with her African heritage and at other times feels closer to her European American heritage.
- A child whose parents have biracial backgrounds feels more multicultural and unique, not identifying with any one ethnicity but rather a sense of loyalty to the geographic culture in which she was raised.

Your Thoughts?

Would someone perceived to be biracial find acceptance in your local area?

These scenarios highlight the ways individuals can adapt to different cultures, a process called ***acculturation***. Those who are low in acculturation choose to identify more with their

ON THE LEADING EDGE
Native American Tribal Colleges

The history of Native American education is, by our current standards of diversity appreciation, shameful and heartbreaking. For example, there was a time when federal agents would take Native American children away from their parents on the reservation and send them to boarding schools, where they were treated horribly. The goal was to take the "savage" out of them and replace it with something "civilized" (Ambler, 2004). Native Americans' long-held distrust of European Americans and the dominant American culture has influenced their way of life, including some reluctance to attend typical American colleges or universities.

In order to provide Native Americans with higher education that honors their history, language, religion, and culture, there is a growing network of tribal colleges. In 2009 the White House Initiative on Tribal Colleges and Universities listed 36 educational institutions spread out from Washington to Michigan across the northern United States, and from North Dakota south to Oklahoma and Arizona (U.S. Department of Education, 2009). First started back in the 1970s (Martin, 2005) these fully accredited colleges emphasize American Indian culture. While many of the colleges have an agricultural and technical focus, some institutions are developing particular specialties. For example, the Southwestern Indian Polytechnic Institute in New Mexico, because of its purposeful location near the Los Alamos National Laboratories, is developing special programs in the sciences. Another mission of the Institute, as well as the other tribal colleges, is to serve as a bridge between the world of higher education and individuals living on the reservations. Many of the internships involve taking information and technology back to the reservation (Reese, 2004).

In some cases potential college students cannot attend a tribal college because of the impractical distance to travel, so most tribal colleges have distance education programs along with their on-site courses (Ambler, 2004). Another issue with more traditional college situations is the high value placed on obligations and responsibilities to extended family members, keeping students away from class. In response, four tribal colleges in Montana are implementing the Family Education Model as a way to incorporate families into the campus support network (Martin, 2005). Tribal colleges are demonstrating openness to the needs of their nontraditional students and communities by seeking creative solutions to various obstacles.

native or racial culture rather than their host culture, while those high in acculturation tend to prefer and adopt the characteristics of their host culture (Miranda, Frevert, & Kern, 1998).

Acknowledging that race, ethnicity, and culture are complex variables, and that studying their influence on other psychological variables is difficult, we will find throughout the text areas of similarity and difference among cultural groups. For example, generally individuals of any cultural background who immigrate to a new culture when they are older have a more difficult time adjusting to the host culture (Angel & Angel, 2006). In the United States, generally elderly members of racial minority groups have less education and lower socioeconomic status, and have dealt with racism and discrimination, resulting in greater suspicion and lack of trust of others (Haber, 2005). Differences among groups have also been found. When considering coping with aging-related issues, for example, African Americans were more likely to rely on their religious beliefs for comfort whereas European Americans were more likely to rely on nonreligious social relationships (Consedine et al., 2004). Also, African Americans named health care as their top concern in old age, whereas European Americans were most concerned with personal finances (Foos et al., 2006). There are also end-of-life differences. African Americans have the highest death rates from major illnesses while Hispanic Americans have the lowest rates with the exception of diabetes. Native Americans also have a very high rate of diabetes (Angel & Angel, 2006).

Your Thoughts?

Is your family's cultural heritage more important to you or your parents?

Part of adopting a multicultural perspective is continued sensitivity to individual differences. As was the case with age and gender, there are many facets of culture to consider. With age and experience individuals are likely to continually grow and evolve in their cultural identity. Although for convenience in data analysis researchers may need to place participants in large categories, such as Hispanic American or African American, it's good to be reminded that there is great diversity within those categories. Cultural backgrounds and lifestyles can vary dramatically. In addition, researchers must be aware that some participants will incorporate more of their ethnic heritage into their identity and lifestyle than others.

Religious Cultures and Practices

Most American adults claim some religious affiliation. According to recent polls only 3% claim to be atheist or agnostic and approximately 10% claim to have no religious preference. About 80% of Americans claim some form of Christianity as their religious preference, with most of those in Catholic or Baptist denominations (Adherents.com, 2005). One could make a compelling argument that until recently, based on the demographics, psychology of religion in America is really psychology of Christianity (Spilka, Hood, Hunsberger, & Gorsuch, 2003). It's important to recognize that there is a great deal of variety among Christian practices, not only in worship choices but also in lifestyle choices and attitudes. It's also important to be reminded that although the minority religions in the United States represent small percentages of the total population, when considered in actual numbers they represent millions of Americans. Judaism, Islam, Buddhism, and Hinduism, when combined, represent an estimated 6.5 million people (Adherents.com, 2005). As the United States population changes in age and ethnicity, it is also changing in terms of religious landscape. Starting in the mid-1960s there has been a dramatic increase in non-Christian religions, particularly among those who practice Buddhism, Hinduism, and Islam (Ecklund & Park, 2007).

Your Thoughts?

Is there much diversity among the religious communities in your area?

The current emphasis on multiculturalism has made social scientists aware that for some individuals their ethnic culture and religion are totally integrated, and for some others their religion alone is their primary cultural influence. Consider again the description of the term culture with religion in mind: *Culture is an enormously broad term including a group's sense of art, science and technology, moral and governance systems, symbols and beliefs, social customs, language and education system, and health care practices*. For some people their religion provides the greatest influence on many of those aspects of culture. We will find that, like the other areas explored in this chapter, religion is multifaceted and complex. Unlike the other areas explored so far, religious beliefs and practices are generally assumed to be more a matter of personal choice.

One might say the field of psychology has had a "love/hate" relationship with religion (Wulff, 1996). Throughout the history of psychology, various therapists and scholars have characterized religious beliefs and practices as both helpful, as in providing comfort and coping mechanisms in difficult times, and as detrimental, as in encouraging delusional thinking. Designing research studies to explore the role of religion in individuals' lives is difficult. Researchers exploring this area will find many of the same challenges as those studying ethnicity. Even simple designs comparing participants who are religious to those who are nonreligious require some criteria to determine who qualifies as religious. As with ethnicity, one option is to let the participants self-identify. If researchers ask, "Do you have a religious preference?" it is likely that some who say "yes" are quite committed to their religion whereas others who also say "yes" have a religious heritage but it has no real effect on their daily lives. If asked, "Are you actively involved in your religion?" there still may be quite a bit of variation in the interpretation of "actively involved." Individuals could interpret that as attendance at religious services on major holidays or two or three times a week, engaging in daily prayer, official membership, or monetary support. This confusion makes any generalizations more suspect.

Some social scientists may want to go a step beyond, asking not only about religion but also exploring spirituality. Once interchangeable, the two words *religion* and *spirituality* have evolved to mean quite different things. The term ***religiosity*** (or *religion*) refers to involvement in religious traditions such as Buddhism or Christianity or institutions, such as the Roman Catholic Church or the Southern Baptist Convention. Religiosity refers to the behaviors encouraged or expected by one's religious affiliation. This definition makes religiosity somewhat easier to measure in that a researcher can find out what is expected by a religious community and gauge a participant's involvement based on that standard. In contrast to religiosity, which is often external and observable, ***spirituality*** refers to an internal state involving one's faith, personal beliefs, and sense of inner harmony. Spirituality can be viewed as one's personal beliefs and feeling of connection to the sacred. With such a broad definition spirituality can include many practices, such as prayer, meditation, fasting, and contemplation, as well as many personal situations, including the individual fully devoted to a traditional spiritual and religious tradition and the person who has no organizational affiliation but projects the wise, caring, and thoughtful manner associated with a spiritual nature (Spilka et al., 2003; Wink & Dillon, 2002, 2003; Wulff, 1997). From a research point of view the confusion over the use of the terms *religiosity* and *spirituality* can create large amounts of error. It is difficult to compare older and more recent research because of the evolution of these terms. It is also difficult when conducting research that includes members of several generations because the researcher must be sure that all participants understand these key terms in the intended ways.

Your Thoughts?

Do you find the distinction between religiosity and spirituality helpful?

To explore religious culture in depth it is often useful to go beyond the distinction between religion and spirituality. Glock (1962) detailed five dimensions of religiosity that have served as the basic dimensions on which one's religiosity can be assessed. In Glock's scheme religiosity can be separated into the following independent aspects:

- Ideological aspect (what you believe)
- Ritualistic aspect (how you worship or show devotion publicly and privately)
- Intellectual aspect (your theological, philosophical, and historical knowledge)
- Experiential aspect (your emotions and feelings)
- Consequential aspect (the effects of your religion in the other areas of your life)

Not only can individuals vary in terms of how much they value or engage in each of these factors, but also religions themselves can vary in terms of the emphasis placed on these dimensions.

Similar to the challenges confronted when working with language variations among Hispanic Americans or Asian Americans, attempting to assess Glock's dimensions across religions or even within Christianity can be difficult. Participants could be responding from the context of one of any number of religious traditions or no religious tradition at all. For example, terms such as *catechism*, *confession*, *sacraments*, *sanctification*, *tongues*, and *prophecy* can have very different meanings or no meaning at all depending on the participant's background. Some investigators try to create separate instruments for various religious traditions, while others attempt to use generic language. For example, a questionnaire may use the phrase "holy writings" with the intention that Christians will think of the Bible, Jews will think of the Torah, and Muslims will think of the Koran. As another example, consider the difficulty in trying to find a generic word for "Higher Power" when some religions have one Deity, such as the Christian God, some have many Deities (or many forms of Deity), such as the Hindus, and others do not have any Deity at all, such as the Buddhists or atheists. Given the many challenges that must be confronted when designing a way to measure or gauge religiosity and spirituality, and in light of the findings that most Americans who claim a religious preference claim some form of Christianity, many researchers in the area of psychology of religion simply designate their participants as religious or nonreligious. Such generalizations are likely to hide important information, ignoring differences among various Christian denominations and those who practice minority religions or adhere to a secular philosophy.

Your Thoughts?

What criteria are most important in determining who qualifies as "religious"?

Recognition of individual and multicultural differences regarding religious cultures raises many of the same issues, concerns, and cautions as were mentioned regarding age, gender, and ethnicity and race. It's good to be mindful of the difference between religiosity and

The numbers of non-Christians in American cities is increasing rapidly.

spirituality, reminding ourselves that just because an individual is engaged in a particular religion, that person's spiritual outlook and practice may be different on Glock's dimensions from official doctrine of the religious group. Similar to attempting to understand an ethnic culture different from one's own, it can be equally as difficult to understand a religious or spiritual culture that is unfamiliar. It takes time to understand new terms, customs, values, internal governance, and lifestyle choices—a difficult task in light of the fact that as American culture changes and evolves, so too will religious organizations and their members. That steady progression of cultural and religious change, along with the mix of gains and losses experienced by individuals with age, creates an area of individual and multicultural differences that is difficult to assess with accuracy.

Intraindividual Variation

To this point we have explored differences in terms of broadly defined cultural perspectives (Western and Eastern cultures), age, gender, ethnicity, racial, and religious cultures. The study of individual and multicultural differences could cover a tremendous number of variables and their interactions beyond what has been covered here, such as differences in education; employment and occupational status; marital, parenting, and family status; sexual orientation and preferences; and physical, mental health, and disability status. Many of those topics are discussed in later chapters. The primary emphasis of this chapter is to raise awareness of the ways individuals can be different from one another. An alternative way to consider individual differences is also gaining attention, that of within-person differences. Variation within individuals that is not known to be related to stable gains and losses is called ***intraindividual variation***. For example, when testing older adults on cognitive tasks twice a week for 7 weeks, Shu-Chen and colleagues (2001) found that fluctuations in performance

Your Thoughts?

If tested weekly, do you think your performance on a memory test would be stable or fluctuate?

were "substantial." There is some evidence suggesting that this inconsistency or intraindividual variation in cognitive performance can be a sign of cognitive aging, with greater fluctuation indicating neurological disorders (MacDonald, Hultsch, & Dixon, 2003).

Such differences, which were once considered to be errors in measurement, secondary findings, or a product of the research design, are now gaining scholarly interest (Anstey, 2004; Nesselroade, 2004). Researchers are finding noteworthy fluctuations in many types of processes, even some thought to be stable in adulthood (Hofer & Sliwinski, 2006). As work in this area continues researchers are distinguishing between fluctuations that fit a pattern, often referred to as *cycles* or *oscillations*, and those with no predictable characteristics (Ram, Rabbitt, Stollery, & Nesselroade, 2005). Some researchers are calling for intense measurement procedures, not only testing an individual each week or each day, but also repeating tests frequently during a session in order to explore attention, fatigue, practice, and motivational effects (Martin & Hofer, 2004). The statistical analysis of this type of data can be very complex, creating new challenges. Researchers are also calling for the development of theories and models of intraindividual change (Hofer & Sliwinski, 2006). It may be useful, for example, rather than considering adult development in terms of an organism seeking equilibrium or balance (the traditional view from early developmental perspectives) to conceptualizing development as a more dynamic process oriented toward change (Nesselroade, 2004). This area of investigation may give scholars a new perspective on aging, filling in a few more pieces of this complicated yet exciting puzzle.

Section Summary

- Individual and multicultural differences are multifaceted, and often interacting with many other areas of life, adding to the complexity of any research effort attempting to be sensitive and inclusive of differences.
- While acknowledging that a global treatment of diversity is beyond the scope of this text, it is good to be reminded that what is written here is primarily based in Western culture as reflected in mainly American psychology.
- This section considers individual and multicultural differences in terms of broad cultural perspectives, age, gender, ethnic, racial, and religious cultures, and intraindividual variation.
- The study of attitudes and stereotypes of age reveals that when only chronological age is known younger adults are judged more favorably than older adults.
- Most of the stereotypes of older adults are negative, though not all are.
- Sensitivity to gender as a source of individual differences requires careful attention to how gender is being measured and categorized.
- Some argue that there is more overlap between genders than differences, and continuing to focus on the differences gives the public and the media a false impression.
- There are many variations of femininism, such as radical feminists, who seek to expose large-scale oppression based on gender.
- When adopting a multicultural approach it is important to remember that individuals within minority categories, such as Hispanic Americans or Asian Americans, may trace their ethnic heritage to different parts of the world with unique customs, lifestyles, religions, and histories.
- For some individuals their sense of culture is highly influenced by their religiosity and personal spirituality.
- Researchers are exploring within-person variation or intraindividual variation as a way to further understand the aging process and individual gains and losses.

Acknowledging Diversity

A recurring theme throughout this chapter is the awareness that generalizations often omit important individual and multicultural differences. Certainly succinct summary statistics or statements are convenient and communicate useful information. It's common when filling out financial, educational, or medical forms to be asked to "check the appropriate box" for gender, ethnicity, race, or religious preference. Researchers often do the same thing, choosing to work with broad categorizations for convenience and to provide brief summaries of findings. While we know that these are not so neat and tidy groupings, it is easy to start thinking of "us" and "them." Often referred to as "in-groups" and "out-groups," social psychologists have found that people tend to recognize more individual differences in their own in-group, and assume that members of the out-groups are very similar to each other (Liu et al., 2003). While we may group all Hispanic Americans together for ease in making general statements, we must be ever mindful that the experience of a third-generation young adult Mexican American woman in an urban setting in the southwestern United States may be very different from the experiences of a first-generation elderly Puerto Rican American man in a rural, farming area in the northeastern United States. This example also highlights the fact that these variables do not exist in isolation, but rather, in this case, gender, age, and location combine to create unique experiences.

Designing ethnically sensitive research studies requires that special attention be given to vocabulary, particular variables, and statistical analysis. As the previous example points out, it is less complicated to simply group all Hispanic Americans together when collecting data, but doing so hides the differences in experiences of Hispanic Americans with distinct ethnic backgrounds. A related issue when considering cultural differences is determining which aspects of culture should be included in data collection (Consedine et al., 2004). For example, are the differences in the experiences, behaviors, and attitudes of Mexican Americans and Puerto Rican Americans stemming primarily from familial or community-based values and customs, religious practices, political backgrounds, or perhaps another unexplored variable? It is clear that ethnically sensitive research can add many new variables and layers of complexity. For example, Haber (2005) suggests that to understand cultural diversity among older adults researchers should routinely include, regardless of the particular variables of interest, lifestyle choices, age, gender, educational attainment, income, marital status, religion, level of physical disability, place of birth, current location in the United States, length of time in the United States, English-speaking skills, and level of acculturation. This encouragement of more complex methodologies that assess multiple cultures across multiples ages (APA, 2003; Bornstein, 2002) would certainly advance our understanding of cultural dynamics. At the same time, however, such techniques require locating and recruiting participants of varying backgrounds, more intensive data collection, and sophisticated data analysis.

Your Thoughts?

What obstacles might keep some researchers from incorporating all these variables?

Section Summary

- In psychology both researchers and counselors (APA, 2003) are encouraged to give the extra effort needed to raise their personal awareness and to develop culturally sensitive practices.
- Generalizations often hide important information.
- Areas of difference often interact, such as age X gender X culture X income.
- Be aware of your own assumptions and stereotyping.
- Though misguided and harmful, not all stereotypical thinking is ill-intentioned or malicious.
- Watch for in-group and out-group thinking.
- Guard against the automatic assumption that what is not "normal" is wrong, sick, or evil and in need of treatment or correction.

Chapter Summary

Early in its history psychologists were interested in developing techniques to measure individual traits, such as intelligence and memory. Beginning in the 1960s American psychologists showed greater interest in the recognition of individual and multicultural differences, eventually bringing that interest into research and therapeutic practice. This chapter focused on age, gender, culture, and religion in terms of difference, while acknowledging that there are many areas worthy of attention and a great amount of interaction between these sources of influence. Here are some of the main points from this chapter:

- Although attempts to measure the ways individuals vary from the average has a long history in psychology, the psychological study of aspects of culture gained momentum in the 1970s.
- Casual use of the terms *average* and *normal* can lead to misunderstanding and misinterpretation of research findings and theories.
- By analyzing data by gender, race/ethnicity, education, or another area of difference social scientists may find that the impression given by broad, general statistics may hide important differences for particular groups of people.
- Recent U.S. Census data reveals more women are receiving higher education, living longer, and living alone in old age than men.
- A global perspective on cultural and individual differences often includes the basic distinction between Western, individualistic cultures (the primary focus of this text) and Eastern, collectivist cultures.
- Most, but not all, stereotypes of older adults are negative, reflecting a focus of the losses that come with age rather than the gains.
- The area of gender differences is highly controversial and complex, including the comparisons of masculine and feminine gender identities, gender roles, and gender role stereotypes as they relate to aging, social and political roles, and performance in numerous areas of life.
- It is estimated that by the middle of the current century approximately half of all Americans will have a cultural heritage that is not European.
- Most of the research on cultural heritage is focused on Hispanic Americans and African Americans, with less targeting Asian Americans and Pacific Islanders or Native Americans and Alaska Natives.
- Multiculturalism is a perspective or ideology that recognizes distinct cultures and strives to treat them with equal respect and status.
- Religious diversity can be found both across religions and within religions, particularly when considering ideological, ritualistic, intellectual, experiential, and consequential aspects.
- Intraindividual variation, or the fluctuations in performance demonstrated by a person when tested repeatedly, promises to bring new insights to the understanding of gains and losses with age.
- Many in the social sciences, including the American Psychological Association, have called on researchers and therapists to deliberately raise their personal awareness of individual and multicultural differences as well as incorporate more culturally-sensitive practices in their work.

Key Terms

Psychometrics **(38)**
Double jeopardy **(43)**
Collectivism **(44)**
Meta-analysis **(44)**
Stereotypes **(45)**
Ageism **(46)**
Elderspeak **(46)**
Gender **(48)**
Gender identity **(48)**
Gender roles **(48)**
Gender role stereotypes **(48)**
Feminism **(49)**
Gender-graded influences **(49)**
Multiculturalism **(52)**
Diversity **(52)**
Culture **(52)**
Cross-cultural **(52)**
Transculturation **(52)**
Ethnicity **(52)**
Race **(52)**
Acculturation **(52)**
Religiosity **(54)**
Spirituality **(55)**
Intraindividual variation **(56)**

Comprehension Questions

1. When did the psychological study of cultural issues gain momentum?
2. What important information is missing when the only data given is the statistical average?
3. Explain some of the problems with dividing thoughts, behaviors, or people themselves into two groups: normal and abnormal.
4. Give an example of what is meant by *hidden* data.
5. Which group is currently the largest minority population within the United States and which group is projected to be in that position in 2050?
6. Explain the basic differences in perspectives between those in Western cultures and those in Eastern cultures in terms of their sense of self and relationships.
7. Give examples of both negative and positive stereotypes of older adults.
8. What are the three areas in which we find most research on gender as it relates to adult development and aging?
9. Explain the reasoning behind the arguments in favor of and against the study of gender comparisons.
10. What is multiculturalism?
11. Explain why it is false to say, "All Hispanic Americans have the same traditions," and why it is equally false to make such a claim about African Americans or Asian Americans.
12. Name and describe each of Glock's dimensions of religiosity.
13. Explain the concept of intraindividual variation and give an example of oscillation.

Answers for Common Sense: Myth or Reality?

1. Myth: The study of cross-cultural and multicultural issues has been a priority in psychology since the discipline began. (See Psychological Study of Human Differences, page 38.)
2. Reality: The U.S. Census data from 2005 revealed that approximately 75% of all men ages 65 years and older were married while approximately 45% of all women in that age range were married. (See Closer Analysis of the Aging Population, page 41.)
3. Reality: Federal agencies estimate that by the year 2050 the Hispanic population will comprise the largest racial minority in the United States. (See Closer Analysis of the Aging Population, page 42.)
4. Reality: Older adults report higher life satisfaction than young adults. (See Age and Ageism, page 47.)
5. Myth: Gender identity is generally formed by about 5 years of age and remains stable throughout adulthood. (See Gender, page 49.)

6. Reality: Researchers have found little differences in the areas of verbal ability and verbal memory in older men and women. (See Gender, page 49.)
7. Reality: When dividing Americans into cultural groups, those whose heritage is Chinese, Pakistani, and Hawaiian are usually put together under the label of "Asian Americans." (See Culture, Ethnicity, and Race in America, page 52.)
8. Reality: The second half of the last century saw a dramatic increase in the number of participants in non-Christian religions in the United States. (See Religious Cultures and Practices, page 54.)
9. Myth: Although religions differ in their specifics, they are basically the same in structure, such as having holy writings, worship of one Deity, and engaging in similar lifestyle choices. (See Religious Cultures and Practices, page 55.)
10. Reality: Humans tend to notice more differences in people in their "in-group" and assume that people in the "out-group" are all quite similar. (See Acknowledging Diversity, page 58.)

Suggested Readings

What an Early Leader in Psychology Says about Educating Women

Hall, G. S. (1904). Adolescent girls and their education. From *Adolescence: Its psychology and its relations to physiology, anthropology, sociology, sex, crime, religion, and education* (Vol. 2, Chapter 17). Accessed at *Classics in the History of Psychology* (http://psychclassics.yorku.ca/topic.htm).

Psychologists Concerned with Racial Issues in 1939

Clark, K. B., & Clark, M. K. (1939). The development of consciousness of self and the emergence of racial identification in negro preschool children. *Journal of Social Psychology, SPSSI Bulletin, 10*, 591–599. Accessed at *Classics in the History of Psychology* (http://psychclassics.yorku.ca/topic.htm).

Decision Making in Individualistic and Collectivistic Cultures

Güss, C. D. (2002). Decision making in individualistic and collectivistic cultures. In W. J. Lonner, D. L. Dinnel, S. A. Hayes, & D. N. Sattler (Eds.), *Online readings in psychology and culture* (Unit 4, Chapter 3), (http://www.edu/~culture), Center for Cross-Cultural Research, Western Washington University, Bellingham, WA. Available online at http://www.ac.wwu.edu/~culture/Guss2.htm.

Twenty-Five Years of Hispanic Psychology

Padilla, A. M. (2002). Hispanic psychology: A 25-year retrospective look. In W. J. Lonner, D. L. Dinnel, S. A. Hayes, & D. N. Sattler (Eds.), *Online readings in psychology and culture* (Unit 3, Chapter 3), (http://www.wwu.edu/~culture), Center for Cross-Cultural Research, Western Washington University, Bellingham, WA. Available online at http://www.ac.wwu.edu/~culture/padilla.htm.

Suggested Websites

Diversity and Immigration in the United States

You can get a great deal of information on ethnic and racial trends in America as well as information on those newly immigrating to the United States at http://usinfo.state.gov/usa/infousa/society/diverse.htm.

Cross-Cultural Psychology

This resource from PsychWeb provides a list of helpful websites focused on cross-cultural studies in psychology at http://www.psychwww.com/resource/bytopic/cross.html.

African American, American Indian, Asian American, and U.S. Latino Websites and Information

This Iowa State University website provides a wealth of information regarding ethnic and racial minority groups and their experiences in the United States at http://www.public.iastate.edu/~savega/divweb2.htm.

Religious Freedom in the United States

You can learn more about the religious diversity and freedom of religion in the United States at http://usinfo.state.gov/usa/infousa/society/religion.htm. Adherents.com provides an enormous amount of data on world religions as well as breakdowns by country and by size of the religion at http://adherents.com.

CHAPTER

3 Healthy Lifestyles and Successful Aging

For many years the study of aging was primarily the study of illness and decline in old age. The application of lifespan developmental theory to the study of aging has enhanced the field in three major ways. First is the acknowledgment that at all points in life we experience gains and losses. Reflecting that, the study of aging has broadened beyond a focus on only areas of decline to include factors involved in optimal or successful aging (Baltes & Baltes, 1990). A second element is the recognition that aging processes vary and occur across the lifespan. Aging does not occur only in late adulthood or in a totally predetermined way. The quality of life experienced in late adulthood reflects the cumulative effect of all the lifestyle choices that preceded it (Settersten, 2006), which is a primary reason why this field is called *adult development and aging*. A third point is the increasing awareness of individual differences. There is dramatic variation in the levels of functioning of aging individuals in many areas, including physical, cognitive, and social abilities. There are also cultural differences that may shape what an individual views as successful aging (Dannefer, 1984).

This particular chapter is focused on improving quality of life and longevity by exploring life expectancy, healthy lifestyles, challenges to healthy living, and successful aging. Later in this book we discuss areas of typical physical aging, physical diseases, and mental disorders. One important theme found throughout the chapter is that optimal or successful aging does not necessarily mean anti-aging. There are a few promising areas of research that may eventually lead to ways to stop or reverse aging, such as caloric reduction in diet and genetic alterations. Generally speaking, however, the vast majority of the so-called "anti-aging products" should be approached with skepticism (AARP Andrus Foundation & International Longevity Center-USA [ILC-USA], 2002). For the time being, a better way to achieve optimal

COMMON SENSE
Myth or Reality?

Mark each of the following items with either an M, if you think it is a myth, or an R, if you think the statement reflects reality. By paying close attention you can find all the answers in this chapter. If needed, the answers are also given at the end of the chapter.

1. _____ Trends in health care indicate that the prevalence of disability among older adults is rising.
2. _____ Most of what determines a person's life expectancy is determined by genetics.
3. _____ In all cultures around the world, women tend to outlive men.
4. _____ The oldest person in recorded history was 122 years old.
5. _____ It is estimated that there are 60 Americans who are 110 years or older.
6. _____ While there are far fewer male centenarians than female, the men who do reach this milestone tend to be stronger physically and cognitively than the women.
7. _____ Most studies find that adult women exercise more than men.
8. _____ It is recommended that adults burn a minimum of 500 calories per day for high-quality physical fitness.
9. _____ Getting regular exercise will improve sleep quality.
10. _____ Lack of sleep has been associated with memory and attention problems.
11. _____ Alcohol helps individuals engage in high-quality sleep.
12. _____ Smoking can reduce one's life expectancy by about 14 years.
13. _____ Less than half of all American adults are overweight.
14. _____ Body mass index (BMI) is a method of determining how much fiber is in certain foods.
15. _____ A pound of body fat is equivalent to 3,500 calories.
16. _____ Alcohol abuse is a greater problem among younger adults than among older adults.
17. _____ Experts view the use of humor as a very poor method of coping with stressors.
18. _____ The primary goal of the movement to promote successful aging is to fight aging in every way possible.

aging is to focus on lifestyle choices. The best path to successful aging is to maintain a healthy diet and exercise regularly, as well as to never smoke or stop smoking and avoid excessive alcohol use (Leventhal, Rabin, Leventhal, & Burns, 2001). While that may sound simple and rather bland, the truth is that many individuals struggle with these issues. Currently, for example, over half of the American population is overweight, and many adults do not get enough regular exercise (AARP Andrus Foundation & [ILC-USA], 2002). Those who are in good physical condition and maintain a healthy diet usually have a higher quality of life in general, and sustain that high level for a longer time in late adulthood.

Before We Get Started . . .

Have you ever wondered about the exact age at which your life will end? Your response to that question may depend on your current age, health status, and recent life experiences. Adults in middle age and late adulthood may ponder that question more than younger adults. Those who are experiencing life-threatening health concerns or those who have recently lost a loved one may find themselves thinking more about end-of-life issues. Many of the points raised in this chapter will likely prompt you to think about your own lifestyle habits and length of life. In this exercise we consider our personal life expectancy and, if that prediction were accurate, how we respond to that information.

Use the Internet to search for terms such as "life expectancy calculator" or "how long will I live?" and you will find several websites with questionnaires that will predict your lifespan. Most of them will ask about your current physical condition, habits, and family history. Take time now to find a calculator to predict your life expectancy.

Subtract your current age from your life expectancy to find the number of years remaining.

Predicted age at death: ________________
Current age: ________________
Years in your future: ________________

What is your reaction to this information? If your calculations indicate you have many years to live I would caution you against thinking that aging is so far away that you have no need to be concerned about it. A more productive approach, whatever your outcome from this exercise, is to realize that what you do now will have an effect on those later years. How can you change your lifestyle so that you can be your mental and physical best for as long as possible? This entire chapter is designed to respond to that question.

Longer Lifespans

Today Americans are living longer than previous generations and living higher quality lives well into late adulthood. While young and middle-aged adults can look forward to a longer lifespan, they can also expect that the lifestyle choices they make will shape their quality of life in late adulthood. The effects of such choices are already evident in older adults.

The older adults of the 21st century are more informed about health issues, are physically healthier, and are more physically active than ever (Rice & Fineman, 2004). Even though older adults are more likely to suffer with chronic illnesses than younger adults (Rice & Fineman, 2004), researchers surveying Medicare records have found that the prevalence of disability among older adults is declining. In the United States approximately 73% of people between the ages of 75 and 84 report no disability, and for those 85 years and older, 40% report no disability. While some of the 60% of older adults reporting disability have very serious conditions, others report only minor problems. In a study of cardiovascular health, involving 5,888 participants, Burke and his colleagues (2001) found that of those who were 85 years or older, 56% of the women and 46% of the men were disease-free and healthy. Based on their review of the literature, Rice and Fineman (2004) have found several factors that may be responsible for the increasing good health of older Americans:

- Better medical care and technology
- Less exposure to disease
- Better behaviors (particularly reduced smoking and better diets)
- Better financial situations
- Willingness to use health aids (such as hearing aids)
- Willingness to engage social support networks

Your Thoughts?

What businesses and industries are likely to benefit from the dramatic increase in the number of Americans over 65 years old?

Others have credited better sanitation practices, cleaner drinking water, better nutrition and food safety, and the discovery of antibiotics with extending the lifespan of older adults (Aldwin, Spiro, & Park, 2006; National Institute on Aging [NIA], 2007a).

It is projected that in 2030 there will be approximately 70 million Americans, roughly one out of every five, 65 years or older (Rice & Fineman, 2004). As concerns grow over the delivery and financing of health care for so many Americans, many believe that promoting healthy lifestyles and preventive measures are the best ways to promote high-quality functioning and longevity.

Longevity and Life Expectancy

Life expectancy is the prediction of how long an individual will live based on personal behaviors and environmental and hereditary factors, while ***longevity*** refers to the number of years a person actually lives. Generally, life expectancy is based on a wide variety of variables that may include family history of illnesses, gender, nutrition, exercise, living situation and social support, levels of stress, coping strategies, quality of sleep, environmental issues such as air quality, and high-risk behaviors such as risky sexual activity or unsafe driving, smoking, and alcohol consumption. Acknowledging that it is difficult to separate the influences of genetic and environmental factors when estimating life expectancy, there is general agreement that the genetic or inherited portion of longevity is between 20 and 30% ([ILC-USA], n.d.; Perls & Terry, 2003). Seventy to 80% of the factors determining length of life are rooted in environmental factors and personal behaviors.

Life expectancies have risen in the United States and many industrialized countries over the last 50 years. Whereas in 1900 less than 1% of the world's population was age 65 or older, today estimates are that over 606 million people, or almost 10% of the world's population, are age 60 or older (DiChristina, 2004). To appreciate how quickly life expectancies are increasing, consider that in the year 1700 the average life expectancy was 35 years old, and 200 years later, in the early 1900s, it had increased by 12 years to 47 years old (Langer & Moldoveanu, 2000). Approximately 100 years later, in 2003, the average life expectancy was 77.5 years old, an increase of 30.5 years (U.S. Census Bureau, 2006b). Trends indicate that life expectancy will continue to rise, though at a slower rate (Ferraro, 2006).

> **Your Thoughts?**
>
> What aspects of women's gender roles might lead them to make choices that result in a longer lifespan?

A case can be made that one of the most consistent and striking areas of gender differences occurs in the areas of longevity and life expectancy (Simon, 2004). Women have gained in both areas faster than men, such that in 2000 in the United States the average lifespan for women was 79.9 years as compared to 74.7 years for men. One of the results of this trend is that for every 100 women who are 65 years old there are only 70 men, and for every 100 women who are 85 years old there are only 38 men. Among all races and ethnicities men have a shorter life expectancy than women (Angel & Angel, 2006). For Americans born in 2003, African American and Caucasian American males have life expectancies of 69.0 years and 75.3 years, respectively. African American and Caucasian American women have life expectancies of 76.1 and 80.5 years, respectively (U.S. Census Bureau, 2006b). Hispanic American women have the highest life expectancy of all, at approximately 88.4 years old (Angel & Angel, 2006). This trend has been noted for some time, not only in the United States but around the world in industrialized and non-industrialized countries as well.

There are many potential contributing factors to these gender-related trends. There may be biological contributors, such as the ways sex chromosomes or sex-related hormones affect the aging process. There are personal and environmental factors to consider. Although the numbers of women engaging in smoking and alcohol abuse are rising, women tend to have healthier lifestyles than men. Women tend to eat healthier foods, consuming less fat than men. Women also take better care of their health and are more likely to see a doctor when something is wrong. While both men and women generally do not get enough exercise and carry too much weight, men tend to be at higher risk for problems due to obesity. Men tend to carry weight around their waist whereas women tend to carry weight on their hips and thighs. Abdominal obesity, seen more often in men, is associated with higher risk of diabetes, hypertension, heart attack, and stroke. Also, women are less likely to be aggressive and take advantage of social support to reduce their stress. Men tend to be more aggressive, involved in violence, and likely to pursue dangerous occupations and hobbies ([ILC-USA]Simon, 2004).

> **Your Thoughts?**
>
> Why might men be more hesitant to see a doctor when something is wrong?

The older women get the more likely they are to be widowed and spending time with other women.

Your Thoughts?

What are the effects on friendship, love, and marriage of the finding that over 85% of all centenarians are women?

Centenarians

Individuals who reach 100 years old and beyond are ***centenarians***. Among the most famous centenarians is Jeanne Calment of Aires, France. When she died in 1997 she was 122 years, 5 months, and 14 days old, making her the oldest person in recorded history at that time (NIA, 2007a). Although the number of centenarians is not growing as fast as the population between 80 and 100 years old, the number is increasing. In the year 2004 there were approximately 50,000 Americans age 100 or older. Approximately 85–90% of centenarians are women.

There is an even more exclusive group, the ***supercentenarians***. To qualify one must be 110 years old or older. Estimates are that there may be as many as 60 individuals in the United States who are supercentenarians. Worldwide estimates place the number of supercentenarians between 200 and 300.

Among the most substantial studies of these exceptional individuals are the ongoing New England Centenarian Study and New England Supercentenarian Study, both sponsored by the Boston University School of Medicine. The Centenarian study began in 1994 with a focus on the New England area, but has now expanded to include centenarians from around the world. Currently, there are approximately 1,500 participants. The Supercentenarian study is a part of this larger study. Since 1994 the supercentenarian study has involved 60 participants, with the oldest participant reaching 119 years old (Boston University School of Medicine, 2004, 2007).

Most of the centenarians in the study have not dealt with age-associated diseases, such as cancer and Alzheimer's disease, and 90% of the sample had been functionally independent until their early 90s. At 100 years old about 15% of those participating still have great health with the exception of arthritis, vision, and/or hearing problems. While the participants vary dramatically in terms of education, socioeconomic status, religion, ethnicity, and diet, there are some consistent commonalities. Few centenarians are obese and very few have a history of smoking, two key factors in longevity studies. The data also indicate that centenarians are better able to handle

ON THE LEADING EDGE

Dancing Their Way to Better Balance

Researchers Giorgos Sofianidis, Vassilia Hatzitaki, Stella Douka, and Giorgos Grouios of the Department of Physical Education and Sport Sciences at Aristotle University of Thessaloniki in Greece were well aware of the concerns older adults have regarding a lack of balance. Many older adults have a fear of falling that often keeps them from getting the exercise they need, which in turn might actually increase their chance of falling. The fear some older adults live with is justified in that falling is one of the principle contributing factors to poor health. Injuries that cause older adults to remain immobile for a long period of time may increase the chances that other life-threatening conditions develop.

Sofianidis and his colleagues recruited 26 elderly adults from five community centers for seniors in their area to take part in a 10-week Greek dance class. The participants, whose average age was 71 years old, were screened to be certain they didn't require walking aids, functioned independently, and had not been diagnosed with a serious medical, physical, or cognitive impairment. In order to have a comparison group, 14 of the participants participated in the first 10-week dance class while the other 12 did not. All the participants were given physical tests for balance before the 10-week class and after. Each of the 14 participants who were selected for the first class completed all 10 weeks of sessions.

When the dance class was over the researchers discovered that the dancers' scores on the balance tests were significantly better than those who didn't get to participate in the first class (Sofianidis, Hatzitaki, Douka, & Grouios, 2009). The dancers had better posture and balance when standing still as well as when moving. Not only did Sofianidis and his colleagues achieve their goal of increasing balance and reducing the likelihood of falling, they also gave the participants an opportunity to meet new people, socialize, and engage in artistic and cultural expression. This program serves as an excellent reminder that adults are much more likely to continue an exercise routine when it involves activities they enjoy.

Your Thoughts?

To put these centenarians in context, what cultural and historical factors were likely to be influential on this generation?

stress and engage in healthy coping mechanisms. Consistent with previous research indicating a genetic component to longevity, extreme longevity seems to run in families. One of the more interesting findings of the study is that rather than aging at a normal pace and simply living longer, it seems that centenarians age at a slower rate than is typical throughout their lives. For example, female centenarians are more likely to have completed menopause at a later age than average, and because of that they are more likely to have had a child after the age of 40. Another interesting finding is that even though there are far fewer male centenarians, those men who do reach this milestone tend to be stronger physically and cognitively than many of the female centenarians (Boston University School of Medicine, 2004, 2007).

Section Summary

- Population trends indicate that, more than ever before in our history, adults are living longer and healthier lives.
- Life expectancy, the prediction of how long an individual will live, has increased dramatically over the last several hundred years, particularly for women.
- In all cultures and ethnicities women live longer than men.
- Women generally take better care of their health and manage their stress better.
- Studies of those who have the greatest longevity, the centenarians and supercentenarians, have found that rather than experiencing a typical aging process and simply living longer, these individuals age at a slower pace throughout adulthood.
- Centenarians generally have controlled their weight, avoided smoking, and handled stress well.
- There seems to be a genetic component to longevity, demonstrated by the findings that long life generally runs in families.

Healthy Lifestyles

Optimal aging is not only about living for many years, but also about the quality of those years. This section focuses on key areas that are influential in determining one's current quality of life, laying the foundation for physical and cognitive functioning in the future. A lifestyle that includes physical fitness, a healthy diet, and restful sleep, maintained through young and middle adulthood, can dramatically increase the likelihood of better functioning in late adulthood. Later in the book we discuss additional "aging decelerators," specifically levels of social support and emotional balance (Aldwin et al., 2006).

When thinking about these health-protective activities it is easy to focus on individual decision making and lose sight of the role of the surrounding environment. For example, it is easy to slip into the assumption that almost any reasonably healthy person can take a walk as a form of exercise, thus if someone does not do so it is a sign of laziness or the absence of willpower. Such thinking neglects many individual differences and variations in personal circumstances. Consider the simple question of where to walk. Research has shown that individuals are much more likely to exercise when they live in a community that is safe, healthy, and offers access to health care services (U. S. Department of Health and Human Services, 2000). Lifestyle choices may be compromised by any number of circumstances, such as inadequate housing, violent neighborhoods, lack of transportation, little discretionary income, or access to quality health care.

Also, when thinking about these health-protective activities it is easy to fall into the thinking that if we follow through with all these recommendations we will be *guaranteed* a healthy life. Of course, such is not the case. All of us need to see a medical professional for appropriate checkups and screenings. While most of us can do more to increase our healthiness and quality of life, we cannot fully prevent disease processes.

Physical Fitness

Most Americans would benefit from engaging in more exercise. The busy lifestyles of many adults, often juggling responsibilities to their families, employers, and communities, while also maintaining homes and vehicles, can leave little time for exercise. Though it is only one part of the formula for a healthy lifestyle, physical fitness is critical to successful aging. In this section we explore just how out of shape American society is, what it means to be physically fit, and some of the many benefits of achieving physical fitness.

Most Adults Are Not Fit. The Centers for Disease Control and Prevention (CDC, 2009b) report that only 32.5% of American adults engage in regular leisure-time physical activity. While some Americans reported inconsistent activity, a staggering 36% reported that they do not engage in any leisure time activities. These findings are consistent with The President's Council on Physical Fitness and Sports (PCPFS, 2010a) report that more than 60% of American adults do not achieve recommended levels of physical activity. The National Institute on Aging (2009c) puts the estimate at more than 66% for older adults. Even college students, who often have access to specialized recreational equipment and safe, enjoyable areas to exercise, generally report inadequate amounts of physical activity. Estimates are that over 50% of all college students do not participate in adequate levels of exercise. For example, in a survey of 493 college students, Buckworth and Nigg (2004) found that only 31 percent engaged in moderate activity 5 or more days a week. Another survey of 736 college students found that most did not exercise 3 or more days a week (Huang, et al. 2003).

Your Thoughts?

What are your primary challenges or obstacles to maintaining a routine exercise program?

Further analysis of the fitness level of most Americans reveals many individual and multicultural differences. One clear trend is that physical activity decreases with age. In a meta-analysis involving 194 research investigations that included over 180,000 participants, Bogg

RESEARCH IN-DEPTH
Descriptive Analysis and Comparing Means

Very often psychologists measure the same variable in two different groups and compare the scores. It is difficult, however, to just look at a list of numbers and decide how different they are, and if the difference is greater than would be seen by chance alone. That was the dilemma faced by Mack and Shaddox (2004) when they measured attitudes toward physical activity among college students. They surveyed 1,625 undergraduate students who were enrolled in a personal wellness course that was required as part of the general education program. The research question was, "Does the experience of taking a wellness/fitness course change attitudes toward physical activity and exercise?" The students were fairly evenly divided among freshmen, sophomores, juniors, and seniors. The questionnaires asked participants to give ratings of 1–5 (strongly agree to strongly disagree) to statements such as "I think exercise is good for me," and "Exercise helps to work off emotional tensions and anxieties." Each student's rating for the 50 items on the survey were added to give a final score. The researchers surveyed the students on the first day of classes (the pretest, prior to the experience) and then again on the last day of classes (the posttest, after the experience). The personal wellness course consisted of lectures and physical fitness activities.

At this point Mack and Shaddox had two sets of scores to compare. They wanted to know if the second set of scores were any different, which would indicate that the course might have influenced attitudes toward physical activity. One way to compare the scores is to consider the average of the scores, called the *mean*, from the pretest and the posttest. The mean of the posttest scores was higher, but the question remained as to whether the difference was meaningful. There were 50 items that could be rated from 1–5, so the range of responses could be between 50 and 250. Mack and Shaddox found that the mean for the pretest was 193 and for the posttest was 195. Is that enough of a difference to view it as important?

In order to answer that question the researchers used a *t-test* procedure, developed by W. Gossett in 1908. Also known as "Student's t-test," this procedure determines whether the differences in the scores are due to experimental error and chance, or if the differences are statistically significant. A *t*-test considers the mean of each set of scores as well as the variation around the mean. For example, the number sets of 50, 50, 50, and 0, 50, 100 will have the same mean of 50, however, the variation around the mean is remarkably different. The first set has no variation because all the scores (50, 50, 50) are exactly the same as the mean. The second set of scores has a great deal of variation because the difference between 0 and 50 or 100 and 50 is rather large. In this case Mack and Shaddox used a *paired-sample t-test* because the pretest and posttest scores were taken from the same participants, not gathered from two separate random samples. Each score was paired with another in that they both came from the same student, one prior to the course and the other after the course. This is also called a *dependent t-test.* By considering the means, variations, and sizes of the number sets, a *t*-test procedure will determine the probability that the results are due to chance. Researchers often report the probability as a *p*-value.

Mack and Shaddox found, using paired-sample *t*-tests, that overall the scores were significantly higher after experiencing the course, with significance at the $p < .01$ level. Generally, when the *p*-value is less than .05 the means are considered to be statistically significantly different. They also compared the mean scores of males and females, and found that females significantly increased their scores, but the males did not. Upperclassmen significantly increased their scores, whereas freshmen and sophomores did not. By dividing the participants into other groups based on prior levels of physical fitness, the researchers found that those with an inactive history and a light exercise history showed significant improvement as well.

When drawing conclusions from descriptive data researchers must be careful with assumptions. It may be that those with a moderate or highly active exercise history already valued physical activities before the class started, thus the class simply reinforced their existing attitudes. The same may be the case for the males, or it may be that the females were genuinely more responsive to the information. It may be the freshmen and sophomores already appreciated the value of fitness, thus their scores remained high, or it may be that the juniors and seniors needed the reminder that fitness is important and exercise time should be added to their busy schedules. All of these possibilities will require further research. (And that is how one study can lead to many more!)

---

and Roberts (2004) found that levels of physical fitness and engagement in physical activities decrease with age, especially after age 30. Another clear trend is that adult men exercise more than women do. The differences are less dramatic in college, with estimates that of the college students who routinely engage in the recommended amount of physically intense exercise, 43% are male and 40% are female (Buckworth & Nigg, 2004). The Centers for Disease Control and Prevention (CDC, 2004) has been documenting exercise activity since 1988, and their findings confirm this trend. CDC surveys are given in 35 states plus the District of

Columbia, with annual sample sizes from 54,685 to 170,423 participants. One question on their survey asks, "During the past month, other than your regular job, did you participate in any physical activities or exercise such as running, calisthenics, golf, gardening, or walking for exercise?" In 2002, 22% of the men and 28% of the women surveyed reported no physical activities during the previous month. Both genders decrease amounts of physical activity with age, such that by the time individuals reach 75 years old approximately 67% of the men are active while only 50% of the women are active (CDC, 2010c). Differences in exercise levels are also found when considering ethnicity and income. African American and Hispanic adults are less active than White adults, and those with less income and education are less active than those with higher incomes or more education (CDC, 2010c; President's Council on Physical Fitness and Sports [PCPFS], 2010b).

Your Thoughts?

What factors might motivate men to exercise more? What obstacles might decrease the opportunities for exercise for women?

Achieving Physical Fitness. What does it mean to be physically fit? The most precise answer to that question should be tailored to individuals, taking into account each person's current physical health and personal characteristics. Generally speaking, to be physically fit adults should establish routines involving regular physical activity, a healthy diet, and appropriate health screenings. Physically fit adults should also refrain from smoking and keep their alcohol consumption low (Chodzko-Zajko, 2000). The physical exercise component of overall fitness should include activities aimed to improve five primary areas of functioning: cardiorespiratory endurance, muscular strength, muscular endurance, body composition (muscle tone compared to fat), and flexibility (National Center on Physical Activity and Disability, 2009).

It's not enough to simply take a walk once in a while, to be at our best physically individuals should pay attention to type and frequency of their activities. Adults should strive to complete a minimum of 20 minutes of vigorously intense activity on at least 3 days of the week, such as bicycling uphill or jogging, or a minimum of 30 minutes of moderately intense activities, such as mowing the lawn or dancing, on 5 or more days of the week. Moderately intense exercise is defined as activities that burn 3.5 to 7 calories per minute, whereas vigorously intense activities burn over 7 calories per minute. See Table 3.1 for more examples. Adults generally need to meet these minimums to burn the recommended 150 calories per day (NIA, 2001, 2009c, 2010f). These are general recommendations, and all of us should seek the advice of a medical professional before we begin or significantly increase an exercise program. We need to start with warm-up exercises, drink plenty of water, and breathe regularly through the exercises. Experts recommend that all adults ease into their program, keep records of their progress, and try to make the experience as enjoyable as possible, which may mean exercising to music or working out with friends (President's Council of Physical Fitness and Sports, 2010c).

Your Thoughts?

Do you think most adults have time for this much exercise?

TABLE 3.1 ***Examples of Moderate and Vigorous Activities***

Moderate Activities	*Vigorous Activities*
Cycling on a stationary bicycle	Climbing stairs or hills
Gardening	Shoveling snow
Walking briskly on a level surface	Tennis (singles)
Mopping or scrubbing the floor	Swimming laps
Golf, without a cart	Cross-country skiing
Volleyball	Downhill skiing
Rowing	Hiking

Adapted from *Exercise: A Guide from the National Institute on Aging*, retrieved from http://www.nia.nih.gov/NR/rdonlyres/25C76114-D120-4960-946A-3F576B528BBD/0/ExerciseGuide_2008.pdf.

Benefits of Fitness. What could be more motivating than to enjoy the benefits of a healthy lifestyle and achieving successful aging? Simply stated, exercise will make just about anyone feel stronger and look healthier (NIA, 2001, 2009c), and who wouldn't want that? Among the many physiological benefits of exercise are improved sleep, flexibility, muscle strength, better balance and coordination, and a stronger immune system (Aldwin et al., 2006; Chodzko-Zajko, 2000). By maintaining a regular fitness program and a desirable weight, individuals may reduce their risk for coronary heart disease, higher blood pressure, osteoporosis, diabetes, arthritis, and some types of cancer (CDC, 2010f; PCPFS, 2010b). Physical fitness can also improve our quality of life in other areas as well, including cognitive functioning throughout the aging process (Chodzko-Zajko, 2000; Rabbitt, 2002). Regular, appropriate exercise has been associated with reduced stress and anxiety, improved mood, and a sense of general well-being. When individuals engage in group or team activities the benefits can also include the opportunities to make new friendships and strengthen existing relationships (Chodzko-Zajko, 2000).

Your Thoughts?

Do you think the benefits would outweigh the costs for an employer to offer an "exercise hour" to employees?

Individuals who engage in adequate exercise during young, middle, and late adulthood also have a greater likelihood of aging well. People of all ages can benefit from regular exercise, even those well into their 90s. It is seldom the case that older people have lost their ability to do things *just because* they are older. Usually, they have become inactive, decreasing their endurance, strength, balance, and flexibility (NIA, 2001, 2009c, 2010f). Regular exercise across adulthood can reduce frailty in older adults by building and maintaining strong bones, muscles, and joints. These benefits will, in turn, help with balance, thus reducing falls and arthritis pain (CDC, 2010f; PCPFS, 2010c). The Cardiovascular Health Study, exploring the role of exercise in successful aging, found that high-intensity exercise was the most powerful predictor of good health at age 65 years and beyond. The study, involving assessments of nearly 6,000 participants from across the United States over a 7-year period, found that among the most powerful factors for increasing the number of healthy years were exercise, higher income, and appropriate weight. Many of the participants who were healthy at age 65 tended to remain healthy during the 7-year study, indicating that establishing a pattern of regular, appropriate exercise is a key in healthy aging (Burke et al., 2001).

Your Thoughts?

How might adults use digital devices and software to increase the likelihood of maintaining an adequate exercise program?

Even with the general awareness of the benefits of exercise there remains a significant portion of American adults who find it hard, if not nearly impossible, to exercise at the recommended levels. In a study involving 502 adults aged 19 to 65 years old, Carroll and Alexandris (1997) found that the most frequently given reasons for not exercising were lack of energy, time, interest, and knowledge about equipment or rules for a particular sport. Inactive participants also indicated that they were concerned about getting hurt. In a study of adults aged 65 and older, Lees, Clark, Nigg, and Newman (2005) found that the most common barriers to exercise were fear of falling or sustaining an injury, lack of interest, and procrastination.

What can be done to overcome some of these obstacles? Choosing the appropriate activities is critical. All adults are more likely to stick to an exercise program when they choose activities they enjoy, can perform safely and correctly, and can afford financially (NIA, 2001, 2009c). Adults are also more likely to exercise outside of their homes when their neighborhoods have sidewalks, trails, traffic signs or lights, and streetlights (Huston, Evenson, Bors, & Gizlice, 2003). Above all, individuals need to be convinced that they will benefit from intense physical activity in order to stay motivated. Keeping an eye on the long-term goal of successful aging has been associated with higher levels of motivation for engaging in vigorous exercise (Hall & Fong, 2003). It is not only the goal of this section or even this chapter, but it is my goal for this entire book to encourage you, no matter your age, to take this long-term view! Successful aging is achievable for all of us who plan ahead, give it effort, and take a long-term perspective.

Nutrition

> **Your Thoughts?**
>
> Would you support a proposal to emphasize nutritional science in K–12 education at the same level as mathematics or English? Why or why not?

The strikingly high estimates of the number of individuals who are overweight or obese indicates that Americans are eating too much for the amount of calories they burn, and are most likely consuming more of those foods that should be taken in sparingly.

The term *nutrition* is often associated with dieting and weight loss, however, it's important to keep in mind that people who are of average weight or even underweight may not have a nutritious diet and suffer from the consequences. Poor nutrition has been linked to general poor health and the onset of several diseases, such as cardiovascular disease, type 2 diabetes, diverticular disease, and some cancers (U.S. Department of Health and Human Services [HHS], 2006). Poor nutrition often occurs along with a sedentary lifestyle, which can compound the negative effects.

The amount of nutrients and calories we should take in depends on our age, activity level, current body weight, and current health status (CDC, 2009e). For example, adults over age 50 generally need a diet rich in calcium, and vitamins B_{12} and D, while women in childbearing years need additional iron and folic acid (HHS, 2006). Speaking generally, most adults would benefit from eating more whole grains, vegetables, and fruits, less sugars and processed foods, and monitoring the calories in their diets. Moderately active young adults should take in approximately 2,400 calories per day, whereas moderately active older adults should take in approximately 2,200 calories. Table 3.2 provides the estimated caloric requirements recommended by the U.S. Department of Health and Human Services and the Department of Agriculture (USDA).

> **Your Thoughts?**
>
> How would you distinguish accurate health information from bogus information on the Internet

There is no shortage of nutrition information available to the American public, whether through the media, educational programs, or food labels. More people are turning to the Internet for health information than ever before, particularly those in the 18- to 29-year-old age range (Hanauer, Dibble, Fortin, & Col, 2004). In the early 1990s the USDA launched a campaign to educate the American public about nutritional needs by using the "food pyramid." The latest version, called *MyPyramid*, was introduced in 2005 with many educational supporting materials and a large, interactive website (*www.mypyramid.gov*). The guidelines are consistent with recommendations by the American Heart Association, American Cancer Society, American Diabetes Association, and other agencies promoting diets designed to lower the risk of various illnesses. In general, MyPyramid was designed to cover a range of activity levels, meet nutrient needs, discourage overeating, and focus on common foods (Krebs-Smith & Kris-Etherton, 2007). It encourages a diet that is high in fruits, vegetables, whole grains, and fat-free or low-fat dairy products, includes lean meats, poultry, fish, beans, eggs, and nuts, and is low in saturated fats, trans fats, cholesterol, salt, and added sugars (USDA, n.d.). Most adults need more calcium, potassium, fiber, magnesium, and vitamins A, D, and E (HHS, 2006), and the best way to get those nutrients is through a healthy diet (NIA, 2008a). As you can see from Figure 3.1, MyPyramid emphasizes physical activity along with a nutritious diet.

TABLE 3.2 ***Estimated Caloric Requirements (in Kilocalories)***

Gender	*Age*	*Sedentary*	*Moderately Active*	*Active*
Female	19–30	2,000	2,000–2,200	2,400
	31–50	1,800	2,000	2,200
	51+	1,600	1,800	2,000–2,200
Male	19–30	2,400	2,600–2,800	3,000
	31–50	2,200	2,400–2,600	2,800–3,000
	51+	2,000	2,200–2,400	2,400–2,800

From U.S. Department of Health and Human Services and U.S. Department of Agriculture (2005).

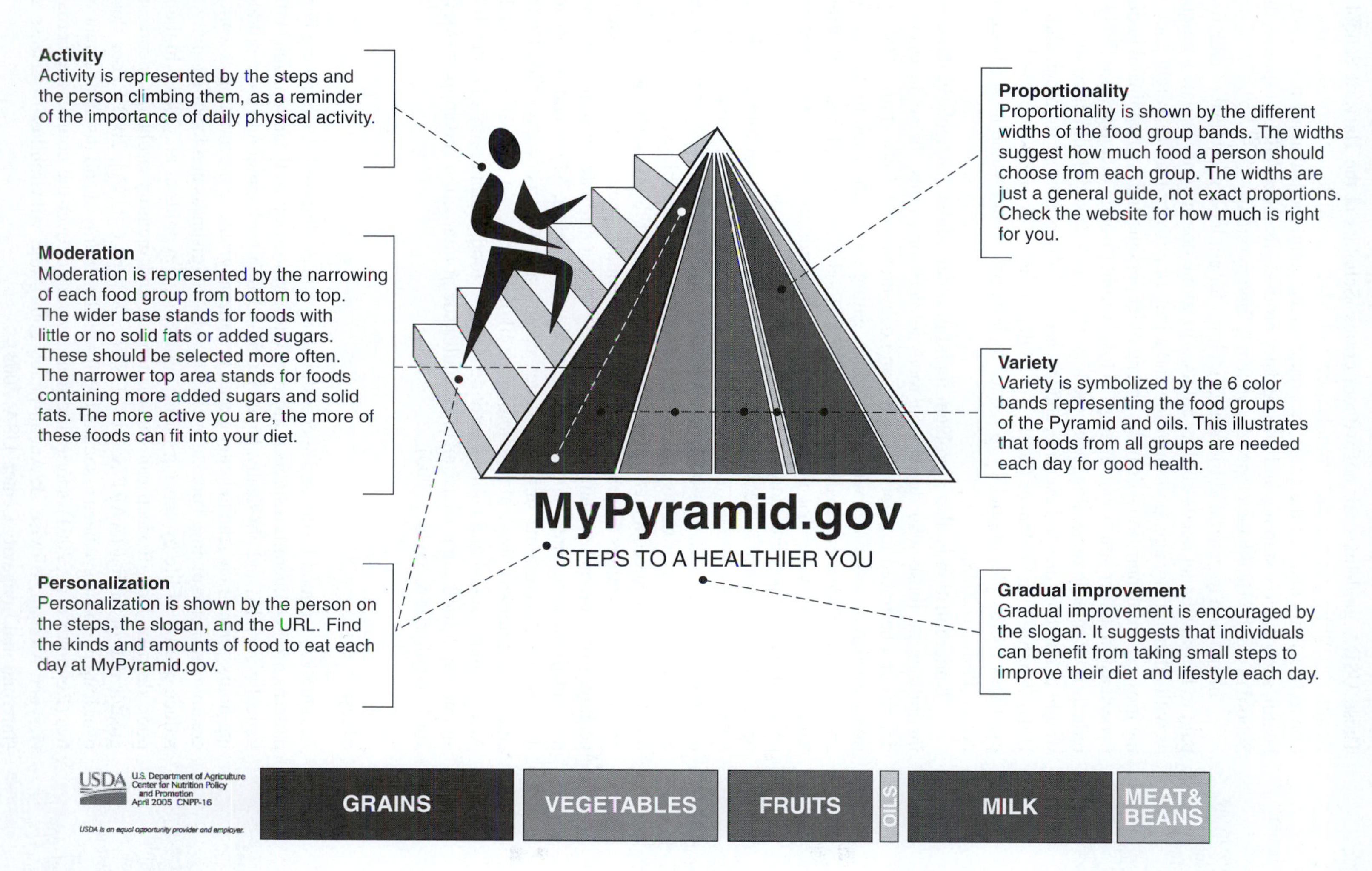

FIGURE 3.1 *The Anatomy of MyPyramid U.S. Dept. of Agriculture (http://www.mypyramid.gov/downloads/MyPyramid_Anatomy.pdf)*

Your Thoughts?

How much consideration should the developers of MyPyramid give to the needs of American agricultural industries and what those industries provide to the public?

These USDA guidelines are not without critics. Scholars at the Harvard School of Public Health (2010b) claim that the symbols used with MyPyramid do not provide enough information to be useful, and that the guidelines recommend some foods that are not essential to good health, such as more starches and low-fat dairy products than needed. In response, the Harvard School of Public Health developed a competing food pyramid.

In addition to general nutritional guidelines for adults, a great deal of attention is being paid to the nutritional needs of older adults. Age alone does not necessitate a unique diet, but as with adults of any age, poor nutrition and a lack of activity lead to weight gain. Obesity is the most common nutritional disorder among older persons and is often linked to diabetes and hypertension. Older adults who attempt to lose weight through diet alone are likely to cause a reduction of muscle mass along with the loss of fat. It is wise for all adults who need to lose weight to combine diet and exercise, and this is especially important for older adults (McCool, Huls, Peppones, & Schlenker (2001). As adults in their 70s or 80s become less mobile and exert less energy they should try to reduce their calorie intake without sacrificing nutritional needs (Phillips, 2003).

Undernutrition is also a problem found in older adults, particularly those who live in institutions or those who depend on food delivery programs. In some cases nutritional deficits can be traced to poor oral health and dehydration (McCool et al., 2000). Poor nutrition may also be associated with eating alone, eating too much or too little, chronic diseases and various medications that affect appetite or food choices, and financial difficulties. In some cases it may be that an elderly individual needs assistance with food preparation (Aldwin et al., 2006). For example, an acquaintance of mine who is in her mid-80s needs help opening cans, jars, and some types of plastic containers. One of our routine activities together involves emptying contents of cans and jars into containers she can open and close easily. (As a side note, she refuses to use the microwave her adult children bought for her because she can't remember how it works and she sees it as too much trouble when the stove works just fine.) Older adults need a diet with an adequate amount of fluids and the appropriate number of calories. A nutritious diet should also contain adequate amounts of proteins, calcium, magnesium, iron, chromium, and vitamins D, C, B_6, B_{12}, and foliate. In some cases older adults may need encouragement and guidance in choosing foods. My friend, if left to her own devices, would consume only cereal, ice cream, and tea every day! Good nutrition can enhance mental and physical functioning for all of us, which in turn raises our quality of life. Also, as many social and cultural activities involve food, maintaining a healthy lifestyle and an interest in food can increase an older adult's social interaction and support (McCool et al., 2001; Wahlqvist & Savige, 2000).

Your Thoughts?

What might community senior centers do to encourage appropriate exercise and nutrition?

Sleep

Another key to good health and successful aging is sleeping well. Maintaining healthy sleep patterns offers numerous benefits at any age. Those who sleep well can function better psychologically, socially, and physically, laying the foundation for happier and more productive waking hours, which may lead to better grades in college, greater concentration at work, and more creative problem solving. Poor sleep can result in sluggishness and lack of activity, which can reduce quality of life by causing further problems (Reynolds et al., 2001). In the short term poor sleep or lack of sleep can cause attention and memory problems, depression, and a greater risk of falling (AARP & [ILC-USA], 2003; [ILC-USA], 2003). Poor sleep patterns over long periods have been associated with social withdrawal and disengagement with activities (Reynolds et al., 2001), shorter lifespans, overuse of over-the-counter and herbal remedies (Kryger, Monjan, Bliwise, & Ancoli-Israel, 2004), and vulnerability to disease and illness (International Longevity Center–USA, 2003).

Your Thoughts?

If an accurate sleepiness test were developed, should drivers be given penalties similar to drunk driving if driving while sleepy? Why or why not?

Some of us who say we are "light sleepers" or that we can't sleep when we are stressed may be causing our own sleep problems by making poor lifestyle choices. Sleep disturbances such as sleeplessness, snoring, or disordered breathing can be the side effects of stress and/or illnesses or medications. Sleeplessness has been associated with obesity, alcohol intake, smoking, nasal congestion, and in women, estrogen depletion during menopause. Snoring, or sleep-disordered breathing, can also be a signal of several health problems, including sleep apnea and high blood pressure or hypertension.

Your Thoughts?

Should individuals in life-or-death situations, such as certain medical staff or airline pilots, be routinely tested for sleep concerns? Why or why not?

Insomnia, reflected in trouble falling asleep and remaining asleep, can have numerous root causes, including medical or psychiatric illnesses, menopause, or lifestyle factors such as the use of alcohol, caffeine, nicotine, some over-the-counter medications, or a poor sleeping environment. Insomnia is also associated with diabetes, obesity, hypertension, and cardiovascular problems (AARP & [ILC-USA], 2003; [ILC-USA], 2003). Estimates are that periods of insomnia or sleepless nights affect between 33% (AARP & [ILC-USA], 2003) and 50% ([ILC-USA], 2003) of all older Americans. Researchers have found that women are more likely to complain of difficulty in falling asleep, while men tend to complain of waking early (Rockwood, Davis, Merry, MacKnight, & McDowell, 2001).

One of the best things individuals of any age can do to help their sleep is to get regular exercise. Another important factor is to keep a regular schedule of going to bed and getting up at the same time every day, making sure to get 7 to 8 hours of sleep. To improve sleep individuals should avoid alcohol, nicotine, overeating, and drinking large amounts of liquid in the evenings. It also helps to create a relaxing routine prior to going to bed. As adults we tend to association a bed-time routine with small children, but the principle is much as the same even when we are older. Our bodies will respond to behaviors such as reading in bed or listening to relaxing music as signals that it is time to fall asleep. In addition to a comfortable and supportive mattress, a sleeping environment should be cool in temperature, quiet, and dark (AARP & [ILC-USA], 2003).

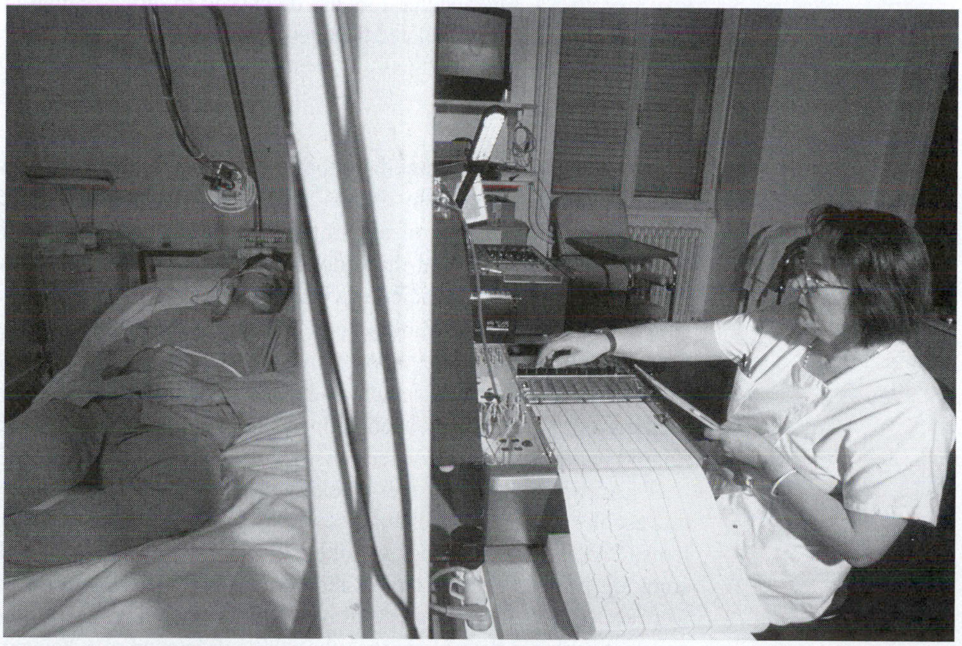

Sleep is so important that routine sleep disturbances should be checked by a health care professional in a sleep laboratory.

Section Summary

- Among the most important components to a healthy lifestyle are a vigorous exercise routine, nutritious diet with appropriate caloric intake, and 7 to 8 hours of restful sleep.
- The benefits of maintaining a healthy lifestyle are both immediate and long-lasting.
- Adults who can complete a minimum of 20 minutes of vigorous and intense activity or a minimum of 30 minutes of moderately intense activity on at least 3 days of the week will find they have enhanced their physiological and psychological functioning as well as reduced the risk of many illnesses.
- Regarding nutrition, most guidelines recommend a diet high in fruits, vegetables, whole grains, and fat-free or low-fat dairy products and low in saturated fats, trans fats, cholesterol, salt, and added sugars.
- Most adults need to alter their diet to include more calcium, potassium, fiber, magnesium, and vitamins A, D, and E. Lack of quality sleep causes psychological and physiological problems that can dramatically affect daily functioning.

Common Challenges to Healthy Lifestyles

Almost any list of destructive choices with the greatest effects on optimal aging will include a sedentary lifestyle and poor nutrition (Ferraro, 2006). Successful aging involves not only engaging in those activities that *decelerate* aging and raise quality of life, such as maintaining an exercise routine and a nutritious diet, but also actively avoiding or stopping those activities that *accelerate* aging. Among the worst habits, in terms of harming major organ systems, general functioning, and reducing healthy aging, are smoking, engaging in substance abuse, and overeating (obesity) (Aldwin et al., 2006; Ferraro, 2006). In this section we focus on several of the more common obstacles to healthy lifestyles: smoking, obesity, alcohol abuse, and high levels of stress. Age accelerators are discussed in other chapters too, including discussions of relationship- and work-related stresses, anxiety, and depression.

Smoking

Your Thoughts?

For those who smoke, what might be the benefits that outweigh the health costs?

Smoking, while in the immediate moment may generate a sense of calmness, has far-reaching and devastating long-term effects. The costs of nicotine addictions are high. Nicotine is responsible for 80–85% of all lung cancer and obstructive pulmonary disease deaths. The CDC (2009c) reports that more deaths are caused by tobacco use than the combined deaths from human immunodeficiency virus, illegal drug use, alcohol use, motor vehicle injuries, suicides, and murders. Smoking is related to a significant percentage of premature deaths as it reduces life expectancy by approximately 14 years (CDC, 2005a). When comparing smoking to other destructive habits such as excessive use of alcohol, overeating, and improper use of medication, smoking has been called "the outstanding performer" as the highest risk health-related behavior in older Americans (Leventhal et al., 2001, p. 188).

Across adults of all ages smoking has been associated with increased rates of cancers, cardiovascular disease, pulmonary disease, stroke, emphysema, asthma, and other lung-related problems (Brook, Brook, Zhang, & Cohen, 2004). In a longitudinal study of young adults who began smoking prior to age 20, Brook and his colleagues (2004) found that by age 29 these smokers were showing more respiratory ailments, difficulties with memory and concentration, headaches, and gastrointestinal problems than those who did not smoke. Focusing on later adulthood, the Cardiovascular Health Study, involving 6,000 participants ages 65 years and older, found that the factor most associated with fewer healthy years was current smoking (Burke et al., 2001).

> **Your Thoughts?**
>
> What factors might contribute to the finding that younger adults are smoking in greater percentages than older adults?

Data collected in 2002 and 2003 indicated that the percentages of Americans who smoked was slowly declining, moving from 22.5% to 21.6%, and while encouraging, these figures indicated that approximately 46 million adults were chronic smokers in 2003 (CDC, 2005b). In 2010 the CDC reported that since the 2002–2003 data collection the decline in smoking rate has stalled at about 20% in spite of the increase in smoke-free zones, higher cigarette prices and many educational and media campaigns. Individuals over 65 years old have a lower smoking rate (about 10%) than young adults (about 33%), with the exception of African American males (20 percent) (Aldwin et al., 2006).

In terms of successful aging, the best plan is to never start smoking. For those who do smoke, seeking the social and medical support needed to stop is well worth the effort. Medical research has shown that anyone who stops smoking, including older adults, will experience immediate health benefits. For those who stop before they develop a smoking-related disease, they can return to the level of health of nonsmokers within 5 to 15 years. For those who quit after a disease process has started, quitting may reduce the rate of disease-related decline (Aldwin et al., 2006). For smokers of all ages the benefits of breaking the habit of smoking and the nicotine addiction are quickly evident and powerful.

Obesity

Obesity has been called an epidemic and one of America's "most challenging public health problems" (Kaplan, 2007). The percentage of obese Americans has more than doubled since 1980 (Tomiyama, Westling, Lew, Samuels, & Chatman, 2007), with more dramatic increases found among men (CDC, 2007b). Using data from 1999 to 2000, the Centers for Disease Control and Prevention (CDC) reported that 30% of adults age 20 years and older were obese, and when the number of overweight and obese were combined the percentage swelled to 64%. These figures were so alarming that the U.S. Department of Health and Human Services has made the goal of reducing obesity among adults one of its highest priorities (HHS, 2000). Another signal of the national concern over obesity came in 2004 when Medicare changed its policy to allow for payment for obesity treatment (Tomiyama et al., 2007). Data collected in 2005–2006 indicated that 34.3% of American adults were obese, a rate similar to that found in 2003–2004 (CDC, 2007).

> **Your Thoughts?**
>
> What aspects of American society have changed since 1980 to contribute to a doubling of the percentage of obese individuals?

In addition to the many difficulties faced by obese individuals in their daily routines, numerous health concerns have been associated with carrying too much weight. These health problems include high blood pressure and high cholesterol, type 2 diabetes, heart disease, stroke, some cancers, and sleep disorders (Aldwin et al., 2006; Kaplan, 2007). Psychologically, extra weight has been linked to increased stress, poor self-image, and lower self-confidence (CDC, 2009a, 2010e; PCPFS, 2010b). Unfortunately, some of these side effects of obesity may also serve as additional obstacles to the regimen of exercise and good nutrition needed to lose weight.

To determine whether individuals are obese, overweight, or within their ideal weight range with precision would require a great deal of information, such as age, percentage of fat and lean muscle mass, and gender. Because most people do not have access to a professional to gather the needed information and make a personal assessment, many experts recommend the use of ***body mass index*** (BMI) scores. One can easily find a BMI calculator on the Internet or work through the calculations as follows:

1. Find your weight (in pounds)
2. Find your height (in inches)
3. Divide your weight in pounds by your height in inches
4. Divide the number from the previous step by your height in inches

5. Multiple the number from the previous step by 703
6. The result is your BMI score

Your Thoughts?

Would you support an employer who would only hire people whose BMI was within a normal range? Why, why not, or under what circumstances?

BMI scores of less than 18.5 are considered underweight, 18.5–24.9 are normal, 25–29.9 are considered overweight, and scores of 30 or more are considered obese. Another way to determine obesity is to consider waist measurement. A general rule is that women with a waist measurement greater than 35 inches and men with a waist measurement greater than 40 inches are obese and at risk for numerous health problems (CDC, 2010e; Harvard School of Public Health, 2010a).

On a societal level, the obesity epidemic is likely to have numerous causes and influences, many of which stem from poor food choices, inadequate physical activity, overconsumption of processed foods, fast foods, larger portions, and increased sugar intake (Kaplan, 2007). On a personal level obesity is likely to be the result of poor lifestyle choices, although it can be a symptom of other health concerns. The good news is that, like smoking, exchanging the unhealthy for healthy habits can produce dramatic physiological and psychological benefits (Aldwin et al., 2006). The bad news is that weight reduction takes discipline, effort, and time. Those who are tempted to try one of the many quick weight-loss products on the market would be wise to check the U.S. Federal Trade Commission and the U.S. Food and Drug Administration websites for the latest information on bogus health claims.

Numerous reviews of research studies on weight loss reveal that most diets result in, first, individuals losing 5–10% of their weight, and second, individuals then regaining the weight they lost (Tomiyama et al., 2007). While the basic formula for weight loss is simple, burn more energy than is taken in, putting that into practice can be difficult. Consider that a pound of body fat is the equivalent of 3,500 calories, and in comparison, walking one mile will use approximately 100 calories (depending on how much an individual weighs, whether the walk is on flat surfaces or hills, and the person's age and general health) (PCPFS, 2010b). In a recent meta-analysis of research on obesity treatments going back to 1970, Powell and Calvin (2007) found that education and awareness are not enough to motivate individuals to lose weight. Considering only studies that observed participants for at least 2 years following their weight-loss program, they found that the best results came when dietary changes (with or without drug treatment) were combined with an exercise program and behavior modification counseling. Across the studies analyzed, approximately 20–40% of the participants were able to keep the weight off (Powell & Calvin, 2007).

Your Thoughts?

Why isn't education enough to get most people to lose weight?

Alcohol Abuse

Another common obstacle to healthy living and successful aging is alcohol abuse and addiction. The National Institute on Alcohol Abuse and Alcoholism (NIAAA; 2007) reports that 1 in every 12 adults, approximately 17.6 million Americans, either abuses alcohol or could be diagnosed with alcoholism. The Centers for Disease Control and Prevention (2008b) report that alcohol is likely to be closely associated with approximately 75,000 deaths each year in the United States. Data indicate that over half of all Americans report drinking some alcohol, with those over 75 years old reporting the lowest rates. Caucasian Americans and multiethnic Americans report the heaviest drinking, followed by Native Americans, African Americans, Hispanics, and Asians (Aldwin et al., 2006). In a large study of over 20,000 Americans, researchers from five universities and the National Institute for Mental Health found that 14% of the adults had experienced alcoholism, most becoming alcoholics before the age of 30. The study also found that those who had or were currently dealing with alcoholism were more likely to be less educated, never married or divorced, and living on a lower income. The number of men who had experienced alcoholism was nearly four times higher than of women, consistent with previous research (Bucholz, 1992).

Your Thoughts?

What factors in American society might contribute to the finding that the alcoholism rate is so much higher for men?

With alcoholic drinks being so common and available we may not realize what medical professionals consider to be excessive alcohol intake. Heavy drinking is defined as more than two drinks per day on average for men, one drink per day on average for women. One drink is any *one* of the following:

- 12-ounce bottle or can of beer or wine cooler
- 5-ounce glass of wine
- 1.5 ounces of 80-proof distilled spirits

Heavy drinking and alcoholism has been associated with a long list of medical problems, including greater risk for several cancers, including cancers of the liver, esophagus, throat, larynx, prostate and breast; numerous liver diseases; immune system problems; neurological problems, such as dementia and stroke; cardiovascular problems; gastrointestinal problems; and, when pregnant, fetal alcohol syndrome. There are also numerous immediate risks for individuals who are intoxicated, such as unintentional injuries (traffic accidents, drowning), violent outbursts, risky sexual behaviors, work-related injuries, and alcohol poisoning (CDC, 2008b: NIAAA, 2007).

Much of the research exploring the influence of alcoholism on adult development has focused on either very young or very old adults. The National Institute on Drug Abuse (NIDA; 2005) reports the use of alcohol, illicit drugs, and cigarette smoking tend to peak during young adulthood. The Substance Abuse and Mental Health Services Administration (SAMHSA; 2005) found that 1.9 million adults, mostly younger adults, engaged in polydrug use, with the most popular drugs being alcohol, marijuana, and cocaine. In interviews with 465 adults in their early 20s, Parker and Williams (2003) found the most popular reasons given for drinking were to celebrate, for pleasure, for the taste, to wind down after work or study, and because it "makes me feel good." Although these young adults experienced many of the negative consequences of their lifestyle, including illness, fights, and arrests for a variety of criminal behaviors including drunk driving, they felt that being intoxicated with alcohol maximized their enjoyment of being in crowded settings, romantic/sexual encounters, and celebrating weekends with their friends.

> **Your Thoughts?**
>
> How might the psychological belief that alcohol maximizes enjoyment be learned and reinforced in the media?

Alcohol abuse among older adults has also gained attention from health care professionals and counselors, as 5–15% of older Americans have alcohol-related problems. Studies show that cigarette smoking and alcohol abuse often begin in adolescence or young adulthood and are continued in middle and late adulthood. Estimates are that government health programs, particularly Medicare, Medicaid, and Veterans Administration Medical Centers, spend about 20% of their health care dollars on problems related to smoking and alcohol abuse (Kirk, Weisbrod, & Ericson, 2002). Even though rates of drug abuse are lower among older adults than younger adults, SAMHSA reports a 32% increase in the number of adults aged 55 and older who are receiving treatment for substance-related disorders, mostly for alcohol-related problems. Once in treatment programs older adults tend to be more motivated and successful than younger adults (Brennan, Nichol, & Moos, 2003).

> **Your Thoughts?**
>
> Do you think it is appropriate to give older adults alcohol as birthday or holiday gifts? Why, why not, or under what circumstances?

Although most older adults consume less alcohol than younger adults, their problems can be just as severe. Estimates are that approximately two-thirds of the older adults with alcohol-related disorders are *earlier-onset problem drinkers*, meaning they developed an alcohol problem prior to age 60. These adults are more likely to develop additional alcohol-related problems, such as cirrhosis of the liver or mood and thought disorders. *Later-onset problem drinkers*, those who develop an alcohol problem as an older adult, are often using a dysfunctional coping method (drinking) to deal with issues surrounding retirement, social isolation, physical and cognitive changes, or the death of a spouse (Hanson & Gutheil, 2004). Whether early or late onset, alcohol abuse can magnify other problems. For example, intoxication can slow reaction times, already slowed by old age, putting older adults at greater risk for falls and other accidents around their home. Older adults are also more likely to take medications or over-the-counter drugs, risking dangerous side effects due to mixing medications and alcohol. In addition, heavy alcohol use can cause more problems for those with high blood pressure and other physical illnesses (NIAAA, 2007).

Stress

The last challenge to healthy lifestyles and optimal aging to be explored here is destructive stress and burnout. Most people live with some level of stress, and some actually thrive on challenges, risk-taking, and adventures that would produce paralyzing stress in others (Veach, Rahe, Tolles, & Newhall, 2003). Stressful situations, when the level of stress is manageable, can prompt self-reflection and personal growth (Park & Fenster, 2004). This section offers a more general perspective on personal stresses, which are overwhelming and detrimental to optimal aging.

Stress and the sources of stress (stressors) can be described in many ways. Stress is usually defined as a negative emotional experience resulting from either the need to change or adapt, or the worry that one will need to change or adapt in the future (Bekker, Nijssen, & Hens, 2001). Stressors can be categorized in terms of ***macrostressors***, major life events, or ***microstressors***, daily hassles or minor events such as misplacing something you need right away (Felsten, 2002). Stressors can results from acute (immediate and temporary) or chronic situations. Even though the experience of overwhelming stress is not pleasant, it is important to remember that stress can stem from events that are very much desired and positive, such as a promotion at work or the arrival of a new baby as well as those unwanted or negative events, such as a car accident or illness. It is likely that stress will always be a part of our lives at some level, thus learning to manage our stress is probably a more productive strategy than waiting for a time in our lives without stress.

Your Thoughts?

How would you design a research study to find if macrostressors or microstressors are more powerful in the lives of college students?

Stressful experiences are highly personal and subjective, varying greatly among individuals. People who have high ***stress reactivity***, meaning they have more intense, emotional reactions to stressful events, tend to view their world as more threatening and feel their coping resources are less effective (Bood, Archer, & Norlander, 2004; Felsten, 2002). Even within individuals stress varies. For example, when people are healthy they can tolerate more stress than when they are not healthy (Cassidy, 2000). As another example of intraindividual change, I notice that the college students in my classes seem to handle stressors much better in the beginning of the semester than toward the end when they are often tired and sleep deprived.

Generally speaking, younger adults perceive greater amounts of stress than is reported by middle-aged or older adults (Hamarat et al., 2001). Hamarat and his colleagues (2001) found that for young adults in their 20s and 30s, self-reported levels of stress were related to their feelings of life satisfaction. Middle-aged and older adults were more influenced by their available coping resources than stress levels when rating life satisfaction. Adults of different ages not only report variations in levels of stress but also report different types of stressors. For example, older adults tend to be more stressed when playing the role of caregiver than middle-aged adults; however, older adults demonstrate less stress over the death of a spouse than middle-aged adults. Older adults tend to report fewer problems and hassles, which may be because they have adjusted to chronic stressors, reporting problems only when they become acute (Aldwin et al., 2006).

Your Thoughts?

What characteristics of young adulthood would lead individuals to perceive or feel more stress even when reporting fewer stressors?

The experience of high levels of stress over time can result in physiological, cognitive, and behavioral changes (Bekker et al., 2001) that many people typically call ***burnout***. While burnout is similar to the clinical terms *anxiety* and *depression*, the term *burnout* in

ON THE LEADING EDGE
Biofeedback 24/7

Researchers Paul Ratanasiripong, Kevin Sverduk, Diane Hayashino, and Judy Prince from California State University at Long Beach recognized the high levels of stress and anxiety most college students deal with routinely and the devastating effects that can have on academic performance. They decided to apply their knowledge of biofeedback to teach students how to reduce their anxiety and stress. Biofeedback involves the use of some type of machinery to give individuals a way to measure physiological responses such as muscle tension, blood pressure, breathing rate, heart rate, and skin temperature. It has been used successfully in the treatment of many different concerns, including stress, anxiety, depression, and hypertension.

In its most traditional sense, biofeedback requires a trained or certified practitioner to work the equipment and guide the process. Until recently most of the equipment has been highly specialized, non-portable, and expensive. Students would go to a lab or clinic for treatment, often imaging a scenario or recalling a high-stress situation.

Ratanasiripong and his colleagues decided to try a new approach. They surveyed the ever-growing collection of new small, portable, and inexpensive biofeedback devices for something they thought college students would feel comfortable with. They chose a device that measures heart rate, giving the students an indication of the effects of positive and negative emotions. Students were shown how to use and maintain the devices and given information about emotions and the feedback from the devices. They were given evidence showing that by maintaining positive emotions they would be able to think more clearly and reduce their blood pressure, reduce muscle tension, and build up their immune system, whereas negative emotions would have just the opposite effect.

The researchers found the students in their study were very comfortable with the technology involved in using the portable devices. The students reported great success not only in reducing anxiety and stress but also in understanding when their anxiety levels were high. By taking portable biofeedback equipment out into their daily world, not only on campus but everywhere they go, they were better able to learn to read their own body signals and see evidence of stress management via the reinforcement from the equipment (Ratanasiripong, Sverduk, Hayashino, & Prince, 2010).

It's important to remember that stress can come not only from the negative events in our lives but also from the positive and greatly desired events.

Your Thoughts?

Would you support an employer who screened employees for high stress and required the same follow-up as employees found with drug and alcohol issues? Why, why not, or under what circumstances?

academic and professional usage is generally associated with highly detrimental work-related stress (McManus, Winder, & Gordon, 2002). High levels of stress, particularly when concentrated in time, can lead to numerous psychological and physiological vulnerabilities. Individuals may react passively by ignoring or avoiding stressors (Bekker et al., 2001), wishing they would simply go away (Tully, 2004). Others respond with high levels of anxiety and aggression (Cassidy, 2000), possibly leading to yelling, losing their tempers, violent actions (Klitzing, 2004), and taking their anxiety out on innocent people around them (Tully, 2004). High levels of stress and burnout have also been associated with difficulties in cognitive functioning (Skowron, Wester, & Azen, 2004), poor work performance, and reduced efficiency (Hannigan, Edwards, & Burnard, 2004). Even more troublesome, high stress has been associated with comfort eating, smoking, alcohol abuse, abuse of other drugs and medications (Tully, 2004), depression (Skowron et al., 2004), and suicide attempts (Klitzing, 2004). The psychological experience of burnout usually involves emotional exhaustion, feelings of depersonalization, cynicism, and lack of productivity or sense of personal accomplishment (McManus et al., 2002). Physiologically, high stress and burnout are most associated with a weakened immune system, making individuals vulnerable to a wide variety of problems and illnesses (Aldwin et al., 2006; Cassidy, 2000; Skowron et al., 2004).

Your Thoughts?

In what types of stressful situations would problem-focused coping be best suited? In what types of stressful situations would emotion-focused coping methods work best?

A primary aspect of successful aging, for adults at any point in life, is the ability to engage in healthy coping mechanisms when dealing with stressors, thus avoiding the destructive outcomes caused by high stress and burnout as much as possible. Healthy coping mechanisms generally fall into two categories, one aimed at problem solving and the other at managing our emotions (Heiman, 2004). ***Problem-focused strategies*** may include talking with peers or mentors about the stressor, changing environments, and working on changing personal behaviors and habits (Tully, 2004). ***Emotion-focused strategies*** may include exercising (Hannigan et al., 2004), spending time in relaxing activities, and building social support networks (Klitzing, 2004). Emotion-focused strategies are designed to help individuals monitor and manage their reactions to stressors (Heiman, 2004).

One of the most popular emotion-focused coping methods is the use of laughter. Humor aimed at something stressful helps to restructure or change the way we think about a stressful situation, thus making it less threatening. Laughing also has physiological benefits, such as muscle relaxation, and psychological benefits, such as creating positive mood states. Individuals with a greater sense of humor generally report the use of productive problem-solving strategies as well as much less stress in their lives (Abel, 2002). The most productive approach to stressful situations may be to use both problem- and emotion-focused strategies when possible. There are times, such as when the stressor is totally out of our control, that emotion-focused strategies are our only option.

For individuals in a Western culture, one of the most important factors in dealing effectively with stress is to establish, as much as possible, personal control and decision-making power over our lives and the stressful situation (O'Connor & Shimizu, 2002). In fact, control is among the most researched constructs in relation to aging decelerators (Aldwin et al., 2006). If an individual has the perception of control, then a stressor or a stressful situation seems more manageable. We can choose better problem-solving strategies if the stressor is viewed more as a challenge than as something overwhelming (Heiman, 2004). For example, Taris and Feij (2004) studied job stress by exploring the role of job demands and sense of personal control among 883 machine operators and office technicians. Those in high demand–low control situations reported the greatest levels of stress and strain, while the lowest levels of stress were reported by employees in low demand–high control situations.

Your Thoughts?

Can you think of other high demand–low control situations? In family situations? College situations?

Section Summary

- Among the worst factors for successful aging, in addition to lack of physical activity and poor nutrition, are smoking, obesity, substance abuse, and overwhelming stress.
- Smoking is often targeted as the worst health-related behavior as it is linked to many illnesses and reduced life expectancy.
- Another area of concern is the strikingly high numbers of adults who are obese, a condition that can increase the risk for many illnesses.
- Researchers have found that the best weight-loss programs include dietary modifications, ample exercise, and behavior-modification counseling.
- Alcohol abuse usually peaks in young adulthood, although the rate of alcoholism among older adults is rising.
- Individuals who are overwhelmed with stresses and engaging in inadequate coping mechanisms are vulnerable to numerous psychological concerns such as anxiety, depression, and even suicide attempts.
- High stress is also associated with a weakened immune system, leading to increased vulnerability to many problems and illnesses.

Aging Well

References to the notion of "successful aging" can be found in social science literature as early as the 1960s, but the concept didn't become popular until the 1980s (Phelan & Larson, 2002; Rice & Fineman, 2004). Prior to the aging of the baby boomers and the scholarly emphases on life satisfaction, quality of life, and positive psychology, most perspectives on aging were pessimistic, basically treating old age as if it were a disease. The concept of successful aging was quite revolutionary when lifespan developmental theorists first proposed that middle and late adulthood could be viewed in terms of growth and development. The current academic field of successful aging is truly interdisciplinary, involving researchers and practitioners from psychology, sociology, social work, biology, and medicine (Phelan & Larson, 2002; Rice & Fineman, 2004).

Although there is general agreement that successful aging is a most worthwhile goal, the factors that actually define what it means to age successfully or optimally are debated. One area of controversy is the role, if any, of "anti-aging medicine" in the quest for successful aging (Binstock, Fishman, & Johnson, 2006). The anti-aging movement is aimed at reducing the amount of time individuals experience the typical characteristics associated with aging. The least controversial approach to anti-aging is to work toward ***compression of functional morbidity***, which is reducing (compressing) the time at the end of life (morbidity) one spends with physical disabilities or is less functional. A more ambitious goal is that of *decelerated aging*. Here the emphasis is on slowing the aging process and extending the years lived. The most aggressive approach is anti-aging in its most complete sense, that of *arrested aging*. This approach seeks to reverse aging and restore the function and appearance of a younger chronological age. There are some promising lines of research in regard to affecting the aging process. In addition to caloric restriction and stem cell research, there are some pharmaceutical interventions that may prove to be helpful in the future (Binstock et al., 2006; NIA, 2007a). On the whole, however, the general public should be cautious with the many so-called anti-aging products on the market. Studies have found that ineffective and potentially harmful products remain unregulated and easily available (Binstock et al., 2006).

Your Thoughts?

What do you think drives some people to take great risks with their health or appearance in order to look younger?

Another area of debate involves the exact factors that should define successful aging (George, 2006). Two meta-analyses of studies on successful aging, one involving 75 empirical studies by Bowling (2007) and another covering 40 years of research by Phelan and Larson (2002), identified the most common view or perspective. Most scholars conceptualized successful aging as containing a social functioning component, reflecting social engagement in life and emotional well-being. Often the definitions included a life satisfaction component, reflecting happiness and meeting personal goals. A psychological or coping component was also emphasized, particularly in terms of adapting and adjusting to change, stresses, and difficulties. The fourth component is the physiological or physical functioning factor. Most definitions of successful aging emphasize good health, absence or minimizing of disease and disability, and independent physical functioning. In her critique of the findings, Bowling (2007) suggested that successful aging be viewed as a continuum that allows for individual differences and variations in environmental opportunities, such as access to health care and safe exercise areas, and cultural values. Another critique of these components is the lack of acknowledgment that, while the goal is to function at the highest level for as long as possible, successful aging also includes coping well with disease processes. In a survey of internists and geriatricians, Snow and Pan (2004) found that these medical professionals included coping well with all life events, including illnesses, disabilities, dying, and death in their understanding of successful aging.

Your Thoughts?

What adaptations to current technologies would help older adults remain socially engaged with friends and family?

With these criteria for successful aging in mind, what is the best strategy for achieving successful aging? As emphasized through this chapter and this entire text, taking a proactive approach to achieve a healthy lifestyle (involving both thoughts and behaviors) throughout adulthood will likely lead to successful aging (Hendricks & Hatch, 2006). While much of this chapter has emphasized physical health, research also points to the powerful role of social support in successful aging. For example, in their meta-analysis Phelan and Larson (2002) found social support, physical activity, high self-efficacy, and high educational achievement to be predictors of successful aging. Similarly, Snow and Pan's survey of physicians (2004) found that they prescribed staying involved in activities and maintaining social networks for successful aging. In a study of elderly citizens, some of whom were in assisted-living residences, Reeker (2001) found that in addition to social resources, those who were aging successfully also had a sense of purpose in their lives. Taking a cross-cultural and more Eastern perspective, a survey of over 5,000 Japanese citizens aged 65 years and older revealed that successful aging was related to higher levels of social interactions, involvement in the community and civic activities, and participation in educational opportunities. Also, the researchers found that successful aging was related to habits developed during middle adulthood, particularly eating well, exercising, engaging in hobbies, and participating in opportunities for continuing education (Ohno et al., 2000).

Your Thoughts?

In what ways might higher educational attainment contribute to successful aging?

Section Summary

- Generally speaking, the criteria for successful aging include high-quality physiological functioning, psychological coping, social interaction, and life satisfaction.
- Achieving successful aging includes using the lifespan developmental principle of plasticity to focus not only on ways to minimize decline and deficit, but also on improvement, adjustment, and coping (Aldwin et al., 2006).
- Individuals who engage in physically, cognitively, and socially active, healthy lifestyles, and who find meaning and purpose in life, are most likely to achieve the goal of aging successfully.

Chapter Summary

The goal of successful aging is not to remain youthful in appearance as long as possible, but rather to remain healthy and active as long as possible, and when not possible, to be able to cope with adverse conditions. Although researchers predict that 20–30% of the aging process is genetically determined, there is a great deal we can do to improve our quality of life throughout adulthood and compress the period of disability at the very end of life. Two of the most important factors are physical fitness and good nutrition, while two of the largest obstacles for Americans are smoking and obesity. Here are some of the main points of the chapter:

- Terms such as "aging well," "successful aging," and "healthy aging" do not imply the need to remain youthful, but rather the goals of good physical and mental health and high life satisfaction.
- As a whole older Americans are healthier and more physically active than ever.
- The trend that women outlive men is found in cultures around the world.
- Individuals in the New England Centenarian and Supercentenarian Studies tend to age at a slower pace than average, and most were of normal weight, avoided smoking, and coped well with stressors.
- Levels of physical activity tend to decline across adulthood, indicating that most adults do not get enough exercise.
- Adults should strive to complete a minimum of 20 minutes of vigorously intense activity on at least 3 days of the week, or a minimum of 30 minutes of moderately intense activities at least 5 days of the week.
- There are numerous and significant health-related, psychological, and social benefits associated with continued physical fitness, which include successful aging.
- Experts encourage adults to find exercises they enjoy that fit in their time schedule and are convenient and affordable.
- While there is debate over the USDA's MyPyramid, there is general agreement that most adults would benefit from eating more whole grains, vegetables, and fruits, less sugars and processed foods, and monitoring the calories in their diets.
- Obesity and undernutrition are problems among older adults.
- To get a better night's sleep, individuals should maintain a sleep routine, avoid alcohol, nicotine, overeating, and large liquid intake in the evenings, and sleep in a cool, quiet, dark location on a supportive mattress.
- Smoking is among the greatest obstacles to a healthy lifestyle, causing numerous health problems and reducing life expectancy.
- Approximately 30% of all adults are obese.
- Treatment programs for obesity work best when dietary changes and exercise programs are combined with behavioral-modification counseling.
- Alcoholism, cigarette smoking, and use of illicit drugs usually peak in young adulthood.
- Older adults with alcoholism are at greater risk for numerous illnesses, falling, automobile accidents, and harmful side effects from interactions with medications.
- Stress is highly subjective and individual, depending on many factors, including the individual's personality, social support, and coping skills.
- Healthy strategies for coping with stress are generally problem-focused and emotion-focused.
- Successful aging involves high-quality social involvement, psychological coping, life satisfaction, and physiological functioning.

Key Terms

Life expectancy **(65)**
Longevity **(65)**
Centenarians **(66)**
Supercentenarians **(66)**
Obesity **(77)**
Body mass index (BMI) **(77)**
Macrostressors **(80)**
Microstressors **(80)**
Stress reactivity **(80)**
Burnout **(80)**
Problem-focused strategies **(82)**
Emotion-focused strategies **(82)**
Compression of functional morbidity **(83)**

Comprehension Questions

1. Give three of the reasons cited by Rice and Fineman (2004) for the increasing good health of older Americans.
2. What is the difference between longevity and life expectancy?
3. Give three of the potential contributors to the consistent finding that women live longer than men.
4. Explain how the aging process for centenarians and supercentenarians differs from that of typical individuals of average longevity.
5. What individual and multicultural trends are found in the data reflecting the amount of exercise most adults engage in?
6. Give several of the benefits of achieving physical fitness.
7. What are some of the reasons older adults give for not exercising?
8. Name several things individuals can do to choose and maintain a successful exercise program.
9. To be the most precise, what variables should be taken into account when considering the amount of nutrients and calories an individual should consume regularly?
10. Generally speaking, what food groups should most Americans increase in their diet, and which ones should be reduced?
11. What can individuals do to improve the quality of their sleep?
12. How do the smoking rates for older adults compare to the rates for younger adults?
13. What are two ways to determine if an individual is obese?
14. What treatment programs work best in reducing weight for obese individuals?
15. How is "heavy drinking" defined and what are some of the immediate and long-term consequences?
16. What are some of the differences in the data collected on alcohol-related issues in young adults and older adults?
17. What are the four characteristics associated with burnout?
18. What are the differences between problem-focused strategies and emotion-focused strategies for dealing with stressors?
19. What are the differences between compression of functional morbidity, decelerating aging, and arrested aging?
20. List the four components found in most definitions of successful aging, and give an example for each.

Answers for Common Sense: Myth or Reality?

1. Myth: Trends in health care indicate that the prevalence of disability among older adults is rising. (See Longer Lifespans, page 64.)
2. Myth: Most of what determines a person's life expectancy is determined by genetics. (See Longevity and Life Expectancy, page 65.)
3. Reality: In all cultures around the world, women tend to outlive men. (See Longevity and Life Expectancy, page 65.)
4. Reality: The oldest person in recorded history was 122 years old. (See Longevity and Life Expectancy, page 66.)
5. Reality: It is estimated that there are 60 Americans who are 110 years or older. (See Centenarians, page 66.)
6. Reality: While there are far fewer male centenarians than female, the men who do reach this milestone tend to be stronger physically and cognitively than the women. (See Centenarians, page 67.)
7. Myth: Most studies find that adult women exercise more than men. (See Most Adults Are Not Fit, page 70.)
8. Myth: It is recommended that adults burn a minimum of 500 calories per day for high-quality physical fitness. (See Achieving Physical Fitness, page 70).
9. Reality: Getting regular exercise will improve sleep quality. (See Benefits of Fitness, page 71.)
10. Reality: Lack of sleep has been associated with memory and attention problems. (See Sleep, page 74.)
11. Myth: Alcohol helps individuals engage in high-quality sleep. (See Sleep, page 75.)
12. Reality: Smoking can reduce one's life expectancy by about 14 years. (See Smoking, page 76.)
13. Myth: Less than half of all American adults are overweight. (See Obesity, page 77.)
14. Myth: Body mass index (BMI) is a method of determining how much fiber is in certain foods. (See Obesity, page 77.)
15. Reality: A pound of body fat is equivalent to 3,500 calories. (See Obesity, page 78.)
16. Reality: Alcohol abuse is a greater problem among younger adults than among older adults. (See Alcohol Abuse, page 79).
17. Myth: Experts view the use of humor as a very poor method of coping with stressors. (See Stress, page 82).
18. Myth: The primary goal of the movement to promote successful aging is to fight aging in every way possible. (See Aging Well, page 83.)

Suggested Readings

Functions of Sleep

Dement, W. C. (2000, October 16). The function of sleep: Regulation or just plain survival? This article can be found at http://www.sleepquest.com/d_column_archive9.html.

Psychology of Sport and Competition

Rushall, B. S. (1999). Some psychological factors for promoting exceptional athletic performance. From Psi Chi National Honor Society in Psychology, Distinguished Lectures Series. This article can be found at http://www.psichi.org/pubs/articles/article_89.asp.

Laughter as Medicine and Stress Relief

Mahony, D. L. (2000). Is laughter the best medicine or any medicine at all? From Psi Chi National Honor Society in Psychology, Distinguished Lectures Series. This article can be found at http://www.psichi.org/pubs/articles/article_81.asp.

Successful Aging in Western and Non-Western Societies

Eyetsemitan, F. (2002). Life-span developmental psychology: Midlife and later years in Western and non-Western societies. In W. J. Lonner, D. L. Dinnel, S. A. Hayes, & D. N. Sattler (Eds.), *Online readings in psychology and culture* (Unit 12, Chapter 2), (http://www.wwu.edu/~culture), Center for Cross-Cultural Research, Western Washington University, Bellingham, WA. Available at http://www.ac.wwu.edu/~culture/Eyetsemitan1.htm.

Suggested Websites

New England Centenarian Study

Learn more about this unique study sponsored by the Boston University School of Medicine, Harvard Medical School, and Beth Israel Deaconess Medical Center at http://www.bumc.bu.edu/centenarian.

Exercise and Physical Fitness

MedlinePlus, sponsored by the U.S. National Library of Medicine and the National Institutes of Health, provides fitness news, nutritional information, and information on specific types of exercise at http://www.nlm.nih.gov/medlineplus/exerciseandphysicalfitness.html.

Good Nutrition

You can learn more about good nutrition habits, food in the news, and weight management at Nutrition.gov, at http://www.nutrition.gov/. You can find resources specifically for older adults at the Center for Nutrition, Physical Activity and Aging at http://nutritionandaging.fiu.edu.

Recreation and Outdoor Activities

The U.S. government also provides leisure and recreational information on auto touring, biking, boating, camping, climbing, fishing, hiking, horseback riding, hunting, and water sports at http://www.recreation.gov.

CHAPTER

4 Identity Development and Personality

Who are you *really*? Who are you on the *inside*? Do you feel like you are the same person now that you were 10 years ago? These are questions of identity and personality. Our sense of personal identity is a critical aspect of our self-concept, as well as a powerful influence on the ways we interact with our environment. The study of identity is often considered part of the study of personality, which is why the two terms are frequently used in similar ways. For example, Erik Erikson, the theorist who inspired a great deal of work on identity, is considered a personality theorist. This chapter begins with a brief overview of personality models, and then focuses on stage models of identity development in adolescence and young, middle, and late adulthood. Based on the work of Erikson and others who expanded his work, these sections explore age-related, general trends thought to be common among adults. It's important to briefly consider identity development in adolescence because it provides the foundation for our entry in young adulthood.

The final sections of the chapter examine other types of models emphasizing lifelong personality traits. While age-related stages may seem at first glance to be more suited to growth and adaptation, we will find that research shows that we can adjust our personality and learn to work with our own traits. For example, someone who is naturally talkative and seeks the center of attention will most likely develop strategies for determining when it is appropriate to be outgoing and when it is not. That individual will learn to be less talkative when necessary, and how to select environments and situations that allow and perhaps even reinforce outgoing behaviors. We revisit some of these topics at the end of this book, exploring changes in our sense of self with age, and the wisdom that often comes from life experiences.

COMMON SENSE
Myth or Reality?

Mark each of the following items with either an M, if you think it is a myth, or an R, if you think the statement reflects reality. By paying close attention you can find all the answers in this chapter. If needed, the answers are also given at the end of the chapter.

1. _____ The standard marker for entry into young adulthood is turning 20 years old.
2. _____ Identity crisis is primarily about choosing a personal value system.
3. _____ Many individuals will move through several of Marcia's identity statuses before reaching identity achievement in adolescence.
4. _____ Identity development is usually worked out in adolescence and then set for the rest of adulthood.
5. _____ Researchers have found that identity statuses in young adulthood influence individuals' abilities to form intimate relationships.
6. _____ Researchers have found that women have a harder time forming a dream of the person they would like to become than men.
7. _____ Most men in their early 40s go through a midlife crisis.
8. _____ Midlife crisis is well accepted among psychologists as a part of middle age.
9. _____ Identity development in middle adulthood involves reassessing and challenging gender roles and expectations.
10. _____ Researchers have found that adolescents and those in late adulthood have very few developmental issues in common.
11. _____ Many researchers view late adulthood as consisting of the younger–old and the very-old.
12. _____ One of the greatest concerns regarding the five-factor model is its success.
13. _____ The developers of the five-factor model believe that personality characteristics reach full development in adolescence.
14. _____ The developers of the five-factor model believe that the five traits are genetic in origin and are universal across all cultures.

Before We Get Started . . .

We will see in this chapter that the things psychologists have learned about personality have come from both theoretical pursuits and research programs. Data on personality can be gathered in several different ways. One way is to use a standard questionnaire. On a scale of 0 to 3, how would you rate yourself on the following items?

0 = I have very little of this trait
1 = I have some of this trait
2 = I display this trait frequently
3 = This is one of my most outstanding traits

_____ Adventurous
_____ Anxious
_____ Assertive
_____ Emotional
_____ Organized
_____ Self-conscious
_____ Self-disciplined
_____ Social
_____ Straightforward
_____ Trusting

Another way to gather information about your personality and self-concept is to ask you to describe yourself, just like you did in the *Before We Get Started* section in Chapter 2. Go back to the list you made at that point and rank the items from the most prominent aspect of yourself to the least demonstrated. If I were to see your ranked list, and particularly if I could interview you to learn more about your choices, I would probably have a good sense of how you perceive your personality. Researchers could use yet another strategy by asking people who know you to describe your personality and to rank your tendencies on the scale above. (Do you think your perception of your own personality is similar to the way your friends see you?)

Personality researchers have many important decisions to make regarding their experimental design. If you were the researcher would you use a questionnaire, a describe-and-rank system, or interviews? Would you branch out to gather data from others regarding your primary participants' personalities? The choices made will affect the quality and depth of your data, but also the amount of time, energy, and resources needed to collect that data from a large number of people.

Models of Personality

There are four primary models of personality, summarized in Table 4.1, which have roots in the metatheories discussed in Chapter 1. Among the most well-known models of personality, such as those developed by Freud and Erikson, are ***stage models*** focused on broad, age-related changes. Also called ***normative-crisis models***, these models are useful when considering the normal and expected challenges met by most adults during young, middle, and late adulthood. For example, younger adults are more likely to be building their identity with many "firsts," such as their first house or first promotion, while middle-aged adults are more likely to be mentoring the young adults and dealing with their own issues of physical aging.

Stage models provide a useful foundation but certainly do not include all that should be considered in personality development. ***Timing-of-events models*** emphasize not only age but also life circumstances, social and cultural expectations, and historical context. Bernice Neugarten, who began promoting timing-of-events models in the late 1960s, wanted an approach that would recognize individual situations within the broad generalizations provided by stage models. For example, rather than simply comparing a 17-year-old woman to a 42-year-old woman based on age, Neugarten was also interested in the life events and context experienced by those two people (Neugarten & Datan, 1973). Suppose that the 17-year-old was single, living with her parents, and still in high school, while the 42-year-old was in a second marriage and fully engaged in a demanding career. If both women had just given birth to their first child, Neugarten would expect the effects of that event to be different for each woman not only because of age abut also because of personal circumstances.

TABLE 4.1 ***Personality Models***

	Stage Models	*Timing-of-Events Models*	*Trait Models*	*Cognitive-Self Models*
Focus	Young, Middle, and Late Adulthood	The effect of the timing of important events	Consistent, stable characteristics	Self-concept, self-esteem, and related areas
Change, Growth, and Development	Based on age	Based on the context and timing of experience	Little significant change	Based on individuals' integration of experiences
Theoretical Foundation*	Organismic	Contextual	Mechanistic	Organismic

*These concepts are discussed fully in Chapter 1.

Your Thoughts?

If you were an employer considering hiring someone, would you rather know about stage of development, individual differences, or traits? Give reasons for your choice.

While acknowledging that our sense of identity and personality will grow and develop with life experiences and age, most people would also agree that there are aspects of personality that remain constant throughout life. ***Trait models*** were developed by those searching for evidence of stable characteristics that are consistent across time, stages, and varying situations. Trait theorists generally focus on basic elements of personality, such as agreeableness or adventurousness. Whereas stage models often arise from theoretical foundations, trait models are more often developed through research findings.

A highly influential facet of personality is captured in ***cognitive-self models***, emphasizing personal thoughts and assumptions. Our self-concept, the way we see ourselves, and our self-esteem, the judgment we make as to whether we are satisfied with ourselves, will likely have an effect on the choices we make as we move through stages of development. Our sense of self may also influence the way we cope with the timing of life events and the ways we modify or manage our lifelong personality traits. Cognitive-self models are explored further in the final chapter as they relate to life satisfaction. Here we explore stage and trait models.

Erikson's Developmental Stage Theory

Many social scientists have cited Erikson's writings as the foundation and inspiration for their own work, including most of those featured in this chapter. In 1950 Erikson first proposed his view of human development as a series of eight crises or struggles to be resolved, and then continued to develop his stage theory throughout his long and productive career. He presented a rather optimistic and healthy view of human development. Each developmental stage is conceptualized as the struggle between a healthy and less-healthy personality characteristic, thus the word *versus* is used. Each struggle or crisis is resolved when one of the two sides becomes a primary part of an individual's personality. For example, the crisis of adolescence, which is ***identity cohesion versus role confusion***, will be resolved when either a unified ***identity*** or role confusion becomes an active and influential personality characteristic. The goal is to resolve each crisis in a way that will ultimately be more productive than destructive. The struggles or crises highlighted at each stage move to the forefront at a particular point in life due to changes in maturity and social interactions generally associated with age. The involvement of social interaction in working through each stage is the reason Erikson's theory is often referred to as a ***psychosocial theory*** (Marcia, 2002a).

Your Thoughts?

How might psychologists measure the influence over time of a person's friends on that person's personality?

When considering Erikson's stages, it is tempting to assume that movement from one stage to the next signals that the previous stage has been dealt with and complete, never to be revisited again. This is not the way Erikson intended it. The potential for each particular stage exists before and after the time when that stage is dominant. There are several important points to gather from this. One point is that while a particular stage of growth or age range may be the optimal time to work through a struggle, such as an identity crisis, that is not the only opportunity to do so. Individuals have the opportunity at any point in life to succeed in working through a crisis from an earlier age (Erikson, 1950; Slater, 2003). Another important point is that developmental crises, such as that of identity, will be revisited many times throughout adulthood (Marcia, 2002a).

It is worth noting before beginning our exploration of identity development through Erikson's stages and those who expanded them that there are numerous exceptions to any broad discussion of identity development. As seen in the other models of personality, identity is quite personal and individual. What is described here is not put forward as the only way to express a healthy identity. In this chapter generalizations are made based on theoretical assumptions and research evidence, while recognizing that there are always exceptions and limitations to even the most conscientious theory or well-designed research.

Adolescence and Emerging Adulthood

There are several reasons for beginning the discussion of adult identity with adolescence, one of which is to explore the transition from adolescence to young adulthood. Aside from the legal definition, it is difficult to point to particular characteristics that clearly mark the distinction between adolescence and young adulthood. In order to fully understand the differences and the transition from one stage to the next, both need to be understood and compared. Another reason to explore the stage of adolescence is to better understand emerging adulthood, the foundation upon which we build adulthood.

Your Thoughts?

Is it unethical to conform to norms or values at work that you don't believe in, thus your words and behaviors may not match your thoughts? Give reasons to support your response.

Erikson: Identity Cohesion versus Role Confusion. The search for identity, involving an ***identity crisis***, is primary in Erikson's understanding of adolescent development. Questions such as "What kind of person do I want to be?" and "How do I want others to perceive me?" highlight the struggles typically faced in this stage. Erikson observed that adolescents are primarily concerned with the degree of discrepancy between how they feel on the inside and how they are seen by others, particularly their peers. Individuals in identity crisis are engaged in self-exploration, trying to learn more about their true self, while at the same time realizing they have some choices to make. Part of the transition from childhood to adulthood is, in Erikson's view, the movement from the morality encouraged and enforced by parents to the personal ethics needed to be a successful adult. Home environments and school settings have most likely provided a needed structure up to this point, and movement to adulthood requires that adolescents now provide their own structure.

In addition to exploring and choosing personal ethics, an adolescent must also begin to choose a career path (Erikson, 1950, 1968). There is much to consider in choosing an occupation, such as the amount of school or training required, the prevalence of job opportunities, and the expected salary level. Adolescents, however, are more likely to focus on

Part of forming an identity is trying on the roles of those you admire.

Your Thoughts?

How important is it that your lifestyle choices are respected by your friends and family?

Your Thoughts?

Is it reasonable to make assumptions based on occupation? For example, do you think a nurse, lawyer, and factory worker would have different values?

how a particular occupation makes them feel and how it is perceived by others. For example, some adolescents may choose an occupation that is perceived to be technical and difficult because that choice makes them feel intelligent and because others will likely assume they are intelligent too.

With each of his stages Erikson described an "adaptive strength" or quality that emerges. The qualitative change experienced through identity cohesion is *fidelity,* or loyalty to the ideals and lifestyle associated with the new identity formed through the struggle or crisis (Erikson, Erikson, & Kivnick, 1986). It can be difficult to be honest in expressing your attitudes, values, and beliefs, especially when doing so is likely to create conflict with loved ones and friends. Imagine the many conflicts and uncomfortable situations an individual may face by choosing to be pro-life regarding the abortion issue in a basically pro-choice family and community. Imagine the conflicts and problems that might arise if an individual chose to have an atheistic attitude toward religion while living in a very religious family. One of the great challenges of adolescence is to discover and create an identity while realizing that some choices will likely cause conflict and disharmony.

Marcia: Exploration and Commitment. Erikson's work has sparked numerous theories and "probably thousands" of studies (Sorrell & Montgomery, 2001), including the work of James Marcia, who began exploring identity crisis with his doctoral dissertation in the 1960s. Erikson felt that often psychological science was too confining and too rigid for his work, thus he preferred to express his ideas through analyses of biographical and autobiographical writings. Marcia decided to use standard research methodology to explore Erikson's adult stages (Marcia, 2002a).

Marcia developed a series of interview questions to assess an adolescent's current state or status in terms of identity development, which is why his findings are called ***identity statuses***. The questions are aimed at understanding an individual's political, religious, and occupational views. Although Marcia's early participants were all males, by the 1970s females were routinely included in the investigations (Kroger, 2000). Marcia found two key elements involved in the struggle with identity cohesion and role confusion, which were the need to explore and consider options and the ability to choose and commit to a particular option. From his perspective, identity is both discovered, through exploration, and constructed, through personal commitments (Marcia, 2001). Marcia also found evidence to show that the pathway to a healthy, productive identity is not the same for all adolescents. Using the two elements Marcia placed participants into one of four identity statuses.

Your Thoughts?

Do you think most adolescents or young adults could accurately say which identity status they are currently in? Why, why not, or under what circumstances?

Identity achievement is the category for those who have explored their various interests and options, and after thoughtful reflection have made commitments to their most comfortable options regarding their political, religious, and occupational or career issues. Having achieved a sense of identity for the time being, these individuals can focus their energy on other endeavors. The label of ***moratorium*** is given to individuals who are intensely exploring and engaged in the personal challenge to develop an identity, but who cannot seem to make decisions and commitments. Moratorium individuals may feel lost in the vast array of options, and may want to investigate and even "try on" most of the choices and options concerning attitudes, beliefs, and even career choices. Often they will seek out information, advice, and opinions from others. Their desire to achieve an identity may bring with it anxiety as well as frustration with their difficulty in making lasting decisions.

Individuals functioning in ***foreclosure*** have chosen an identity early in their adolescence. Often their values, attitudes, beliefs, and even career choices reflect those of their parents or close adult role models. Adolescents in foreclosure tend to be rigid and stubborn regarding their choices, with little tolerance for alternatives. In fact, these individuals can be quite defensive when challenged regarding their choices. While displaying confidence in their choices, research would suggest that these individuals have not yet worked through their identity crisis but have actually postponed it. Their time of exploration and struggle with decisions and commitments will likely arrive later in their lives.

The fourth category of identity statuses Marcia developed is ***identity diffusion***. Much like foreclosure individuals, those in identity diffusion have postponed their identity crisis. Unlike those in foreclosure, however, those in diffusion have little or no interest in exploring or committing to particular values, attitudes, beliefs, or career paths. Individuals in identity diffusion are often described as aimless, directionless, and wandering. With no goals and no desire for direction, their lives often appear chaotic and disorganized. Researchers have also found that individuals in identity diffusion have lower self-esteem (Marcia, 2001, 2002a, 2002b).

Extensive work has been done with Marcia's identity statuses, comparing them to many other variables. Kroger (2000) reviewed a large number of research studies published from the mid-1960s to 1999 that explored other psychological aspects of individuals in each of the four identity statuses. Table 4.2 summarizes her findings.

Compared to the others, those in identity achievement have reached the highest levels of morality, ego development, independence, and self-esteem. The outstanding features of those in moratorium reflect their sense of urgency in working through their identity issues. The individuals in foreclosure are the most rigid, have the greatest need to conform to social expectations, and are the most vulnerable to external authorities. The least healthy individuals, based on this research summary, are those in identity diffusion.

Similar results were found when exploring cultural identity development (Miville, Koonce, Darlington, & Whitlock, 2000). When surveying 104 African American college students researchers found a relationship between racial identity and identity statuses. In particular, Miville and her colleagues (2000) found that those who were functioning in identity achievement expressed a positive racial identity. Participants who were found to function in moratorium or identity diffusion were found to have "more naive and White-oriented racial identity attitudes" (p. 219). They did not find any relationship between foreclosure and racial identity for African American college students. In a second study involving 195 Mexican American college students, however, Miville and her colleagues found that those functioning in foreclosure completely adopted Hispanic/Latino values, attitudes, and outlook. Those who were functioning in moratorium and identity diffusion expressed cultural identity conflicts.

Your Thoughts?

How similar or different do you think these findings would be for individuals who were in a minority due to their religious preference? Sexual orientation? Political outlook?

TABLE 4.2 ***Research Findings on Identity Statuses***

Identity Statuses	*Research Findings*
Mature Statuses*	Higher levels of moral development, intimacy, ego development, self-esteem, and personal autonomy Healthier defense mechanisms
Moratorium	Highest levels of anxiety Highest levels of openness to new experiences
Foreclosure	Highest levels of authoritarianism Highest levels of external locus of control Greatest use of normative approaches to personal problem solving
Identity Diffusion	Highest levels of nonadaptive defense mechanisms Low levels of intimacy, self-esteem, personal autonomy, and ego development

*Mature Statuses = Identity Achievement and Moratorium

Adapted from Kroger J. (2000). Ego Identity status research in the new milennium. *International Journal of Behavioral Development, 24*(2), 145–148. Reprinted with permission of sapp publications.

ON THE LEADING EDGE
Internet Identities

Anastasia Panagakos (2003) has been monitoring the various ways ethnic groups can become or remain connected through the use of the computer. Her particular focus is on Greek ethnic communities in Canada. Traditionally, ethnic groups would settle in communities where they could provide the cultural experiences needed to teach young children their ethnic background. Some theorists had predicted that the European ethnic groups that moved west would lose their ethnicity and their connections to the traditions. Panagakos is finding, however, that younger generations, who are more comfortable with computer-based communications, are actually drawing closer to their heritage. Rather than rely on local communities, or in the absence of local communities, individuals of Greek heritage can connect directly to the "homeland" via the Internet.

Panagakos (2003) has conducted numerous interviews both in person and online. She found that many Greek young adults became interested in exploring their culture through the music-swapping features available via the Internet. Greek music became the starting point for numerous conversations about Greek culture and Greek identity. Those conversations then led to friendships and virtual communities.

Not only might Internet communities allow someone to draw close an ethnic identity but the communication may also allow those far away to maintain their ethnic identity. Plaza (2009) found that second generation Caribbean-origin university students are creating websites to act as a "symbolic bridge" between their educational home in the United States, Canada, or Great Britain and their Creole homeland. In analyzing the content of the websites Plaza determined that the authors felt their identity was fluid and changing with their immersion in two cultures. In the study of Greek identity Panagakos found that knowledge and information gained via the computer occasionally makes its way back to the local ethnic communities. For example, information shared about festivals over the Internet will sometimes bring change to the local community festivals. It will be interesting for social scientists to observe the ways personal technologies and the Internet will change how we view our ethnic backgrounds and our attachments to places and cultures in the future.

Just as with the African American college students, the Mexican American students functioning in identity achievement expressed a positive cultural identity. It is reasonable to assume for those whose culture is a prominent part of their lives, working through their sense of cultural or racial identity would be just as important as working through religious identity or occupational identity.

Understanding these four identity statuses is only part of understanding the pathway to developing a healthy identity. Some individuals will move through several identity statuses in their quest for identity. The most common progression is to begin with foreclosure or identity diffusion, move into moratorium, and then to identity achievement (Kroger, 2000). Marcia viewed the foreclosure–moratorium–identity achievement pathway as the optimal progression (Marcia, 2002a). To illustrate this journey to identity formation let's consider a hypothetical adolescent named Jennifer. Her parents are teachers and she admires them for their profession. Also, Jennifer is the oldest of four children, so she has had a lot of experience tutoring her younger siblings. Following this typical pattern, Jennifer may begin adolescence in foreclosure with a decision to become a math teacher and work in the same school district as her parents. After high school she enters college very confident of her choice to be an education major. While in college she takes many different courses and finds that she has many interests and talents. She also learns of career choices she never even knew existed before college, and starts to consider other majors. She enters moratorium with a sense of exploration and uneasiness. She was so sure that she wanted to be a math teacher, and now she is not sure at all. In her junior year of college she begins to make some decisions about her future. She decides to drop her education major and switch to math and computer science. Jennifer now sees herself as a global citizen ready to participate in international business. She is now in identity achievement, settled in her new sense of direction and looking forward to a career in a corporate setting.

Jennifer's progression from foreclosure to moratorium, and then to identity achievement, illustrates the role that identity crisis can play in adolescence and into young adulthood. It is important to realize that when we move into young adulthood it could be that we have not achieved identity and need to work through issues of exploration and commitment to attitudes, beliefs, values, and goals. For those who did attain identity achievement, it is also important to remember that they will continue to grow and develop their identity with each new stage of life.

Your Thoughts?

Setting aside legal definitions, would you argue that traditional-aged college students are adolescents or young adults?

Your Thoughts?

Do you think that, generally, women and men experience identity development in young adulthood differently? Why, why not, or under what circumstances?

Young Adulthood

As much as individuals may think they have life figured out at age 16 or 18, things certainly seem to be different at ages 25 and 35. There are many life events that are typically experienced in young adulthood that can alter our sense of identity. The first time you see your name on a business card with a title you've waited to see for a long time, maybe "manager" or "owner," your identity will change. The first time you have a business card with the profession you have dreamed about, such as "teacher" or "lawyer," your identity will take a leap in a new direction. Other such identity-changing experiences may be the first time you sign papers to purchase a home or when you become a parent. While there is no clear division between adolescence and young adulthood, these first-time adult experiences are certainly signals that one has entered a new phase of life. This section focuses on three views of identity development in young adulthood.

Erikson: Intimacy versus Isolation. Through a productive resolution to the ***intimacy versus isolation*** stage we learn a new facet of commitment, the mutual give-and-take that sustains long-term love relationships. The adaptive strength gained in this stage is mature love (Erikson et al., 1986). In Erikson's view, individuals must have addressed their identity before they are ready to move into intimate, mature love relationships. In other words, you must be aware of your own goals and values before you can love someone else in a mature way. The core of this young adult stage is trust and vulnerability. Individuals who have developed intimacy are comfortable in relationships. They trust themselves and others, which allows them to form close emotional ties without fear. They are also quite giving of themselves in relationships. On the other hand, those who are functioning in isolation have not fully developed their identity and they have little tolerance for those who are different. They are afraid and hesitant to trust anyone else or form close relationships. Whereas those in intimacy are more cooperative, those in isolation are more competitive and less willing to contribute or give of themselves (Hamachek, 1990).

Marcia: Depth and Commitment. Each of Erikson's stages of adulthood can be viewed as an internal reorganizing or identity reformulation. While the period of adolescence may be the primary time in life to work through identity issues, it appears that adults revisit and cycle through identity issues with each new phase of life (Marcia, 2002a, 2002b).

Hundreds of research studies have been conducted since the mid-1980s to explore and extend the concept of identity statuses into young, middle, and late adulthood (Kroger, 2002a, 2002b). For example, based on interviews with 53 male college undergraduates, researchers found that those who functioned in identity achievement were able to establish the healthiest intimate interpersonal relationships. Both the foreclosure men and the identity diffusion men displayed relationships that were more stereotypical and superficial. The most isolated and least intimate of the four groups were the identity diffusion men, while the foreclosure men displayed the greatest need to be socially accepted. The most diverse group, in terms of difficulty in describing or categorizing, was the moratorium men. Perhaps because individuals in moratorium are exploring various mindsets, when faced with negotiating interpersonal, intimate relationships they continue to explore and try different options (Orlofsky,

Marcia, & Lesser, 1973). After many such studies a pattern has emerged linking adolescent and young adult identity statuses.

Whereas the key elements in adolescence were exploration and commitment, in young adulthood the two key elements are depth in relationships and the ability to make lasting personal commitments (Marcia, 2002b; Orlofsky, 1993). Marcia has designed the following parallel identity statuses:

- Identity Achievement–Intimate
- Moratorium–Preintimate
- Foreclosure–Pseudointimate
- Identity Diffusion–Stereotyped or Isolated

An intriguing aspect of this stage is that the level of satisfaction in personal identity development is directly shaped by a partner or lover who is likely to be developing his or her own sense of identity. Individuals in the *intimate* status value depth in personal relationships. They trust themselves and others, are comfortable establishing intimacy, and now have the ability to establish long-term commitments. As with identity achievement, the intimate status is ultimately the healthiest of the four.

The other three identity statuses of young adulthood also parallel the adolescent model. Just as moratorium adolescents are in the midst of exploring, the *preintimate* young adults are searching for and desiring depth in their relationships. The preintimate individuals are not yet able to make long-term commitments, possibly because of their own issues yet to be worked through and possibly because their partner or lover is not ready to make a commitment. Operating from a completely different perspective, *pseudointimate* individuals believe that there is no reason to strive for depth in relationships because they have already made long-term commitments. Although these individuals may claim to have established intimacy, their commitments are empty facades without the element of depth. The least adaptive of the young adulthood identity statuses, *stereotyped* or *isolated*, includes individuals with little interest or experience in establishing depth or long-term commitments. The *stereotyped* individual keeps all relationships at a superficial level by responding in the expected ways rather than with genuine emotion and authenticity. The *isolated* person may avoid close relationships whenever possible. Either way, these individuals are emotionally isolated (Marcia, 2002b; Orlofsky, 1993).

Your Thoughts?

Aside from two people with intimate status, which combinations of identity statuses would produce a stable love relationship? Which combinations would likely be unstable?

Just as Marcia's work on adolescent development sparked many new research efforts, his work in young adulthood has also been the catalyst for many new studies. One such longitudinal study done by Josselson (1987, 1996) followed 30 female college students for 22 years. The women were interviewed at 21, 33, and 43 years old. The data analysis suggested four "trajectories" similar to Marcia's identity statuses. Josselson used the label of *pathmaker* to distinguish the women who were able to face risks, balance their needs with those of others, and were able to make commitments. These women were experiencing Marcia's intimate status. *Searchers*, those who were preintimate, were idealistic and often paralyzed by choices and options, and as such had great trouble making commitments. The *guardians*, operating in the pseudointimate status, were quite set in their outlook and tended to be high achieving. They also highly valued their family's expectations. Josselson used the term *drifters* for those in isolation who seemed to be living for the moment with little concern for the future or their identity development.

Your Thoughts?

How might Levinson's choice of participants have influenced his results?

Levinson: Early Adulthood Stage. Daniel Levinson, another well-known researcher and theorist inspired by Erikson's work, responded in a fashion similar to Marcia by choosing a research-oriented approach to explore stages of personality development (Levinson, 1978; Minter & Samuels, 1998). The participants in Levinson's original study were 40 men,

Among the challenges of young adulthood one of the most prominent is establishing a loving, intimate relationship.

recruited when they were between 35 and 45 years old. The men were equally distributed among four occupations: blue-collar workers, business executives, biologists, and novelists. Based on his research Levinson divided the Early Adulthood stage into the Novice Phase and the Settling Down Period.

Your Thoughts?

In what ways do you think a mentor is helpful? Are there any drawbacks to having a mentor?

The ***Novice Phase*** is composed of the Early Adult Transition (ages 17–22), Entering the Adult World (ages 22–28), and the Age Thirty Transition (ages 28–33). His participants described four important tasks or issues that determined satisfaction in the Novice Phase and later provided the most productive entrance into middle adulthood. The first of these four tasks was *forming a dream*. This was not a concrete plan, but rather it was a vision or abstract sense of the kind of life an individual hoped to have in the future. This future identity was a powerful influence in terms of decision making and lifestyle choices. The second task was to *form a mentor relationship*. Mentors provided support, advice, and inspiration that moved the individual closer to realizing the dream of the future. Levinson described the mentor as a transitional figure who mixes parental and peer roles. The third task was to *form an occupation*. This involved trying several different types of work as well as taking on the mindset of a particular occupation. Most of the men in Levinson's study tried various types of jobs before settling into their careers. The fourth task of the novice phase was to *form a marriage and family*. Even though Levinson chose the term *marriage* it seems reasonable that this concept can be extended to heterosexual and homosexual, married and nonmarried partners. Much like Erikson's description of developing intimacy, this task was focused on forming intimate friendships and love relationships. Also like Erikson, Levinson found that those who had not developed their own identity at the time they made love commitments generally had more difficult and less stable relationships.

Your Thoughts?

Why is it that forming a love relationship before forming a dream may be detrimental to a love relationship?

The ***Settling Down Period***, occurring in one's mid-30s to around age 40, was a time when the men in Levinson's study started to "get serious" about their commitments and responsibilities. This last period of the Early Adulthood stage represents the culmination of all the productive and destructive choices made during the Novice Phase. Levinson found two tasks that need to be completed during the Settling Down Period: to establish one's place in society and to work at advancement (Levinson, 1978). While many psychologists have been interested in Levinson's research, there have been relatively few follow-up studies. Part of the reason for this may be the large time commitment required by the researcher and the participants to complete Levinson's intense interview research design.

One of the immediate concerns regarding Levinson's work is that his initial study involved only males. Recognizing this, Levinson had begun work on women's development but did not have a chance to complete it before he died. Several of his colleagues later took over the research work and published their findings. The greatest difference found between women and men involved forming a dream. Levinson found that while men's dreams were more ambitious and career-focused, women's dreams conveyed the competing desires for homemaking and parental dreams as well as occupational dreams (Kittrell, 1998). Levinson's findings were similar to those of Roberts and Newton (1987), reflecting data collected at a similar point in history and using Levinson-type interviews with 39 women, who found that women were much more focused on dreams that involved relationships, marriage, and family concerns.

Minter and Samuels (1998) not only found gender differences regarding the forming of a dream, but also found that the process was more complex for women. In their study of 355 women, the researchers found that for women who formed a dream and that dream became reality, their transition into middle adulthood was satisfying. However, for those who formed a dream and gave up on it, the transition into middle adulthood was much more difficult. Whereas Levinson believed that the absence of a dream would lead to meaninglessness at midlife, Minter and Samuels found that women without a dream displayed moderately high levels of life satisfaction. Thus, the women who did not form a dream were doing much better than those who did form a dream but the dream was never fulfilled. Aside from forming a dream, researchers have found that the other three tasks of the Novice Phase tend to apply to women as well as men (Minter & Samuels, 1998; Schiller, 1998).

Your Thoughts?

Considering the research presented, do you think it is wise to encourage women to form a dream? Why or why not?

The quest to create and understand our identities, which begins in adolescence, continues through young adulthood. Many of the life choices and events common to young adulthood, such as completing formal education, forming a love relationship and family, establishing a career, and settling into a community, also give rise to new and challenging aspects of personal identity. With each new role or transition individuals add new dimensions and complexities to their personal identity. The progress individuals make in building their young adult identities will carry them into middle adulthood.

Middle Adulthood

Just as adolescents may feel they are in limbo between childhood and adulthood, those in middle age may feel they are in an ill-defined time between young and old. Unlike adolescents who are waiting for their adult lifestyles to begin, however, those in midlife are often trying to keep up with the demands of adulthood. Middle adulthood is a time of responsibility as well as change. For many people in this age range their own children and adolescents are depending on them for resources and advice, while at the same time their older parents and relatives may need some assistance and extra care. This is also the time when jobs and career opportunities can be the most rewarding, but also the most challenging and demanding.

Middle-aged people find themselves in an identity transition. While they are not a part of the younger adult generation, they are also not yet in the late adulthood world of their parents. As a middle-aged woman I'm often aware of these distinctions. Around the university I hear students talking of video games, songs, or technologies I've never heard of. When I tell them that I remember when all music was on vinyl albums or that the first time I used a simple computer I was a junior in college, they look at me like I'm an alien. On the other hand, I have dinner frequently with a group of older friends ranging in age from mid-60s to 80s. They usually discuss their health issues and medical care, brag about their adult children and grandchildren, and discuss any new gadgets designed to make cooking or gardening easier. Although I greatly enjoy the company of my older friends I find that they have little interest in the technologies I use in my classrooms or the grind of the work-a-day world.

One major change in thinking that usually marks middle age is the transition from feeling as if all of life is ahead to realizing that, based on the average lifespan, life is about half over. This change in outlook does not have to be one of "doom and gloom," but rather it can be a motivating and clarifying force. Midlife adults may ask themselves, "What can I do to get everything I want out of the second half of life?" I find that the older I get the more I enjoy things I used to consider mundane or routine, something I've gained from hearing my older friends lament the things they've had to give up. And while I'm continually reminded by my college students to dream of the future, I find I'm much more deliberate in choosing how best to spend my time and energy in achieving my goals.

Erikson: Generativity versus Stagnation. In Erikson's view the challenge of midlife can be described as the struggle of ***generativity versus stagnation***. The word *generativity* sounds much like *generous, generation*, and *generate*, and with good reason. Middle-aged individuals who are developing generativity are concerned about the next generation and anxious to find creative ways to share their own resources. By this point midlife adults have experienced many events that are yet to come for younger generations. Generative individuals are motivated to mentor, train, and share their advice and wisdom, whether it be with their own children, family, or those involved in the same business or community. Erikson also found that individuals in generativity are often interested in expressing their creativity. The adaptive strength developed through generativity is *care*. It is important to note that this level of caring is mature and generously given. While it may seem natural to care for those who care about you, Erikson's notion of care in this case has been broadened to include those who cannot or will not return similar concern.

Stagnation is, in Erikson's model, the opposite of generativity. Whereas generativity leads to concern for others, stagnation leads to a concern for oneself. Individuals functioning in stagnation may feel that they have nothing special to offer the next generation or that just taking care of themselves is all they can manage. Their focus is more on what they want and need, often stifling creativity (Erikson et al., 1986). To illustrate the differences between generativity and stagnation, consider a hypothetical family gathering that includes Jerry, who is experiencing generativity, and Stan, who is experiencing stagnation. Jerry may spend time with a nephew giving advice on how to find a summer job, and then chatting with his aunt about getting her car fixed. Jerry may tell folks about his role in building a children's park in his hometown, or he may be working on the family genealogy so that everyone can have complete records. Stan, on the other hand, may spend a good part of his day telling people about his health problems. He might get frustrated when others do not take his health issues as seriously as he does. If someone asks, "So what's new with you, Stan?" he reply might be, "Nothing. I'm still doing the same old thing. Just working day after day so I can retire, get old, and die." Stan's reply would likely push others away, leaving him isolated by the end of the day.

Your Thoughts?

If your relative seemed to be moving toward stagnation, what might you suggest that could potentially move that person toward generativity?

Marcia: Inclusivity and Involvement. The struggle between generativity and stagnation may initiate yet another cycle of reorganizing aspects of personal identity (Marcia, 2002a, 2002b). Marcia and his colleagues found evidence to support the notion that, just as in adolescence and young adulthood, there are different pathways or identity statuses to work through in the struggle to develop generativity and avoid stagnation. Whereas depth and commitment were key elements in young adulthood, in middle adulthood the key elements are inclusivity and involvement (Bradley & Marcia, 1998; Marcia, 2002a, 2002b; McAdams & St. Aubin, 1998). The four midlife identity statuses parallel the adolescent statuses as follows:

- Identity Achievement–Generative
- Moratorium–Pseudogenerative (Agentic and Communal)
- Foreclosure–Conventional
- Identity Diffusion–Stagnant

The healthiest way to move to Erikson's generativity is to be fully inclusive and actively involved with others, leading to the identity status labeled *generative.* Individuals who achieve generativity are balanced, tolerant, growth-focused, and concerned with a wide range of projects, topics, and people.

There are also less healthy ways to move through midlife identity development. Paralleling adolescent moratorium, Marcia used the label of *pseudogenerative* for those individuals who appear to be generous and inclusive but are actually quite restrictive in their involvement with others. There are two types of pseudogenerative individuals. *Agentic-pseudogenerative* individuals are generally self-absorbed but will engage in caring for those who offer such care in return. *Communal-pseudogenerative* individuals are less self-absorbed and more community focused, however, their tendency is to care about those who show appropriate gratitude in return. Those functioning in a communal-pseudogenerative status have a strong desire to be needed and to feel indispensable. The middle adulthood status similar to adolescent foreclosure is labeled *conventional.* Adults functioning in this status feel no need to be inclusive outside of the boundaries they have already established. They primarily care for others with similar values and standards and often have difficulty accepting or tolerating differences. Marcia and his colleagues also noted that those in the conventional status generally had the attitude that the younger generations need firm guidance to develop as "proper" adults. The last of the four identity statuses for middle adulthood is labeled *stagnant*, serving as the parallel to identity diffusion. Adults functioning in the stagnant status feel no desire for inclusivity or involvement with other projects or persons. Researchers have found that this group also reports little life satisfaction (Bradley & Marcia, 1998; Marcia, 2002b). Erikson and Marcia emphasized the ways individuals relate to others in their social environment, through generativity and inclusivity. Levinson, on the other hand, highlighted internal changes.

Your Thoughts?

How might knowing that a financial contributor to the local library is pseudogenerative help the fundraising director increase the chances of more donations?

Levinson: Middle Adulthood Stage. Levinson's research indicated that Middle Adulthood consists of the Midlife Transition (ages 40–45), Entering Middle Adulthood (ages 45–50), Age 50 Transition (ages 50–55), and Culmination of Middle Adulthood (ages 55–60). During the ***midlife transition*** individuals must reassess the past, make appropriate changes in mindset and lifestyle, and work through the "four polarities" of individuation. Levinson described the conflicting polarities that dominate midlife as:

- Young–Old
- Destruction–Creation
- Masculine–Feminine
- Attachment–Separateness

Your Thoughts?

If you were asked to create a picture or a video clip of someone in midlife crisis, what hypothetical scenario would you create?

Those who resolve these conflicts by finding a comfortable place within each polarity will likely have an easy transition through middle adulthood. Those who cannot come to terms with these, however, will likely find themselves in a difficult midlife transition that may develop into a midlife crisis. For example, the contented, basically happy individual will find a point of view regarding aging that makes sense and is comfortable, successfully managing the young–old polarity. People in middle adulthood must find a functional identity in the time between young and old age. Whenever I ask my college students to verbally paint a picture of midlife crisis it almost always involves a middle-aged male dressed like someone half his age, driving in a red sports car, and doing everything possible to show off and gain attention. What this scene really communicates is that midlife crisis is partly a crisis of age and identity. The man in this scenario cannot find a productive middle ground in the young–old polarity and has chosen to act much younger than his age. This hypothetical character could have displayed his crisis by opting to act much older than his chronological age, thinking of himself as almost elderly. Finding a comfortable place on the age continuum is a key to midlife happiness.

In addition to working with age, midlife individuals must find a balanced view of destruction and creation. People in their 40s and 50s often become more aware of the finiteness of life as they see members of the older generation dying. It is important for midlife individuals to plan for their own care when they are the oldest generation, while at the same time not allowing such concerns to dominate their thoughts and destroy their quality of life. The goal is to find balance between planning for the end of life (destruction) and exploring creativity (creation). Often people in midlife want to try new things and renew interests they had before their lives became so busy. They may explore new challenges in their work, hobbies, or community activities. Returning to the scenario of the man in the red sports car, he may be ignoring the signs of aging, such as facial wrinkles and balding, and trying to look younger through his dress and lifestyle. He is also likely to engage in destructive behaviors, possibly putting his body, marriage and family, or career at risk.

Your Thoughts?

How might you measure emotional sensitivity in young adult and middle-aged men to see if it changes over time? What behaviors might you track?

Finding a balance between feminine and masculine gender roles is also an important task of middle adulthood. Levinson found that the men in his study who were comfortable with themselves in midlife had learned to appreciate their feminine qualities as well as their masculine ones. By finding a comfortable place between traditional gender roles we can truly develop into the best *person* we can be. For example, men can enhance their emotional and self-expressive side and women can learn to be more assertive and ambitious. By developing their most valued male and female qualities they are becoming ***androgynous***. Midlife crisis is experienced when individuals cannot find that comfortable place and instead move toward an ultra-masculine or ultra-feminine gender role. This ultra-masculine appearance may be the illusion maintained by the now infamous man in the red sports car.

Finally, midlife adults must find balance between attachment and separateness. Midlife brings some unique relationships to most adults. Their own children, now adults themselves, are somewhat like peers. It is difficult for parents of adult children to balance their attachment (i.e., "I'm still your mother!") with the recognition that their children are independently functioning citizens. At the same time, midlife adults can see that their own parents, who have been separate, may now need more attachment, support, and assistance as they age. Returning to the man in the red sports car, it may be that he has emotionally and/or literally divorced himself from his attachments to his family in order to embark on some new adventure. He may be experiencing a self-inflicted separation.

Levinson's research on midlife crisis captured the attention of many people, including the many social scientists who have furthered his work. Although he found that approximately 80% of his participants experienced a midlife crisis, there has been little support for the generalization that *most* adults have a midlife crisis. In fact, researchers still debate the very existence of midlife transitions and crises. The primary criticisms of Levinson's research on midlife crisis focus on his use of a narrow age range, his choice of participants (who were too few, too specialized in their work, and of similar ages), the fact that Levinson undertook his original study to better understand his own issues with midlife, and issues regarding the way he scored and coded the information from his interviews with participants (Whitbourne, 2005). There is also debate over the meaning and best use of the term *crisis*. Just how difficult does a transition have to be in order to call it a crisis? Many psychologists and researchers agree that midlife is time for reflection and transition, but the notion of a tumultuous crisis is met with skepticism and debate.

Levinson's Middle Adulthood begins with the Midlife Transition, and continues to include the next phase, Entering Middle Adulthood. Levinson viewed this period as a time to modify the four aspects of the life structure: the dream, occupation, mentoring, and family life. It is time to reevaluate the dream now that early adulthood has passed. Our attitudes, values, beliefs, and goals can be quite different when we're in our 40s than they were in our 20s. My husband is a perfect example of this. His goals in his 20s were all about climbing the corporate ladder and making money. In his late 40s and early 50s his vision of himself changed from corporate executive to artist, his "uniform" changed from a suit to jeans, and his working place from an office to an artist's studio. Like most of us in midlife, his guiding dream and vision needed to reflect his identity changes. People in midlife are usually at a different place in their career, and it is likely that much has changed since they started working. It is typical to reevaluate occupational goals. As for the task of forming a mentor relationship, most likely that was a transitional relationship that served its purpose in young adulthood. It may be time for the midlife individual to become a mentor for the next generation. The fourth part of the life structure, love and family relationships, have most likely changed dramatically in the 15 or 20 years since the beginning of young adulthood as well. All of these adjustments need to be integrated into our life structure in preparation for Late Adulthood (Levinson, 1978).

Your Thoughts?

How do you think the point in history in which these women and men lived affected the results of these studies?

Gender Identity Development. Levinson's research indicated that balancing masculine and feminine qualities is part of the midlife identity transition. Two well-known ***longitudinal*** studies, the Mills Longitudinal Study of women and the Grant Study of Harvard University men, support this move toward androgyny. Both studies followed college students through young adulthood and into midlife. The Grant Study began with college men in 1938, while the Mills Study began much later, in 1958, with female students at Mills College. The results indicated that while men and women move through distinctive developmental stages, both involved challenging gender roles.

Women in the Mills Longitudinal Study were described as increasing in femininity during their 20s, and then decreasing in femininity during their 30s and 40s. The women felt they spent their 20s learning to fulfill their roles as women, and then in their 40s experienced the freedom to expand their gender role. With age the women gained more confidence, new perspectives, and a sense of power. When reflecting back on their early 30s, the women were doing so much for other people that they felt exploited, weak, alone, and depressed. In their 40s they felt more influential, productive, effective, and satisfied with their lives (Helson & Moane, 1987). In their 50s the women believed they were in the "prime of their lives." They expressed confidence, involvement with others, and a sense of personal security. They also developed more androgynous personalities that integrated both feminine and masculine characteristics. Most of the women who felt empowered in their 50s were living with a partner only (no children or other relatives in the house), rated their health as good, and generally reported high incomes. In most cases their children had moved out and concerns had shifted to their aging parents (Helson & Mitchell, 1990). For the women in the Mills Longitudinal Study, midlife was a time of integration, self-development, and developing a stronger sense of commitment to their values and goals (Helson & Wink, 1992).

ON THE LEADING EDGE
Technology-Friendly Personalities

Will individuals with particular sets of personality traits embrace technology more than others? This research question has been posed several times with participants of different backgrounds. Bostjan Antoncic, faculty in the area of Management at the University of Primorska in Solvenia, wondered if entrepreneurs who develop new technologies or use technologies in new ways had a unique personality profile. He recruited 160 business developers, mostly men, to answer questions during a face-to-face interview. The entrepreneurs, all based in Slovenia, were typically 30 to 40 years old and had 10 to 20 years' experience. Most of the businesses were small with 50 or fewer employees. Using an instrument measuring the five factors of personality, two factors seemed to be the keys to success in technological development. Those who were successful were high in openness to experience and low in neuroticism. For the entrepreneurs it is important to be willing to explore new ideas and trends while also remaining low in anxiety and willing to take risks. It is interesting to notice not only the personality factors that were influential but also to consider those that were not involved. Extraversion, conscientiousness, and agreeableness were not influential in predicting technological developments.

The notion of technology-friendly personalities was also explored by Chambers, Hardy, Smith, and Sienty (2003) with a group of school teachers. Rather than the five factor personality model, Chambers and her colleagues chose the well-known Myers–Briggs Type Indicator (MBTI), which places individuals on four dimensions. For this particular study the researchers used only two of the dimensions: Sensory/Intuitive and Feeling/Thinking. People who score high in sensing (S) are ones who rely heavily on information gained through personal experiences and their five senses. On the other end of that dimension, intuitive (N) personality types rely heavily on their internal hunches and "gut reactions." The feeling/thinking dimension places a strong reliance on emotional responses (F) at one end and a strong reliance on logical processing (T) on the other. These two dimensions can be combined to form four groups: SF, ST, NF, and NT.

Chambers and her colleagues (2003) recruited 164 intermediate and secondary school teachers who were just beginning their teaching careers to participate in the study. The teachers took both the MBTI and a technology questionnaire. The results indicated that those with an Intuitive/Thinking (NT) personality type were the most receptive to technology.

Together these two studies contribute to a profile of technology-friendly and innovative personalities as those who are open to new ideas, have good intuition about which ideas to develop, are low in anxiety and willing to take risks, and able to logically think through the development process and follow through. As personal technologies become even more varied and pervasive it will be interesting to observe personality preferences. For instance, will the same personalities who are drawn to computer games also be drawn to business software?

The men of the Grant Study were focused on establishing their occupations and lifestyles during their 20s, and continuing to consolidate their positions during their 30s. In young adulthood these men needed to further separate from their parents' control, and settle into a career, a marriage, and start a family. These men also spent time deepening friendships. In their 30s the men worked to be their best in their many roles, such as employee, husband, father, and friend. Similar to the men in Levinson's midlife study, the men in the Grant Study experienced a midlife transition that eventually led to peacefulness and satisfaction in their 50s. Although the men did not experience a traumatic crisis in midlife, they did begin to question the decisions and commitments they had made to corporations, spouses, neighborhoods, and so on, as well as their own priorities. Researchers found that most of the men moved through this questioning phase to develop generativity. In their 50s the men of the Grant Study were more nurturing and expressive, indicating that they too were able to challenge gender roles and develop more androgynous personalities (Vaillant, 1977).

Identity development in middle adulthood has been characterized as the struggle with generativity versus stagnation, inclusivity and involvement, and the quest for balance in attitude toward young–old, destruction–creation, separateness–attachment, and masculine–feminine characteristics. Having established a lifestyle, set goals, and made commitments during young adulthood, individuals in middle adulthood are reassessing those earlier decisions. In midlife individuals have the opportunity to reinvent themselves in a way that is less tied to gender roles and other social conventions. They also have the opportunity to share their wisdom and resources, and thus influence the future.

Late Adulthood

Late adulthood, both as an area of research and as an experienced phase of life, is undergoing quite a change. There was a time when psychologists considered late adulthood or old age to begin at retirement. It was a time to slow down and prepare for the end of life. Today, late adulthood is often viewed as a series of stages. There is a qualitative difference in abilities, lifestyles, and viewpoints between those who are newly retired and very active, those who are older and slower but still relatively healthy, and those who are ill and/or in the final months of life. Kroger (2002a, 2002b), one of the proponents of a divided late adulthood, views the beginning of late adulthood as a transition much like adolescence. She notes that both adolescents and older adults are:

- Dealing with biological changes
- Renegotiating relationships with their families
- In positions that may require them to rely on their families more than they would prefer to
- Questioning and reflecting on their purpose in life
- Fighting stereotypes
- Valuing a driver's license as confirming autonomy

Levinson (1978) also viewed this time of life as movement between periods of stability and transition. He described late adulthood as beginning around age 65 and "late late adulthood" as beginning around age 80.

Based on interviews with participants aged 65 years and older, Kroger (2002a) found several distinct differences between the "younger old" participants who were between the ages of 65 and 75, and the "very old" who were over 75. The younger old individuals were challenging themselves with creative endeavors that involved the reworking of their own life story, often involving memorabilia and items around the house. While these individuals were likely to be adjusting to lessened physical abilities and perhaps with illness, they were also maintaining involvement in leisure activities, vocational and volunteer interests, friendships, and their community. Kroger found that, in contrast, the very old individuals were using much of their energy to focus on the present moment. They were concerned with finding meaningful ways to spend their days. Much of their attention was given to rebalancing relationships and finding meaning in their simple lifestyle. Although many of the standard, classic developmental theories were created when late adulthood was viewed as a uniform stage, these views are changing. This section explores the last stage of Erikson's and Marcia's identity development theories. Table 4.3 summarizes the key features for these theories and Levinson's work across young, middle, and late adulthood.

Erikson: Integrity versus Despair. Erikson's final stage, ***ego integrity versus despair***, is one of life review and the challenge of integrating all of life's experiences into a cohesive identity. Those individuals who can achieve integrity are content and approach the end of life with a sense of gratefulness and gratitude. They have confidence in themselves, and even in late adulthood they are not easily pushed around. Integrity comes to those who can synthesize their life story in a way that generates meaning and purpose, while despair comes to those who cannot generate such meaning and purpose. Individuals functioning in despair often blame others

TABLE 4.3 ***Identity Development in Adulthood***

	Erikson	*Marcia*	*Levinson*
Young Adulthood	Intimacy vs. Isolation Focus: Love commitments Adaptive Strength: Love	Depth and Commitment Statuses: Intimate Preintimate Pseudointimate Stereotyped or Isolated	Novice Phase Tasks: Forming a Dream Forming a Mentor Relationship Forming an Occupation Forming a Marriage and Family
Middle Adulthood	Generativity vs. Stagnation Focus: Concern for Others Adaptive Strength: Care	Inclusivity and Involvement Statuses: Generative Pseudogenerative Conventional Stagnant	Midlife Transition Challenges: Young–Old Destruction–Creation Masculine–Feminine Attachment–Separateness
Late Adulthood	Ego Integrity vs. Despair Focus: Life Review and Integration Adaptive Strength: Wisdom	Wisdom and Continuity Statuses: Integrated Nonexploratory Pseudointegrated Despairing	(did not address late adulthood)

Adapted from Marcia, J E., (2002), Identity and psychosocial development in adulthood. Identity *An International Journal of Theory and Research (2)*, 7–28. Used with permission from Taylor & Francis; and Levinson, D. (1978). *The Seasons of a Man's Life.* New York: Ballantine Books. Used with permision of Random House, Inc.

Your Thoughts?

If an older relative was in despair (as Erikson describes it) would you help pay for counseling for that person? Why, why not, or under what circumstances?

for their situation and tend to be more easily pushed around. Despair is often displayed as regret, pessimism, and a fear of death. It is important to note that those functioning in integrity are not necessarily the opposite in that they are always upbeat and optimistic (Hamachek, 1990). For Erikson, the key in developing integrity is to acknowledge the regrets, the reasons for pessimism, and the things that cause pain, but to keep those negative aspects in balance by also remembering the many good things enjoyed and reasons for optimism. The adaptive strength that comes from working through this stage is wisdom. In this context wisdom is the ability to hold paradoxes and contrasting items in balance, such as regrets and achievements. The wise person can enjoy life while realizing that, now in late adulthood, death will likely come sooner rather than later (Erikson et al., 1986).

Marcia: Wisdom and Continuity. In the last of Marcia's identity reformulations of Erikson's stages, the key elements in late adulthood are the commitment to developing wisdom and establishing continuity in the cycle of life. As was done in the previous stages, Marcia and his colleagues observed the following parallels:

- Identity achievement–Integrated
- Moratorium–Nonexploratory
- Foreclosure–Pseudointegrated
- Identity diffusion–Despairing

The late adulthood identity status that parallels identity achievement, *integrated*, includes individuals who have a strong sense of historical as well as current connection to others, thus they have continuity in their life cycle. They also have a well-developed set of beliefs and values that gives them a strong foundation in wisdom. The *nonexploratory* identity status, similar to that of moratorium, is found in individuals who display little interest in wisdom, beliefs, or values. Their focus tends to be on the routine and mundane aspects of life. Individuals functioning in the nonexploratory status also tend to be narrow in their perspective and outlook, which gives them very little sense of continuity and connection to others. The late adulthood identity status most closely matching foreclosure is *pseudointegrated.* These individuals tend to use slogans, clichés, and superficial sayings as a substitute for wisdom, and because of that they feel no need to develop wisdom. Without wisdom to understand their place in the life cycle, the pseudointegrated have a sense of resignation regarding their connections to others. The final identity status, paralleling identity diffusion, is labeled *despairing*. These individuals are lacking in wisdom and continuity. Marcia (2002b) and Hearn (1993; cited in Marcia, 2002b) found that despairing individuals show inconsistent values and beliefs, and very little concern for themselves or others.

Your Thoughts?

Do you view the integrated identity status as the only "good" one and all the others as dysfunctional? Give reasons to justify your response.

Marcia and his colleagues have investigated identity statuses throughout adolescence and adulthood for many years. In his more recent work Marcia (2002b) is investigating lifelong patterns regarding identity statuses. While there is much research yet to be done with these hypotheses, there is some indication that those who acquire identity achievement in adolescence will continue into the intimate, generative, and integrated statuses. The pattern of healthy, productive adjustment will likely continue throughout life for these adults. Those individuals functioning in moratorium, preintimate, pseudogenerative, and nonexploratory may still transition into the identity achievement statuses. It appears that those in foreclosure, adolescents who have rigidly and stubbornly taken on an identity without exploration, may continue into pseudointimate, conventional, and to pseudointegrated in late adulthood. And, unfortunately, there are also indications that those who cannot move toward establishing an identity in adolescence, those in identity diffusion, may continue into stereotyped/isolated, stagnant, and despairing identity statuses.

One of the most satisfying aspects of late adulthood is sharing knowledge and wisdom.

Gerotranscendence. Taking the work of Erikson, along with other instrumental writers in psychology such as Carl Jung and Robert Peck, Lars Tornstam has developed and popularized a level of development building on this last stage, which he calls ***gerotranscendence***. Achieving this level requires a shift in perspectives from a physical, rational, and practical approach to one that is more spiritual, universal, and transcendent in nature. These shifts take place in terms of our sense of self, our relationships, and our sense of place in historical time and in the universe. Whereas some have characterized gerotranscendence as a process that may even begin in midlife (Degges-White, 2005; Tornstam, 1997), others view it more as a process found in old age (Wadensten, 2005).

Criticisms of Erikson's Stage Theory

Erikson's stages of psychosocial development, and the many research theories and investigations they inspired, provide a useful profile of adult identity development. Helpful and enlightening as they are, these stages are only generalizations, and certainly there are individual differences and circumstances that can influence or alter a particular person's identity development. In other words, at a grand level these stages describe many people, but at the individual level they may not describe any one person perfectly. Some have criticized these stage models for that very characteristic, being too broad and general to be useful. Hamachek (1990), writing from the point of view of a counselor, finds it difficult to evaluate or diagnose a client based on Erikson's work because of the absence of behavioral indicators. Most of Erikson's writings focus on the internal, psychological transitions rather than the specific behaviors that indicate one's identity development. This same critique could be made of most of the other theories discussed in this section as well.

Your Thoughts?

Do you agree with Hamachek? Do think stage models, such as Erikson's, are useful?

Another aspect of identity theories that often draws criticism is the emphasis on our sense of self. Erikson highlighted the importance of self-development by referring to each stage as a crisis, which conveys the feeling that these stages demand immediate and full attention. Other researchers, such as Marcia and Levinson, were not as dramatic in their descriptions of stage struggles. In collectivistic cultures, such as many Eastern cultures that emphasize family and community, one's sense of self would not seem so important, and certainly not be worthy of the term *crisis*.

A final point to keep in mind is that because these stage models have become so accepted it is tempting to treat them as facts and give the theory a higher priority than any research data. For example, when approaching a research study, should the primary goal be to determine how well the participants fit Erikson's theory (emphasis on the theory as "right") or to find out how well Erikson's theory fits the data collected from the participants? Sorrell and Montgomery (2001), in their critique of Erikson's work, worry that the model is often given the higher priority.

Section Summary

- The psychosocial view of personality development provided by Erikson, Marcia, and Levinson, summarized in Table 4.3, is filled with challenges and opportunities for growth as individuals move through a series of age-related normative crises.
- Following the struggle to achieve a level of personal identity in adolescence is the young adulthood desire to establish intimacy and make a commitment to another person.
- Erikson viewed the individual in middle adulthood with a healthy adjustment as engaging in generativity, generously sharing resources and knowledge, rather than stagnation and self-absorption.

- Marcia explored the drive toward inclusivity and involvement in the many domains of life, while Levinson explored the stagnant, blocked status often referred to as midlife crisis.
- Researchers have found gender differences in midlife development for several college samples participating in lengthy longitudinal studies.
- In the final stage of Erikson's model individuals are challenged to put together a satisfying cohesive story of their lives, and from this gleaning the wisdom that comes when reflecting on a lifetime of experiences.
- Marcia further explored the ways older adults manage their newly established "wise one" status, including those who are coping by presenting an imitation of true wisdom.
- The construct of gerotranscendence, sometimes viewed as an additional stage in Erikson's developmental sequence, emphasizes a shift in thinking to a more cosmic and universal perspective.
- The popularity of this stage model of personality development may have caused some to fully accept the reality of Erikson's theory without searching for behavioral indicators or alternate explanations of age-related changes.
- It is important to remember that Erikson's theory was built on observations from particular generations, as is some of the longitudinal research used to support it.
- Critics are wise to point out the likelihood of cultural and generational bias in Erikson's work.

Five-Factor Model of Personality Traits

Whereas Erikson's work represented primarily a theoretical exploration of large-scale age-related transitions, the five-factor personality model represents an empirical or data-driven search for evidence of stable traits. Erikson's background, studying with Sigmund Freud, and his interest in lifelong development led him to create a psychosocial model of personality growth over time that is strikingly different from the study of personality outside of such influences. The five-factor model represents the quest to understand personality with few, if any, preconceived theoretical notions.

The study of ***personality*** includes many diverse areas, such as characteristics and traits, emotions, moods, motivations, coping strategies, and goals. Personality characteristics play a major role in predicting satisfaction or dissatisfaction in many areas, such as in relationships and parenting and work roles, and because of that developmental psychologists have a great interest in personality studies. There are five general ways in which personality theory and research is rather distinctive or unique from other areas of psychology (Hall & Lindzey, 1978):

- It was often in disagreement or conflict with the other areas of psychology.
- It is generally functional in orientation.
- It is often concerned with motivational processes.
- It emphasizes a need to understand the whole person (not just behavior).
- It tends to be more broad than specific, and thus integrative.

Often in academic literature the terms *self* and *identity* are grouped with many other topics under the heading of *personality*. While some scholars draw clear boundaries between these terms, in everyday language those words are practically interchangeable. In their chapter "Personality and Aging" in the *Handbook of the Psychology of Aging*, Ryff, Kwan, and Singer (2001) ask, "Where does personality end and self begin?" (p. 487). It is important that

Your Thoughts?

How might a career counselor benefit from knowing which personality traits are likely to be permanent?

researchers, theorists, therapists, and other practitioners agree on terms and definitions in order to communicate through conference presentations, journal articles, and other writings. An area of particular interest is the exploration of stability and change among various personality characteristics. As individuals move through developmental stages, and adjust to the life events that occur along the way, which personality characteristics are most likely to remain stable, and which ones might change? This is an important question when predicting current and future thoughts and behaviors.

The five-factor model, proposing that basically all personality characteristics can be reduced to five categories or factors, first gained popularity in the 1980s. McCrae and his colleagues (2002) believe that these factors can account for all "emotional, interpersonal, experiential, attitudinal, and motivational styles" (p. 1457). While it has been challenged and criticized, the model has remained one of the most popular ways to conceptualize personality dimensions, particularly in the fields of clinical, industrial/organizational, and health psychology. Whereas many studies of personality are grounded in theory, these five factors were discovered through research efforts resulting in large amounts of data (McCrae & John, 1992). The factors were produced by a statistical procedure called ***factor analysis***, which detects groups of personality characteristics that appear to operate in a cohesive way. Based on many years of research involving thousands of participants from around the world, the five basic personality factors that have emerged are Extraversion, Agreeableness, Conscientiousness, Neuroticism, and Openness to Experience (McCrae & John, 1992). Each factor is summarized in Table 4.4. McCrae and his colleagues believe that the model can enhance communication among researchers and therapists because it integrates a wide variety of personality tests and models. They also believe that it is comprehensive and yet efficient in that it requires only five dimensions or scores on a personality test.

The Factors

Your Thoughts?

Would you support an employer who selected employees based on their extraversion scores? Why, why not, or under what circumstances?

The first factor, and perhaps the most well known, is ***Extraversion***. *High extraversion* is the label given to individuals who are talkative, energetic, outgoing, and friendly. These highly social people are cheerful, fun-loving, and spontaneous. Those who are low in extraversion, sometimes called ***Introversion***, tend to be quiet and passive, and may even be shy, reserved, and withdrawn. They are often considered more serious, aloof, and inhibited. The Extraversion factor has generated some controversy because of its closeness to another of the five factors, Agreeableness. McCrae and his colleagues prefer to view extraversion as containing more nonrelational aspects while agreeableness contains traits that have to do with interpersonal relationships.

TABLE 4.4 ***Five-Factor Personality Traits***

Trait	*Descriptive Characteristics*
Extraversion	Warmth, gregariousness, assertiveness, activity, excitement seeking, positive emotions
Agreeableness	Trust, straightforwardness, altruism, compliance, modesty, tender-mindedness
Conscientiousness	Competence, order, dutifulness, achievement striving, self-discipline, deliberation
Neuroticism	Anxiety, hostility, depression, self-consciousness, impulsiveness, vulnerability
Openness to Experience	Fantasy, aesthetics, feelings, actions, ideas, values

Based on McCrae & John (1992).

RESEARCH IN-DEPTH
Correlational Analysis

In an ideal world psychologists would be able to find the causes of all human thoughts, emotions, and behaviors through controlled experimentation. In the real world the best alternative is to rely on creating a controlled environment for smaller animals such that cause-and-effect can be established. When working with a laboratory animal experimenters can know the animal's genetic background, its diet and habitat since birth, and everything the animal has ever been exposed to. With those factors known researchers can manipulate the environment or the animal in some way and then observe what effect the manipulation caused. Human beings are much less willing to be controlled or manipulated! In many cases social scientists, doing the best they can responsibly and ethically, choose not to use experimental methods that establish cause-and-effect but rather search for associations or relationships between various characteristics.

As an example of such a study, consider the research questions that Stober (2003) presented in his study of self-pity, which is feeling sorrowful about one's own condition. Rather than attempting an extremely difficult (if even possible) study of what the possible causes of self-pity might be, Stober was interested in the relationship between self-pity, the five personality factors, and styles of anger. In order to explore these potential relationships Stober recruited 141 German college students to take several different questionnaires. The questionnaires were scored so that each student had a score for each variable. Then a statistical procedure called a ***correlation*** was performed to find the relationships. Correlations range in numerical value from –1.00 to +1.00, with numbers approaching either end reflecting a stronger relationship. The closer the numerical value is to 0.00 the weaker the association, with 0.00 indicating no relationship at all.

The results indicated that self-pity was correlated with only one of the five factors, Neuroticism, with a numerical value of +0.59. This ***positive correlation*** indicates that the scores are moving in the same direction and that the trends are parallel. Participants who scored higher in self-pity also scored higher in neuroticism, as well as the opposite, that those who scored lower in self-pity also scored lower in neuroticism. Self-pity was also found to be positively correlated with inward-focused and outward-focused anger. Displaying the opposite trend, however, was the relationship between self-pity and anger control, which produced a correlation of –0.22. This ***negative correlation*** indicates that the trends in the data are moving in an opposite way. Participants with higher scores on the self-pity scale tended to have lower scores on the anger control scale, and the reverse, those with higher anger control scores reported less self-pity.

One of the most important things to remember about correlations is that they do not provide evidence for a cause-and-effect relationship. For example, it could be that neuroticism causes self-pity, however, this research methodology does not prove that. It also could be the case that variables that were not even considered in this study, such as depression or a neurological condition, may be at the root of this finding. Even without the value of establishing causation, correlational research is very popular in the social sciences. By understanding more about the relationships between various thought patterns and behaviors, researchers can create better studies, theories, and predictive models. Also, by giving information on related psychological characteristics to counselors and therapists, those practitioners can be more effective with their clients.

The second of the five factors, ***Agreeableness***, provides a sense of how humanistic or hostile one might be in interpersonal situations. Those individuals who score high in agreeableness are usually described as good-natured, warm, and gentle. These soft-hearted, trustworthy people are altruistic and caring. As the name of the factor implies, these individuals have a helpful, sympathetic, and cooperative nature. On the other hand, those who are low in agreeableness tend to be more argumentative, antagonistic, and suspicious. Their cold disposition toward others is sometimes described as ruthless and vindictive. Some critics of the five-factor model find the label of "agreeableness" too mild for a factor that is focused on humanitarian altruism versus ruthless antagonism.

Your Thoughts?

What might be some negative aspects or consequences to being highly agreeable?

High scores in ***Conscientiousness*** reflect the characteristics of responsibility and self-discipline. Those who are high in this factor tend to be organized and are often achievement-oriented. They are careful and diligent. People who are low in conscientiousness are much the opposite, often referred to as lazy and irresponsible. Other characteristics associated with low conscientiousness are impulsive, disorganized, and undependable. A criticism of this factor and the Agreeableness factor is that they have a judgmental or morality component to them. The Agreeableness factor may be exaggerated to become a "good versus evil" category, while the Conscientiousness factor may be conceptualized as "willpower versus weakness."

Your Thoughts?

Would you support an employer who selected employees based on their neuroticism scores? Why, why not, or under what circumstances?

Those individuals who are high in ***Neuroticism*** tend to be high-strung, anxious, nervous, and moody. They often experience feelings of guilt, along with worry and self-pity. Studies have found that those high in neuroticism are more prone to psychiatric disorders. Those who are low in neuroticism tend to be emotionally stable and even tempered. These individuals are usually calm, easygoing, and relaxed. Rather than dealing with frequent distress, low-neuroticism individuals are generally content. McCrae and his colleagues have found that Neuroticism is the least controversial of the five factors among personality psychologists.

Your Thoughts?

Would it be useful for a romantic couple to share their personality profiles before making a long-term commitment? Why, why not, or under what circumstances?

The final factor, ***Openness to Experience***, creates a continuum between those who are curious, adventuresome, and daring, and thus high in openness, and those who are routine and conventional, or low in openness. Those who are high in openness to experience are imaginative, original, artistic, and open to new ideas. Those who are low in openness are down-to-earth and practical, while at the same time less artistic or aesthetically sensitive, less interested in cultural pursuits, and more narrow in their interests. This factor is the most controversial of the five (McCrae & Costa, 1987; McCrae & John, 1992), possibly because it seems to imply that a person wouldn't be creative and open to new ideas while at the same time valuing tradition and predictability.

While numerous studies and literature reviews have confirmed the statistical evidence for the five factors, the model is not without criticism. Although this may seem counterintuitive at first, one of the major concerns about the model is its very success. Similar to the criticism made of Erikson's theory, some psychologists are concerned that because the five-factor model is so popular others will simply assume that the model demonstrates the truth about personality, and thus stop trying to modify or critique the model. Others have criticized the model because it does not provide a complete theory of personality. Having been developed from research efforts the five-factor model is not as unified and extensive as theoretical models, such as Erikson's stages of identity development. Some researchers find that five factors are too many, while others find five to be too few. Occasionally, a sixth factor has been proposed, such as culture, values, gender, or self-evaluation, but none of these factors have the statistical power of the major five factors (McCrae & John, 1992). McCrae and his colleagues have continued to work with the ever-growing collection of data and with suggestions for revisions (Costa & McCrae, 1997).

Current Research: Gender, Age, and Culture

Some of the more recent research involving the five-factor model has focused on the issue of stability and development throughout the lifespan. McCrae and his colleagues theorize that the personality traits have biological origins. If this is true, it raises the question as to when, in terms of biological maturity or age, will these personality traits reach full development? McCrae and his colleagues estimate that personality traits continue to develop until young adulthood, with only slight changes after age 30. Earlier findings, largely based on longitudinal studies, indicated that conscientiousness and agreeableness tend to increase in adulthood, while neuroticism, openness, and extraversion tend to decrease (McCrae et al., 2002). A more recent review of the literature (Roberts, Robins, Caspi, & Trzesniewski, 2003) indicated support for the findings that conscientiousness and agreeableness tend to increase, and that neuroticism tends to decrease. No clear pattern could be established for openness and extraversion (McCrae et al., 2002).

What Do You Think

What events happen to most adults in their 20s that may shape or influence their personality development?

Srivastava, John, Gosling, and Potter (2003) further explored the question of change and stability in adulthood by considering change in personality traits between young and middle adulthood, specifically before and after age 30. Their study was quite large, involving 132,515 adults between ages 21 and 60 from the United States and Canada. The results, as summarized in Table 4.5, were generally consistent with previous findings, with the major exception that gender differences were noted. Srivastava et al. found that both men and women demonstrated patterns of increases in conscientiousness and agreeableness, which is consistent with previous research. Women and men demonstrated a slowing in the increase in conscientiousness after age 30, and both displayed the greatest increase in agreeableness after age 30. Women generally reported higher scores overall than men in conscientiousness and agreeableness. Results for neuroticism indicated that women show a consistent decline in adulthood while men demonstrated little change in their levels of neuroticism. Younger women demonstrated a much higher level of neuroticism, such that the consistent decline during adulthood brought them to similar levels as the men. The results for openness and extraversion were less clear, which is also consistent with previous research. Women demonstrated a rate of change in openness that is similar both before and after age 30; however, the change was in opposite directions. Women tended to increase in openness to experience prior to age 30 and decrease after age 30. Overall men had higher scores in openness than women did. Finally, gender differences were found in extraversion scores. Women, who overall had higher scores than men, tended to increase slightly prior to age 30 and decrease slightly after age 30. Men demonstrated a slight increase in extraversion across adulthood, such that men and women had very similar scores later in adulthood.

Your Thoughts?

How might the gender expectations in American society encourage the gender differences found by Srivastava et al.?

In terms of personality and aging, scholars are now calling for more research into the role of personality in the ways people cope with health-related issues and for further exploration of the relationship between personality and cultural and socioeconomic influences (Ryff, et al., 2001).

In addition to the research questions of development and stability of personality traits, others have questioned the usefulness of the model in other cultures. To explore this concern, McCrae (2001) and his colleagues collected and analyzed data from participants representing 26 different cultures on five different continents. Questionnaires were translated into the appropriate languages, including Chinese, Estonian, Norwegian, Serbian, and Russian. The results were similar to American samples for both age and gender trends. In a similar study Allik and McCrae (2004) compared data gathered from 36 different cultures and also found similar results. When comparing particular cultures to each other they concluded that cultures that are geographically close tend to have greater similarities in personality traits. Their findings also suggested that European and American cultures were distinct from Asian and African cultures in terms of the level of each trait. For McCrae (2001, 2004) these findings reinforce the belief that the five personality factors are genetic and universally found in all cultures.

Your Thoughts?

What would be the biggest challenges involved in accurately translating a personality questionnaire into another language?

Section Summary

- The factors Extraversion, Agreeableness, Conscientiousness, Neuroticism, and Openness to Experience have stood up well to continued researched studies involving thousands of participants over many years.
- McCrae and his colleagues have demonstrated that some facets of personality remain fairly stable and consistent over time.
- There is evidence to suggest that the five factors are common across cultures while demonstrating some gender differences.

TABLE 4-5 ***Gender Differences in the Five-Factor Model Across Adulthood***

Personality Factor	*Population*	*Trends*
Conscientiousness	Previous research	Increasing across adulthood
	Women	Increasing across adulthood Change slows but does not stop after age 30
	Men	Increasing across adulthood Change slows but does not stop after age 30
Agreeableness	Previous research	Increasing across adulthood
	Women	Increasing across adulthood Greatest amounts of increase occurred after age 30
	Men	Increasing across adulthood Greatest amounts of increase occurred after age 30
Neuroticism	Previous research	Decreasing across adulthood
	Women	Decreasing across adulthood Consistent decline across adulthood
	Men	No significant change across adulthood No significant change before or after age 30
Openness to Experience	Previous research	No clear pattern had emerged
	Women	Increasing prior to age 30; decreasing after age 30 Change is of similar strength across adulthood
	Men	Increasing prior to age 30; decreasing after age 30 Change at a faster rate after age 30 than before age 30
Extraversion	Previous research	No clear pattern had emerged
	Women	Increasing prior to age 30; decreasing after age 30 Change is of similar strength across adulthood
	Men	Increasing across adulthood Change slows but does not stop after age 30

Adapted from Srivastava, John, Gosling, & Potter (2003).

Chapter Summary

Personality, both in terms of age-related development and stable traits, provides an important part of the profile from which psychologists and counselors can predict an individual's thoughts and behaviors. Stage theories offer a structure that can serve to organize what psychologists have learned about the ways people change across adulthood, while personality traits offer further insight into the ways adults will cope with age-related challenges. Here are some of the main points of the chapter:

- The four primary models of personality are stage models, timing-of-events models, trait models, and cognitive-self models.
- Erikson's view of development involves a series of eight normative psychosocial crises or stages.
- The stage of identity cohesion versus role confusion is focused on choosing what type of person an adolescent wants to be, and being true to that identity.
- Marcia found four identity statuses—identity achievement, moratorium, foreclosure, and identity diffusion—based on adolescents' sense of exploration and commitment in the areas of beliefs and attitudes in the areas of politics, religion, and career choices.
- Marcia has found that a productive pathway to developing an identity is through the foreclosure–moratorium–identity achievement sequence.
- Erikson's young adult stage of intimacy versus isolation is the quest to trust and truly love another person.
- Marcia's model applied to Erikson's young adulthood stage centered on depth in relationships and long-term commitment, and produced four identity statuses: intimate, preintimate, pseudointimate, and stereotyped or isolated.
- Levinson found that in the Novice Phase young adults need to form a dream, form a mentor relationship, form an occupation, and form a loving relationship.
- Erikson's middle-age stage of generativity versus stagnation reflects the struggle between giving wisdom and resources to others and turning inward to self-preservation.
- Marcia's version of Erikson's middle adulthood stage centered on inclusivity and involvement, and has four statuses: generative, pseudogenerative (which can be agentic or communal), conventional, and stagnant.
- Levinson found that the Midlife Transition is the search for balance between the identity concepts of young–old, destruction–creation/masculine–feminine, and attachment–separateness.
- Although the Mills Longitudinal Study and the Grant Study found that men and women experience identity development somewhat differently, both found that individuals challenge gender roles in midlife and both experience more freedom and enjoyment in their 50s.
- Late adulthood is now viewed as containing several phases, often with a focus on the newly retired, the "young–old" who are active and growth-focused, and the "old-old" who are less active and focused on a very simple lifestyle.
- Erikson's final stage, integrity versus despair, involves the challenge of integrating life experiences to produce either meaningfulness and contentment, or regrets and pessimism.
- Marcia's identity statuses for Erikson's last stage, centered on wisdom development and continuity, are integrated, nonexploratory, pseudointegrated, and despairing.
- Gerotranscendence, which may reflect the final stage in Erikson's developmental theory, involves a view of life that is more cosmic in orientation.

- The most common criticisms of stage theories are that as generalizations they ignore too many individual differences, are too broad to be useful, lead to a self-centered view, and that they dominate data interpretation in research.
- The five-factor model, containing Extraversion, Agreeableness, Conscientiousness, Neuroticism, and Openness to Experience, has been dominant in personality research since the 1980s.
- Among the five factors, Neuroticism is the least controversial while Openness to Experience is the most controversial among scholars.
- Research with the five-factor model indicates that personality traits can continue to develop, both increasing and decreasing throughout adulthood.
- Research with the five-factor model indicates some gender differences across the lifespan, but very similar patterns in cross-cultural studies.

Key Terms

Stage models **(91)**
Normative-crisis models **(91)**
Timing-of-events models **(91)**
Trait models **(92)**
Cognitive-self models **(92)**
Identity cohesion versus role confusion **(92)**
Identity **(92)**
Psychosocial theory **(92)**
Identity crisis **(93)**
Identity statuses **(94)**
Identity achievement **(94)**
Moratorium **(94)**
Foreclosure **(94)**
Identity diffusion **(95)**
Intimacy versus isolation **(97)**
Novice Phase **(99)**
Settling Down Period **(99)**
Generativity versus stagnation **(101)**
Midlife Transition **(102)**
Androgynous **(103)**
Longitudinal design **(104)**
Ego integrity versus despair **(106)**
Gerotranscendence **(109)**
Personality **(110)**
Factor analysis **(111)**
Extraversion **(111)**
Introversion **(111)**
Correlation **(112)**
Positive correlation **(112)**
Negative correlation **(112)**
Agreeableness **(112)**
Conscientiousness **(112)**
Neuroticism **(113)**
Openness to Experience **(113)**

Comprehension Questions

1. Name the four types of personality models and describe how each is unique.
2. Explain the use of the term *crisis* in Erikson's stage model.
3. Describe the characteristics of an identity crisis as experienced in identity cohesion versus role confusion.
4. Describe Marcia's four adolescent identity statuses.
5. Explain what Marcia believes to be the optimal progression through the identity statuses.
6. Name and describe Erikson's young adulthood stage.
7. Name and describe the four identity statuses Marcia associated with young adulthood.
8. What are the four important tasks of the Novice Phase found by Levinson?
9. What have researchers found when comparing the ways men and women move through Levinson's Novice Phase?
10. Name and describe Erikson's middle adulthood stage.
11. Name and describe the four identity statuses Marcia associated with middle adulthood.
12. Explain the dilemmas found in Levinson's four polarities that characterize midlife transition.
13. Give several examples of criticisms of Levinson's research on midlife transition.

14. Compare and contrast the findings of the Mills Longitudinal Study and the Grant Study.
15. What are the parallels Kroger makes between adolescents and individuals in late adulthood?
16. What is the primary difference between the "young–old" and the "old-old," and why is that an important distinction?
17. Name and describe Erikson's late adulthood stage.
18. Name and describe Marcia's four identity statuses associated with late adulthood.
19. Explain the common criticisms of Erikson's stage model.
20. What are the five generalizations Hal and Lindzey make regarding personality theory?
21. Name and describe each of the factors of the five-factor model developed by McCrae and his colleagues.
22. Summarize the cross-cultural studies done using the five-factor model.

Answers for Common Sense: Myth or Reality?

1. Myth: The standard marker for entry into young adulthood is turning 20 years old. (See Adolescence and Emerging Adulthood, page 93.)
2. Myth: Identity crisis is primarily about choosing a personal value system. (See Erikson: Identity Cohesion versus Role Confusion, page 93.)
3. Reality: Many individuals will move through several of Marcia's identity statuses before reaching identity achievement in adolescence. (See Marcia: Exploration and Commitment, page 96.)
4. Myth: Identity development is usually worked out in adolescence and then set for the rest of adulthood. (See Young Adulthood, page 97.)
5. Reality: Researchers have found that identity statuses in young adulthood influence individuals' abilities to form intimate relationships. (See Marcia: Depth and Commitment, page 97.)
6. Reality: Researchers have found that women have a harder time forming a dream of the person they would like to become than men. (See Levinson: Early Adulthood Stage, page 100.)
7. Myth: Most men in their early 40s go through a midlife crisis. (See Levinson: Middle Adulthood Stage, page 103.)
8. Myth: Midlife crisis is well accepted among psychologists as a part of middle age. (See Levinson: Middle Adulthood Stage, page 103.)
9. Reality: Identity development in middle adulthood involves reassessing and challenging gender roles and expectations. (See Levinson: Middle Adulthood Stage and Gender Identity Development, page 104.)
10. Myth: Researchers have found that adolescents and those in late adulthood have very few developmental issues in common. (See Late Adulthood, page 106.)
11. Reality: Many researchers view late adulthood as consisting of the younger-old and the very-old. (See Late Adulthood, page 106.)
12. Reality: One of the greatest concerns regarding the five-factor model is its success. (See The Factors, page 113.)
13. Myth: The developers of the five-factor model believe that personality characteristics reach full development in adolescence. (See Current Research: Gender, Age, and Culture, page 113.)
14. Reality: The developers of the five-factor model believe that the five traits are genetic in origin and are universal across all cultures. (See Current Research: Gender, Age, and Culture, page 114.)

Suggested Readings

Early Work on Personality Traits, 1921

Allport, F. H., & Allport, G. W. (1921). Personality traits: Their classification and measurement. *Journal of Abnormal and Social Psychology, 16*, 6–40. Accessed at *Classics in the History of Psychology* (http://psychclassics.yorku.ca/topic.htm).

Thoughts on Personality and Therapy in 1947 by Carl Rogers

Rogers, Carl R.. (1947). Some observations on the organization of personality. *American Psychologist, 2*, 358–368. [1947 APA Presidential Address.] Accessed at *Classics in the History of Psychology* (http://psychclassics.yorku.ca/topic.htm).

Cross-Cultural Research on the Five-Factor Model

McCrae, R. R. (2002). Cross-cultural research on the five-factor model of personality. In W. J. Lonner, D. L. Dinnel, S. A. Hayes, & D. N. Sattler (Eds.), *Online readings in psychology and culture* (Unit 6, Chapter 1), (http://www.wwu.edu/~culture), Center for Cross-Cultural Research, Western Washington University, Bellingham, WA. Available at http://www.ac.wwu.edu/~culture/mccrae.htm.

Studying Personality in the Philippines

Church, A. T., & Katigbak, M. S. (2002). Studying personality traits across cultures: Philippine examples. In W. J. Lonner, D. L. Dinnel, S. A. Hayes, & D. N. Sattler (Eds.), *Online readings in psychology and culture* (Unit 6, Chapter 2), (http://www.wwu.edu/~culture), Center for Cross-Cultural Research, Western Washington University, Bellingham, WA. Available at http://www.ac.wwu.edu/~culture/church_katigbak.htm.

Suggested Websites

Personality and the Big Five

Find more information and online personality tests at the Personality Project, http://www.personality-project.org/.

Diversity in Approaches to Personality

You can find more information about areas of personality studies, such as Interpersonal Theory and Personality Disorders, at the Great Ideas in Psychology site, http://www.personalityresearch.org/.

African American Racial Identity Research Lab

At the AARI Research Lab, part of the Department of Psychology at the University of Michigan, you can find many sources about racial identity as a general construct as well as an enormous amount of information on African American identity. See http://www.lsa.umich.edu/aari/index.htm.

More on Research Studies in Personality

To learn more about current research go to the Institute of Personality and Social Research at the University of California at Berkeley, at http://ls.berkeley.edu/dept/ipsr/ or the National Institute on Aging and National Institutes of Health website for the Laboratory of Personality and Cognition, at http://www.grc.nia.nih.gov/branches/lpc/lpc.htm.

CHAPTER

5 Friendships and Love Relationships

What would life be like without supportive friends, lovers, and family members? Most of us would not want to find out. This chapter surveys several types of social relationships, including research on friendships and love relationships, and the following chapter explores parenting and intergenerational family relationships. Even though what we want and need from friendships as adults is certainly different from what we desired as children, we still benefit from friendships and social support no matter what age we are. This chapter is focused more on friendships during young and middle adulthood. Friendships and social support networks are also discussed later in the book as sources of comfort and means of coping with the challenges of late adulthood.

Traditionally, textbook chapters on these topics would be arranged in a chronological, linear progression moving through friendships, heterosexual love relationships, marriage, parenting, grandparenting, and perhaps caring for elderly relatives. Although the outlines for this and the following chapter look somewhat similar to that traditional scheme, any review of current research will quickly reveal that Americans and many others around the world are deviating from that traditional path. For example, while love relationships are of primary importance to most adults, many are choosing less traditional lifestyles that include cohabiting (living together outside of marriage). Also, while the debates surrounding gay marriage continue around the world, the numbers of gay partners receiving legal recognition is increasing, and in some parts of the world same-sex marriages are openly celebrated. Another factor bringing diversity and change to the once traditional life adult trajectory is the acceptance of divorce and remarriage. It is not only young adults who are cohabiting and possibly marrying, but also middle-aged and older adults who find themselves divorced or widowed and looking for another primary love relationship.

COMMON SENSE
Myth or Reality?

Mark each of the following items with either an M, if you think it is a myth, or an R, if you think the statement reflects reality. By paying close attention you can find all the answers in this chapter. If needed, the answers are also given at the end of the chapter.

1. _____ Physical appearance is an important characteristic in choosing friends for both young and middle-aged adults.
2. _____ One of the functions of friendship is to develop intimacy.
3. _____ Men and women tend to have circles of friends that are similar in size and closeness.
4. _____ Never-married adults often cite their freedom as one of the greatest advantages of their lifestyle.
5. _____ Researchers have found that people in intimate relationships report that a sense of commitment is one of the most important aspects of a love relationship.
6. _____ A popular theory of love relationships states that the type of attachment infants develop with their caregivers will be the type of attachment those infants, when they are adults, will develop with their lovers.
7. _____ Most heterosexual couples who live together view it as a trial period prior to marriage.
8. _____ The *cohabitation effect* is the common research finding that couples who cohabit prior to marriage are more likely to divorce.
9. _____ Researchers have found that heterosexual and gay couples are more alike in terms of satisfaction and stability than different.
10. _____ Currently, there are no countries in the world that legally recognize same-sex relationships.
11. _____ Marital satisfaction increases throughout adulthood for most couples.
12. _____ Love, loyalty, and shared values are key factors in a healthy marriage.
13. _____ Approximately half of all marriages end in divorce.
14. _____ Adultery is the most common reason given for divorce.
15. _____ Less than half of all divorced individuals will remarry.

Before We Get Started . . .

Do you think of some of your family members like friends? Researchers have found that adult siblings are often highly valued sources of social support and advice. If you have siblings or stepsiblings, do you consider them to be your friends? (If you do not have siblings in your life perhaps you can consider cousins or other relatives in your generation.) Before we consider friendships and interfamily relationships, consider how well matched you and your siblings are in terms of *friendship* characteristics. In a recent research study Johnson (2001) found that adults generally have friends who are similar in the areas listed below. How similar are you to each sibling in terms of the following characteristics?

Age
Career choice
Educational achievement
Marital status
Parental status
Physical appearance
Religious views
Residential proximity
Self-esteem
Social activity
Social skills
Social–political attitudes
Sports participation
Hobbies
Income
Leisure activities

Do you feel closer, more like friends, with those family members who are more similar to you in those areas? Johnson found that close friends are generally similar in terms of education, income, hobbies, and sports and leisure activities, and they tend to live close to each other or in similar types of neighborhoods. Do you think there are other characteristics that influence friendship among family members more than the items listed above?

It would be interesting to ask your friends to analyze their family relationships in this way, particularly those with biologically intact families and those with blended families that include stepsiblings. It would also be interesting to ask people of different ages to rate their siblings in this way. How might cultural background, age, and/or generational influences make a difference?

Friendships

Your Thoughts?

In what ways might personality development, particularly regarding identity, influence the roles friends play in our lives?

Even though the characteristics of friendships change with age (Gurucharri & Selman, 1982) such relationships are no less important in adulthood than they were in childhood. Often as children we are limited in our choice of friends based on who our parents allow us to associate with. As adults we have much more freedom in choosing our friends—an opportunity we should take seriously. While we are generally not able to choose our coworkers, neighbors, or relatives, we can choose the people we want to spend our leisure time with. We can build a supportive network of close, trustworthy friends who share each others' good fortune and difficult times. Cultivating and maintaining close, supportive social networks can be helpful at all ages, and is particularly important for successful aging in late adulthood.

Developing Friendships

What characteristics do you look for when choosing friends? Johnson (2001) set out to answer that question by comparing the characteristics of pairs of friends, acquaintances, and nonfriends among middle-aged adults. He found that his participants tended to be friends with others who have similar values, interests, leisure activities, and backgrounds. Friends are also more likely to be similar in age, income, and parental status. When considering the differences between casual friends and close friends, Johnson found that close friends usually have similar levels of educational attainment and live close by or live in a similar type of neighborhood. Interestingly, physical appearance, which is often listed as important in friendships among young adults, was not related to friendship for middle-aged adults. Johnson's research may provide some insight into the reasons why some friendships are lifelong and others come and go. Considering those characteristics that distinguish close friends, when individuals achieve a higher level of education, become a parent, or even gain or drop a hobby, such personal changes may also bring changes in friendships.

Your Thoughts?

How might a large difference in educational attainment affect friendships adversely?

Americans often use the term *friend* to refer to many relationships from the most casual acquaintance to the most dear or closest friend. A close relationship, or what one might call a *true* friendship, can provide many benefits and offer opportunities for reciprocity. Based on a review of friendship studies involving adult participants, Mendelson and Aboud (1999) identified six primary functions of these close relationships. The first function, *stimulating companionship*, refers to the ways friends enhance experiences and activities. Friends can make celebrations special and memorable, as well as make even routine activities more enjoyable. It is the companionship aspect of friendship that prompts the Centers for Disease Control and Prevention (CDC; 2008a) to encourage those with problems getting motivated to exercise to enlist the help of a friend. The second function is to *provide help* when needed. When facing difficult events or hard decisions, friends can provide advice as well as tangible forms of aid,

Friends are good companions, making even mundane chores more fun.

such as transportation or money. *Intimacy*, the third function of friendship, refers to the role that friends play in listening to personal concerns or problems and in giving honest feedback. Secrets should be safe with close friends. The fourth function is the making of a *reliable alliance*. Friends stick together in good and bad times, bonded by a sense of loyalty. Often it is close friendships that help individuals cope with difficult work or marital situations. The fifth function, *self-validation*, is focused on the role friends play in promoting a healthy self-image. True friends help us feel good about ourselves. They contribute to our sense of pride in the things we do well, and they support us when we are trying to change the less desirable aspects of ourselves. The final function is *emotional security*. Friends provide the secure base needed to try something new or to face something that is anxiety-provoking. These six functions can be combined to create a definition of ***friendship*** as intimate, stimulating companionship that is a source of help, reliable alliance, self-validation, and emotional security. Any relationship, whether with friend, relative, lover, spouse, or adult child, that fulfills all six of these functions is incredibly beneficial and valuable.

Your Thoughts?

How might the value we place on each of the functions change across young, middle, and late adulthood?

Convoy Model of Friendship

The ***convoy model of friendship*** and social support, developed by Antonucci in the 1980s, continues to be one of the primary theories pertaining to friendships across adulthood. It is often conceptualized as three protective layers or concentric circles around an individual.

Your Thoughts?

How many different types of relationships would be represented in your convoy? Familial, intimate, social, work-based, school-based, others?

The innermost circle contains those people, whether friends or family, who are the closest and provide the most support. These individuals are so close that it would be hard to imagine life without them. The middle circle contains people who are important but not as close or as supportive as those in the inner circle. The outer circle contains those individuals who are supportive or close primarily because of the role they play, such as a coworker or a neighbor (Antonucci, 2001; Levitt, Weber, & Guacci, 1993; Seibert, Mutran, & Reitzes, 1999). Convoys are not fixed but rather evolve with age and life experiences. Consistent with Johnson's research on choosing friends, as individuals move through various experiences in life, such as graduating from college, entering an occupation, or creating a family, the people they place in the inner, middle, and outer circles will likely change. Levitt and colleagues (1993) found this to be the case when comparing the convoys of three generations of women, finding that the young adult women included more friends in their networks, whereas their mothers and grandmothers included more family members. Even with the members of the convoys changing, most people maintain the size of their social support network until very late in life, usually in their 80s, when convoys start to decrease in size (Antonucci, 2001; Seibert et al., 1999). When considering the quality of convoy relationships across adulthood in American and Japanese participants, Akiyama, Antonucci, Takahaski, and Langfahl (2003) found that frequency of negative relationships decreases with age, with the exception of marriage relationships. The American sample showed the most negative interactions with spouses during middle age while negative interactions in Japanese couples remained at a steady level throughout adulthood. Akiyama et al. also found that for both samples negative interactions with fathers and mothers increased with age.

Convoys have also been found to differ by gender, indicating that women and men often build their social support structure differently. Researchers who study closeness and intimacy, either as a function of friendships or love relationships, tend to agree that women grow closer to others through self-disclosure and emotional conversations, but the pathway men take to establish close relationships is less clear. Some scholars believe that men simply do not develop closeness to the degree that women do, while others argue that men create intimate social relationships through shared activities other than conversations (Fehr, 2004). Women also tend to have more extensive support networks, more intense relationships, and provide and receive more support from their social networks (Antonucci, 2001; Antonucci et al., 2001). While women appear to benefit from expanded, intimate social networks, researchers have also found that these close relationships can cause distress. When members of their social network become smothering or demanding, women are more likely to be affected by the negativity (Antonucci, 2001; Antonucci, Lansford, & Akiyama, 2001).

Your Thoughts?

In what ways might male/male and female/female friendships differ?

Section Summary

- As adults we can choose our friends, and if we choose wisely we can build for ourselves a strong network of support individuals.
- Most adults choose friends who are similar in age, income, and parental status, with closest friends sharing similar neighborhood characteristics and educational accomplishments.
- True friendships can be characterized as intimate, stimulating companionship that is a source of help, reliable alliance, self-validation, and emotional security.
- Gender and age differences in friendships have been found using the convoy model of friendship, which conceptualizes three levels of closeness.
- Women tend to create larger convoys and are more involved in them than men are in their convoys.

Single Lifestyles

Some adults find it more appealing to maintain a lifestyle that does not involve most of the topics explored in this chapter. Rather than cohabiting or marrying, these adults choose to spend their lives as single adults. In a strict sense the term *single* refers to someone who is not married. In common usage, however, the label could be applied to legally single individuals who may or may not be in love relationships as well as people who are divorced or widowed. This particular section focuses primarily on those adults who have never married and are not in or seeking a love relationship.

Research on never-married individuals indicates that this is not a homogeneous group, with some enjoying their lifestyle and others finding it dissatisfying. In a study of 51,000 people in Norway, Mastekaasa (1995) found that single, never-married individuals had a poorer sense of well-being and a higher suicide rate than those who were cohabiting or married. On the other hand, Robinson-Rowe (2002) found a group of never-married women who were quite happy with their lifestyle choice. The women, ranging in age from 40 to 52 years old, felt that their "never-married" status was not forced on them or given to them by default, but rather it was their personal lifestyle choice. In their view the most satisfying part of the single life was the freedom from responsibilities to others, sense of personal control, and the ability to pursue exciting opportunities, such as educational or career options or opportunities to travel. These never-married women also felt that the most important factor in maintaining a satisfying single life was to create a personally meaningful lifestyle that included strong social networks.

Your Thoughts?

How might the reasons for choosing to be without a romantic partner change with age?

Regardless of whether individuals feel their single status is due to choice or circumstances, single adults often deal with stereotyping and stigma. To learn more about this, Zajicek and Koski (2003) interviewed 28 single adults, ranging in age from 22 to 88 years old, who were living in Britain. The participants indicated that they felt odd socially because the general expectation was that everyone of a certain age ought to be in a relationship. They also felt pressure from their families and friends to "find someone." Participants reported that while some people seemed to imply "there must be something wrong with you," other individuals with partners or spouses gave the impression that they were afraid the single adult would "steal" their partner. The men and women in Zajicek and Koski's study learned to cope by replacing negative terms, such as "unattached," with positive ones, such as "career-focused," emphasizing advantages of their status. They also spent time and effort creating personally meaningful and social lifestyles.

Your Thoughts?

How would you design a study to determine if young adults have a positive, negative, or neutral attitude toward other young adults who choose not to be in a relationship?

Building Love Relationships

The often used closing line in romantic fairy tales, "and they lived happily ever after," gives the impression people who are truly in love should experience ultimate bliss every day. Most of us learn over time that we do not live in fairy-tale worlds, and that even the happiest of relationships cycle through more and less satisfying times. Rather than viewing love as one unified construct, many researchers view love as multifaceted and complex. For example, one theory of ***love styles***, developed by Lee in the early 1970s (as cited in Montgomery & Sorell, 1997), focused on several types of love reflecting intentions or motivation:

- *Eros*—an intense emotional and physical attraction
- *Ludus*—a game, just playing around
- *Storge*—a deeply committed friendship
- *Pragma*—a practical choice
- *Mania*—possessiveness
- *Agape*—selflessness, putting the other first

Your Thoughts?

Which style(s) of love would you predict are associated with divorces? Why? How might you test your hypothesis?

Continuing with the notion that the term *love* can include many distinct variations, this section focuses on two popular theories of love, both of which emphasize types or patterns of love. The first, the triangular theory of love, emphasizes the ways primary elements in love interact. The second theory, attachment styles, considers variations in our first primary love relationship, that between an infant and caregiver, and then projects those experiences on to adult love relationships.

Triangular Theory of Love

Your Thoughts?

How would you predict the balance between the three parts of love would change with age? Give reasons to support your response.

Sternberg's (1997a) ***triangular theory of love*** emphasizes intimacy, passion, and decision/commitment as the primary forces in a love relationship. *Intimacy* is the emotional part of love that involves feelings of warmth, comfort, closeness, and understanding toward the other person. Similar to that called for by Erikson in his young adult stage of personality development, intimate relationships have established trust and open lines of communication. *Passion* is the motivating or driving part of love that is both the longing for and involvement in sexual activity. The third component, *decision/commitment*, reflects the cognitive aspects of love. Even

ON THE LEADING EDGE
Online Dating

Do people who use online dating services have unrealistically high expectations? Do they really think they can find a perfectly matched mate through the Internet? These were the questions explored by James Houran, who is affiliated with an online matching service, and Rense Lange from the Illinois State Board of Education. They asked 222 nonmarried participants to imagine the pool of dating candidates they may have access to through a dating service, and to consider how many in that pool would be determined by the service to be good matches. Participants were asked to estimate the percentage of candidates the service would find to be *perfectly compatible*, *exceptional*, *favorable*, *marginal*, and *totally incompatible* with the research participant. The category of *perfectly compatible* was designed to reflect the common concept of soul mates as two people who are totally and genuinely compatible. The researchers found that most participants estimated the percentage of candidates selected by the service to be perfectly compatible to be about 10%. The participants thought that most of the candidates would be in the middle category or *favorable*.

Perhaps a question Houran and Lange should have added is "How many of your estimated 10% of perfectly compatible candidates are likely to be telling the truth?" This was a question Catlina Toma and Jeffrey Hancock from the Department of Communication at Cornell University recently explored. They recruited men and women from the New York City area who were subscribed to any one of several mainstream online dating services. Using this strategy the researchers had access to the primary information the participants had given to the dating services, such as age, physical appearance, relationship status, habits and interests, and beliefs.

Out of 489 people contacted 40 men and 40 women met the selection criteria and were willing to visit a university laboratory for data collection. The researchers asked individuals to rate the accuracy of the data on their dating profile. Addition data collected were ages taken from driver's licenses, and height and weight measurements. After a photograph was taken the participants were debriefed regarding the real purpose of the study.

Toma and Hancock were then able to compare the data collected to the information they had placed on their dating profiles. They also had independent raters assign attractiveness scores to the photographs taken in the lab as well as those posted on the dating service websites. The results indicated that those individuals whose lab photographs were judged to be less attractive were more likely to post self-enhanced photographs that increased their attractiveness and to lie about their physical characteristics. Although some of these participants did enhance their social status in the online dating profile, they were much more likely to improve their physical characteristics. The results also indicated that women were more likely to enhance their profile than men (Toma & Hancock, 2010).

Dating services may find they are struggling with the same issues as instructors in distance-education courses and others involved in online interactions, "How do I know that is really *you*?" As communication increases via the internet, and important personal, employee-, education- and health-related information is exchanged, the need for accurate and honest information is critical.

though some people talk of "falling" in or out of love, the triangular theory emphasizes the cognitive, decision-making process through which one concludes, "Yes, I do love this person" and then makes the commitment to love during the good and not-so-good times in the future.

An important feature of the triangular theory of love is that it provides a way to describe love relationships as they evolve over time. Let's consider a hypothetical example of two heterosexual adults, Louis and Lekeesha, who fell in love and spent their lives together. They first met at a party and were immediately attracted to each other. The relationship began as passion only. Over time intimacy developed, but passion remained primary in the relationship. As they spent more time together they decided to make a commitment to each other. When Louis and Lekeesha had their first child it seemed that their lives, which were already busy, became much more so. Their commitment to each other remained strong, but they didn't have as much time or energy for passion as they did in the past. When the couple was in middle age, and the last child left home, they found themselves spending much more time together, and intimacy became prominent. Passion and commitment were still there, but those components were not as important as the close "best-friend" relationship they had developed. In late old age Louis developed cancer, and as he became more and more ill he was unable to provide the passion or the intimacy that he once had. It was their commitment that kept their love strong through those troubling times.

Sternberg's (1997a) theory provides ways to discuss the different types or kinds of love experienced by Louis and Lekeesha as well as considering various intensities of love. The patterns of love, summarized in Table 5.1, include everything from close friendships to lust, romance, and companionship (Sternberg, 1986). It is important to note that the patterns are created by the elements that are emphasized in the relationship. The theory is called "triangular" because the three parts can represent three points on a triangle in which love can move around (Sternberg, 1997a). For example, in companionate love, the emphasis is on intimacy and commitment. A couple will likely still have a sexual relationship but it is not as important in their lives as the closeness they have developed over many years and their sense of dedication to each other's needs and goals. Falconi and Mullet (2003), in a study involving 400 French adults ranging in age from 18 to 93 years old, found that the triangle operates as a "compensatory schema" in which a decrease in one element results in the increase in another. For example, if intimacy is decreased due to an extremely busy and demanding schedule, a couple may compensate by placing more emphasis on commitment. Sternberg's triangular theory is useful in that it provides a way to characterize changes in relationships as well as a way to consider the facet of love that may be primary or lacking at any given time.

Your Thoughts?

What might be some of the obstacles keeping adults from maintaining consummate love?

The participants in Falconi and Mullet's (2003) study reported that of the three parts of love, decision/commitment was the least important. This is consistent with an earlier study by Aron and Westbay (1996), who found that college students also viewed decision/commitment as the least important element. It may be that if forced to choose most people believe that if intimacy and passion are strong then commitment will follow. It might also be the case that decision/commitment is equated with legal marriage, thus those who are cohabiting outside of marriage view that element as less important.

Attachment Styles

The study of attachment styles adds the dimension of personal history to the study of love relationships. The triangular theory considers current circumstances and perspectives, whereas the study of ***attachment styles*** considers the effects of our earliest love-based relationships, that of infant and primary caregiver, on our current love relationships. The research on infant–caregiver attachment styles was promoted in the late 1960s by Bowlby, and was extended to adult love relationships in the 1970s (Kenny & Barton, 2003).

TABLE 5.1 *Sternberg's Patterns of Love*

Pattern of Love	*Emphasized Elements*	*Description*
Non-Love	None	Absence of love
Liking	Intimacy	Close, warm, and trusting relationship
Infatuated Love	Passion	Intense psychophysiological or sexual relationship that may feel like "love at first sight"
Empty Love	Decision/Commitment	Relationship held together by a personal sense of determination and obligation
Romantic Love	Intimacy and Passion	An emotionally close and sexual relationship that may be moving toward the point of commitment
Companionate Love	Intimacy and Decision/ Commitment	A very close, dedicated couple, often best of friends, who do not view passion as a priority
Fatuous Love	Passion and Decision/ Commitment	A rapidly developing, whirlwind, sexual relationship in which individuals make commitments before intimacy has had time to develop
Consummate Love	Intimacy, Passion, and Decision/Commitment	The ultimate combination of all three elements for the most satisfying love relationship

From Sternberg (1986). Copyright by the American Psychological Association. Reprinted with permission.

The blending of this infant and adult research has resulted in discovery of four attachment styles based on levels of anxiety and avoidance in relationships (see Table 5.2). Adults with a ***secure attachment style*** are the most stable in terms of maintaining relationships. They view themselves and their lover as worthy of respect, care, and affection. When in romantic relationships securely attached individuals are responsible, dependable, and comfortable with intimacy. The remaining three types of attachment styles are variations of insecure attachments. Looking to the future, research indicates that those with secure attachments are more likely to have successful relationships, whereas those with nonsecure attachments are more vulnerable to relationship problems (Treboux, Crowell, & Waters, 2004).

Adults with an ***anxious-ambivalent attachment style***, sometimes labeled ***preoccupied attachment style***, find themselves experiencing competing feelings. They are focused on

TABLE 5.2 *Adult Attachment Styles Categorized by Anxiety and Avoidance*

		Attachment-Related Anxiety	
Attachment-Related Avoidance		HIGH	LOW
	HIGH	Avoidant-Fearful	Avoidant-Dismissing
	LOW	Anxious-Ambivalent (Preoccupied)	Secure

From Collins, N. L. & Feeney, B. C. (2004). An attachment theory perspective on closeness and intimacy. In D. J. Mashek and A. Aron (Eds.), Handbook of Closeness and Intimacy (pp. 163–187). Mahwah, NJ: Lawrence Erlbaum Associates. Reprinted with permission.

establishing closeness, intimacy, and approval in relationships while at the same time they tend to view themselves as unworthy of the care and affection they seek. This dilemma leads to anxiety-provoking situations. Those with an anxious-ambivalent attachment style live with a persistent fear of rejection and abandonment. For example, this person may say to a romantic partner, "There are so many people who are better than me that I'm afraid you'll leave me."

> **Your Thoughts?**
>
> How would you design a study to find out if anxious-ambivalent attachment style or poor self-esteem is the greater contributor to this approach to love?

Another type of attachment, the ***avoidant attachment style***, can take two forms. Adults with an ***avoidant-dismissing attachment style*** also find themselves with competing feelings. They believe they are desirable romantic partners worthy of respect, but are suspicious of lovers, characterizing them as unreliable and uncaring. Individuals with an avoidant-dismissing attachment style value personal independence and sense of worth. This creates a situation in which they seek love relationships, while at the same time they do not trust others to be loyal and love them in return. Adults with an ***avoidant-fearful attachment style*** take the dismissing approach even farther. They have so much anxiety and suspicion that they avoid any type of intimate relationship. Those with an avoidant-fearful attachment style take the view that the threat of rejection or abandonment is so great that entering a romantic relationship is simply not worth the risk. In their view, relationships are more trouble than they are worth (Collins & Feeney, 2004).

Researchers have found that most individuals display secure attachments. In a survey of heterosexual couples, Volling, Notaro, and Larsen (1998) found that 74% of the women and 76% of the men displayed secure attachments, and 94% of the couples surveyed had at least one securely attached partner. Of those without a secure attachment, 19% of the women and 22% of the men displayed an avoidant style, and a very small percentage, 7% of the women and 2% of the men, displayed an ambivalent style. Other researchers have found that those with anxious-ambivalent or avoidant-fearful styles have the most negative views of themselves and display more symptoms of depression (Van Buren & Cooley, 2002). Those with anxious-ambivalent styles are also the most distressed when a relationship ends (Barbara & Dion, 2000). Those with a secure or avoidant-dismissing attachment style have the most positive view of themselves and display fewer depressive symptoms (Van Buren & Cooley, 2002). Interestingly, researchers have not found outstanding or consistent gender differences regarding attachment styles (Gallo, Smith, & Ruiz, 2003).

> **Your Thoughts?**
>
> Which combinations of attachment styles do you predict would be the most stable? The most dysfunctional?

Section Summary

- Rather than thinking of love as a unified state one has either fallen in or fallen out of, it is more productive to think of love as multifaceted, varying in patterns and types, and changing or evolving over time.
- Sternberg's triangular theory describes love as varying in terms of intimacy, passion, and commitment.
- The proportions of intimacy, passion, and commitment are dynamic, changing in response to environmental and personal circumstances.
- Attachment styles bring individuals' past histories into an understanding of love relationships.
- While there are a small percentage of adults with ambivalent or avoidant attachment styles, most couples have at least one securely attached partner.

Cohabitation

In the 1970s theorists Duvall and Hill proposed a family life cycle paradigm, which described the expected sequence of falling in love, getting married, having children, and establishing a career (Erickson, 1998). The dramatic cultural changes occurring in Western culture since that

Your Thoughts?

How might the reasons for cohabiting be different for never-married, divorced, or widowed couples?

time have blurred such simple characterizations. Many adults are choosing to live with their romantic partners, in some cases prior to an eventual marriage and in other cases in the place of marriage. More and more often gay male and lesbian adults are "coming out of the closet" to openly share their cohabiting lifestyle with their romantic partners. This section explores both straight and gay cohabiting relationships.

Heterosexual Cohabiting Couples

For many years ***cohabitation***, or living together as a romantic couple outside of marriage, has been gaining popularity in Western countries, including the United States, where estimates are that more than half of all couples cohabit before getting married (Dempsey & deVaus, 2004; Kline et al., 2004). According to U.S. Census Bureau estimates, the number of couples cohabiting increased from about one-half million in 1970 to over 5 million in 2001 (Brown & Snyder, 2006, jumping to 51 million in 2007. In 2005 the U.S. Census Bureau reported that the majority of the households had shifted from married to unmarried households (Alternatives to Marriage Project, 2009). In an international survey involving over 22 countries, the percentages of those cohabiting varied widely, with 3.3% in Japan, 5.2% in Italy, 23.6% in the United States, 26.3% in Canada, 32.1% in the Czech Republic, and 32.4% in Sweden (Batalova & Cohen, 2002).

Researchers have found that the relationships among couples who are cohabiting range from casual to intimate and committed. For example, Sassler (2004) found that among college undergraduate and graduate students the most common reasons for living together were financial and for convenience. By sharing expenses couples could live in more desirable places and avoid the need to travel between two locations and duplicate household and personal items. The reason mentioned the least often was cohabiting as a way to test a relationship prior to marriage. Sassler found that most of the students did not talk about the future of the relationship with their partner prior to cohabiting, and most did not discuss marriage for several years after moving in together. While the students in Sassler's study gave less intimate reasons for living together, other studies have indicated that some cohabiting relationships are based on long-term commitments. In a study of couples across Canada, LeBourdais and Lapierre-Adamcyk (2004) found that cohabiting served as the childless phase in a committed relationship. Once the couples decided it was time to have children they married. In a similar study of Scottish adults researchers also found that those who were cohabiting had a strong sense of commitment to their partners and viewed their relationships as permanent (Jamieson et al., 2002).

Your Thoughts?

How might the reasons for cohabiting differ when considering young, middle-aged, and older cohabiting adults?

While the number of cohabiting couples of all ages swells, and their reasons for their lifestyle choice vary, most of the research on cohabitation has focused on one question: Does cohabitation cause divorce? Numerous research studies have found the ***cohabitation effect***, that cohabiting prior to marriage is associated with reports of less satisfying marital relationships and higher rates of divorce (Dush, Cohan, & Amato, 2003; Kline, et al., 2004). There are several competing theories as to why the cohabitation effect occurs. The ***causal theory*** suggests that cohabitation changes individuals' attitudes about marriage and relationships. While this is one possible explanation, it is important to remember that correlation or association does not prove or establish causation. It *may* be that cohabiting causes divorce, but it may also be the case that something else causes both cohabiting and divorce, which is the basic premise of the ***selection theory***. This second theory proposes that people who choose to cohabit may have certain characteristics or may choose partners with certain characteristics that cause the couple to be more likely to divorce. Those who promote selection theory focus on characteristics such as personality traits, religiosity, age, educational level, income level, number of previous marriages, and the number of children living in the home (deVaus, Qu, & Weston, 2003; Kline et al., 2004). For example, Kline and her colleagues (2004) found that cohabiting couples who were not engaged to be married displayed more negative interactions, less commitment, and less relationship confidence than couples who began cohabiting after becoming engaged (Kline et al., 2004). Other studies have found that cohabiters are more likely to have poor communication and problem-solving skills than noncohabiting couples (Cohan & Kleinbaum, 2002).

> **Your Thoughts?**
>
> Based on the three theories, what questions would you ask and what advice would you give friends who are cohabiting and concerned about a future divorce?

The third theory attempting to explain the cohabitation effect is the ***measurement theory***. This perspective suggests that when studying the duration of a relationship researchers should consider the cohabiting years along with the marriage years (deVaus et al., 2003). This strategy was used in an analysis of over 14,000 Australian adults. Researchers found that when considering the entire amount of time couples had lived together there was no difference in divorce rates between premarriage cohabiters and noncohabiters. It may be that it takes several years for an unstable relationship to end, and those who cohabit prior to marriage start that process earlier, thus they divorce earlier than an unstable couple who waits until marriage to begin living together.

To further explain the measurement theory, suppose you are a researcher who is gathering public legal records of couples who were married 3 years ago. Your sample includes Alvin and Alice, who lived together for 5 years prior to marriage, and Brenda and Brian, who did not cohabit prior to marriage. You decide to take a commonly used approach by sending out questionnaires asking participants (1) did you live together prior to marriage and (2) are you currently married or divorced? At the time participants receive your questionnaire, Alvin and Alice had been living at the same residence for a total of 8 years (5 years cohabiting + 3 years of marriage). On the other hand, Brenda and Brian have been living at the same residence for only 3 years at the time they received your questionnaire (0 years cohabiting + 3 years of marriage). The measurement theory suggests that to be fair you should check to see if Brenda and Brian are still married after living at the same residence as long as Alvin and Alice have.

It is likely that the study of cohabiting couples will separate into different lines of research beyond the cohabitation effect. Those who are cohabiting prior to their first marriage may have different characteristics than those cohabiting who have been married and divorced in the past or are widowed. Taking a developmental perspective, it is interesting to consider the reasons why a college couple or a young adult couple without children would choose to cohabit, and how the reasons might be different for a middle-aged cohabiting couple with children or an older cohabiting couple. As the numbers of cohabiting couples increase so will the difficulty in making any generalized statements about this lifestyle choice.

Gay Cohabiting Couples

> **Your Thoughts?**
>
> What is the law in your state regarding the granting or recognition of gay marriages or civil unions?

While the research on cohabitation for heterosexual couples has focused on the cohabitation effect, much of the research on gay and lesbian cohabiting has been on intimate cohabiting relationships as a substitute for marriage. When comparing gay, lesbian, and heterosexual married couples, numerous studies have found many more similarities than differences in terms of relationship quality, satisfaction, and duration. In a longitudinal study beginning in the 1980s, Kurdek (1998) gathered data on 66 gay male, 51 lesbian, and 236 married couples for over 5 years. He found that relationship satisfaction was high for all three groups at the beginning of the study, and all three groups declined in relationship satisfaction, at generally the same rate, over the 5 years. By the end of the study 7% of the married couples had divorced, and 14% of the gay couples and 16% of the lesbian couples had ended their relationships (Kurdek, 1998). In a separate study of relationship conflict, Kurdek found that married, gay, and lesbian couples experience conflict over many of the same things, primarily sharing power, dealing with personal flaws, issues related to intimacy and sexuality, and personal distance, such as spending too much time with other commitments (Kurdek, 1994). Other studies comparing gay and straight couples have found similar types of problem-solving styles, levels of productive and destructive communication behaviors, emotional behaviors, and other indicators of relationship health (Gottman et al., 2003; Julien, Chartrand, Simard, Bouthillier, & Begin, 2003; Kurdek, 1998, 2004).

Your Thoughts?

Do you think a marriage and family therapist who is gay could provide high-quality services to heterosexual couples?

Although the similarities are more numerous than the differences, there are some important differences between heterosexual and gay couples, as well as between gay and lesbian couples. In his longitudinal study Kurdek (1998) found that lesbian partners reported the highest levels of intimacy and the most equality as compared to gay or straight couples. Both gay and lesbian partners reported more autonomy as individuals than spouses. Other differences were noted by Solomon, Rothblum, and Balsam (2004), who compared the quality of relationships among gay and lesbian couples who had engaged in a civil union, gay couples without a civil union, and heterosexual married couples. In this case the gay couples with civil union status had taken advantage of Act 91, passed by the Vermont legislature in 2000, giving gay couples legal status and benefits. The primary differences between the three groups involved child care and housework, levels of family support, relationship satisfaction, and stress levels. Married women reported the most time spent with child care and housework, whereas lesbian women from both civil union and nonunion relationships reported equally balanced time spent with child care and housework. Lesbian women reported the least amount of family support, whereas the gay and heterosexual married couples reported similar levels of family support. Levels of relationship satisfaction were similar for all participants except for gay males in nonunion relationships. They were less satisfied and more likely to have considered ending their relationship (Solomon et al., 2004).

Your Thoughts?

What factors might contribute to the finding that lesbian couples receive less family support than gay male couples?

As the focus of this chapter shifts from cohabiting to marriage, it is important to note that cohabitation, and in some cases civil unions, may be the only options for gay and lesbian couples. In 2001 only Belgium, Canada, and the Netherlands legally recognized same-sex relationships as marriages (Solomon et al., 2004). By early 2010 the world situation had changed such that same-sex couples had some degree of legal recognition, which could be a recognized marriage, civil union, or registered partnership, in numerous countries around the world. The political climate in the United States in early 2010 remained unsettled, with several states performing same-sex marriages, others recognizing marriages but not performing them, some banning gay marriage, and still others changing their stance with each voting cycle.

In 2004 the American Psychological Association (APA), the primary professional organization for psychologists, adopted an official policy supporting same-sex civil marriages. This was not just an emotional or empty political statement, but rather it was the conclusion of a great deal of research and consultation. In addition to giving support to the notion that gay male and lesbian couples are "remarkably similar to heterosexual couples," the APA statement expressed concerns over the continued negative impact of discrimination. Researchers have been able to link higher levels of depression with gay lifestyle–related stressors, such as societal stigma, homophobia, destructive stereotypes, and numerous types of discrimination (Lewis, Derlega, Griffin, & Krowinski, 2003). The APA was also concerned that gay and lesbian couples cannot take advantage of the more than 1,000 federal statutory provisions that guarantee married individuals particular rights, benefits, and privileges (APA, 2004a). Offering gay and lesbian couples the basic rights given to married heterosexuals would provide needed legal privileges and protections, which ease many stresses and increase quality of life.

Your Thoughts?

Do you agree with the American Psychological Association's position? Why or why not?

Section Summary

- As the number of cohabiting couples increases so does the difficulty in making generalized statements about adults who are living with a romantic partner outside of marriage.
- The causal, selection, and measurement theories are possible explanations of the cohabitation effect, the findings that those who cohabit are more likely to divorce if they choose to marry.

- It may be that research will diversify to focus on cohabiting couples of various ages and with various circumstances, such as when younger children are involved.
- In contrast to heterosexual cohabitation, the focus on gay and lesbian couple households has been to compare their relationships to those of heterosexual married couples.
- While there are differences, most of the research indicates that gay and lesbian couples deal with many of the same stressors and issues as married couples.
- The political climate is changing as more nations give legal recognition to same-sex couples and as powerful organizations like the American Psychological Association offer support to the call for marital status for gay couples.
- It is important to consider that regardless of the sexual orientation of individuals in a romantic relationship, we can all learn from those who live in harmony in satisfying relationships and from those whose relationships do not survive.

Marriage

In spite of the rise in the numbers of cohabiting couples and divorces, living in a married relationship remains a very popular lifestyle among adults in American society. The growing emphasis on positive psychology has propelled social scientists to consider not only those marriages with problems but also happy, satisfying marriages. Marriage is still a popular area of study because of its importance in adult life but also because the study of marriage has an enticing facet for researchers that few variables relating to relationships have: marriage is easy to measure. You are either legally married or not. That makes it an easy item to place on any questionnaire or survey of adults. That also makes it somewhat easier to gather information because of the legal records available to the public, and thus available to social scientists as well.

Marital Expectations

Even though we know our spouses are not perfect human beings, and neither are we, there might still be within us that desire to live like the "happily ever after" couples in fairy tales or blissfully happy couples we might see in the media. An older developmental model of marital relationships, developed by Tamashiro (1978), may offer some insight into such expectations for both married and committed-cohabiting couples. The four developmental stages for marital relationships are:

- Magical Stage
- Idealized Conventional Stage
- Individualistic Stage
- Affirmational Stage

During the magical stage spouses are focused primarily on behaviors, such as spending money together and establishing a home. Even the simplest of things, such as writing both names on an envelope for the return address, is a statement that these individuals are now functioning as one unit. Much of the excitement and enchantment of the magical stage comes from merging their lives together. Once their married lifestyle becomes more routine, couples move into the idealized conventional stage. Here the energy given to marriage focuses on following expectations, social rules, and conventions. In this stage many couples move toward traditional husband and wife roles. It feels important to couples at this stage to develop a good reputation as a happy, romantic married couple. Tamashiro hypothesized that some couples will spend their entire marriages in this stage, while others will move to the individualistic stage. At this point couples' married lifestyles have become comfortable and predictable, thus the spouses turn

Your Thoughts?

What social and family influences might encourage or demand that a couple stay in the idealized conventional stage?

During the magical stage of marriage we are filled with excitement and enthusiasm for our new lifestyle.

their attention toward mutual companionship. Spouses support each other in areas of self-improvement and in the expression of their personal values. The final stage of marriage, the affirmational stage, involves unconditional respect and support within the marriage. The relationship has evolved into a safe place from which spouses can manage the uncertainties in life. In this final stage spouses can focus on their highest values and principles, and explore the meaning and purpose of life. Tamashiro's stages have some striking similarities to several patterns described by Sternberg's triangular theory of love. The primary difference between the two theories is that Tamashiro's stages appear to be linear, building on one another, whereas the triangular theory of love allows for movement in many directions within the triangle as well as repeating or cyclical patterns.

Expectations are of critical importance when considering self-reported marital satisfaction. For many years social scientists reported that marital satisfaction, when graphed over time, followed a "U-shaped curve" (Van Laningham, Johnson, & Amato, 2001), such as that found by Akiyama et al. (2003) in their analysis of spouses within convoys. Research data indicated that satisfaction was generally very high, perhaps unrealistically so, at the beginning of a marriage during Tamashiro's magical stage. As the relationship became more comfortable and routine, marital satisfaction then declined. This trend continued until marital satisfaction reached a low point when the spouses were middle-aged. The up-side of the U-shaped curve occurred as some of the demands of careers and child care lessened and the couple moved into late adulthood.

As more longitudinal data became available an interesting difference was found. The U-shaped pattern was found using cross-sectional research, which is vulnerable to generational differences. When examining marital satisfaction with longitudinal data, the increase in marital satisfaction after midlife disappeared. Figure 5.1 illustrates the difference. For example, data from a 17-year longitudinal study involving nearly 6,000 participants indicated a decline in marital satisfaction throughout life, with no increase in late adulthood. The steepest periods of decline generally occurred in the earliest stage, as the magical phase declined, and the end of the marriage, which may be just prior to death or divorce (Van Laningham et al., 2001). These findings were based on data gathered through phone interviews involving questions on many topics, such as the amount of love and understanding shown by their spouse and the level at which they agreed with their spouse on key issues. It may be that marital satisfaction is unusually high in the early years, and then decreases to a comfortable, maintainable level for much of adulthood. It is interesting to consider whether this decrease indicates dissatisfaction based on unmet expectations or an adjustment to a more realistic assessment of marital relationships.

Your Thoughts?

What factors in American society and culture might lead newlyweds to expect more than what is reasonable from their spouse?

Happy and Healthy Marriages

Happy and healthy marriages have been associated with many benefits beyond the higher quality of life and general contentment a good relationship brings. Those who are married are also more likely to have higher job satisfaction, higher incomes, better physical health (Rogers & May, 2003; Stack & Eshleman, 1998), and better mental health (Horwitz, White, & Howell-White, 1996). Researchers have even linked long-term marriage to an intelligent spouse as one of the factors in preserving adequate cognitive functioning into old age (Rabbitt, 2002).

In addition to self-reported ratings of marital happiness, healthy and happy marriages have been characterized in several ways. The Healthy Marriage Initiative (HMI; U.S. Department of Health and Human Services, 2004) defines a healthy marriage as one that is mutually enriching, respectful, and satisfying, and one in which the spouses are committed to growth, effective communication, and successful conflict management.

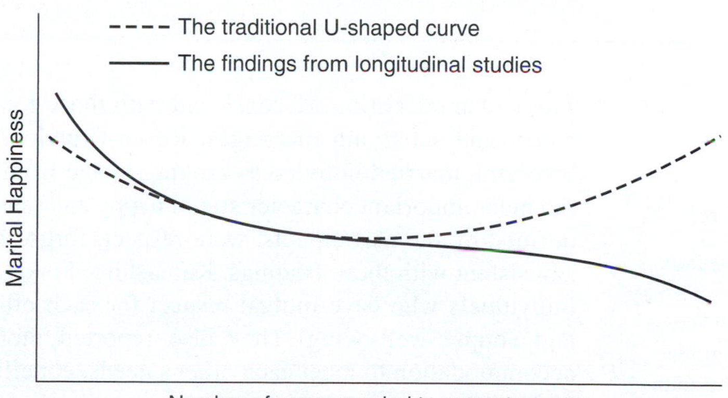

FIGURE 5.1 ***Marital Satisfaction in Cross-Sectional and Longitudinal Data.***
Adapted from Van Laningham, Johnson, & Amato (2001). Reprinted with permission of UNC Press.

RESEARCH IN-DEPTH
Reliability

Researchers Norm O'Rourke of the Gerontology Research Centre and Programs of Simon Fraser University and Philippe Cappeliez of the School of Psychology at the University of Ottawa wanted to find a way to measure just how much married couples distort their responses on questionnaires. Psychologists have found that few people seem to want to admit that they are bored or unhappy with their marriage, thus when responding to questionnaires about marital satisfaction individuals will often answer as if their marriages were idealistically perfect. For example, some individuals will agree with statements such as "If my spouse has any faults, I am not aware of them" or "I have never regretted my marriage, not even for a moment." While there may be some rare individuals who can fully agree with those statements, most married individuals, when honest, would need to qualify those statements to some degree. O'Rourke and Cappeliez (2002) decided to create a new test to estimate the amount of distortion in marital satisfaction questionnaires. To people who are unaware of the process, it may appear that when psychologists need a questionnaire to measure something they just make one up. Actually, when done appropriately, the process of creating a questionnaire and demonstrating that it is accurate is quite involved. In fact, so much is involved that there is an entire area of psychology devoted to testing and measurement called ***psychometrics***. In this segment the focus is on the first step in developing a questionnaire, which is establishing reliability. Another *Research In-Depth* segment focuses on the second half of the process, which is establishing validity.

The first step for O'Rourke and Cappeliez was to review studies that have explored this phenomenon known as ***marital aggrandizement***, and to develop a clear definition of the concept. Different from marital satisfaction or marital contentment, marital aggrandizement is the inability or lack of willingness to acknowledge any interpersonal negative experiences with one's spouse. The second step was to locate any existing questionnaires measuring something similar to marital aggrandizement and study them thoroughly. The researchers decided to work with items from an older questionnaire, the Marital Conventionalization Scale, developed by Edmonds. The third step was to give the questionnaires out for practice trials. Using feedback from the practice sessions O'Rourke and Cappeliez were able to refine and, when needed, add, subtract, or rewrite items. As the questionnaire changed from the original to a new form, the name was changed to the Marital Aggrandizement Scale.

Once a good draft of the test has been written, the next step is to demonstrate ***reliability***. The researchers needed to know that the level of marital aggrandizement was stable or reliable for particular individuals. If marital aggrandizement is found to fluctuate quickly and dramatically, then the concept is of little use. What good is a measurement if it cannot be trusted an hour later? In order to show reliability, O'Rouke and Cappeliez used a common technique called a "test–retest" procedure, resulting in test–retest reliability. They gave the new questionnaire to 200 participants who had been married at least 20 years and who were at least 50 years old. The participants were asked 15 months later to complete the same questionnaire. The scores were then compared to find out how similar they were for each participant. The results indicated that yes, the Marital Aggrandizement Scale did demonstrate reliability. O'Rourke and Cappeliez continued the process of test development, demonstrating validity as well. The process of test development is long and complex, involving many rounds of collecting data and making adjustments based on statistical procedures. Now that the process is complete, any researcher can use the Marital Aggrandizement Scale with confidence that it is reliable.

These characteristics are consistent with those found in research with couples who report happy and satisfying marriages. Rosen-Grandon, Myers, and Hattie (2004), in a study involving married individuals ranging in age from 20 to 75 years old, found that love was the most important characteristic in happy and healthy marriages. The key aspects of love, defined by the participants, were respect, forgiveness, romance, sensitivity, and support. Consistent with these findings, Kumashiro, Finkel, and Rusbult (2002) found that married individuals who have mutual respect for each other reported greater marital satisfaction and couple well-being. They also reported more pro-relationship behaviors, such as accommodation to meet each other's needs, conciliation and compromise, and willingness to forgive.

Your Thoughts?

How might the factors contributing to a happy marriage be different for younger, middle-aged, and older adults?

Rosen-Grandon et al. (2004) found that loyalty was the second most important characteristic in healthy marriages. In this case loyalty referred to a sense of trust in the lifetime commitments made to the marriage by both partners. This finding has also been supported by

Your Thoughts?

Is loyalty as important in cohabiting as it is in marriage? Why, why not, or under what circumstances?

other research studies. In a longitudinal study involving 3,627 married couples from across the United States, Impett, Beals, and Peplau (2001) found that when either a husband or a wife demonstrated a high level of commitment to a marriage, the resulting relationship was more likely to be stable and satisfying. Clements and Swensen (2000) found that commitment was a stronger predictor of marital quality than ego development, length of marriage, church attendance, or gender. Couples with higher levels of commitment also reported fewer marital problems and greater levels of verbal expression, moral support, and love.

The third characteristic important to marital happiness, following love and loyalty, was labeled "shared values" (Rosen-Grandon et al., 2004). This referred to sharing similar beliefs on important issues, such as parenting practices, financial planning, and religious activities. By comparing currently married and recently divorced couples, Skaldeman and Montgomery (1999) demonstrated that those who remained married held similar views in key areas, whereas those who were divorced did not. All of the participants felt that their values had changed over time, and those who remained married believed that they and their spouses had changed in compatible ways. One area of particular interest regarding shared values is that of religious beliefs. Researchers have found that couples with similar views on what they consider to be important religious beliefs or practices tend to have greater marital satisfaction and stability (Fiese & Tomcho, 2001). Chinitz and Brown (2001) found that spouses in ***interfaith marriages***, where each spouse claims a different religious preference, such as Jewish-Christian or Jewish–No Religion, demonstrate high marital satisfaction when the spouses were in agreement on what they consider to be key issues, such as the role of family religious celebrations and religious education of their children.

Your Thoughts?

What might couples do to increase the likelihood that they change in compatible ways?

Section Summary

- The movement toward positive psychology has encouraged researchers to consider not only those marriages with problems but also those that are satisfying.
- Tamashiro's four stages of marital development are the magical, idealized conventional, individualist, and affirmational stages.
- As Tamashiro pointed out, some couples may expect to stay in the magical stage of marital development, while others may never reach the lofty stage of personal support described in the highest stages of marital development.
- Research shows that marital satisfaction declines rapidly during the first years of marriage, then stabilizing in a slight decline, with another drop at the end of the marriage (due to death or divorce).
- Happy and healthy marriages are based on the communication and demonstration of love, loyalty, and shared values, along with respect, forgiveness, romance, sensitivity, support, and a strong commitment to conflict resolution and mutually enhancing growth.
- It is clear that not only do both spouses need to give effort and attention to the establishment of a healthy marriage, but also to continue those efforts across time to maintain a satisfying relationship.

Endings and New Beginnings

While it is difficult to estimate the numbers of cohabiting couples, whether straight or gay, who decide to end their relationships, the legal documentation required for divorce makes it much easier to track the numbers of marriages that have ended. In 2003 the National Center for Health Statistics (NCHS) reported that there were slightly more than half as many divorces as marriages. Recent projections are that 40–50% of all first-time marriages will end in divorce (Stanley, 2005). The high divorce rate has prompted many social scientists to explore the characteristics more common among those who divorce, the adjustment process following divorce, and the long-term adjustment that often includes remarriage. It is important to keep in mind that while the primary cultural response to divorce is that it is an undesirable and difficult outcome, there are situations in which divorce may be the appropriate choice, such as in an abusive situation, and that positive personal growth and development may be initiated or accelerated by the divorce process.

Your Thoughts?

Would you estimate the rate of breakups for cohabiting couples to be similar, higher, or lower? Give reasons to support your response.

Characteristics of Couples Who Divorce

Which couples are more likely to divorce? There have been numerous longitudinal studies focused on this question, some observing couples during marriage and others beginning even earlier in the premarital relationship. One of the consistent findings is that couples who have high levels of conflict prior to marriage or in the earliest stage of marriage are at a higher risk for divorce (Gottman & Levenson, 2000). For example, after following 100 couples for 13 years as part of the Denver Family Development Study, Clements, Stanley, and Markman (2004) found that those who divorced had married at a younger age and rated themselves as having serious problems in areas such as sex, money, and communication. Those who divorced also indicated higher levels of emotional invalidation, which includes habits of insulting, being sarcastic, and making negative comments toward each other. In another study of 500 married couples over 8 years, Kurdek (2002) found that quick separations and divorces could be predicted by low levels of love, liking, and trusting a partner and high levels of psychological distress at the beginning of the marriage.

Your Thoughts?

What factors might lead someone to marry a person he or she didn't trust or like?

Researchers have also found that those who divorce rather quickly have different characteristics than those who divorce after many years of marriage. Huston, Caughlin, Houts, Smith, and George (2001) followed 164 couples for the first 13 years of marriage, and during that time 56 of the couples divorced. Those who divorced within 2 years of marriage reported weak romantic ties, less love, and more antagonism toward their spouse from the beginning of the relationship. Those who divorced after a marriage lasting 2–7 years had become ambivalent about their marriage. As the years passed they felt less in love and viewed their partners as less responsive to their needs. The couples that divorced after 7 years of marriage were among the most affectionate as newlyweds. Beginning in the first year of marriage, however, their ratings of love and affection dropped dramatically. Huston and his colleagues suggested that these couples took longer to divorce due to personal attachment or the hope that their relationship would become enjoyable again.

Your Thoughts?

Do you think the pattern would be the same for cohabiting couples who end their relationships? For gay and lesbian couples? Why or why not?

Although researchers have found that couples who indicate increased conflict and less love and trust are more likely to divorce, those items are generally not the reasons given for divorcing. Based on a survey of over 200 divorced couples, Amato and Previti (2003) found that infidelity or adultery was the most commonly reported cause of divorce. Using data from the General Social Surveys conducted by the National Opinion Research Center, researchers found that those reporting an extramarital encounter at some point in their lives were more likely to be unhappily married, male, employed, and have a higher income. Those who were happy with their marriages and those who attended religious activities were much less likely to report infidelity (Atkins, Baucom, & Jacobson, 2001). In interviews with 205 recently separated or divorced individuals, Spanier and Margolis (1983) found those who were involved in an extramarital relationship believed that the infidelity was not the primary problem but rather a side effect of a troubled relationship. Other common reasons for divorce were incompatibility, drinking or drug use, and simply growing apart. More than half of the time it is the wife in a marriage who will initiate the divorce (Amato & Previti, 2003).

Your Thoughts?

What factors might contribute to the finding that wives are more likely to initiate divorces than husbands?

ON THE LEADING EDGE
Infidelity in Cyberspace

Is it possible to be unfaithful or "cheat" on your lover via the Internet? Your response may depend on how infidelity is defined. Generally researchers focus on sexual infidelity, sometimes called *adultery*, which involves intimate sexual activity with someone other than your lover, and emotional infidelity, which is falling in love with someone other than your lover. Previous research has shown that while most people believe that both emotional and sexual relationships via the Internet can be transgressions, not all agree that these transgressions should be considered infidelity (Whitty & Quigley, 2008).

Whitty and Quigley (2008) explored both types of infidelity with a group of college students by giving them hypothetical scenarios to judge. The scenarios varied in terms of online and offline infidelity and in terms of emotional and sexual involvement. When exploring infidelity in general, the researchers found that the male college students said they would be more upset over sexual infidelity, while female college students found emotional infidelity more upsetting. Although the online transgressions were upsetting, every participant in the study thought the offline (real-life) infidelities were more upsetting. Whitty and Quigley suggest that because the Internet is assumed to be a mixture of reality and fantasy, and because it is a fairly new medium, the "rules" or acceptable boundaries are not yet established. Some participants may view cyber-infidelity as less harmful fantasies whereas others view it as seriously as offline betrayal. Another interesting difference between offline and online infidelities is that many participants link sexual activity and love when considering offline infidelities, whereas when considering online transgression those two are not linked. Engaging in cyber-sexual activities does not imply emotional love, nor does engaging in cyber-based emotional love–centered dialog imply the likelihood of sexual involvement (Whitty & Quigley, 2008).

Research efforts such as this one are critical for marriage and family therapists who are now seeing clients for whom cyber-infidelity is a problem. Recent studies suggest that many therapists feel ill-equipped to diagnose and work with these clients as the area is so new (Goldberg, Peterson, Rosen, & Sara, 2008).

Adjusting to Divorce

While it is important to understand the interpersonal dynamics and the reasons for divorce, it is also important to understand how people who have recently divorced recover and adjust to their new lifestyle. In addition to possibly helping children, extended family members, and friends adjust to the ending of a marriage, ex-spouses must also change their ways of thinking, their lifestyles, and begin the process of establishing new routines (Ahrons, 1980). By following 208 divorced couples across 17 years, Wang and Amato (2000) found that better adjustments were made by those who had one or more of the following characteristics:

- Younger age at the time of divorce
- Been the one to initiate the divorce
- Wanted the divorce more than the other spouse
- Has steady employment
- Has a satisfactory income
- Has formed a new romantic relationship

Your Thoughts?

Do most people treat the breakup of a cohabiting couple with the same level of sympathy as a divorce? Should they? Why, why not, or under what circumstances?

Among those in Wang and Amato's study, 25% of the former wives and 7% of the former husbands experienced a substantial decrease in income. Participants reported that they lost friends due to the divorce, and 66% of participants moved to a different residence. In comparing adjustment to divorce in Western culture to Eastern culture, Cohen and Savaya (2003) explored adjustment to divorce by Muslim Arab women (147 participants) and men (165 participants) in Israel. They found that those with higher levels of education and employment made better adjustments. Overall, the men adjusted better to their divorce than the women.

It appears that adjusting to changes brought on by a divorce is particularly difficult for those without sufficient resources, particularly people without adequate income, employment, education, or social support.

Remarriages

Most of the research on building new romantic relationships is focused on ***remarriage***, a broad term that includes all marriages that are not a first marriage for one or both spouses. After examining the results of over 850 research articles, Coleman, Ganong, and Fine (2000) determined that about 75% of all divorced individuals will remarry and that men are more likely to remarry than women. Remarriages that do end in divorce tend to do so more quickly than first marriages, particularly when the spouses are young adults. Among adults over age 40, remarriages are just as stable if not more so than first marriages (Coleman et al., 2000). Both remarried and first married couples believe it is important to share the same attitudes and preferences in the areas of leisure, religion, household tasks, decision making, communication styles, and sexual activities. Remarried individuals usually differ from those in their first marriages by preferring greater autonomy and independence (Allen, Baucom, Burnett, Epstein, & Rankin-Esquer, 2001).

Your Thoughts?

What factors might contribute to the finding that remarriages with spouses over age 40 are more stable than even first marriages?

Your Thoughts?

What factors might contribute to the finding that men are more likely to enter into a relationship quickly and to remarry faster than women whose spouses have died?

Some remarriages or new cohabiting situations include individuals who are widowed. Previous research has found that widowed individuals are much less likely to remarry than those who are divorced (Bishop & Cain, 2003), although, since the early 1980s there has been an increase in the numbers of widowed individuals who are cohabiting. Men are more likely to enter a romantic relationship, and to do so more quickly, than women following the death of a spouse. The average amount of time until remarriage for a widowed man is 4 years, whereas the average for widowed women is just over 6 years. As in divorce situations, financial stressors are often of primary concern for widowed individuals, particularly women.

Researchers have found that remarriage among couples over 40 years old is usually stable and satisfying.

Section Summary

- The ending of what was intended to be a long-term love relationship can be a life-changing event, bringing with it psychological and physical distress.
- Currently, it is predicted that nearly half of all first-time marriages will end in divorce.
- Researchers have found that couples who have high levels of conflict, poor communication, emotional invalidation, or a general lack of trust or love during their premarital interactions or early married life are more likely to divorce.
- The most common reason cited for divorce is adultery, which is often viewed by those involved as a side effect rather than the main cause of the marital breakup.
- Generally, better adjustments are made by those who divorce at a younger age, have steady employment, and a good income.
- As disruptive and painful as divorce can be, research indicates that most people will remarry.
- The most stable remarriages tend to occur when the spouses are middle-aged or older.

Chapter Summary

This chapter explores some of the ways friendships, love relationships, and living arrangements change with age. Although the people we might list as part of our friendship convoy will likely change with age and circumstances, our social network can provide strength, support, advice, and help throughout our lives. As adults we find ourselves with the privilege and responsibility of choosing not only friends but our intimate partner and lifestyle. Researchers have focused on the choice of cohabiting rather than marriage for heterosexual couples as well as cohabiting as the only option for most gay and lesbian couples. Research efforts have also focused on the characteristics of happy love relationships, unhappy relationships, breakups, and new relationships and remarriages. Here are some of the main points of the chapter:

- The six functions of friendships in adulthood are stimulating companionship, help, intimacy, a reliable alliance, self-validation, and emotional security.
- The convoy model of friendships describes three concentric circles or layers of closeness and support through which friends move in and out during our lifetime.
- A popular view of gender differences in relationships is that women grow close by talking and self-disclosure while men grow close through sharing activities.
- Despite the negative stigma faced by never-married adults, many enjoy their freedom and independence.
- Sternberg's triangular theory of love involves three primary components—intimacy, passion, and decision/commitment—which can combine in various ways to create patterns of love.
- The four types of attachment styles (secure, anxious-ambivalent, avoidant-dismissing, and avoidant-fearful) reflect individuals' attitudes regarding their own worthiness of love and the abilities of their lover to return love.
- Heterosexual cohabiting couples express many reasons for their lifestyle, ranging from casual to intimate and committed.
- Three theories offered to explain the cohabitation effect are the causal theory, selection theory, and measurement theory.
- Researchers have found that cohabiting gay couples are quite similar to cohabiting and married heterosexual couples in terms of satisfaction and stability.
- The American Psychological Association supports the movement to provide legal same-sex unions for gay couples.

- Tamashiro's stages of marital development move from the magical stage to the idealized conventional stage, the individualistic stage, and finally to the affirmational stage.
- Whereas cross-sectional data indicates marital satisfaction starts high, dips in midlife, and then rises again, longitudinal data indicates marital satisfaction starts high, declines to a sustainable level, and then declines at the end of the marriage.
- Some of the primary factors involved in marital satisfaction are love, loyalty, and shared values.
- In longitudinal studies researchers have found that couples who divorce often show more negativity and conflict earlier in their marriage or even in their premarital interactions.
- The most common reason cited for divorce is adultery.
- Researchers have found that better adjustment to divorce is related to steady employment, a satisfactory income, higher levels of education, and building a new romantic relationship.
- Remarriages are more successful when the individuals are older.

Key Terms

Friendship **(123)**
Convoy model of friendship **(123)**
Love styles **(125)**
Triangular theory of love **(126)**
Attachment styles **(127)**
Secure attachment style **(128)**
Anxious-ambivalent attachment style **(128)**
Preoccupied attachment style **(128)**
Avoidant attachment style **(129)**
Avoidant-dismissing attachment style **(129)**
Avoidant-fearful attachment style **(129)**
Cohabitation **(130)**
Cohabitation effect **(130)**
Causal theory **(130)**
Selection theory **(130)**
Measurement theory **(131)**
Psychometrics **(136)**
Marital aggrandizement **(136)**
Reliability **(136)**
Interfaith marriages **(137)**
Remarriage **(140)**

Comprehension Questions

1. Name and describe the six functions of friendship in adulthood.
2. Describe the convoy model of friendships.
3. Describe how the convoys of men and women differ.
4. Give an example of the negative stigma often applied to never-married adults.
5. Name and describe the six styles of love developed by Lee.
6. Describe the three elements in Sternberg's triangular theory of love and explain the ways they can combine to form patterns of love.
7. Name and describe the four types of attachment styles.
8. Name and explain each of the three theories given to explain the cohabitation effect.
9. What have researchers found when comparing married straight couples, cohabiting gay or lesbian couples, and gay or lesbian couples who have a civil union?
10. What is the position of the American Psychological Association on same-sex civil unions?
11. Name and explain Tamashiro's developmental stages for marital relationships.
12. Explain the differences in the results of cross-sectional and longitudinal studies of marital satisfaction.
13. What characteristics have been found to contribute to healthy marriages?
14. What have researchers learned about premarital and early marriage interaction that may predict later divorce?

15. What have researchers learned about the differences between those married couples who divorce very quickly versus those who divorce after many years of marriage?
16. What factors are important in facilitating a better adjustment to divorce?
17. What have researchers learned about successful remarriages?

Answers for Common Sense: Myth or Reality?

1. Myth: Physical appearance is an important characteristic in choosing friends for both young and middle-aged adults. (See Developing Friendships, page 122.)
2. Reality: One of the functions of friendship is to develop intimacy. (See Developing Friendships, page 123.)
3. Myth: Men and women tend to have circles of friends that are similar in size and closeness. (See Convoy Model of Friendship, page 124.)
4. Reality: Never-married adults often cite their freedom as one of the greatest advantages of their lifestyle. (See Single Lifestyles, page 125.)
5. Myth: Researchers have found that people in intimate relationships report that a sense of commitment is one of the most important aspects of a love relationship. (See Triangular Theory of Love, page 127.)
6. Reality: A popular theory of love relationships states that the type of attachment infants develop with their caregivers will be the type of attachment those infants, when they are adults, will develop with their lovers. (See Attachment Styles, page 127.)
7. Myth: Most heterosexual couples who live together view it as a trial period prior to marriage. (See Heterosexual Cohabiting Couples, page 130.)
8. Reality: The *cohabitation effect* is the common research finding that couples who cohabit prior to marriage are more likely to divorce. (See Heterosexual Cohabiting Couples, page 130.)
9. Reality: Researchers have found that heterosexual and gay couples are more alike in terms of satisfaction and stability than different. (See Gay Cohabiting Couples, page 131.)
10. Myth: Currently there are no countries in the world that legally recognize same-sex relationships. (See Gay Cohabiting Couples, page 132.)
11. Myth: Marital satisfaction increases throughout adulthood for most couples. (See Marital Expectations, page 134.)
12. Reality: Love, loyalty, and shared values are key factors in a healthy marriage. (See Happy and Healthy Marriages, page 136.)
13. Reality: Approximately half of all marriages end in divorce. (See Endings and New Beginnings, page 138.)
14. Reality: Adultery is the most common reason given for divorce. (See Characteristics of Couples Who Divorce, page 138.)
15. Myth: Less than half of all divorced individuals will remarry. (See Remarriages, page 140.)

Suggested Readings

Learning about Love by Observing Harlow's Monkeys

Harlow, H. F. (1958). The nature of love. *American Psychologist, 13*, 573–685. Accessed at *Classics in the History of Psychology* (http://psychclassics.yorku.ca/topic.htm).

Sexual Orientation

American Psychological Association. (2008). *Answers to your questions: For a better understanding of sexual orientation and homosexuality*. Washington, DC: Author. Retrieved from http://www.apa.org/topics/sorientation.pdf.

Cross-Cultural Views of Family Systems

Georgas, J. (2003). Family: Variations and changes across cultures. In W. J. Lonner, D. L. Dinnel, S. A. Hayes, & D. N. Sattler (Eds.), *Online readings in psychology and culture* (Unit 13, Chapter 3), (http://www.wwu.edu/~culture), Center for Cross-Cultural Research, Western Washington University, Bellingham, WA. Available at http://www.ac.wwu.edu/~culture/georgea.htm.

Adjustment Following a Divorce

Iowa State University. (1996). *Divorce matters: Coping with stress and change*. Ames, IA: Author. Retrieved from http://www.extension.iastate.edu/Publications/PM1637.pdf.

Suggested Websites

Online Dating Services: Caution

Just as with any online service or purchase, consumers need to do their homework before giving personal information over the Internet. The Attorney General's Offices in several states have posted guidelines for consumers, such as http://www.atg.wa.gov/ askcolumn.aspx?id=11936 (Washington State) and http://www.michigan.gov/ag/0,1607,7-164-17278-62279—,00.html (Michigan).

Sexual Health Issues

Sexually active adults of all ages should be aware of sexual hygiene, illness prevention, and sexual health issues. Medline Plus, an online service of the National Library of Medicine, has a wealth of information on sexual health issues listed at http://www.nlm.nih.gov/medlineplus/sexualhealthissues.html.

Marriage

Learn more about marriage and divorce at the National Marriage Project at Rutgers University at http://marriage.rutgers.edu/, or for more on the Healthy Marriage Initiative, see http://www.acf.hhs.gov/healthymarriage/.

Divorce

For advice on coping with divorce as an adult, parent, or child, see the Medline Plus page on divorce, sponsored by the National Institutes of Health, at http://www.nlm.nih.gov/medlineplus/divorce.html.

CHAPTER

6 Families, Generations, and Communities

Our lives as adults change dramatically when children enter our household. As we take on the new identity of "mom" or "dad" we often find that suddenly time and energy are limited and precious resources. Our priorities may change and even our circle of friends may evolve to include primarily those with children the same ages as ours. Our parents, now grandparents, may become heavily involved in the lives of their grandchildren, bringing new joys and challenges. Becoming a parent may also lead us to see our neighborhood and social community in a whole new way. What are the local parks like? Are the schools good? Is this the area I want my children to grow up in? We may find ourselves volunteering for community roles in order to provide quality experiences for our children.

Referring back to the timing-of-events model of personality development, it is important to remember that first-time parents who are in their 20s may see things differently than first-time parents in their late 30s. Americans and many others in Western cultures are finding their family structures developing in unconventional ways. The commonplace occurrences of divorce and remarriage, changing cohabitation partners, parenting stepchildren, and parenting children in a first marriage, and then again in a subsequent marriage, have changed what people used to expect in a family. As a society we are learning to be careful in assuming the roles various family members play. For example, a middle-aged woman might be a mom, stepmom, cohabiting partner and/or fiancé, or grandma.

COMMON SENSE
Myth or Reality?

Mark each of the following items with either an M, if you think it is a myth, or an R, if you think the statement reflects reality. By paying close attention you can find all the answers in this chapter. If needed, the answers are also given at the end of the chapter.

1. _____ Infertility problems are found more often in women than in men.
2. _____ In vitro fertilization is the most common treatment for infertility.
3. _____ None of the states in the United States will allow an openly gay couple to adopt a child.
4. _____ Most parents cite the love and affection children bring as the greatest rewards of parenting.
5. _____ Most parents cite the financial burden children bring as the greatest cost of parenting.
6. _____ One of the most influential factors in predicting parental satisfaction is the age of the parents.
7. _____ The number of American adults choosing not to be parents is rising.
8. _____ Research shows that there are no differences in quality of life between adults with children and adults who are choosing not to have children.
9. _____ In divorce situations it is more common for the maternal grandparents to get more involved with their children.
10. _____ Within a family system an individual is generally at retirement age before being seen as an authority in the family.
11. _____ Among adult siblings, brothers tend to have the closest relationships.
12. _____ Residents who move from a suburban area to an urban area often do so for the racial diversity.
13. _____ In the United States more adults rent their homes rather than own them.
14. _____ Most Americans live in metropolitan suburbs.
15. _____ Nearly one-quarter of American households include an elderly individual.
16. _____ Urban residents are more likely to view communities as geographic locations than rural residents.
17. _____ New Jersey is one of the top six states in terms of destinations for adults older than 60 who are moving for their post-retirement years.
18. _____ More than one-third of adults older than 85 live in nursing homes.

The ways we view and interact with our families, neighborhoods, and communities will continue to change as we move through young, middle, and late adulthood. Our lives will most likely change as we move into the role of the middle-aged children of older adults who need assistance in their daily lives. Again we may turn to our community for resources and support. As time continues to pass it is likely that we will eventually become grandparents striving to be a supportive and stable influence in our grandchildren's lives. We will become the retirees seeking volunteer opportunities to stay active in the community. And we will become the older citizen needing some assistance in our lives and perhaps a special housing situation. Although it is necessary in a structured book like this to explore topics in isolation and in some ordering scheme, the reality of adult life is that our roles as friends, parents, stepparents, adult children of aging parents, workers, volunteers, retirees, and community members are closely related and intertwined. They may occur simultaneously and in varying sequences as we move through life's journey.

Before We Get Started . . .

Have you ever considered how many communities you are a part of? Write down all the groups of people that you are associated with or feel a connection to. Remember to include the groups of people you affiliate with in a face-to-face setting, those you identify with but may not know personally (such as fans of a musician or a sports team), and those you are associated with via the Internet. To help with your brainstorming, consider your communities in terms of:

- Extended family networks
- Neighborhoods, towns, cities, regions, country

- Academic groups, clubs, organizations, graduates, alumni
- Employee groups, professional organizations, associations
- Ethnic, racial, cultural, or religious groups
- Groups formed around political issues or government-related issues
- Special interests, hobbies, entertainment, and sports-related groups
- Groups meeting around health, medical, abuse, or recovery issues
- Groups meeting around age-related issues

Are you surprised by the length of your list? Once you have your list together, pick out the three communities you consider the most important. Which do you value the most? Now shift your thinking and consider the three you are *engaged in* the most. In other words, which three communities consume the most time and effort? Are the most important ones the same as the ones you spend the most time with? Why or why not?

Now that you have given some thought to your communities in terms of involvement and importance, consider the differences in terms of the types of interactions. What differences do you notice between the face-to-face communities, like your neighborhood, and those that seldom meet as a group, such as sports fans? What differences do you notice between the Internet communities, which generally have no expectation of meeting in person, and face-to-face communities? Do you think Internet communities, or communities that you seldom meet, can be just as powerful as face-to-face communities? If so, under what circumstances? If not, then why not?

Parenting

From an adult development and aging perspective the study of parenting is challenging for several reasons. One complication is that parenting is such a long, pervasive, and almost universal process that parental development is difficult, if not impossible, to separate from general adult development (Azar, 2003). Another factor in studying parenting is that most of the focus is, as it should be, on the children. Most of the social science resources are aimed at understanding how parents influence their children rather than the parents' personal development. Taking an adult development and aging perspective, this section focuses primarily on parenting from the parents' point of view. The topics include the choice to become a parent, role changes that come with parenting, and the interaction of parental and marital satisfaction.

Pathways to Parenting

Although the small percentage of adults choosing not to be parents is growing, most of us will at some point in our lives become parents. There are many ways to become a parent, all of which deserve careful consideration and planning. For example, any woman who may be pregnant should heed the recommendations made by the National Center on Birth Defects and Developmental Disabilities (2004) for healthy pregnancy. Some of these recommendations include:

- Avoid toxic substances, such as cleaning solvents, lead, mercury, some insecticides, and paint and paint fumes
- Avoid alcohol, caffeine, and cigarette smoking and secondhand smoke
- Eat healthy, drink extra fluids, and get plenty of sleep
- Be careful with over-the-counter drugs that contain harmful substances
- Take extra iron and folic acid

Your Thoughts?

How might you design a study to test the accuracy of college students' knowledge in this area?

The most important piece of information to remember is that prenatal care is critical to a baby's healthy development.

For couples who have been trying to conceive for over a year, or for women who have had multiple miscarriages, infertility treatments may be considered. ***Infertility*** is a medical disease affecting approximately 6.1 million individuals, about 10% of those in the reproductive-age population (American Society of Reproductive Medicine [ASRM], 2004). The cause of infertility is found approximately one-third of the time to be a female problem, one-third of the time attributed to a male problem, with the remaining cases attributed to either both partners or simply an "unexplained" cause (ASRM, 2004; National Infertility Association, 2010). Generally, male infertility problems are related to lack of or low numbers of sperm cells while female infertility problems are related to ovulation disorders, such as blocked fallopian tubes or endometriosis (tissue outside the uterus, often forming cysts). Most infertility disorders are treated with drug therapy or surgical procedures. In vitro fertilization (IVF), which involves fertilizing eggs in the laboratory and placing them in the woman's uterus, accounts for less than 5% of the infertility treatments in the United States (ASRM, 2004).

Another pathway to parenting is through adoption. The adoption process can vary dramatically depending on the practices of particular agencies and the various legal concerns, both in terms of national laws as well as state and local laws. For example, some states have different requirements for new parents than for stepparents. It is imperative that potential parents take the time to educate themselves on the laws and the options available in their area (National Adoption Information Clearinghouse [NAIC], 2003, 2004). Couples or individuals may choose to seek an independent adoption directly from the pregnant parent, or choose to go through a private or public agency in order to adopt a child from within the country (domestic) or from outside the country (international). Those who adopt children from other cultures will typically face different types of stresses, such as dealing with racial discrimination toward their child; however, researchers find that their stresses are no greater than those associated with "traditional" parenting (Judge, 2003). In planning an adoption decisions must also be made in terms of choosing to adopt an infant or older child who is healthy or a child with special needs or developmental disabilities. Yet another decision point relates to ***open adoption*** in which the birth family and the adopted child may have some contact with each other. Researchers have found that open adoption arrangements are generally positive experiences (Siegel, 2003).

Your Thoughts?

Setting aside adopting stepchildren, what factors might keep adults from adopting?

For gay and lesbian couples who choose to have a family, the choices are even more complex. A lesbian woman may choose artificial insemination or a gay male may choose artificial insemination with a surrogate mother. In terms of adoption, the NAIC reported in 2004 that most states are "largely silent on the issue of adoption by gay and lesbian persons," with some banning gay adoption, some allowing gay couples to adopt, and others allowing one partner to adopt, with the other adopting the child at a later date (Craft, 2004; NAIC, 2004). While some individuals may have some reservations about gay males or lesbians in parenting roles, there is growing research evidence to support the view that there are no significant differences between children raised by straight or gay parents. In 2002 the American Academy of Pediatrics (AAP) gave its support to gay parents in general, and specifically encouraged agencies and lawmakers to allow both parents in a gay couple to adopt their children. The AAP's statement has since been endorsed by several other important groups, such as the American Academy of Child and Adolescent Psychiatry, the National Association of Pediatric Nurse Practitioners, and the Canadian Pediatric Society. In 2004 the American Psychological Association (APA), the National Association of Social Workers (NASW, 2004), and the American Anthropological Association (2004) gave their support as well. Whatever means adults choose, and whatever their circumstances, the pathway to becoming a parent is the first step in the life-changing process of parental development.

Your Thoughts?

Considering that people may lie on a questionnaire, how might you design a study to gauge whether gay parents might be accepted in a particular neighborhood?

Parental Satisfaction

What do parents consider to be the rewards or benefits of parenting? One way to consider parental satisfaction is to compare the positive aspects of parenting with the not-so-positive. Waldron-Hennessey and Sabatelli (1997), in a survey of 439 parents, found the most important benefits are the happiness, love, and affection they feel as well as the sense of meaning, purpose, fulfillment, and achievement experienced in their parenting role. The participants also included the sense of "being a family" and watching their children grow and develop as highlights. Other positive aspects cited were the pleasure, fun, and stimulation that children bring into the lives of their parents. Waldron-Hennessey and Sabatelli also asked parents to list the greatest costs or challenges involved in parenting. Participants indicated that parenting restricts their personal freedom, social life, and activities outside of the home, as well as their privacy. While most parents believed the benefits far outweighed the costs, parents of younger children reported greater rewards than those parenting adolescents and young adults.

Your Thoughts?

What factors may contribute to the finding that parents of younger children report more personal rewards?

Although informative, you may find a cost–benefit analysis of parental satisfaction rather crude, arguing that parenting should not be reduced to something similar to a business decision. Parenting is often a central part of our identity, perhaps even more so than the role of spouse or partner. Parental identity has also been found to be more important than career or professional roles (Rogers & White, 1998). From Erikson's view of adult development, after establishing identity and creating a love relationship, individuals are then ready to experience generativity. Parents have a direct and full-time role in shaping the next generation by sharing their resources, knowledge, and wisdom. One of the differences found between adults who choose to be parents and those who do not is that the adults without children were less generative, although they may express generativity through mentoring or caring for other family members (Butler, 2003).

What is at the heart of parental satisfaction? While family processes, parent–child interactions, and child behaviors are influential, researchers have found the most powerful factors to be marital quality and level of role conflict (Rogers & Matthews, 2004). In a national survey involving 1,200 parents, Rogers and White (1998) found that marital happiness and parental satisfaction are not only related, but they influenced each other. A happy marriage may provide many of the resources needed for successful parenting and high levels of parental satisfaction can then strengthen one's commitment to a marriage. Also, when one feels successful in parenting, that sense of pride can "spill over" to satisfaction in marital and family life. Parents without the support of a high-quality marital relationship report much lower levels of parental satisfaction (Rogers & White, 1998).

Your Thoughts?

Where might parents who are without the support of a high-quality marital relationship go for support and advice regarding parenting issues?

A similar and even stronger trend relating marital and parental satisfaction was found for stepparents. In studies comparing the parental satisfaction of parents in first marriages parenting their biological children with parents in remarriages parenting stepchildren, the stepparents routinely report lower levels of parental satisfaction (Ishii-Kuntz & Ihinger-Tallman, 1991; Rogers & White, 1998). Whereas biological parents are more likely to view their parent–child tensions as separate from their marital relationship and look to the marital relationship for strength, stepparents are more likely to view conflict with their stepchildren as a marital issue (Fine & Kurdek, 1995). This difference may occur because when parenting biological children the parents had some time to develop a relationship prior to children entering the family. Stepparents, on the other hand, most likely developed relationships with their spouses and their stepchildren simultaneously.

The second factor closely associated with higher parental satisfaction is reduced levels of role conflict (Rogers & Matthews, 2004). ***Role conflict theory*** states that role strain occurs when the demands and expectations of important roles are in conflict (Twenge, Campbell, & Foster, 2003). For example, a survey of over 600 male and female physicians found that their

RESEARCH IN-DEPTH

Questionnaires and Standardized Tests, Part 2: Assessment Validity

Researchers from the Department of Psychiatry at the State University of New York at Stony Brook have developed a checklist parents can complete to help professionals diagnose children with behavioral and emotional problems. The items correspond to symptoms for numerous disorders as indicated in the fourth edition of the *Diagnostic and Statistical Manual of Mental Disorders*, published by the American Psychiatric Association (1994). Before the researchers can promote their test, however, they need to follow a strict procedure to make it a standardized test. As was discussed in the previous *Research In-Depth* section, the first steps include rewriting and refining the items and establishing reliability, which means a test is stable. Once reliability is established, the next step in the process is to establish ***validity***, which is to make sure the test is *really* measuring the appropriate concept.

The test, called the Child Symptom Inventory–4: Parent Checklist (CSI-4PC), is a 97 item questionnaire that highlights symptoms for 12 childhood disorders, including oppositional defiant disorder and attention-deficit/hyperactivity disorder. The checklist asks parents to mark each symptom they have observed, how often it occurs, and how severe it is. In order to begin the standardization process the researchers surveyed 247 mothers of boys with various childhood disorders on two different occasions, between 1 and 4 months apart, to establish test–retest reliability. To establish validity the researchers needed to show that the items measuring separate childhood disorders were truly measuring something distinct (discriminant or divergent validity), and second, that each distinct set of items predicted the severity of a disorder in the same accurate way as other tests or methods of diagnosis (convergent validity). In order to achieve this, the researchers compared the parents' ratings on the CSI-4PC with other standardized and well-established tests, such as the Child Behavior Checklist. Parents' ratings on the CSI-4PC were also compared to diagnoses made through standard interview procedures. As a final check, children and their parents were tested 4 years after the initial study in order to show the predictive power of the CSI-4PC (criterion validity).

Once all the data were collected, extensive statistical procedures were used to show that the CSI-4PC met the criteria for each type of validity. By demonstrating criterion, discriminant, and convergent validity, the researchers had met their goals of establishing the questionnaire as a standardized test. The researchers then took the final step in the process. They gave the test to even more parents, some with children with disorders and some with healthy children, in order to establish typical scores for children with no disorders, mild disorders, and severe disorders. At this point the researchers can encourage professionals to use the CSI-4PC along with interviews, teacher observations, and other methods of data collection in order to make the most accurate diagnoses (Sprafkin, Gadow, Salisbury, Schneider, & Loney, 2002). Although it may seem as if the professionals who create such tests, as experts, should be able to simply create a useful test in an hour or two, the many months of work involved in standardizing a test works as a filter to pull out much of the hidden bias, mistakes, and not-so-well-worded items. Psychology, with its scientific foundation, demands that evidence beyond someone's opinion be given in order to give credibility to material or information. Establishing validity is a necessary part of that scientific process.

---

parental satisfaction was primarily determined by their level of marital satisfaction and the amount of conflict they felt in terms of their profession interfering with their responsibilities as a parent (Warde, Moonesignhe, Allen, & Gelberg, 1999). Those physicians, both female and male, with the highest parental satisfaction reported very supportive spouses who helped to alleviate role conflict. Twenge and her colleagues (2003), after reviewing 148 research investigations involving over 47,000 participants, determined that role conflict and restriction of freedom best explained the differences in parental satisfaction.

For those individuals in a marriage or similar relationship who are trying to maintain housework, child care, and employment, the stresses related to the many demands of each role may be severe (Lorensen, Wilson, & White, 2004). Costigan, Cox, and Cauce (2003) found that among 83 sets of dual-earner parents, fathers' work experiences were generally unrelated to parenting whereas mothers' negative work experiences were related to an increase in negative parenting behaviors and negative observations of father's parenting. In a longitudinal study of 150 married women, Goldberg and Perry-Jenkins (2004) found that women who returned to part-time work after maternity leave experienced the greatest role strain. They felt that they were not involved in their work enough to feel that they were "good" employees, and yet they felt that when they left their child they were not a "good" parent either. Goldberg and Perry-Jenkins also

Your Thoughts?

What factors in American gender and cultural roles and expectations may be affecting the findings regarding mothers' and fathers' role conflict?

ON THE LEADING EDGE
Prison Dads and Moms

The incarcerated fathers at the North Idaho Correctional Institution are learning about their children and themselves from parenting classes offered through the prison system. The classes are offered along with other life skills courses designed to help the inmates adjust and lead productive lives once they have finished their sentences (Bushfield, 2004). Similar programs have proven to be effective with mothers as well (Kennon, Mackintosh, & Myers, 2009). These programs not only benefit the inmates, but will likely benefit their children as well. Among the prison population, previous research has indicated that children of prisoners are more likely to be prisoners themselves in the future.

The parenting course for fathers was designed by the staff at the institution to address the specific needs of incarcerated fathers. The program involves daily classes in parenting over a 4-week period. There are four content areas that make up the course: child development, role of fathers, appropriate discipline and communication, and creating a family learning environment. Through this course inmates explore the social, emotional, and moral development of children while considering the place for fathers as role models and teachers. The emphasis on a learning environment is designed to show fathers that family literacy and educational development are among the best ways to reduce the risk of incarceration of their own children in the future.

Dr. Suzanne Bushfield, a social work educator and researcher, surveyed 32 male prisoners who had completed the parenting course. The participants were primarily White males in their late 20s. More than half of them did not complete high school. The inmates were surveyed regarding their knowledge and attitudes toward parenting at the beginning and again at the end of the course. Following the course the inmates indicated that they were less likely to use corporal punishment, such as spanking or "forcing" children to respect authority. They were also less likely to rely on their children for emotional care, such as expecting a child to comfort a parent who is sad. Many of the inmates said they had learned the most about discipline and their own attitudes toward children. The fathers also said they developed a better sense of why fathers' involvement is important in children's lives (Bushfield, 2004).

Suzanne Kennon of the Virginia Correctional Center for Women and her colleagues investigated the outcomes of a similar program for incarcerated mothers. The researchers surveyed 57 women before and after a 12-session class focused on parenting issues. Similar to the father's course at the North Idaho Correctional Institution, these women followed a curriculum designed by a developmental psychologist. The results of the study showed that the mothers gained a better understanding of the needs of their children. The women also gained better parenting attitudes, self-esteem, and a more accurate and in-depth understanding of the legal system regarding parents rights and responsibilities (Kennon, Mackintosh, & Myers, 2009).

found that the women placed a great deal of role expectations on themselves. Those who reported engaging in less child care and housework displayed lower levels of well-being and greater distress. Those who reported greater amounts of child care and housework displayed a greater sense of well-being in fulfilling their role expectations, yet at the same time they reported frustration and stress over their difficult lifestyle. This frustration will most likely affect other areas of their lives, including their marital satisfaction.

Choosing Not to Parent

Although most Americans will find themselves in a parenting role at some point in their adult lives, there are a growing number of individuals who are choosing not to be parents. This trend is particularly strong among highly educated and career-oriented women (Lee & Schaninger, 2003). In a recent analysis of the 2001 General Social Survey data collected from Canadians ages 20 to 34 years old, 7% of the women and 8% of the men said they do not plan to have children (Stobert & Kenny, 2003). As this minority gets larger the commonly applied term for this lifestyle, ***childless***, has become problematic. Some view the term to mean that an individual is "less" or missing something necessary to be whole. For those who are voluntarily choosing not to be parents, and who do not feel they have a deficit, the term ***childfree*** is often applied.

Critics argue that the term *childfree* sounds too much like *carefree*, and thus implies a lack of responsibility or maturity, which supports many of the associated negative stereotypes. Often childfree individuals are judged to be selfish and deviant (Letherby, 2002), showing less warmth, caring, and kindness than individuals with children (LeMastro, 2001). Childfree women are thought to be "unfeminine" (Letherby, 2002) and childfree men less powerful or capable (LeMastro, 2001).

Your Thoughts?

What similarities and differences would you predict when considering men's and women's reasons for choosing not to have children?

Although those characteristics are often associated with a childfree lifestyle they are not reflective of the sentiments voiced by childfree adults. In a recent study Stobert and Kemeny (2003) found that individuals who choose not to parent are doing so for a wide variety of reasons, including engaging in fulfilling or demanding careers, environmental reasons related to rising world population figures, and that they or their partners simply do not enjoy children. When comparing parents and childfree couples, researchers find no differences in terms of quality of life (Skutch, 2001), self-esteem, or depression (Nomaguchi & Milkie, 2003).

Section Summary

- Among the majority of adults who do choose to become parents, some will need medical assistance to treat infertility while others may choose to adopt.
- For most adults their role as a parent will become central in their sense of identity, thus parental satisfaction becomes critical to personal happiness.
- The primary factors contributing to parental satisfaction are marital quality and level of role conflict.
- While most American adults will be a parent at some point, it is important to recognize that there is a minority of adults who choose a childfree lifestyle and find it satisfying.
- These adults often choose a lifestyle without children because they are engaged in fulfilling and demanding careers or they simply do not enjoy children.

Grandparenting

Grandparents donate many hours of care as well as financial and material resources to their grandchildren. While the typical grandparents are in their early 50s, married, and not yet retired, there are many who do not fit that average profile. Grandparents vary in many ways, including age, financial situation, social status, and in their degree of interest in and approach to their grandparenting role.

Grandparenting Styles and Roles

In what is now classic research in developmental psychology from the 1960s, Neugarten described several approaches to the role of grandparenting. Based on a sample of 70 grandmothers and 70 grandfathers, 5 styles or types of grandparents emerged (Neugarten & Weinstein, 1964):

- ***Formal:*** proper, not interfering with parenting, and setting clear boundaries
- ***Fun Seeker:*** informal, playful, and keen on mutual satisfaction
- ***Surrogate Parent:*** taking on most or nearly all parents' responsibilities
- ***Reservoir of Family Wisdom:*** authoritarian, dispenser of skills and resources
- ***Distant Figure:*** distant and remote, generally appearing on holidays

In a similar effort to explore grandparent–grandchild relationships, Mueller, Wilhelm, and Elder (2002) also found five categories of grandparents:

- ***Influential:*** highly involved and often physically present
- ***Supportive:*** somewhat less involved and takes a less parental stance than the influential
- ***Passive:*** Moderately involved, engage in few activities with grandchildren
- ***Authority-Oriented:*** Moderately involved and sees primary role as an authority figure
- ***Detached:*** Least involved

Your Thoughts?

What characteristics are captured in Neugarten's list that are not in Mueller's list? What characteristics are in Mueller's list but not Neugarten's?

Mueller and her colleagues found that grandparents who were more involved in various aspects of their grandchildren's lives reported higher-quality relationships. They also found that these grandparenting styles were specific to relationships with particular grandchildren, thus grandparents may display different styles to different grandchildren. Interestingly, there are various situations that seem to be associated with detached grandparents, such as geographic distance, no encouragement from parents to get involved, being on the paternal side of the family, a lack of shared interests with their grandchildren, and having a large number of grandchildren (Mueller et al., 2002).

Rewards of Grandparenting

Your Thoughts?

What might grandchildren say are the rewards of having grandparents?

When asked about the benefits of grandparenting, many adults will cite the freedom to be involved in pleasurable activities with grandchildren without much of the work involved in actual parenting (Dellmann-Jenkins, Blankemeyer, & Olesh, 2002). In essence, grandparents can have fun with their grandchildren without many of the responsibilities of parenting (Glass & Huneycutt, 2002). Peterson (1999) found, through a survey of 146 Australian grandparents, that the most rewarding aspects of grandparenting were the opportunities to share in activities and watch their grandchildren develop. Another important benefit of grandparenting is the sense of meaning and purpose found in the role of wise elder. Grandparents often maintain the family history and traditions, give advice to younger family members, and share resources (Strom, Carter, & Schmidt, 2004). In a study involving more than 200 grandparents, participants who found the greatest sense of meaning and purpose in their role also displayed the highest levels of grandparenting satisfaction, personal well-being, and physical health (Hayslip, Henderson, & Shore, 2003).

Difficult Issues in Grandparenting

Not all grandparenting situations are ideal, and as the number of grandparents increases we are becoming more aware of grandparents' problems and concerns. For example, a study of African American grandparents indicated that they seldom had as much information about the abilities, feelings, or needs of their grandchildren as they would like. The grandparents reported a lack of understanding of the pressures, conflicts, and goals of younger generations (Strom et al., 2004). In an Australian study Peterson (1999) found that grandparents reported the lack of contact with their grandchildren when desired, worrying about them, and having little control over what their parents say or do as frequent concerns. The grandparents also reported problems regarding parents' expectations of frequent child care, making them feel imposed upon and often wearing them out physically (Peterson, 1999).

Your Thoughts?

What factors might contribute to the reluctance of grandparents to say they are doing too much babysitting?

Much of the recent research, legal, and political activity involving grandparents has focused on two areas of difficulty, both of which involve grandparents' legal rights. One area focuses on grandparents who are taking on the parental role of raising their grandchildren and the other considers the role of grandparents following a divorce. There are numerous reasons why grandparents may be put in the role of substitute parents, or ***surrogate parents***, such as when a single parent or both parents need to work outside of the home (Gray, Mission, & Hayes, 2005). This may involve grandparents who have legal custody or protection while their grandchildren live with them, grandparents whose grandchildren live with them but they do not have custody, and grandparents who provide day care (Jendrek, 1993). In some cases the custodial parent is very young, single, and unable or unwilling to perform as a parent. In other situations a grandparent may feel the need to assume the role of surrogate if the parent is suffering from a physical or mental illness. Other reasons for surrogate parenting include drug, domestic, or child abuse involving the parent or grandchildren, or a parent who is absent due to incarceration or death (Reynolds, Wright, & Beale, 2003).

Much of the focus on grandparents who are providing the bulk of the child care is on grandmothers and more often in urban areas, though it is important to remember that similar situations occur with grandfathers and in rural communities as well (Bullock, 2005). In 2000 there were approximately 5.5 million children living in grandparent or other-relative households, and of those 2.1 million children were being raised with no parent present (Generations United, 2004). Many of these grandparents find that not only is surrogate parenting unanticipated and exhausting, it often reduces their financial resources. They may have retired early, reduced work hours, used savings, or postponed a new career in order to raise their grandchildren (Reynolds, Wright, & Beale, 2003).

Grandparents who serve as surrogate parents may find themselves worn out physically and out of sync socially.

Acting in the capacity of a surrogate parent can be stressful and difficult on many levels. When coerced or forced to take on parental responsibility researchers find that grandparenting satisfaction often declines. The stresses associated with primary child care may contribute to poor general health or intensify existing health problems for grandparents. At a time when they may need social support the most, these older adults often feel out of place among their friends and peers who do not have small children around all the time. Grandparents may feel a sense of intrusion and deprivation from the lifestyle they intended for this point in their lives. These grandparents may also have to deal with parenting conflicts with their adult children regarding their grandchildren, as well as conflicts involving lawyers, teachers, and other family members (Glass & Huneycutt, 2002). They may be in need of legal and financial help as well as parenting training and social support (Dellmann-Jenkins et al., 2002). These grandparents are likely to be in the emotionally difficult situation of feeling love for their grandchildren and intense frustration over their role as surrogate parents.

Another situation that may cause emotional difficulty is when parents divorce. Grandparents are in a vulnerable position when their adult children decide to divorce. Consider the following hypothetical scenario:

> Tony and Denise have relied on Tony's mother and father to help with child care for many years. Because Tony and Denise both work afternoon shifts, Tony's parents pick up their grandchildren from school each day. Grandma and Grandpa fix snacks and an evening meal, help the children with their homework, watch television, get them ready for bed, and stay up with them until one of their parents arrives.

What might happen if Tony and Denise were to divorce? In an effort to learn more about these family dynamics Lussier, Deater-Deckard, Dunn, and Davies (2002) studied 192 families in England who were either intact, stepfather families, stepmother families, or single-mother families. They found that most of the children reported more contact with maternal grandparents than paternal grandparents and the most contact with maternal grandmothers. Most of the children felt close to their grandparents, although there was tension in the relationship with grandparents on the noncustodial side. Lussier and her colleagues found that children who maintained close relationships with their grandparents were better adjusted following a divorce and the related subsequent changes, such as changing residences and changing schools. As more grandparents find themselves dealing with this difficult situation, more questions are being raised regarding the legal rights of noncustodial grandparents to secure visitation privileges with their grandchildren. Custodial parents, whether divorced or not, are the gatekeepers between grandparents and their grandchildren. Grandparents, like Tony's parents in the hypothetical scenario, are turning to the legal system to allow them to maintain the relationship they had developed with their grandchildren.

Your Thoughts?

If you were a judge would you ever give grandparents visitation rights? If not, why not? If so, under what conditions?

Your Thoughts?

How might the situation with Tony and Denise be perceived or treated differently if they were a lesbian couple dissolving their relationship?

Section Summary

- With the increase in longevity and the numbers of multigenerational families, it is more likely than ever that older adults are grandparents and perhaps even great-grandparents.
- Many adults enjoy the role of sharing activities and watching their grandchildren develop while having the freedom of limited involvement.
- In some cases grandparenting situations are not ideal, causing grandparents to feel imposed upon and overwhelmed by too much childcare.

- Some grandparents become surrogate parents without the legal rights and options of legal parents.
- Parents, particularly custodial parents, are often the ones who decide whether grandparents may remain active in their grandchildren's lives following a divorce.

Family Role Transitions

Time brings changes in families, roles, and responsibilities. Young children become adults and, with time, may become guardians and caregivers for their parents. At one time role transitions were treated like problems, with much of the related research focused on retirement and widowhood. Now many social scientists have shifted their perspective from a problem-centered emphasis to a life-cycle perspective that emphasizes expected stages of growth and development. Even with this shift, adjustment to retirement and widowhood continue to be among the most researched, along with transitions to parenting, grandparenting, and adult caregiver roles. Researchers in Western cultures are also growing more aware that family role transitions are likely to be influenced by culture and tradition. Whereas in some cases it may feel like something "extra" or even a burden to care for aging parents, in other cultures or traditions it may be viewed as simply an expected part of adult life or even as a privilege that brings with it high social admiration and approval.

> **Your Thoughts?**
>
> In addition to those listed here, what other adult family role transitions can you think of?

Transition Models

Several models have been applied to the study of family role transitions, including the compensation model, the life-course model, and the cumulative disadvantage model (Ferraro, 2001). Each model emphasizes a unique perspective, and it may be useful in some cases to use several models to best understand particular role transitions. Similar to the selection–optimization–compensation (SOC) model, the ***compensation model*** focuses on the ways we try to compensate for the losses as our families change with age. This may be evident when a young couple is overwhelmed by the time and energy demands of parenting and subsequently compensates by decreasing social commitments and accepting help from grandparents. This might also be seen when an older adult who is forced to give up driving begins using the phone much more often and encourages others to visit.

The ***life-course model*** emphasizes the decisions one makes across the lifespan, the timing of those decisions, and how those decisions are influenced by history, society, and culture. When considering, for example, the way a widow is coping with her new lifestyle, her thoughts and behaviors would be viewed in terms of her choices and her context. She may have adjusted well because she created a community of friends prior to her husband's death, or she may be lonely because she chose a solitary lifestyle. If she is an older adult she may be comfortable financially because her adult children gave her good advice regarding her retirement planning, or she may be struggling financially because prices are rising and she is on a fixed income.

> **Your Thoughts?**
>
> How might the transition be different if this hypothetical widow is young and her husband died while in military service?

Another model, the ***cumulative disadvantage model***, focuses on the ways early life circumstances influence later life role transitions. Those individuals who begin adulthood with key advantages often have more resources later in life. Advantages such as advanced education and higher incomes often lead to better jobs with less physical risk, better health care, and better housing, all of which may contribute to more options and better decision-making in late adulthood. On the other hand, those who begin adulthood with disadvantaged circumstances may find that problems in one area of life then cause other problems, all of which accumulate to lead to difficulties in late adulthood (Ferraro, 2001). Some adults whose only options for employment are physically demanding jobs with a higher risk for injury may find themselves in need of early retirement due to health problems. The resulting physical disabilities may lead to problems with mobility, transportation, and housing.

Shifting Status in the Family

Among the many changes in the roles family members play, one of the most significant involves the relationship between parents and their adult children. Since the late 20th century there has been a dramatic increase in the number of adult children returning to live with their parents for an extended amount of time after being away from home (Goldscheider, Goldscheider, St. Clair, & Hodges, 1999; Lippert, 1997). This trend further extends the length of time of parental authority. Generally, between the ages of 30 and 45 years old, adult children transition from child or adolescent status to authority status within their family. Until that point many young adults report an intimate relationship with their parents, still seeking parental advice and relying on parental resources (Lawson & Brossart, 2004), while also reporting tension and conflict in their relationships. In a study involving 474 individuals who composed 158 family triads (father, mother, and adult child ranging in age from 22 to 49 years old), Birditt, Miller, Fingerman, and Lefkowitz (2009) found that parents were more upset over individual issues, such as finances or education, whereas adult children focused more on relationship tensions, such as personality differences. They also found as the age of the adult children increased in their sample so did the level of intensity in terms of relationship tension.

Your Thoughts?

What factors or events may contribute to finding that this role transition occurs when adult children are between 30 and 45 years old?

Middle-aged adult children have usually established their own independent lifestyle and are more likely to see themselves as peers with their parents. They are more likely to report withholding information about personal problems and hiding their true feelings in discussions with their parents. This shift toward ***personal authority in the family system*** is expected and generally healthy. It allows middle-aged adults to enjoy their place as fully functioning adult family members. Their authority status also allows them to give their aging parents advice and guidance in planning for the future (Lawson & Brossart, 2004). Conflict and tension still exist in these relationships (Birditt et al., 2009), and it tends to be more intense when there are more adult children in the family. Relationships also seem to be less positive when adult stepchildren are involved (Ward, Spitze, & Deane, 2009).

Although expected, it can be awkward when this transition in status occurs. Often the first steps in the process are made by middle-aged adults offering social support and advice to their parents. To learn more about this process, Ikkink, van Tilburg, and Knipscheer (1999) surveyed 365 Danish adults and 634 of their children regarding social support. The researchers found that adult children were more likely to offer support when they lived closer to their parents and when the parents offered some support in return. Of the various types of interpersonal relationships, they found that adult daughters with young children offered the most support. The results also indicated that the adult children reported giving more support than their aging parents indicated they received. One possible reason for this finding is that adult children overestimate the support they offer because finding additional time and energy is difficult in the midst of busy lifestyles. While it may feel like a serious commitment for an adult child to visit a parent one evening a week, the adult parent may feel as though a week is a long time to wait. Another factor may be that parents underestimate the support given because they expect to receive more support than they do. Taking a different point of view, another possibility is that parents underestimate the support given because they want to believe they are independent and not in need of much help, whereas adult children overestimate the support because they want to believe they are gracious and caring individuals.

Your Thoughts?

How might new technologies increase the support adult children are able to offer their parents from a distance?

As the authority in the family shifts adult children find themselves providing more support for their parents.

At some point after the authority status has shifted these middle-aged adults will slowly transition to the role of caregiver for their parents. According to the ***caregiving trajectory theory*** developed by Cicirelli (2000), there are three major stages leading to active caregiving. Adults begin with the *Concern Stage*, which occurs when they first begin to observe some decline in the mental and/or physical health of their parents. Although there are usually no major problems at this point, such observations often trigger the awareness in adults that they cannot take their parents' good health for granted. Adult children may respond by contacting their parents more often, watching more closely for any symptoms or signals of serious problems, and possibly begin conversations about future care with their siblings. The second stage in the caregiving trajectory theory, the *Urging Stage*, occurs when symptoms and signals of problems are frequently appearing. In this stage the adult children begin to openly attempt to persuade their parents to take better care of themselves. These adult children may encourage their aging parents to take medications as prescribed, maintain a healthy diet, and get enough exercise. The final stage, the *Action Stage*, requires the adult children to take action to provide their aging parents with the assistance they need. At this point their parents may be displaying mobility problems as well as a general inability to maintain household routines, complete daily activities, or solve typical problems (Cicirelli, 2000).

Supportive Family Members

Although this section is primarily focused on the transition of authority from parents to their adult children, it is important to remember that older adults often have other sources of social support in addition to their adult children. It's also important to keep in mind that some older adults do not have children and even some who do have unreliable or absent adult children. Spouses, siblings, close friends, and members of their religious communities are often part of an older adult's social support network (Krause, 2001). Spouses are the most important source of support. When they are not able or available, adult children and siblings are sought out for advice and assistance when needed (Antonucci, 2001).

Although siblings are generally a part of each other's lives throughout the lifespan, research trends indicate that during the years when each is giving attention to spouses and children sibling relationships are not as close as they are likely to be later in adulthood. They may call on each other for emotional or instrumental support, such as babysitting, during these years; however, their priorities lie with their own families. With age and fewer family responsibilities siblings often grow closer (Myers & Bryant, 2008). Issues relating to aging parents may serve as a catalyst, prompting adult siblings to communicate more frequently (Moyer, 1992). In a survey of over 7,000 adults, White and Riedmann (1992) found that 63% of the participants said they considered at least one sibling to be a close friend, and 53% indicated that they talked to their siblings at least once a month. Among siblings researchers have found that sister/sister relationships are the strongest, whereas brother/brother relationships are the weakest (Lee, Mancini, & Maxwell, 1990; White & Reidmann, 1992). Connidis and Campbell (1995) found the same closeness among sisters in a study of 528 siblings in Canada. Also, as one might predict, those individuals who were not married and those without children reported greater closeness to their siblings. Not only is gender a factor, proximity is also important. Siblings who live closer to each other tend to have much stronger relationships (Lee et al., 1990; White & Reidmann, 1992).

Your Thoughts?

What factors might contribute to the findings that sister/sister relationships are stronger than brother/brother relationships?

Section Summary

- As family members age their roles and relationships change.
- Older adults may begin to see the consequences of their previous life circumstances (cumulative disadvantage model) and choices (life-course model), and begin to make deliberate choices in order to compensate for losses (compensation model).
- Whereas younger adults often rely on their parents for advice and resources, middle-aged adult children see themselves as peers to their parents.
- Over time, most middle-aged adult children will likely transition to the role of caregiver for their elderly parents.
- Older adults will look not only to their children for support, but also to their siblings, friends, and community.

Living Arrangements Across Adulthood

Closely related to creating a family is creating a feeling of being "at home." The level of comfort found in the place we call home can have a strong influence on our personal sense of security and well-being. As we consider the role of the environment on psychological growth and development it is important to consider not only where people live, but also those characteristics that transform a location into the place that feels like home. Chances are there will be several places across our lives that we think of as home. The home(s) we grew up in, the first place that was "ours" (and not our parents' place), the home(s) our children grow up in and the places we live in retirement will all be special to us. In this section we consider trends in the typical living arrangements for adults of all ages in the United States while keeping in mind those special qualities that make a place feel like home.

Creating a Home Atmosphere

What is the psychological difference between *housing* in its most practical sense and *home* in its most comforting sense? What makes a dwelling a home? While the many individual and environmental differences involved are likely to lead to numerous responses (Doyle, 1992), there are some notions of home that are common. One of the primary indicators that a physical living space has acquired our abstract label of *home* is that it has become a part of our identity (Dobbs, 2004; Doyle, 1992; Groger, 1995). We have personalized it to reflect our personality and interests. Home is also the primary place where we learn some of our most important roles, perhaps as spouse, partner, mom, or dad, and express the resulting changes in our identity through various symbols, such as wedding pictures or children's art displayed on the wall. Acquiring a feeling of home takes time, familiarity, and the exercise of personal control and choices (Dobbs, 2004). Over time we build memories that contribute to our home–self connection. Our sense of home gives a physical location an emotional atmosphere that creates the feeling of uniquely personal and private space (Doyle, 1992).

Your Thoughts?

How might homeless parents or those who are transient and move frequently approximate a sense of home for their children?

The characteristics that contribute to the sense of being "at home" are likely to change as we transition through young, middle, and late adulthood. For young adults their choice of housing may be directed by how they would like to be seen by others. Young adults are also building their personal identity as they establish themselves as workers, community members, lovers, spouses or partners, and as parents. Home is the place they learn some of these new roles. Middle-aged adults are likely to be household managers, trying to balance the many demands placed on them. For these adults home may be a retreat from the chaos of the outside world. Home may also become the place for loved ones to gather, serving as the center of family life. As older adults are evaluating all the many changes occurring in their own bodies and their environment, they may look to home as a safe place physically, financially, and psychologically. As they transition to different housing arrangements with relatives or as part of an institution their notion of home may become primarily memories of the place they left behind (Doyle, 1992).

Your Thoughts?

How might an assisted-care facility or nursing home create a sense of home for the residents?

Typical Housing Arrangements

Relying on U.S. Census Bureau data we can get a general idea of the living arrangements of typical American adults. We should always be mindful, however, that such generalizations hide many individual differences, and that the housing market is fluid, changing with the economy and individual needs. For example, a look at the typical housing situation in the United States will not bring out the U.S. Census Bureau (2006a) finding that just over 1% of American households lack adequate plumbing and nearly 7% lack adequate heating. Regarding the fluidity of the market, just over 17% of Americans surveyed had moved in the past year. Another bit of useful information missing in a statistical snapshot is the reasons for such moves. In a study of households moving between urban and suburban locations, Pellegrini and Gibson (1998) found that most residents who left an urban area for a suburban area were parents with small children. Their primary reason for moving was to enroll their children in safer schools with higher quality academic programs. Those who moved from urban to suburban areas were more likely to be married, in their 30s, have at least a bachelor's degree, earn a reasonably high income, and have children younger than 5 years old. Those who moved from a suburb to a more urban area, on the other hand, were usually interested in the racial and cultural diversity an urban location offers, as well as staying close to family and friends. Generally, those who moved to urban areas from suburban locations were older than 50 years old and divorced.

Your Thoughts?

What might make an urban setting attractive to an adult older than 50 years old? What might be concerns or disadvantages?

While acknowledging the limitations of general statements, it is still useful to ask, "What is the typical American housing situation?" The American Housing Survey for the United States in 2005 (U.S. Census Bureau, 2006a) found that 78% of Americans live in what would be classified as an urban location, with most of those living in metropolitan suburbs. The remaining 22% live in rural areas. Of the nearly 125 million households surveyed, 75% were single-family structures while the other 25% were multi-unit structures, such as apartment buildings or condominiums. Thirty-one percent of the homes were being rented 69% were owner-occupied. The Census Bureau found that slightly more than 50% of the homes included a married couple, while 35% included children and 23% included an elderly individual. Approximately 15% of those surveyed were living on an income below the poverty line, while in contrast, approximately 28% owned homes valued at $200,000 or more. Most of the homes had two or three bedrooms, one or two bathrooms, and an outside area (a porch, deck, balcony, or patio). Approximately half of those surveyed had a separate dining room and about one-third had two or more living rooms or a recreation room.

Neighborhoods and Communities

Several trends have emerged from the study of personal interaction and level of satisfaction with our neighborhoods and communities. One consistent finding is that residents of rural areas report the highest levels of community satisfaction. By analyzing the data collected from 4,629 urban and 853 rural participants in the General Social Surveys (GSS), sampled from across the United States, Toth, Brown, and Xu (2002) found that while both rural and urban participants were generally satisfied with their communities, the rural participants reported the highest levels of satisfaction. In a similar study Prezza and Constantini (1998) interviewed Italian residents from a very small town and rural area of 1,700 residents, a small town of 21,000 residents, and a large city of 52,000 residents, and also found that the residents of the small town and rural area were the most satisfied.

Your Thoughts?

Would you predict an association between personality traits and a tendency toward place-centric or experience-centric attitudes? Why or why not?

The second trend, noted by Toth and his colleagues (2002) when analyzing the GSS data, is that rural residents generally have *place-centric* attitudes and expectations toward their communities while urban residents generally have *experience-centric* attitudes and expectations. Rural residents value the close geographic proximity of family members, friends, and neighbors. Prezza and Constantini (1998) found that rural residents, particularly mothers, were likely to be directly involved in local activities, organizations, school functions, and community meetings. The rural residents felt that as their community involvement increased so did their sense of community satisfaction and personal life satisfaction. Most believed that if they weren't satisfied with their communities then their personal life satisfaction would not be as high.

Your Thoughts?

What factors might keep an urban neighborhood from developing a place-centric view of community?

The experience-centric view of the urban residents leads to a different set of expectations. Toth and his colleagues found that urban residents defined communities by interpersonal relationships, regardless of geographic location or distance. Prezza and Constantini (1998) found that urban residents frequently traveled outside of their own neighborhood or geographic area for social activities. There were no expectations that neighbors would provide social support. In fact, when evaluating local areas urban residents focused not on other people but rather on the quality of services, such as health care facilities, schools, road and park maintenance, and other recreational services. Rather than finding community in place-centric situations, urban residents looked to gathering places for people with social similarities with little regard to geographic closeness.

Another trend noted is that community satisfaction involves not necessarily the size or location of the community but rather the way it functions. Even though residents of rural areas tend to report higher levels of community satisfaction (Pellegrini & Gibson, 1998), Leyden (2003) found that residents of *complete neighborhoods*, whether urban, suburban, or rural, were more likely to know and trust their neighbors, be socially and politically active, and demonstrate a stronger sense of community than those in *modern neighborhoods*. Studying neighborhoods in Galway, Ireland, Leyden defined complete neighborhoods as those with easily accessible sidewalks that connect all the primary facilities, thus encouraging residents to walk to the grocery store, post office, their children's schools, religious activities, doctors' offices, community events, and parks and recreational areas. Modern neighborhoods, in contrast, are designed to meet residents' needs at megastores and large shopping malls, which are usually connected by multilane highways and large parking lots. In modern neighborhoods it is essential that residents travel by car or public transportation as walking is dangerous and often prohibited by laws and by physical structures.

Your Thoughts?

Can you think of any advantages of the modern neighborhood over the complete neighborhood?

RESEARCH IN-DEPTH
Naturalistic Observation

One of the most difficult aspects of psychological research is to design studies in a way that encourages participants to be honest in their responses to questions. There are many reasons why participants change or withhold the truth, such as risk of embarrassment or potential problems if the information were made public. Imagine, for example, an adult who is afraid to be alone in the dark. If that should come up on a questionnaire the individual may deny that fear because it is embarrassing. As another example, consider a study of marital happiness that asks if the participants have ever had an extramarital affair. The participants who have had an affair may choose to withhold that information due to the potential problems that might arise if that information was given to their spouses.

One way to try to find out what people are actually doing is to engage in a field study. Researchers using this methodology will observe people in natural, public settings and record their behaviors. Imagine a researcher who wants to learn more about prejudice toward people with physical disabilities. If the researcher simply asks participants, "Do you engage in prejudicial behaviors toward people with physical disabilities?" it is highly likely that they will all respond "no," whether they actually engage in those behaviors or not. The researcher is likely to get more accurate results by observing the ways people respond to others with physical disabilities in a natural setting, such as a shopping mall or an amusement park.

Researchers from the Fund for Scientific Research and the Katholieke Universiteit (Catholic University) in Belgium used naturalistic observation to study the phenomenon of "basking-in-reflected-glory" (Boen et al., 2002). This occurs when people associate themselves with others who are successful, such as wearing the logo of a winning soccer team or displaying a picture of themselves and someone famous. To observe this in a natural setting, the researchers compared the political signs people placed in their yards prior to an election, and then checked again to see who still had their sign up the day after the election. The researchers first recorded the location of political signs in three distinct towns, specifically a university town, a provincial town, and a section of a large, industrial town. Five teams of observers recorded the addresses of all the residents who had a political sign in their window or on their lawn 2 days before a major election for members of parliament. At the end of the day they had recorded 462 addresses with signs supporting four different political parties.

To determine whether residents were basking-in-reflected-glory, the research teams returned the day after the election to see if residents of the winning parties were more likely to leave their signs up. The data revealed that those residents who supported winning parties did indeed leave more signs in their windows or on their lawns. Compared to those supporting the losing parties, supporters of the winning parties were basking-in-reflected-glory. The researchers also found that the residents who supported the party that won the most seats in parliament were most likely to have their signs out the day after the election. Residents who supported a party with a modest number of members elected were less likely to display signs; however, they did have more signs out than the residents supporting the party with the least number of members elected.

Using naturalistic observation the researchers were able to show that residents were basking-in-reflected-glory by continuing to associate themselves with the winning party. In addition to their primary findings, the researchers found anecdotal evidence to further support their conclusions. For example, the observers found that there were six new signs added since the election in support of the winning party. Also, the observers noticed that some of the residents kept their signs visible for over 2 weeks beyond the election (Boen et al., 2002). One of the advantages of naturalistic observation is that, rather than relying on participants to explain what they would do in a situation, the researchers can observe what people actually do. One of the disadvantages is that there is no control over a naturalistic setting. For example, when the researchers returned after the election to observe which signs were still displayed they found that 13 of the residences could not be checked because shutters blocked the windows where the posters had been displayed. Another disadvantage is that often there are no opportunities to ask participants why they engaged in such behavior. Did the residents supporting the winning party keep their signs up as a way of celebrating? Did they leave the signs up due to arrogant motives, possibly to show their superiority and to make those supporting the losing party feel bad? Did some of them just forget to take them down? Were the women, men, younger or older adults more likely to want the signs to remain up? These questions make it clear that researchers need to be careful in their interpretations of observed behaviors. Often it is the "why did you do that?" question that leads researchers to take what they have learned to naturalistic observation and apply that knowledge to new research involving questionnaires or interviews.

Having lived in rural, urban, complete, and modern neighborhoods I can see the value and challenges in each setting. I grew up in an urban setting in the fourth largest city in the United States. I enjoyed the options available in the general area if I (or my family) were willing to travel. As a young adult I could find just about any resources, activities, or gatherings of like-minded people I wanted. The lack of neighborly interaction didn't concern me in a modern neighborhood because I was a busy professional looking to excel in my career. At that time I didn't recognize the value of community activities or neighborhood organizations, and I didn't realize how keenly aware of potential crime and personal safety I had become. As my life changed I found myself, in my early 30s, living for the first time in a rural area. At first I noticed everything I missed about urban life, such as the availability and diversity in shopping, restaurants, resources, and facilities. Over time I came to appreciate the natural beauty of my new surroundings as well as the devotion of those long-time residents striving to make their community better. I realized the power of the local town council and school board, and the value of friends and neighbors who step in when social services are not available. Now I spend much of my time in a complete community where walking is the norm and many of the residents know one another. While it is true that it feels as if "everyone knows your personal business" in a small town, there is also a comforting sense of belonging and familiarity. As a small but cooperative group of residents we feel empowered and motivated to work toward transforming our little town into the community we want it to be.

Housing Options for Older Adults

Older adults are diverse in their abilities and resources, and this variation is reflected in their housing. The "young-old," often the newly retired, usually have good health, adequate resources, and upon retirement, a newfound freedom. There are also older adults who are not as well functioning as the young-old, showing some elderly qualities, but are still quite capable of independent living. With age and increased disability these independent older adults will most likely need more direct assistance and care. In this section we explore the migration of older adults through various stages of independence and assistance. This journey affects not only older adults but also their adult children and extended families, possibly involving physical, social, spiritual, and financial support.

Your Thoughts?

Do you think it is wise for those newly retired to move to a new location far from the friendships and social support they have developed? Why or why not?

Post-Retirement Migration Models. The young-old, the newly retired who have adequate health, energy, and material resources, frequently choose to move once they are no longer tied to a location due to employment. Based primarily on analysis of many years of U.S. Census Bureau data, three models of housing migration have emerged. One model, the *migration decision model*, emphasizes the decision to move once the things that keep adults in a certain area are overwhelmed by things that pull them toward relocation, particularly after retirement. For those with the means to move, the characteristics that tend to draw older adults are mild climates, lower taxes, a growing economy, and scenic (coastal or mountainous) areas generally near a metropolitan area (Longino & Bradley, 2006).

A second model, the *place identity migration model*, emphasizes attachment to a particular location, especially the location lived in prior to the current one. This model addresses those individuals who may live in one location but *home* is somewhere else, usually a place they left behind. In some cases it is the area in which they grew up or where many family members live.

The *life-course migration model* emphasizes how the characteristics that qualify as attractive features of a location change with age. Younger adults are more likely to move to an area that meets their desires in terms of educational and work opportunities and family needs. Litwak and Longino (1987) identified three primary moves for older adults, with the first coming right after retirement. Generally moving from a more urban to a less urban environment,

ON THE LEADING EDGE
Community Learning Centers

In January 2002 the No Child Left Behind Act put into place several incentives for businesses and community-based organizations to become partners with local public schools to create 21st Century Community Learning Centers (CCLCs). Part of the vision for CCLCs was to create centers that are open year-round with activities occurring all hours of the day and night. One example of a thriving CCLC is the Rosa Parks School in Portland, Oregon that provides space for the Boys and Girls Club after school (Butler, 2010). CCLCs are encouraged to have activities designed to meet the educational and social needs of community members of all ages and backgrounds. In order to qualify for the government program schools or school districts must create a partnership with at least one other organization to provide academic assistance and family support. Options for partnering organizations include youth development organizations, community centers, faith-based organizations, businesses, and colleges and universities.

In her 2004 work, Dawn Anderson-Butcher, Professor in the College of Social Work at The Ohio State University, found that CCLCs were providing academic assistance to students, such as tutoring, enhanced summer school and night courses, and expanded library hours. Some programs included homework clubs, career exploration, and job training workshops. A current example of this trend, the Mound Fort Junior High School in Ogden, Utah, serving as a CCLC, has offered student tutoring, mental health counseling, courses in English as a second language, and GED classes taught in Spanish in 2008. The center also provides child care during courses to make it easier for parents to attend (Butler, 2010). To increase community ownership, pride, and social cohesion, as well as to broaden their offerings, community members often share their talents by offering classes in areas such as quilting, tai chi, and photography. Dr. Anderson-Butcher sees great potential for the CCLCs to serve as effective centers of activity for students, family members, and the community. Her vision includes continuing education courses, family health clinics, and counseling and social work services. She views school-based social workers as the leaders in observing and documenting the needs of students, their families, and others in the communities, as well as facilitators in creating and implementing new programs. The schools of the past, which were totally focused on the children attending, are now becoming family and community centers that can bring as much enrichment to residents and parents as they do to the children and adolescents.

this first move often involves choosing the amenities that come in an environment that caters to new retirees (Litwak & Longino, 1987; Longino, 1990, 2001). Those who migrate to a new state, in contrast to those who do not move or move within their current state, tend to be younger retirees, married (rather than widowed), homeowners, and have higher education and income (Longino & Bradley, 2006). The top six states receiving the highest numbers of new residents older than age 60 during the last 40 years are Florida, California, Arizona, Texas, Pennsylvania, and New Jersey (Longino, 2001), though the percentages of those moving to Florida and California have declined (Longino & Bradley, 2006). There are also adults in this first move stage who prefer a cyclical migration to a different location for only part of the calendar year. For example, trends in the data show that adults living in the United States near the Canadian border are more likely to migrate seasonally to warmer temperatures during the winter months. Analysis of international migration reveals that most of those older adults are either from Canada and Mexico, or they are the parents of individuals from another country who have become U.S. citizens and are now ready to bring their parents over (Longino & Bradley, 2006).

Your Thoughts?

Is the area in which you currently live appealing to the newly retired? Why or why not?

The second move in the life-course model occurs when older adults experience moderate forms of trouble with everyday tasks due to aging or disease-related disability. In order to remain as independent as possible, the purpose of this second move is to get closer to resources, such as adult children or other relatives, public transportation services, and needed health care services. This second move, as well as the third one, is more likely to be to a metropolitan setting. The third move occurs when older adults are coping with chronic disability and health and dependency issues, thus it generally involves the transition to an assisted-care facility. In contrast to the first move in the life-course model, the third move is usually a local move (Litwak & Longino, 1987; Longino, 1990, 2001).

Aging in Place. The second and third moves in the life-course migration model signal the need for additional assistance and services, ranging from minimal adjustments, such as moving items around the house to avoid frequent trips up and down stairs to full around-the-clock personal care. These migration moves can be difficult on many levels, and it is in these steps that adult children may be most involved, trying to find the best solutions based on everyone's needs, desires, and financial resources. Many older adults would prefer to ***age in place***, meaning they would like to choose where they live and have services change within that setting as their personal needs change. Most would rather not make that third move in the migration model to a final location, even when increased levels of assistance or additional health care are required for daily living (Joint Center for Housing Studies [JCHS], 2001). This was evident in a 2005 survey of Medicare recipients 85 years and older that found 76% continued to live in traditional communities, and many wanted to remain in community settings. Among the others in the 2005 survey, 7% lived in some type of community housing with services and 17% lived in a long-term care facility (Federal Interagency Forum on Aging-Related Statistics, 2008). The Harvard University Joint Center for Housing Studies (2001) concluded after extensive research that four components are critical for successful aging in place. They are:

Your Thoughts?

How might bringing generations of different ages together increase the ability of older adults to age in place?

- Giving older adults choices regarding housing and health-care options in their community
- Flexible services within the community that can accommodate older adults' changing needs
- Individuals of different ages and generations living in the same community
- Efficient and monitored care so that assistance is not overdone or inadequate

Many older adults would prefer to age in place, staying rooted in their private home in a traditional community setting.

Aging in place presents many challenges depending on the resources in the area, such as the lack of public transportation in many rural areas. Successful aging in place also requires good communication and coordination of those providing housing assistance, social services, and medical services. Managing these challenges may fall on the shoulders of the adult children and extended family members of those aging in place.

To get a better sense of how this might work, imagine Jean, the 55-year-old daughter of Gladys who has dementia and fairly extensive arthritis. Gladys remained in her own home as long as Jean felt it was safe, but recently it has become obvious that Gladys can't be left alone. Now Gladys spends her evenings at Jean's, sleeping in a spare bedroom. Because Gladys doesn't always know where she is and gets restless at night, Jean keeps a baby monitor in Gladys's room so she knows when Gladys is up in the middle of the night. Jean wakes Gladys up early in the morning, helps her dress for the day, and gets her some breakfast and her various medications. When it is time for Jean to go to work she'll drop Gladys off at her 30-year-old niece's house where Gladys will spend the day with Tracy, her two young children, and her dog. Gladys seems nervous around the active children, but she loves to pet the dog. Tracy keeps up with Gladys's medical and dental appointments, physical therapy, prescription needs, and tries to get her out to see relatives once in a while. Jean keeps up with all of Gladys's finances, bills, and insurance papers. Gladys will spend most of her day watching television and petting the dog, occasionally shuffling around the house. At this point Gladys can't fully manage the restroom by herself, so Tracy frequently has to stop what she's doing to help. Gladys has a habit of moving things around the house, and Tracy's always finding odd things in the trash or the refrigerator. Just before the evening meal Jean will return to take Gladys to her house, prepare a meal, and settle in for the evening. All of this is intrusive but manageable until something interrupts the routine, such as when Gladys gets sick and is in the hospital, one of Tracy's children is ill, or Tracy or Jean simply need a vacation from caregiving.

Housing with Assistance and Services. Residential settings that offer ***assisted-living*** services can vary dramatically, making the term hard to define with precision. Part of the variation is due to the wide array of potential services required to accommodate individuals who need a minimum level of assistance to those who are just a step away from full-time care. Long-term care can include social, medical, and housing services that allow individuals to approximate their lifestyle prior to disability (Stone, 2006). For example, some older adults may need assistance with *instrumental activities of daily living (IADLs)*, such as managing household chores and grocery shopping, while others may need help with basic *activities of daily living (ADLs)*, such as dressing and eating. Another reason for the lack of precision is that each state in the United States has its own definitions and guidelines for assistance and public funding (Stone, 2006). Yet another complicating factor is the difficulty in separating daily living needs from health care needs (JCHS, 2001).

In terms of actual structures, assisted-living settings may include single-unit houses, condominiums, or apartments. As needed, residents are generally provided help with meals, housekeeping, transportation, social and recreational activities, extra security, and health care (American Association of Retired Persons [AARP], 2004). Residential group living can vary as well. Adult foster care facilities generally involve only a few full-time residents cared for in a home-like setting, whereas adult day care centers usually offer services on a per-hour basis. A typical, full-time board-and-care facility has 10 or more residents, and provides meals, 24-hour staff, housekeeping, and assistance with bathing, dressing, and medications (Stone, 2006). The use of nursing homes, providing around-the-clock professional medical care, is declining due partly to the increased assisted-living options and the declining rate of disability in older adults. Generally, those in nursing homes have the most

Your Thoughts?

Would you predict that a person with a place-centric view or an experience-centric view would have an easier transition to assisted living? Give reasons for your response.

severe disabilities (Rice & Fineman, 2004; Stone, 2006; Wahl, 2001). No matter which type of facility, the residents will likely feel better if it can be made to feel like home. Studies investigating the transition to full-time care have found that a feeling of *home* can develop when residents are given choices creating a sense of control, have outlets for self-expression, social involvement, and a comfortable routine (Wahl, 2001). Residents feel more at home when they have a comfortable yet stimulating place that takes on personal meaning (Scheidt & Windley, 2006).

One popular response to the desire for as much independence as possible, continuity in the transition to additional care when needed, and a sense of being at home is the creation of ***continuing care retirement communities*** (CCRCs). These are small communities or villages that provide structures for independent household living to full nursing home care. A campus may have a section of single-unit homes, an apartment complex, an assisted-care facility, and a hospital-like nursing home. Residents who join a CCRC can move from one type of facility to another, depending on their needs (AARP, 2004). The transition to a CCRC will be easier for those who can bring treasured items with them and continue many of their habits, such as engaging in their usual recreational, social, and religious activities (Wahl, 2001). Older adults are more likely to move into a CCRC they are familiar with in an area close to their former home, consistent with the third move in the life-course migration model (Litwak & Longino, 1987; Longino, 1990, 2001).

Your Thoughts?

How might a CCRC staff keep older adults engaged in the outside community? What community groups are likely to reach out to CCRC residents?

Section Summary

- One of the most important aspects of transforming a house into a home is the way we personalize the environment so that it becomes part of our identity.
- Home often serves as the comfortable place where individuals learn new roles, such as spouse or parent.
- As we move through young, middle, and late adulthood our home–self interactions change as our roles change.
- The American Housing Survey of 2005 finds that most Americans live in single-family structures they own in the metropolitan suburbs.
- It is important to remember that generalizations about housing, as with any topic, hide many individual differences, and may create a false sense that such information is static.
- Residents of rural areas often report higher community satisfaction, though their criteria for evaluation is different from that of urban residents.
- Residents of larger cities tend to evaluate community satisfaction on the quality of resources, and not personal life satisfaction or relationships with neighbors.
- It is common for adults to migrate after retirement to a more desirable location, usually a scenic place with mild climates and a better economy, though some return to a place they left behind.
- Eventually many older adults will need some type of assistance or services to remain functional, which is likely to prompt the move to another location and perhaps a residence with assisted-care services.
- Many adults would like to age in place, which is to choose where they want to live and have any needed assistance in that place.
- For those seeking or needing housing with assistance they may choose adult day care, adult foster care, residential homes, nursing homes, and continuing care retirement communities.
- Efforts are being made to view assisted living less like a nursing home and more like a traditional residence that feels like home.

Chapter Summary

Individuals make many decisions, such as choosing to be parents or to be childfree. They make decisions about living arrangements and possibly blending families. As individuals move into late adulthood they may transition through the roles of grandparent and great-grandparent, retired, and eventually elderly family member. Social environments, whether they are the personal family dwellings in traditional neighborhoods, assisted-care facilities, or the larger political and societal environment, can have a profound influence on personal growth and development. Here are some of the main points of the chapter:

- It is important to remember that in addition to biological pregnancy, an adult may become a parent through stepparenting or adoption.
- Many parents cite the happiness, love, and sense of purpose children bring as the greatest rewards of parenting, and cite the loss of freedom as the greatest cost.
- Parental satisfaction is greatly influenced by marital quality, particularly in families with stepparents.
- Increased role conflict is associated with decreased parental satisfaction.
- Childless individuals are those who want to have their own biological children but cannot, whereas childfree individuals are those who are voluntarily choosing not to have children.
- There seems to be little difference among childfree and parenting adults in terms of life satisfaction.
- Grandparents may take on many different roles, including those labeled as formal, fun seeker, surrogate parent, reservoir of family wisdom, distant figure, influence, supportive, passive, authority-oriented, and detached.
- The greatest rewards of grandparenting are the joys of sharing activities and watching grandchildren grow up while having the freedom to be involved only when desired.
- Much of the research on grandparenting difficulties has focused on the stresses of grandparents who are acting as surrogate parents and strained relationships with grandchildren following a divorce.
- Three models can be applied to the study of family role transitions: compensation model, life-course model, and cumulative disadvantage model.
- As adult children move into personal authority in the family system, they move through the caregiving trajectory of concern, urging, and action when providing support for aging parents.
- Siblings are often a source of advice and emotional support for older adults.
- The American Housing Survey of 2005 finds that most Americans live in single-family structures they own in the metropolitan suburbs.
- The abstract experience of home is related to the personalization and experiences we have in a physical structure that shapes our sense of identity.
- Rural residents generally report higher community satisfaction than urban residents.
- Rural residents tend to have place-centric attitudes and value the close geographic proximity of family and community activities.
- Urban residents tend to have experience-centric attitudes and tend to think of communities as coalescing around experiences or special interests rather than one geographic location.
- It is common for older adults to move following retirement, often to a more desirable climate or a place that feels more like home.
- Many adults want to age in place, meaning they want to choose where they live and have any needed assistance brought to that place.

- Assisted-living services range from basic activities of daily living, such as help dressing to assistance with instrumental activities of daily living, such as grocery shopping.
- Residential living centers range from adult day care services to continuing care retirement communities.

Key Terms

Infertility **(148)**
Open adoption **(148)**
Role conflict theory **(149)**
Validity **(150)**
Childless **(151)**
Childfree **(151)**
Surrogate parents **(154)**
Compensation model **(156)**
Life-course model **(156)**
Cumulative disadvantage model **(156)**
Personal authority in the family system **(157)**
Caregiving trajectory theory **(158)**
Age in place **(165)**
Assisted living **(166)**
Continuing care retirement communities (CCRC) **(167)**

Comprehension Questions

1. What are the most common reproductive problems for infertile men and women?
2. What do parents cite as the greatest rewards and costs of parenting?
3. Explain how marital satisfaction is related to parental satisfaction differently for parents raising their own biological children versus stepparents.
4. Explain the role conflict theory and give an example involving parenting.
5. What is the difference between childless and childfree?
6. Give examples of the contrasting roles grandparents may play in the lives of their grandchildren.
7. What do grandparents generally cite as the benefits of grandparenting?
8. Give several examples of the stresses faced by grandparents who are acting as surrogate parents.
9. Explain the differences between the compensation model, the life-course model, and the cumulative disadvantage model regarding family role transitions.
10. Explain what it means for an adult to gain personal authority in the family system.
11. Explain what happens during the concern, urging, and action stages of the caregiving trajectory theory.
12. How is one's sense of identity related to the concept of home?
13. What were the reasons found for households moving from urban to suburban areas, and from suburban to urban areas?
14. According to the American Housing Survey of 2005, what are the characteristics of the typical American housing situation?
15. What differences did researchers find in the attitudes and expectations of residents of rural/small town and urban areas regarding their communities?
16. Name and explain the differences between three models of older adult migration.
17. According to the Joint Center for Housing Studies, what are the four components needed for successful aging in place?
18. Describe and give examples of basic activities of daily living and instrumental activities of daily living.
19. What are continuing care retirement communities?

Answers for Common Sense: Myth or Reality?

1. Myth: Infertility problems are found more often in women than in men. (See Pathways to Parenting, page 148.)
2. Myth: In vitro fertilization is the most common treatment for infertility. (See Pathways to Parenting, page 148.)
3. Myth: None of the states in the United States will allow an openly gay couple to adopt a child. (See Pathways to Parenting, page 148.)
4. Reality: Most parents cite the love and affection children bring as the greatest rewards of parenting. (See Parental Satisfaction, page 149.)
5. Myth: Most parents cite the financial burden children bring as the greatest cost of parenting. (See Parental Satisfaction, page 149.)
6. Myth: One of the most influential factors in predicting parental satisfaction is the age of the parents. (See Parental Satisfaction, page 149.)
7. Reality: The number of American adults choosing not to be parents is rising. (See Choosing Not to Parent, page 151.)
8. Reality: Research shows that there are no differences in quality of life between adults with children and adults who are choosing not to have children. (See Choosing Not to Parent, page 152.)
9. Reality: In divorce situations it is more common for the maternal grandparents to get more involved with their children. (See Difficult Issues in Grandparenting, page 155.)
10. Myth: Within a family system an individual is generally at retirement age before being seen as an authority in the family. (See Shifting Status in the Family, page 157.)
11. Myth: Among adult siblings, brothers tend to have the closest relationships. (See Supportive Family Members, page 159.)
12. Reality: Residents who move from a suburban area to an urban area often do so for the racial diversity. (See Typical Housing Arrangements, page 160.)
13. Myth: In the United States more adults rent their homes rather than own them. (See Typical Housing Arrangements, page 160.)
14. Reality: Most Americans live in metropolitan suburbs. (See Typical Housing Arrangements, page 160.)
15. Reality: Nearly one-quarter of American households include an elderly individual. (See Typical Housing Arrangements, page 160.)
16. Myth: Urban residents are more likely to view communities as geographic locations than rural residents. (See Neighborhoods and Communities, page 161.)
17. Reality: New Jersey is one of the top six states in terms of destinations for adults over age 60 who are moving for their post-retirement years. (See Post-Retirement Migration Models, page 163.)
18. Myth: More than one-third of adults over age 85 live in nursing homes. (See Aging in Place, page 165.)

Suggested Readings

A Female Psychologist Reflects on Women Choosing Not to Have Children, 1916

Hollingworth, L. S. (1916). Social devices for impelling women to bear and rear children. *American Journal of Sociology, 22*, 19–29. Accessed at *Classics in the History of Psychology* (http://psychclassics.yorku.ca/topic.htm).

Family and Socialization Factors in Brazil

Dessen, M. A., & Torres, C. V. (2002). Family and socialization factors in Brazil: An overview. In W. J. Lonner, D. L. Dinnel, S. A. Hayes, & D. N. Sattler (Eds.), *Online readings in psychology and culture* (Unit 13, Chapter 2), (http://www.wwu.edu/~culture), Center for Cross-Cultural Research, Western Washington University, Bellingham, WA. Available at http://www.ac.wwu.edu/~culture/DennenTorres.htm.

Living Long and Well in the 21st Century

Published in November 2007 by the U.S. Department of Health and Human Services. Available at http://www.nia.nih.gov/AboutNIA/StrategicDirections/.

Aging in Place

Coordinating Housing and Health Care Provision for America's Growing Elderly Population, published by the Joint Center for Housing Studies of Harvard University and the Neighborhood Reinvestment Corporation in 2001. Available at http://www.jchs.harvard.edu/publications/seniors/lawler_w01-13.pdf.

Suggested Websites

Becoming a Parent

For any questions or concerns regarding infertility, see the Infertility section of Medline Plus at http://www.nlm.nih.gov/medlineplus/infertility.html for many helpful links. For questions regarding adoption, the National Adoption Information Clearinghouse provides valuable information and links to other sites at http://naic.acf.hhs.gov/pubs/f_start.cfm.

Parenting Questions

Parenting issues are covered extensively at the Medline Plus website for parenting, at http://www.nlm.nih.gov/medlineplus/parenting.html, and the U.S. Government's Parenting Directory at http://www.firstgov.gov/Topics/Parents.shtml.

Inspired to Volunteer?

Find out about many different volunteer opportunities in your area through volunteer.gov at http://www.volunteer.gov/.

Resources for Older Adults

Eldercare Locator is a service of the U.S. Administration on Aging that helps you find local resources at http://www.eldercare.gov/Eldercare/Public/Home.asp. Regarding housing in particular, the AARP website will get you started with pertinent information at http://www.aarp.org/families/housing_choices/.

CHAPTER

7 Education, Careers, and Retirement

Just as the pathway through relationship and family development has grown less linear and more cyclical, as with cycles of marriage and remarriage, so has the pathway through education, employment, and retirement. While many young adults will commit several years to full-time education or training before moving into their careers, it is likely that they will return to educational settings often. The number of older-than-traditional-aged students is growing on most college campuses as young and middle-aged adults look to improve their current career or switch to something different. Also growing in number are the individuals seeking training or employment after they retire from their primary employer. Often these retirees desire the extra income as well as the physical, mental, and social stimulation a work environment can provide.

The term *work* can refer to many different activities, from household chores to traditional away-from-home employment to at-home telecommuting. While fully acknowledging that many nonpay situations, such as raising children or caring for elderly parents, can be as meaningful and challenging as paid work (if not more so in some situations), this chapter is focused primarily on those who are gainfully employed or retired. Several topics are explored here, including factors involved in choosing a career and establishing job satisfaction, along with some of the primary areas of concern, such as the stress workers may bring home to their families. Other areas of concern include gender-related issues and ageism in the workplace. Technological advances are continually changing the way work is performed, and older adults in particular need to be able to keep up with the changes.

COMMON SENSE
Myth or Reality?

Mark each of the following items with either an M, if you think it is a myth, or an R, if you think the statement reflects reality. By paying close attention you can find all the answers in this chapter. If needed, the answers are also given at the end of the chapter.

1. _____ Approximately one-fifth of the students who begin college at a 4-year public institution will never complete their degree program.
2. _____ Researchers have found that student–parent relationships have little influence on traditional college students' academic success.
3. _____ A strong preoccupation with academic failure in college has been associated with higher grades.
4. _____ Data from the last decade indicate that more women than men are attending college.
5. _____ Older college students generally perform better academically than traditional-aged students.
6. _____ The most common education program for prison inmates is computer literacy.
7. _____ Over half of all American citizens cannot read beyond an eighth-grade level.
8. _____ Higher incomes have been associated with better cognitive functioning in old age.
9. _____ Government studies indicate that the average worker will have four different jobs between the ages of 18 and 34.
10. _____ The U.S. Department of Labor predicts that jobs involving health care services for older adults will show increases in wages and salaries over the next few years.
11. _____ Researchers have found that proficiency in technical skills is more likely to result in higher wages than proficiency in general cognitive abilities.
12. _____ The U.S. Census Bureau has determined that women have achieved equal pay for equal work when comparing women's and men's incomes.
13. _____ Research indicates that female nurses make more money than male nurses.
14. _____ Sexual harassment, according to the Equal Employment Opportunity Commission (EEOC), does not include incidents between same-sex individuals.
15. _____ Most research shows that with age the job performance of older workers declines.
16. _____ Older adults who volunteer live longer than those who do not.
17. _____ Age is a key factor for people in deciding when to retire.
18. _____ Employer-based retirement or pension programs have been a part of the American workforce since the late 1880s.
19. _____ In 2008 the average Social Security monthly benefit for a retired worker was just over $24,000 per year.
20. _____ In 2005 more than half of American employees had some type of IRA.
21. _____ Most women find that widowhood results in a significant loss of income.
22. _____ Medicare is used primarily for inpatient hospital costs.
23. _____ Social Security, Medicare, and Medicaid are insurances that cover only older adults.
24. _____ Data from 2008 show that Medicare, Medicaid, private insurance, and other federal and state programs usually cover the costs of older adults in residential nursing home facilities.
25. _____ Older adults seldom vote as a unified group on age-related political issues.

Just as the term *work* can refer to many different tasks and situations, the term *retirement* can also refer to many diverse situations. It was once the case that retirement came only when an individual was simply too old or physically unable to do meaningful work. With increased longevity, the need to stay active, and the need to finance health care and possibly assisted living, many older adults who wear the label *retiree* are still very active. Some retirees will keep themselves busy with hobbies and travel, while others may become child care providers for grandchildren or volunteers in their community. Some people will retire from one employer and begin work for another. It is common to see retirees work in part-time jobs, seasonal employment, or start their own business. As this chapter deals with financial matters we end by exploring the reality of financing retirement and associated health care needs.

Before We Get Started . . .

One day at work I received some very wise counsel that I want to pass along. On this particular day it seemed that everything was going wrong. Not only that, I had what felt like a mountain of work to do in a very short time. I was complaining about this to one of my colleagues, and he asked, "What would be the perfect week for you?" I found that question surprisingly hard to answer. It was much easier to tell him all the things I did not like about my current situation. I took his question to heart, and eventually created a vision of my perfect work week. Over time I have been careful to make choices that have moved me closer to my ideal work situation.

Now, I would like to challenge you to consider what would be a perfect week *for you* at work. If you could have any work situation you desired, what would you choose? Working:

- with older adults
- with adults of all ages
- with adolescents
- with children
- with infants
- with animals
- with numbers
- with data and information
- with objects or merchandise
- with computers
- with large machines
- with precise instruments
- in a laboratory
- at night
- on weekends
- in a setting that requires local travel
- in a setting that requires cross-country travel
- at home
- outdoors
- in an office setting
- in a hospital setting
- in an educational setting
- in a military setting
- in a religious setting
- in a large city
- in the suburbs
- in a rural setting
- close to home
- an 8-to-5, Monday to Friday schedule
- in a setting that requires international travel
- in a setting that is competitive
- in a position that is routine and predictable
- in a position that has a lot of variety

You may think of other characteristics that are not listed here, and by all means, add them to your list. Rather than thinking of what you would like to *be*, in terms of titles or positions, it is useful to think about what you want to *do*. How would you like to spend your work-related time and energy? Is your current career choice compatible with your vision of enjoyable work?

Education Across Adulthood

Your Thoughts?

Do you think in-person courses are generally better, worse, or just different from media-based courses? Give reasons to support your response.

Educational opportunities for adults of all ages are taking many different forms. In addition to traditional college classes held on campuses during the 8:00 A.M. to 5:00 P.M. work week, some colleges and universities offer evening and weekend classes as well as courses taught via television, podcasts, DVDs, and website-based interactive software. There are part-time residential programs and distance education for those who can't make it to a campus routinely. On-site courses are gaining popularity as employers are continually challenged to keep their employees up-to-date. Part of the push to provide many types of learning opportunities comes from the desire to meet the needs of the increasingly diverse population seeking more education. Institutions of higher education now serve those seeking a first career as well as those who want to change careers. Community colleges are serving their area residents of all ages and situations not only by providing academic courses, but also by providing services such as child care and life-skills courses. Educational opportunities are also increasing for students whose first language is not English. The variety in the types of educational opportunities available and among students' circumstances is the focus of this section.

Traditional College Students

> **Your Thoughts?**
>
> How do the stresses of traditional college freshmen differ from traditional college seniors?

> **Your Thoughts?**
>
> What might be some of the most frequent reasons why students never complete their college education?

The National Center for Education Statistics (NCES, 2002) defines traditional college students are those who have a high school diploma, began full-time college directly after high school, depend on parents, grants, and loans for financial support, and who are employed only part time or only in the summer. These students are immersed in the college experience, usually living on campus or very near it, and are not married or acting as parents themselves. These students are often called ***traditional college students***, primarily because of their age and their full-time, on-campus status. The three most common areas of stress for these students are social, financial, and academic (Skowron, Wester, & Azen, 2004). Among the greatest areas of interest and concern for those working with traditional college students is the academic adjustment to college-level work and eventual academic success. The college experience is designed to be challenging academically, and one of the unfortunate realities of college life is that not everyone will be academically successful, at least in their early attempts at completing a degree. The American Council on Education (ACE, 2003) found that of the students who begin their college experience at a 4-year public institution, approximately 51% will transfer to another institution or leave college coursework for a period of time. Overall, the ACE estimates that approximately 21% of those who begin college at a 4-year institution will never complete their degree program.

Numerous factors have been found to influence academic success, including supportive parental relationships (Holahan, Valentiner, & Moos, 1994; Strage & Brandt, 1999) and successful social adjustment to college life (Paul & Brier, 2001; Woosley, 2003). Strage (2000) found that rapport with instructors and peers was also related to college adjustment and academic success. She was particularly interested in the ways students of different ethnic backgrounds performed in college. Her investigation revealed that the way academic adjustment and success are measured influences the conclusions drawn from the data. For example, she found that based on grade points the white students excelled beyond Hispanic and Southeast-Asian Americans. However, the Hispanic students excelled in persistence, task involvement, and confidence, even though their grades were not as high. The Hispanic students were focused on "mastery" of the material more so than grades.

Perry, Hladkyi, Pekrun, and Pelletier (2001) explored academic adjustment with 234 undergraduate students by measuring levels of perceived academic control and failure preoccupation. Students with high levels of perceived academic control put more effort into their studies, as compared to those with low academic control, primarily because they believed that they could influence their grades by the amount of effort or work they put into studying and completing assignments. Those high in academic control monitored their behaviors in terms of what helped them get better grades and what did not, and made appropriate adjustments. In comparing levels of failure preoccupation, those with high levels took more notes and often obtained better grades than those who were lower in failure preoccupation. Perry and his colleagues put the participants into one of four groups, as described in Table 7.1, based on each student's perceived level of academic control and failure preoccupation. When comparing the grade points and other indicators of academic achievement, the researchers found that students in the high academic control/high failure preoccupation group consistently outperformed the other three groups. The reasoning that effort makes the difference, combined

TABLE 7.1 ***Research Groups Designed by Perry et al. (2001)***

Characteristics	*Description*
High Academic Control/High Failure Preoccupation	I can basically control my grades through effort and hard work, and I need to give it all the effort I can because I could fail just like anyone else.
High Academic Control/Low Failure Preoccupation	I can basically control my grades through effort and hard work, and as long as I do my best I do not need to worry about failing.
Low Academic Control/High Failure Preoccupation	I cannot control my grades because I do not control the difficulty of the tests, the course, or the professor, which worries me because I could fail the course and not be able to do anything about it.
Low Academic Control/Low Failure Preoccupation	I cannot control my grades because I do not control the difficulty of the tests, the course, or the professor, but I doubt that those things would be so bad that I would fail the course.

Your Thoughts?

How might a student's sense of academic control been shaped by parents and teachers prior to college?

with the belief that failure is a possibility if enough effort is not applied, creates the motivation needed to produce high grades (Perry et al., 2001). Similar studies have also found that students with a greater sense of academic control set higher goals (Boulter, 2002) and viewed academic struggles as challenges rather than threats (Chemers, Hu, & Garcia, 2001). Adjustment to the college experience for students following the traditional path can be challenging. Those who are optimistic and believe they are competent are more likely to find academic success (Boulter, 2002; Chemers, Hu, & Garcia, 2001).

Adult Students

Historians often point to World Wars I and II as the time when the academic world became interested in adult education. Psychologists and educators were called upon to create aptitude tests that could quickly determine a soldier's strengths and determine what type of work or placement would be best. This drew attention to both intelligence testing and adult learning. After World War II many soldiers took advantage of the financial incentives included in the GI Bill that allowed them to enter colleges and other postsecondary schools (Smith & Pourchot, 1998).

Over the years many labels have been used to distinguish these nontypical students from traditional college students. They have been called *nontraditional students* by those who see them as operating outside the norm for college students, *mature students* in many European settings (Murphy & Roopchand, 2003), and *adult learners* by the National Academic Advising Association (Skorupa, 2002) in the United States. Unfortunately, problems can be found with all of those terms. Dividing students into traditional and nontraditional is too reminiscent of the terms *normal* and *abnormal*. At the same time, *mature students* may imply that the others are immature, and *adult learners* may imply that others are not adults, or they are adults who are not learning. Depending on the criteria used to determine traditional and nontraditional status, it has been estimated that as many as two-thirds of all college students are nontraditional (NCES, 2002). The lack of consistency in the use of labels and the defining criteria causes problems when comparing data and research results. Though none of the terms are ideal, for clarity this text uses the terms *traditional college students* and ***adult students*** when the distinctions are important.

Your Thoughts?

What historical events or national trends have likely contributed to the increase in older students attending or returning to college?

The number of adult students has been increasing over the last 30 years. The National Center for Education Statistics (2002) has noted several trends, specifically that more students are enrolling on a part-time basis, entering 2-year colleges, and more women are enrolling than men. They also found that the number of older college students has risen from 28% of the college population in 1970 to 39% in 2002. This trend is occurring in other countries as well. For example, in the United Kingdom the government expects 50% of all citizens over 30 years old to have some involvement in higher education (Murphy & Roopchand, 2003).

A great deal of the current research on adult students has focused on the ways their needs and personal situations are different from traditional college students. Often adult students want to be recognized for their life experiences. It may be difficult to listen to a lecture on something they have personally experienced and not share their story. They often begin or return to higher education with a strong desire to apply what they are learning immediately to their current life or work situation, rather than using it in the future after graduation. In addition, adult students often highly value the classroom experience because it is their primary, and in some cases only, contact with college life (Donaldson, 1999). In a national survey of more than 4,600 college students, Lundberg (2003) found that traditional college students reported engaging in more peer-to-peer teaching and higher quality peer relationships outside of the classroom whereas the adult students reported engaging in more discussions with peers in-class and higher quality relationships with faculty. A similar study involving more than 65,000 college students also found that adult students reported less involvement in campus activities (Graham & Donaldson, 1999). Though less involved, Graham and Donaldson (1999) found that adult students felt they were making more progress than traditional college students did, particularly in areas such as writing and problem solving. Adult students often perform better overall than traditional college students. They are more likely to reorganize information, integrate it with what they already know, and elaborate on it as needed (all of which are great memory enhancers and study techniques). Adult students are also more likely to design their own study strategy to process difficult information.

Your Thoughts?

What might contribute to the findings that adult students report higher quality relationships with faculty?

Another obvious and tremendous difference between traditional and adult students is found in their lifestyles. Not to diminish the very real demands and stresses of traditional college life, outside of the classroom adult students may be involved in full-time work, family life, parenting, household maintenance, and commuting issues. In some cases, when dealing with tensions at work, divorce situations, single parenting, illnesses, inadequate housing, or an unreliable vehicle, it may be difficult for an adult student to give the needed attention and energy to college classwork (Alford, 2000). Researchers have found the stresses involved in balancing school, work, and home demands can be lessened when adult students feel satisfied with their academic program, and when they feel supported by their family, coworkers, and classmates (Kirby, Biever, Martinez, & Gomez, 2004).

Your Thoughts?

Do you think this shift in education is more likely a result of the technology revolution or a changing economy in the United States? Give reasons to support your response.

Lifelong and Life-Wide Learning

Lifelong and *life-wide learning* are broad terms that may refer to a wide range of educational settings and topics. Although these areas may overlap, generally ***lifelong learning*** is focused on work-related topics whereas ***life-wide learning*** encompasses non-employment-related topics. The demands of global, information-based economies have prompted governments, educational institutions, and industries to join the lifelong learning movement in order to maintain a competitive edge. Universities and colleges are responding with "cradle to grave" programs, research programs focused on adult students, and new journals, such as the *International Journal of Lifelong Education*.

In some professions the topic of lifelong learning is closely associated with lifelong *earning*. Many professional associations require their members to pursue coursework and continuing education units (CEUs), and to attend in-house programs, conferences, and workshops.

ON THE LEADING EDGE
Computer Counseling

Social scientists, such as industrial/organizational psychologists, human resource managers, educators, career counselors, and others who monitor changes in the workforce, need a way to organize the many occupations available in the United States, especially the newly created careers. One option has been the Dictionary of Occupational Titles sponsored by the Department of Labor. A more recent index, also sponsored by the Department of Labor, is the Occupational Information Network (O*NET, http://online.onetcenter.org/) which provides a wide range of details for approximately 1,000 distinct occupations. Each occupation is rated in 52 areas, such as "worker characteristics," which contains information regarding workers' abilities, interests, work values, and work styles. Some examples of the types of occupations listed are:

- business and financial operations occupations
- education, training, and library occupations
- food preparation and service-related occupations
- life, physical, and social science occupations
- protective services occupations
- transportation and material-moving occupations

Within each of those categories there are many specific jobs, such as biologist, shipping clerk, physician assistant, and electrician. Examples of the types of characteristics associated with each occupation are verbal abilities, mathematical abilities, attention span, psychomotor and sensory skills, and physical abilities.

Researchers from the Department of Psychology at Michigan State University and consultants from the Career Vision/Ball Foundation recently explored the ways a career counselor might use the O*NET information to match clients' characteristics to those assigned to particular occupations. The researchers were primarily interested in matching abilities, such as level of vocabulary, memory skills, and writing speed. By assessing a client's characteristics, and then finding a match to worker characteristics provided in the O*NET, career counselors would have a much greater chance of achieving a good "person–occupation fit." Previous research has shown that when individuals are well matched to their occupation there are positive outcomes for both the employee and the employer. The researchers recruited 219 adults who were seeking career advice in order to begin their study of the matching process. After assessing each client's strengths the information was entered into the databases, which produced a number reflecting the level of person–occupation fit. The career advisors and the clients found the information useful and informative. It is likely that such databases will, in the future, allow many educational and vocational counselors to not only find the best person–occupation fits for their clients, but also be able to introduce their clients to satisfying occupations that the clients were unaware of (Converse, Oswald, Gillespie, Field, & Bizot, 2004).

In the health care field, for example, the topic of lifelong learning has become "one of the most frequently discussed concepts in professional education" (Hojat et al., 2003, p. 436). A study of physicians, ranging in age from 29 to 82 years old, found the most important reason for lifelong education was the need to remain up-to-date in order to best advise their patients. The second most important reason given was the many benefits that come from remaining active in professional conferences. The physicians also expressed their desire to keep up with new information, maintain their technological skills, and engage in the understanding and resolving of difficult medical issues (Hojat et al., 2003). Of course, physicians are not the only professionals expected to stay current in their field. In order for individuals in almost any industry to remain competitive in the global marketplace they must continually keep up with the latest technology and most current information (Glastra, Hake, & Schedler, 2004; Tuijman, 2003).

Your Thoughts?

Can you think of anything negative or troublesome regarding this move toward life-wide education?

Life-wide learning programs, which are generally focused on topics outside of paid employment, may be offered by colleges or universities, community centers, health clinics and hospitals, local libraries, religious communities, or even bookstores and coffee shops (Tuijman, 2003). Life-wide programs focus on a vast array of topics, such as hobbies, leisure and recreational activities, parenting and family issues, basic education, and health concerns. In a survey of community college offerings, Johanyak (2004) found many life-wide programs focused on age-related and developmental topics such as childbirth preparation, child care for new parents, and supplemental programs for school-age children. Programs were available for older adults as well, emphasizing exercise, fitness, nutrition, and health education. Older adults are seeking life-wide programs for social and cognitive stimulation (Kim & Merriam, 2004; Laanan, 2003) and to learn ways to adjust to the challenges of aging while remaining independent as long as possible (Ballard & Morris, 2003; Mehrotra, 2003).

The popularity of lifelong and life-wide education has expanded both the range of topics in the domain of education and the notion of where such learning can take place. For example, General Education Development (GED) classes, vocational training, college courses, and literacy tutoring are among the most popular life-wide learning programs offered to prison inmates. Educational training has been found to improve the psychological well-being of inmates and reduce the likelihood of returning to prison later. In fact, educational achievements are better predictors of recidivism than work training (Foley & Gao, 2004).

Another expanding area of lifelong and life-wide education is focused on types of adult ***illiteracy***. The National Assessment of Adult Literacy (NAAL, 2004), sponsored by the U.S. Department of Education, defined literacy as "using printed and written information to function in society, to achieve one's goals, and to develop one's knowledge and potential." Estimates are that nearly one-fourth of the adults in the United States are functioning well below this literacy standard, with more than half of the American adult population unable to ready beyond an eighth-grade level (National Institute for Literacy [NILF], 2004; Roman, 2004). While some of these individuals need assistance with English as a second language (ESL), this is not reflective of the majority of the adults with literacy issues. Many of these adults never completed high school.

Your Thoughts?

What general, societal, and personal factors may have contributed to this high illiteracy rate?

In addition to general reading and comprehension levels, those in medical fields are concerned about the health literacy of their patients. Studies have found that many people have trouble understanding general medical information, as well as more specific items such as consent forms for procedures, prescription instructions, and recovery/care instructions. It is estimated that the health care costs of health-illiterate patients are 50% higher due to mistakes and misunderstandings. One action medical professionals are encouraged to take is to provide health care information at a sixth-grade level and to provide as many pictures as possible (Erlen, 2004; Kohn, Henderson, & Walton-Brooks, 2003). There are similar concerns among professionals regarding financial literacy. Many employees do not understand the principles or vocabulary related to their investing options, creating many mismanaged accounts vulnerable to catastrophe (Schulz & Borowski, 2006).

Your Thoughts?

While there are benefits to providing patient information written at a sixth-grade level, what might be the costs?

Section Summary

- In this information age it is clear that educational needs continue throughout adulthood, and that these needs vary based on the situations of the learners involved.
- Traditional college students—those who attend college right out of high school as a full-time student, single with no children, unemployed, and living on campus—must deal with social, financial, and academic stresses.
- Academic adjustment and achievement for traditional college students has been linked to parental support, supportive friends, a sense of personal academic control, and a fear of failure.
- Estimates are that as many as two-thirds of all college students are adult students who do not fit the profile of the traditional college student.
- Adult students need the support of those close to them in order to cope with the demands related to college, work, family, parenting, household issues, and other stressors that come along.

- Lifelong and life-wide learning, often occurring outside of a traditional college lecture hall, cover a vast array of situations and topics, including professionals who want to remain up-to-date in their field, community members seeking help with family or parenting issues, and adults seeking help learning English as a second language.

Jobs and Careers

Understanding the role of work in the lives of adults is important for many reasons, not the least of which is its impact on almost every other facet of life. Consider that for those who sleep 8 hours a night, work 40 hours across a 5-day work week, and spend one hour traveling to and from work each day, 40% of their waking hours are spent on work. It is likely that a fair amount of the remaining 60% of their waking hours are spent thinking about work-related issues. Much like love relationships, the pervasiveness of work in many adults' lives requires developmental psychologists to give work situations a great deal of attention. This section focuses on jobs and careers as they relate to well-being and personal satisfaction, as well as work-related difficulties and areas of work-related stress.

Income, Socioeconomic Status, and Successful Aging

When I ask my college students, "Why do people work?" the first and most obvious response is "to make money." This provides another reason for developmental psychologists to consider the influence of work in adults' lives: Income and its related characteristics have been found to influence long-term physical and mental health. For example, income is the strongest predictor of subjective well-being among young and middle-aged adults, and is the second strongest predictor behind health issues for older adults (George, 2006). While those findings do not prove cause-and-effect, they do indicate a strong relationship between income and well-being. Higher incomes have been credited with the overall improvement in women's health over the last several decades.

Your Thoughts?

What opportunities might a higher income provide that could lead to better cognitive functioning in late adulthood?

Recently Schnittker (2007) analyzed data from the General Social Survey collected from 1974 to 2004 and concluded that improvements in women's health during that time were related to the corresponding improvements in educational and income opportunities for women. Higher incomes have even been associated with healthier cognitive functioning in late adulthood (Rabbitt, 2002).

Often when analyzing the influence of income researchers will broaden their study to focus on ***socioeconomic status*** (SES), which is generally based on educational attainment, occupational status, and income (Antonucci, 2001). While SES has become a standard characteristic in many social science studies this summary variable does hide some important individual differences. For example, someone might have a high income but little social status, such as an executive in a disliked corporation or a currently-out-of-favor politician. On the other hand, someone might have very high social status but little income, such as a beloved community or religious leader. Measuring SES in terms of older adults also presents some problems. Educational attainment was not emphasized or as available when the current elderly were young adults. In addition, it may be hard to determine occupational status for jobs that have lost status over the decades or simply no longer exist. Finally, regarding income, the current elderly may live on much less income than they did earlier in their adult lives (Antonucci, 2001; Berkman, 1988). That being said, SES is a common research variable frequently applied to all age groups.

Your Thoughts?

What factors might cause the association between SES and self-esteem to weaken after retirement?

As a measure of our working life, SES has been associated with numerous psychological and physical signs of successful aging. For example, a recent meta-analysis of more than 400 studies found that higher SES is related to healthier self-esteem in young adulthood and

Data indicates that dramatic improvements in women's physical health can be linked to their movement in professional roles and higher SES.

even more strongly related for middle-aged adults (Twenge & Campbell, 2002) before decreasing in association after retirement.

Higher SES has also been related to better physical health. When adults have a stronger educational background, a job that allows them more personal control over their time and pays better wages, they usually have more resources to devote to maintaining good health. In a recent review of adults with diabetes, for example, those with higher SES were able to purchase better foods, afford gym fees and other costs associated with exercise, and take the time away from work for medical concerns (Johnson & Drueger, 2005). Income and SES have been associated with well-being, self-esteem, cognitive functioning, and overall health and management of health problems, all of which play a role in successful aging.

Changing Nature of Work

As demonstrated in the older theories of career development, it was once the case that a successful work trajectory was a linear path through predictable stages. In the middle and late 20th century many Americans expected to work for only one or two employers for their entire careers. At that time loyalty was thought to be the key to success, demonstrated by promotions and salary increases. Such an attachment often fostered a personal sense of identity with the organization (Sullivan, 1999). It was anticipated that individuals would spend their 20s choosing a career, and once settled in their 30s, were well established and ready for high-level authority and responsibility (Thomas & Kuh, 1982). This same path is described in the stage theory of career development proposed by Super in the late 1950s. This very popular model details four career stages. The first stage is *exploration*, which involves educational training and opportunities to survey career options. The second stage is the time of *establishment* where one becomes employed, builds a reputation, and advances in the organization. *Maintenance*, the third stage, reflects the middle-aged employee who is working to maintain expertise and search for new innovations. The final stage, *disengagement*, reflects preparation for retirement and the end of meaningful work (Sullivan, 1999; Super, Osborne, Walsh, Brown, & Niles, 1992).

The work experience of many Americans in the 21st century is quite different from this earlier structure. In order to compete in the global economy employers must respond quickly to changing technologies, demands, and markets (Moen & Spencer, 2006), changing the nature of work and the lifestyle of employees. Data suggests that most Americans will change jobs every 4½ years (Sullivan, 1999), and the average person will hold nine different jobs between the ages of 18 and 34 years old (U.S. Department of Labor [DOL], 2000). This ebb and flow of bringing in and releasing employees as needed has prompted workers to feel personally independent and less loyal to employers. Rather than being directed through their careers by leaders in a company or organization, many current workers are self-managed, taking responsibility for their own career and financial planning. Employees are focused less on titles and promotions and more on personal training (lifelong learning) and personal marketability (Sullivan, 1999).

Your Thoughts?

When you consider these changes, what strikes you as positive and healthy? What might be negative and unsettling?

Similar to the life cycles mentioned in other chapters, such as marriage–divorce–remarriage, or child care–empty nest–grandchild care, theories of work are moving toward career recycling or career renewal. While acknowledging that the old theories of the late 20th century are outdated, new theories have not kept pace with the rapidly changing nature of work. Currently the focus is on cycles of novice-to-mastery as each wave of new technology brings even more change (Sullivan, 1999). Those who are continuing Super's work have moved away from terms such as *career development* or *career maturity* to focus on *career adaptability* across adulthood (Super et al., 1992).

Person/Employment Fit

As the American workplace adjusts to a new paradigm it is beneficial for potential employees to consider their own skills, needs, and personality and how well those characteristics will fit in available work environments (Super et al., 1992). Based on current observations, the U.S. Department of Labor (2000) predicts that most jobs in the future with above-average earnings will require substantial training, and many will require a bachelor's degree. Looking beyond the year 2010, the DOL (2004) predicts that the industries with the fastest wage and salary growth will be in five areas:

- Computer-related areas, such as software publishers, computer systems design, Internet services, and data processing
- Management, scientific, and technical consulting services
- Employment services
- Health care services, rehabilitation services, and community care facilities for older adults
- Child day care services

Your Thoughts?

Would you advise colleges to develop majors in all these areas? Why, why not, or under what circumstances?

Recognizing the changing nature of work, how might an adult prepare to excel in the American and global workforce? While it makes good sense to focus on a college major or area of study, researchers have found that developing only one or two skills may not be the best strategy for success. Several large studies have indicated that general mental or cognitive abilities are among the best predictors of job success and earning potential, even more so than specific technical or physical skills. Based on their analysis of several large databases containing information on more than 1,000 jobs, Rotundo and Sackett (2004) recommend that individuals

ON THE LEADING EDGE
Workplace Deviance

Researchers from the Universities of Iowa, Nebraska, and New Orleans, and The Gallup Organization, are exploring the role of personality and attitudes toward work environments in the occurrence of workplace deviance. The term *workplace deviance* refers to the voluntary violation of a workplace rule or norm that potentially has serious consequences to the employer or employees. Workplace deviance includes behaviors such as deliberate rudeness, slacking off or withholding effort, sabotaging processes, withholding key information, and stealing. Traditional wisdom in this area has been that most employees view employment as an exchange or an agreed-upon bargain: I give you effort and loyalty and you give me benefits (pay, vacation time, etc.) and fair treatment. When that bargain is not maintained and employees feel they do not receive adequate benefits and/or fair treatment, they are less likely to give effort and loyalty and more likely to engage in workplace deviance. While the researchers believe this point of view is common, they also believe that it is influenced by personality traits.

In one particular study the research team involved 853 participants who were store managers, assistant managers, nonmanagement employees, sales and customer service workers, and clerical workers from several different companies (Colbert, Mount, Harter, Witt, & Barrick, 2004). Analysis of data from several questionnaires indicated that there was a tendency for employees to engage in workplace deviance, particularly withholding effort, when they held negative perceptions regarding their work environment. They also found that workplace deviance was more likely in situations where the employees felt little organizational support, particularly in terms of helpful resources. However, when the researchers considered personality traits, they found that employees who are high in conscientiousness or agreeableness did not engage in workplace deviance even when holding negative views about their employment situation. Conscientious workers are achievement oriented and dependable, while those high in agreeableness are kind and nurturing. The strongest relationship between negative perceptions of the work environment and withholding effort was found for employees who are low in emotional stability which is reflected in the neuroticism factor. Those workers are moody and anxious, while those high in emotional stability are calm, easygoing, and relaxed. The personality traits of extraversion and openness to experience were not related to workplace deviance.

A more recent study further explored these personality differences. Stephanie Hastings and Thomas O'Neill (2009) of the Social Science Centre at the University of Western Ontario found that it was important to consider the subcategories of the five personality factors for a clearer understanding. They found that the anger component of the neuroticism factor was significantly predictive of workplace deviance.

Based on these findings and others, one preventive measure regarding workplace deviance is for employers to improve employees' perceptions of their work environment and level of support received from the company or institution. Another suggestion is to include personality measures as a part of the application process, with the goal of hiring employees who are higher in conscientiousness, agreeableness, and emotional stability for particular positions. Finally, employers may want to initiate programs for employees with anger management issues (Hastings & O'Neill, 2009) as well as add programs that raise their awareness of the traits of conscientiousness, agreeableness, and emotional stability, and encourage these traits through rewards programs (Colbert et al., 2004).

Your Thoughts?

Would you support a college curriculum that removed many opportunities for electives in order to require courses in these areas? Why, why not, or under what circumstances?

training for high-wage positions focus on a wide range of skills, such as mathematics, logic, writing, reading comprehension, critical thinking, and presentation skills. These findings are consistent with a meta-analysis involving 89 international studies, which found that individuals with better cognitive skills were more successful, due primarily to their ability to manage high levels of job complexity (Salgado et al., 2003). Realizing that the nature of work is changing, to create the best person/employment fit it is advantageous to develop broad skills that will transfer to new settings as the market changes.

While staying up-to-date on the trends in employment is important, we should also consider the "person" part of the person/employment fit. The notion of matching personality traits with particular areas of employment was made popular by John Holland, who developed a theory of job–personality fit in the late 1950s (Furnham, 2001). His theory, which still serves as the basis for numerous career-orientation questionnaires, involves six different personality themes: Realistic, Investigative, Artistic, Social, Enterprising, and

Conventional. Individuals in the *realistic* category generally prefer working outdoors, such as a landscaper or farmer. They usually work with machines or engage in manual activities, preferring to work with objects rather than people. Many carpenters and those who build large-scale items would fit in the realistic category. Those preferring an *investigative* theme are curious about the natural world, and prefer a scientific, logical method to their exploration. These interests and skills are needed for a great deal of medical research and practice, as well as work in other sciences. The *artistic* personality is focused on self-expression, beauty, and creativity, as shown through materials and ideas. While we may think of the more traditional arts, such as sculpture or painting, this category may also include writers, musicians, and interior and fashion designers. Both the investigative and artistic themes are more focused on ideas, concepts, and hypotheses, rather than physical materials or machinery, facts or data.

Your Thoughts?

While it is ideal to match personality and career characteristics, what might be the detrimental effects of a great mismatch between personality and career characteristics?

Individuals with a *social* theme prefer interacting with people in a nurturing and caring way, while valuing service, fairness, and understanding. Some of the most fitting areas of work for the social personality are counseling and social work. Whereas individuals with a social theme are focused on human services, the *enterprising* theme is focused on initiative, persuasion, social responsibility, and social status. The enterprising personality would do well in a business setting as well as positions that rely heavily on persuasion, such as some areas of law and politics. The final theme, the *conventional* personality, is for those who work well with detailed tasks and thrive in a structured environment. Work that requires precise attention to details, procedures, and information, such as some areas of the insurance industry, banking, and law, would suit the conventional personality well. Both the enterprising and conventional themes include individuals who are more focused on details and data. It is important to note that individuals may find that their interests fit well in one of Holland's six themes, or that their work personality is a blending of several themes (Jones, 1995; Prediger, Swaney, & Mau, 1993).

Person/employment fit includes not only matching personality types and skills with available employment positions, but also the goal of finding a position within a career field that an employee will be satisfied with. Reflecting common findings, a study of health care professionals found that career satisfaction and desire to stay with a particular employer were primarily influenced by:

- valued input on key decisions
- recognition of accomplishments
- opportunities for intrinsic professional growth
- congruence between work environment and personal values

Your Thoughts?

Is it realistic to expect most employers to provide these opportunities? Why, why not, or under what circumstances?

These factors, found to be more powerful predictors of job investment than pay (Randolph, 2005), are echoed in other recent studies. Employees have a greater sense of ownership in their work when they are given decision-making power (Pierce, O'Driscoll, & Coghlan, 2004) and when their involvement is authentically important and taken seriously by their employer (Posig & Kickul, 2003). Staying with an employer for all of these positive reasons can bring a strong sense of ***affective work commitment***. Such employees have high job satisfaction and find their personal identity in their affiliation with the organization (Culpepper, Gamble, & Blubaugh, 2004). Unfortunately, there are those employees who do not have such a positive work experience but feel they have no realistic choice but to stay in their current position. Labeled a ***continuance work commitment***, these employees may feel that the costs of leaving are greater than the costs of enduring their current position or that there are no other reasonable positions available.

Work-Related Stresses

All of us who are employees desire the benefits of a good income and the satisfaction of finding a good person/employment fit. Realistically we know that any employment situation is likely to have both satisfying and stressful aspects. There are many sources of work-related stresses, ranging from the temporary loss of a computer system that's down to the most serious of issues, such as drug, alcohol, or sexual abuse at work (Knudsen, Roman, & Johnson, 2004; Zhiwei & Snizek, 2003). Here the discussion focuses on only a small sample of work-related stressors, targeting both those that may be more and less under an employee's control.

One potential source of work-related stress is wage discrimination. There are numerous types of discrimination to consider regarding work and employment issues, including those based on age, disability, national origin, religion, gender, or sexual orientation, as well as discrimination that occurs in hiring, performance evaluations, and promotion practices. Wage discrimination is the injustice that occurs when individuals are not given comparable wages for comparable work. Due to the work of the Equal Employment Opportunity Commission (EEOC), the U.S. government agency created to deal with wage discrimination, some areas of wage discrimination are improving. ***Within-job wage discrimination***, unequal pay for employees in the same position, is much less common than in previous years (Petersen & Sporta, 2004). Current laws also require equal pay for those who are engaged in different jobs that are "substantially" equal or of ***comparable worth*** within the same company or organization. The EEOC (2005) considers such factors as skill level, physical and mental effort, responsibility, and working conditions and hazards to determine if particular jobs are comparably and substantially equal.

Your Thoughts?

What factors might keep employees from challenging employers regarding equal pay? What might keep them from filing complaints with the EEOC?

In spite of such laws, women continue to earn less than men. The U.S. Census Bureau reported that women earned about 73% of men's earnings in the year 2000 (Lips, 2003). Not unique to the United States, in the United Kingdom, the National Statistics Office (2004) reported that women earned approximately 86% of what men earned in 2003. The gender difference in pay is evident even in situations where one might not expect it, such as in professions requiring advanced education and prestige. For example, within the highly powerful profession of legal practice, the Bureau of Labor Statistics reported that in 2002 female lawyers working full-time received 69.4% of that earned by male lawyers in similar positions, a figure that had increased to 77.5% by 2005 (Diaz, 2009). Another circumstance in which it may seem reasonable to expect women to earn as much as men if not more is in those occupations that have been dominated by women. Even there, men continue to have higher wages. For example, female nurses make approximately 88% of what male nurses make, and female bookkeepers make approximately 94% of what male bookkeepers earn (Lips, 2003). Regardless of the awareness of wage discrimination for more than 10 years now, the gender gap in pay remains prevalent. As recently as 2009 the Lilly Ledbetter Fair Pay Act was signed into law to, yet again, address gender discrimination in pay (Diaz, 2009).

Your Thoughts?

Is the changing nature of work likely to increase or decrease gender-related wage discrimination? Give reasons to support your response.

Social scientists investigating these differences have found that gender-related wage discrimination has evolved through various mechanisms. One concern is ***allocative discrimination***, which occurs at the point of hiring. Women are often hired for less prestigious positions, which have lower pay ranges. Another concern is ***valuative discrimination***, referring to the findings that traditionally female occupations, even those requiring skills and other wage-relevant factors, are valued less and are paid less (Lips, 2003; Petersen & Sporta, 2004). While much of the focus on wage discrimination centers on female–male pay gaps, it is important to remember that age discrimination (Henretta, 2001) and racial discrimination (Huffman & Cohen, 2004) often lead to valuative and wage discrimination as well.

Perhaps one of the most well-publicized and discussed work-related stressors is sexual harassment. Not only are most employees made aware of the sexual harassment policies of their employer, but also the topic is frequently in the news. In 2003 the EEOC and state and local Fair Employment Practices Agencies (FEPAs) received 13,566 claims of sexual harassment, with 14.7% of those charges being filed by men. In 2009 the number was slightly lower at 12,696 charges with 16.0% of those being filed by men (EEOC, n.d.). It is important to notice that all cases are not situations of male perpetrators and female victims. Sexual harassment complaints are filed by men and women, with accusations being made against the other and the same-sex perpetrators (EEOC, 2004). The EEOC defines ***sexual harassment*** as "unwelcome sexual advances, requests for sexual favors, and other verbal or physical conduct of a sexual nature" that occur in the workplace, and "when submission to or rejection of this conduct explicitly or implicitly affects an individual's employment, unreasonably interferes with an individual's work performance or creates an intimidating, hostile or offensive work environment" (EEOC, 2002). Based on various court decisions the EEOC definition has been divided into two legal terms reflecting two types of sexual harassment. ***Quid pro quo sexual harassment*** occurs when sexual activity is requested as a condition for something in the workplace, such as a promotion or to avoid being fired. ***Hostile environment sexual harassment*** occurs when the work environment is so stressful due to behaviors of a sexual nature that one cannot perform his or her job adequately. Numerous things could make the environment hostile, such as offensive language, jokes, literature, pictures, gestures, or touching.

Your Thoughts?

Can you think of examples of language, music, objects, or gestures that older adults might find offensive but younger adults would not?

The topic of work-related stressors is broad, including more than discrimination and harassment. Another area of stressors highlights role conflict, a source of work-related stress when trying to manage work and family needs. Some of the work/family role conflict studies have focused on work-interfering-with-family (Noor, 2004). Consider, as an example, those who label themselves "workaholics." Kemeny (2002), analyzing data from the 1998 General Social Survey, found that individuals who identified with that term spend more hours working than others, think about work more during "off" times, report higher levels of stress, and were concerned over their lack of family time. Generally, those who are experiencing work-interfering-with-family are also experiencing family-interfering-with-work stressors as well (Noor, 2004). Employer attitudes toward work/family issues can ease or escalate the associated stress levels (Judge & Colquitt, 2004). One line of research aimed at reducing work/family conflict is successfully utilizing the selection, optimization, and compensation model (SOC). Baltes and Heydens-Gahir (2003) recruited 241 adults, ranging in age from 21 to 64 years old and representing a wide variety of occupations, including accounting, education, health care, counseling, and building maintenance, to participate. The adults were given training in identifying desires and goals (selection), recognizing and using resources (optimization), and practicing flexibility when facing obstacles or the unexpected (compensation). Participants who were better at utilizing the SOC strategy in both their work and family roles reported less stress in both work-interfering-with-family and family-interfering-with-work. The SOC strategy, as judged by its success in work/family stress situations, may be useful to employees dealing with other work-related stressors as well.

Your Thoughts?

While it is clear that stresses transfer from work to family, what productive skills might also transfer from work to family?

Older Workers

The changing nature of work, influenced by technology and the changing demographics in Western countries, is creating new challenges for older workers. As the general population ages, so, too, is the age of the average employee (DOL, 2000). It is predicted that by the middle of this century one of every five workers in the United States will be 55 years old or older, and about half will be white non-Hispanic (Hardy, 2006). Concerns over the viability of the Social Security system, along with increased and healthier lifespans, have prompted many older adults to remain in the workforce as long as they can. Older workers receive competing and conflicting messages in that it is widely acknowledged that employers need

RESEARCH IN-DEPTH
Self-Report Diary Entries

Researchers Nicole Roberts and Robert Levenson, from the Psychology Department at the University of California at Berkeley, were interested in learning more about the impact of job stress on marital interactions. They first sought a group of participants with high-stress occupations, choosing 19 male police officers and their spouses. As they read previous studies to determine the best way to collect data they realized that almost all of the findings were based on self-report questionnaires. While there are many advantages to using questionnaires, such as the anonymity of the participants and the ability to survey many people quickly, there are also some concerns. Researchers must keep in mind that some participants may not remember information accurately, thus what they report may not reflect reality. Also, some participants may choose to withhold information or give false information. For example, when taking a questionnaire on marital interactions some adults may be embarrassed or ashamed to admit that their marital interactions are poor, and instead report that their conversations are enjoyable and helpful. Rather than continue with only self-report questionnaires, Roberts and Levenson added the use of diaries and laboratory observations to their research methodology.

In addition to completing several questionnaires at the beginning of the 4-week study, participants were asked to complete a diary entry at the end of each day. They were asked to comment on the amount of job-related stress and job-related pleasure they experienced that day, as well as the amount of marriage-related stress and marriage-related pleasure. Participants were also asked to list the number of hours they worked and the number of hours they spent with their spouse each day. By asking police officers and their wives to complete diary entries each day the researchers were, assuming the participants were honest, gaining a more accurate picture of each day's experience. If the researchers simply asked, "How many stressful work days have you had in the past month?" the participants may estimate much higher or lower than the actual number of days. By requiring daily entries the participants do not have to rely on their memory and their "best guess" during the 30-day study. In addition to the diaries the participants were asked to attend a 90-minute session each week for 4 weeks during which their interactions would be videotaped. The tapes were then scored based on the positive and negative interactions observed.

Roberts and Levenson (2001) found that job stress can "spill over" to create negative interactions in marital relationships. Even those couples who reported high levels of marital satisfaction were affected by the husband's work-related stress. As would be expected, on the days of highest stress the couples displayed less pleasurable feelings regarding their interactions. By using daily diary entries the researchers were able to chart day-to-day changes as well as each couple's overall perceptions. Roberts and Levenson believe their findings provide a warning for those in high-stress positions that a continual pattern of negative interactions may lead to a higher than normal risk of divorce. They encourage couples with high-stress positions to develop stress management techniques, find ways to talk about job stress with spouses, and make an effort to include positive emotions in marital conversations. In terms of research methodology, the daily diary entries reduced the need to rely on memories, providing data that is less likely to be as distorted as questionnaires asking about experiences over the previous week or month.

---

them in the workforce, so much so that they are protected by laws, on the other hand older workers are often met with the stereotypes and myths suggesting that they are too old to be valuable.

Laws, such as the 1967 Age Discrimination in Employment Act and the 1990 Older Workers Benefits Protection Act in the United States, are designed to prevent discrimination in hiring and forced retirement based on age. An Internet search on "mandatory retirement" will quickly reveal that such laws have been enacted in several countries around the world. Aimed at workers ages 40 years and older, these laws have been strengthened over the years so that, with only a few exceptions, it is illegal to establish a mandatory retirement age (Hardy, 2006). Certainly, there are ways organizations can create aversive situations so that older employees choose to quit or retire earlier than planned, such as downsizing, lack of work, or restructuring that leads to the elimination of their position and the transfer to a less desirable one. Unfortunately, older workers who do lose their jobs are less likely than younger employees to find employment, and if they do it is likely to pay less than their previous position (Henretta, 2001).

Older employees are usually perceived to be more mature and responsible than younger employees. They are more likely to arrive on time, take pride in their work, and display a good attitude (Hardy, 2006). Why, then, is it so difficult for older workers to find and maintain employment? Older employees are also thought to cost more money in terms of health and retirement benefits and assumed to be resistant to learning new skills (Hardy, 2006). In a recent review of the literature, Czaja (2001) compiled a list of the more common myths about older employees. This false view indicates that older employees are likely to:

- be physically unable to do their job
- have a high rate of absenteeism
- have a high rate of accidents
- be less productive
- be less motivated
- be resistant to change and innovation
- be unable to learn new skills

While it is true that older adults may not be suited for work involving heavy physical demands, Czaja found little support for the belief that age is related to a decline in job performance. A more recent review also concluded that research on older workers shows that age accounts for only a fraction of the difference in performance, and much more variance is accounted for by experience (Hardy, 2006). While it is clear that cognitive processing slows with age, areas of expertise are generally not affected by aging. Various studies have shown that when adults have developed an expertise in an area over a lifetime, they remain competitive in that field in later adulthood (Czaja, 2001). Regarding training, older adults may need more practice time, particularly with technologies that they are unfamiliar with (Cutler, 2006; Czaja, 2001). While additional training may cost more, data suggests that the costs are offset by the lower rates of absenteeism displayed by older workers as well as their loyalty in remaining with a supportive employer (Culter, 2006).

Your Thoughts?

What factors have likely contributed to these false stereotyped assumptions about older workers?

Section Summary

- There are many reasons for developmental psychologists to study the changing nature of work.
- Not only do most adults spend a large percentage of their waking hours focused on work, researchers have found that income and the related variables of education and occupational status are associated with well-being, self-esteem, and overall physical health.
- Career development used to depend on loyalty to an organization, as Super described in his four stages of exploration, establishment, maintenance, and disengagement.
- Today most Americans change jobs often, cycling through the processes of personal career development and career adaptability.
- It is useful to consider the person/employment fit, particularly in terms of available positions, growth industries, general skills, personality traits, and job satisfaction.
- Work environments often bring stress, and in some cases the stressors are serious and powerful, such as wage discrimination and sexual harassment.
- Work-related stresses may also come from individuals' difficulties in blending work and family life.
- Older workers, despite all the research to the contrary, still face the perception that they are unable and unwilling to learn new skills and contribute fully in an employment setting.

Volunteer Work and Community Involvement

Whether during our formal education, career, or in retirement, many of us as adults will find ourselves involved in volunteer and community work. On the most basic level, neighborhood and community involvement can be as simple as informally helping your neighbors. Farrell, Aubry, and Coulombe (2004) found that engaging in neighboring activities, such as lending yard tools or offering transportation, increased a sense of community for 345 residents from a metropolitan area in Canada. In another study involving participation in a community garden, 195 gardeners from urban neighborhoods reported a strong sense of belonging and connection to their neighborhood, community, and larger city (Shinew, Glover, & Parry, 2004). Most of the residents chose to participate in community gardening to relax, to enjoy nature, and to improve their neighborhood. Not only did gathering to garden meet those needs, it also enhanced neighbors' willingness to trust each other and form social bonds, particularly among neighbors of different racial backgrounds. Community involvement can also be encouraged by participation in more formal community organizations. For example, a study of 2,490 individuals in Chicago found that residents who belong to religious organizations are more likely to bond with their community and take advantage of community resources (Barnes, 2003). ***Social cohesion*** results from the belief that neighbors share some common values and goals, trust each other, and are willing to help each other (Fisher, Li, Michael, & Cleveland, 2004). Researchers have found that social cohesion is highly related to social bonding and supportive interactions among neighbors.

Your Thoughts?

Would you support a town council who voted to slightly raise taxes to provide more community opportunities for social cohesion? Why, why not, or under what circumstances?

Another means of neighborhood and community involvement is through volunteer service. Volunteering can take many forms, which makes it difficult to precisely define and measure. Informal volunteering could be defined in a broad way to include just about any helpful behaviors whereas formal volunteering generally involves an organization or agency that coordinates individual efforts. Formal volunteer organizations can include local, state-wide, national, or international agencies, such as:

- educational organizations, libraries, and schools
- political organizations
- military-related support organizations
- religious organizations
- hospitals, nursing homes, and other care facilities
- health care and medical research organizations
- humanitarian and community social services organizations
- environmental and animal-care organizations
- senior citizens organizations
- historical societies

In formal volunteer situations the process of contacting an agency and arranging to participate may resemble the process of applying for employment. Table 7.2 gives a summary of the rights and responsibilities of volunteers and the organizations that coordinate volunteer efforts. Whether a volunteer experience is more or less formal in structure and commitment, the points summarized in Table 7.2 provide good guidelines for volunteer situations (Volunteer.Gov, 2004).

Adults of all ages can be found contributing incredible numbers of hours of service to their friends, family members, and local and larger communities. A closer look will reveal that, though they may work side-by-side on the same projects or with the same organizations, individuals' motivations and benefits are likely to vary based on their age. A study of 724 young adults, ages 18 to 30 years old, revealed that those who engage in volunteer work were

TABLE 7.2 ***Rights and Responsibilities of Volunteers and Agencies***

	Rights	*Responsibilities*
Volunteer	Clear Assignment and Duties Enjoyable Work Orientation and Training Supervision, Support, and Help Respect, Fair Treatment Worthwhile Tasks Safe, Healthy Working Conditions Terminate an Agreement if Needed	Be Honest about Strengths, Limitations, Motivation, and Time Commitment Participate in Training Fulfill Your Commitment Abide by the Rules of the Organization Cooperate with Staff Be Flexible and Keep an Open Mind Stay Informed Regarding the Organization and Your Position Ask for Help or Clarification if Needed
Agency	Place Volunteers in the Best-Suited Situations and Reassign When Needed Request References Require Volunteers to Attend Training Expect Volunteers to be Responsible Receive Notice of Leaving Terminate a Volunteer Agreement if Needed	Interview Candidates Provide Volunteers with a Written Position Description Treat Volunteers with Respect and Worth Inform of Special Events for the Workforce Provide Supervision Seek and Respect Volunteer Contributions Conduct an Exit Interview When an Agreement is Terminated

From Volunteer.Gov/Gov (2004).

more likely to have higher educational attainment, a good income, and many years of previous volunteer work (Oesterle, Johnson, & Mortimer, 2004). These findings lend support to the long-term value of service-learning programs, which encourages high school and college students to volunteer in their communities. To further support students in their service-learning endeavors many colleges and universities now offer *co-curricular transcripts* that officially document internship and volunteer experiences for employers and graduate schools.

Your Thoughts?

How might employers or graduate schools benefit from receiving official co-curricular transcripts? How might students benefit?

The peak number of volunteer service hours and effort usually occurs in middle adulthood. Adults in their 40s and 50s are more likely to have family ties, school-age children, and personal investments in their work and communities—all of which may bring many volunteer opportunities to their attention. In an analysis of the personal motives of 458 executive-level volunteers who were encouraged to volunteer by their employers, Farmer and Fedor (2001) found that some were altruistic in their efforts, whereas others were interested in social networking or learning new skills to further their careers. In another study of middle-aged volunteers, Rotolo and Wilson (2004) compared data collected over a 15-year period from 3,141 women from the "civic generation" who were born between 1923 and 1937, and 3,196 women from the "baby boom generation," born between 1944 and 1954. While both groups of women donated large amounts of time and effort, the older, civic generation women were more interested in volunteering through churches, service clubs, and ancillary organizations serving hospitals and schools, whereas the baby boom generation women were more interested in political action and community empowerment.

Your Thoughts?

What societal changes occurred between these two generations that may have contributed to the preferences in volunteering?

While middle-aged adults may provide the most donated hours, older adults may benefit the most from volunteering. Fully retired adults who engage in volunteer efforts often feel better about themselves, report greater life satisfaction, demonstrate better physical health (Van Willigen, 2000), and live longer than older adults who do not volunteer (Shmotkin, Blumstein, & Modan, 2003). The social involvement that comes with volunteering serves as a guard against isolation and depression, and contributes to a new sense of identity and purpose. It also allows older adults to engage in useful work by staying busy with meaningful and socially valued activities (Li & Ferraro, 2006). In a study comparing thousands of adults ranging in age from 55 to 74 years old, Mutchler, Burr, and Caro (2003) found that those who reported volunteering prior to retirement generally continued volunteering at the same level after retirement. Some older adults may view volunteering as a bridge between full-time employment and complete retirement.

Your Thoughts?

Considering the benefits and potential problems, do you think it is generally a good idea for older adults to volunteer? Why, why not, or under what circumstances?

In spite of all the benefits, there are some concerns regarding older adults and their involvement in ongoing volunteer activities. While they may receive a great deal of praise for their involvement, some advocates for older adults worry that seniors will begin to think that they must engage in meaningful activities to justify their existence (Martinson, 2006). Volunteer work may begin to feel more like an obligation rather than a choice. Knowing that people and organizations are counting on continued contributions may cause older adults to ignore signs that they should slow down or cut back on their volunteer hours (Li & Ferraro, 2006).

Section Summary

- Social cohesion, the belief that neighbors are friendly, can be trusted, and will help each other, can be fostered through social and supportive interactions, such as engaging in neighboring activities and shared participation in community programs.
- Volunteering as a means of community involvement can include almost any form of informal help as well as formal opportunities through local, national, or even international agencies.
- Young adults may be encouraged to volunteer through their high school or college, whereas middle-aged adults are more likely to feel encouragement from their employers, their children's school, and various community organizations.
- Volunteering can provide meaningful work, social engagement, and influence functioning in terms of better physical and mental health for older adults.

Retirement

Along with the changing nature of work, our concept of retirement has diversified and changed over recent years as well. Following World War II Americans developed an ideal view of retirement as the shift from work to a life of leisure, occurring around age 65 (Moen & Spencer, 2006). Retirement was perceived as a life event that occurred once and generally signaled the end of paid work (Hardy, 2006). In the 21st century retirement among Americans has developed into a multifaceted, less predictable situation that may include adults who are gainfully employed. This section focuses on the transition to retirement and the earlier, healthier post-retirement years.

Difficulties in Characterizing Retirees

Many of the same complexities arise in attempting to accurately define the term *retirement* as occurs when attempting to define *late adulthood*. Many people view retirement and late adulthood as beginning simultaneously, usually in our early to mid-60s. With the exception of returning to paid employment, is there a point at which retirement ends? Should we stop calling people "retired" when they are too disabled in old age to work? Does retirement end, as late adulthood does, at the end of life? If we label people as "retired" until the end of life, then it is nearly impossible to make any generalizations about this group of adults ranging from the healthiest, active 65-year-old to the very old. Although clear terms have not emerged to distinguish periods of retirement, social scientists have suggested that the years just after retirement represent a distinct and unique time in life. It may be that, similar to the way adolescence became recognized as a unique phase of life among scholars in the early 20th century, retirement will emerge as a unique phase as well (Moen & Spencer, 2006).

Your Thoughts?

Do you think the term "retired" will transition to be a generalized term referring to a period in life like adolescence? Why or why not?

In addition to the difficulties in establishing boundaries to retirement as a developmental stage, there are many other issues that make it difficult to characterize retirees. With age adults grow more distinct in terms of individual differences. Retirees vary in numerous ways, including age, personality, marital status, health status, cognitive abilities, financial status, and living arrangements. They are likely to be influenced by their various life experiences, including the years they spent working in particular fields and with particular employers. They may be influenced by their generational and corresponding social expectations. For example, historically men have moved through the traditional work trajectory of education–work–retirement. Husbands chose the right time to retire and wives retired whenever their husbands did (Moen & Spencer, 2006). Retirees may also be shaped by current concerns, such as African Americans who report more concern over retirement issues than Caucasian Americans. African Americans are more likely to be forced into retirement and deal with disabilities (Foos, Clark, & Terrell, 2006). Without established parameters or a specific focus, it is difficult to make generalizations or characterize "most retirees."

Retirement as a Process

Rather than conceptualizing retirement as a one-time life-changing event it may be more useful to view retirement as a process or series of adjustments for retirees and their families (Rosenkoetter & Garris, 2001). Pre-retirement, starting at about age 45 (Moen & Spencer, 2006), is the time to begin the process of planning ahead for the transition to retirement. While age is a key factor in anticipating retirement, employees are likely to consider their health as well (Taylor & Shore, 1995). One of the most influential pre-retirement activities, in terms of increasing the likelihood of a successful adjustment to retirement, is involvement in pre-retirement programs (Lo & Brown, 1999; Rosenkoetter & Garris, 2001). Employees who participate in pre-retirement planning sessions feel better about themselves post-retirement, report less loneliness and boredom, more enjoyment, and slightly more activity in retirement (Rosenkoetter & Garris, 2001).

A common image of newly retired adults can be found in the characterizations of the "young-old" in late adulthood. They are old enough to have left primary employment but young enough to have an active lifestyle. For some adults it can be a time of increased companionship with loved ones and friends, sharing mutual interests and hobbies (Krause, 2006). Leisure activities can grow in importance to the point of replacing work identities (Settersten, 2006). For example, the retired teacher may now be known in the community as a master craftsman in restoring antique furniture or as a master gardener. Many retirees also take advantage of the time and resources to travel (Staats & Pierfelice, 2003). In a study that involved 795 retired physicians and 455 of their spouses, Austrom, Perkins, Damush, and Hendrie (2003) found that those who were happiest in retirement reported better health, a sense of financial security, participation in activities and hobbies, a good marital and sexual relationship, and an overall sense of optimism. The retired physicians indicated that the most

Your Thoughts?

How might the SES of retired physicians influence these findings? Do you think the results would be similar for the general population?

enjoyable part of being retired is the freedom from work and the time for activities, whereas their spouses focused on the opportunity to spend time with family.

Adjustment to retirement also has its obstacles and challenges. Austrom and her colleagues (2003) found that the major challenge cited by the retired physicians was the loss of their professional role. Some adults not only feel the loss of their career in terms of identity, but also in terms of the challenges, new experiences, and camaraderie it provided (Price, 2000). In interviews with a group of retired professional women Price (2000) found that not only did these women miss their professional identity, they found the stereotypes applied to "old, retired women" to be frustrating and degrading.

Similar to the way the changing nature of work has resulted in a shift from an emphasis on career development to career adaptability, flexibility has become one of the keys to successful retirement. Rather than an abrupt shift from full-time work to no gainful employment there is a growing trend for individuals who have retired to continue working in some capacity (Hardy, 2006). It is common for retirees to use their expertise and talents in short-term or part-time paid arrangements (Gerardi, 2003; Pointon, 2004), thus cycling through phases of retirement and unretirement. ***Bridge employment***, the term for work that serves as the transition from full-time work to permanent withdrawal from the workforce, has been linked to retirement satisfaction and psychological well-being (Kim & Feldman, 2000).

Your Thoughts?

What might be the negative effects or difficulties, if any, related to bridge employment?

Researchers have found that willingness to be proactive in seeking meaningful activities will influence post-retirement life satisfaction (Carter & Cook, 1995; Lo & Brown, 1999). Those who are active, whether engaging in bridge employment, volunteer work, or leisure activities, report high life satisfaction (Kim & Feldman, 2000). Adjusting to retirement is a process that may involve cycling through several lifestyle options before settling into a satisfying routine in late adulthood.

Rather than making an abrupt shift from working full time to retirement many older adults are engaging in partial retirement or finding bridge employment.

Section Summary

- The many individual differences in response to retirement along with the many lifestyle choices make it difficult to characterize retirees.
- The period of retirement is often viewed as a time simultaneous with late adulthood, though some scholars believe it will emerge as a unique time period much like the period of adolescence.
- It is helpful to conceptualize retirement as a flexible process that may cycle through several periods of full-time work, part-time work, and no work.
- Researchers have found that pre-retirement planning is often a predictor of high life satisfaction in post-retirement.
- Many of the factors associated with post-retirement satisfaction are similar to those predicting general life satisfaction in late adulthood, including good health, adequate financial resources, enjoyable activities, and high-quality social relationships.

Economic Issues and Aging

In the 2008 U.S. presidential election the economy, health care, and Social Security were much discussed topics—as they should have been. Those who were close to retirement were listening anxiously to determine if they could financially afford to make the lifestyle switch from employee to retiree. They were also wondering about the risks they may take in terms of insurance coverage of their current and future health care costs. Middle-aged adults were listening to the discussions of these topics as they wondered what the future might hold for them in 20 or 30 years. In 2006 there were approximately 37 million people in the United States who were 65 years or older (Federal Interagency Forum on Aging-Related Statistics, 2008), a sizeable group that continues to influence the economy. As that age group continues to grow, projected to be 71.5 million in 2030 (NIA, 2008b), the needs of this generation cannot be overlooked. As those individuals age they will need increasing amounts of physical assistance, transportation, social support, and health care. While many families try to manage care of their older loved ones, it can be expensive and exhausting when maintained for years.

Your Thoughts?

In what ways might major industries change as the population of older adults grows? How might the job market shift for those employed?

In this section we explore some of the issues surrounding the typical financial state and economic well-being (or lack of) for older adults. These issues raise a simple and yet profound and fundamental question: Should the government, and if so to what extent, assist citizens with retirement, housing, and health care needs (Walker, 2006)? This is a question not only being asked in the United States but in many industrialized countries around the world (Holden & Hatcher, 2006).

The Evolution of Retirement Programs

It may seem to younger generations or those who haven't explored the history of care for older adults that employers and government organizations have always provided financial assistance to retirees and older adults for living and health care needs. Actually, these benefits are a fairly recent development. Pension programs were first established in Europe in 1889 and then in the United States in 1935 (Schulz & Borowski, 2006; Walker, 2006). While pension programs were designed to reward long-term employees, they were also used as leverage for employers and in some cases as tools in negotiations with employee unions.

The Social Security Act of 1935 came after many veterans and organized labor groups actively campaigned for financial support in late adulthood (Binstock & Quadagno, 2001). These early retirement and health care programs aimed at financial help for older adults were seen as worthwhile because they had worked hard all their lives. Older adults were characterized as the "deserving poor" who were often passive politically, isolated socially, and unable to care for themselves. As years have passed the spotlight has shifted from the plight of these older individuals, a humanitarian focus, to the stress on the economy caused by the amount of public money spent on health care and housing needs. Rather than a source of pride and civic duty, caring for older adults is now conceptualized as a problem (Walker, 2006). As more adults take money out of the Social Security program than contribute, it is clear that a problem looms in the future. The Social Security Administration (SSA) reported in 2008 that the average benefit for a retired worker was $1,079/month, for a widow or widower was $1,041/month, and for a retired couple was $1,761/month.

Your Thoughts?

Do you think most older couples could meet their medical and other financial needs on $21,132 per year? If not, where might the additional money come from?

Before the 1974 Employee Retirement Income Security Act (ERISA) was passed there was a greater likelihood that retirement pensions would be lost due to employer bankruptcy or poor management and investing of funds. While ERISA helped protect those who were promised pensions it created additional financial and operational burdens for employers (Schulz & Borowski, 2006). To adjust to the changing laws and economy, employers have responded by shifting away from *defined benefits retirement programs* in which employers pay retirees a specific benefit based on a formula that usually involves years of service and average earnings to *defined contribution retirement programs* in which employers make contributions to an employee's pension account. Rather than an amount an employee could count on with defined benefits in retirement, the amount one receives with defined contributions depends on many dynamic factors, such as investment decisions, returns, and management fees. Another recent change is the addition of 401(k) accounts (or 403(b) for nonprofit and educational organizations), named after sections of the Revenue Act of 1978. These programs allow employees to voluntarily contribute to tax-deferred retirement accounts. In some cases employers offer matching funds or profit-sharing to employees' 401(k)s. Beyond government and employer-based programs, the financial industry has responded by creating Individual Retirement Accounts (IRAs) to which any individual can contribute (Schulz & Borowski, 2006).

Your Thoughts?

What factors might discourage young adults from understanding their future retirement needs or contributing to their retirement savings?

The Reality of Financing Retirement

Currently, the primary sources of income for people ages 65 and older may include a combination of Social Security benefits, earnings from post-retirement work, retirement benefits (from personal plans or employer-based plans), and other assets (Holden & Hatcher, 2006). Post-retirement financial well-being has been related to accumulated wealth, which is usually based on:

- The value of one's home (after mortgages and debts are paid)
- The value in IRAs
- Income from investments in stocks and bonds
- Other assets (businesses, farms, real estate, vehicles, cash, and other valuable items)

The reality is, however, that many Americans will have only a few of those resources. Just as the physical and cognitive individual differences are great among older adults, so are the differences in financial support. The U.S. Census Bureau (2008b, Table 537) found that in 2005 approximately 47 million people representing 41.5% of the U.S. households had some type of IRA. Approximately 45% of American employees are covered by an employee pension plan, which is low among industrialized countries (Schulz & Borowski, 2006).

In contrast to those with some retirement coverage, the National Institute on Aging (NIA, 2007b) reports that a significant number of Americans have saved little or nothing for retirement. Surveys of various demographic groups show that those who have lower incomes

While most adults dream of the perfect retirement situation, financing the many years after our work income ceases can be difficult for many Americans.

Your Thoughts?

Would you support a law that required adult children to pay the balance of their parents' health care costs? Why, why not, or under what circumstances?

Your Thoughts?

Do you support the option of personal control in investing versus requiring citizens to save in a government program? Why, why not, or under what circumstances?

also have fewer resources to put toward retirement, and are less likely to have IRAs or employer-based pension plans. Approximately 9% of individuals ages 65 and older have incomes low enough to place them at or below the poverty line (DeNavas-Walt, Proctor, & Smith, 2007; NIA, 2008b). For women, widowhood usually results in a significant loss of income (NIA, 2007b). In terms of ethnicity, about one-third of all Hispanic and African Americans depend completely on Social Security benefits for their income, as compared to about 1/16 of non-Hispanic whites (Angel & Angel, 2006).

These financial concerns are causing many experts to evaluate the retirement plans of currently employed adults, both personal and employer-based plans, trying to gauge if current plans will provide adequately for employees when they retire (Holden & Hatcher, 2006). One of the many debates surrounding retirement funding is whether to give more responsibility and control to individuals for managing their own retirement accounts, as opposed to keeping the bulk of retirement money in the Social Security system. Experts worry that while some individuals would do quite well managing their own retirement nest egg, some recipients may spend their savings too quickly. Experts also worry that many adults will simply be overwhelmed by the details, technical language, and amount of choices, resulting in poor decisions and little money available to manage housing and health care in late adulthood (NIA, 2007b; Schulz & Borowski, 2006).

Managing Health Care Costs

A central and difficult to predict factor in financing retirement is financing health care. To fully appreciate the economic issues of aging it's helpful to have an understanding of the primary source(s) of health insurance for older adults and how they have evolved over the decades.

Medicare and Medicaid were established in 1965 as Title XVIII of the Social Security Act. Medicare was intended to be used for acute care involving physician and hospital charges and other related costs. At that point in history it was rare to have health insurance as part of retirement benefits, and a hospital stay could be quite costly. Currently, Medicare covers approximately 97% of adults ages 65 and older, and is primarily used for outpatient care, office visits, skilled nursing facilities, and home health services. Whereas Medicare is a federal program controlled by the U.S. government, Medicaid is state-controlled program designed for low-income Americans and those who need long-term care. Allowing each state to control Medicaid creates a great deal of confusion as programs can vary dramatically (Moon, 2006).

Medicare has been and continues to be controversial. It has been the target of budget cuts, peaking in 1997 with the Balanced Budget Act, but also has had expansions, such as the 2003 addition of the Medicare Prescription Drug, Improvement, and Modernization Act. The current critical debates are focused on two key areas: the implementation and the funding of the program. In terms of implementation, the fees assigned to various procedures and services and the ways medical professionals are paid are continually debated and adjusted. From a funding standpoint, Medicare has been called a "runaway" program that was responsible for nearly 13% of the federal budget in 2004. Another concern is that the Federal Insurance Contributions Act (FICA) payroll tax, which funds Medicare, is not replacing the amount of money taken out for medical care each year. There are many predictions as to when this fund might be exhausted based on many complex economic models (Moon, 2006). While Social Security, Medicare, and Medicaid are generally associated with aging, it should be emphasized that these are largely encompassing programs that serve many Americans with various needs, including individuals with disabilities and family members of recently deceased workers (Binstock & Quadagno, 2001).

Your Thoughts?

Considering these possibilities, how do you feel about contributing more to FICA as an employee?

In addition to Medicare and Medicaid, about one-third of Americans have employer-sponsored retiree health plans for themselves and possibly their spouses or partners. It is usually the highest income retirees who have an opportunity for employer-sponsored retiree health plans, and those individuals are often in the best financial position in retirement. Some insurance companies offer individual supplemental coverage, often called Medi-gap insurance, which is helpful when there is a catastrophic situation resulting in enormously high medical costs. An option that is decreasing in popularity is to join a private plan, essentially opting to channel Medicare benefits into a health maintenance organization (Moon, 2006).

Even though the average household income has remained fairly steady since the beginning of this century (DeNavas-Walt et al., 2007), between 1992 and 2004 the average health care costs for older Americans (adjusted for inflation) rose from $8,644 to $13,052 (NIA, 2008b). Consider older adults who are attempting to age in place who want to have an aide come to their home to offer minimal assistance. The average cost for someone providing homemaker services to an older adult, such as cleaning and fixing meals, is $18 an hour, whereas the average per hour rates for a home health aide is $29. For an older adult who needs 2 hours of homemaking and 1 hour of health assistance per day, the average cost would be $455 per week, which is over $23,000 per year. While most individuals have some health care coverage and would not pay that entire amount themselves, the out-of-pocket expenses can add up. For example, imagine a family that realizes that a loved one needs to be in a residential medical facility. On average Medicare provides for about 10%, and Medicaid approximately another 40% of the money spent on nursing homes (Long-Term Care, 2008). Other financial support often comes from various federal, state, private insurance, and other private funds (Stone, 2006). Data from 2008 indicate that, on average, 18% of the cost of such facilities is paid out-of-pocket. As shown in Table 7.3, the out-of-pocket costs for several years of care may financially strain an individual or that person's family (Long-Term Care, 2008). In some cases those costs shown in Table 7.3 do not cover additionally prescribed therapies, medications, or treatments off-site.

Your Thoughts?

How much money is a family saving by taking 24/7 care of aging parents?

TABLE 7.3 ***Cost of Long-Term Housing in the United States, 2008***

	Average Per Day Average Out-of-Pocket	*Average Per Week Average Out-of-Pocket*	*Average Per Year Average Out-of-Pocket*
Adult day health care center	$59 *$11*	$413 *$75*	$21,535 *$3,898*
Nursing home, semi-private room	$187 *$34*	$1,309 *$237*	$68,255 *$12,354*
Nursing home, private room	$209 *$38*	$1,463 *$264*	$76,285 *$13,807*

National Clearing House for Long-Term Care Information (2008).

Older Adults as a Political Force

Your Thoughts?

Do you think older adults will be more unified politically as their number increases and their funding decreases? Why or why not?

Older adults are often assumed, simply because of their age, to be a cohesive group with similar, traditional views on issues that affect them directly. There are some reasons for making these assumptions, such as the data showing that retirees in local settings often vote to increase funding for services they use, such as public transportation, and are less concerned with services they do not plan to use, such as public education (Longino & Bradley, 2006). (That is not unique to retirees; many constituencies vote to improve their personal circumstances.) In light of the many difficulties older adults face in financing retirement and health care it would seem reasonable that this growing population would be a political force for change. Such is not the case. The combined effort of older adults is seldom consistent in influencing public policy and funding. Although older Americans tend to be active in voting and feel loyalty to their political party, their opinions are quite diverse. To draw some contrast, older adults across the European Union countries are much more politically active and effective (Walker, 2006).

When it comes to voting as a block in ways that may alter Social Security, Medicare, or Medicaid, it is important to remember that age is only one factor among many, and similar to adults of all ages, it may be that gender, SES, ethnic culture, religious views, political party, or some other characteristic is much more influential on an older adult's voting record. Also, individual differences exist in terms of economic well-being, usually gauged by accumulated wealth, personal control over financial matters, goods and services purchased, and the amount of leisure time one has (Holden & Hatcher, 2006). These trends may change as the number of individuals older than 65 years old increases and as their adult children struggle to help them with emotional and financial support.

Section Summary

- It is clear that the number of older adults is increasing, and as they age they will need costly health care and housing.
- Whereas older adults were once viewed as the "deserving poor," the focus has shifted from a humanitarian perspective to an economic one.
- Over the years there have been changes in Social Security, Medicare, Medicaid, and employer-based pension plans as these entities have adjusted to increasing demands and shrinking resources.
- While nearly 42% of Americans have an IRA and 45% have some type of employer pension plan, a significant number of Americans have saved little or nothing to fund their retirement and increased health care needs.

- Even with additional coverage beyond Medicare and Medicaid the out-of-pocket expenses for health assistance in a private home or a residential facility can be significant.
- While it would seem that these worries and concerns would motivate older adults to vote as a block to change their situations, voting patterns indicate the older adults are widely diverse in their political opinions.

Chapter Summary

Most adults spend a great percentage of their waking hours engaged in education or paid or unpaid work. While the traditional college experience is a popular path beyond high school, the college landscape is changing due to increasing numbers of adult students that enter the system and the expansion of technologies and providers of higher education. Lifelong and life-wide programs have brought education into many new areas, such as prison education and health-related patient education. Twenty-first century employees who excel in high-paying jobs are seeking personal training as they move toward a lifestyle of self-managed careers and a satisfying person/employment fit.

Even those workers with higher job investment and satisfaction are likely to be challenged by job-related stresses and problems. Among such issues are wage discrimination, sexual harassment, work/family role conflicts, and age discrimination aimed at older workers. Retirement, once considered a one-time event that ended paid employment, now is best conceptualized as a process cycling through periods of work and no work. A major factor in the reluctance to stop working completely is the concern over financing health care and housing assistance when the time comes. Here are some of the main points of the chapter:

- Traditional college students are those who enter full-time college directly from high school, live in campus housing, and finish their degree in 4 to 5 years.
- Academic success for traditional college students has been linked to high parental and social support, along with a high sense of academic control and a healthy preoccupation with failure.
- Adult students often differ from traditional college students in terms of campus social involvement, personal lifestyles, motivation, and goals, and they often outperform traditional students academically.
- Lifelong and life-wide learning can include life skills courses, such as parenting and fitness classes, as well as GED classes and tutoring in English as a second language.
- The focus on literacy includes reading, comprehension, and using information to function productively in general society as well as in specialized areas such as health literacy.
- Income and SES can influence well-being, self-esteem, cognitive functioning, overall health, and management of health problems, all of which play a role in successful aging.
- Super's theory of career development, involving the four stages of exploration, establishment, maintenance, and disengagement, is being replaced with a focus on career recycling, renewal, and career adaptability.
- General abilities and overall cognitive skills are highly related to earning potential and occupational success.
- Holland's theory of job–personality fit highlights six personality types: Realistic, Conventional, Social, Artistic, Investigative, and Enterprising.
- Affective work commitment involves identity, pride, and involvement in one's job, whereas continuance work commitment is based on feeling there are no reasonable options but to stay in an unsatisfatying job.

- While within-job wage discrimination is much less common, women still earn less money than men.
- Sexual harassment incidents include any situation in which unwanted sexual behaviors occur in the workplace, particularly when such behavior is connected to employment status (quid pro quo) or creates an offensive work environment (hostile environment).
- The SOC strategy—selection, optimization, and compensation—has been found to reduce both work-interfering-with-family and family-interfering-with-work stresses.
- Despite the research to the contrary, older workers face age discrimination based on stereotypes that they are less able to learn new skills and will cost more than younger employees.
- Some volunteer opportunities are informal, such as when neighbors help one another, while others are formal arrangements, involving organizations, position descriptions, and supervision similar to a work situation.
- Young adult volunteers are more likely to be well educated, have a good income, and have a history of volunteer service.
- The peak of volunteer service generally occurs in middle adulthood.
- Older adults benefit the most from volunteering, through social involvement, participation in meaningful work, and indirectly better mental and physical health.
- It is difficult to characterize retirees because of the numerous individual differences and situations presented in late adulthood.
- Adjustment to retirement is best viewed as a process of cycling through various phases of work and no work.
- Satisfaction in post-retirement, similar to satisfaction in late adulthood, is linked to good health, enjoyable activities, and good relationships.
- Retirement programs, such as Social Security and employer pension programs, were seen as ways to reward adults for a lifetime of hard work and to help them when they became part of the "deserving poor."
- Social Security, Medicare, Medicaid, and employer pension plans have adapted over the decades to increasing demands and shrinking resources.
- Many employer-based pension plans have shifted from defined benefits programs to defined contribution programs.
- While just over 40% of American employees have an employer-based retirement plan or an IRA, many Americans have saved little or nothing for retirement.
- Medicare was originally intended to cover acute health costs, whereas most of it is now spent on outpatient care, office visits, skilled nursing facilities, and home health services.
- Data from 2008 regarding payment for residential facilities shows that after contributions from Medicare, Medicaid, and other resources, on average 18% of the costs are paid out-of-pocket.
- Older adults show tremendous individual differences and seldom vote in a unified fashion.

Key Terms

Traditional college students **(175)**
Adult students **(176)**
Lifelong learning **(177)**
Life-wide learning **(177)**
Illiteracy **(179)**
Socioeconomic status **(180)**
Affective work commitment **(184)**
Continuance work commitment **(184)**
Within-job wage discrimination **(185)**
Comparable worth **(185)**
Allocative discrimination **(185)**
Valuative discrimination **(185)**
Sexual harassment **(186)**
Quid pro quo sexual harassment **(186)**
Hostile environment sexual harassment **(186)**
Social cohesion **(189)**
Bridge employment **(193)**

Comprehension Questions

1. What are the typical characteristics that define a *traditional college student*?
2. Describe the study conducted by Perry and his colleagues involving academic motivation and failure preoccupation, and give the results.
3. How do adult students and traditional college students differ in terms of peer interaction and social involvement?
4. What is the general difference between lifelong and life-wide learning?
5. Give examples of the kinds of programs offered in community-based lifelong and life-wide learning programs.
6. What does it mean for an adult to be literate?
7. Name three areas of successful aging that have been related to income or SES.
8. Contrast Super's theory of career development with the current trends in American employment.
9. What are the five areas the U.S. Department of Labor predicts to have the greatest growth in the near future?
10. What have researchers found when exploring the role of specific versus general cognitive skills in terms of earning potential and occupational success?
11. Describe each of Holland's six job-personality themes and give examples of careers associated with each.
12. What is the difference between affective and continuance work commitment?
13. Explain the terms "within-job wage discrimination" and "comparable worth."
14. What are the differences between allocative and valuative discrimination?
15. What is the difference between quid pro quo and hostile environment sexual harassment?
16. Explain how the SOC model was applied to work/family role conflict.
17. Name three of the common myths associated with older workers.
18. What are the differences between informal and formal volunteer opportunities?
19. How might social cohesion develop from volunteer experiences?
20. How do young, middle, and older adults vary in terms of their volunteer activities?
21. What did Farmer and Fedor find regarding the personal motives of executives who were required by their employers to volunteer?
22. What are the benefits and the concerns expressed for older adult volunteers?
23. Explain why it is hard to characterize or make generalizations about retirees.
24. Explain the concept of bridge employment.
25. When and why were employer-based pension programs started?
26. When and why was Social Security started?
27. What is the difference between defined benefits and defined contribution retirement programs?
28. What four pieces of information are usually used to determine accumulated wealth as it relates to post-retirement financial well-being?

29. What percentages of Americans have some type of IRA (as reported by the U.S. Census Bureau for 2005)?
30. How has the focus of Medicare changed from what it was originally intended to cover and what it primarily covers now?
31. How is FICA, the Federal Insurance Contributions Act payroll tax, related to concerns regarding the longevity of Medicare?
32. What is the average percentage of out-of-pocket expenses after Medicare, Medicaid, and other resources have been maximized to pay for residential care for older adults?
33. What explanations are given for why older Americans do not vote as a unified group for their own age-related interests?

Answers for Common Sense: Myth or Reality?

1. Reality: Approximately one-fifth of the students who begin college at a 4-year public institution will never complete their degree program. (See Traditional College Students, page 175.)
2. Myth: Researchers have found that student–parent relationships have little influence on traditional college students' academic success. (See Traditional College Students, page 175.)
3. Reality: A strong preoccupation with academic failure in college has been associated with higher grades. (See Traditional College Students, page 175.)
4. Reality: Data from the last decade indicate that more women than men are attending college. (See Adult Students, page 177.)
5. Reality: Older college students generally perform better academically than traditional-aged students. (See Adult Students, page 177.)
6. Myth: The most common education program for prison inmates is computer literacy. (See Lifelong and Life-Wide Learning, page 179.)
7. Reality: Over half of all American citizens cannot read beyond an eighth-grade level. (See Lifelong and Life-Wide Learning, page 179.)
8. Reality: Higher incomes have been associated with better cognitive functioning in old age. (See Income, Socioeconomic Status, and Successful Aging, page 181.)
9. Myth: Government studies indicate that the average worker will have four different jobs between the ages of 18 and 34. (See Changing Nature of Work, page 182.)
10. Reality: The U.S. Department of Labor predicts that jobs involving health care services for older adults will show increases in wages and salaries over the next few years. (See Person/Employment Fit, page 182.)
11. Myth: Researchers have found that proficiency in technical skills is more likely to result in higher wages than proficiency in general cognitive abilities. (See Person/Employment Fit, page 182.)
12. Myth: The U.S. Census Bureau has determined that women have achieved equal pay for equal work when comparing women's and men's incomes. (See Work-Related Stressors, page 185.)
13. Myth: Research indicates that female nurses make more money than male nurses. (See Work-Related Stressors, page 185.)
14. Myth: Sexual harassment, according to the Equal Employment Opportunity Commission, does not include incidents between same-sex individuals. (See Work-Related Stressors, page 186.)
15. Myth: Most research shows that with age the job performance of older workers declines. (See Older Workers, page 188.)
16. Reality: Older adults who volunteer live longer than those who do not. (See Volunteer Work and Community Involvement, page 191.)
17. Reality: Age is a key factor for people in deciding when to retire. (See Retirement as a Process, page 192.)
18. Myth: Employer-based retirement or pension programs have been a part of the American workforce since the late 1880s. (See The Evolution of Retirement Programs, page 194.)
19. Myth: In 2008 the average Social Security monthly benefit for a retired worker was just over $24,000 per year. (See The Evolution of Retirement Programs, page 195.)
20. Myth: In 2005 over half of American employees had some type of IRA. (See The Reality of Financing Retirement, page 195.)

21. Reality: Most women find that widowhood results in a significant loss of income. (See The Reality of Financing Retirement, page 196.)
22. Myth: Medicare is used primarily for inpatient hospital costs. (See Managing Health Care Costs, page 197.)
23. Myth: Social Security, Medicare, and Medicaid are insurances that cover only older adults. (See Managing Health Care Costs, page 197.)
24. Myth: Data from 2008 show that Medicare, Medicaid, private insurance, and other federal and state programs usually cover the costs of older adults in residential nursing home facilities. (See Managing Health Care Costs, page 197.)
25. Reality: Older adults seldom vote as a unified group on age-related political issues. (See Older Adults as a Political Force, page 198.)

Suggested Readings

Matching Men and Work, 1913

Münsterberg, H. (1913). *Psychology and industrial efficiency*. Accessed at *Classics in the History of Psychology* (http://psychclassics.yorku.ca/topic.htm).

The Changing Nature of Work

U.S. Department of Labor, *Working in the 21st Century*, at http://www.bls.gov/opub/working/home.htm.

Retirement in America

National Institute on Aging, (2007, August). *Growing older in America: The Health and Retirement Study*, at http://www.nia.nih.gov/ResearchInformation/ExtramuralPrograms/BehavioralAndSocialResearch/HRS.htm.

Health Care in the United States

The U.S. Health Care System: Best in the World, or Just the Most Expensive? Prepared by the University of Maine for the Bureau of Labor Education in 2001. Available at http://dll.umaine.edu/ble/U.S.%20HCweb.pdf.

Suggested Websites

SES and Poverty in the United States

To further explore SES and poverty go to the U.S. Census Bureau website to find collections of data and summaries at http://www.census.gov/hhes/www/poverty/poverty.html.

Need a Career Guide?

Learn more about career choices and industries with the *Career Guide to Industries*, produced by the U.S. Department of Labor at http://www.bls.gov/oco/cg/.

What is Sexual Harassment?

To learn more about sexual harassment read the article by the U.S. Equal Employment Opportunity Commission and browse the links at http://www.eeoc.gov/types/sexual_harassment.html.

Social Security and Financial Security in Retirement

For those who want to know more about the financial aspects of retirement, the Social Security Administration has an informative website at http://www.ssa.gov/, with an informative introduction at http://www.ssa.gov/understanding.htm.

CHAPTER

8 Memory and Basic Cognition

The ability to transfer information from the environment to our brain, encode it into a form we can understand, and then store, manipulate, and retrieve it when needed is foundational to every thought that passes through our mind. When memory processes are working well they are generally taken for granted and go unnoticed. It is when the system falters, such as when we cannot remember someone's name or the password we assigned to a software program, that we take notice. It is obvious that memory systems are not perfect or totally under our control; otherwise, we would remember everyone's name and all our software passwords accurately and on-demand. Also, if we could control these processes we might choose to erase some of the embarrassing or painful memories that we cannot seem to forget.

This discussion explores models of memory and brain structures with an emphasis on the areas that change with age for those who are healthy and without a memory-altering illness. Attention will be given to various types of memory as well as particular aspects of memory functioning, such as processing speed. Cognitive research, both in psychological and neurological laboratories, further supports our common observation that all memories are not the same nor are they perfectly accurate. Common memory errors and ways of enhancing memory functioning are explored here as well.

COMMON SENSE
Myth or Reality?

Mark each of the following items with either an M, if you think it is a myth, or an R, if you think the statement reflects reality. By paying close attention you can find all the answers in this chapter. If needed, the answers are also given at the end of the chapter.

1. _____ According to information processing theory, information can stay in short-term memory for several hours.
2. _____ Short-term and working memories are the same thing.
3. _____ Under normal circumstances our brains lose 2–3 grams of weight per year after age 60.
4. _____ In some cases younger and older adults use different parts of their brains to process the same information.
5. _____ Researchers have found that the neurological organization of male and female brains is somewhat different.
6. _____ Selective attention involves focusing on two things at one time.
7. _____ Particular aspects of working memory decline with age, beginning in young adulthood.
8. _____ Memories for life events and experiences tend to deteriorate with age.
9. _____ Older people are more likely to remember who told them something interesting but forget what the interesting information was.
10. _____ Memories for procedures, such as playing an instrument or typing, tend to deteriorate with age.
11. _____ Memories for facts, knowledge, and concepts tend to decline with age.
12. _____ It is relatively easy to convince individuals that they remember something that, in reality, did not happen.
13. _____ Even though the amount of improvement declines with age, older adults can improve their memories with training and practice.

Before We Get Started . . .

One of the many interesting areas of memory research focuses on the detail and accuracy found in personal memories for very specific events. Consider as an example your memories for your personal experience and the factual information related to the attacks on the World Trade Center towers in New York City on September 11, 2001. How many of these questions can you answer?

1. Personal Memories
   a. When did you hear the news?
   b. Who told you?
   c. Where were you?
   d. How did you feel?
   e. What did you do in the next few hours following the moment when you heard the news?

2. Factual Details
   a. What day of the week was September 11, 2001?
   b. What time did the first plane crash into the World Trade Center tower?
   c. What time did the third plane crash into the Pentagon?
   d. Where did the fourth plane crash?
   e. Did the north tower or the south tower of the World Trade Center collapse first?
   f. What were the flight numbers and carriers of the four planes involved?

Which of the two types of information, factual or personal, was easier to remember? Do you have confidence that your personal memories are accurate? Do you think your responses to the factual questions are accurate? You can find the answers to the factual questions in the section on flashbulb memories.

Memory Models

Memory is among the most researched of all areas of psychology, beginning in the first psychological laboratories in the late 1800s (Schneider, 2000). Memory research remained common until the rise of ***behaviorism***, which focused on observable behaviors rather than mental processes. From the mid-1930s until the ***cognitive revolution*** American psychologists paid little attention to memory processes. Several factors converged in the 1960s that directly influenced the study of memory and promoted the study of cognition. One such factor was that American psychologists were beginning to take note of the now well-known work of Swiss psychologist Jean Piaget, whose theory of cognitive development raised questions about the growth of memory skills in children. Also, an emerging interest in language development raised questions regarding the organization of words and concepts in memory storage. Another primary movement in the cognitive revolution was the convergence of the fields of computer science, artificial intelligence, and neuroscience. As scientists began to consider the brain-as-computer-hardware and brain-as-computer-software metaphors, numerous models of memory were proposed (Schneider, 2000). This section considers two models popular among cognitive and developmental psychologists: the information processing and parallel distributed processing models. These models are part of the foundation from which researchers have explored changes in memory processing in healthy aging individuals as well as those with disease or illness.

Your Thoughts?

Can the brain-as-computer metaphor be taken too far? How might it be limiting?

Information Processing

While there are many theories that focus on particular aspects of memory, such as auditory and visual memories, there are relatively few comprehensive theories of memory. One of the standard and most popular comprehensive models is the ***information processing theory***, developed by Atkinson and Shiffrin, and later expanded by Baddeley and Hitch. In the late 1960s Atkinson and Shiffrin proposed that memory involves a series of connected storage areas through which information is brought in, stored, and later retrieved. Before we consider changes with age and the effects of disease and illness on memory we will review the basic flow of information when all conditions are optimal.

The first step in the information processing model is our ***sensory registers***, which are the physiological structures involved as information is transferred from the environment into our awareness, primarily through our five senses. Information can be held in the sensory registers for approximately 1–4 seconds, depending on which of the five senses is involved. The process of translating the sensory information into brain signals is called ***encoding***. Once encoded the information then moves to ***short-term memory***, where it must be given some attention or it will fade away rather quickly (Cohen, Kiss, & LeVoi, 1993). In common usage the phrase "short-term memory" can refer to information gathered in the last couple of hours or even the last few days. Cognitive and experimental psychologists, however, define short-term memory as lasting less than half a minute (Craik, 2003). So what happens when, following a trauma, a person can't remember what they did today or yesterday? Cognitive psychologists would not say that person has lost their short-term memory but rather that the ability to make new long-term memories has been lost. Short-term temporary storage holds items for approximately 6–12 seconds without any rehearsal, longer if the individual is focused on the information. One of the most consistent research findings regarding short-term memory is that most individuals can hold about five to nine items, which is sometimes stated as 7 plus or minus 2 items, at a time in this storage area.

If information in short-term memory is given the appropriate attention, under healthy circumstances, it will move into relatively permanent memory, which is called ***long-term memory***. Information in long-term storage can be retrieved, used in cognitive processing, and translated into the appropriate form, such as speech or another specialized movement, in order to communicate information back to the environment. The key to quick and accurate retrieval appears to be efficient organization of information in memory storage (Cohen et al., 1993).

Long-term memory appears to be a set of interacting modules or networks rather than one unitary system. The most researched of these modules are procedural, semantic, and episodic memories. ***Procedural memories*** support tasks that we repeat so often they become routine. For example, accomplished musicians, as well as people who do a lot of typing, find that the movements become automatic such that they can play their instrument or type without giving their actions any attention. When we are recalling facts, concepts, and knowledge-based information, such as the type of information often learned in educational or work settings, we are retrieving ***semantic memories***. ***Episodic memories*** are those for personal experiences, which are often stored with time and contextual information as episodes in our life story. Even though these modules are distinct in terms of function they often work simultaneously. For example, if you are telling a friend about your last vacation while driving, you are retrieving episodic memories as you describe your experiences and procedural memories as you remember how to operate your car. If the conversation switches to figuring out how many miles remain to your destination, the mathematical problem solving would require the use of semantic memories (Mitchell, Brown, & Murphy, 1990; Tulving, 1985).

Your Thoughts?

Considering procedural, episodic, and semantic memories, which would take the least amount of effort to retain? The most effort? What makes the difference?

Baddeley and Hitch (1994) modified the Atkinson and Shiffrin model by replacing short-term memory with ***working memory***, which they envisioned would encompass temporary storage or ***primary memory*** and serve as the central processing center for all types of thinking and remembering. Working memory contains the ***central executive processes*** that direct attention and coordinate all information coming into working memory through the sensory registers and that being retrieved from long-term memory. It is in the working memory that individuals can hold needed information while transforming it into something new (Baddeley, 2002; Baddeley & Hitch, 1994). To experience processing in working memory try to answer the following question using only your mental abilities (no paper and pencil or calculator):

- Think of the numbers that are a part of your address, including your zip code, and add those numbers together as single digits.
- Now, think of your phone number, and add those as single digits to your previous sum.
- Finally, add your age to this number. What is the total?

Your Thoughts?

Sometimes it's easier to "think out loud" when solving problems like this. Why might that be?

In this exercise you must read and understand the task, retrieve the information, hold it in your working memory, manipulate and transform it, and hold the new information while you read the next. This task is similar to those used on the Wechsler Adult Intelligence Scale, an IQ test, to measure working memory. To further illustrate the flow of information through the model, consider the verbal exchange detailed in Table 8.1.

Parallel Distributed Processing

Another model inspired from the brain-as-computer metaphor is the ***parallel distributed processing***, or PDP, theory. It is not as comprehensive as the information processing theory, however, it provides a way of understanding long-term memory and is useful when interpreting research on memory decline with age. The PDP theory states that individuals store mental representations of very specific units of information and build connections between those units. Memories are formed when mental energy activates the appropriate units and connections to create a concept. Does this sound familiar? The PDP model is part of the connectionist approach, discussed in detail in Chapter 1, as one of the major approaches to the study of adult development and aging.

TABLE 8.1 ***A Verbal Exchange to Illustrate the Information Processing Model***

Location	*Example*
Environment	A mother calls her teenage son on the phone and asks, "Did you remember to walk the dog?"
Sensory Registers	Her son's five senses are taking in a great deal of information, including her voice.
Working Memory	His working memory is holding the important information, his mother's words, while needed information is retrieved from long-term memory.
Long-Term Memory	He must retrieve episodic memories to determine if he does have memory of walking the dog. Procedural memories will automatically activate the needed understanding of word meaning and sentence structure.
Working Memory	Here her son processes his memories and formulates the words and sentences needed to respond.
Output	"Yes, I remembered to walk the dog. We were out for about 20 minutes."

To illustrate the PDP model, consider a hypothetical character, Mattias, who is looking through a cookbook for something to take to a party. He turns the page and sees "Jambalaya." Energy begins moving through his mental network, connecting each letter (*j, a, m, b, l,* and *y*) and the appropriate sounds used to pronounce the word. His mental energy also travels down the strong bonds associated with "jambalaya," which brings to his mind other concepts, such as Creole, spicy, stew, and southern United States. The energy may follow strong bonds to memories of a trip he took to New Orleans while in college, which may then lead to more college

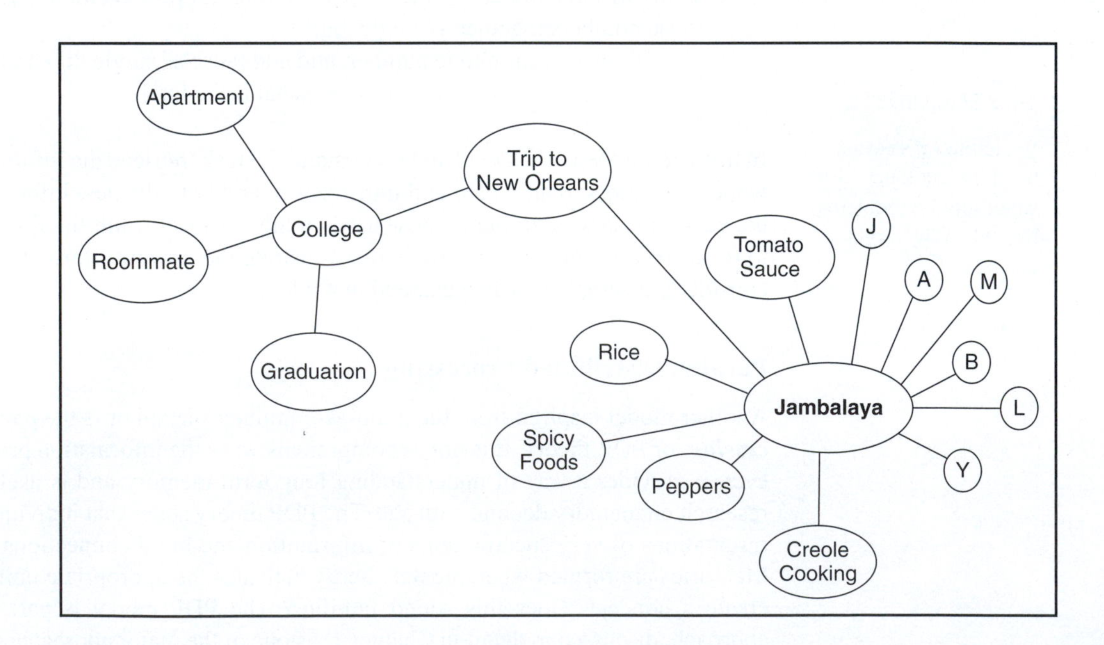

FIGURE 8.1 ***Illustration of Parallel Distributed Processing Model.***

Your Thoughts?

Did you think of the aftermath of Hurricane Katrina when you saw *New Orleans* in the text?

memories coming to mind. As he reads over the recipe he strengthens the bonds between the word *jambalaya* and the ingredients, such as rice, peppers, and tomato sauce. See Figure 8.1 for a diagram of how this process might work. If Mattias decides to make jambalaya often, he will likely strengthen the bonds between the word and the ingredients, making it easier to remember the ingredients in the future. If he closes the cookbook and doesn't think about jambalaya again for a long time, the bonds between the word and the ingredients will become weak, and he may have trouble remembering the ingredients in the future.

The *parallel* nature of the PDP theory comes from the assumption that the mental energy needed to follow connections and pull together information can occur in many directions or pathways at once (Cohen et al., 1993). There is a great deal of research evidence to support the existence of different types of memory and multiple memory systems (Hoyer & Verhaeghen, 2006; Kramer, Fabiani, & Colcombe, 2006). The PDP model provides a way to explain how it is that Mattias could access procedural memories (language), semantic memories (ingredients), and episodic memories (college trip) simultaneously. The PDP model also represents an efficient organizational structure by reducing all information to its smallest parts and then creating connections or bonds between related units.

Your Thoughts?

How might the PDP model explain the tip-of-the-tongue phenomenon?

Section Summary

- The study of memory is among the oldest fields in psychology.
- The information processing model offers a framework for following information as it moves from the environment to our permanent storage, to be retrieved when needed.
- In the information processing model the working memory serves as the central location for all cognitive processing.
- The parallel distributed processing (PDP) model, part of the connectionist approach, provides a way to envision the simultaneous processing needed to fully comprehend a situation and respond to it.
- The PDP model proposes a structure in which energy travels along many pathways of connected units of information at once, allowing for the retrieval and manipulation of procedural, semantic, and episodic memories simultaneously.

Memory and the Aging Brain

The U.S. Congress declared the 1990s the Decade of the Brain (National Institute of Neurological Disorders and Stroke [NINDS], 2007), highlighting the scientific community's long-standing fascination and respect for the complex workings of the human brain. Biological theories have been prominent in the field of lifespan development, and particularly influential in the study of adult development and aging. Two recent developments have converged to even further elevate the status of neuropsychology in the study of aging: New technologies that allow for greater precision in brain imaging, and the increased research efforts aimed at understanding disorders related to changes in brain tissue such as Alzheimer's disease. With safe, accurate technologies, increased research funding, and longitudinal designs researchers can monitor changes in individuals across time. Understanding typical neurological changes with age is critical to anticipating expected changes in cognitive processing as well as recognizing pathological changes (Salthouse, 2006b).

Your Thoughts?

How might counselors and therapists benefit from an understanding of brain anatomy?

Brain Imaging

For centuries doctors and scientists who studied the human brain were greatly limited in what they could observe, often learning by watching the behaviors of patients with brain damage or examining a patient's brain after death. Current technologies involving noninvasive, safe brain imaging techniques provide enormous amounts of data to add to patient observations. One category of brain imaging technologies is the ***structural scans***, such as ***computerized tomography (CT)*** and ***magnetic resonance imaging (MRI)***. These methods produce detailed anatomical images of brain structures. CT scans utilize x-ray technology to highlight variations in density, distinguishing primarily between bone, soft tissue, and fluids. Through the use of CT scans researchers have noted ***brain atrophy***, which is a decrease in the amount of brain tissue detected over time (Albert & Killiany, 2001). Brain weight, on average 1,400 grams for men and 1,250 grams for women, decreases by 2–3 grams per year after age 60. Measuring the volume of the brain as compared to the size of the skull, at age 60 individuals' brains generally take up about 95% of the skull area, whereas by the time people get into their 90s their brains generally take up about 80% of the skull area (Vinters, 2001). Rather than a uniform reduction in size, particular brain structures change at different rates, with some structures starting to reduce in size around age 30. As might be expected, those structures that reduce the most in size show the greatest reductions in performance as well (Kramer et al., 2006).

MRIs are different from CT scans in that MRI technology utilizes magnetic and radio waves to detect different types of soft tissue that form brain structures (Albert & Killiany, 2001; Vinters, 2001). The largest and most developed brain structure is the ***cerebrum***, which is divided into the left and right hemispheres. The entire surface of the cerebrum (both hemispheres) is covered in a darker layer, about the thickness of three dimes, called the ***cortex***. This area, the location of most cognitive processing in the brain, gets it name from the Latin word for "tree bark" because of its characteristic folds and wrinkles. The cortex is also referred to as ***gray matter*** because the nerves in this area lack the insulation that makes other parts of the brain look white (NINDS, 2005). Brain scans indicate that both gray and white matter decrease with age (Kensinger & Corkin, 2003).

Soft tissue in each hemisphere of the cerebrum is separated into four distinctive lobes or regions (see Figure 8.2). It is in the ***frontal lobe*** of each hemisphere where a great deal of

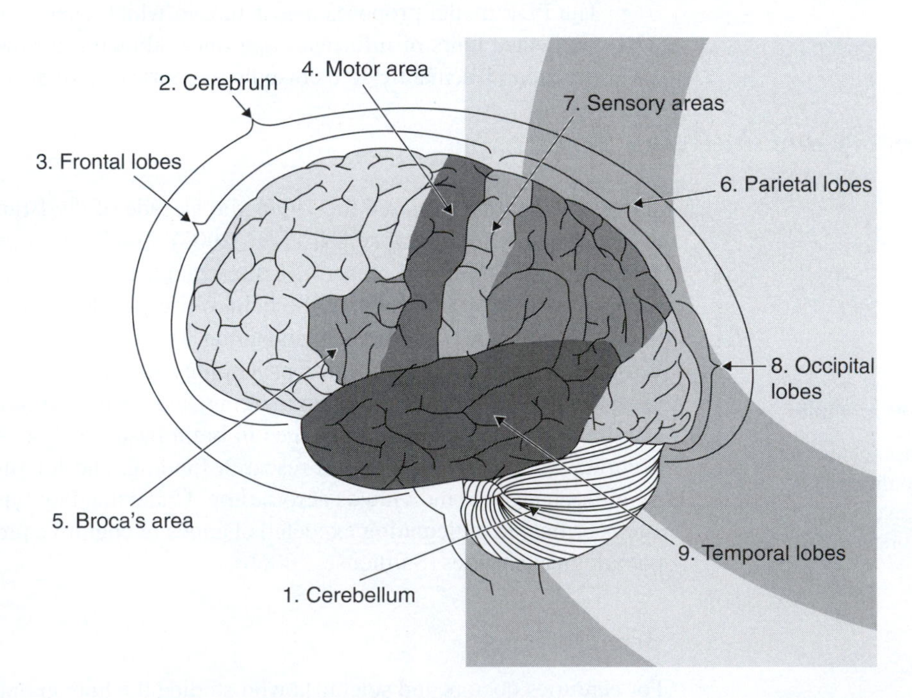

FIGURE 8.2 ***Four Lobes Found in Each Hemisphere.***
From National Institute of Neurological Disorders and Stroke (2007).

thinking occurs, including reasoning, planning, memory processes, and problem solving. For instance, when you are planning the next dinner party at your home, considering what to serve and how best to spread out the food and drinks on the table, you are engaging your frontal lobes. The frontal lobes also contain a motor area for controlling voluntary movement. Behind the frontal lobes are the ***parietal lobes***, which are involved in sensory processing, particularly taste, touch, and temperature. Once the party you planned with your frontal lobe occurs, the taste and texture of the food is registered by your parietal lobes. Interestingly, the parietal lobes are also the location of reading and arithmetic processing. In the very back of the brain are the ***occipital lobes***, which are involved in visual processing. As you look around the room at your party to make sure everyone is having a good time your occipital lobes are processing that information for you. Underneath these three lobes are the ***temporal lobes***, which are involved in processing sounds. As you enjoy the music at your party you are engaging the top of each temporal lobe. As you and others at your party try to remember the words to a song popular several years ago, talking about cover art for CDs and concerts along with trying to remember the words, your temporal lobes are the doing most of the processing (NINDS, 2005). The ability to safely observe differences in brain tissue in healthy brains and those with various diseases as people age has greatly improved our understanding of both brain structures and expected cognitive changes with age.

Another category of brain scan technologies are the ***functional scans***, such as ***positron emission tomography (PET) scans*** and ***functional magnetic resonance imaging (fMRI)***, which provide valuable information regarding the ways brain structures function. The focus on function distinguishes these from the structural scans that highlight anatomical details. PET scans monitor brain functioning by analyzing blood flow, based on the assumption that a greater amount of blood flow in a specific part of the brain indicates greater processing activity. PET scans require patients or research participants to have injected or inhaled a radioactive isotope, which is then followed as an indicator of the changes in blood flow in the brain. Studies utilizing PET scans have indicated that the frontal lobes are active during the encoding and retrieval of information. fMRIs, in contrast to using a radioactive substance, involve the observation of the magnetic quality of water molecules, indicating the ratio of oxygenated to deoxygenated blood in the brain, which is also considered an indirect indicator of processing activity (Albert & Killiany, 2001).

Your Thoughts?

Would you participate in a brain imaging research study? Would you let your child participate? Why or why not?

These brain imaging technologies have added to our understanding of how our brain changes with age. Researchers have found, for example, that aging affects the frontal and temporal lobes more than the others (Albert & Killiany, 2001; Kensinger & Corkin, 2003; Vinters, 2001). PET scans and fMRIs have shown that the prefrontal lobes are active when older individuals are engaging their memory, although the activation pattern is somewhat different from that of younger adults (Albert & Killiany, 2001; Craik, 2003; Kensinger & Corkin, 2003). Brain imaging of younger adults shows that recalling information activates regions that are predominantly lateralized in the right prefrontal cortex, whereas older adults activate both right and left prefrontal regions (Craik, 2003). The use of both hemispheres by older adults appears to increase their memory span, thus proving to be an adaptive change with age (Cherry, Adamson, Duclos, & Hellige, 2005). Although incorporating a healthy lifestyle and cognitively stimulating activities can help our brains function at their best, older adults can expect a gradual decline in some areas of cognitive functioning as they age, much of which is linked to overall decreased activity in the frontal lobes (Craik, 2003).

In terms of memory and cognition, one of the most studied parts of the ***inner brain*** is the ***hippocampus***. Although it is relatively small, it can be thought of as the librarian for all thoughts and memories. It sends information to the appropriate parts of the brain for long-term storage, and then retrieves the information when needed. Brain imaging technologies have shown that hippocampal functioning decreases with normal aging. Healthy older adults often take longer to learn something new than younger adults; however, once information is

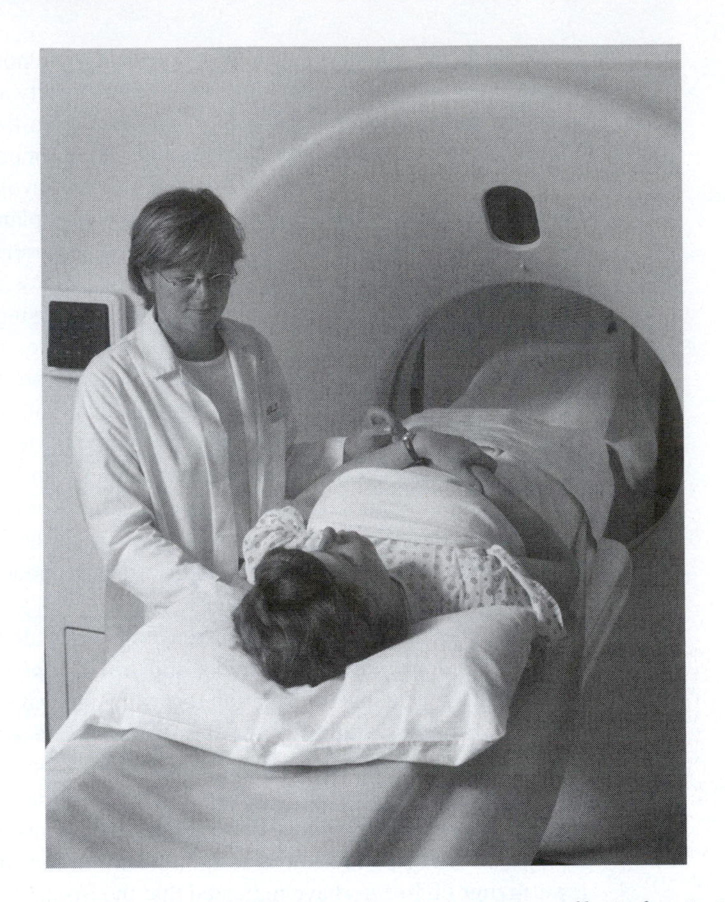

Use of fMRI equipment has dramatically increased our understanding of brain functioning and aging.

learned older adults retain and remember it when needed (Kensinger & Corkin, 2003). In contrast, individuals with Alzheimer's disease have difficulty transferring information from short-term to long-term memory and later retrieving it. Postmortem and MRI studies have found that individuals with Alzheimer's disease have severe damage in the hippocampal area (Albert & Killiany, 2001).

Individual Differences in Brain Development

Though it is tempting to make sweeping generalizations regarding brain imaging findings, there are other key points to consider. For example, although researchers can demonstrate associations between what is found studying brain images and cognitive processing, these relationships do not *prove* cause-and-effect. It is clear that the workings of the human brain are complex and there is much yet to discover. Another important point is that individuals can vary greatly in their aging process, including in their brain activity (Fabiani, Friedman, & Cheng, 1998). Not only are gender differences noted in brain functioning (Albert & Killiany, 2001; Sinnott & Shifren, 2001), researchers have found individual and intraindividual differences in processing speed and performance on various memory tasks (Li, Aggen, Nesselroade, & Baltes, 2001; Zimprich, Hofer, & Aartsen, 2004). Aging individuals also vary in their level of environmental stimulation, social support, personal experiences, physical abilities and activity levels, personal health, quality of health care, nutrition, and amount of cognitive stimulation

Your Thoughts?

How might inexpensive and accessible technologies be adapted to be more user-friendly and cognitively stimulating for older adults?

(Albert & Killiany, 2001). Acknowledging these variations, a new view of developmental neuropsychology is emerging that highlights the awareness that brain structures and functions are likely to be predictable, but not in a precise way. Currently, there is an emphasis on ***equifinality***, the notion that the same neurological function may be achieved by different individuals' brains through somewhat different paths, and ***equipotentiality***, the assumption that brain cells may develop to take on new functions or tasks (Gottlieb, 2001). There is also a growing interest in exploring ways to stimulate brain plasticity to prevent or reduce age-related cognitive decline. ***Plasticity*** refers to the brain's potential to reorganize and structure itself due to environmental stimulation and demands, resulting in improved functioning (Jessberger & Gage, 2008; Li et al., 2008). In some cases when neurons are no longer able to function due to age or injury other neurons will demonstrate plasticity by changing in order to start performing the functions that were lost.

Section Summary

- Researchers have found, using numerous imaging techniques, that healthy brains do change with age, particularly in the frontal areas and in the hippocampus, and that these neurological changes are associated with changes in cognitive processing.
- Structural scan technology, such as CT and MRI, distinguish between types of tissue, fluid, and bone.
- Structural scans assist researchers in charting the shrinking or reduction in size of various parts of the brain that occur with age.
- PET and fMRI technologies reveal more about the functioning of parts of the brain by charting activity.
- Functional scanning techniques have highlighted the changes in the hippocampal areas and the frontal and temporal lobes, which correspond to changes in cognitive processing and memory skills.
- Although the data collected from brain images are remarkable and have contributed greatly to our understanding of brain functioning and aging it is important to note the high occurrence of individual and intraindividual differences are often hidden when general summary statements are made.

Memory Performance Across Adulthood

The information processing and parallel distributed processing models provide ways to conceptualize the flow of information through encoding, transformation, storage, and later retrieval. Although the models present a hypothetical ideal, the reality of the aging brain is that structures, functioning, and performance do change across adulthood. While it may seem that all aspects of memory would be affected by age, that's actually not the case. Researchers have found through brain imaging and cognitive testing that while some areas are more vulnerable, showing decline in performance with age, other areas remain stable across adulthood. This section explores stability and change in memory skills and performance across adulthood, specifically in terms of attention, working memory and processing speed, and episodic and nonepisodic memory. In some cases deficits in sensory registers, such as visual and hearing problems, may contribute to the inaccuracies and slow cognitive processing found with age (Hoyer & Verhaeghen, 2006; Thornton & Light, 2006). If you become concerned over gaps in an older adult's memories or information processing skills it is wise to encourage a discussion with a health care professional about any medical conditions, drugs, or needed check-ups that may shed some light on the cognitive changes. It is also wise to encourage vision and hearing examinations to find out if accurate and complete information is flowing beyond the sensory registers for processing.

Attention

Younger adults are more efficient and successful in their use of attention processes than older adults, although the relationship between aging and attention is quite complex. One aspect that adds to the complexity is that attention is not one function but rather many specific processes. For example, ***selective attention*** is used when choosing to focus on a conversation rather than music playing in the background, or choosing to read something on the Internet while animated advertisements are playing. Although the term *selective* highlights the primary goal of this function selective attention actually involves two simultaneous tasks: choosing or selecting the stimuli to focus on, and the ability to inhibit or ignore all other irrelevant items. ***Vigilance***, another attention process, refers to sustained attention over time. This attention process would be active when waiting for soup to boil or listening for one's number to be called at the deli. Another type of attention process is ***search***, which involves searching for a stimulus, much like scanning the grocery store shelf for a specific product or a parking lot for a particular car.

Your Thoughts?

When you are trying to read, what is the hardest background noise to block out? What is it about those noises that commands your attention?

One of the most researched areas of attention is ***divided attention***, which involves simultaneously maintaining focused energy on more than one stimulus (Rogers & Fisk, 2001). Older adults show both a decline in the amount of available attentional energy and increased difficulty processing all the necessary information in dual-task situations (Craik, 2003). For adults of all ages, but especially for older adults, dividing attention when taking in new information is more problematic than dividing attention when retrieving already learned information (Neveh-Benjamin, Craik, Guez, & Kreuger, 2005; Whiting, 2003). For example, it would be more difficult to concentrate on preparing food from a new recipe and simultaneously engaging in an intense conversation than to drive to a familiar location while engaging in the same intense conversation.

Attention studies done in laboratory settings can be quite complex. Often attention is measured by asking participants to attend to stimuli on a computer monitor and when a response is triggered to immediately press a specifically designated key on the keyboard. The reaction time, measured from the time of the presentation of the stimulus to the time a key is pressed, includes both the time taken for cognitive processing and the amount of time needed for sensory adjustment and physical responses. Imagine, for example, that you are in an

Most adults have difficulty dividing attention when engaging two sensory modes, such as visual attention needed while driving and auditory attention needed while on the phone.

attention study requiring you to watch a screen full of appearing and disappearing color squares. Your task is to press the "c" key on a computer keyboard if an orange square appears and the "n" key if a light green square appears anywhere on the keyboard. The researchers must estimate how long it takes your brain to process the signal "there's an orange square," as well as how long it takes your finger to respond once your brain gives the command "press the 'c' key." In studies involving switching attention from one focal point to another, researchers have found that older adults are slower in response time than younger adults by about one-half of a second. Older adults who are not familiar with computers may be shy or cautious with their responses until they are given some practice time. It may also make a difference if older adults are allowed to simplify their responses, such as by saying a particular word when the target item appears on the screen rather than finding a key on the keyboard (Rogers & Fisk, 2001).

Your Thoughts?

How many years do you think it will be until most people in their 70s are comfortable with computer technology?

Working Memory and Processing Speed

As described earlier regarding the information processing model, information that passes through sensory registers and receives appropriate attention will move to short-term or primary memory. Studies have shown very little decline in primary memory with age (Backman, Small, & Wahlin, 2001; Kensinger & Corkin, 2003). For example, the task of repeating a set of numbers immediately after hearing them shows little change with age (Craik, 2003).

Information is usually held in short-term or primary memory until it can be manipulated or transformed in working memory. For example, the following requires primary memory: *Repeat these words until you can look away and recite them in order: peach, banana, plum, apple, orange, pear.* To involve working memory, imagine a follow-up task: *Look away while reciting the words in order from your most favorite to your least favorite fruit.* Beginning in young adulthood individuals gradually have more trouble with executive control functions, such as processing complex information, large amounts of information, or using elaborate strategies to process information. Working memory deterioration has been found in many tasks, including reading, computing, and listening. It has also been shown in many studies that interference, which requires an inhibitory process to ignore the interfering stimuli as happens with selective attention, can also decrease the effectiveness of working memory in older adults (Backman et al., 2001; Berg & Sternberg, 2003; Craik, 2003; Kensinger & Corkin, 2003; O'Connor & Kaplan, 2003; Thornton & Light, 2006). Neuropsychological studies have found that often these changes in memory are associated with changes in the frontal and temporal regions of the brain (Souchay, Isingrini, & Espagnet, 2000).

Your Thoughts?

How might an employer use this information to train older employees for new positions?

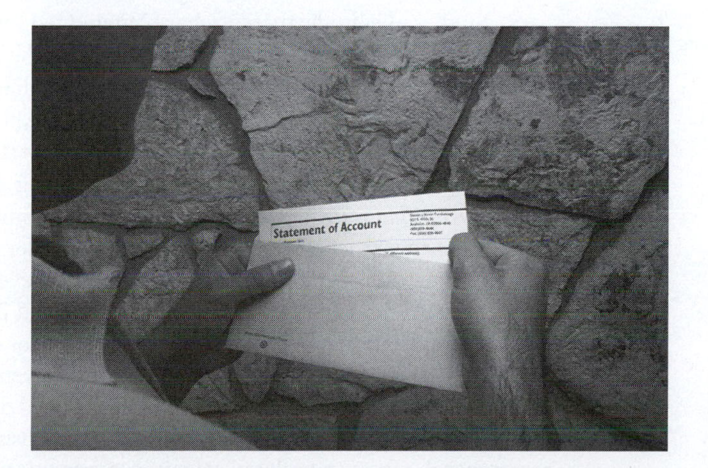

With age most adults will need a longer amount of time to process complex information.

There is much confidence in the robust findings that both the executive control functions and the processing speed in working memory slow with age. In fact, decrease in processing speed is the most popular hypothesis as the primary reason for cognitive decline with age (Craik, 2003; Hoyer & Verhaeghen, 2006; Kensinger & Corkin, 2003; Thornton & Light, 2006), though other possible reasons have been suggested. Other hypotheses include a decrease in memory storage capacity (Kensinger & Corkin, 2003), less ability to coordinate cognitive tasks and processes, and less ability to switch cognitive tasks (Hoyer & Verhaeghen, 2006). Using the PDP model, another possibility is that deficits in the transmission of energy among memory representations are causing weak connections between bits of information (Thornton & Light, 2006).

Episodic Memory

Once information has been processed as needed in working memory it is stored in long-term memory for later retrieval. As discussed earlier in the information processing model, one way of conceptualizing long-term memory is in terms of episodic memory, which is discussed here, and other types of nonepisodic memory, which are discussed in the next section. Episodic memories are those for personal experiences or life episodes. The pieces of information that make up these memories are connected by time and place, which is often referred to as *environmental context* (Craik, 2003). You are retrieving episodic memories when you describe all you can remember about:

- one of your favorite vacations
- the last family gathering you attended
- your activities 4 days ago

Memories for life experiences generally deteriorate in a steady fashion from early to late adulthood, becoming noticeable for most individuals in their 60s (Backman et al., 2001; Hoyer & Verhaeghen, 2006). The decline in episodic memory is thought to be associated with the reduction in processing speed and decreased efficiency observed in working memory (Hertzog, Dixon, Hultsch, & MacDonald, 2003). Although it has been commonly accepted that episodic memories decline with age, some studies have demonstrated otherwise (Veiel & Storandt, 2003). For example, by comparing data collection methods Ronnlund, Nyberg, Backman, and Nilsson (2005) were able to show while cross-sectional data demonstrates a decline in the retrieval of episodic memories, longitudinal data reflect stability until age 60.

Your Thoughts?

What kind of memory training program would you design to help with this problem? How might you design a research study to test the success of the program?

Studies of episodic memory have highlighted some interesting patterns. For example, older adults have more trouble accurately remembering the source of a particular piece of information or memory (Kensinger & Corkin, 2003). Often they can remember the content but cannot remember who said it or when they heard it. This can lead an older adult to repeat stories to the very person who was the source of their information (Craik, 2003; Hoyer & Verhaeghen, 2006).

Another interesting and consistent finding in studies of episodic memory is the ***autobiographical memory bump***, which is sometimes referred to as the *reminiscence bump.* Researchers consistently find that when asking older participants for a list of "most important" personal memories the responses are generally for events, more positive than negative, that happened when the participants were in their teens and 20s (Birren & Schroots, 2006). This reminiscence pattern begins for adults in their late 30s or 40s. It is referred to as a *bump* because of the way it looks when graphing the number of events recalled as among the most important across the decades (see Figure 8.3). One age-related difference noted is that younger adults tend to recall their personal thoughts about these early events whereas older adults are more likely to remember the facts and related semantic information (Backman et al., 2001; Levine, Svoboda,

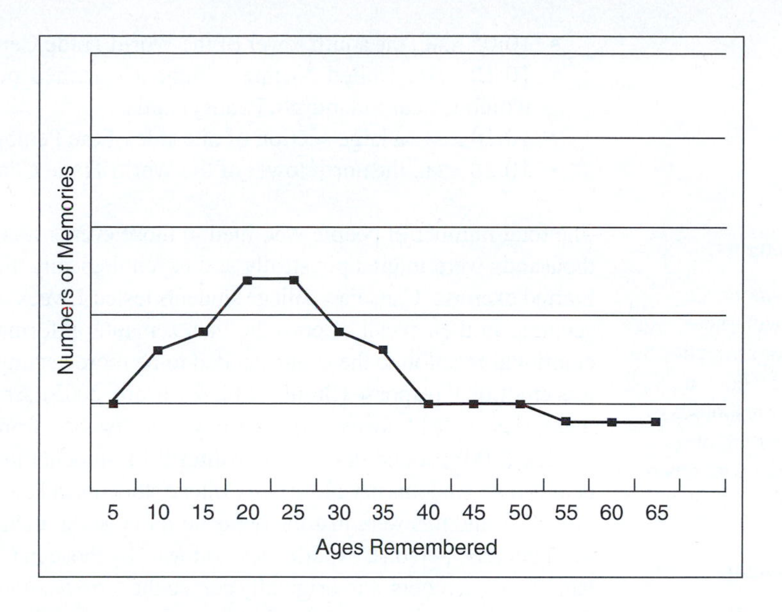

FIGURE 8.3 ***Autobiographical Bump.***

Hay, Winocur, & Moscovitch, 2002). There are several hypotheses regarding the cause of the autobiographical memory bump. One suggestion is to take the data at face value and conclude that the most important events in life are concentrated in adolescence and young adulthood. (While that is a viable hypotheses it is a little disheartening for those of us beyond young adulthood!) Another reason might be that many first-time events, such our first car, first apartment, wedding, or child, are powerful because of their first-time status and therefore stand out in memory (Jansari & Parkin, 1996). Another hypothesis is that adults have more time to rehearse older memories, which strengthen the bonds or connections between the units of information, thus allowing for easier and quicker retrieval. Individuals who are in their 60s or 70s have had many years to retell the stories of their significant young adulthood experiences (Bernsten & Rubin, 2002). Yet another line of reasoning is that the memories recalled are significant in that they contribute to our sense of identity (Birren & Schroots, 2006; Conway, 2003). These self-defining memories confirm our view of ourselves and our personality (Conway, 2003). Supporting this hypothesis, some studies have shown that adults remember events that were associated with their psychosocial stage at the time the memory was formed (Conway & Holmes, 2004). Keep in mind that the autobiographical memory bump is likely to be the result of a complex set of factors that may involve the blending of several of these hypotheses.

Your Thoughts?

If you were given grant money and staff to study one of the autobiographical memory bump hypotheses, which would you choose? Why?

A third pattern unique to episodic memories is the occurrence of ***flashbulb memories***, which are made when unexpected, shocking events occur. For memory researchers the events of September 11, 2001, often referred to as simply "9/11," created the perfect opportunity to study flashbulb memories. In the Before We Get Started section of this chapter there were several questions regarding personal experiences (episodic memories) and some factual details (semantic memories) regarding 9/11. How well did you do with the factual information? Here is a summary of what happened on that Tuesday morning. All the times given are approximate, and presented in Eastern Standard Time.

- 8:46 A.M., American Airlines Flight 11 crashed into the north tower of the World Trade Center in New York City
- 9:03 A.M., United Airlines Flight 175 crashed into the south tower of the World Trade Center
- 9:45 A.M., American Airlines Flight 77 crashed into the Pentagon in Washington, D.C.

- 10:05 A.M., the south tower of the World Trade Center collapses
- 10:10 A.M., United Airlines Flight 93 crashed near Shanksville in Somerset County, which is near Pittsburgh, Pennsylvania
- 10:10 A.M., a large section of one side of the Pentagon collapses
- 10:28 A.M., the north tower of the World Trade Center collapses

Your Thoughts?

Were you more accurate with the episodic or semantic items? Why do you think your responses were consistent or inconsistent with other findings?

Your Thoughts?

Do you think 9/11, Hurricane Katrina, or the oil spill in the Gulf of Mexico in April 2010 will create the most flashbulb memories?

The total number of people who died in those events was estimated to be over 3,000, and many thousands were injured physically and psychologically. In a study similar to the Before We Get Started exercise, Canadian college students tested 1 week and then 6 months after 9/11 were more accurate in their recall of episodic than semantic information. Students who reported a greater emotional reaction to the events tended to be more accurate with the facts than those reporting a less emotional response (Smith, Bibi, & Sheard, 2003). Another study involving college students' memories of 9/11 focused on the physical distance from the site of the World Trade Center. Pezdek (2003) found that 7 weeks after 9/11 students in Manhattan remembered more factual details than students in California. College students in Hawaii retained the least semantic information. The findings were just the opposite for episodic memories. Students in Hawaii reported the most detailed personal experiences, followed by those in California, and then by those in Manhattan. The researchers who originally coined the term *flashbulb memory,* Brown and Kulik, believed that the place or location, the duration of the event, the characteristics surrounding the way an individual learns of the information,and the emotionality involved were key factors (Tekcan, Ece, Gulgoz, & Er, 2003). Historical events, which meet these criteria for large numbers of people, provide psychologists with unique opportunities to learn more about flashbulb memories.

Just as with so many topics in adult development, it is important to note that individual differences in memory performance can be dramatic. Individuals with higher levels of education tend to perform better on many memory tasks, including episodic retrieval. Researchers have also found that women tend to have better episodic memories than men (Backman et al., 2001). Certainly episodic memories are affected by deterioration; however, the extent of the effects will vary among individuals.

Nonepisodic Memory

Even though procedural and semantic memories are considered separate modules of permanent storage, they demonstrate a similar pattern with age that is distinct from episodic memory. Procedural memories often involve motor, perceptual, and/or cognitive operations, such as the skills needed for reading or driving. For those who become skilled at a task, such as typing or playing an instrument, it may seem as if their responses occur with little or no attention or mental effort. From a PDP model perspective, successful procedural memories are those that have developed extremely strong bonds between units of information such that working memory easily and quickly finds and retrieves appropriate information. Most research indicates that procedural memory remains strong through the aging process, particularly for skills learned at a younger age (Backman et al., 2001; Mitchell et al., 1990; Rogers & Fisk, 2001). Also, the ability to develop new procedural memories tends to remain strong throughout adulthood (O'Connor & Kaplan, 2003).

Semantic memories, long-term memories for general knowledge, facts, and concepts are stored without any need to remember time or place (Craik, 2003). You are retrieving semantic memories when you attempt the following tasks:

- Name as many types of birds as you can.
- Starting with the number 105, subtract 7, give the answer, subtract 7 again, give the answer, and continue giving all the answers until you reach zero.
- Give the past-tense forms of the words *speak, buy,* and *say.*

ON THE LEADING EDGE
Intrusive Memories

Therapists who work with clients with posttraumatic stress disorder (PTSD) are continually seeking new insights that may help in the healing and recovery process. One aspect of PTSD that has gained the attention of several researchers is the involuntary reliving of intrusive memories. Researchers from Duke University Medical Center and the Durham Veterans Affairs Medical Center teamed up to further understand the mechanisms behind intrusive memories. Rubin, Feldman, and Beckham (2004) recruited 50 male veterans, ranging in age from 25 to 78 years old, who were diagnosed with PTSD and seeking treatment. In addition to numerous questionnaires, the men were asked to recall four memories: one from 2 years before service, one noncombat memory from their time in the service, one from combat, and one from service that had become an intrusive memory. For each memory the men were asked to fill out a questionnaire that rated the sensory experience of reliving the memory as well as the the emotional content.

The researchers found that the experience of reliving a memory, whether voluntarily or by experiencing an intrusive memory, is heavily grounded in the emotional content of the memory. Their findings indicated that emotions work on both a cognitive level as well as a physiological or visceral level. When comparing the preservice, noncombat, combat, and intrusive memories, the researchers found that the key factor in the vividness and "feeling of realness" in reliving an experience is the emotional intensity.

Although the criteria for diagnosis with PTSD requires that the traumatic events evoke intense fear, horror, or helplessness, researchers have explored the power of other emotions to create intrusive memories. Donald Robinaugh and Richard McNally (2010) of Harvard University found that some traumatic events leading to PTSD symptoms are centered around intense feelings of shame, also producing intrusive, vivid memories. In this case shame was defined as a moral emotion involving a negative self-evaluation, operating in contrast to guilt which involves a negative evaluation of an action. Whereas feelings of guilt prompt the thought "I did a bad thing" feelings of shame prompt the thought "I'm a bad person." Robinaugh and McNally found that when the memories that prompted the shame are central to one's identity and life story they are more intrusive and vivid. By learning more about the mechanisms that bring to mind these intrusive and involuntary memories, particularly those aspects that contribute to the feeling of reliving the experience, researchers hope to find better ways to ease the suffering of individuals with PTSD.

You may not remember when and where you learned the names of particular birds or the past-tense form of *buy,* but it's likely that you do remember the information. Most models of semantic memories propose that information is organized and stored hierarchically, starting with a general concept and moving to specific items. For example, in remembering the birds you may have started with a general category like "large birds," naming those, and then moving to smaller birds.

Research has shown that semantic memories retrieved regularly remain strong with age, as do their organization and structure (Backman et al., 2001). In a cross-sectional study involving 345 participants ranging in age from 20 to 92 years old, Park and her colleagues (2002) found that verbal knowledge remained strong as working memory, short-term memory, long-term memory, and processing speed declined (see Figure 8.4). Other studies have also demonstrated that word knowledge may remain strong until individuals reach their 90s (Hoyer & Verhaeghen, 2006). In a study designed to compare cross-sectional and longitudinal data on memory, Ronnlund et al. (2005) tested 829 participants ranging in age from 35 to 80 years old across a 5-year span. Cross-sectional analysis of semantic memory for 35- to 60-year-old participants demonstrated stability, while the longitudinal data actually showed increases in the amount of semantic knowledge retained. For participants older than age 60, both cross-sectional and longitudinal analysis revealed only a slight decline in semantic memory. These findings are consistent with earlier studies demonstrating that middle-aged adults performed the best on tests of semantic memory (Backman & Nilsson, 1996). From a PDP perspective it appears that, just as with procedural memory, the conceptual bonds that connect units of information remain strong throughout most of adulthood, allowing for quick and accurate retrieval. One area of semantic memory that does show decline with age is the ability to remember new facts, such as remembering the names of people recently met (Craik, 2003; Kensinger & Corkin, 2003).

Your Thoughts?

Based on these findings how much of a risk is an employer taking when hiring an older adult with expertise in a desired area?

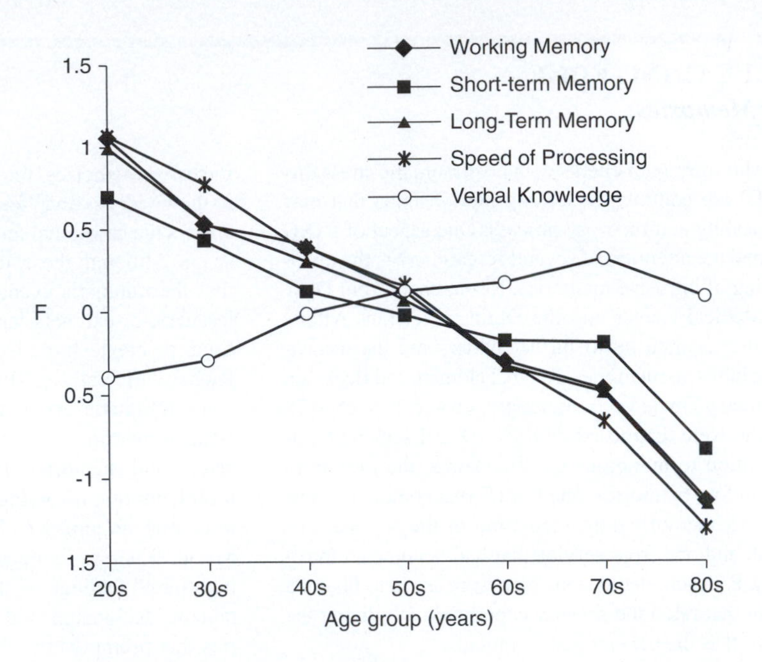

FIGURE 8.4 ***Changes in Working Memory, Short-Term Memory, Long-Term Memory, Speed, and Verbal Knowledge from the 20s to the 80s.***

From Park, Lautenschlager, Hedden, Davidson, Smith, & Smith (2002, p. 305). Copyright by the American Psychological Association. Reprinted with permission.

Section Summary

- It is somewhat misleading to make the broad assertion that memory worsens with age.
- Research shows that some memory skills and performance actually improve with age, others remain stable, and some do decline in accuracy and efficiency (Craik, 2003).
- Older adults have reduced attentional energy and are less accurate with some attention-related tasks.
- Among the more robust findings in memory research are the decreases in processing speed and executive control functions in working memory.
- Episodic memories, those for personal experiences, are much more vulnerable to deterioration and loss than procedural or semantic memories.
- Among the interesting age-related patterns noted in research on episodic memories are inability to recall the source of information, the tendency to recall memories from adolescence and young adulthood (autobiographical memory bump), and the ability to form flashbulb memories for personally shocking events.
- Procedural and semantic memories remain strong with age.

Memory Errors, Improvement Strategies, and Training

When considering memory and aging an interesting trend emerges regarding memory errors and failures. Studies show that the same memory problems that are dismissed in younger adults are considered worthy of much more attention and concern when attributed to older adults (Hess, 2006). Most adults, no matter what age, realize that their memory processes are not perfectly accurate and complete. In a survey of adults between the ages of 20 and 83,

Your Thoughts?

Thinking in evolutionary terms, what might be the advantages of having a less-than-accurate memory?

Reese and Cherry (2004) found many memory deficits common to all adults. Participants of all ages wished they were better at remembering precise verbal information, such as the punch lines in jokes or specific medical terms. Another common complaint was problems with recall of spatial location information, such as remembering directions to a certain location or where an item was left (Reese & Cherry, 2004). Fortunately, there is good news in that most adults, even those well into late adulthood, can improve their memory skills with effort and practice (Hoyer & Verhaeghen, 2006; Kramer et al., 2006), as well as by maintaining good physical health. Physical fitness and a healthy diet have been linked to improvements in many cognitive functions, including speed of processing and working memory functions (Hoyer & Verhaeghen, 2006).

Common Memory Errors

One of the differences between computer memory and human memory is that, assuming the hardware and software are working properly, computer memory is always accurate; the information entered is the exact information retrieved. Imagine how frustrating it would be to save a word processing document, and then have the following happen when you tried to retrieve it:

- Only key words and phrases were retained, and all the "filler" had to be recreated
- Other, similar documents had blended with the particular document retrieved
- An error message appeared saying "This document cannot be accessed at this time"

These sorts of memory problems happen with human memory all the time, regardless of age. Whether it is *absentmindedness,* failing to remember something routine such as where we left our cell phone, or *blocking,* when we cannot bring to mind information we are confident we know (Schacter, 1999), all adults struggle with common types of forgetfulness.

In addition to retrieval problems, most adults are vulnerable to the imperfections and delicate nature of memory. Over the last two decades research on ***false memories*** has highlighted the ease with which individuals can be led to confirm information that, in reality, never

Research on the prevalence of false memories has raised many questions about the accuracy of eyewitness testimony.

occurred. For example, by comparing personal accounts to actual events, Pezdek (2003) found that college students held many false memories related to the events of September 11, 2001. Although some participants had great confidence in the accuracy of their memories, some of them had the sequence of events out of order, the timing of events distorted, and even the locations of the plane crashes wrong. False memories can be prompted by many sources, such as personal bias that leads an individual to insert new information into memories and *suggestibility,* the term used when false but often repeated information seeps into personal memories (Schacter, 1999). One laboratory method for inducing false memories is called the *DRM paradigm,* with "DRM" being the initials of the developers, Deese, Roediger, and McDermott (Dehon & Bredart, 2004). Try this version of the technique:

Your Thoughts?

How might crime investigators use this information on common memory errors?

- Find a place where you can write or type a set of words and number from 1 through 10.
- Read the following 10 words to yourself once, shut the book, and write down as many of the words as you can remember: *water, float, fish, cruise, row, paddle, motor, ship, ski, sail.*
- Did you come up with 10 words or was your list shorter?
- Compare your list to the list above. How many of the 10 words did you get correct?

Did you put the word *boat* as one of the remembered words? If you did you are not alone. More than just a memory test, the DRM paradigm is designed to send energy through a network of connected words that are related to a larger target concept. The word *boat* is the target for many of the words presented. Although adults of all ages produce the false memory for the target word, older adults demonstrate false memories more often (Backman et al., 2001; Dehon & Bredart, 2004).

Individual Memory Improvement Strategies

Most adults use a combination of internal strategies, such as memorization techniques, and external methods, such as making a note of something to be remembered, in order improve our daily functioning. One of the most studied internal strategies is ***mnemonics***, which involves creating artificial bonds or connections in order to increase the likelihood of memory retrieval. For example, a popular mnemonic called an ***acronym*** involves making a word out of the first letters of the items to be remembered. Many schoolchildren learn to associate the word ***HOMES*** with the Great Lakes in the northern part of the United States. The five great lakes are ***H***uron, ***O***ntario, ***M***ichigan, ***E***rie, and ***S***uperior. Although the true meaning of the word *homes* is generally unrelated to the Great Lakes, the acronym provides an artificial way of associating the terms. Another popular mnemonic is an ***acrostic***, which involves making sentences using words that start with the same letters as the to-be-remembered words in the same order as the to-be-remembered words. One common acrostic is ***P***lease ***E***xcuse ***M***y ***D***ear ***A***unt ***S***ally, which is associated with the order of arithmetic operations, ***P***arentheses, ***E***xponent, ***M***ultiply, ***D***ivide, ***A***dd, and ***S***ubtract. Songs and rhymes can also serve as mnemonics. It is likely that many American adults still sing a familiar alphabet song learned by most preschool children when putting information in alphabetical order or recite a common rhyme to remember how many days are in each month.

Another popular mnemonic strategy often used is to link information to mental images or pictures, a technique called a ***pictorial mnemonic***. Dretzke (1993) found that adults instructed to study pictures that illustrated words remembered the words better than those who were told to mentally create their own picture. Younger and middle-aged adults benefited more from the use of pictorial mnemonics than the older adults (Kennet, McGuire, Willis, & Schaie, 2000). A method that combines the strengths of acrostics, rhymes, and pictorial visualization is the

RESEARCH IN-DEPTH
Deception

When recruiting participants, researchers should provide enough information for people to decide whether they want to participate. This information may include the topics involved and the nature of the study, the level of anonymity, any activities involved, and the time frame and any special arrangements. Informed consent is especially important when the variables being studied are personally or socially sensitive, or when the activities involved are strenuous, lengthy, or in some other way risky. Informed consent is required by all universities, medical centers, government agencies, and professional groups such as the American Psychological Association and the American Medical Association. All of these institutions have Institutional Review Boards that must approve all human research.

That said, in some cases true informed consent will likely cause interference. There are times when a study simply could not be carried out unless the participants were somewhat deceived. This was the dilemma facing Porter, Spencer, and Birt (2003) who wanted to try to create false memories in participants by giving them misleading questions about an emotional scene. If they told the participants prior to the study "we are studying false memories and we plan to give you misleading questions to do that," then participants would be ready for the challenge. The researchers, seeing the need for the use of deception, sought and gained permission from their local Institutional Review Board to be initially less-than-truthful with their participants.

Porter and his colleagues (2003) recruited 90 Canadian undergraduate college students as participants. After being given a partially accurate description of the study, participants signed forms indicating their "informed" consent. Each participant then filled out a questionnaire and saw one of eight randomly mixed photographs. The eight photographs included three with highly positive scenes, three with highly negative scenes, and two with nonemotional or neutral scenes. Each participant was asked to describe the scene while viewing the pictures. That was followed by about 20 minutes of filling out questionnaires. At this point some of the research procedure changed. Some of the participants were given additional questionnaires on the emotional quality of the pictures while other participants were exposed to misleading questions before filling out the emotional quality questionnaires. Some of the misleading questions emphasized major items that were not in the original scenes. For example, in a picture in which there was no dog involved, one of the misleading questions used was "Was the German Shepherd dog in the background lying down or standing?" Whether in the misled group or the non-misled group, all the participants were then asked to describe as much as they could remember about the original scenes. After they reported all they could remember the participants were asked some direct (nonmisleading) questions, such as "Was there a dog in the scene?" This represented the end of the laboratory experiment, but not the end of participant involvement.

Before the participants were finished with the process they needed to be *debriefed*. All of the participants had a right to know what was really happening in the study, thus all were told the real point of the experiment when it was over. The debriefing process involved an explanation of the true nature of the study and a chance to ask questions.

Porter and his colleges (2003) found that none of the participants in the non-misled group recalled misinformation, although 53% of the participants in the misled group displayed false memories. They also found that the level of false recall varied by the emotions displayed in the scene, with most of the false memories occurring in the negative scenes.

Psychologists try to keep the use of deception to a minimum, recognizing that in some cases the benefits of what will be gained from the study outweigh the ethical violation and any associated risks. When studying topics that initiate a strong sense of social correctness or appropriateness, such as gender or racial issues, psychologists will gain a more accurate understanding of how people *really* think when using deception. For example, deceptive language such as "The purpose of this study is to explore teacher–student interactions in math and science classes" will likely bring a more accurate understanding of gender bias than stating "The purpose of this study is to explore gender bias among math and science teachers toward boys."

The use of deception raises many ethical questions that should be explored thoroughly before an experiment begins. This responsibility lies first and foremost with the researchers. They must demonstrate to their various review boards that deception is necessary, that it is done in the least offensive way possible, and that the benefits gained from what would be learned from the study outweigh any potential problems caused by the deceptive technique.

peg-word mnemonic, useful when the to-be-remembered items must be recalled in a particular order. The first step in the strategy is to associate words that rhyme with the numbers, such as *one* and *bun* or *one* and *gun, two* and *shoe* or *two* and *zoo,* and so on, for as many items as need to be remembered. The second step is to visualize the first item to be remembered as, for example, being shot out of a gun, while the second item is visualized in the context of a zoo. Another mnemonic that emphasizes pictorial visualization is the ***method-of-loci***, using a strategy that involves associating the to-be-remembered items with various familiar locations. For example, to remember to get chips, dip, and soda at the grocery store you might visualize cans of soda exploding in your living room, popping and covering the walls with sticky liquid, so you avoid the exploding cans and run into the kitchen only to find you almost fall because the floor is covered in crunchy chips and the faucet is flowing with dip that has filled the sink and is dripping down the cabinet. Internal strategies, whether word-based like an acrostic or picture-based like the method-of-loci, can be extremely helpful in creating long-term memories. Some mnemonics are so powerful that they take on their own meaning. I find, for instance, that my college students know what the acronym *SCUBA* refers to even though they cannot tell me what the *S, C, U, B,* and *A* stand for.

Your Thoughts?

What individual characteristics might contribute to a person's preference for verbal or pictorial mnemonics?

In addition to internal strategies, adults also cope with memory deficits and errors through external strategies. Among the more popular external memory tools are calendars and written (Reese & Cherry, 2004) and digital notes on smart phones and other devices. Following routines can also help in remembering important items. For example, by establishing a routine set of things to do before leaving home in the morning we are less likely to forget

ON THE LEADING EDGE
Memory Training for Older Adults

Erin Hastings and Robin West (2009) wanted to explore different methods of helping older adults improve their memory. They recruited 185 adults between the ages of 54 and 92 to be in one of three conditions: group training, self-training with a manual, and the group told they had to wait for a spot to open which actually served as the control group. The members of the group training condition met for 2 hours over a period of 6 weeks to work through the same manual that the self-training group received to work through as homework. Follow-up memory tests indicated that both groups improved their memory skills. The group condition felt more in control of their memory processes than the self-training group, although even that group improved in levels of confidence.

In a similar study but with a different research question, a group of researchers representing the Karolinska Institue, the Department of Psychology at the University of Umea, and the Stockholm Gerontology Research Center in Sweden, along with the Max Planck Institute for Human Development in Berlin, Germany, wanted to learn more about the value of teaching older adults various mnemonic strategies as compared to asking them to create their own strategy. The researchers were particularly interested in techniques that allow adults older than 60 years old to encode and retain information for several months. A total of 60 individuals were recruited for the study.

One group of participants was given 10 one-hour sessions to learn a particular mnemonic to help in remembering numbers. The participants memorized a code that matched the numbers 0 to 9 with an equal number of consonants. In order to remember a four-digit number, the participants would match the numbers with the corresponding consonants and try to make a word or sentence based on the letters. If the number to be remembered was 2894, and the corresponding consonants were C, S, T, G, the participants might remember "cast-g" or "Cars Stop, Then Go." Another group of participants were given the same number of training sessions; however, they were encouraged to create their own meaningful way of remembering the numbers. If the numbers to be remembered were 4824, one individual might focus on "4 doubled is 8, 2 doubled is 4," whereas another participant might think "when I was 48 my son was 24." At the end of the training sessions for both groups the participants were given the task of memorizing 6 four-digit numbers. The researchers test the participants' accuracy in recalling the 6 items at 30 minutes after learning them, and then again at 24 hours later, 7 weeks later, and for the last time at 8 months later.

Although the two groups performed equally well with the recall of the numbers at 30 minutes and 24 hours, the group that created personally meaningful strategies significantly outperformed the other group at 7 weeks and 8 months beyond the time of learning. The researchers were able to show that when attached to personally meaningful information, older adults can learn and retain specific information for a rather long time (Derwinger, Neely, MacDonald, & Backman, 2005). These findings, combined with those of Hastings and West (2009), are encouraging for family members, health care professionals, and others who are working with older adults in terms of remembering important items, such as phone numbers and personal identification numbers (PIN).

something important (American Academy of Family Physicians, 2000). Another strategy is to use your environment itself as a memory aid by keeping specific items in consistent places. This involves such strategies as keeping remote controls and rechargers in a certain basket, placing items for a trip by the front door, and even parking in a similar location at frequently visited stores (Reese & Cherry, 2004). Creating this familiar pattern will increase the likelihood of remembering important information (Craik, 2003). It will be interesting to observe how comfort levels with technology will change the ways adults use external memory tools. As I see more and more middle-aged and young adults using their smart phones for email, text, and calendar reminders I wonder if that will continue into late adulthood. Also, although not a specific external memory strategy, engaging in cognitively stimulating and complex activities will help us retain the good internal memory skills we developed over the years (Hoyer & Verhaeghen, 2006; Mayo Clinic, 2004).

Your Thoughts?

How would you set up a study to learn about generational differences in the use of common technologies as external reminders?

Memory Training

Although the amount of improvement will lessen in old age (Hoyer & Verhaeghen, 2006), with some effort, attention, and practice, older adults can learn various memory improvement techniques (O'Connor & Kaplan, 2003; Rogers & Fisk, 2001). For example, by keeping attention focused, rather than divided among tasks, and by using more elaborative encoding strategies, older adults can perform many memory tasks as well as younger adults (Whiting, 2003). In a large-scale meta-analysis involving 33 different memory studies and 1,539 older adults, Verhaeghen, Marcoen, and Goossens (1992) found that training programs can substantially improve memory processes for older adults. Research comparing training in different types of mnemonic strategies shows that almost any mnemonic, when taken seriously and practiced, can improve memory. To demonstrate this, Woolverton, Scogin, Schakelford, Black, and Duke (2001) asked 77 participants, ranging in age from 66 to 88 years old, to work with various mnemonics and memory aids, such as physical reminders (such as notes), categorizing information in meaningful groupings, and various strategies for associating names and faces. They found that all the strategies worked, although all were less effective for the older participants. Rasmusson, Rebok, Bylsma, and Brandt (1999), performing a similar study with 53 residents of a continuing care retirement community, also found all the strategies to be successful in improving memory retrieval.

Your Thoughts?

How can a health care professional use this information to help older patients remember their medications?

Researchers have also found that a positive attitude both in general and about one's cognitive processes is related to memory performance (Mayo Clinic, 2004). Adults who believe that memory strategies can improve their memory tend to perform better on memory tasks (Jennings & Darwin, 2003). Also, adults who receive confidence-building feedback on their memory performance along with mnemonic training perform better than those who receive mnemonic training alone (Hastings & West, 2009; West, Bagwell, & Dark-Freudeman, 2008). For example, in a memory training program involving adults ranging in age from their 50s to their 90s, West et al. (2008) found that participants' individual sense of self-efficacy and control over memory were powerful influences on memory performance.

In this chapter we come full circle beginning with memory models and brain functioning and ending with the concept of brain plasticity. In this context plasticity is reflected in the ways personal experience, in this case memory training, can influence the structure and function of neurons and neural networks resulting in improvements in cognitive performance (Li et al., 2008; Ulrich, 2008). While it is debated whether enough substantial research evidence exists to support the folk wisdom of "use it or lose it," often referred to as the *mental-exercise hypothesis* as it relates to long-term memory decline (Salthouse, 2006a, 2007; Schooler, 2007), it does appear that adults of all ages can benefit from memory training.

Section Summary

- Adults of all ages complain of memory errors and failures.
- Memories are delicate and sometimes inaccurate, so much so that false memories can be easily induced in a laboratory setting.
- One way to improve memory skills is to learn internal strategies, such as using mnemonics to create meaning among items to be remembered.
- External strategies, such as writing notes and keeping items in only one location, can also improve the likelihood of memory retrieval.
- Memory performance benefits from appropriate physical fitness and a healthy diet.
- Numerous studies have shown that memory skills improve with training, even among older adults.
- It appears that almost any mnemonic or improvement strategy will improve memory as long as it is taken seriously, given attention and effort, and practiced.

Chapter Summary

The psychological understanding of memory includes the blending of data collected from brain imaging technologies and theoretical models of information processing. Using technology that analyzes the changes in the amounts of tissue, blood flow, and oxygen in the brain, along with carefully designed cognitive tests, researchers are seeking to understand the differences between normal, expected memory changes due to age and those caused by disease. Generally, whereas primary or short-term, procedural, and semantic memories tend to remain strong with age, the processing components of working memory and episodic memories tend to deteriorate with age. It is important to note, however, that there are many individual differences that make such generalizations less helpful. It is also important to remember that there are many common memory errors that all individuals are susceptible to, and that memory performance can often be improved through personal effort and the use of memory aids. Here are some of the main points of the chapter:

- Information processing theory states that information from the environment enters our awareness through our sensory registers, is held in short-term memory for processing in the working memory, and continues to long-term memory where it is stored and retrieved by the working memory when needed.
- The parallel distributed processing theory states that memory is organized as a large, intricate network of units connected by associations or bonds, and that retrieval of information involves sending energy down numerous pathways at once.
- Brain imaging produced by structural scans, such as CT and MRI scans, have demonstrated brain atrophy, beginning for most people after age 60.
- Measures of brain functioning, such as PET scans and fMRIs, have indicated that older adults may engage different brain structures when involved in cognitive processing, particularly in the frontal lobes, than they did when they were younger.
- Although some attention processes decline in speed and accuracy with age, most older adults perform better when they are familiar with the task, have time to practice, and can simplify their responses.
- Whereas the short-term or primary memory does not show decline with age, processing speed and the efficiency of the executive control functions in working memory do show deterioration with age.
- Episodic memory demonstrates a great amount of loss and deterioration with age.

- The autobiographical memory bump refers to the consistent finding that older adults recall more important events from their adolescent and young adulthood years than any other time in life.
- Flashbulb memories, containing both semantic and episodic information, occur when shocking, unexpected events occur.
- Procedural and semantic memories tend to remain strong throughout adulthood, with many areas remaining strong for individuals into their 90s.
- Memories can be delicate and distorted, sometimes displaying errors prompted by absentmindedness, bias, or the introduction of false information.
- Strategies to enhance memory include the use of mnemonics, keeping notes, and placing items in routine locations.
- Researchers have found almost all mnemonics and memory improvement strategies work as long as the individual invests time, energy, and commitment into the process.

Key Terms

Behaviorism **(206)**
Cognitive revolution **(206)**
Information processing theory **(206)**
Sensory registers **(206)**
Encoding **(206)**
Short-term memory **(206)**
Long-term memory **(206)**
Procedural memories **(207)**
Semantic memories **(207)**
Episodic memories **(207)**
Working memory **(207)**
Primary memory **(207)**
Central executive processes **(207)**
Parallel distributed processing theory (PDP) **(207)**
Structural scans **(210)**
Computerized tomography (CT) **(210)**
Magnetic resonance imaging (MRI) **(210)**
Brain atrophy **(210)**
Cerebrum **(210)**
Cortex **(210)**
Gray matter **(210)**
Frontal lobes **(210)**
Parietal lobes **(211)**
Occipital lobes **(211)**
Temporal lobes **(211)**
Functional scans **(211)**
Positron emission tomography (PET) scans **(211)**
Functional magnetic resonance imaging (fMRI) **(211)**
Inner brain **(211)**
Hippocampus **(211)**
Equifinality **(213)**
Equipotentiality **(213)**
Plasticity **(213)**
Selective attention **(214)**
Vigilance **(214)**
Search **(214)**
Divided attention **(214)**
Autobiographical memory bump **(216)**
Flashbulb memories **(217)**
False memories **(221)**
Mnemonics **(222)**
Acronym **(222)**
Acrostic **(222)**
Pictorial mnemonic **(222)**
Peg-word mnemonic **(223)**
Method-of-loci **(224)**

Comprehension Questions

1. Describe how information moves from the environment to permanent memory according to the information processing theory.
2. What are the differences between procedural, semantic, and episodic memories?
3. According to the parallel distributed processing theory, how are memories stored and retrieved?
4. What have researchers found regarding brain atrophy by using CT scans?
5. When comparing the fMRI results from younger and older adults, what have researchers found regarding cognitive activity?
6. Explain the differences between selective attention, vigilance, search, and divided attention.
7. What would be the error in equating reaction time with mental processing time when giving older adults attention-related tasks?
8. Which part(s) of working memory remain stable with age and which part(s) deteriorate?

9. How does episodic memory change with age?
10. What is the autobiographical memory bump?
11. What did researchers find when studying the flashbulb memories made by the events of 9/11?
12. How do procedural memories change with age?
13. How do semantic memories change with age?
14. Explain the concept of false memories and the DRM paradigm.
15. Define and give an example of an acronym and an acrostic.
16. Give three examples of external memory improvement tools or techniques.
17. What have researchers found regarding older adults and memory training programs?

Answers for Common Sense: Myth or Reality?

1. Myth: According to information processing theory, information can stay in short-term memory for several hours. (See Information Processing, page 206.)
2. Myth: Short-term and working memories are the same thing. (See Information Processing, page 207.)
3. Reality: Under normal circumstances our brains lose 2–3 grams of weight per year after age 60. (See Brain Imaging page 210.)
4. Reality: In some cases younger and older adults use different parts of their brains to process the same information. (See Brain Imaging, page 211.)
5. Reality: Researchers have found that the neurological organization of male and female brains is somewhat different. (See Individual Differences in Brain Activity, page 212.)
6. Myth: Selective attention involves focusing on two things at one time. (See Attention, page 214.)
7. Reality: Particular aspects of working memory decline with age, beginning in young adulthood. (See Working Memory and Processing Speed, page 215.)
8. Reality: Memories for life events and experiences tend to deteriorate with age. (See Episodic Memory, page 216.)
9. Myth: Older people are more likely to remember who told them something interesting but forget what the interesting information was. (See Episodic Memory, page 216.)
10. Myth: Memories for procedures, such as playing an instrument or typing, tend to deteriorate with age. (See Nonepisodic Memory, page 218.)
11. Myth: Memories for facts, knowledge, and concepts tend to decline with age. (See Nonepisodic Memory, page 218.)
12. Reality: It is relatively easy to convince individuals that they remember something that, in reality, did not happen. (See Common Memory Errors, page 222.)
13. Reality: Even though the amount of improvement declines with age, older adults can improve their memories with training and practice. (See Memory Training, page 225.)

Suggested Readings

Forgetting as a Sign of Psychopathology, According to Freud

Freud, S. (1901). *The psychopathology of everyday life* (A. A. Brill, Trans.). Accessed at *Classics in the History of Psychology* (http://psychclassics.yorku.ca/topic.htm).

Classic Memory Research

Miller, G. A. (1956). The magical number seven, plus or minus two: Some limits on our capacity for processing information. *Psychological Review, 63,* 81–97. Available at http://psychclassics.yorku.ca/Miller/.

Bilingualism and Memory

Altarriba, J. (2002). Bilingualism: Language, memory, and applied issues. In W. J. Lonner, D. L. Dinnel, S. A. Hayes, & D. N. Sattler (Eds.), *Online readings in psychology and culture* (Unit 4, Chapter 4), (http://www.wwu.edu/~culture), Center for Cross-Cultural Research, Western Washington University, Bellingham, WA. Available at http://www.ac.wwu.edu/~culture/altarriba.htm.

Cultural Factors in Complex Decision Making

Strohschneider, S. (2002). Cultural factors in complex decision making. In W. J. Lonner, D. L. Dinnel, S. A. Hayes, & D. N. Sattler (Eds.), *Online readings in psychology and culture* (Unit 4, Chapter 1), (http://www.wwu.edu/~culture), Center for Cross-Cultural Research, Western Washington University, Bellingham, WA. Available at http://www.ac.wwu.edu/~culture/Strohschneider1.htm.

Suggested Websites

Interactive Tour of the Brain

To learn more about the brain in an entertaining way, you can take a tour of the brain at http://www.braintumor.org/anatomy/, sponsored by the National Brain Tumor Foundation.

Want a More In-Depth Understanding of the Brain?

For more detailed descriptions of brain anatomy, visit the "Anatomy of the Brain" at http://www.neurosurgerytoday.org/what/patient_e/anatomy1.asp, sponsored by the American Association of Neurological Surgeons.

Concerned About Memory Loss?

Medline Plus offers a large assortment of articles that focus on memory health and deficits at http://www.nlm.nih.gov/medlineplus/memory.html.

Fragile Memories, False Memories

The American Psychological Association provides the latest research on false memories and memories of childhood abuse at http://www.apa.org/pubinfo/mem.html.

CHAPTER

9 Complex Cognition

Complex cognition involves transforming information into something different from its initial form (Hoyer & Verhaeghen, 2006). Whereas the last chapter focused primarily on the processes needed to encode signals from the environment, make sense of them, store them, and retrieve the information when needed, this chapter focuses on integrating and transforming information. Consider, for example, the task of deciding whether to acquire an expensive new coat that you've wanted for some time. Intellectual and mathematical skills are needed to figure out the cost, particularly if the coat is on sale and if there is a tax on clothing. Everyday problem solving may be involved in pondering whether you should gamble that the coat will be there when winter is over and you might get it at a discount. Another possible strategy is to make those around you aware that you'd really like to receive the coat for your birthday or another special celebration, and wait to see if that solves your problem. Creativity may be involved if you consider selling some items you own or making some items to sell to raise some money to buy the coat. Creativity might also be involved if you decide to do something to make the coat hanging in your closet look better. If you start wondering whether the coat is worth the money, if you will feel guilty about spending so much money on a new coat, and wondering if you should just save the money, you are engaging in moral reasoning.

While it is necessary to understand the basic workings, both physiological and cognitive, of memory processing, it is also important to realize that such processing seldom takes place in isolation. Our assumptions, desires, and values may be swayed by social, emotional, or moral considerations (Hoyer & Verhaeghen, 2006). For example, a grandchild might ask "Grandpa, what is 5 x 5?" Even though Grandpa knows the answer he may choose to plead ignorance and lead the child through the process of figuring it out herself. This chapter explores several types of complex cognition that reflect not only academic processing but some of the more everyday or real-world cognitive processing most people engage in routinely.

COMMON SENSE
Myth or Reality?

Mark each of the following items with either an M, if you think it is a myth, or an R, if you think the statement reflects reality. By paying close attention you can find all the answers in this chapter. If needed, the answers are also given at the end of the chapter.

1. _____ IQ tests are generally used for diagnostic purposes in clinical settings.
2. _____ Studies show that IQ peaks in middle adulthood and remains stable through late adulthood.
3. _____ Intelligence and memory are affected differently by aging.
4. _____ In areas of expertise adults will show little if any cognitive decline while at the same time they will show cognitive decline in other areas.
5. _____ There is an accepted academic theory of intelligence that promotes common sense as a key facet of general intelligence.
6. _____ People who are gifted are good at everything.
7. _____ There is an accepted academic theory of intelligence that recognizes athletic ability as intelligence.
8. _____ Most researchers define creativity in terms of whether the final product, such as a song or a piece of pottery, has been judged to be creative.
9. _____ Older adults with higher educational achievement tend to be better at everyday problem solving than those with less education.
10. _____ Motivation is one of the major elements in moving from moral thoughts to moral behaviors.
11. _____ When faced with a moral dilemma, using the question "How will I benefit from this?" is a mature approach.
12. _____ Research shows that the moral development of most journalists is higher than the average adult.
13. _____ Researchers find that men and women consistently emphasize different values in moral reasoning.
14. _____ A person's values tend to be stable throughout life.
15. _____ People are generally consistent in applying their values no matter in what area of life a moral conflict occurs.

Before We Get Started . . .

There are many ways to measure adult cognition. To get a better sense of how some of these assessments differ, try the following problems.

> Problem 1: Which of the following words is the antonym of *aberrant? constricted, deviant, pernicious,* or *universal*
>
> Problem 2: If a store owner wants to make 20% profit on a book that costs $86.00 wholesale, what should the retail selling price be?
>
> Problem 3: At work a top manager, several steps ahead of you in rank, asks you what you think of the new employee team-building program he initiated last month. You think it's ineffective and a terrible waste of time and money. Would you respond truthfully?
>
> Problem 4: You are a 72-year-old adult, living alone, with 3 grown children and 7 grandchildren who live close by. You are often lonely and wish your family would spend more time at your home. What are some things you can do to encourage them to visit more often?

Do all of these problems require intelligence? Common sense? Emotional sensitivity? Values or moral reasoning? These items highlight various kinds and types of intelligence psychologists measure. While one or more of these questions might be useful to measure academic ability, other items might be more useful in determining the cognitive functioning of older adults.

Intelligence

The term *intelligence* is used in casual conversation to refer to just about anything smart, clever, or creative. We may talk about many types of intelligence ranging from common sense to "book smarts." Psychologists generally approach intelligence in four primary ways, with each one highlighting particular facets or functions (Berg & Sternberg, 2003). The approach explored in this section, the ***psychometric perspective***, emphasizes the measurement and assessment of intelligence. Another view, the ***cognitive perspective***, focuses attention on information processing and the divisions of fluid and crystallized intelligence. Both the psychometric and cognitive perspectives are discussed in this section, along with some recent theories of intelligence that draw from several perspectives. Later in this chapter the focus moves to the third perspective, the ***contextual perspective***, with an emphasis on everyday problem solving and person–environment interactions. Finally, the fourth perspective, the ***neo-Piagetian perspective***, is discussed in the last chapter of the book. The approach, labeled to reflect adult growth beyond the series of stages proposed by Jean Piaget, a famous scholar in cognitive development, highlights the development from formal, analytical thinking to wisdom.

Your Thoughts?

Should everyday problem solving be considered a form of intelligence? Why or why not?

Assessment of Intelligence

Although intelligence tests are generally used for diagnostic purposes in clinical situations and less so with the general public, many people have some idea of what IQ represents even if they are not familiar with actual IQ tests or the field of *psychometrics.* The term ***intelligence quotient (IQ)*** refers to the comparison of an individual's mental age or level of cognitive abilities as compared to his or her chronological age. While chronological age can be easily determined with accurate birth records, determining mental age is much more difficult. To date, the best way of assessing age-appropriate cognitive skills is through the use of IQ tests. One popular measure of mental age for adults, the *Wechsler Adult Intelligence Scale (WAIS),* assesses cognitive abilities with tasks that address four key areas: verbal comprehension, perceptual reasoning, working memory, and processing speed (Bowden, Weiss, Holdnack, & Lloyd, 2006).

Your Thoughts?

Do you think most people expect or hope that their IQ is above average? What societal, cultural, or educational factors support your opinion?

Many of the early versions of intelligence tests, first created about a century ago, were aimed at assessing the cognitive abilities of school-age children. A second wave of development came about a half-century ago with the need to assess the cognitive abilities of American men who were entering the military. When the field of developmental psychology gained interest in adult development and aging, these tests were given to middle-age and older adults as well. Generally these adult studies found a serious decline in intelligence beginning in young adulthood, with cross-sectional studies indicating greater age differences than longitudinal studies (Ackerman & Rolfhus, 1999). For example, using data collected every 7 years from 1956 to 1984 from participants in the Seattle Longitudinal Study, Hertzog and Schaie (1986, 1988) found that intelligence increases in young adulthood, stabilizes in middle age, and then begins to decline for participants in their early 60s. Interestingly, they found that those who started with the highest scores in young adulthood tended to maintain their top position even when scores for the entire group started to decline. They also found significant individual differences and deviations from this general pattern (Hertzog & Schaie, 1986, 1988).

Your Thoughts?

Considering the cognitive skills usually measured in a standard IQ test, what would contribute to the findings that IQ peaks in young adulthood?

Current research examining intelligence IQ across adulthood has prompted changes in the ways older adults are tested as well as the way intelligence is conceptualized. For example, a recent revision of the WAIS includes larger pictures and other visual stimuli to meet the needs of older adults with vision deficits. Publishers are also providing more data on older

With age, adults find their strengths often shift from traditional IQ test information to that of everyday problem solving.

clients, allowing clinicians and others to determine the range of expected scores for older adults (Kaufman, 2000). As these modifications are made researchers are gaining a better understanding of the influence of age on IQ. Consistent with our understanding of information processing and brain functioning, intelligence tasks designed to engage working memory and assess processing speed show the expected decline with age (Ackerman & Rolfhus, 1999; Berg, 2000), whereas other skills, such as size of vocabulary, do not (Uttl & Van Alstine, 2003). It is important to remember that the primary use for IQ tests is not the simple measure of how "smart" someone is, but rather to assess strengths and weaknesses in primary cognitive areas.

Your Thoughts?

Under what circumstances might it be helpful to give an older adult an IQ test?

Fluid and Crystallized Intelligence

The cognitive approach, complementary to the psychometric determination of IQ, examines the ways neurological changes influence intelligence. In addition to changes in information processing, the cognitive perspective has emphasized two simultaneously functioning but independent types of intelligence: fluid and crystallized. ***Fluid intelligence*** is comprised of the skills needed to transform and process information, such as abstract reasoning and perceptual speed (Ackerman & Rolfhus, 1999; Berg & Sternberg, 2003), and is similar in function to working memory. For example, Zimprich and Martin (2002) measured fluid intelligence by asking participants to identify the missing piece in a picture and to arrange colored blocks to match a diagram. It is often activated when adapting to and drawing conclusions from new and complex information (Berg, 2000; Masunaga & Horn, 2001). The concept of ***cognitive mechanics***, developed by Baltes and his colleagues, is also similar to fluid intelligence. Cognitive mechanics refers to the biological processes involved in thinking, such as the processing of sensory information and physical cues involved in body coordination.

Cognitive research, some of it spanning more than 70 years, has found that cognitive mechanics and fluid intelligence tend to decline with age (Baltes & Staudinger, 1992; Leventhal, Rabin, Leventhal, & Burns, 2001; Masunaga & Horn, 2001; Schaie & Willis, 1993; Zimprich & Martin, 2002). We should be careful of jumping to conclusions because the findings may not be as grim as our assumptions. Using data from the Seattle Longitudinal Study, Schaie (1993) and his colleagues found that the skills used in fluid intelligence decline, but at a very slow rate. Participants in the Baltimore Longitudinal Study reported that cognitive decline did not become noticeable in everyday life until around age 70 (Giambra, Arenberg, Zonderman, Kawas, & Costa, 1995). One noteworthy exception to the decline in fluid intelligence has been found regarding areas of expertise. Rather than decline, experts tend to demonstrate stable working memory skills in their specialty area, even though otherwise they display a general decline in fluid intelligence (Masunaga & Horn, 2001).

Your Thoughts?

How might this information on expertise be useful to an employer?

Crystallized intelligence consists of the knowledge gained through educational and cultural systems, such as common vocabulary and mathematical skills (Berg, 2000). These semantic memories are analogous to Baltes's work in ***cognitive pragmatics***, referring to the cultural and social nature of thinking. Skills that rely primarily on cognitive pragmatics include reading, language comprehension, and wisdom. In contrast to the decline of cognitive mechanics and fluid intelligence, cognitive pragmatics and crystallized intelligence remain stable through most of adulthood (Baltes & Staudinger, 1993; Berg, 2000). In some cases, particularly in areas of expertise, the information learned and retained by older adults may exceed that of younger adults (Leventhal et al., 2001). Participants in the Baltimore Longitudinal Study demonstrated increases in crystallized intelligence until middle age, followed by a plateau until very late adulthood. Most did experience a slow decline in crystallized intelligence in old-old age (Giambra et al., 1995). Participants in the Seattle Longitudinal Study also displayed stable levels of crystallized intelligence until their late 70s (Schaie, 1993).

The concepts of fluid and crystallized intelligence have been helpful to psychologists in understanding patterns of cognitive change with age. Just as with memory and IQ research, it is important to note that researchers often find a wide range of individual differences. College professors, for example, who routinely engage in intellectually stimulating activities do not show the change in fluid intelligence that other individuals often do (Compton, Avet-Compton, Bachman, & Brand, 2003). Individuals may also vary in areas of expertise, which can alter the general patterns found with fluid and crystallized intelligence across adulthood (Leventhal et al., 2001; Masunaga & Horn, 2001). Schaie and Willis (1993) reported great variation in cognitive abilities among participants in the Seattle Longitudinal Study, often associated with individual differences and how a cognitive skill was measured. These findings are consistent with other studies indicating that fluid and crystallized intelligence can be influenced by educational achievement, type of occupation, the intellectual stimulation level of daily activities, and the incidence of chronic disease (Berg & Sternberg, 2003).

Your Thoughts?

After college graduation, what intellectually stimulating activities are available to most adults?

Alternative Theories of Intelligence

The perspectives highlighted here, the triarchic theory and the theory of multiple intelligences, emphasize the multidimensional nature of intelligence and emphasize some aspects of intelligence that are distinct from the psychometric and cognitive models. The ***triarchic theory of intelligence***, proposed by Sternberg in the 1980s, consists of analytical, creative, and practical elements. Consistent with common findings, most of us will excel in only one or two of the elements, though it is possible to excel in all three (Callahan, 2000; Sternberg, 1994, 1997b; Sternberg, Castejon, Prieto, Hautamaki, & Grigorenko, 2001). Analytical intelligence involves abstract thinking, reasoning, and the cognitive skills needed to be successful with typical academic-type exercises. Traditional intelligence tests and measures of fluid intelligence are primarily assessing analytical intelligence. While intelligence is often equated with academic or IQ test performance, the triarchic theory raises to an equal level of importance two other areas. Creative intelligence relies on experiential learning and adaptation through trial and error. The ability to respond to tasks, challenges, or new situations in insightful and productive ways is also part of creative intelligence. The third area, practical intelligence, is similar to common sense. Individuals who are high in practical intelligence can adapt to different contexts and thrive in real-world situations. It might be said that individuals who are high in practical intelligence "know how to work the system" and shape their environment (Davidson & Downing, 2000; Sternberg, 1994, 1997b; Sternberg et al., 2001). Imagine for a moment the rare person who is high in all three elements. Consider a hypothetical woman, Allison, who is an architect and engineer. She clearly excels in academic and analytical intelligence. Being high in the creative element, Allison has the insight to design in new and daring ways. She is likely to be a risk-taker, learning from her attempts at designs that work well and those that don't. Finally, being high in practical intelligence and "street smarts," Allison is able to persuade clients to try her daring designs, and most importantly to pay top money for her work.

Your Thoughts?

Does common sense fit in your understanding of intelligence? Why or why not?

Your Thoughts?

Do most careers or jobs facilitate or support development of all three elements? What career or job might serve as an example of supporting all three?

While Sternberg and others have applied the triarchic theory to many domains, the fields of education and business have been primary targets. Within education, one particular area of interest is the relationship between intelligence and giftedness. Sternberg (2000b) views gifted individuals as those whose intelligence can be described as excelling in one or more of the three parts of the triarchic theory. His theory, summarized in Table 9.1, describes the ways single elements and various combinations of intelligences might be expressed. Research suggests that very few people excel in and balance analytical, creative, and practical intelligence. These truly gifted consummate balancers can determine which of their strengths to combine in particular situations to produce the best result (Callahan, 2000; Sternberg, 2000b). One of the lessons to be learned from Sternberg's triarchic theory is that because most individuals are not strong in all three areas, a teamwork approach to problem solving, gathering individuals with various strengths, may be the best strategy.

Another alternative to the traditional view of intelligence is Gardner's theory of ***multiple intelligences***. Although the theory includes traditional areas, such as linguistic and mathematical intelligences, it highlights more and different types of intelligences than the triarchic theory. Based on a strict set of criteria, Gardner has isolated eight intelligences: logical-mathematical, linguistic, spatial, musical, bodily-kinesthetic, interpersonal, intrapersonal, and naturalistic. (See Table 9.2, on page 237, for a description of each.) In order for a set of skills to be considered a separate intelligence they must be associated with activity in specific locations in the brain. Gardner also considers intellectual skills that are found in gifted individuals, such as experts and leaders in various fields, as well as in individuals with unusual mental abilities, such as those with autism. In addition, separate intelligences should follow a unique course of development. Another key to a separate intelligence is that an area or domain must develop its own unique symbol system, such as music and mathematics, or its own unique vocabulary. In addition to all these criteria Gardner also considers research on intelligence from other cultures and historical data that provide clues to evolutionary development in cognitive areas (Davidson & Downing, 2000; Gardner, 1993; Wagner, 2000). Gardner continues to seek evidence of other types of intelligence based on this set of criteria. Currently, there is work to determine if enough evidence exists to support an existential or spiritual intelligence.

Your Thoughts?

Which of these intelligences are emphasized in a typical K–12 curriculum in American education? Which are ignored?

TABLE 9.1 ***Sternberg's Patterns of Giftedness***

Pattern of Giftedness	*Elements Involved*	*Description*
Analyst	Analytic Intelligence	High in ability to evaluate and analyze Great memory skills Average or below in creativity and practical application
Creator	Creative Intelligence	High in ability to generate useful ideas Often thought of as dreamers Trouble making ideas concrete and with implementing them
Practitioner	Practical Intelligence	High in practical skills Persuasive and entertaining Lacks creative idea generation and substance in thinking
Analytic Creator	Analytic and Creative Intelligences	High in ability to generate ideas and to evaluate them Average or below social skills Trouble in getting their good ideas recognized and appreciated
Analytic Practitioner	Analytic and Practical Intelligences	High in ability to analyze and implement information Often very successful in conventional terms Lacks new insights and creativity
Creative Practitioner	Creative and Practical Intelligences	High in creative ideas and persuasive social skills Great at creating and selling ideas to others Lacks ability to discern which ideas are practically useful
Consummate Balancer	Analytic, Creative, and Practical Intelligences	High in analytical, creative, and practical intelligence Able to make truly outstanding contributions to society

Based on Sternberg (2000b).

Work with Gardner's multiple intelligences has been particularly popular in the field of education, including higher education and programs aimed at adult students. While many psychologists find Gardner's work fascinating, others find it frustrating. It has proven difficult to design accurate measures of the multiple intelligences and to create programs to develop or enhance all the intelligences.

Section Summary

- Two of the four approaches to intelligence (psychometric, cognitive, contextual, and neo-Piagetian) along with some alternative theories are discussed in this section.
- IQ tests, representative of the psychometric approach, are designed to measure mental and cognitive abilities through tasks focusing on verbal comprehension, perceptual reasoning, working memory, and processing speed.

TABLE 9.2 ***Gardner's Multiple Intelligences***

Type	*Talent*	*Examples*
Logical-Mathematical	Confronting and assessing objects and abstractions and discerning their relations and underlying principles	Mathematicians, scientists, philosophers
Linguistic	A master and lover of language and words with a desire to explore them	Poets, writers, linguists
Spatial	An ability to perceive the visual world accurately, transform and modify perceptions, and re-create visual experiences even without physical stimuli	Architects, artists, sculptors, mapmakers, navigators, chess players
Musical	A competence not only in composing and performing pieces with pitch, rhythm, and timbre but also in listening and discerning	Composers, conductors, musicians, music critics
Bodily-Kinesthetic	Controlling and orchestrating body motions and handling objects skillfully	Dancers, athletes, actors
Interpersonal	Accurately determining moods, feelings, and other mental states in others and using the information as a guide for behavior	Politicians, anthropologists
Intrapersonal	Accurately determining moods, feelings, and other mental states in oneself and using the information as a guide for behavior	Psychiatrists, religious leaders
Naturalist	Recognizing and categorizing natural objects	Biologists, naturalists
Existential (possible intelligence)	Capturing and pondering the fundamental questions of existence	Spiritual leaders, philosophical thinkers

Gardner (1998).

- Even though IQ scores show decline with age, it is important to note that while tasks involving working memory and processing speed decline, other cognitive skills remain stable with age.
- Representative of the cognitive approach, fluid intelligence and cognitive mechanics show a decline with age whereas crystallized intelligence and cognitive pragmatics are generally stable until very late in adulthood.
- One exception to the pattern of cognitive decline is in the area of expertise where adults can continue to excel in both fluid and crystallized intelligence.
- Alternative theories of intelligence have added to the traditional notion of intelligence by emphasizing new and distinct areas.
- The triarchic theory of intelligence acknowledges traditional models of intelligence through the analytical element, but also emphasizes creativity and practical intelligence.
- Based on a strict set of criteria, Gardner has isolated eight multiple intelligences: logical-mathematical, linguistic, spatial, musical, bodily-kinesthetic, interpersonal, intrapersonal, and naturalistic.

Creativity

> **Your Thoughts?**
>
> Do you think of creativity as a subset of intelligence or something separate from intelligence?

Similar to the debated issues surrounding the study of intelligence, ***creativity*** has also proved to be a difficult concept to define and measure. The question of whether creativity is a dimension of intelligence has also been debated since the psychological study of creativity began in the early 1950s (Sawyer, 2003). While some theories of intelligence fully embrace creativity, such as Sternberg's triarchic theory of intelligence, others involve creativity minimally if at all. Rather than approach creativity as a type of intelligence, other perspectives have focused on various aspects of creativity, including personality traits common in creative individuals, thinking processes that facilitate creative ideas, and characteristics of creative products (Cropley, 2000). Measures of creative people have emphasized cognitive characteristics such as imagination, cognitive flexibility, curiosity, openness to new ideas, and willingness to consult with others (Cropley, 2000).

> **Your Thoughts?**
>
> What careers or jobs might value these cognitive characteristics? In what careers or jobs might these characteristics be detrimental?

Although the rate of production of creative pieces generally peaks in young or middle adulthood, the development of creative thought processes and talents often continues throughout adulthood. In a series of interviews with visual artists, such as those who paint, make pottery, and design jewelry, Reed (2005) found that creative individuals progress through a series of stages similar to the selection, optimization, and compensation model developed by Baltes (1997). Early in young adulthood, the *selection* stage, the artists made their creative talents their priority by beginning their careers as artists. During the *optimization* stage, occurring later in young adulthood and into middle adulthood, the artists were focused on productivity. They found joy in challenging themselves to be the most efficient in producing as much as they could. Later in middle adulthood, they moved into the *compensation* stage during which they learned to adjust their artistic work around various life situations and issues of physical aging. For example, some of the artists mentioned that as young adults they could work 10 hours a day, and with age that had reduced to 6 or 7 hours. The *integration* stage, which may start in middle or late adulthood, involved a shift from a focus on the items produced to an enjoyment of the process. For some of the artists the process working with clay or paint was similar to a spiritual experience. In this stage the artists were less concerned about public approval of their work. The final stage, the *motivation* stage, occurred in late adulthood when the desire to create becomes the primary life passion for the artists (Reed, 2005). Many artists produce great works during this time, which has been labeled the ***swan song phenomenon***. For example, by analyzing the works of great classical music composers, Simonton (1989) found that those who were in the last years of their lives were driven to produce their "master works." Although researchers have found that creative behaviors, measured by the level of productivity, often declines through middle and late adulthood, creative skills, cognitive complexity, and personal motivation may continue to grow across adulthood.

> **Your Thoughts?**
>
> Do you think these stages would be the same for musicians? Fiction writers? Other types of artists? Why or why not?

Although this section on creativity is embedded in the larger context of complex cognition, it is important to note that creative endeavors may influence many domains, particularly personality. For example, Dollinger, Dollinger, and Centeno (2005) found that young adults who show evidence of creative accomplishments and the greatest potential on instruments that predict future creativity were also among the more nonconforming and the most active in exploring their own identity development. The influence of creativity can be found in middle age as well. In analyzing interviews with 29 women ages 31 to 64, Adams-Price and Steinman (2007) found that the creative activity of making jewelry provided a sense of generativity and society connection while also enhancing self-esteem and reducing stress during midlife. Continuing into late adulthood, Feist and Barron (2003) found that in a group of 80 male graduate students first assessed in 1950 when they were 27 years old, across the years to their current age of 72, two variables on the California Personality Inventory proved to be the strongest predictors of lifelong creativity. One of those items was tolerance, similar to open mindedness, and the second was psychological mindedness or the ability to do well at figuring out what other people are thinking and feeling.

Section Summary

- The study of creativity has moved in many directions, including its relationship with intelligence, personality traits, thinking patterns, and characteristics of creative products.
- Reed (2005) found that creative individuals progress through a series of stages consisting of the selection, optimization, compensation, integration, and motivation stages.
- Although creativity productivity slows in middle and late adulthood, creative skills, cognitive complexity, and personal motivation may continue to grow.

Everyday Problem Solving

The contextual approach to intelligence highlights everyday problem solving by bringing together cognitive research on formal problem solving and practical intelligence, while also considering clinical research on coping and adapting to changes in our environment (Marsiske & Margrett, 2006). Rather than focus on an individual's performance on pencil-and-paper measures of analytical and verbal skills, as with IQ tests, or on the changing (fluid) and stable (crystallized) aspects of general intelligence, the contextual approach emphasizes skills similar to the creative and practical intelligences in the triarchic theory of intelligence and the interpersonal and intrapersonal intelligences isolated in the multiple intelligences theory. It highlights the ways adults *function* in their social and physical environment. Whereas traditional problem-solving tasks have one correct answer, everyday problem solving involves commonly occurring, multidimensional problems that often have many possible outcomes, with some solutions being better than others (Thornton & Dumke, 2005). The interest in everyday functioning is, in part, a response to the apparent contradiction between age-related decline on tests of fluid intelligence and IQ and the fact that many adults continue to function at satisfactory or even extraordinary levels as they age (Marsiske & Margrett, 2006; Patrick & Strough, 2004).

Your Thoughts?

Would everyday problem solving be a good measure of a person's wisdom? Why, why not, or under what circumstances?

Factors in Problem-Solving Performance

Just as IQ test questions come in numerous forms and require knowledge from various domains, so too do everyday problems. ***Well-defined problems*** are clearly structured so that the starting point, ending point, and procedures for solving the problem are exactly defined. Our challenge as problem solvers in this case is to discover or retrieve key information in order to solve the problem. For example, Allaire and Marsiske (2002) tested performance on well-defined everyday problems by showing research participants nutrition labels and asking questions such as "Which item has more fat?" In this case the beginning information is clear (data on the labels), the form of the solution is clear (the answer is one of these items), and to solve the problem one needs a procedure (find the grams of fat for each item and compare). They also gave participants ***ill-defined problems***, which offer little clarity, such as "What would you do if you just realized that you lost your blood pressure medication?" The question doesn't specify where the participant is when realizing this (starting point), what options are available (procedures), or what an acceptable solution might be (ending point). The strategy to solve the problem may be different depending on whether the individual is at home or work or on vacation, has access to a car or cell phone, and the estimated probability of finding the medication versus getting a new prescription filled. Allaire and Marsiske found that the best predictor of competence in everyday functioning was the combined performance on both well-structured and ill-structured problems. They also found that the ability to solve everyday problems was a better predictor of participants' quality of daily functioning than age or standard intelligence scores.

ON THE LEADING EDGE
Putting a Face on Intelligent Robots

Service robots are finding their way in to hospitals and nursing homes as nurses assistants. Most of these robots do not interact directly with patients, but rather deliver items from one station to another, such as from the pharmacy or food service to nursing stations. While the developers understand that the software running the robot and the mechanics of the robotic movement must run smoothly, they also understand that eventually these robots will be used to interact with patients. The research team of Tao Zhang of the Department of Electrical Engineering and Computer Science at Vanderbilt University, along with David Kaber, Biwen Zhu, Mandia Swangneir, and Lashanda Hodge of the Edward P. Fitts Department of Industrial and Systems Engineering and Prithima Mosaly from the Industrial Extension Services, both at North Carolina State University (2010), have begun the process of introducing the feeling of humanness, called perceived anthropomorphism, to the current robot technologies. In a recent study they tested the emotional responses to a facial configuration, a voice message, and an interactive PC tablet in terms of increasing the perceived anthropomorphism.

Twenty-four older adults, ranging in age from 64 to 91 years old, were recruited from two local senior centers. Each participant pretended to receive medicine from the robot while seated in a small room. Several trials were conducted with several different robot conditions: abstract face (just big eyes), human-like face (mask), synthesized voice, human voice (digital recording), visual interaction (read a message on a screen), and physical contact (press a button on a touch screen). In addition to measuring the participants' heart rate and galvanic skin response they also asked the individuals involved to rate the robot's humanness.

When the data was analyzed the research team discovered that the human-like features (human face, human voice, and physical contact) created the strongest positive emotional response in the patients and the highest rating of humanness. When offering different combinations of the robot characteristics the data revealed that even the more abstract additions were better than simply a machine with wheels, and as the complexity and humanness of the features were increased so too increased the participant's positive response.

As personal technologies continue to fill our lives, such as smart phones and car electronics, it is interesting to think of what the future holds in terms of technology-smart homes, schools, workplaces, and hospitals. In a few years we might find that a trip to Grandma's house, which we may have thought of a trip back in time, becomes a trip to the future.

Research findings have supported the contextual approach in that success in solving everyday problems is associated with our social and environmental context. Several studies have found, for example, that adults perform better in solving everyday problems when the issue, topic, or people involved are of interest to them (Patrick & Strough, 2004; Thornton & Dumke, 2005). One way to categorize people in terms of social context is to place them in the general categories developmental psychologists use all the time: young, middle, and late adulthood. Artistico, Cervone, and Pezzuti (2003) used these simple distinctions and found that younger adults performed better on problems involving school exams and computer use, while older adults were better with problems involving grandparenting issues, such as requests for babysitting. Research aimed at older adults often presents problems typical for their age, such as dealing with medications, food preparation, housekeeping, financial management, transportation, and family issues (Marsiske & Margrett, 2006; Patrick & Strough, 2004; Strough, Patrick, Swenson, Cheng, & Barnes, 2003).

Your Thoughts?

What areas or categories of problem solving would you expect middle-aged adults to excel in?

Differences in problem-solving strategies also reflect self-awareness and the wisdom that comes with understanding our social context. Younger adults are often better with well-defined and abstract problems (Vukman, 2005), and usually generate a greater number of possible solutions to a problem. Middle-aged and older adults tend to generate fewer but more targeted responses (Marsiske & Margrett, 2006). Middle-aged and older adults are also more aware of their own problem-solving styles (Vukman, 2005) and can compensate for personal tendencies, such as deliberately countering a habit of making impulsive decisions. In a study comparing the problem-solving strategies of participants 19 to 80 years old, Haught, Hill, Nardi, and Walls

(2000) found that the younger adults took the least amount of time to generate responses, thus reflecting faster processing speed. Although the older adults took longer they did not make more errors than the others. Generally, the middle-aged adults were the best at finding potential solutions to practical, everyday problems (Haught et al., 2000; Vukman, 2005).

Another key aspect of everyday problem solving, different from traditional, formal problem solving, is that we often consult with others when trying to solve everyday problems (Krause, 2006; Marsiske & Margrett, 2006). In most formal situations, such as when taking an IQ test or a college entrance exam, we would be labeled "cheaters" if we consulted someone else about the probable solution to a question. In our everyday lives, however, we ask for others' opinions all the time when trying to solve a problem, and usually that is a helpful strategy. As found in a study involving 249 older African Americans who were part of the Baltimore Study on Black Aging, social support was associated with the generation of better solutions to everyday problems (Whitfield & Wiggins, 2003). Studies show that our collaboration is more effective when we feel emotionally close to the person we are confiding in (Cheng & Strough, 2004; Strough et al., 2003). Strough and her colleagues (2003) found, for example, that most married adults collaborate with their spouses when trying to resolve a problem. When a spouse is not available, the next choice for collaboration is adult children. The order of preference expressed by these older adults for collaboration in problem solving was found to be spouse, adult children, siblings, friends, and finally neighbors. In addition to contributing to the best solutions to everyday problems, collaboration with family or friends can also partially compensate for cognitive decline, optimize everyday performance, enhance relationships, and reduce stress and tension (Meegan & Berg, 2002).

Your Thoughts?

What would your order of preference for advice be? In what ways would you predict your order will be different in 10 years?

Selection, Optimization, and Compensation Strategy

The selection, optimization, and compensation (SOC) model is a popularly applied strategy for everyday problem solving as well as an overall approach to life management. This process involves selecting the highest priorities or goals in a situation and then optimizing one's resources while compensating for losses or deficits in order to reach those identified goals. To illustrate the process, consider the hypothetical character Darrell, a rising star in a management position at a local bank. He's become frustrated over work-interfering-with-family stresses, primarily problems caused by working long hours and weekends, and family-interfering-with-work stresses, usually stemming from his wife calling to say he needs to leave work to take care of a problem with one of the children. The SOC model would first of all encourage Darrell to examine his goals and priorities and select the most important ones. If Darrell chooses to focus on career goals he's likely to make a different set of changes than if he chooses to focus on family goals. For the sake of this example let's say Darrell decides that involvement in the lives of his young children is more important than his career aspirations at this point. With the decision made, Darrell now needs to optimize his resources to achieve his selected goals. Increased involvement with his family will mean less time at work, thus Darrell must figure out ways to be more time-efficient at work and to curb his habit of volunteering to take on new responsibilities. He might also increase his time with his children by hiring someone to do his lawn work at home rather than taking time to do it all himself. The compensation part of the SOC would encourage Darrell to try to compensate for the things he's losing or giving up because of his selected focus. He is used to being the star performer at work, and cutting back will mean that someone else will become the top employee. How can he compensate? Perhaps he can trade "Employee of the Year" by taking on the title of "Coach" for his son's baseball team or his daughter's soccer team. Taking pride in the accomplishments and successes of his children may soon compensate for the loss of the high praise at work.

Your Thoughts?

How might the SOC model apply to the tension between college demands and other areas of your life?

RESEARCH IN-DEPTH
True Experiments

True ***experimental research designs*** involving people are less common than descriptive or associative studies, but do occur. It is difficult to say with known accuracy that one thing *caused* another when discussing the behaviors of human beings, primarily because we and our environments are so complex. Persuaded by the potential benefit of the findings, Nezu, Nezu, Felgoise, McClure, and Houts (2003) were determined to find out if training in problem solving for cancer patients would cause a reduction in their daily hassles and stress levels, and raise their overall quality of life.

To participate in the problem-solving study patients had to meet strict physical, psychological, and education criteria. It is very important to try to make sure all the participants had as similar a set of circumstances as possible, so that any change in their condition could be attributed to the problem-solving therapy. For example, all the participants had to be diagnosed with cancer sometime within the 6 months prior to starting the study. If some patients were newly diagnosed while others were quite advanced in their illness, then it would be difficult to determine if the stage of the disease had any influence on the outcome. After all the screening tests were completed, 150 well-matched participants were selected for the study.

The next step in the procedure was to randomly place participants in groups. Random placement is one of the most important characteristics in a true experiment. Each participant should have an equal chance of being assigned to any group. Assuming the participants were similar in characteristics to begin with, this further equalizes the groups prior to the experimental treatment. Nezu and his colleagues established three groups: PST, PST-SO, and WLC. Participants in the PST group received problem-solving therapy, while those in the PST-SO group received problem-solving therapy along with their significant others. The WLC group, the "wait-list control" group, received no therapy during the actual study. The group was called "wait list" because the participants were told that the program had filled up and they would have to wait for the next set of therapy sessions. The WLC group plays a vital role serving as the ***control group***. By incorporating a group of very similar patients who are not receiving problem-solving therapy, the researchers can compare the two experimental groups (PST and PST-SO) to the WLC group to determine just how much difference the therapy made.

A true experimental research design also involves independent and dependent variables. The actual training and the three-group design are ***independent variables*** controlled by the researchers. The therapy focused on defining the problem, generating options, selecting an option, and monitoring the outcome. It required extensive training lasting over many sessions. The ***dependent variables***, in this case the level of stress and depression, are the outcomes that are dependent on the quality and type of the therapy.

The results indicated that at the 6-month and 12-month follow-up the patients in the PST and PST-SO groups reported less stress and depression than the WLC group. These findings allow Nezu and his colleagues to say with confidence that the training did cause a reduction in levels of stress and depression. The researchers also found that at a 6-month follow-up those who had problem-solving therapy with their significant others reported less stress than those who received the therapy alone, though by the 12-month follow-up differences between the PST and PST-SO groups had faded.

While involving a control group is necessary to judge success, it may not seem fair that some patients were given an opportunity to improve the quality of their daily lives and others were not. There are ethical guidelines set up by all major organizations, such as the American Psychological Association and the American Medical Association, and by local hospitals, universities, and other research institutions, to make sure that patients are treated fairly. Most guidelines require that control groups be offered any treatment or therapy found to be beneficial after the research is completed. Consistent with these policies, Nezu and his colleagues offered the therapy to the participants in the control group when the study was over, as well as to those who did not meet the original criteria for participation.

Baltes and Heydens-Gahir (2003) tested the SOC model with 241 adults, ranging in age from 21 to 64 years old, who were similar to our fictional character Darrell in trying to handle many everyday problems related to balancing the demands of full-time employment with family needs. The participants represented a wide variety of occupations, including accounting, education, health care, counseling, and building maintenance, and on the average had worked for their organization for 8 years. Participants who were better at utilizing the SOC strategy in both their work and family roles reported less stress in both areas and less role conflict in both work-interfering-with-family and family-interfering-with-work. Use of the SOC strategy was successful in reducing stress regardless of the levels of job involvement, supervisor support, family involvement, social support, the number of hours worked, or the gender of the participant. Baltes

The SOC model can be used to help individuals with life management concerns, such as when parents struggle to balance work and family needs.

and Heydens-Gahir also found that in work situations the selection component seems to be most important, while in family situations the optimization component is most effective in reducing stress. Blending work and family roles appears to be a continual challenge in the daily lives of many adults. The SOC model offers some insight in the ways adults can maximize their family and work satisfaction.

Section Summary

- The contextual approach to intelligence emphasizes the application of cognitive skills to the kinds of real-world problems adults confront in their daily environments.
- The type of problem, age of the individual, topic or domain, and level of social support are among the most influential factors on everyday problem-solving skills.
- Studies have shown that middle-aged adults are among the best in finding high-quality solutions to practical problems.
- Although intelligence in the sense of traditional IQ testing decreases with age, it appears that age brings a shift in focus from academic or school-type intelligence to that of everyday problem-solving and experience-based expertise.
- One example of a problem-solving strategy, the SOC model, involves identifying priorities and goals, and then using available resources to overcome deficits and achieve those goals.
- Use of the SOC model may increase the likelihood of successful problem solving in everyday situations and contribute to overall successful aging.

Moral Reasoning

In an effort to find how "ordinary" people perceived intelligence, Berg and Sternberg (1992) asked participants ranging in age from 22 to 85 years old to list the characteristics they would expect to find in a highly intelligent 30-year-old, 50-year-old, and 70-year-old.

While the 30-year-old was characterized as one who showed curiosity, an open mind, original thinking, and adaptability, the 50- and 70-year-old highly intelligent person was described as demonstrating communication skills, common sense, maturity, responsibility, problem-solving skills, and moral reasoning. As a well-researched area of complex cognition, moral reasoning represents a blend of many aspects of intelligence, creativity, everyday problem solving, and personal value systems.

Resolving Everyday Personal Moral Problems

Your Thoughts?

Pause after reading the short scenario and consider what advice you would give Terry.

There are many questions that arise when seeking to understand how individuals apply their values systems to everyday situations. Consider this hypothetical situation:

> Pat suggests to Terry that they have lunch together at the nearby deli. Terry does not want to be seen with Pat, much less spend time over lunch. Terry believes that in most situations it is better to just speak the truth, but this situation seems more difficult than most.

Would it be better for Terry to be honest with Pat or to make up a reason why having lunch together is not possible? Are there additional facts you want before giving advice, such as the nature of Terry and Pat's association, their age, or gender? Would it matter if Terry and Pat were coworkers? Family members? Children? Significantly different in age? Of different genders? Would it make a difference if you knew why Terry did not want to spend time with Pat? Researchers in the area of ***moral development*** study these types of questions with participants of all ages, seeking to understand both their complex cognition and behaviors. The study of moral development provides insight into the ways an individual determines the right course of action when in a moral dilemma, and how those methods change across the lifespan (Blasi, 1980; Kristiansen & Hotte, 1996; Smith, 1991). Based on years of research Narvaez and Rest (1995; Rest & Narvaez, 1991) have proposed a ***four-component model of moral behavior***:

- Moral sensitivity
- Moral reasoning
- Moral motivation
- Moral character

Although this ordering follows a logical sequence Narvaez and Rest maintain that these components may occur simultaneously or independently in a different order. They also maintain that an individual can be skilled or lacking in any combination of the four components, thus one may be very concerned with moral reasoning but lacking in sensitivity, or highly motivated but lacking in sound moral reasoning.

The first component in the production of moral behavior is *moral sensitivity.* It may seem obvious that we must be aware a problem exists before we can start to solve it, but that awareness is critical to achieving moral actions. This could be something mild, such as wishing "Merry Christmas" to someone who is Jewish, or major, such as remaining ignorant of personal actions that are polluting the environment. *Look at that last sentence closely—am I lacking in moral sensitivity by calling an environmental issue more important than a religious issue?* I continually struggle with moral sensitivity as I write this book. I know I am shaped by my social and political views and those views influence my judgment in terms of topics I choose to discuss, the tone with which I present particular topics (positive, negative, matter-of-fact, etc.), and issues I decide to leave out. Moral sensitivity may involve several types of intelligence, including practical and interpersonal. We must pay attention to the sometimes subtle verbal and nonverbal cues in the environment in our effort to maintain moral sensitivity.

Your Thoughts?

How might you design a workshop on moral sensitivity training for employees of a local hospital?

Once an individual is aware of a moral dilemma, the next step is to figure out the best course of action. *Moral reasoning* is the process by which we decide what we should do in a particular situation. While there are likely to be many influences on moral reasoning, such as societal norms and laws, personal value systems, and the seriousness of the issue(s) at stake, one of the most important factors influencing the process is cognitive functioning (Narvaez & Rest, 1995; Rest & Narvaez, 1991). The way a person reasons and justifies moral actions changes with growth in cognitive sophistication and complexity, which generally corresponds to one's level of education (Dawson-Tunik, Commons, Wilson, & Fischer, 2005). Moral reasoning requires us to choose a course of action that is consistent with our values and our assessment of the situation.

Moral motivation comes from the desire or need to perform the best course of action once it is determined through moral reasoning. Often the motivation we need to take action in a moral dilemma comes in the form of an emotion. That's why the appeal made by many organizations raising money for a cause is an emotional one. I would guess that all of us are sensitive to the fact that people are starving in some parts of the world. I would also guess that most of us, reasoning about this international situation, would want someone to help us if we were without enough food. What will actually motivate us to take action? Usually, it is emotional pictures or an emotional story. Seldom, if ever, do difficult situations or moral dilemmas involve only one value or one emotion. Thinking of this international situation may bring to mind issues of justice and fairness. We may be moved by compassion to donate money. We think of issues of privilege and find that our sense of guilt motivates us to donate money. We may also think of our own loved ones' needs, and perhaps not donate to the international cause but make a commitment to not spending money frivolously. We might think of the needs of our own community, and not donate money to the international cause but rather donate time and labor in our own neighborhood. Notice that the same behaviors, to donate money or not, could result from different lines of reasoning and emotions. The emotions most often considered basic to achieving moral behaviors are guilt, shame, and empathy (Eisenberg, 2000).

Your Thoughts?

Is it morally appropriate for an organization to appeal to your emotions? Would you feel manipulated if you made an emotional choice? Why or why not?

Moral character relies on ego strength and conviction to do the right thing, particularly when the consequences are predicted to be uncomfortable (Narvaez & Rest, 1995; Rest & Narvaez, 1991). Even when we are sensitive to a moral issue, have thought it through, and chosen the moral values upon which to act, it can still be hard to follow through with the necessary actions and maintain our commitment. Going back to the question of donating money to an organization to provide food to starving people around the world, it seems likely that some of us may be made aware of the problem, reason that donating is the right thing to do, find motivation in compassion and the good feeling that comes from helping others . . . and then forget all about the experience the next day! (Which is why those appeals usually end with the phrase "make that phone call now.") *Moral character* is the label given to the persistence to follow through on our decision to take action.

Your Thoughts?

If you wanted to compare people high in moral character to those who are not, how would you go about finding participants?

Currently, there is no single test that measures all four components of the model. Most of the research has focused on moral reasoning, with some attention given to moral sensitivity and motivation, and little consideration given to moral character (Walker, 2002). Even though Kohlberg's theory of moral reasoning has gained the most attention for many years, the four-component model provides the context by which moral reasoning relates to moral behaviors.

Moral Cognition Across Adulthood

Of the four components, the most researched and debated is that of moral reasoning, which is also referred to by some as *moral judgment.* Beginning with Kohlberg's work in cognitive-developmental theory in the late 1950s, studies have shown that with age and education adults grow in their ability to reason through complex situations involving values and moral issues

(Dawson-Tunik et al., 2005). This growth has been charted in stages that usually occur in a predictable sequence, although they may be experienced in slow or quick progression. It is also the case that many adults will not achieve or demonstrate the highest stages of moral reasoning (Gibbs, 1995).

Kohlberg's (1976, 1984) six stages of ***moral reasoning*** are grouped into three levels according to social perspective. The progression he detected began with a preconventional focus on self-centered needs and desires, moving to a conventional level focusing on significant individuals' opinions and the interests of larger groups, and eventually arriving at the post-conventional level with an emphasis on core values and principles.

The first level, *preconventional moral reasoning,* involves resolving moral dilemmas with reasoning based on self-centered, concrete thinking. At this level society's rules and expectations are viewed as external and imposed by authorities. The first stage in preconventional moral reasoning, *punishment/obedience morality,* involves a focus on avoiding physical punishment and obedience for obedience's sake (i.e., just because you're supposed to). This is an egocentric perspective that evaluates dilemmas from a perspective of personal pleasure and punishment, usually centered around physical, here-and-now issues. This stage may come into play when taking advantage of a work situation when the boss is away, knowing that the likelihood of negative repercussions are much less likely, or when driving, gauging whether to speed and just how much faster than the speed limit one can go based on the predicted likelihood of punishment from law enforcement officers. Stage 2 in preconventional moral reasoning, *instrumental purpose and exchange,* adds a layer of complexity by considering the perspectives of others. At this stage we are still focused on egocentric needs, but now we realize that others have needs too, and sometimes working together can allow all of us to get what we desire (Kohlberg, 1976, 1984). Imagine a situation in which a group of employees are told that if performance increases each person will all get a bonus. Stage 2 reasoning may lead some employees to be helpful to their coworkers only because they, personally, want the bonus.

Your Thoughts?

How might you set up a study to learn more about whether adults operate at a lower stage than they usually do when driving?

The second of the three levels, *conventional moral reasoning,* demonstrates an advance in maturity in that we have internalized social rules and dominant values, thus we will now look beyond egocentric needs to the needs of others. Most adolescents and adults are functioning in this level, which contains stages 3 and 4. *Mutual interpersonal expectations,* the third of Kohlberg's stages, brings to focus the need to consult and include others in solving everyday personal moral problems. In this stage we place a high priority on being viewed as a good person in the eyes of those whom we have selected as important, particularly friends, family members, role models, and mentors. The fourth stage, *social systems and conscience,* enlarges the need to consider the opinions of people we know and trust to consider the larger group or the big picture. The focus has now shifted to the good of everyone in the group, which may refer to everyone in the company, university, city, society, or in the world. According to Kohlberg (1984), when we are operating in stage 4 we realize and respect the fact that without laws, rules, and social expectations, anarchy and chaos would destroy our quality of life.

Post-conventional moral reasoning represents the highest level of moral maturity in Kohlberg's theory. This level involves a shift from giving the greatest consideration to others' opinions or the common good to a perspective emphasizing personal values, which are self-chosen, life-guiding principles. The fifth stage, *utility and individual rights,* involves the recognition that not all values are of equal power and importance, and that laws cannot always dictate the highest or most important values. For those of us who reach this stage we are engaged in the most complex cognitive processing by considering all of the perspectives of the previous stages while framing ill-structured moral problems in terms of values. Part of the growth in stage 5 is the realization that in some situations values may lead to conflicting behavior choices and one must determine which value is most important. For example, an individual may be passionate about public education, and thus willing to pay more in taxes to

Your Thoughts?

What factors might contribute to the findings that Kohlberg's post-conventional level is so rare?

support it, while feeling conflicted knowing that raising taxes may cause some poorer homeowners to move, which violates that person's passion toward helping the poor. The ultimate stage in Kohlberg's theory, *universal ethical principles,* reflects the culmination of all the previous stages. This very rare individual displays a total commitment to self-chosen ethical principles. The few individuals who achieve this level of cognition have integrated their highest values into every part of their lives to the extent that their values are their most prominent characteristics. Their values have become their identity—it is who they are.

To bring these stages together for comparison, imagine the basic moral dilemma of watching someone shoplift several items in your local grocery store. What is the best course of action? That depends partly on the line of reasoning that seems most persuasive to you at the time. For example:

- Stage 1: Will I get in trouble for not notifying authorities? Will the shoplifter try to hurt me or retaliate?
- Stage 2: Will I get a reward for turning the shoplifter in? Will I be a local hero?
- Stage 3: What would my best friend tell me to do? What would my minister tell me to do?
- Stage 4: What if everyone started shoplifting? We can't allow that to start or we will lose some of our freedoms.

ON THE LEADING EDGE
Moral Excellence

Early work in the area of morality often focused on individuals who appeared to lack morality. The focus of psychologists and sociologists tended to be on antisocial and destructive behaviors, often involving individuals who were involved in criminal activity. There is a growing trend rooted in the movement toward positive psychology, however, to balance this work by giving attention to individuals who excel in moral development. One way to approach the study of moral excellence, as Lawrence Walker of the Department of Psychology at the University of British Columbia and Karl Henning of the Department of Psychology at the University of Guelph did, is to ask a large group of adults from the general population for their characterization of moral exemplars.. Specifically, they asked over 1,400 adults ranging in age from 18 to 92 to list the characteristics they associated with justice, bravery, and caring. Walker and Henning (2004) found that while there were some overlapping descriptions, participants generally viewed each type of exemplar as unique. The moral exemplar demonstrating justice was primarily characterized by honesty, fairness, and as one who follows principles. The brave exemplar was viewed as primarily intrepid, excelling in courage and risk-taking. The moral exemplar excelling in caring was viewed as primarily loving and empathic.

In a more recent study Lawrence Walker, along with Jeremy Frimer and William Dunlop (2010) of the University of British Columbia extended their understanding of moral excellence by conducting interviews and collecting questionnaire data from 50 individuals who received either the Canadian Medal of Bravery or the Caring Canadian Award and 50 comparison individuals. The results indicated that there is not one personality type that is associated with a moral exemplar or hero, but rather three different types emerged. One profile Walker and his colleagues discovered is the *communal* type, demonstrated by social interdependence, nurturance, and a desire for relationships and opportunities for giving. The second personality profile was the *deliberative* type who was independent, thoughtful with a well-developed sense of personal ethics, and focused on self-development. The third personality profile, what Walker and his colleagues labeled the *ordinary* type, appeared to be unremarkable. They concluded that this group represented those individuals who are taken by situational factors and simply act in a heroic way.

Walker and his colleagues are working to help psychologists and others understand the personality and characteristic profile of those who excel in moral reasoning and behavior. This work can help us not only understand what might be lacking in those who have immature moral reasoning or antisocial behaviors but also how better to identify and cultivate moral excellence.

- Stage 5: Several things are coming to mind: Driven by poverty, May have hungry children, Store owner's right to be paid, Societal order and responsibilities. What action achieves my highest value?
- Stage 6: My identity is built on my highest principles, which are justice and fairness. I will react quickly and follow through because living my principle is the most important choice I can make.

In this hypothetical scenario you can see the shift in thinking from preconventional thinking (self-focused) to conventional (focused on others), and finally to post-conventional (focus on principles).

Advancing in Moral Cognition

Current research indicates that adults are not uniform in their moral development, with some staying in a particular stage as others continue to transition to new perspectives. The Center for the Study of Ethical Development, for example, found that medical school students generally demonstrate higher stages of moral reasoning than some other students in health professions, notably dental and veterinary students (Rest & Narvaez, 1994). Coleman and Wilkins (2002) found the average level of moral reasoning of a group of journalists to be higher than the general adult population average but slightly less than that of medical students. The journalists demonstrated a wide range of moral stages, including about 24% of the sample who scored below the average adult level. While these types of comparisons are interesting, many researchers are more interested in *why* these group variations and individual differences occur.

Your Thoughts?

Which college major(s) might stimulate the most growth in moral reasoning? Give reasons to support your response.

According to Kohlberg (1976) at least two criteria are *necessary but not sufficient* for moral growth. In other words, these criteria create the foundation for growth but do not *cause* moral growth to occur. The first foundational element is cognitive development. A person must have the cognitive maturity to think in abstract ways in order to function at the higher levels of moral reasoning. The second criterion is a type of social stimulation that Kohlberg labeled ***role-taking opportunities***. These opportunities occur when we mentally or physically place ourselves in someone else's position and actively consider the other's perspective (Higgins, 1995). Role-taking opportunities can occur in many settings, particularly educational, occupational, and cross-cultural settings. Gaining insight into a perspective different from your own can also come through various types of media, such as books, film, and theater. For those who have cognitive maturity and role-taking opportunities, research suggests that the potential exists for progression to the higher stages of moral reasoning. Functioning as a type of crystallized intelligence, evidence suggests that there is very little decline in moral reasoning due to age (Dawson, 2002).

Gender Differences in Moral Cognition

In the 1980s scholars began to challenge and refine Kohlberg's theory on many fronts. One particular area of focus was gender differences in reasoning. More specifically, researchers were exploring the hypothesis that two orientations or trajectories of moral stage development can lead to maturity in moral reasoning and that those two paths are primarily gender-related (Gilligan, 1982; Walker, 1995). Gilligan (1982), a leader in this effort, asserted that Kohlberg's emphasis on justice and equality represented a male view of ethics emphasizing personal and universal rights. Women, as she found in her research, often operate with a view of ethics that emphasizes care and responsibility. Anyone, female or male, who focuses on personal relationships in response to questions on Kohlberg's Moral Judgment Interview will be scored at a lower stage of moral reasoning (Pratt, Diessner, Hunsberger, Pancer, & Savoy, 1991).

At the heart of this controversy is Kohlberg's third stage, mutual interpersonal expectations, in which one wants to be seen favorably by significant others, and the fourth stage, social systems and conscience, in which the individual places greater importance on the needs of the larger group. Imagine the hypothetical but realistic dilemma faced by an employee who must choose between the competing responsibilities of work-related obligations and taking an elderly aunt to a medical appointment. One response is "My aunt has always helped me out. I want to hear firsthand what the doctor says so we know how best to help her." Another response would be "I can't just take off work and neglect my responsibilities. People are depending on me and the company would never survive if everyone did that." The first example emphasizes a strong personal relationship and caring attitude (stage 3) while the second example highlights the good of the larger organization and need for reliable organizational loyalty (stage 4).

Your Thoughts?

Do any of these statements sound stereotypically male? Female? Why?

Based on data collected through many interviews, Gilligan (1982) proposed an alternative path of moral growth comprised of three phases or levels. The first level is similar to Kohlberg's preconventional level with the focus on our own needs and desires. Gilligan viewed this level as emphasizing practicality and personal survival. The transition to the second level involves a shift from selfishness to responsibility for others. As our perspective widens to target the needs of others, we develop an attitude of self-sacrifice, putting all others ahead of ourselves. A final transition then moves us from a focus on self-sacrifice for others to what Gilligan conceptualizes as our personal truth. In this mature level we learn to balance our own needs with the needs of others. At this highest level we treat ourselves with the same respect and care that we give to others. Gilligan's criticism of much of the research in moral reasoning is that studies often use measures based on Kohlberg's six stages, which are not sensitive to an ethic of care (Gilligan, 1982; Jaffee & Hyde, 2002).

Your Thoughts?

In what areas might women be more likely to show self-sacrifice? In what areas might men be more likely to show self-sacrifice?

The issue of gender-related moral reasoning has been extensively debated and investigated. Walker (1991, 1995) has conducted numerous literature reviews and performed his own investigations, only to find no empirical evidence for Gilligan's claims. Walker maintains that

Gilligan's theory predicts that women in the second level will focus on self-sacrifice, doing as much as they can for others while neglecting their own needs.

there are more similarities than differences in the justifications of males and females. In another effort to uncover or clarify gender differences, Dawson (2002) reanalyzed data from several pioneering studies of Kohlberg's stages using the most current statistical modeling techniques. This technique revealed age and educational level were strong predictors of stage of moral reasoning and that the effect of gender was very small and inconsistent. In addition, researchers have found that a personal preference toward emphasizing justice or care is not related to cognitive complexity (Pratt et al., 1991; Skoe & von der Lippe, 2002) but rather strongly related to personality (Glover, 2001).

Values Systems and Moral Cognition

Whether considering complex cognition, everyday problem solving in general, or more specifically resolving a moral dilemma, the question remains as to which personal values or principles will guide the reasoning process. Applying the selection–optimization–compensation model to values-based reasoning, we could frame this question in terms of "Which values are likely to be selected from the various competing and conflicting personal preferences?" Kohlberg's stages 5 and 6 rely on the highest value(s) being selected and acted upon.

Values, the principles that guide our actions (Schwartz, 1996, p. 2), have been categorized and approached in several different ways. Some investigators have worked with a *general framework approach,* which assumes that as adults we have a stable, core set of values that can be applied to any situation. This type of research, now considered a more traditional approach, was pioneered by Rokeach (1973) and made popular through the use of the Rokeach Values Survey. The questionnaire consists of values reflecting states of being or endpoints, called *terminal values,* such as *equality* and *happiness,* along with *instrumental values,* which reflect ways of being or acting, such as *ambitious* and *cheerful.* Those taking the survey are challenged to rank the values in terms of the most important guiding principles they use in their lives to the least important. While it is interesting to consider differences in ranking for specific values, such as *true friendship* and *mature love,* researchers are finding more usefulness in a focus on themes. In a meta-analysis involving studies from 41 different countries, Schwartz (1996) found two patterns in the data. One pattern highlighted the conflict between *self-enhancement,* such as personal achievement and power, and *self-transcendence,* such as tolerance and benevolence. The second pattern focused on *openness to change,* which involves independent thought, creativity, and challenge, and *conservation values,* which include conformity, tradition, and security. Over the years two primary areas of concern have emerged from using the general framework approach. One source of frustration is that the data generated by ranking values provides fragmented information with little opportunity for theory-building. Another problematic area is the assertion in the general framework approach that values systems are stable across context and with age. Schwartz (1996) has found evidence indicating that the way we prioritize items in our values systems will change with time and experience, findings that are consistent with research on stages of moral reasoning.

Your Thoughts?

Do the patterns found by Schwartz offer any insight into Gilligan's concerns regarding moral reasoning?

More recent approaches to values systems have accounted for greater flexibility and change over time. The *contextual approach* to values emphasizes the influence of the social and physical environment in shaping the ways individuals prioritize their values in that moment. Seligman and Katz (1996) found, consistent with the contextual approach, that when participants are asked to rank the importance of personal values such as the sanctity of life and environmental issues, the same participants would give contradictory opinions depending on the context. Another recent perspective, the *source approach* to values, allows for individuals to look to different domains for values. This approach, developed by Lewis (1990), states that individuals may look to one or more of the following six sources for guidance when resolving everyday personal moral conflicts:

Your Thoughts?

Would younger adults be more likely to look to different sources than older adults? Why, why not, or under what circumstances?

- Respected authority
- Logic
- Sensory experience
- Feelings
- Intuition
- Scientific method

An individual may, for example, seek an authority in a religious context, use intuition in a parenting context, and use logic in work situations. While the academic study of values systems has not produced a formula for predicting which values will rise to the level of a "guiding principle" in particular stages or contexts, the research in this area has given researchers insight into the various ways values may be selected.

Section Summary

- As a type of complex cognition, resolving personal moral dilemmas brings together several types of intelligence and everyday problem-solving skills.
- Moral behaviors, reflecting the resolution of a problem, are dependent upon moral sensitivity, reasoning, motivation, and character.
- Moral cognition can be described using Kohlberg's three levels and six stages of moral reasoning.
- Across adulthood most individuals will move through a series of stages that increase in levels of cognitive complexity, engaging self-centered, other-centered, and values-centered perspectives.
- Research suggests that stimulation prompting advancement through stages of moral reasoning comes primarily from cognitive development and role-taking opportunities.
- The criticism of gender bias in Kohlberg's assessment of moral reasoning, specifically favoring a male-oriented justice system over a female-oriented value system based on care, remains controversial in that it has gained much support while the research evidence generally does not support it.
- Regarding values as a general topic of study, some view value systems as stable, general frameworks whereas others view them as changing with the context and varying based on source.

Chapter Summary

The areas of complex cognition emphasized in this chapter are intelligence, creativity, everyday problem solving, and moral reasoning. In all these areas the changes in neurocognitive functioning and information processing that come with age have an effect. While the slowing of working memory and processing speed are evident in traditional IQ testing and in measures of fluid intelligence, it is also clear that some adults develop skills that respond much like expertise in their resistance to decline. By moving the application of cognitive skills from traditional and hypothetical tasks to the domain of everyday experience, researchers find that adults generally improve in their cognitive performance with age. Here are some of the main points of the chapter:

- Four primary approaches to cognition are the psychometric, cognitive, neo-Piagetian, and contextual perspectives.
- The Wechsler Adult Intelligence Scale, one of the most popular IQ tests used, includes tasks of verbal comprehension, working memory, perceptual organization, and processing speed.
- Using IQ scores across adulthood, cross-sectional studies find that intelligence begins to decline in young adulthood, while longitudinal studies find that IQ peaks in young adulthood, stabilizes in middle adulthood, and declines in late adulthood.
- Fluid intelligence, which involves processing information, tends to decline with age, while crystallized intelligence, which is the information gained from education and enculturation, tends to increase through most of adulthood.
- Sternberg's triarchic theory of intelligence emphasizes the interaction of analytic, creative, and practical intelligences.
- The triarchic theory of intelligence has been applied to types of giftedness, with the most gifted being the individual who excels in all three intelligences.
- Gardner's eight multiple intelligences, stemming from a strict set of criteria, are logical-mathematical, linguistic, spatial, musical, bodily-kinesthetic, interpersonal, intrapersonal, and naturalistic.
- Creativity has been studied using many different techniques, with some aimed at creative products, creative personalities, and creative processes.
- Studies of creativity indicate that, much like expertise and everyday problem-solving skills, the quality and complexity of creative processes and products generally grow with age.
- A better predictor of older adults' competence in daily living is their everyday problem-solving skills, rather than their scores on tests of fluid intelligence or general IQ.
- The type of problem, topic area, age of the individual, and level of social support are among the most influential factors in resolving everyday problems.
- The selection, optimization, and compensation model of life management can also be applied to everyday problem solving.
- Narvaez and Rest have developed a four-component model leading to moral behavior, which consists of moral sensitivity, moral reasoning, moral motivation, and moral character.
- Kohlberg's theory of moral reasoning, involving six stages, describes the movement from the motivation to avoid punishment, through exchanges, valuing others' opinions, obeying laws and conscience, to developing a lifestyle around a person's highest values.
- Researchers find that moral reasoning is facilitated by cognitive development, role-taking opportunities, and intellectually or ethically stimulating situations, as can occur in formal education or profound life experiences.
- Gilligan and others have challenged the gender-neutrality of Kohlberg's stages by asserting that it favors a justice and fairness orientation (masculine values) over an emphasis on caring and responsibility (feminine values).
- There are various perspectives on the makeup and influence of values systems in moral cognition, such as the stable general framework approach, and the perspectives that emphasize the context of the moral conflict, such as the contextual and source approaches.

Key Terms

Psychometric perspective on intelligence **(232)**
Cognitive perspective on intelligence **(232)**
Contextual perspective on intelligence **(232)**
Neo-Piagetian perspective on intelligence **(232)**
Intelligence quotient (IQ) **(232)**
Fluid intelligence **(233)**
Cognitive mechanics **(234)**
Crystallized intelligence **(234)**
Cognitive pragmatics **(234)**
Triarchic theory of intelligence **(234)**
Multiple intelligences **(235)**
Creativity **(238)**
Swan song phenomenon **(238)**
Well-defined problems **(239)**
Ill-defined problems **(239)**
Experimental research designs **(242)**
Control group **(242)**
Independent variables **(242)**
Dependent variables **(242)**
Moral development **(244)**
Four-component model of moral behavior **(244)**
Moral reasoning **(246)**
Role-taking opportunities **(248)**

Comprehension Questions

1. What are the four perspectives on intelligence and how is each one unique from the others?
2. What are the four areas of mental abilities measured by the WAIS?
3. What have researchers found regarding changes in IQ across adulthood?
4. What are the differences between fluid and crystallized intelligence?
5. What are the differences between cognitive mechanics and pragmatics?
6. How do fluid and crystallized intelligences change across adulthood?
7. Name and explain the functions of each of the three elements in Sternberg's triarchic theory of intelligence.
8. Explain how Sternberg applied the triarchic theory of intelligence to giftedness.
9. What are the eight multiple intelligences and how is each one unique?
10. What are the criteria Gardner uses to determine that a talent is a separate intelligence?
11. Describe the overlap of creativity and the various perspectives on intelligence.
12. Name and describe the lifespan stages of creativity discovered by Reed (2005).
13. What personal and situational factors would predict better everyday problem-solving abilities for older adults?
14. Create an example applying the SOC model to an everyday problem encountered by most adults.
15. Explain each of the four components in the model of moral behavior developed by Narvaez and Rest (1995).
16. Describe the levels in Kohlberg's theory of moral reasoning, emphasizing how each is distinct.
17. Describe each of the stages involved in Kohlberg's theory of moral reasoning.
18. What are the two factors most important in stimulating movement in stages of moral reasoning?
19. Explain the controversy over gender differences in moral reasoning.
20. How is the general framework approach to values different from the contextual and source approaches?
21. Describe the pairs of conflicting values found by Schwartz (1996).
22. What are the six sources of values highlighted in the source approach?

Answers for Common Sense: Myth or Reality?

1. Reality: IQ tests are generally used for diagnostic purposes in clinical settings. (See Assessment of Intelligence, page 232.)
2. Myth: Studies show that IQ peaks in middle adulthood and remains stable through late adulthood. (See Assessment of Intelligence, page 232.)
3. Myth: Intelligence and memory are affected differently by aging. (See Assessment of Intelligence, page 233.)
4. Reality: In areas of expertise adults will show little if any cognitive decline while at the same time they will show cognitive decline in other areas. (See Fluid and Crystallized Intelligence, page 234.)
5. Reality: There is an accepted academic theory of intelligence that promotes common sense as a key facet of general intelligence. (See Alternative Theories of Intelligence, page 235.)
6. Myth: People who are gifted are good at everything. (See Alternative Theories of Intelligence, page 235.)
7. Reality: There is an accepted academic theory of intelligence that recognizes athletic ability as intelligence. (See Alternative Theories of Intelligence, page 235.)
8. Myth: Most researchers define creativity in terms of whether the final product, such as a song or a piece of pottery, has been judged to be creative. (See Creativity, page 238.)
9. Myth: Older adults would rather collaborate with their siblings in problem solving than with their own adult children. (See Factors in Problem-Solving Performance, page 241.)
10. Reality: Motivation is one of the major elements in moving from moral thoughts to moral behaviors. (See Resolving Everyday Personal Moral Problems, page 244.)
11. Myth: When faced with a moral dilemma, using the question "How will I benefit from this?" is a mature approach. (See Moral Cognition Across Adulthood, page 246.)
12. Reality: Research shows that the moral development of most journalists is higher than the average adult. (See Advancing in Moral Cognition, page 248.)
13. Myth: Researchers find that men and women consistently emphasize different values in moral reasoning. (See Gender Differences in Moral Cognition, page 249.)
14. Myth: A person's values tend to be stable throughout life. (See Values Systems and Moral Cognition, page 250.)
15. Myth: People are generally consistent in applying their values no matter in what area of life a moral conflict occurs. (See Values Systems and Moral Cognition, page 251.)

Suggested Readings

The Best Mental Tests, 1890

Cattell, J. M. (1890). Mental tests and measurements. *Mind, 15,* 373–381. Accessed at *Classics in the History of Psychology* (http://psychclassics.yorku.ca/topic.htm).

Culture and Human Intelligence

Sternberg, R. J. (2002). Cultural explorations of human intelligence around the world. In W. J. Lonner, D. L. Dinnel, S. A. Hayes, & D. N. Sattler (Eds.), *Online readings in psychology and culture* (Unit 5, Chapter 1), (http://www.wwu.edu/~culture), Center for Cross-Cultural Research, Western Washington University, Bellingham, WA. Available at http://www.ac.wwu.edu/~culture/Sternberg.htm.

Creativity in Brazilian Culture

Fleith, D. S. (2002). Creativity in the Brazilian culture. In W. J. Lonner, D. L. Dinnel, S. A. Hayes, & D. N. Sattler (Eds.), *Online readings in psychology and culture* (Unit 5, Chapter 3), (http://www.wwu.edu/~culture), Center for Cross-Cultural Research, Western Washington University, Bellingham, WA. Available at http://www.ac.wwu.edu/~culture/Fleith.htm.

Classic Article Examining Maternal Values, 1916

Hollingworth, L. S. (1916). Social devices for impelling women to bear and rear children. *American Journal of Sociology, 22,* 19–29. Available at http://psychclassics.yorku.ca/Hollingworth/children.htm.

Suggested Websites

Historical and Current Controversies in Intelligence

Human Intelligence, http://www.indiana.edu/~intell/, provides information on the historical influences and current controversies in the study of human intelligence.

IQ Testing

For general information and numerous websites to explore, check out IQ testing at About.com, http://psychology.about.com/blsub_int_iqtest.htm.

Howard Gardner and Multiple Intelligences

You can learn more about Gardner and his research at http://www.infed.org/thinkers/gardner.htm, as well as by exploring multiple intelligences at About.com, http://psychology.about.com/od/intel/a/multi_intel.htm.

Research in Moral Reasoning and Ethics

The Association for Moral Education maintains a lengthy list of links to groups that study moral development at http://www.amenetwork.org/links.html.

CHAPTER

10 Typical Physical Aging

It is obvious that as we age our bodies change. Fortunately, the promotion of successful aging has raised awareness that all of adulthood, including late adulthood, can involve periods of growth and personal development. The ever-increasing research evidence continues to indicate that physical fitness, good nutrition, and psychological and social well-being can dramatically improve quality of life throughout adulthood. Ultimately, though, no matter how well we follow a plan for successful aging, there are inevitable physical changes we must adjust to. This chapter focuses on areas of normal, expected physical changes, specifically in terms of external appearance, sensory and motor functioning, body systems, and sexuality. Changes in brain physiology and functioning are covered in the chapters on cognition.

Exploring the boundaries between normal and abnormal aging is insightful for several reasons. When we understand what to expect with age we can anticipate coping strategies. While some of the typical changes involve attitudinal adjustments, such as tolerating or accepting "gray hair" or "wrinkled skin" as a part of our identity in a society that often values youth, other normal age-related developments may trigger changes in the way we live, such as learning to use a hearing aid or adding support rails for the bathtub. Another useful insight gained from the comparison of normal and abnormal aging is a better sense of when developments are normal and when to be concerned over physical or cognitive changes and seek a medical evaluation. For example,

COMMON SENSE
Myth or Reality?

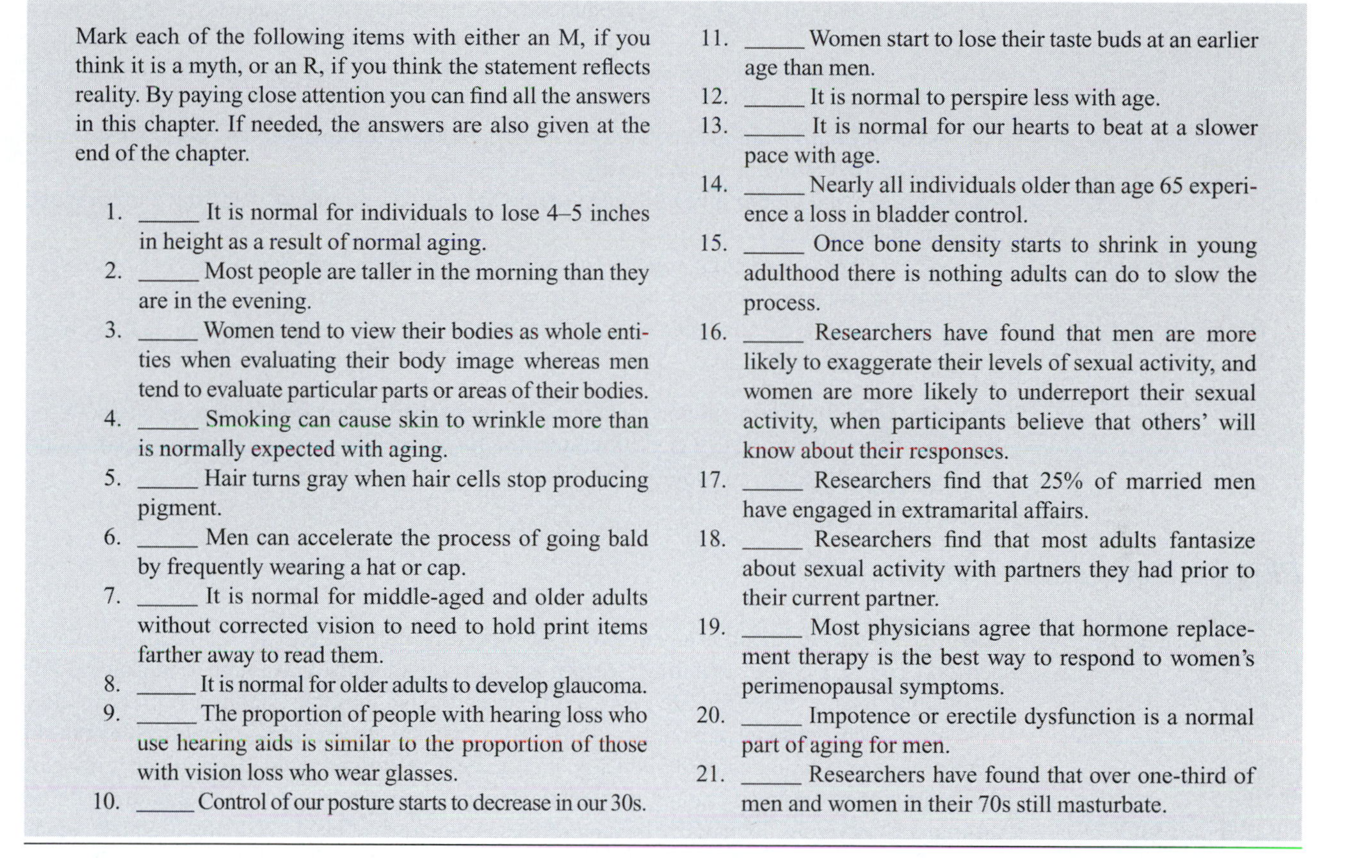

Mark each of the following items with either an M, if you think it is a myth, or an R, if you think the statement reflects reality. By paying close attention you can find all the answers in this chapter. If needed, the answers are also given at the end of the chapter.

1. _____ It is normal for individuals to lose 4–5 inches in height as a result of normal aging.
2. _____ Most people are taller in the morning than they are in the evening.
3. _____ Women tend to view their bodies as whole entities when evaluating their body image whereas men tend to evaluate particular parts or areas of their bodies.
4. _____ Smoking can cause skin to wrinkle more than is normally expected with aging.
5. _____ Hair turns gray when hair cells stop producing pigment.
6. _____ Men can accelerate the process of going bald by frequently wearing a hat or cap.
7. _____ It is normal for middle-aged and older adults without corrected vision to need to hold print items farther away to read them.
8. _____ It is normal for older adults to develop glaucoma.
9. _____ The proportion of people with hearing loss who use hearing aids is similar to the proportion of those with vision loss who wear glasses.
10. _____ Control of our posture starts to decrease in our 30s.
11. _____ Women start to lose their taste buds at an earlier age than men.
12. _____ It is normal to perspire less with age.
13. _____ It is normal for our hearts to beat at a slower pace with age.
14. _____ Nearly all individuals older than age 65 experience a loss in bladder control.
15. _____ Once bone density starts to shrink in young adulthood there is nothing adults can do to slow the process.
16. _____ Researchers have found that men are more likely to exaggerate their levels of sexual activity, and women are more likely to underreport their sexual activity, when participants believe that others' will know about their responses.
17. _____ Researchers find that 25% of married men have engaged in extramarital affairs.
18. _____ Researchers find that most adults fantasize about sexual activity with partners they had prior to their current partner.
19. _____ Most physicians agree that hormone replacement therapy is the best way to respond to women's perimenopausal symptoms.
20. _____ Impotence or erectile dysfunction is a normal part of aging for men.
21. _____ Researchers have found that over one-third of men and women in their 70s still masturbate.

research has shown that the same common memory errors and mistakes that are ignored in younger adults are often attention-grabbing and taken as reasons for concern with older adults (when there is no need for concern) (Hess, 2006). That said, when in doubt a medical evaluation is always a wise decision whether the result is a serious diagnosis or peace-of-mind that there are no major problems. There are individuals, particularly men, who will ignore physical or cognitive problems which should be taken as signs of concern (Bertakis, Azari, Helms, Callahan, & Robbins, 2000).

Before We Get Started . . .

In a chapter focused on typical physical changes with age it is appropriate and important to discuss sexuality. Later in this chapter we consider sexuality across adulthood, but here we consider studies involving young adults. Researchers have found an interesting trend among college students. When asking students about their own sexual behaviors the frequency and number of partners is often much less than what those students estimate regarding the sexual activity of their peers (Scholly, Katz, Gascoigne, & Holck, 2005). Take a minute to give your best responses to the following questions, listing as many different sources of information as you can think of:

1. Who or what would give college students the idea that everyone else is having sex more often?
2. Who or what would give college students the idea that everyone else has many more sexual partners?
3. Who or what would give college students the idea that more students contract sexually transmitted infections than actually do?
4. Who or what would give college students the idea that more students have unintended pregnancies than actually do?
5. What could be advantageous about college students' beliefs that others are more sexually active?
6. What could be disadvantageous or destructive about college students' beliefs that others are more sexually active?

Finally, pretend for a moment that you are a college administrator who is concerned about the physical health of students. Based on your thoughts on the previous questions, what would you suggest colleges do to promote sexual health and more accurate perceptions of college student behaviors?

Physical Aging Across Adulthood

Generally, young adulthood is a period of high energy. It is a time to make major life decisions, such as choosing a college, entering a career, and starting a family. It is a time to be "on the go" and pushing toward cherished life goals. While individuals in middle adulthood still have busy lives, substantial goals, and amazing personal drive, they are also beginning to notice changes in their bodies and a mild decrease in energy. For example, I noticed in my early 40s that my hair was turning gray, I needed reading glasses, it was harder to lose weight, and I couldn't pull an "all-nighter" anymore. Even though many of these changes had been occurring gradually since my mid-20s, it wasn't until my 40s that these changes were noticeable. Like most middle-aged adults, I adjusted. Changes in appearance and sensory and body functioning will continue through middle and late adulthood, with another noticeable shift usually occurring in our 70s. Recognizing this shift, Neugarten suggested a distinction between the *young-old* and the *old-old,* with the transition taking place around 70 years old (Kensinger & Corkin, 2003).

Your Thoughts?

Considering sensory and major body systems, in what ways has your body changed over the last 10 years?

Aging is multifaceted and not necessarily detrimental. In order to make useful distinctions the term *aging* is generally qualified in more specific ways. ***Primary aging,*** the focus of this chapter, is the term used to refer to changes with age that are normal and nonpathological. Changes associated with puberty when we are young, and changes in our vision as we age, are both examples of primary aging. The signs of aging that are directly linked to disease, detrimental lifestyles, or environmental factors are called ***secondary aging.*** In many contact sports that rely primarily on physical strength and agility, for example, the effects of years of training, playing, and surviving injuries will show as professional players reach middle age. While the life of a professional athlete may be glamorous and productive on many levels, from the perspective of secondary aging, it can be detrimental to the aging process. Risky behaviors and unhealthy habits, such as smoking, can also contribute to secondary aging. A third distinction, ***tertiary aging,*** refers to the rapid loss of physical and cognitive functioning just before death.

Your Thoughts?

What jobs or occupations would likely accelerate secondary aging?

Not only is aging multifaceted within an individual, showing both primary and secondary aging, but also across individuals. It's important to remember that aging results from a complex interaction of personal and environmental factors, bringing to light numerous individual differences over time (National Institute on Aging [NIA], 2007a).

ON THE LEADING EDGE
Performance Enhancing Drugs

Just about anyone who plays sports or follows a favorite professional athlete or team will have heard of controversies surrounding the use of performance enhancing drugs. While the general public often hears sports figures say "I didn't know I was taking a banned substance" Andrea Petroczi of the School of Life Sciences at Kingston University in Australia and Eugene Aidman of the School of Psychology at the University of Adelaide in Australia contend that doping is deliberate, requiring planning and ongoing strict adherence to a regimen. Doping behaviors have been found at the preadolescent level and continuing through high school, college, amateur, and professional sports. The National Institute on Drug Abuse (2009) reports that the use of anabolic steroids, a common type of performance enhancing drug, can cause extreme mood swings, paranoia, delusions, and aggressive behaviors. Anabolic steroids, which should only be purchased by prescription for an appropriate medical condition, also have an addictive quality. Withdrawal from the use of these performance enhancing drugs can cause fatigue, mood swings, insomnia, and depression which may lead to suicide attempts. Considering the fact that the use of doping can bring with it life-and-death consequences, it is critically important that we better understand the psychological aspects of doping.

Vanessa Lentillon-Kaestner of the Institute of Sport and Physical Education Sciences at the University of Lausanne in Switzerland and Catherine Carstairs from the History Department at the University of Guelph in Canada set out to learn more about how doping practices get started for young elite cyclists. Based on semi-structured interviews with 8 cyclists ranging in age from 21 to 27, they discovered that the young cyclists held two very different standards for amateur racers and those who were professional: amateurs should remain clean, professionals should be allowed to use anabolic steroids. Through the interviews Lentillon-Kaestner and Carstairs (2010) discovered that those around the amateur athletes also worked to protect them from doping, but once turned professional it was the more experienced professionals who taught the novices what to do. When asked about their concern over the health risks of using performance enhancing drugs the athletes generally ignored it and compensated by saying that professional sports are inherently dangerous.

While we often think of terms such as "typical aging" and "successful aging" as referring to people in middle age or late adulthood, when considering those who push their bodies to their physical limits, the signs of typical aging can start to appear in early adulthood. Adding to that the drive to be a competitor and not wanting to let the team down, many of the cyclists interviewed believed their only chance to compete and win is with the use of performance enhancing drugs.

Section Summary

- Changes in appearance and sensory and body functioning are common throughout adulthood; most notice them more starting in middle adulthood.
- Primary aging refers to changes with age that are normal and nonpathological, while secondary aging refers to changes caused by disease, detrimental lifestyles, or environmental factors.
- While general statements are often made regarding physical health, it is important to remember that there are many individual differences.

Changes in Appearance

Often when we think of the markers of aging we think of changes in physical appearance. Typical of many Americans, when a group of middle school students were asked to give signs of aging, their most frequent responses were "wrinkles" and "gray hair" or "baldness" (Lichtenstein et al, 2003). This section explores changes in body shape, skin, and hair. While there are some treatments that may slow some of the aging processes or hide the changes, eventually we must acknowledge these physical signals that we are getting older. The psychological components of that adjustment in identity can be just as important as physical adjustments in terms of quality of life.

Changes in Body Shapes

Generally, body shapes morph with age due to changes in height, muscle mass, and body fat. Everyone loses some height as they age, on the average 4 cm (1.57 inches) between young adulthood and the young-old age of around 70 years old, with another 3.5 cm (1.38 inches) between young-old and old-old age of mid-90s (Sagiv, Vogelaere, Soudry, & Ehrsam, 2000). Why do we get shorter? When we are younger the disks that cushion spinal vertebrae compress during the day and then expand and rehydrate during sleep. (That's why people are often taller in the morning than in the evening.) Over the years the disks become less flexible, causing less expansion and resulting in less height for most people (NLM, 2008b). Along with a shorter profile, everyone loses muscle mass and gains body fat with age as well. The expected decrease in muscle mass, approximately 20% from age 30 to age 70, will bring changes in our body shape (NIA, 2007a). Primarily due to metabolism decreases, body fat tends to increase during middle age (Mayo Clinic, 2008a). As a result, middle age and older adults cannot eat as much as they did in young adulthood and maintain their weight. Just like modifying any long-held habit, it can be very difficult for some of us to learn to say "no" to certain foods or admit our situation and choose from the "senior" portion of the menu when eating out. In late adulthood we will need to be even more mindful of our physical health as both our body fat and muscle mass start to decrease (NIA, 2007a).

Your Thoughts?

How might an employer encourage employees to maintain a healthy weight?

Research focused on the psychological transition and adjustments associated with changes in body shape, often referred to as the part of our identity called *body image,* shows that men and women generally react in different ways. For example, in interviews with 42 adults, ranging in age from 22 to 62 years old, Halliwell and Dittmar (2003) found that the men tended to view their bodies as one whole entity, whereas the women divided their bodies into parts or areas. Thus, when asked about their body image, men emphasized a general impression of how well their bodies as a whole were aging, while women gave many critiques of different parts of their bodies. Also, the men tended to highlight how well their bodies functioned, while appearance was the primary concern of the women in the study. When asked

Even under the healthiest of circumstances our bodies change with age.

specifically about appearance, most of the men felt that aging had a neutral or positive impact on their appearance, while most of the women felt aging had a negative impact on their appearance. The women in this study were not alone in their perspective. Many researchers and social commentators have noted different standards for men and women as they age. Often people want to look good, however they might define "looking good," in order to feel attractive and desirable. Although men may look distinguished and handsome with a little gray hair and weathered skin, women often perceive a different standard, requiring a youthful figure, perfect skin, and perfect hair. The drive to look like the models, actresses, and other celebrities who are viewed as examples of the ideal female body shape is unrealistic and doomed to frustration. Models represent the thinnest 5% of the female population (Saucier, 2004). One of the challenges of successful aging is to accept the benign changes in our bodies, and to realize that whether we are male or female, we do not have to meet unrealistic societal standards or be of a certain age to be desirable, attractive, or even sexy.

Your Thoughts?

What industries or manufacturers gain from women's drive to look youthful? What industries or manufacturers would gain if women's attitudes were more like the men's?

Changes in Skin

Like many other areas of primary aging, skin changes that become noticeable in midlife actually began in our mid-20s. The most common skin changes include the development of wrinkles, dryness, and age spots. Also with age our skin becomes thinner, less elastic and firm, and more fragile, contributing not only to more wrinkles, particularly around the eyes and forehead, but also more bruises and cuts (American Academy of Dermatology [AAD], 2008a; National Library of Medicine Medline Plus [NLM], 2010d). Age spots, sometimes called "liver spots," are flat brown areas that may resemble large freckles. Many people have an inherited predisposition to develop age spots, however, continued exposure to the sun can bring them out as well. Although they may look unappealing, age spots are not related to liver disease, nor are they cancerous or precancerous (AAD, 2008b). There are changes in the skin other than sunspots that can be signals of a more serious problem. It is always a good idea to have a professional look at any changes in your skin to make sure the condition is the harmless one you believe it to be.

While skin changes due to primary aging are inevitable, sun exposure and smoking are among the most common causes of damaged skin, resulting in excessive wrinkling and increasing the risk of skin cancer (Mayo Clinic, 2008a). The benefits of quitting smoking are numerous, with less skin wrinkling and risk of skin cancer among them.

What are the best ways to protect your skin from ***photoaging***, the dermatological term for aging caused by sun exposure (AAD, 2008a)? According to the National Institute on Aging (2009a), try to stay out of direct sun even on cloudy days, and when you are in the sun wear protective clothing and use an appropriate sunscreen. The NIA also warns against artificial tanning. Though most people are aware of such warnings, many people ignore them. A recent study of female college students revealed that their primary reasons for engaging in sunbathing and tanning were to enhance their general attractiveness, increase the appearance of physical fitness, and because of the influence of media, family, and friends (Cafri et al, 2006). While the reinforcements may seem to be worthwhile in young adulthood, when those college women are older they will likely see the effects of their behaviors in wrinkles and greater skin cancer risk.

Your Thoughts?

Do you think college males would give the same reasons for tanning? If different, what might their reasons be?

Changes in Hair

Perhaps one of the most telling signs of aging is the appearance of gray and/or thinning hair. While it is a safe assumption that the previous sentence is referring to hair on our heads (and it is), as human beings we have hair all over our bodies except for our lips, palms, and soles of our feet (NLM, 2010b). The transition to gray or white hair is the result of genetically programmed changes in special root cells that produce hair color pigment. The process of graying

> **Your Thoughts?**
>
> Why isn't hair color for men as popular as it is for women?

is gradual because the hairs tend to reduce pigment production at differing rates. When the cells produce no pigment at all the hair is white. There is no way to prevent hair from graying or to adjust the age at which graying begins, which is also genetically determined. The age ranges for the transition to gray hair are quite varied. Some people start turning gray in their 30s, while others may not start graying until their 60s (NLM, 2008a).

The medical term for baldness, or hair loss from the scalp, is ***alopecia.*** Generally associated with older men, it can occur in men and women of all ages. Although the myths still circulate that frequently wearing a hat or using a blow dryer can cause hair loss (American Osteopathic Association, 2008), about 95% of the cases of baldness are ***androgenetic alopecia,*** or *male pattern baldness,* which is genetic in origin. Hereditary factors also affect the age, speed, and pattern of hair loss. Women with alopecia usually experience thinning hair at the front, top, or on the sides, but rarely complete baldness. While hair loss may be caused by hereditary factors, it is important to note that alopecia can occur as a result of many health conditions, such as poor nutrition or undergoing surgery; from certain diseases, such as diabetes; or the medications used to treat certain problems, such as depression, high blood pressure, cancer, and arthritis (American Academy of Physicians, 2002; NLM, 2010b). While it's most likely that hair loss is nothing more than a sign of aging, alopecia along with all physical changes should be discussed with medical professionals.

American society and its media have a history of promoting youthful appearances at all costs (Calasanti, 2007), leaving many individuals with gray hair and/or alopecia quite self-conscious about their condition. For those with graying hair who want to cover it up the treatments are plentiful, relatively safe, and easy to self-administer. Those with alopecia are not as fortunate in this regard. Their situation is often viewed as a disease that needs to be treated. It is important to thoroughly research any hair replacement treatments before trying any of them. While there are some medically approved options available for alopecia, there are also many bogus products, which do not work and may cause harmful side effects (Mayo Clinic, 2010d).

> **Your Thoughts?**
>
> Why isn't hair replacement for women as popular as it is for men?

Section Summary

- Starting in young adulthood, though generally not noticeable until middle age, our bodies start to change their shape, particularly due to changes in height, lean muscle mass, and distribution of body fat.
- By middle age individuals start to notice more wrinkles, age spots, and general skin dryness.
- Avoiding sun exposure, artificial tanning, and smoking are the best ways to reduce the amount and speed of skin aging.
- Graying and thinning hair are primarily genetically determined, benign processes that show wide variation in terms of age.
- Whether it is body shape, skin, or hair issues, the psychological adjustment both within the individual and in the ways others choose to respond to those signals of aging can be dramatic.

Changes in Sensory Systems

Along with wrinkles and gray hair, other typical signs of aging may include the growing need for reading glasses and hearing aids. This section focuses on changes involving *exteroceptive senses,* primarily vision, hearing, and balance. As we age our sensory thresholds increase, requiring more energy and stronger signals for detection. The most dramatic changes occur in terms of vision and hearing, although all the senses are affected by aging (University of Maryland Medical Center [UMMC], 2009). Just as with gray hair or wrinkled skin, we need to make successful physical and psychological adjustments to adapt to our changing abilities in regard to vision, hearing, and other senses. While some adjustments, such as wearing glasses, are generally accepted, other adjustments, such as wearing a hearing aid or carrying a walking cane, may have a strong impact on our own self-concept and personal identity as well as cause others to treat us differently.

Changes in Vision

Our eyes are complex organs with many features that change as we age. Some of the changes have mild consequences, such as the reduced ability to produce tears, leading to dry and irritated eyes. Though annoying, this condition is easily controlled with eye drops and perhaps using a humidifier when the climate is dry (Mayo Clinic, 2008a, 2010b). Other changes are more serious. The cornea, as seen in Figure 10.1, increases in curvature, which adds to the amount of scattered intraocular light. The lens becomes less flexible and less transparent with age, which also leads to poorer vision. One of the most common signs of aging eyes, the need to hold items farther away in order to read or see details, is a direct result of changes in the lens. By the time most adults are in their 40s they have developed ***presbyopia***, the condition in which the lens cannot accommodate or focus clearly on objects that are only a short distance away (Mayo Clinic, 2009f; Schieber, 2006). Other expected changes include ***papillary miosis***, a decrease in the average diameter of the pupil, and ***ptosis***, drooping eyelids, both of which limit the amount of light and information coming into the eye (Schieber, 2006). For those with aging eyes the most commonly reported vision problems are blurriness and inability to see fine details, the length of time it takes to adjust to changes in light intensity (such as moving indoors on a bright day), difficulty tolerating and seeing when a bright glare is present, seeing in low light conditions, making distance judgments (Fozard & Gordon-Salant, 2001) and difficulty in detecting moving objects (NIA, 2007a).

Your Thoughts?

How might these common changes affect driving ability?

The three most common eye *pathologies*—cataracts, glaucoma, and age-related maculopathy or macular degeneration (Mayo Clinic, 2008a; Schieber, 2006)—are so frequently occurring in the general population that many people view them as inevitable or expected with

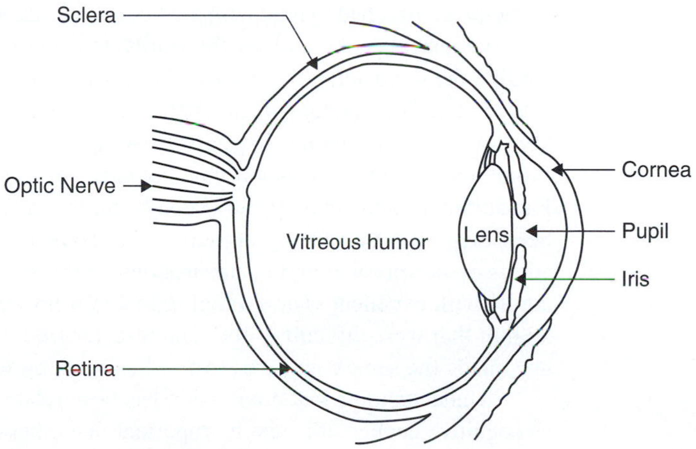

Sclera
Optic Nerve
Vitreous humor
Lens
Cornea
Pupil
Iris
Retina

FIGURE 10.1 ***Basic Eye Anatomy.***

From the National Eye Institute, National Institutes of Health. (2006).

age when such is not the case. Cataracts are the leading cause of age-related visual impairment (Schieber, 2006), affecting about half of all Americans over age 65. When individuals are bothered with ***cataracts*** they have a clouded eye lens that is similar to trying to look through a fogged-up window. Fortunately, cataract surgery is relatively safe and effective (Mayo Clinic, 2010a). ***Glaucoma,*** another common cause of vision loss, affecting approximately 3 million Americans, is actually a group of diseases that cause unusually high pressure inside the eyeball and related damage to the optic nerve. These conditions can usually be controlled through eye drops or surgery (Mayo Clinic, 2008c; Schieber, 2006). ***Age-related maculopathy*** or ***macular degeneration*** occur when the part of the retina responsible for central vision deteriorates, causing blurred vision or a blind spot in the center of the visual field. Macular degeneration is also a leading cause of severe vision loss in older adults, affecting more than 1.6 million Americans. Unfortunately, this disease is progressive (Schieber, 2006) and difficult to treat (Mayo Clinic, 2008b).

Age-related visual impairment can cause significant problems, requiring extra attention and effort, and consequently adding stress to even routine daily activities (Schieber, 2006). For example, interview data from 155 adults between the ages of 65 and 92 years old revealed that poor vision had caused problems preparing meals, using public transportation, writing checks, handling money, and taking medications (Travis, Boerner, Reinhardt, & Horowitz, 2004). Older adults may feel isolated when vision problems cause them to stop trying to read the newspaper or the closed captioning on the television, drive, or travel to see their family and friends. It is not a surprise that poor vision has often been linked to depression (Horowitz, 2004; Wahl, Becker, Burmedi, & Schilling, 2004). The blunders caused by poor vision and the accompanying frustration and depression may lead friends and family to falsely conclude that their loved ones are suffering from cognitive or memory decline. For example, a woman in her 80s might purchase the wrong kind of soup not because she was confused or forgot her favorite recipe but because she couldn't read the labels while at the store and simply guessed. An elderly father may ask his adult children to sort his mail and pay his bills not because the task is too challenging mentally but rather because it takes so much effort to read and comprehend all the fine print.

Your Thoughts?

What might a social worker do to better distinguish between a cognitive and a sensory deficit when working with clients over age 60?

Several researchers have designed studies to demonstrate that poor vision rather than declining cognitive processing may cause older adults to make cognitive mistakes. In one such study, Anstey, Dain, Andrews, and Drobny (2002) asked 94 participants from New South Wales, Australia, ranging in age from 60 to 87 years old, to try a version of the Stroop task. The participants first had to read names of colors aloud, in order to establish a baseline of just how fast each participant could say the words. In the next task, the participants had to refrain from reading the word, but rather they had to say the name of the color of the ink in which the word was printed. For example, if shown the word "blue" printed in green ink, the participant should say "green." They found that performance on the Stroop task was related more to level of visual acuity and color vision than cognitive processing. Using a different strategy, Berardi, Parasuraman, and Haxby (2001) conducted several cognitive tests in which the stimuli had been degraded by varying amounts. Rather than comparing the cognitive performance of adults of various ages and visual abilities, in this case Berardi and her colleagues recruited 62 adults with excellent vision, ranging in age from 20 to 73, and then gave all the participants stimuli that were difficult to see. The researchers found that all the participants, regardless of age, made the same cognitive errors when working with the same incomplete stimuli.

Understanding that poor vision has been related to depression and can be misunderstood as cognitive decline, it is vitally important that older adults have routine visual evaluations, get the appropriate glasses or treatments, and remain creative and flexible in their efforts to deal with vision impairment. How do older adults cope with poor vision? That was the question posed to 26 visually impaired seniors, ranging in age from 65 to 93 years old, by Ryan, Anas, Beamer, and

Bajorek (2003). Although the participants still struggled to read important items, most had switched to large-print versions of printed material or opted to listen to audio recordings when possible. When neither was available the participants used high-powered magnifiers and special lights. To better manage grocery shopping and banking the participants chose smaller establishments, developed relationships with the employees, and asked for help when needed.

Experts would add to those findings that older adults make sure the prescription for their glasses is correct, purchase large-print clocks and phones, and that they have proper lighting around their house. It may be useful for a family member or friend to mark important settings on dials that are hard to read. Computer monitor settings can be adjusted for large font sizes, which often helps those with vision problems find important medical information, stay informed on the latest news and weather, and communicate with others through websites and e-mail (Mayo Clinic, 2008b). Many advocates for older adults, including social workers and public health officials, are working to bring changes that would make restaurants, public transportation, and retail and grocery stores more user-friendly for older adults, allowing them greater independence and social involvement (Crews, 2003).

Your Thoughts?

What modifications could a restaurant make in order to be more user-friendly to adults with visual impairment? Hearing impairment?

Changes in Hearing

The most dramatic sensory changes associated with aging (UMMC, 2009), and thus the most studied, occur with vision and hearing. Similar to various components in our eyes, parts of our auditory system show natural changes with age, leading primarily to hearing impairment. Damage to the hair cells in the inner ear, changes in the auditory canal and ear drum, the natural loss of hair cells in the cochlea, and the loss of neurons in the auditory nerve (see Figure 10.2) are the most common sources of age-related hearing impairment (Fozard & Gordon-Salant, 2001; Mayo Clinic, 2008a). ***Presbycusis***, the broad term for hearing loss that is part of the normal aging process, is difficult to measure because it is often impossible to distinguish normal hearing loss from the gradual deterioration caused by other factors, such as environmental noise, hereditary factors, or even some disease processes (Fozard & Gordon-Salant, 2001). For example, for the

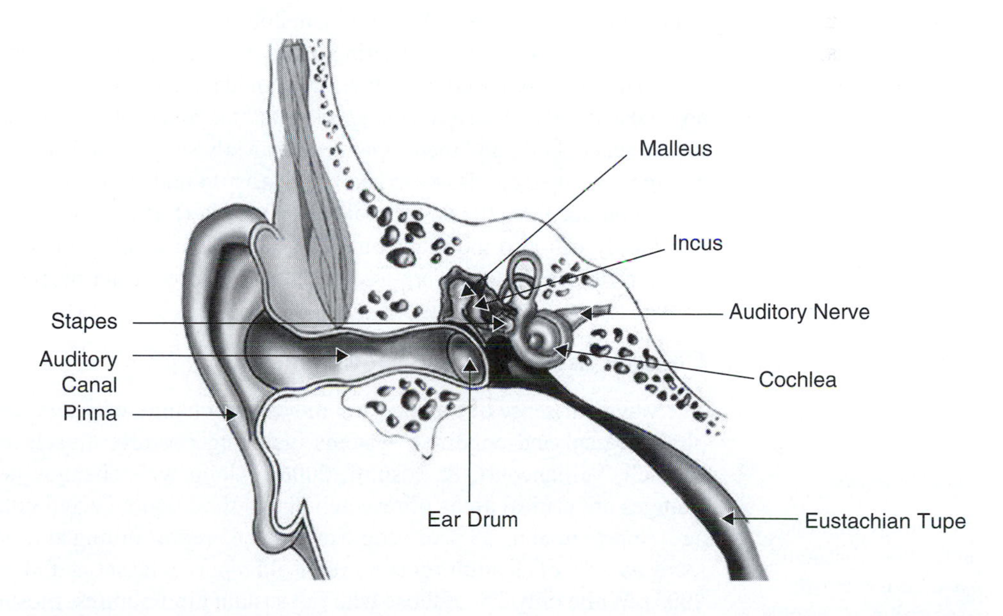

FIGURE 10.2 ***Basic Anatomy of the Ear.***
From the National Institute on Deafness and Other Communication Disorders (2008).

Your Thoughts?

Do you think personal music devices should have a built-in limit so the music in the ear buds cannot be loud enough to cause hearing loss over time?

individual who rides a loud motorcycle frequently, it is difficult to discern what percentage of hearing loss would have occurred due to aging and what has been accelerated due to the repeated close proximity to a loud engine. Presbycusis may also be worsened by other physical health issues, such as heart disease, high blood pressure, or diabetes (National Institute on Deafness and Other Communication Disorders [NIDOCD], 2010a).

Approximately 33% of adults over 60 years old and 50% of those over 85 years old have some hearing impairment (NIDOCD, 2010a, 2010c). The most common complaints are the inability to hear higher frequencies, difficulty picking out one person's voice or one sound when there is background noise, and ***tinnitus*** or ringing in the ears (Fozard & Gordon-Salant, 2001; Mayo Clinic, 2008e; NIDOCD, 2010a). Researchers have found that hearing declines faster in men (NIA, 2007a); however, women worry more about hearing loss (Espmark, Rosenhall, Erlandsson, & Steen, 2002), complain more when they cannot hear well, and adjust better to hearing aids than men do (Fozard & Gordon-Salant, 2001).

Presbycusis cannot be reversed, but there are ways to cope with the changes. The primary mode of adjustment is through the amplification of sounds with various types of hearing aids (Fozard & Gordon-Salant, 2001). Even though the hearing aids that fit in the ear are programmable in terms of acoustic changes, require minimal adjustment, and come in a variety of styles and sizes (Montano, 2003), the NIDOCD (2010b) reports that only 20% of the American adults who need hearing aids actually get them. Isn't it interesting that Americans accept glasses much more readily than hearing aids? Glasses, which signal a deficit in vision, are viewed as a fashion accessory. Hearing aids, which signal a deficit in hearing, are, however, viewed as a sign of weakness, frailty, and physical decline. Other reasons individuals give for rejecting hearing aids are the cost, the need for regular maintenance, and difficulty in handling the small devices (Montano, 2003). Unfortunately, this phenomenon is not limited to Americans. In interviews with 154 Swedish participants between the ages of 70 and 91 years old, Espmark et al. (2002) found that of those who did display some hearing loss, only 8% were interested in hearing aids. A similar study of 291 80-year-old Finnish adults found that one-fourth of the men reported hearing impairment, and of those 10% used a hearing aid, while only 10% of the women reported a hearing impairment, and of those 8% wore a hearing aid (Hietanen, Era, Sorri, & Heikkinen, 2004).

Your Thoughts?

What could the media do to encourage more adults to wear hearing aids?

Whether an adult with hearing impairment is wearing a hearing aid or not, there are things we can do to assist in a conversation. We should reduce any background noise, face the individual and speak clearly, and avoid elderspeak or talking to the adult like a child. Sensory deficits are not intellectual deficits, and there is no need to overly simplify information. If you find that individuals are not using their glasses or hearing aids, try to find out if there is a problem you can help with, and encourage them to use these aids consistently (LeJune, Steinman, & Mascia, 2003). Friends and family can also inquire about devices that can amplify phone calls, televisions, computer speakers, door bells, and warning devices, such as smoke alarms (Mayo Clinic, 2009c).

Changes in Balance and Movement

The ways our sense of balance and movement change with age are complex, involving many physiological and cognitive systems including posture, muscle strength, and reaction time (Newell, Vaillancourt, & Sosnoff, 2006). Along with changes in vision and hearing, these changes are critical areas of research due to the frequency and potential severity of falls with age. Approximately 33% of people over age 65 report falling at least once within a year, and as many as 50% of all adults over 80 years old report at least one fall per year (de Rekeneire et al., 2003). While only 2% of those who fall sustain hip fractures, most of those who do will not be able to return to independent living, and approximately 33% of those who are hospitalized due to falling will die within a year (Newton, 2003).

Your Thoughts?

What items might be on the floor that could cause someone with poor vision or unstable balance to trip?

Balance involves maintaining control and equilibrium while orienting to gravity, the quality of the support beneath you, and objects in the environment (Newton, 2003). We will likely use different muscles, movement, and weight adjustments to balance while going up or down stairs, across a hard floor or soft dirt and grass, and when walking through our living space versus a crowded grocery store aisle. Among the various types of movements studied in relation to aging, walking is the most frequently analyzed. It requires moving from stability to instability and back to equilibrium without losing control (Newell et al., 2006) and may involve anticipatory and compensatory balance responses. Anticipatory balance responses are adjustments made to maintain balance, such as holding on to a rail while going up or down stairs or leaning on the grocery cart for balance while shopping (Newton, 2003). Although older adults may feel more need to anticipate being caught off balance, adults of all ages routinely make such adjustments.

Your Thoughts?

How might pregnancy or dramatic weight gain or loss affect balance?

Compensatory balance responses are those that occur in response to an event, such as stepping on an uneven surface or tripping (Newton, 2003). It is here that older adults may feel the effects of age and, unfortunately, may not be able to compensate fully without injury. Several factors are to blame. Postural control, which begins to decrease in our 30s, is critical for still and moving positions (Newell et al., 2006). ***Proprioception***, the ability to sense where body segments or parts are based on signals from joints and muscles, is also needed for balance and movement. Decreasing postural control, proprioception, muscle mass, and strength, along with a general slowing of movements with age (Ketcham & Stelmach, 2001), are likely contributors to the findings that physical movements become slower depending on the level of complexity involved. It takes older adults longer to reestablish stability when walking (Newell et al., 2006). Another complicating psychological factor may be that older adults are more concerned with accuracy in their movements, knowing the potential risks associated with falls, causing them to give more attention and concentration to moving and as a result, move slower (Ketcham & Stelmach, 2001).

While it is certain that with age our skills in balance and movement will weaken, there are other variables that influence the rate and level of decline as well as our ability to successfully adjust. For example, our brain coordinates information from many sensory systems, allowing for creative compensation and problem solving as skills in particular areas maintain or decline at differing rates (Ketcham & Stelmach, 2001). For adults who are able to successfully compensate, the rate of decline may not produce dramatic changes until very late in their lives. For example, Hunter and Thompson (2001) tested the rate of change in reaction time and muscle strength in 217 healthy Australian women between the ages of 20 and 89 years old. The women were asked to tense their knee muscles in response to the flash of a light. The results indicated that the amount of reaction time was progressively longer with age, at a rate of about 0.57 milliseconds per year—that's *one half of one thousandth of a second.* Finally, as with so many aspects of physical development, regular exercise and an active lifestyle can lessen the rate of change in balance and movement (Mayo Clinic, 2008a; Phillips, 2003). Hunter and Thompson found that participants who engaged in physical activity regularly were faster in reaction time than nonactive women, particularly for women between the ages of 79 and 89 years old. Unfortunately, some older adults are hesitant to exercise because of their fear of falling, and yet, the more they remain sedentary the more likely they are to lose their balance (Newton, 2003).

Your Thoughts?

What can medical professionals and loved ones do to alleviate these fears of exercise?

Other Sensory Changes

Along with changes in vision, hearing, and balance older adults will also experience normal changes in taste, smell, and touch. It is difficult to separate the sensations of taste and smell because they are closely integrated in terms of experience. In early adulthood most individuals have about 9,000 taste buds that detect the sensations of sweet, salty, sour, and bitter. The number

ON THE LEADING EDGE
Aging Drivers

The issue of driving is a sensitive one for many older adults as their children start paying more attention to Mom or Dad's physical and cognitive skills. Mom and Dad know that at some point this freedom will be taken away. The ability to drive at any time to get what they need is a way to maintain control of their schedules, tasks, privacy, and independence, particularly in areas where public transportation is not available or user-friendly for elderly citizens. Driving also provides opportunities to travel to social events, religious services, exercise classes, medical appointments, shopping centers, and other locations and events that greatly enhance quality of life. Older adults who are not able or have the resources to drive must rely on public transportation, other drivers, walk, or simply try to do without needed items. Even when others seem willing to drive, older adults may feel like their requests are burdensome and may reduce their traveling to only the most important appointments, which can greatly reduce quality of life.

While many older adults want to continue driving as long as possible, data indicates that older drivers and teenagers are at the greatest risk of being involved in a fatal accident (Henderson, 2004). Older adults are different from teenagers in that they are more likely to be involved in an accident during the day, with another car, and to die in the accident. (Teenagers are more likely to be in a single car accident at night and their youthful age increases their chances of surviving a crash.) As the number of older drivers increases the need to keep them safe while allowing them to maintain a high level of independence for as long as possible has prompted many researchers, health care professionals, law enforcement agencies, and others to examine this circumstance and propose changes. For example, Susan Henderson (2004), from Memorial Hospital Outpatient Therapy Services, suggests that changing all two-way stops to four-way stops would reduce accidents involving older drivers by as much as 50%. She also advocates changing the sequencing of traffic lights so that all directions are stopped for a brief time before the traffic cycle repeated. It would also be helpful for car manufacturers to consider older drivers by creating larger controls, such as turn signals, and developing larger displays with high contrast colors.

Melissa O'Conner and Jerri Edwards of the School of Aging Studies at the University of South Florida, Virginia Wadley of the Division of Gerontology, Geriatrics, and Palliative Care at the University of Alabama, and Michael Crowe of the Department of Psychology at the University of Alabama took a different focus by examining cognitive processing as it relates to driving. They were particularly interested in the effects of cognitive changes on driving for those individuals who develop mild cognitive impairment (MCI), a syndrome that can be detected and is thought to be a transitional phase from healthy functioning to various types of dementia (O'Conner, Edwards, Wadley, & Crowe, 2010). Data collection came from 2,355 participants, all at least 65 years old and community dwelling, who reported that they had driven a car in the last year and believed they were still capable of driving. O'Conner and her colleagues found that participants with MCI demonstrated poorer visual acuity and less physical ability and also reported more difficulty driving, less frequent driving, and driving less distance from home than cognitively healthy participants. It is encouraging that those with MIC were somewhat aware of their difficulties and reduced their driving frequency and range. This research offers another way to determine when driving should cease based on cognitive changes. Regardless of the focus, whether it is cognitive and physical abilities (O'Conner et al, 2010), changing the way we drive, or instituting special driving tests for older adults (Henderson, 2004), the segment of the population without driving privileges who need transportation and services will continue to grow. Along with the many resources focused on determining driving abilities and how to prolong safe driving, it might also be of benefit to consider alternative means of transportation for older and cognitively impaired drivers (Carr and Ott, 2010).

of taste buds slowly decreases, beginning for women in their 40s and men in their 50s. The rate of decrease differs for sweet, salty, sour, and bitter taste receptors, which is why foods that taste good to us at one point in life may not taste good years later. While the decrease in taste buds is important to note, much of what we often think of as the flavor of food actually comes from the smell, which doesn't begin to diminish until our 70s. A significant loss in taste and smell can lead to malnutrition (Nordin et al., 2003; UMMC, 2009). There are many reasons why older adults may eat less, including the need for fewer calories due to a sedentary lifestyle, the need to lose weight, mouth pain due to tooth decay or poorly fitting dentures (Mayo Clinic, 2009b, 2008a), as well as the combined decrease in taste and smell that simply takes the enjoyment

Your Thoughts?

What practical things can friends and family do if they think an older adult is risking malnutrition?

out of eating. All of these factors could result in the attitude that food preparation is more trouble than it is worth. A significant loss in smell can lead to other problems as well, such as not sensing that food has spoiled or detecting a gas leak (Nordin, Razani, Markison, & Murphy, 2003; UMMC, 2009).

Older adults also experience a reduced sense of touch, which can lead to reduced or confused responses to pain, vibration, cold, heat, or pressure. At this point in our lives we may scratch or cut ourselves, or develop a small sore and not feel any pain, and thus not take care of the problem appropriately. Adults with remarkably decreased touch perception are also at risk for frostbite, hypothermia, and burns. It may be important for family members or friends to adjust the water heater so that bath water cannot get too hot, and to have a thermometer with large numbers handy to judge how warm or cool to dress (UMMC, 2009). Regarding adjusting to high air temperatures, it is common with age to perspire less, which makes it harder for the body to cool itself. This creates a situation of increased risk of heat exhaustion and heat stroke (Mayo Clinic, 2008a).

Your Thoughts?

What kinds of household technologies could be developed to address a reduced sense of touch?

Section Summary

- With age our eyes change in ways that contribute to many common complaints, such as blurriness, presbyopia, and difficulty with changing light conditions, adjusting to glare, and seeing in low light conditions.
- While glasses, large print, extra lighting, and other adjustments may help, older adults with impaired vision may feel frustrated, isolated, and even depressed over their physical and social situation.
- The most common complaints regarding hearing loss are difficulty concentrating on specific sounds when there is background noise, difficulty hearing high frequency sounds, and tinnitus.
- Although hearing aids have improved technologically, many people who could benefit from a hearing aid will not wear one.
- Many of the sources of sensory input required for balance and movement decline with age, including postural control, proprioception, muscle strength, and reaction time.
- To reduce the risk of falling due to loss of balance experts recommend maintaining a routine exercise program.
- A reduced sense of taste and smell can cause older adults to eat less, running the risk of malnutrition, or to eat food that has spoiled.
- A reduced sense of touch can include a lack of sensitivity to pressure, pain, cold, or heat, any of which may allow a small problem, such as dressing for outdoor temperatures or caring for a small cut, to turn into a major problem.

Changes in Body Systems

This section highlights changes in our cardiovascular system, digestive system, and bones as we move from young adulthood to middle and late adulthood. Generalized summaries of trends across age are useful as long as we remember that such wide-ranging statements neglect individual differences and inherent complexities. For example, as has been observed with several different sensory systems, particularly hearing, it can be difficult to separate the effects of primary and secondary aging. To further complicate the discussion of primary aging, it is tempting to make the false assumption that conditions that are common, such as cataracts or high cholesterol levels, are a part of normal aging when in fact they are frequently occurring

Your Thoughts?

Working with lab animals, how might you maximize the contrast between primary and secondary aging?

pathologies. A third layer of complexity comes with the recognition that individuals age at very different rates, and that even within one person, organs and organ systems show different rates of decline (NIA, 2007a).

In spite of the complexities, there are some generalizations that can be made about aging body systems. For example, aging is associated with a somewhat weakened immune system, which can make older adults more vulnerable to illness and may cause them to take longer to recover (Phillips, 2003). Aging is also linked to a decrease in breathing capacity as lung tissues lose some flexibility and rib cage muscles shrink (NIA, 2007a), though the nonpathological changes in our lungs generally do not affect the daily lifestyle of older adults (Aldwin & Gilmer, 2004). As was detailed in the chapter on memory, our brain shows signs of change with age as well. Also applicable to most people regardless of individual variations in aging are the recommendations for successful aging: routine exercise, healthy diet, no smoking, avoiding excessive alcohol, and regular medical checkups.

Aging Cardiovascular System

Although our hearts are less efficient and do show signs of age, the normal, expected cardiovascular changes do not have major effects on the lifestyle of older adults. That said, the pathologies of the cardiovascular system are, unfortunately, rather common and extremely serious. Generally, with age our hearts become enlarged and beat at a slower rate due to a reduction in pacemaker cells (Aldwin & Gilmer, 2004). Not only does the pumping rate decline but also does the body's ability to extract oxygen from the blood. The combined effects of these changes into late adulthood are that the maximal oxygen consumption during exercise declines by about 10% for men and 7.5% for women. Also, arteries tend to stiffen with age, resulting in the need for more force to move blood through the body (NIA, 2007a) and increased blood pressure (Mayo Clinic, 2008a, 2008c). Experts recommend that in addition to eating well, exercising, maintaining a healthy weight, and avoiding smoking, we should also routinely monitor our blood pressure, cholesterol, and triglycerides for warning signs of heart disease (NLM, 2010c).

Your Thoughts?

Would you support an employer who gives bonuses to employees with good medical checkups?

Most people experience an increase in blood pressure with age.

Aging Digestive System

> **Your Thoughts?**
>
> How has the media reinforced the association between older people and bladder control problems?

Many small changes in our digestive system occur naturally as we age and are likely to go unnoticed (Mayo Clinic, 2008a). With age the breakdown and absorption of food diminishes as a result of decreased production of digestive enzymes and our kidneys become less efficient at filtering waste products from the blood (NIA, 2007a). Small changes in our stomach, liver, pancreas, and intestines do not disrupt the digestive process but can cause more constipation. Although among individuals 65 years and older, approximately 30% will develop some loss of bladder control (Mayo Clinic, 2008a), aging does not cause urinary incontinence (NIA, 2009b). Women are more likely than men to develop incontinence, particularly after menopause (Mayo Clinic, 2008a).

Aging Bones

> **Your Thoughts?**
>
> How can someone routinely engage in weight lifting and other strength training exercises at home for little or no cost?

As many of us know from the successful efforts to educate the public about osteoporosis, reduction in bone density is expected with age. Bones go through a normal cycle of *resorption,* the process of removing old bone tissue, and *formation,* the laying down of new bone. This process is regulated in part by estrogen in women and testosterone in men (National Institute of Arthritis and Musculoskeletal and Skin Diseases [NIAMSD], 2009). Bone mass usually reaches its maximum between the ages of 25 and 35 years old and then begins to shrink in density. For most individuals the balance in this process will shift in young adulthood, such that the resorption of old bone tissue begins to occur faster than the formation of new bone, causing the reduction in density (NIAMSD, 2009). For women, bone loss tends to accelerate after menopause, when estrogen production declines (Phillips, 2003). Engaging in regular weight-bearing exercises, such as walking, running, and strength training, can slow bone loss as well as avoiding smoking and excessive alcohol intake, and maintaining a diet rich in calcium and vitamin D (NIA, 2007a; NIAMSD, 2009).

Section Summary

- Although generalizations can be made regarding changes in body systems due to normal aging processes, these summary statements must be considered along with the findings that it is sometimes impossible to separate primary and secondary aging, it is easy to make false assumptions that common pathologies are inevitable, and individuals age at differing rates, and even within individuals different systems age at different rates.
- With age our hearts become enlarged, slow in beating rate, and lessen in muscle flexibility, resulting in increased blood pressure.
- The many expected changes to our digestive systems due to normal aging are small and generally go unnoticed.
- Our bones will start losing density in young adulthood, and if unchecked, could lead to serious consequences in late adulthood.

Changes in Sexuality

Few things are as personal or as complex as sexuality. It is a basic part of the human experience, contributing to our sense of self and personal well-being. In a loving relationship sexual expression can bring intense pleasure and emotional satisfaction. Depending on how we choose to define "sexiness" for ourselves and our partner(s), sexual expression may be a source of affirmation that one is loved and valued, or it may be a source of anxiety, bringing feelings of inadequacy and inferiority. As our bodies change with age so does our sense of sexiness and ability to engage in some sexual activities. This section discusses some of the issues involved in the psychological study of sexuality, the effects of aging on reproductive systems, and sexual attitudes and activities for individuals across adulthood.

Issues in Sexuality Research

It seems that when it comes to sex research, some people are quite curious about who's doing what with whom and how often. They may want to know what is normal and abnormal in terms of sexuality. Those are difficult questions to answer with confidence as data on socially taboo topics can be difficult to collect, trust, and report accurately. Healthy skepticism regarding any research is wise, and even more so when considering socially-sensitive topics such as sexual thoughts, attitudes, and behaviors.

Risk of Heterosexism in Sexuality Research. The scientific study of sexuality is a relatively recent endeavor. The ground-breaking work of Alfred C. Kinsey, who published *Sexual Behavior in the Human Male* in 1948 and *Sexual Behavior in the Human Female* in 1953, as well as William Masters and Virginia Johnson, who published *Human Sexual Response* in 1966, opened the door for the scientific and public discussion of healthy heterosexuality. That early work, along with the predominant societal and religious premise that monogamous heterosexual behavior was the norm, made it easy to assume that nonheterosexual feelings, thoughts, and behaviors were deviant. Rather than seeking to understand different sexual orientations and preferences, much of the interest in these groups revolved around questions of just how deviant they were and to what extent they tried to mimic "normal" relationships. For example, while some prior scientific work was conducted on gay sexuality, the area was not well researched until the HIV epidemic of the early 1980s. Once some data was available, ***heterosexism,*** reflected in the attitude that the healthiest or most appropriate sexual practices are those of heterosexuals, was revealed in some cases. Whereas vaginal intercourse and mutual orgasm are central to many heterosexuals' experiences, studies have shown that many gay males do not enjoy penetrative sex, placing more emphasis on types of contact, oral sex, and masturbation (Campbell & Whiteley, 2006).

Your Thoughts?

Would you trust researchers to keep details of your personal sexual experiences confidential? Why, why not, or under what circumstances?

This example highlights another contributing factor to the risk of heterosexism, which is the lack of data describing sexual activity of nonheterosexual individuals. In addition to all the many reasons why heterosexual individuals may falsify data, those who are gay, lesbian, bisexual, transgendered, or feel they don't fit in any of those categories, may view the risk of losing confidentiality as being much too high for participation in any research study. As was the case regarding intimate relationships and lifestyles, much of the data available, and thus most of the information presented here, came from heterosexual participants. It's important that we acknowledge that and do our best to guard against heterocentric assumptions.

Risk of False Data in Sexuality Research. Trustworthy data is difficult to collect when researchers rely on self-reported information on questionnaires or in interviews. When questions are asked about private sexual thoughts or behaviors for which honest responses could be embarrassing, stigmatizing, or even illegal, participants may withhold the truth and give what they believe to be socially appropriate responses. What can researchers do to have confidence in the accuracy of their data? One option is to conduct laboratory studies using specialized equipment to measure sexual responses. (See Research In-Depth for an example of such a study.) Another option would be to place video cameras in certain places for naturalistic observation of sexual behaviors—if that were legal, you could get it approved by the ethics committees, and you could find participants!

RESEARCH IN-DEPTH
Physiological Measures

All researchers, and particularly those studying socially charged and personal topics such as sexual arousal, are continually working on the problem of how to acquire the most honest and accurate information from participants. Researchers at Boston University have found a method that they believe produces fairly accurate results (Nobre et al, 2004). The technique used, called penile plethysmography (PPG), measures any changes in the circumference of a penis, which is a signal of arousal. (And you thought research was boring!) With this technique, no matter what a male adult might say is arousing or not, a PPG can give exact measures that indicate sexual interest. The research team was specifically interested in how men's estimates of sexual arousal compared to the physiological measures of arousal using the PPG. Their hope was to apply what they found to better understand some of the issues surrounding sexual dysfunction and erectile difficulties.

The potential participants were put through a great deal of screening before being asked to join the study. During the first session the participants were given numerous questionnaires, screened for psychological disorders and any sexual dysfunction, and after visiting the laboratory and becoming familiar with the equipment, asked about their comfort level regarding the procedures. In the second session, the PPG equipment was used to measure a full erection achieved while watching erotic films. Those who did not achieve a full erection could not continue with the study. The researchers continued to recruit participants and conduct screenings until they had 60 participants, ranging in age from 18 to 45 years old. During the actual study participants watched a total of five erotic films. The five films used in the study were intended to induce varying levels of arousal. A small table was placed over participants' laps so that they could not observe their own penile reaction. After each film they were asked to respond to several questionnaires. Following each film the men were given a 3-minute recovery time for their penile erection to return to baseline.

As intended, the participants reported varying levels of arousal to the different films, with the least arousing producing, on average, 40% of a full erection, and the most arousing producing 88% of a full erection. The researchers found that the participants tended to indicate less penile erection than the PPG indicated. Among the most important findings for the purposes of their study related to the men's emotions and attitudes. Participants expressing negative emotional patterns on the prescreening questionnaires achieved less physiological arousal and gave lower self-reported levels of arousal than those with positive emotional patterns. Although negative emotional patterns were related to less arousal, positive emotions were not related to increased arousal above the baseline. The researchers also found that those who had more positive attitudes about watching erotic films gave self-reported arousal estimates that corresponded more accurately with their PPG measurements. The researchers plan to extend this work to learn more about this gap between men's psychological assessment of their arousal and their actual physiological reaction. They also intend to explore the ways negative emotions surrounding sexual performance in men with sexual dysfunction may affect what they expect in performance (less self-reported arousal) and how those expectations may then affect physical arousal.

It is clear in this case that physiological measurements gave important information that participants apparently could not accurately assess. There are many potential sources of error in self-report data, including whether participants paid attention to the questions, took them seriously, and responded honestly. Instruments like the PPG allow researchers to get a better gauge of physiological responses, and from that they can infer psychological responses. Studies like this one, however, are not without sources of error. For example, it may be that individuals who were willing to participate in such a study were "self-selected," that is to say that only men with certain personality or psychological profiles were willing to participate.

Your Thoughts?

What, if any, generational differences would you expect to find across adulthood regarding willingness to be honest and respond fully to research questions regarding sexuality?

While some researchers have specialized equipment and laboratories, others look for ways to increase the likelihood of honest responses using more traditional methods. Based on the premise that participants are more likely to be honest if they have confidence that their responses can never be traced to them (complete anonymity), questionnaires are the only option. To test this premise, Durant, Carey, and Schroder (2002) compared the responses of 155 male and 203 female college students who were placed in either a completely anonymous situation or one in which confidentiality was verbally assured. Questionnaires were designed to ask about both neutral sexual behaviors, such as holding hands, and very sensitive topics regarding sexual behaviors. Durant and her colleagues found that those in the confidentiality-assured conditions, and thus at some risk of exposure, were more likely to refuse to participate in the study. The researchers compared the groups based on the assumption that the behaviors of the college students as a whole were likely to be similar, implying that the responses from the complete-anonymity and the confidentiality-assured groups should be similar. Durant and her colleagues found that the confidentiality-assured group reported less masturbation, fewer sexual partners, and left more sensitive items blank than the complete-anonymity group.

Alexander and Fisher (2003) used a slightly different way of assessing the risk of misrepresentation among 201 college students who were asked to fill out questionnaires about sexual experiences and behaviors. Some of the students were allowed to fill out questionnaires and place them in a locked box, assuring complete anonymity. Other students were placed in an "exposure threat" condition in which the participants thought they would have to hand in their questionnaires to a student assistant who could possibly look at the responses. The researchers wanted this group to respond to the questionnaires with the threat in mind. (When the students in this condition tried to hand in the questionnaire the assistant told them to put their papers in a locked box, thus in reality the student assistant did not see the questionnaires). A third group of students were assigned to the ***bogus pipeline*** condition in which participants were asked to take questionnaires while connected to a polygraph or lie detector machine. Although in reality the machine was not working, participants were led to believe that it was on and could detect their false responses. Again the researchers made the assumption that, on average, the college students' responses should be about the same, such that differences between the three groups might be attributed to the test-taking condition. Alexander and Fisher found that the largest differences occurred in the exposed threat situation involving the student assistant. Males were more likely to inflate their level of sexual activity and females were more likely to reduce their sexual activity levels when they thought someone might see their responses. In contrast, females reported more partners in the bogus pipeline (lie detector) condition than males did. Differences were also found for age of first intercourse depending on the condition. Males reported an earlier age in the exposed threat condition, while females reported a lower age in the anonymous condition. Both of these studies confirm the warning to view data regarding sexual thoughts and behaviors with some skepticism.

Your Thoughts?

What social and cultural factors might have contributed to these gender differences?

Risk of Misunderstanding Research Findings. Another issue to consider is that, even when researchers believe research data is relatively accurate, the way the results are reported can lead to inaccurate assumptions. For example, frequencies, such as the number of times participants engage in sexual intercourse over a certain period of time, are often reported in averages. The results should be interpreted carefully because averages give a view of the center of the range, but they do not indicate anything about the range. For example, if a survey showed that adults have sexual intercourse an average of three times a week, that does not necessarily mean that most of the participants indicated three times a week. It could be that some indicated zero or one, while others indicated five or six times a week.

Sexuality in Young Adulthood

As individuals move into young adulthood a wide variety of options for sexual expression become available. Some of us will choose a celibate lifestyle, while others will choose monogamy. Although the term "monogamy" is used casually to refer to almost any couple, the term actually refers to someone who has only one sexual partner for his or her entire life. Most of us will choose or find ourselves practicing ***serial monogamy***, which occurs when an individual moves through a series of primary relationships throughout his or her lifetime, maintaining loyalty to each partner while in that particular relationship. Some of us may openly maintain several sexual relationships at the same time, while in other cases an individual may secretly maintain more than one relationship, such as when engaging in extramarital affairs.

Your Thoughts?

What personal and social factors might be contributing to the high percentage of extramarital affairs?

Data indicate that approximately 25% of married men and 15% of married women have engaged in extramarital affairs. Young adults will choose lifestyles based on their sexual orientation and their desire or tolerance for various behaviors. For example, researchers have found that most heterosexual adults engage in vaginal intercourse and oral–genital sexuality, whereas approximately 25% engage in anal intercourse, and approximately 10% routinely engage in masturbation (DeLamater & Friedrich, 2002).

Taking a closer look at current trends in sexual behaviors, Traeen, Stigum, and Sorensen (2002) surveyed 2,135 urban Norwegians between the ages of 18 and 49 years old. Most of the participants were heterosexual (88%), reporting, on average, 16 partners across their lifetimes and two partners within the last year. When asked about specific behaviors, this group reported, on average, having masturbated six times and engaged in oral sex three times in the last month. The heterosexual group rarely engaged in anal sex. Approximately 2% of the participants indicated that they were gay, and had engaged in sexual activity exclusively with same-sex partners. This gay group reported, on average, 54 partners across their lifetimes and three partners within the last year. The gay group also reported more masturbation than the heterosexual group (12 times in the last month), and an equal amount of oral sex. When asked about experiencing attraction to same-sex and other-sex individuals, approximately 8% indicated attraction and approximately 5% indicated sexual activity with both. When the data was analyzed by age, bisexual experiences increased from 4.8% among those 18 to 24 years old to 11% among those 40 to 44 years old. The bisexual group reported 37 partners across their lifetimes and three partners within the last year. Regarding specific behaviors, the bisexual group reported having masturbated 11 times; engaging in oral sex, on average, four times; and engaging in anal sex once in the last month.

Your Thoughts?

What personal and social factors may be contributing to the findings that the reports of bisexual experiences increase with age?

Reflective of current research on sexual thoughts, Hicks and Leitenberg (2001) surveyed 349 heterosexual adults ranging in age from 18 to 70 years old to assess their sexual fantasies. They found that 98% of the men and 80% of the women reported *extradyadic fantasies,* which is fantasizing about someone other than their current partner, during the previous 2 months. The findings were basically the same for those who were married as compared to those cohabiting. Men reported greater numbers of fantasies per month than women did. Both men and women were more likely to fantasize about individuals who had never been their partners rather than fantasizing about former partners. For both men and women, the number of extradyadic fantasies increased as the length of their current relationship increased. Those who reported more previous sexual partners, and those who reported having an affair while with their current partners, also reported more fantasies. This finding was stronger for women than for men.

Sexuality in Middle Adulthood

Your Thoughts?

From an evolutionary point of view, why would it be advantageous to have our sexual activity decrease with age?

When romances are new, no matter where the individuals are in their life cycle, couples put more energy into a relationship, including ways to keep their sex life exciting. Over time, as the newness of the relationship passes, stresses emerge and priorities change, sexual interaction may not be as frequent or as exciting. In recent years the topic of sexuality in middle-aged and older adults has gained more attention as the baby boomers become older, and as they have more "tools" such as drugs that improve penile erections and increase sexual desire. While it is certainly possible to maintain a satisfying sex life through middle adulthood, it usually requires some effort (Kingsberg, 2000).

The frequency of sexual activity in middle adulthood is lower than in young adulthood, but not absent. In a study of over 3,000 heterosexual women in middle adulthood, Cain and her colleagues (2003) found that 60% reported regular sexual intercourse, 24% regular oral sex, and about half engaged in masturbation. The participants who were not sexually active cited the lack of a partner as their primary obstacle. Most women in the study indicated that their primary reasons for having sex were to express love and for pleasure. Most of the women (77%) indicated that having sex was important to them. The participants also indicated that the early stages of the menopausal process were, for most of them, only minimally influential on their sex lives (Cain et al., 2003). In a similar study of men, researchers also found that sexual activity declines as compared to young adult levels, but continues through middle adulthood. The Massachusetts Male Aging Study monitored the sexual activity of 1,085 men ages 40 to 70 years old over a 9-year period. The researchers found that during the study men in their 40s reported, on average, three less erections per month and a decrease in sexual intercourse by once per month. Those in their 60s reported a decrease in erections by 13 per month, and a decrease in sexual intercourse by three times per month (Araujo, Mohr, & McKinlay, 2004).

Your Thoughts?

What are the advantages of a longitudinal rather than cross-sectional study of sexual activity?

Changes in Female Sexual Health

Physical development in middle adulthood brings with it changes in sexual feelings and behaviors. Whereas pregnancy is generally associated with young adulthood for women, changes associated with menstrual cycles and perimenopausal symptoms are associated with middle age. For some women the midlife changes will require some adjustments and may be frustrating at times, but little more. For other women these changes may be physiologically and psychologically dramatic (Kingsberg, 2000).

Managing Menopause. It is difficult to consider sexuality in middle adulthood without considering the process women experience leading to menopause, usually across their late 40s and early 50s. Menopause, which is the cessation of menstruation, does not happen quickly. It is not the case that a woman will experience her periods as usual and then suddenly menstruation ceases, but rather there is a process leading to menopause. ***Perimenopause*** begins when a woman's body first signals that the processes leading to menopause have begun, and it ends one year after her last period, when she has reached ***menopause.*** It is common for the perimenopausal process to last anywhere from 2 to 8 years. The most common signs and symptoms are menstrual irregularities, hot flashes (lasting between 30 seconds and 10 minutes), sleeping problems, mood changes, vaginal and bladder problems, decreased fertility, some body and skin changes, and loss of bone. While some women will seek medical attention during this time, particularly if their symptoms are severe, other women are able to work through the perimenopausal symptoms without medical intervention (Mayo Clinic, 2008d; NIA, 2010b).

Your Thoughts?

Would you support an employer who denied a woman a leadership position because it was assumed that she was or would be approaching menopause in the near future?

Prior to 2002 conventional wisdom and medical advice regarding perimenopause was that hormone replacement therapy (HRT) was the best approach for dealing with the symptoms. It was believed that HRT would relieve hot flashes, vaginal dryness, and even protect against osteoporosis and heart disease. However, in 2002, a study done by the National Institutes of Health, called the Women's Health Initiative, found that HRT introduced more risks than benefits. In fact, the study found that some HRTs actually increased the risk of heart disease, breast cancer, stroke, blood clots, and dementia. Following the announcement of the results of the study many doctors advised their patients to stop the HRT. While most experts agree that HRT is probably not the best choice for many women, there may be special cases in which short-term use of HRTs may be helpful, such as with severe hot flashes or extreme vaginal discomfort. Rather than using HRT many doctors are now recommending the same lifestyle changes that are encouraged for healthy aging in general:

Your Thoughts?

What might the medical community do to reassure women that their advice is trustworthy?

- Consistent physical exercise
- Stop smoking
- Eat healthy foods

Prior to the year 2002 women were routinely prescribed hormone replacement therapy to ease the symptoms of perimenopause. We know now that such therapy can be dangerous and should be carefully explored and researched.

- Avoid caffeine
- Maintain a healthy weight
- Avoid excessive alcohol
- Practice stress reduction techniques, such as meditation or yoga

Along with some products that may be helpful for particular symptoms, there are many bogus products marketed as well. It is important to research any product thoroughly before trying it. Even some herbal products, which some women have found helpful, may interact with other medications (Mayo Clinic, 2010e, 2008b) or may be helpful only in controlled amounts.

Women, Sexuality, and Aging. Women's psychological responses to perimenopause vary dramatically. Some women, particularly those who are comfortable with aging, may view perimenopause as a sign of maturity, becoming more self-confident and assertive in communicating with their sexual partner. Some women find menopause to be quite liberating in that the risk of pregnancy is gone as well as the monthly hassles of menstruation (Kingsberg, 2000; NIA, 2010c). In a study involving over 3,000 heterosexual women in the perimenopausal age range of 42 to 52 years old, Cain and her colleagues (2003) found that most of the women maintained an active sex life.

Your Thoughts?

What specific personal and cultural factors might predict a positive or negative response to perimenopause?

For some women, perimenopause adds intensity to the other signals that they are aging, such as gray hair and increasingly wrinkled skin. Not only are they feeling less sexually desirable on an emotional level, but also their body may feel uncooperative. As vaginal fluid production decreases and sexual tissues atrophy with age (NIA, 2007a), many women experience *dyspareunia,* painful intercourse caused by poor vaginal lubrication. In fact, this is the most common sexual problem for older women (NIA, 2010c). While it is expected that women will experience some reduction in their interest in sex when compared to their adolescent and early adulthood levels, in some cases the disinterest may develop into *female sexual dysfunction.* This common disorder, affecting 4 out of every 10 women, is associated with little or no sexual interest, arousal, or orgasm, and physical pain during sexual activity (Mayo Clinic, 2010c).

Changes in Male Sexual Health

Most men between the ages of 35 and 65 years old experience changes resulting from a gradual reduction in hormone levels, particularly testosterone. This transition has been called many things, including ***andropause***, male menopause, and *aging male syndrome* (National Women's Health Information Center [NWHIC], 2009b). Although men do not lose their fertility as women do in menopause, sperm production will decrease (NIA, 2007a). Most men will experience some characteristics similar to female menopause, such as problems with sleeping, memory, and concentration, as well as depression, anxiety, irritability, loss of energy, and bone and hair loss. During this time men also have less interest in sex and develop erection problems (NWHIC, 2009b). Most men will find it takes longer to gain an erection; however, some will develop impotence or erectile dysfunction, meaning they cannot sustain a hard erection long enough to engage in sexual intercourse (NIA, 2010c). While this condition is somewhat common, affecting 15–25% of men over age 65, it is not a normal part of aging.

Your Thoughts?

What personal and cultural barriers might keep a man from discussing these issues with his health care provider?

Men may also experience some discomfort due to enlarged prostate glands, a common condition called *benign prostatic hyperplasia* (National Kidney and Urological Diseases Information Clearing House, 2006). For most men their prostate will begin to enlarge in early adulthood, though it is usually after age 50 before the symptoms are bothersome. Across adulthood the prostate starts out about the size of a walnut and grows to be the size of a lemon. This puts pressure on the urethra and may cause problems when urinating (National Cancer Institute, 20094).

Sexuality in Late Adulthood

Levels of sexual activity usually continue to decline in late adulthood but may not stop completely. There is evidence that sexual activity continues on some level for many people into their 70s and 80s (Mayo Clinic, 2009g). A survey of 98 adults between the ages of 50 and

Older adults can, and do, have an active sex life.

80 years old suggests that erectile dysfunction in men and a lack of interest in women often combine to bring about the decline in sexuality (Mazur, Mueller, Krause, & Booth, 2002). Unfortunately, some illnesses can decrease sexual function and desire, such as arthritis and other types of chronic pain, diabetes, heart disease, and stroke. Some medications, such as those taken for high blood pressure, depression, weight control, diabetes, and ulcers, can also decrease sexual function and desire (Mayo Clinic, 2009g; NIA, 2010c). Regardless of these obstacles, many older adults can and do maintain an active sex life. Unfortunately, the reason for the lack of an active sex life may not be physiological, but rather the lack of a suitable partner or the reluctance to begin another relationship after the death of a spouse. Researchers have found that approximately 33% of women age 70 and older still masturbate, as well as 43% of men age 70 and older (Willert & Semans, 2000).

Your Thoughts?

What personal and cultural barriers might keep older adults from discussing sexuality with a health care provider?

Maintaining good health, communication, flexibility in expectations, and engaging in some creativity will greatly increase the likelihood of a satisfying sex life in late adulthood. Older couples who are open to having sex when they are most energetic, such as in the morning, creative in setting the mood and in sexual play, and those who expand their definition of sex beyond intercourse are more likely to be happier with their sex life as they age (Mayo Clinic, 2009g). In addition to the development of new medications to increase sexual function, therapists and physicians are now educating and encouraging older couples to move beyond their conventional idea of what a sexual encounter should include to explore the involvement of oral sex, manual stimulation, sexual aids, massage, or erotic media (Kingsberg, 2000).

Your Thoughts?

Would you support an assisted-living center that offered sex education workshops for the residents? Why, why not, or under what circumstances?

Older adults are growing more proactive in fulfilling their desires for sexual activity by becoming more involved in Internet dating services, chat rooms, and placing personal ads as ways of meeting other older single adults. Older adults are using the Internet to find medical information, sex education, and pornography, as well as information on sexual aids, drugs, and other products (Adams, Oye, & Parker, 2003). It certainly appears that older adults are pursuing active sex lives now more than ever (Kingsberg, 2000).

Section Summary

- It is wise to view data on sexuality with some caution, allowing for the likelihood that some groups of individuals will be absent, choosing not to participate in research, while others may provide false or misrepresentative data.
- Most young adults are heterosexual, engage frequently in vaginal and oral sex, and less frequently in masturbation or anal sex.
- Most adults fantasize about sexual activity with someone who has never been their partner.
- Researchers find that middle-aged adults are sexually active, though somewhat less active than their younger counterparts.
- Some women in middle age may find the menopausal process, highlighted by hot flashes and vagina dryness, to be ultimately liberating and requiring minor adjustment, whereas others may have such difficulty with the process that they eventually develop female sexual dysfunction disorder.
- Recent studies have indicated that hormone replacement therapy for women can be harmful and should be used only in special cases.
- Most middle-aged men will experience andropause and the related symptoms including problems with sleeping, memory, and concentration, as well as depression, anxiety, irritability, loss of energy, and bone and hair loss.

- Complete impotence or erectile dysfunction is not a normal part of male aging.
- Sexual activity will continue to decline in late adulthood, although it is not absent for all older adults.
- Those who are creative and willing to broaden their view of sexual interaction beyond intercourse can maintain a satisfying sex life.

Chapter Summary

Changes in external appearance, sensory and body systems, and sexuality are to be expected with age. While these changes may require some attention and possibly some attitudinal or behavioral adjustments, they should not be viewed as a disease process. Much of the distress over these normal changes, such as graying hair or menopause, is fueled by an emphasis on youthfulness in American society. Here are some of the main points of the chapter:

- The term "aging" can be divided into primary, secondary, and tertiary aging, distinguishing between external or environmentally caused aging (secondary), normal or expected aging (primary), and the decline seen just prior to death (tertiary).
- A number of physiological factors, such as reduced height and changes in lean muscle and body fat, contribute to the overall changes in body shape that accompany age.
- Men tend to evaluate their bodies in terms of how they function while women tend to focus more on appearance.
- The speed and extent of skin aging, particularly dryness, wrinkles, and age spots, can be accelerated by smoking, sun exposure, and exposure to artificial tanning.
- Whether hair is turning gray, thinning, or falling out, the processes are usually benign and genetically determined.
- Among the most common vision problems are blurriness and inability to see fine details, the length of time it takes to adjust to changes in light intensity (such as moving indoors on a bright day), difficulty with glare, and seeing in low light conditions.
- Many adults cope with mild visual impairment by using glasses, good lighting, magnifying aids, audio books, large fonts on computer screens, and by going to familiar stores, banks, etc., where they know people who can help them.
- The most common complaints regarding presbycusis is difficulty hearing a particular person when there is background noise and high-frequency sounds, and tinnitus.
- While hearing aids can help in many situations, they are often rejected by older adults because of expense, maintenance, difficulty of use, and the sense that they signal frailty.
- Consistent exercise can help older adults maintain a better sense of balance, proprioception, muscle flexibility, and reaction time, all of which can reduce the risk of serious injury due to falling.
- Reductions in the ability to taste and smell increase the risk that older adults will eat less and suffer from malnutrition.
- Diminishing ability to sense hot and cold temperatures puts older adults at risk of frostbite, hypothermia, and burns.
- While there are changes expected in major body systems with age, many are relatively easy to adjust to.
- With age our hearts become enlarged, slow in beating rate, and lessen in muscle flexibility, resulting in increased blood pressure.
- Changes in our digestive systems due to the normal aging process are small and likely to go unnoticed.

- To avoid the expected decrease in bone density with age individuals are encouraged to engage in regular weight-bearing exercises, such as walking, running, and strength training, avoid smoking and excessive alcohol intake, and maintain a diet rich in calcium and vitamin D.
- Based on testing conditions that are anonymous, confidential, likely to be exposed, and subject to the bogus pipeline, researchers have found that participants sometimes give misinformation in studies of sexual thoughts and behaviors.
- Researchers find that most sexually active adults engage in a wide variety of sexual thoughts and behaviors, practice serial monogamy, and frequently engage in sexual fantasies involving someone other than their partner.
- Although most middle-aged adults have less sex than young adults, most maintain an active sex life.
- Recent research has made physicians cautious in prescribing hormone replacement therapy for women's perimenopausal symptoms, and many now recommend lifestyle changes.
- Men experience a reduction in hormone production and related symptoms.
- For those who are relatively healthy and creative, elderly individuals can maintain a satisfying sex life.

Key Terms

Primary aging **(258)**
Secondary aging **(258)**
Tertiary aging **(258)**
Photoaging **(261)**
Alopecia **(262)**
Androgenetic alopecia **(262)**
Presbyopia **(263)**
Papillary miosis **(263)**
Ptosis **(263)**
Cataracts **(264)**
Glaucoma **(264)**
Age-related maculopathy **(264)**
Macular degeneration **(264)**
Presbycusis **(265)**
Tinnitus **(266)**
Proprioception **(267)**
Heterosexism **(272)**
Bogus pipeline **(274)**
Serial monogamy **(274)**
Perimenopause **(276)**
Menopause **(276)**
Andropause **(278)**

Comprehension Questions

1. What are the differences between primary, secondary, and tertiary aging?
2. What is the average amount of loss in height from young adulthood to late adulthood?
3. Give an example of a gender difference found when comparing men's and women's attitudes toward aging.
4. Aside from inherited predispositions, what are the primary causes of skin aging?
5. What causes hair to turn gray?
6. What is androgenetic alopecia?
7. What physiological changes contribute to poorer vision with age?
8. How is glaucoma different from cataracts?
9. What physiological changes contribute to poorer hearing with age?
10. What are some of the reasons given by individuals with hearing impairments for not wearing hearing aids?
11. What changes in body systems can increase the risk of falling?
12. What is proprioception, and how might it influence anticipatory and compensatory balance responses?

13. What factors may contribute to an older adult's loss of interest in eating?
14. Give examples of the types of problems that may result from a decrease in touch sensitivity.
15. Give three reasons why making generalizations about normal or expected changes due to age in large body systems is difficult.
16. What changes occur in the cardiovascular system due to normal aging processes?
17. What changes occur in the digestive system due to normal aging processes?
18. What changes occur in bone health due to normal aging processes?
19. What is heterosexism?
20. Explain the difference between anonymity and assurance of confidentiality in research methodologies.
21. What is serial monogamy?
22. What is perimenopause and its associated signs or symptoms?
23. Why is hormone replacement therapy, as a response to perimenopause, controversial?
24. Give some examples of ways older adults can modify or expand their views of sex in order to maintain an active sex life in late adulthood.

Answers for Common Sense: Myth or Reality?

1. Myth: It is normal for individuals to lose 4–5 inches in height as a result of normal aging. (See Changes in Body Shapes, page 260.)
2. Reality: Most people are taller in the morning than they are in the evening. (See Changes in Body Shapes, page 260.)
3. Myth: Women tend to view their bodies as whole entities when evaluating their body image whereas men tend to evaluate particular parts or areas of their bodies. (See Changes in Body Shapes, page 260.)
4. Reality: Smoking can cause skin to wrinkle more than is normally expected with aging. (See Changes in Skin, page 261.)
5. Myth: Hair turns gray when hair cells stop producing pigment. (See Changes in Hair, page 261.)
6. Myth: Men can accelerate the process of going bald by frequently wearing a hat or cap. (See Changes in Hair, page 262.)
7. Reality: It is normal for middle-aged and older adults without corrected vision to need to hold print items farther away to read them. (See Changes in Vision, page 263.)
8. Myth: It is normal for older adults to develop glaucoma. (See Changes in Vision, page 263.)
9. Myth: The proportion of people with hearing loss who use hearing aids is similar to the proportion of those with vision loss who wear glasses. (See Changes in Hearing, page 266.)
10. Reality: Control of our posture starts to decrease in our 30s. (See Changes in Balance and Movement, page 267.)
11. Reality: Women start to lose their taste buds at an earlier age than men. (See Other Sensory Changes, page 268.)
12. Reality: It is normal to perspire less with age. (See Other Sensory Changes, page 269.)
13. Reality: It is normal for our hearts to beat at a slower pace with age. (See Aging Cardiovascular System, page 270.)
14. Myth: Nearly all individuals over age 65 experience a loss in bladder control. (See Aging Digestive System, page 271.)
15. Myth: Once bone density starts to shrink in young adulthood there is nothing adults can do to slow the process. (See Aging Bones, page 271.)
16. Reality: Researchers have found that men are more likely to exaggerate their levels of sexual activity, and women are more likely to underreport their sexual activity, when participants believe that others will know about their responses. (See Risk of Misunderstanding in Research Findings, page 274.)
17. Reality: Researchers find that 25% of married men have engaged in extramarital affairs. (See Sexuality in Young Adulthood, page 275.)
18. Myth: Researchers find that most adults fantasize about sexual activity with partners they had prior to their current partner. (See Sexuality in Young Adulthood, page 275.)

19. Myth: Most physicians agree that hormone replacement therapy is the best way to respond to women's perimenopausal symptoms. (See Managing Menopause, page 276.)

20. Myth: Impotence or erectile dysfunction is a normal part of aging for men. (See Changes in Male Sexual Health, page 278.)

21. Reality: Researchers have found that over one-third of men and women in their 70s still masturbate. (See Sexuality in Late Adulthood, page 279.)

Suggested Readings

Older Adults and the Challenges of Driving

National Highway Traffic Safety Administration. (n.d.). Driving safely while aging gracefully. This article can be found at http://www.nhtsa.dot.gov/people/injury/olddrive/Driving%20Safely%20Aging%20Web/.

More on Menopause

National Institute on Aging. (2008). Menopause: Time for a change. This article can be found at http://www.nia.nih.gov/HealthInformation/Publications/Menopause/.

Myths of Aging, Including Myths about Sex

Denmark, F. (2002). Myths of aging. From Psi Chi National Honor Society in Psychology, Distinguished Lectures Series. This article can be found at http://www.psichi.org/pubs/articles/article_38.asp.

International Sexuality Description Project

Schmitt, D. P. (2002). Are sexual promiscuity and relationship infidelity linked to different personality traits across cultures?: Findings from the International Sexuality Description Project. In W. J. Lonner, D. L. Dinnel, S. A. Hayes, & D. N. Sattler (Eds.), *Online readings in psychology and culture* (Unit 6, Chapter 4), (http://www.wwu.edu/~culture), Center for Cross-Cultural Research, Western Washington University, Bellingham, WA. Available at http://www.ac.wwu.edu/~culture/Schmitt.htm.

Suggested Websites

Conditions Affecting Vision and Hearing

To find out more about vision and hearing topics, see Medline Plus' website for Eyes and Vision Topics, at http://www.nlm.nih.gov/medlineplus/eyesandvision.html, and for Hearing Disorders and Deafness, at http://www.nlm.nih.gov/medlineplus/hearingdisordersanddeafness.html.

Anti-Aging/Longevity News

To read the latest on ways to slow or halt the aging process, go to the Anti-Aging/Longevity section for WorldHealth.net at http://www.worldhealth.net/.

Sexual Orientation

Read frequently asked questions about sexual orientation answered by the American Psychological Association at http://www.apa.org/pubinfo/answers.html, or find out more about the American Psychological Association's work on Lesbian, Gay, and Bisexual Concerns, at http://www.apa.org/pi/lgbc/.

Sexual Health

Learn more about sexual health across adulthood and sexual orientation at http://www.nlm.nih.gov/medlineplus/sexualhealthissues.html.

CHAPTER

11 Disease, Illness, and Disorders

At some point in our adult lives most of us will be forced to cope with a chronic illness, as indicated by the results of a National Institute on Aging (NIA, 2007b) study showing that only 17% of adults age 85 and older reported no major health problems. The New England Centenarian Study offers two key observations in this regard: (1) only a small percentage of us are likely to age without developing a chronic illness, and (2) most of the centenarians in the study have managed for years with a chronic illness (Boston University School of Medicine, 2004). These observations serve as a reminder that the goal of successful or optimal aging is not to attempt to halt the aging process but rather to maximize one's potential for good health and to cope well with disability and loss when it develops.

While the emphasis of this chapter is to profile some of the most frequently experienced physical illnesses and psychological disorders in adulthood, it will begin with several important reminders regarding the less-than-precise dichotomy between *physical* and *psychological* concerns and the omission of important points that occur in any generalized view of disease. For the sake of the chapter organization it is helpful to place illnesses in the physical or the psychological category, but some illnesses demonstrate strong effects in both areas. Also, in a chapter like this one there is limited space in which to explore an illness or disorder, allowing for only a brief overview. Short, generalizing summaries will likely ignore individual differences such as many variations of the same illness, and differences in the experience of living with the illness or disorder based on age, health status in other areas, or quality of medical care. Following a discussion of these limitations and others concerns, the chapter turns toward physical illnesses, including cardiovascular disease and Alzheimer's disease, followed by psychological disorders, including depression.

COMMON SENSE
Myth or Reality?

Mark each of the following items with either an M, if you think it is a myth, or an R, if you think the statement reflects reality. By paying close attention you can find all the answers in this chapter. If needed, the answers are also given at the end of the chapter.

1. _____ The American Psychiatric Association prefers the term mental or psychiatric *illness.*
2. _____ Hispanic Americans report less illness than African Americans.
3. _____ Among the top 10 causes of death for Americans, more people die of cardiovascular disease and cancer than the other eight causes combined.
4. _____ Cold sweat, nausea, and light-headedness are some of the symptoms of a heart attack.
5. _____ Women are more likely to survive a heart attack than men.
6. _____ Early symptoms of cancer generally don't cause pain.
7. _____ More women develop and die from breast cancer than men who develop and die from prostate cancer.
8. _____ Some strokes are so mild that the symptoms are undetected or ignored.
9. _____ Adults who are recovering from a stroke often have trouble speaking, reading, and writing.
10. _____ American Indians have one of the highest rates of diabetes in the world.
11. _____ Diabetes can cause blindness.
12. _____ Alzheimer's disease and dementia are two names for the same condition.
13. _____ The most reliable means of determining if an older adult has Alzheimer's disease is through a blood test.
14. _____ Well over half of all those age 80 and older have Alzheimer's disease.
15. _____ Depression is the most common psychological disorder.
16. _____ Women are more likely to be diagnosed with depression than men.
17. _____ Electroconvulsive therapy, also called shock therapy, is no longer used as a treatment for depression.

Before We Get Started . . .

For better and for worse we all live with our genetic predispositions. You may not have given it much thought, but at some point in the future you may want to know about your biological family's medical history. In some cases, such as with adoption, the information may be unavailable. In other cases important information may have been lost when older family members died without leaving a written account of their own medical history and that of others in the family. It may be that your collective family memory is accurate in terms of basic information such as what a relative died from, and perhaps even the age at which that person died, but if that's all the information passed along there are key items missing. For example, you may know that your uncle died of a heart attack, but do you know if he had glaucoma or diabetes? You may know that your great grandmother died of cancer, but do you know what type of cancer? Do you know if she had high blood pressure or cholesterol problems?

Begin by making a list of your extended biological family members on a sheet of paper or in a word processing document. On the left-hand side list the names of your biological relatives:

- Your father
- Your father's siblings
- Your father's parents (your grandparents)
- Your father's aunts and uncles
- Your mother
- Your mother's siblings
- Your mother's parents (your grandparents)
- Your mother's aunts and uncles

Now for each of those persons can you answer the following:

- Have or ever had heart disease, stroke, diabetes, or cancer?
- Have or ever had any other chronic conditions?
- Currently do or ever did take medication for a chronic condition?
- If that person has died, do you know at what age and what the cause was?

At any point in your life having this information can help determine if you should consider preventive measures or extra screening. If you do experience a medical emergency, knowing the medical history of your extended family can reduce the time it takes medical professionals to determine your correct diagnosis and treatment.

A quick online search will indicate many forms you can use to record your family medical history. Regardless of how you collect the information, it's important for you and your children to be aware of the conditions that are more frequent in your biological family.

Distinctions and Wholeness

While providing an overview of physical illnesses and psychological disorders it is all too easy to slide into a fact-focused, distant perspective, reading through the descriptions as if they were case studies. The distinctions between disease processes are important for understanding the ways they alter an individual's body and mind, but we shouldn't lose sight of the whole person or the whole picture. It is less threatening for us to think of cancer, for example, in a matter-of-fact way than to personalize it by thinking of ourselves or our parent coping with cancer. The concept of successful aging includes a focus on the whole picture, including the biological, psychological, and social adjustments that are associated with chronic illnesses. A friend of mine who was diagnosed with cancer several years ago made it clear that he did not want his friends to refer to him as a "cancer patient," nor were we to say that he was "dying of cancer." He insisted that we say he was "a person living with cancer." His concerns reminded me that as the lifespan increases and medical technologies and treatments improve there are more and more older adults who are living with a chronic condition, in some cases for many years, and maintaining a high quality of life.

Determining Health and Illness

What may seem at first glance to be a relatively simple question, "Are you healthy?" is proving to be rather complex and difficult. If healthiness is defined as existing in a state purely free of anything one might consider disease, illness, disorder, or sickness, then few of us would qualify. If we eliminated from our list of healthy individuals all those who smoke, are overweight, have any medical or psychological diagnosis, or have any common headaches, flu, cold, infection, allergies, cuts or scrapes, bruises, anxiety, insomnia, or anything else considered not healthy, the remaining group of individuals would likely be quite small. The Health and Retirement Study sponsored by the National Institute on Aging (2007) found that about half of their participants ages 55–64 said they had very good or excellent health, whereas only one-quarter of those 65 years and older rated their own health as very good or excellent. When considering adults in their 60s and older the question of healthiness takes on another layer of complexity. Can an older adult who is experiencing the expected changes with age, such as poorer vision, hearing, balance, and cognitive processing speed, be considered healthy (Rabbitt, 2002)? Are there any circumstances under which an adult who has a chronic or terminal disease can be considered healthy if he or she is functioning well (Aldwin, Spiro, & Park, 2006)?

Your Thoughts?

How might you design a study to find out if young and older adults tolerate equal or different amounts of discomfort before seeking medical attention?

One factor in deciding whether to consult a medical professional about discomfort is the option of trying to treat the symptoms with over-the-counter products.

Related to the question "Are you healthy?" is another important question, "How do you determine that you are not healthy and need to seek medical care?" Researchers have found that one factor used in this process is our perception of how severe our symptoms are as compared to symptoms we've had in the past or what we've observed in other people (George, 2001). Another factor is our perceived susceptibility to disease. For example, whereas younger adults are less likely to think they have a major illness, older adults believe they are much more likely to receive the diagnosis of a major illness. In determining whether to see a medical professional we also weigh the costs and benefits of medical care. Some of us may find ourselves in a situation in which our symptoms are so painful, aversive, or even life-threatening that medical care is favored and sought out. Sometimes we may experience symptoms that are mild, prompting us to wait to see if the symptoms fade and/or try to treat the symptoms with over-the-counter or alternative medicines. Older adults may ignore mild symptoms, considering them a sign of old age rather than a sign of illness. In other cases, some older adults may fear that seeing a medical professional may lead to the discovery of some currently undetected problem (George, 2001).

Definitions and Categories

Several terms commonly used in everyday language have rather specific meanings when used in a technical or scientific context. In general language people often use the terms *disease* and *illness* interchangeably. In a strict sense, the term ***disease*** refers to physiological characteristics, symptoms, and changes that are diagnosed and given a disease name. The term ***illness*** refers to the general physical, psychological, emotional, and social discomfort caused by or associated with the disease (George, 2001). A third term, ***disorders***, is preferred by the American Psychiatric Association when referring to psychopathology or mental illness (American Psychiatric Association, 1994).

Most citizens are aware of medical distinctions when it comes to seeking medical care. Most of us have had reason to learn that the medical profession is divided into various specialties, such as internal medicine or cardiology, and we are aware that therapists, counselors, psychologists, and psychiatrists vary in specialty and background as well. Some therapists may be marriage and family therapists, while others may specialize in eating disorders or substance abuse. Following in the tradition of dividing diagnoses and treatments into categories, this chapter is divided into physical diseases and illnesses and psychological disorders. Such distinctions, though helpful in organizing information, are not as useful when observing lived experiences. Often diseases have psychological components and vice versa. In recognition of this interconnection many health care providers often work as part of a team of professionals that may include physicians, nurses, psychologists, psychiatrists, physical therapists, occupational therapists, nutritionists, and social workers. This treatment team model has also grown out of the awareness that when a disease or disorder occurs there may be many facets to the illness and surrounding side effects that need to be addressed. For example, an individual who is being treated for heart disease may also need psychological treatment for depression, physical therapy for daily activities and exercise, as well as nutritional counseling for weight loss.

Your Thoughts?

How might the distinction between symptoms of disease and illness be useful in data analysis?

Your Thoughts?

What factors in American society might contribute to the findings that women are more likely to try self-care and alternative methods of health care?

Individual Differences and Diversity

Another set of factors that are easily ignored when engaging in brief summaries are the many individual differences that influence our health and the likelihood of seeking and receiving medical attention. Gender differences, for example, are found among older adults. Women in late adulthood are more likely to try self-care to reduce symptoms of poor health through the use of over-the-counter and alternative methods whereas men are more likely to simply endure the symptoms (George, 2001). Depending on the health issues involved, an individual's sexual orientation may be a factor in the decision to seek medical attention (Knight, Kaskie, Shurgot, & Davis, 2006). Regarding personality differences, those who are health optimists are likely to live longer, compare their health to their peers more often, and attribute symptoms to old age as compared to health pessimists and health realists (George, 2001). Individual differences in terms of coping skills, quality of social support, living arrangements, educational background and financial status, and quality of health insurance can factor into our decision to seek medical attention.

Your Thoughts?

What personality factors might contribute to an individual's motivation to seek medical attention?

Another source of individual differences associated with health issues is that of ethnic and racial diversity. As an example of how this diversity can be neglected or overlooked, earlier in this section is the statement, "The Health and Retirement Study sponsored by the National Institute on Aging (2007) found that about half of their participants ages 55–64 said they had very good or excellent health, whereas only one-quarter of those 65 years and older rated their own health as very good or excellent." While the statement is accurate and informative, it does not note that among those in the latter group, whites were twice as likely as blacks or Hispanics to rate their health very good or excellent, with much of the difference also related to socioeconomic status. That same study found that approximately 1 out of every 14 white participants did not have private health insurance to cover them from the time they retired until they qualified for Medicare, whereas that number increased to one out of every eight blacks and one out of every four Hispanics (NIA, 2007b). While African Americans and Hispanic Americans as demographic groups have very similar socioeconomic profiles, Hispanic Americans report much less illness and higher longevity. Studies have found that African Americans tend to be diagnosed at later stages in physical disease, have less aggressive treatment, and show higher rates of mortality (Angel & Angel, 2006).

Your Thoughts?

If you wanted to learn more about these differences, where would you start? What resources would you consult?

ON THE LEADING EDGE
Counseling for Individuals with Limited English Proficiency

Daneille Rose, Ph.D., of the Center for the Study of Healthcare Provider Behavior for the VA Greater Los Angeles Healthcare System and colleagues from other university and medical institutions in the area published a summary of 2004 data collected from physicians working with women with breast cancer who also had limited English proficiency (LEP) (Rose et al., 2010). Less than half of the physicians reported good availability of trained interpreters. Rose and her colleagues also found that smaller health care practices found the cost of training the staff and hiring the interpreters to be an obstacle to providing that type of assistance. Without adequate communication these women with LEP are at a much higher risk for problems in understanding what is happening to them, the next steps, drug regimens and other treatments, and how to manage health insurance needs.

In 2007 two members of the Center for Mental Health Services Research at the University of California, Berkeley, and a representative of the Office of Multicultural Services for the California State Department of Mental Health echoed the call of the U.S. Surgeon General for additional resources for individuals with limited English proficiency (LEP) (Snowden, Masland, & Guerrero, 2007). Many individuals with LEP come from homes where another language is dominant. Estimates are that 26 million American citizens speak Spanish at home and almost 7 million speak an Asian or Pacific Island language. Snowden and her colleagues (2007) used the forum of the *American Psychologist* journal to highlight the progress programs in California had made to meet the needs of mental health clients with LEP. State practices were designed to respond to a *threshold language policy,* requiring that when the number of individuals using services in a geographic area who have LEP and speak the same primary language reaches an established level or threshold then additional services must be offered. Among the many implementations were the requirements that documents, phone-based services, and crisis hotlines should be available in several languages, and that local agencies serving a substantial population of individuals with LEP should have sufficient staff who speak that language (including sign language) to translate as needed. There was also an effort to let those who may need these services know they are available. Snowden, Masland, and Guerrero (2007) found what Rose and her colleagues found in analyzing the 2004 data; the primary obstacle to implementation is funding.

One strategy that may offer some relief is to provide training to those individuals who are already serving as nonprofessional or ad hoc interpreters. This strategy was described by Christopher Larrison, Daniel Velez-Ortiz, and Lisette Piedra of the School of Social Work, Pedro Hernandez of the Children and Family Research Center at the University of Illinois at Urbana-Champaign, and Andrea Goldberg of the Frances Nelson Community Health Center in Champaign, Illinois. They found that some of the informal interpreters demonstrated a high level of commitment to their ethnic community and willingness to engage in training toward professional status. Rather than seeking to relocate interpreters from other areas it may be cost effective and efficient to begin working with individuals who already show dedication to helping community members with LEP.

Section Summary

- Realizing that very few of us are totally healthy for long periods of time, it is useful to consider the concepts of *health* and *illness* as related and overlapping.
- Regardless of scientific distinctions between health and illness, individuals use various criteria for determining whether they are ill enough to seek medical attention, including perceived severity of the symptoms and the costs and benefits of health care.
- In a strict medical context, *disease* refers to the symptoms involved in making a diagnosis and *illness* refers to the side effects and related problems.
- Another point that often gets neglected in the analyses of health and disease are the many individual differences, particularly in terms of ethnic diversity, that are associated with quality of health and disease management.
- For the sake of brevity and summarization it is necessary to make general statements; however, it is critical to remember that the actual experience of these diseases and disorders varies greatly.

Physical Illnesses

According to the Centers for Disease Control and Prevention (CDC, 2010a), more Americans died of heart disease and cancer than any other diseases. As can be seen in Figure 11.1, which lists the top 10 causes of death for Americans in 2007, more people died from heart disease and cancer (1,178,942) than from the other top eight causes of death combined (667,589). The number of deaths registered in 2007 was just over 2.4 million, thus heart disease and cancer were responsible for nearly half of all deaths in the United States (CDC, 2010a). Further analysis by age group revealed that the most frequent causes of death for adults ages 25–44 years old, starting with the most frequent, were accidents, cancer, heart disease, suicide, and homicide whereas for those 65 years old and older the top causes were heart disease, cancer, stroke, chronic lower respiratory diseases, and Alzheimer's disease (Minino, Xu, Kochanek, & Tejada-Vera, 2009).

Your Thoughts?

What might lead some people to think Alzheimer's disease causes more deaths than cancer or heart disease among older adults?

As reflected in the shifting focus of Medicare from acute to chronic illnesses, the primary causes of death have shifted to chronic illnesses (Aldwin et al., 2006). Experts anticipate that medical research and treatment will continue to focus on chronic conditions such as heart disease, stroke, chronic lung disease, and arthritis (Gatz & Smyer, 2001).

Cardiovascular Disease

The term ***cardiovascular disease,*** often called *heart disease,* refers to a broad category of diseases and conditions that affect the functioning of your heart, such as high blood pressure, coronary artery disease, and heart attack (Mayo Clinic, 2009d). *Coronary artery disease,* also called *coronary heart disease,* is the most common type of cardiovascular disease, occurring when the arteries that supply blood to the heart muscle become hardened and narrow due to plaque buildup. ***Atherosclerosis,*** the term for that condition, is illustrated in Figure 11.2. Plaque, made of fatty substances including cholesterol, may build up to the point that an artery is so blocked the heart can't get the blood or oxygen required to function. Often blood clots form, increasing the potential for further blockage (CDC, 2010b). When our heart cannot pump blood the way it should we may experience *arrhythmias* (irregular heartbeats), *angina* (chest pains), and *myocardial infarction* (heart attack).

The ultimate worry is that heart disease will lead to a heart attack. The major symptoms of an attack for men and women are discomfort in your chest and other areas of your upper

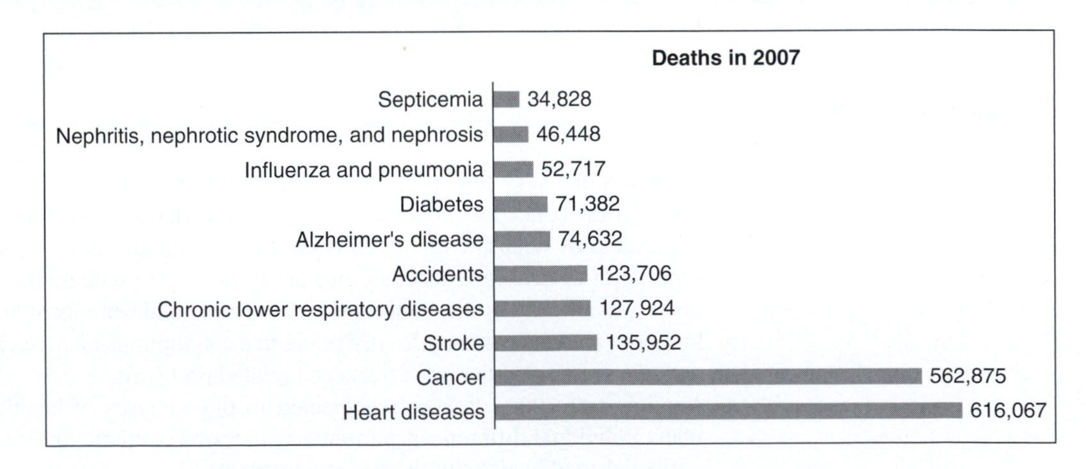

FIGURE 11.1 ***Top 10 Causes of Death in 2007***

Adapted from Centers for Disease Control and Prevention. (2010, June 28). Faststats: Deaths and mortality. Atlanta, GA: Author. Retrieved July 14, 2010 from http://www.cdc.gov/nchs/fastats/deaths.htm

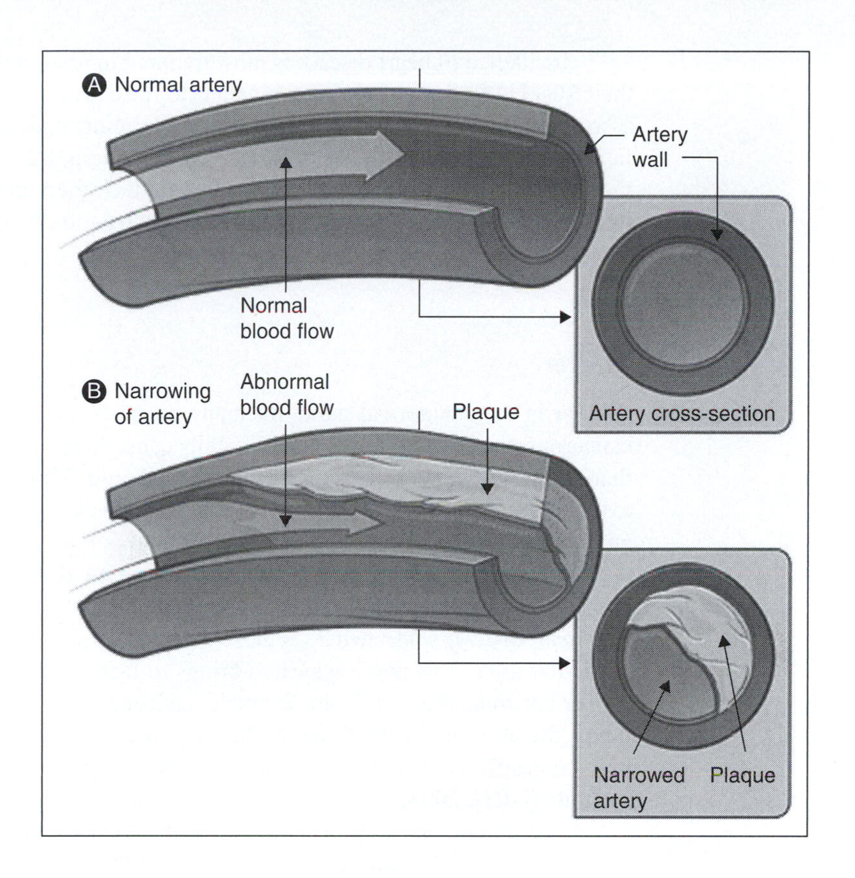

FIGURE 11.2 *Atherosclerosis*

From the National Heart Lung and Blood Institute, U.S. Dept. of Health and Human Services and NIH (2009).

Your Thoughts?

What factors might lead an adult to turn down opportunities to learn CPR or to use a defibrillator?

body including your arms, neck, and jaw, shortness of breath, cold sweat, nausea, or lightheadedness (CDC, 2010b). Along with those signs women often report heartburn, loss of appetite, fatigue and weakness, coughing, and heart flutters (National Women's Health Information Center, 2009a). A heart attack is a true emergency that should alert bystanders to call 9-1-1 and do all they can to get help immediately. Individuals trained in CPR (cardiopulmonary resuscitation) and defibrillation (electrical shock) may be able to help until medical personnel arrive (CDC, 2010b; Mayo Clinic, 2009d).

There are tests medical professionals can use to better estimate the condition of a person's heart, including exercise stress tests, electrocardiograms (EKG; measuring electrical function), and echocardiograms, which create a picture of the heart. If heart disease is detected there are various treatments ranging from surgery to medications to changes in lifestyle. One of the best ways to address cardiovascular disease, as well as to prevent it, is to address the risk factors:

Your Thoughts?

Would you support an insurance company who required therapy for clients with anger issues to reduce the risk of cardiovascular disease? Why, why not, or under what circumstances?

- high blood cholesterol, high blood pressure, or diabetes
- demonstrate tobacco use, physical inactivity, excessive alcohol use, obesity
- a diet high in saturated fats, cholesterol, and salt

are at higher risk (CDC, 2010b, May Clinic 2009d). Cardiovascular disease has also been related to personality characteristics that lead to greater hostility, anxiety, and depression. In fact, some studies indicate that frequent hostility and anger can be as severe a risk factor as smoking, particularly for middle-aged men (Aldwin et al., 2006).

Incidence of heart disease is most frequent in men in their 50s and 60s and for women in their 70s. Until recent national campaigns to raise awareness, cardiovascular disease was most associated with men, resulting in the disease being underrecognized in women by patients, families, and medical professionals (Leventhal, Ragin, Leventhal, & Burns, 2001). Women are more likely to die within a year after a heart attack than men (38% to 25%, respectively), and within that group of women the death rate is substantially higher for black women (American Heart Association, 2008).

Cancer

Cancer is the categorical name for many diseases that begin with abnormal cell growth. In cancerous circumstances the genes in cells cause them to either multiply more often or faster than they should, or to live longer than they should. This buildup of cells creates tumors and extra tissue. In some cases these tumors are *benign,* meaning noncancerous, nonspreading, and non–life threatening. In other cases the tumors are *malignant,* meaning they will destroy the tissue around them and metastasize or spread throughout the body. Cancer is usually named for the place that it starts. Those that start in the blood are called *leukemia, multiple myeloma,* or *lymphoma,* whereas those that start in solid tissue and organs are named for that particular area. This naming system brings to light a key point in understanding whether the cancer has metastasized. If, for example, cancer begins in breast tissue and then moves to the lungs, the abnormal cells found in the lungs are cancerous breast tissue cells. The most common places for cancer cells to move to are the lungs, bones, liver, and brain (National Cancer Institute [NCI], 2004).

The precursors for cancer may be inherited or triggered by certain lifestyle and environmental factors. For example, certain diets, use of tobacco, and exposure to ultraviolet radiation from the sun increase the risk of developing cancer. ***Carcinogens*** (cancer-causing substances) in the workplace, such as asbestos, asphalt fumes, diesel exhaust, secondhand tobacco smoke, and many other chemicals also increase cancer risk (NCI, 2005; CDC, 2009d). The risk of developing cancer does increase with age as well (NIA, 2010a). There are two critical strategies to employ in reducing your personal risk of developing cancer. One is to make smart lifestyle choices, including not using tobacco products, consuming less fatty foods and more vegetables, fruits, and whole grains, exercising regularly, keeping a lean weight, and avoiding ultraviolet sun rays by using sunscreen and wearing appropriate clothing, including hats. The other strategy is to get regular medical checkups regardless of whether cancer seems to run in your family or not (NCI, 2005).

Your Thoughts?

What jobs or situations might put employees at a greater risk of developing cancer?

Just like the causes or triggers can vary dramatically, so can the symptoms depending on the type of cancer. Early symptoms may include a lump, thickening, new mole, or changes in an existing wart or mole. Unexplained changes in weight, unusual bleeding or discharge, or changes in bowel or bladder habits may also be early signals of cancer. Cancer treatments are much more effective when the disease is found early; however, these symptoms may be ignored because they usually don't cause pain and can be similar to those caused by infections, benign tumors, or other less alarming problems. The National Cancer Institute also cautions that a nagging cough, hoarseness, difficulty swallowing, or persistent indigestion should be taken seriously as potential early warning signs (NCI, 2005). Only medical professionals, through the use of physical examination, blood tests, and imaging techniques, and ultimately by analyzing some of the actual tissue (a biopsy), can determine if a condition is cancer. Treatments may include surgery to remove the cancer, radiation, chemotherapy, hormone therapy, other biological therapies to destroy the cells, or some combination of those actions (NCI, 2005).

Your Thoughts?

How might the media raise citizens' awareness of these potential early warning signs?

RESEARCH IN-DEPTH
Quasi-Experiments

The most important aspects of a true experiment, primarily the establishment of cause-and-effect through the random assignment of well-matched participants, can be difficult to achieve in research with human beings. ***Quasi-experimental designs***, ones in which the participants are not randomly assigned, are much more common in psychology. For example, in any study comparing the responses of males and females the design is quasi-experimental because participants cannot be randomly assigned to gender groups. The same situation arises when comparing adults by age. Young adults cannot be in the late adulthood group, nor can older adults be in the young adulthood group. The loss of randomization results in much less clarity and certainty when interpreting the results.

Gwen Wyatt and her colleagues at Michigan State University used a quasi-experimental design in their study of the effects of reflexology and guided imagery during chemotherapy with cancer patients (Wyatt, Sikorskii, Siddiqi, & Given, 2007). This study was designed to provide foundational information for true experiments in this area in the future. In the quasi-experimental study Wyatt and her colleagues (2007) offered cancer patients the option of participating in a complementary therapy group, specifically reflexology (deep massage of hands and feet), guided imagery (soothing mental images), guided imagery plus reflexology, or simply an interview. The interview-only group served as the control group. *Complementary therapies* are nonconventional treatments used along with conventional medical therapy (in this case chemotherapy) while *alternative therapies* are nonconventional therapies used in the place of conventional therapies. The researchers were looking for the influence of the independent variables (type of complementary therapy) on the dependent variable of quality of life.

One outcome of allowing the patients to choose their own treatment group was that the groups were not balanced in number of participants. In this case 22 participants opted for guided imagery, 21 selected reflexology, 40 desired both, and 13 participants chose the interview only. Allowing participants to choose their groups did lead to some interesting observations, such as the finding that the guided imagery group had more patients with lung cancer than other groups. Also, the interview-only group included patients who were more likely to be in the early stages of cancer while the treatment groups were more likely the choice of those with later stages of cancer. Consistent with those findings, those in the treatment groups started with lower quality of life scores than the interview-only group prior to the treatments. The interview-only group was also younger in age and reported more education than the other groups.

Wyatt and her colleagues found more patients stayed with the reflexology-only group as compared to the others, whereas the guided imagery–only group showed the highest attrition or dropout rate at 41%. Those who dropped out of the guided imagery–only and the guided imagery plus reflexology displayed higher anxiety and depression as well as lower physical and emotional well-being. The patients who chose the reflexology group were interesting in that comparisons of those who stayed in the reflexology group versus those who dropped out of the group showed that the patients with the higher quality of life dropped out, while those with lower quality of life stayed in the group. It may be that those who dropped out felt they didn't need the extra therapy, whereas those who stayed with the group were struggling (lower quality of life) but felt the reflexology was worth the effort.

Quasi-experimental designs can certainly add to the knowledge base in psychology and offer interesting and helpful insights. The loss of true randomization, however, limits the interpretation of the findings and prohibits any conclusions regarding cause-and-effect. It is interesting to find, for example, that the patients who dropped out of the guided imagery–only and the guided imagery plus reflexology displayed higher anxiety and depression, but without true randomization the researchers cannot say that guided imagery *caused* increased anxiety and depression. The same is true regarding the finding that a greater percentage of patients dropped out of the guided imagery–only group. It is an interesting finding, but the researchers cannot make the assumption that something about the guided imagery therapy *caused* participants to drop out.

Analyses of data on death rates due to cancer in 2006 reveals that the most deadly form is lung cancer, with the second being prostate cancer in men and the third being breast cancer in women. Others near the top of the list were cancers of the colon and rectum, pancreas, ovary, and blood cancers. In terms of the number of cases reported in 2006 National Program of Cancer Registries (CDC, 2010c) data indicated that prostate cancer was the leader, followed by breast and then lung cancer. Comparing by ethnicity whites report the highest number of cancer cases (NIA, 2007b). Among the promising signs in the treatment of cancer is that survival rates have improved in recent years. The National Cancer Institute estimates that approximately 64% of the people diagnosed with cancer will be alive 5 years later (NCI, 2005).

Your Thoughts?

How might this information on survival rates help an individual who was just diagnosed plan for the future?

Cerebrovascular Disease

Just as *cardio*vascular disease is a broad category of diseases that cause problems with blood flow through the heart, ***cerebrovascular disease*** is a broad category of diseases that cause problems with blood flow to and through the brain, resulting in the immediate destruction of brain cells and tissue once the flow of oxygen and nutrients stop. Also, just as we think of the seriousness and possible loss of life with a heart attack, we can think of any disruption in blood flow to the brain as a *brain attack,* which is just as serious and worthy of the same level of alarm (National Institute of Neurological Disorders and Stroke [NINDS], 2003). Cerebrovascular disease and Alzheimer's disease, a type of dementia, are the most common brain afflictions of older adults. Alzheimer's disease usually results in more widespread brain changes, whereas cerebrovascular disease can cause well-defined and isolated damage (Vinters, 2001).

The condition most associated with cerebrovascular disease is stroke. *Hemorrhagic* strokes occur when a blood vessel in the brain breaks and bleeds, creating a disruption of blood flow to the rest of the brain and a great deal of pressure where the bleeding occurs (NINDS, 2003). One of the most common causes of a hemorrhagic stroke is a weak or thin spot on an artery wall that allows blood to collect and expand the artery, called an ***aneurysm,*** that can leak blood or rupture. Again comparing to cardiovascular disease, just as plaque can build up and cause blockages and narrowing of the passageways to the heart, it can do the same to the passageways to the brain. Cerebrovascular disease, like cardiovascular disease, is aggravated by high blood pressure.

Your Thoughts?

Do you think most people would respond to these symptoms of "brain attack" as rapidly as they would the symptoms of a heart attack? Why, why not, or under what circumstances?

Most strokes are *ischemic,* usually caused by one of three primary problems: (1) ***thrombosis,*** the formation of a clot within a blood vessel in the brain or neck; (2) an ***embolism,*** the movement of a clot from another part of the body to the brain; or (3) ***stenosis,*** the severe narrowing of an artery in or leading to the brain (NINDS, 2010a). The primary symptoms associated with strokes are the *sudden* appearance of:

- Numbness or weakness in limbs or face on one side of the body
- Confusion and trouble communicating
- Difficulties with vision
- Severe headache

Ischemic strokes range in intensity from severe to attacks so mild that the symptoms may be ignored or even go undetected. During a mild stroke, often called a *mini-stroke,* it may appear to others as if the individual is daydreaming, unaware, or confused (NINDS, 2003). These mild ischemic strokes may only last a few moments and be dismissed rather than recognized as mini-strokes and cause for alarm (NINDS, 2010a).

There are three steps in the treatment and management of strokes. The first is to recognize the risk factors and work to prevent the actual occurrence of a stroke. Prevention involves living a healthy lifestyle and managing or avoiding the primary risk factors of heart disease, high blood pressure, high cholesterol, diabetes, smoking, a family history of strokes, and a history of experiencing mini-strokes. Age is also a factor in that well over half of all strokes occur to adults over age 65 (NINDS, 2003, 2010a).

Those who survive a stroke will likely be forced to cope with immediate and long-term challenges. The second step in stroke management is coping with the emergency and the immediate recovery. Initial treatments will often involve various medications and in some cases surgery. Hemorrhagic strokes will require immediate life-saving procedures. In the case of ischemic strokes there are drugs available that can dissolve the blood clots. For the best results these drugs should be administered as soon as possible, and within 3 hours of the stroke to be most effective. Three hours is not very long when factoring in the time it takes for the individual

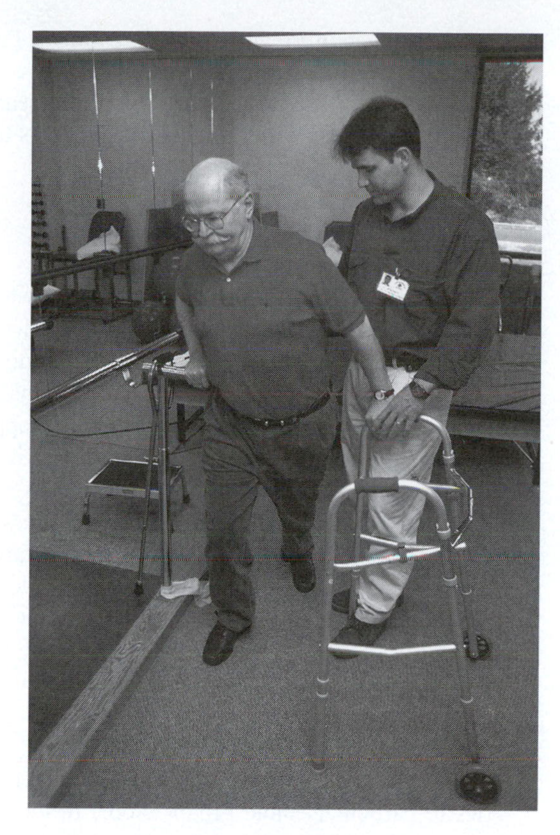

Rehabilitation following a stroke often involves relearning very basic movements and tasks.

Your Thoughts?

How might the response time be influenced by the location (rural, suburban, or urban) of the adult who has just had a stroke?

to recognize what has happened, get some help, get transportation to a hospital, and go through any emergency admissions procedures, the initial evaluation, diagnosis, and finally receive the treatment (NINDS, 2003). Diagnosis can involve a neurological examination, blood tests, and brain scans. Using any number of medical imaging techniques medical professionals will be able to see where brain tissue is dying and where blood may be collecting on the brain.

The third step in managing a stroke is to work to prevent another occurrence while also engaging in long-term rehabilitation. The type and amount of therapy needed will depend on the severity of the stroke and the residual damage. Strokes often leave weakness or paralysis on one side of the body as well as brain damage in the areas that control balance and coordination. Recovery may involve physical therapy to relearn simple activities like sitting up and walking as well as occupational therapy to relearn how to perform personal tasks such as dressing, eating, and toileting. Following a stroke adults often engage in neurocognitive therapy to regain reasoning skills, attention span, and some types of memory function. Often they need speech therapy to regain as much of their communicative abilities as they can. Strokes may cause slurred speech as well as various types of *aphasia,* the inability to speak, read, or write clearly. Another facet of the rehabilitation process involves coping with the many emotions related to the entire experience, which may include depression, anxiety, and anger. Psychotherapy may be helpful in learning to manage emotions and sustain motivation to work through the long rehabilitation process (NINDS, 2003, 2010a).

Your Thoughts?

How might an adult's family and social support network assist in this rehabilitation?

Strokes are the third leading cause of death (NINDS, 2010a) and the cause of more serious long-term disabilities than any other disease (NINDS, 2010a). With estimates of over 700,000 new strokes each year in the United States (NINDS, 2010a), researchers are investigating many avenues of prevention and treatment. For example, one interesting area of research is focused on animals that hibernate and survive with such a decreased flow of blood to the brain it would kill a nonhibernating animal. Researchers hope that by learning how their brains function scientists can find ways for humans to cope better with decreased blood flow in the brain (NINDS, 2010a).

Diabetes

Diabetes is the name given to conditions in which our bodies do not process insulin in the way they should. Under fully healthy circumstances our bodies turn the food we eat into glucose (sugar), which is then used by cells for growth and energy. When someone has diabetes either the pancreas doesn't produce insulin to transform the glucose to a useable substance or the cells that need nourishment do not respond appropriately. The result of either situation is that glucose builds up in the bloodstream, which is why tests for diabetes essentially check for elevated levels of blood glucose. In some cases several measures of blood glucose may be taken over time while an individual's body is processing a glucose drink (NDIC, 2008).

Your Thoughts?

Would it be unethical for a health insurance company to penalize a client who has risk factors for Type 2 diabetes and continues an unhealthy lifestyle? Why or why not?

Diabetes has several features that distinguish it from the other diseases profiled to this point. It is unique in that, for some cases, following the detection of early signs of pre-diabetes adults can actually stop the disease from developing (Johnson & Drueger, 2005). The occurrence of Type 2 diabetes can be dramatically reduced by losing weight, controlling your diet, and exercising regularly. By losing 5–7% of your body weight if you are overweight and engaging in 30 minutes of exercise 5 days a week you can lower your risk of developing diabetes by nearly 60% (NDIC, 2008).

Diabetes is also different from the other diseases in that it demonstrates unusually strong ties to particular ethnic groups. Some of the highest rates of diabetes in the world are found among Alaska Natives and American Indians (Angel & Angel, 2006; NDIC, 2008). Type 2 diabetes is much more common among Hispanics, African Americans, Asian Americans, Native Hawaiians, and other Pacific Islander Americans than among whites (NDIC, 2008; NIA, 2007b).

A third unique feature of diabetes is that it may be statistically misrepresented. Some people have no symptoms and in other cases the symptoms are mild and ignored, thus medical attention is not sought. Also, diabetes may be statistically undetected as a cause of death because well over half of all individuals with diabetes die from heart disease or stroke (CDC, 2010d; NDIC, 2008).

There are three main types of diabetes: Type 1, Type 2, and gestational diabetes. Type 1 diabetes occurs when, for some unknown reason, the body's immune system that fights infection destroys the insulin-producing cells in the pancreas. Unfortunately, the individual with Type 1 must take insulin everyday in order to survive. This type usually develops in childhood and is sometimes called *juvenile-onset diabetes* or *insulin-dependent diabetes.* Adults with this condition have most likely been coping with it for years (CDC, 2010d; NDIC, 2008). Gestational diabetes develops late in pregnancy in 3–8% of pregnant women in the United States. Although this condition usually fades after birth these women are at higher risk of developing Type 2 diabetes later (NDIC, 2008).

Your Thoughts?

What might an employer do to encourage employees with these characteristics to get checked for Type 2 diabetes?

Type 2 diabetes is more common, sometimes milder than Type 1, and slower to develop. With Type 2 the pancreas is producing insulin but the body has insulin resistance and doesn't use it well. Type 2 diabetes has been called *non-insulin-dependent diabetes mellitus* or *adult-onset diabetes.* Type 2 is often associated with middle and late adulthood, obesity, physical inactivity, and family history of diabetes (CDC, 2010d; NDIC, 2008). The National Institute of Diabetes and Digestive and Kidney Diseases estimates that approximately 7.8% of the American population, or about 23.6 million people, have diabetes, though not all of those are currently diagnosed cases (NDIC, 2008). As illustrated in Figure 11.3 the percentages are higher in those 60 years and older.

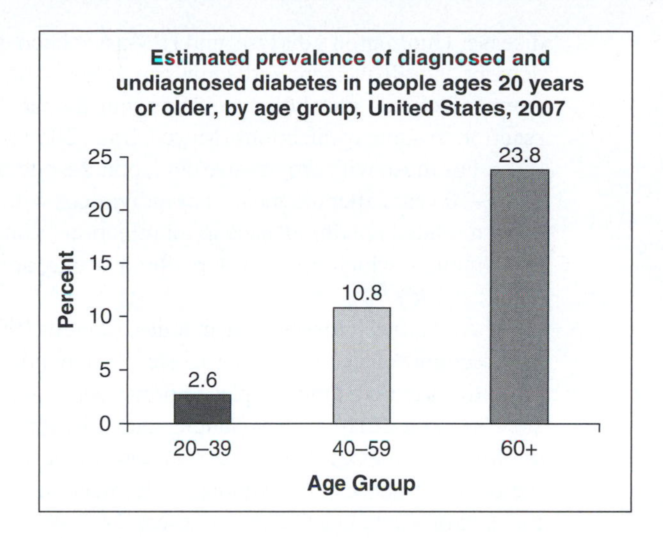

FIGURE 11.3 ***Prevalence of Diabetes by Age***

From the National Diabetes Information Clearinghouse. (2008).

The symptoms of Type 1 and Type 2 are essentially the same, though they develop more slowly with Type 2. They include fatigue, frequent urination, increased thirst and hunger, weight loss, blurred vision, slow healing of wounds or sores, numbness or tingling in hands or feet, dry skin, and higher frequency of infections. Long-term diabetes is associated with several potentially life-threatening conditions, including blindness, heart disease, stroke, kidney failure, lower-extremity amputations, and nerve damage (CDC, 2010d; NDIC, 2008).

The primary treatments for diabetes involve active monitoring and healthy maintenance of weight, diet, blood glucose levels, insulin, and other medications as needed. Those with diabetes should have routine checkups with ophthalmologists for vision health and podiatrists for foot care. Currently, the National Institutes of Health and the Centers for Disease Control and Prevention are researching potential cures for diabetes, including possible pancreas transplants, cell transplants, and cell manipulation (CDC, 2010d).

Alzheimer's Disease

The illnesses summarized in this section, including Alzheimer's disease, are connected by their ranking as leading causes of death and their primarily physical characteristics. Alzheimer's disease is probably the most associated with aging in terms of public perception. Due to its strong physical and psychological characteristics it provides a bridge, serving as the last in the section on physical diseases and leading to the next section exploring psychological disorders.

Alzheimer's disease is one of many diseases that can cause ***dementia,*** a group of symptoms or conditions that result from brain-related diseases. Dementia symptoms, previously called *senility* (Vinters, 2001), vary in type and severity depending on the cause. Common symptoms include memory loss and difficulty communicating, learning new information, planning, organizing, and reasoning. Not only do these symptoms frustrate individuals with dementia and those around them, the personality changes, inappropriate behavior, paranoia, agitation, and hallucinations can make it more challenging to care for them. Some types of dementia will progress in severity along with the disease that is causing it, such as Alzheimer's disease, Huntington's disease, and HIV-associated dementia. It is important to note that not all dementias will worsen, and some can actually be reversed. Dementia symptoms can result from infections, metabolic problems, nutritional deficiencies, poisoning, brain tumors, and reaction to some medications (Mayo Clinic, 2009a).

Your Thoughts?

Why might it be important for people to know that Alzheimer's disease is only one type of dementia?

For those with progressive dementia the rate of decline can vary, with death coming usually 3–10 years after diagnosis. For individuals with progressive dementia the cause of death is often a related condition, such as an infection (Vinters, 2001). Alzheimer's disease and vascular dementia, which may develop after a stroke, are the two most common forms of dementia (NIA, 2010d).

Alzheimer's disease was first described in 1907 as a very rare condition. By the 1960s it was recognized as the leading cause of dementia (Vinters, 2001). Alzheimer's disease is a brain disease involving misplaced proteins that get clumped and tangled with other brain tissue (NINDS, 2010b). These tangles then disrupt connections between nerve cells, accelerate the loss of synapses (Vinters, 2001), lower levels of neurotransmitters, and eventually lead to the death of nerve cells. Although a tremendous amount of time and resources are currently focused on Alzheimer's disease, researchers are still searching for the cause(s) (NIA, 2010d), the cure (NINDS, 2010b), and a reliable and relatively simple test for the disease (NIA, 2003). Criteria designed by the National Institute of Neurological and Communicative Disorders and Stroke and the Alzheimer's Association have established a way to determine "probable" Alzheimer's disease by confirming dementia, finding symptoms beginning between ages 40 and 90, showing the progressive worsening of memory and cognitive functioning, detecting no lapses in consciousness, and eliminating all other diseases or conditions that may account for the dementia (NIA, 2003).

Your Thoughts?

What are some potential problems with a diagnosis that rests on eliminating all other diseases or conditions that may account for dementia?

Although the length of life once Alzheimer's disease begins can range from 5 to 20 years (NINDS, 2010b), the progression of Alzheimer's disease is predictable, following a trajectory through four stages. The first stage, *preclinical Alzheimer's disease,* actually starts 10–20 years before diagnosis as parts of the brain begin to atrophy (shrink). Many of the changes at this point, which could be described as very mild cognitive impairment, are often thought to be just signs of age (NIA, 2003). One branch of research on Alzheimer's disease is searching for

Estimates are that just over 50% of all individuals with Alzheimer's disease are cared for at home, often by loved ones with little training or support.

ways to detect these changes as early as possible. For example, because advanced Alzheimer's disease causes the deterioration of language, some researchers are focusing on the earliest changes in adults' language-based mistakes. The disease doesn't affect grammar or sentence construction, but does affect vocabulary choices and semantic understanding (Kemper & Mitzner, 2001). Another branch is focused on the genetic markers of Alzheimer's disease. Interestingly, the three genes associated with the development of familial or early-onset Alzheimer's disease are different than those associated with late-onset dementia. Current research indicates that the genetic pattern that seems to lead to the development of Alzheimer's disease in whites has less effect in Hispanics and does not have the same effect in African Americans (Vogler, 2006).

Your Thoughts?

What would be the advantages and disadvantages of knowing that you have genetic markers of Alzheimer's disease?

The second step in the process is called *mild Alzheimer's disease.* The symptoms include memory loss, confusion over familiar things and places, difficulty with routine tasks, poor judgment, loss of spontaneity, loss of initiative, increased anxiety, and mood and personality changes (NIA, 2003). Usually at this point the symptoms have become strong enough that the adult or their loved ones are concerned, medical professionals become involved, and a diagnosis is made. By the time an adult reaches the third stage, *moderate Alzheimer's disease,* the brain damage has spread to areas that control sensory processing and conscious thought. Extra care or supervision of the individual is often necessary. In addition to the symptoms of stage two worsening, these adults will now have difficulty learning new things, problems recognizing family and friends, agitation, hallucinations, suspiciousness or paranoia, episodes of wandering, loss of impulse control, repetitive movements, and perceptual-motor problems, such as trouble getting out of a chair. Adults at this stage may get angry when they are confused and can't remember what to do. These adults may also seem to cling to their caregiver as a source of security and comfort (NIA, 2010d; NIA, 2003; Vinters, 2001).

Your Thoughts?

If you were hiring health care professionals to work with Alzheimer's disease clients, what personality characteristics would you look for?

Many of us worry about our older relatives, and when they forget simple things we worry even more. Are these early signs of dementia? An elderly relative of mine who has Alzheimer's disease taught me that the types of forgetting and confusion seen in stages two and three are much more than the typical "Where did I put my keys?" or "What was it I wanted to tell you?" For example, I would stop in to visit her while she was still well enough to live with her adult daughter. One time while visiting I noticed the kitchen trash can was missing, so I asked her where it was. She went to her room and returned, handing me a pair of boots. Later I asked her where I might find some tape to use on wrapping paper for a birthday gift and she brought me a tea bag. On other visits I found the remote control for the television in the freezer and folded clothes in the refrigerator. On occasions when I was there while she was trying to get dressed I noticed that she would sometimes forget to take her pajamas off before putting daytime clothes on. Sometimes she would put her shoes on before her pants, and then, of course, not be able to get her pants on over her shoes. She would get frustrated, start over, and often do the very same thing unless someone intervened. I also noticed that my relative worried about objects that were unfamiliar, like my cell phone. Lying on the table where she could see it, she asked repeatedly what it was and kept trying to put it in a drawer or in the trash.

In the fourth and final stage, *severe Alzheimer's disease,* all the symptoms reach their peak. Many patients have little if any awareness of themselves, their loved ones, or their surroundings. Without memories they have no identity or sense of self. In some cases their language functions have deteriorated to the point that they cannot communicate clearly, but rather groan or grunt. Adults at this point may spend most of their time in bed sleeping. They are likely to experience seizures, lack bladder and bowel control, and have difficulty swallowing. Patients with Alzheimer's disease usually die from complications caused by the disease, with the most frequent cause being pneumonia (NIA, 2003).

Alzheimer's disease is not an evitable part of aging even though the incidence does increase with age, affecting an estimated 20–40% of those over 80 years old (Vinters, 2001). Although younger adults can develop the disease, it is rare to find it in individuals under 60 years old (NIA, 2010d). Current estimates place the number of Americans with Alzheimer's disease between 2.4 and 5.1 million, and with numbers of adults over age 65 growing it is likely that those estimates will rise over the next decade (NIA, 2010e).

Section Summary

Your Thoughts?

Has reading about these illnesses prompted you to take better care of yourself? If not, why not? What may be needed beyond education?

- Cardiovascular disease, the leading cause of death among women and men, includes diseases and conditions that affect the functioning of the heart, including high blood pressure, coronary artery disease, and heart attack.
- A good diet and a healthy weight, adequate exercise, yearly checkups, and monitoring of cholesterol and blood pressure are some of the best means of prevention of cardiovascular disease (and many other concerns too!).
- Cancer includes conditions that begin with abnormal cell growth that destroys healthy tissue and may metastasize throughout the body.
- Cerebrovascular disease includes conditions that interrupt blood flow to the brain, destroying brain tissue, which then causes many types of lifelong disabilities.
- Diabetes, occurring when the body doesn't have or use insulin to transform glucose into fuel, is unique in that it can be prevented in some cases through diet and exercise.
- Dementia is the name for a group of symptoms, including the deterioration of memory processing, reasoning ability, decision making, judgment, language processing, and communication skills.
- Alzheimer's disease, one of the leading causes of dementia, is a brain disease that progresses through four stages of cognitive and physical deterioration.

Psychological Disorders

The distinction between physical diseases and psychological disorders is useful in categorizing problems by their sources or primary symptoms and characteristics. One risk of using such a system is that it gives the false impression that a physical disease doesn't have much to do with psychological concerns and vice versa. Alzheimer's disease is a perfect example of the interaction of physical brain deterioration and cognitive deficits, fear, anxiety, paranoia, and dysfunctional behaviors. In some cases psychological disorders and symptoms can be traced to physiological sources, particularly areas of the brain or specific neurotransmitters. Presenting physical diseases first in this chapter may also give the impression that they are the more prevalent or the most important concerns. That, too, would be a misinterpretation. The National Institute of Mental Health (NIMH, 2010b) estimates that about one out of every four Americans age 18 and older suffer from a diagnosable mental disorder at some point during a calendar year. They estimate that the most serious mental illnesses affect about 6%, or 1 in every 17 Americans. In this section we explore the standard system for diagnosing psychological disorders, and then explore anxiety disorders and depression.

Your Thoughts?

What factors in American culture might contribute to such a high number of cases?

Classifications and Individual Differences

The standard guide for defining and classifying psychological disorders is the ***Diagnostic and Statistical Manual of Mental Disorders.*** The fourth edition of the DSM, DSM-IV, was published by the American Psychiatric Association in 1994, and later minor text revisions were

Your Thoughts?

What are the advantages and disadvantages of allowing DSM-IV information to be readily available on the Internet and in bookstores?

published in 2000. The next edition, DSM-V, is currently being developed. DSM-IV provides everyone in the therapeutic, research, medical, and insurance fields with defining criteria for all mental disorders. It is divided into five sections, Axis I–V, reflecting various aspects of mental health and dysfunction. Axis I, clinical syndromes, is the largest section and contains what most people think of as psychiatric disorders. Both of the topics explored here, anxiety and depression, are found in Axis I. Developmental and personality disorders make up Axis II. These are generally long-lasting conditions that must be taken into account when treating any Axis I disorder, such as mental retardation. Axis III covers physical or medical conditions that might influence the primary diagnosis. For example, an adult may have a diagnosis of generalized anxiety or depression that may be directly related to a diagnosis of cancer or Alzheimer's disease. Axis IV emphasizes sources of psychosocial stress, such as transitioning to a new job or coping with the death of a loved one. Again, it may be that an adult is diagnosed with depression (Axis I), however, that condition is directly tied to the death of a parent (Axis IV). Axis V is designed to give a global or overall sense of how the person is functioning (American Psychiatric Association, 1994).

It is important that all professional therapists stay current in terms of new research and maintain their own continuing education. The American Psychological Association (APA) has issued several sets of policies requiring therapists to stay up-to-date, such as the 2002 *Guidelines on Multicultural Education, Training, Research, Practice, and Organization for Psychologists* (APA, 2002) and the 2003 *Guidelines for Psychological Practice with Older Adults* (APA, 2004). Without extra effort and deliberate study it may be difficult for a therapist to understand the vocabulary and worldview of a client who has a different geographic, economic, educational, generational, ethnic, religious, or cultural background. Part of the response to this cultural awareness is the growing trend for therapists to not only specialize in particular disorders but also to specialize in therapy with people who have particular sets of common characteristics. The specialty of *geropsychology* in clinical therapy is a perfect example of this trend (APA, 2004c).

The DSM classification system allows therapists to document major life events that are likely to influence other diagnoses and treatment.

Your Thoughts?

How might gender roles and expectations for men and women influence these findings?

As is the case with any general overview, summaries of mental disorders often overlook individual differences. For example, consider the common finding that women are much more likely to be diagnosed with anxiety disorders and depression whereas men are much more likely to be diagnosed with substance use and antisocial disorder (George, 1990). It is important to determine how these data are collected. Are researchers considering only Axis I diagnoses and not others? Could it be that women are more likely to seek help from medical professionals, thus they receive a diagnosis of an anxiety or depressive disorder; however, men are more likely to cope with alcohol or display angry outbursts that lead to diagnoses of substance use and antisocial disorder? These questions are discussed further in the section on mood disorders. Consider as a second example an older adult with Alzheimer's disease who has been diagnosed with depression. Depending on the way the data is collected, that individual's data may or may not be counted among the number of adults with depression. It could make a tremendous difference if those collecting data recorded only Axis I diagnoses and not the others, or if they recorded only psychological or psychiatric records and not medical records (Gatz & Smyer, 2001). While use of the DSM-IV has certainly brought structure and standardization to the study of mental disorders, there remains room for interpretation of criteria and areas for further refinement in the future.

Anxiety Disorders

Some psychological disorders can be described as severe, intense, or disruptive versions of feelings most people have from time to time. Anxiety, such as that experienced before taking some type of test or speaking to a large group if you aren't used to it, is common in its mild form and usually fades once the target event has passed. An ***anxiety disorder*** can produce feelings just as intense if not worse and last for months. Adults with panic attacks, for example, often feel terrified, experiencing hot flashes and chills, tingling in their hands, nausea, chest pains, and difficulty breathing. The pain and distress can be so great in some cases that individuals may believe they are having a heart attack (NIMH, 2010a). One of the many disruptive characteristics of anxiety disorders is the worry over how embarrassing an episode may be in a public place, which can make it difficult to work or socialize (NIMH, 2010a). Another difference between typical feelings of anxiety we all have at times and an anxiety disorder is that there may not be a clear source causing the anxiety. If you are nervous because you are taking a test then you know the reason why you are nervous. With an anxiety disorder individuals may have all the feelings of anxiety without an understanding of why they are anxious.

Your Thoughts?

What are some destructive but common ways adults try to cope with anxiety?

The DSM-IV category of anxiety disorders, which includes *panic disorder, social anxiety disorder, generalized anxiety disorder, posttraumatic stress disorder,* and *obsessive–compulsive disorder,* are the most common psychological disorders in the United States (Anxiety Disorders Association of American [ADAA], 2010a.d.-c). The National Institute of Mental Health (2010a) estimates that about 40 million American adults will suffer with an anxiety disorder at some point in a calendar year. Women are more likely to be diagnosed with generalized anxiety disorder, panic disorder, posttraumatic stress disorder, and specific phobias, whereas obsessive–compulsive disorder and social anxiety disorder are equally likely in either gender (ADAA, 2010a).

Your Thoughts?

How might gender roles and expectations for men and women influence these findings?

The causes of anxiety disorders have not been discovered, although it is likely that our genetics, brain chemistry, personality, and particular set of life events are all factors (ADAA, 2010c). At one time it was thought that anxiety decreased with age, partly due to the findings that while anxiety disorders are found in approximately 16% of adults of all ages, the percentage drops to 11% among adults over age 65 (Harwood, Mark, McKusick, Coffey, King, & Genuardi, 2003). The current perspective is that older adults are less likely to report psychological symptoms and are more likely to emphasize their physical concerns (ADAA, 2010b).

ON THE LEADING EDGE
Art Therapy for Posttraumatic Stress Disorder

Upali Nanda and Kathy Hathorn of the American Art Resources in Houston, Texas teamed up with Lea Barbato Gaydos of Beth-El College of Nursing and Health Sciences at the University of Colorado and Nicholas Watkins of HOK Product Design and are calling upon art therapists and researchers to explore the impact of visual art on war veterans with posttraumatic stress disorder (PTSD). Their concerns grew out of compassion and the realization that approximately 1.64 million American military personnel have been deployed as part of Operation Enduring Freedom and Operation Iraqi Freedom, and of those approximately 29% have or will develop PTSD. These soldiers will experience severe anxiety and panic with an intensity that affects their sensory perception and ability to communicate, and at a frequency such that it affects their routine daily functioning. Not only is there a growing need for counselors to work with these soldiers but also a need to find the most effective and low-cost therapeutic methods.

Previous research has shown that visual art, and particularly art with nature content, can reduce stress and anxiety in psychiatric patients. Even patients recovering from surgical procedures have better results if they have a window with a nature view or even a picture with a nature scene to gaze upon. As a result of these and similar findings, groups such as the Society for the Arts in Healthcare have formed and many hospitals invest in art programs (Nanda, Hathorn, Gaydos, & Watkins, 2010). The American Art Therapy Association states that as a form of therapy artistic expression can not only help individuals work through problems and conflicts but also facilitate personal development and growth (2010).

Recently, there have been some efforts to explore the use of art therapy with combat soldiers with PTSD. Gregory Lande, Vanita Tarpley, Jennifer Francis, and Rebecca Boucher of the Department of Psychiatry at Walter Reed Army Medical Center in Washington, DC, have begun work on the Combat Trauma Art Therapy Scale that can be used to identify themes associated with combat experiences. Lande and his colleagues asked participants to rate emotional pictures as a way to identify coping difficulties (Lande, Tarpley, Francis, & Boucher, 2010). The American Art Therapy Association states that as a form of therapy artistic expression can not only help individuals work through problems and conflicts but also facilitate personal development and growth (2010). Returning to the call put forth by Nanda, Hathorn, Gaydos, and Watkins (2010), perhaps it is time to involve more soldiers with PTSD in art therapy.

In terms of diagnosing and treatment it may be difficult to determine if anxiety is present in older adults who have dementia or other cognitive deficits. Also, anxiety may be a side effect of one or several medications being taken for other concerns (ADAA, 2010a).

Anxiety disorders are highly treatable, though only about one-third of those who suffer with the disorder will receive treatment (ADAA, 2010c). Anxiety disorders are often associated with other mental disorders and physical diseases and are usually treated with medication and psychotherapy. It is common for psychiatric medications to have some side effects and take several weeks to begin working as well as taking a while to wear off if they are stopped. One of the primary reasons adults with psychological disorders believe treatments failed is that they didn't give their medications enough time to start causing a noticeable change. In terms of therapy, one of the most popular choices is cognitive-behavioral therapy, which focuses both on changing destructive thoughts and modifying behaviors. Stress management skills (NIMH, 2010a) and relaxation training can also be helpful in coping with an anxiety disorder (Gatz & Smyer, 2001).

Your Thoughts?

What factors might keep an adult from seeking diagnosis and treatment for an anxiety disorder?

Mood Disorders

Although many people use the term *depression* in a way that communicates well in everyday situations, professionals use more specific vocabulary designed to highlight particular characteristics of depression. The DSM-IV category of ***mood disorders*** encompasses not only *major depressive disorder,* but also *dysthymic disorder* (chronic, mild depression), and *bipolar disorder* (cycling between depression and extreme highs or mania). The National Institute of Mental

Health (2010b) estimates that mood disorders affect about 9.5% of the population, with most of those cases being major depressive disorder.

> **Your Thoughts?**
>
> What factors might contribute to the view that depression is not a disability but rather something we should snap out of?

Similar to some anxiety disorders, the characteristics of some mood disorders can be described as intense and long-lasting versions of the mild, transient "low" or "down" moods we all have from time to time. Major depressive disorder, however, can last for weeks at a time, bringing not only a sense of sadness, hopelessness, and pessimism, but also feelings of worthlessness and loss of interest in the things that were once fun. Fatigue, aches and pains, insomnia, and changes in eating habits can accompany major depressive disorder as well (NIMH, 2009). Among adolescents and adults ages 15–44 in the United States, major depressive disorder is the leading cause of disability (NIMH, 2010b).

Mood disorders become evident for most people in their late 20s or early 30s (NIMH, 2010b) and are often diagnosed in adults with anxiety disorders (ADAA, 2010a). Mood disorders are strongly associated with substance abuse (NIMH, 2010b). Much like anxiety disorders, it is likely that mood disorders have multiple causes including genetic and environmental factors. Evidence associating brain changes and mood disorder has been detected using brain-imaging technologies (NIMH, 2009).

> **Your Thoughts?**
>
> What questions would you want answered before allowing your spouse or parent to receive ECT?

As a set of characteristics, general depression is highly treatable, usually with a combination of medications and psychotherapy. Adults undergoing treatment are also encouraged to exercise, socialize, set reasonable goals, and think positive thoughts. When the treatments are unsuccessful, a condition called *resistant depression,* the technique of electroconvulsive therapy (ECT) may be used. Once thought to be barbaric and inhumane, technologies and procedures have improved to the point that yearly, monthly, or even weekly ECT treatments are options for those with severe and resistant cases (NIMH, 2009).

In terms of individual differences, major depressive disorder is much more common among women than men. Among the many potential factors contributing to this gender gap are the findings that women may be more sensitive to psychosocial or relationship factors that facilitate depression as well as need to adjust to hormone changes throughout puberty, monthly cycles, pregnancy, and menopause. Also, women are more likely to admit to depressive feelings. Generally, men who do seek treatment tend to focus more on their physical symptoms than women. Men who don't seek treatment are more likely to turn to alcohol or drugs when depressed (NIMH, 2009).

Depressive disorders in older adults may be neglected because the symptoms are assumed to be characteristics of a physical illness or side effects of a medication or treatment. In some cases major depressive disorder may be overlooked or dismissed simply based on the assumption that depression is expected in old age. Aging is not, by itself, a cause of major depressive disorder (NIMH, 2009). Among those age 85 and older who participated in the Health and Retirement Study sponsored by the National Institute on Aging (NIA, 2007b) only 20% experienced severe depression. Rather than simply focusing on advancing age, it may be that some of the psychosocial changes that accompany aging (Yang, 2007) prompt depressive episodes. For example, the circumstance of giving up driving was strongly associated with depression among those who participated in the study (NIA, 2007b).

> **Your Thoughts?**
>
> Do you think most people expect older adults to be depressed? If so, why?

Section Summary

- The National Institute of Mental Health estimates that nearly 25% of American adults age 18 and older suffer from a diagnosable mental disorder at some point during a calendar year.
- The standard for making these diagnoses is the fourth edition of the *Diagnostic and Statistical Manual of Mental Disorders.*

- Anxiety disorders are the most common psychological disorders in the United States, affecting approximately 40 million Americans per year.
- The category of anxiety disorders, which includes panic disorder, social anxiety disorder, generalized anxiety disorder, posttraumatic stress disorder, and obsessive–compulsive disorder, are highly treatable once diagnosed.
- The classification of mood disorders includes major depressive disorder, dysthymic disorder, and bipolar disorder.
- Depressive disorders in older adults may be neglected because the condition is assumed to be a part of old age and/or a side effect of a disease or medication.

Chapter Summary

When exploring the most frequent diseases and disorders of adulthood it is important to pay attention to both the biological and psychological processes and the many individual differences that influence those processes. Among the most frequent causes of death in adulthood are cardiovascular disease, cancer, cerebrovascular disease, diabetes, and Alzheimer's disease. Among the most frequent psychological disorders are anxiety disorders and depression. Successful aging involves not only maximizing one's health potential through habits intended to maintain good health, it also involves coping well with illness and disability when presented with it. Here are some of the main points of the chapter:

- Individuals use various criteria to determine if they are ill enough to seek medical attention, including their evaluation of the severity of the symptoms and their personal vulnerability to disease.
- In a strict medical context the term *disease* refers to the actual symptoms and processes used in diagnosing and labeling a disease, whereas *illness* refers to the side effects and related problems.
- It is important to remember while reading general accounts of diseases and disorders that there are many individual differences influencing an individual's life with a particular condition, including differences in gender, personality, race and ethnicity, and access to quality medical care.
- Cardiovascular disease is a broad category of conditions that affect the functioning of the heart, including high blood pressure, coronary artery disease, and heart attack.
- Cancer, diseases characterized by abnormal cell growth, are thought to be caused by changes in the cell genes that may be hereditary or caused by environmental factors, such as a fatty diet, use of tobacco products, exposure to ultraviolet radiation, or exposure to environmental carcinogens such as asbestos or diesel exhaust.
- Cerebrovascular disease is a broad category of conditions that affect blood flow to and through the brain, such as hemorrhagic and ischemic strokes.
- Diabetes, occurring when the body doesn't have or use insulin to transform glucose into fuel, can lead to blindness, heart disease, stroke, kidney failure, lower-extremity amputations, and nerve damage.
- Dementia is the name for a progressive group of symptoms, including the deterioration of memory processing, reasoning ability, decision making, judgment, language processing, and communication skills, which can be caused by various diseases and conditions.
- Alzheimer's disease, one of the leading causes of dementia, is a brain disease that progresses through four stages of cognitive and physical deterioration.
- Psychological disorders are diagnosed based on criteria specified in the *Diagnostic and Statistical Manual of Mental Disorders,* which allows for categorizing on five levels called axes.

- Anxiety disorders, the most common psychological disorder in the United States, are thought to be just as common among older adults even though they are less likely to be diagnosed.
- Mood disorders, the most common cause of disability among those 15 to 44 years old, are highly treatable.
- A key to successful aging is coping productively with the changes caused by physical disease or psychological disorder.

Key Terms

Disease **(287)**
Illness **(287)**
Disorder **(288)**
Cardiovascular disease **(290)**
Atherosclerosis **(290)**
Cancer **(292)**
Carcinogens **(292)**
Quasi-experimental design **(293)**
Cerebrovascular disease **(294)**
Aneurysm **(294)**
Thrombosis **(294)**
Embolism **(294)**
Stenosis **(294)**
Diabetes **(296)**
Alzheimer's disease **(297)**
Dementia **(297)**
Diagnostic and Statistical Manual of Mental Disorders **(300)**
Anxiety disorders **(302)**
Mood disorders **(303)**

Comprehension Questions

1. What criteria do individuals use to determine if they are ill enough to seek medical attention?
2. What are the differences between the terms *disease, illness,* and *disorder?*
3. Give examples of the differences of perceived health and availability of health insurance among blacks, Hispanics, and whites.
4. What are the primary signs or symptoms of a heart attack?
5. What are the risk factors for cardiovascular disease that can also be viewed as targets for prevention of heart disease?
6. Explain what happens when cancer has metastasized.
7. What are the two strategies for reducing the risk of developing cancer?
8. What are the three most common causes of ischemic stroke?
9. What are the three steps in the management and treatment of cerebrovascular disease?
10. What are the symptoms of Type 2 diabetes?
11. What is dementia?
12. Name and describe the four stages of Alzheimer's disease.
13. Describe the five axes of the *Diagnostic and Statistical Manual of Mental Disorders.*
14. How are anxiety disorders different from the typical nervousness everyone has from time to time?
15. Explain the debate over whether anxiety decreases with age.
16. Describe the many similarities between anxiety disorders and major depressive disorder.
17. What is "resistant depression" and what can be done about it?
18. How do women and men respond differently to depression?

Answers for Common Sense: Myth or Reality?

1. Myth: The American Psychiatric Association prefers the term mental or psychiatric *illness*. (See Definitions and Categories, page 288.)
2. Reality: Hispanic Americans report less illness than African Americans. (See Individual Differences and Diversity, page 288).
3. Reality: Among the top 10 causes of death for Americans, more people die of cardiovascular disease and cancer than the other eight causes combined. (See Physical Illnesses, page 290.)
4. Reality: Cold sweat, nausea, and light-headedness are some of the symptoms of a heart attack. (See Cardiovascular Disease, page 291.)
5. Myth: Women are more likely to survive a heart attack than men. (See Cardiovascular Disease, page 292.)
6. Reality: Early symptoms of cancer generally don't cause pain. (See Cancer, page 292.)
7. Myth: More women develop and die from breast cancer than men who develop and die from prostate cancer. (See Cancer, page 293.)
8. Reality: Some strokes are so mild that the symptoms are undetected or ignored. (See Cerebrovascular Disease, page 294.)
9. Reality: Adults who are recovering from a stroke often have trouble speaking, reading, and writing. (See Cerebrovascular Disease, page 295.)
10. Reality: American Indians have one of the highest rates of diabetes in the world. (See Diabetes, page 296.)
11. Reality: Diabetes can cause blindness. (See Diabetes, page 297.)
12. Myth: Alzheimer's disease and dementia are two names for the same condition. (See Alzheimer's Disease, page 297.)
13. Myth: The most reliable means of determining if an older adult has Alzheimer's disease is through a blood test. (See Alzheimer's Disease, page 298.)
14. Myth: Well over half of all those age 80 and older have Alzheimer's disease. (See Alzheimer's Disease, page 300.)
15. Myth: Depression is the most common psychological disorder. (See Anxiety Disorders, page 302.)
16. Reality: Women are more likely to be diagnosed with depression than men. (See Classifications and Individual Differences, page 304.)
17. Myth: Electroconvulsive therapy, also called shock therapy, is no longer used as a treatment for depression. (See Mood Disorders, page 304.)

Suggested Readings

Older Adults and Mental Health

Psychology and Aging: Addressing Mental Health Needs of Older Adults. Publication of the American Psychological Association. Available at http://www.apa.org/pi/aging/psychandaging.pdf.

Anxiety Disorders

Barlow, D. H. (2003). The nature and development of anxiety and its disorders: Triple vulnerability theory. From Psi Chi National Honor Society in Psychology, Distinguished Lectures Series. This article can be found at http://www.psichi.org/pubs/articles/article_340.asp.

Cultural Aspects of Depressive Disorders

Marsella, A. J. (2003). Cultural aspects of depressive experience and disorders. In W. J. Lonner, D. L. Dinnel, S. A. Hayes, & D. N. Sattler (Eds.), *Online readings in psychology and culture* (Unit 9, Chapter 4), (http://www.wwu.edu/~culture), Center for Cross-Cultural Research, Western Washington University, Bellingham, WA. Available at http://www.ac.wwu.edu/~culture/Marsella.htm.

Cultural Psychopathology

Ryder, A. G., Yang, J., & Heini, S. (2002). Somatization vs. psychologization of emotional distress: A paradigmatic example for cultural psychopathology. In W. J. Lonner, D. L. Dinnel, S. A. Hayes, & D. N. Sattler (Eds.), *Online readings in psychology and culture* (Unit 9, Chapter 3), (http://www.wwu.edu/~culture), Center for Cross-Cultural Research, Western Washington University, Bellingham, WA. Available at http://www.ac.wwu.edu/~culture/RyderYangHeine.htm.

Suggested Websites

You can learn more about Alzheimer's disease at the Alzheimer's Resource Room, sponsored by the U.S. Department of Health and Human Services, at http://www.aoa.gov/alz/public/alzcarefam/disease_info/questions_to_ask.asp.

The National Library of Medicine offers an interesting summary of the interaction of emotions and diseases at http://www.nlm.nih.gov/hmd/emotions/emotionshome.html.

The National Center for Chronic Disease Prevention and Health Promotion website for Mental Health, at http://www.cdc.gov/mentalhealth/.

To learn more about drug abuse you can explore the website for the National Institute on Drug Abuse, at http://www.drugabuse.gov/.

CHAPTER

12 Coping and Support in Late Adulthood

Much of our time and energy as human beings is spent coping with change. Whether it is less significant, such as changing clothes because we're too hot or too cold, or more significant with long-lasting implications, such as moving to a new residence or adjusting to new medications, adapting to change is a constant process in our lives. Moving through middle age into late adulthood is a journey full of changes. We will transition through relationships, perhaps from spouse to widow, and from parent to grandparent and even great-grandparent. During this time we will move through the employment to full retirement transition. We'll notice changes in our cognitive, sensory, and major body systems. Physical changes from the relatively minor, such as graying hair, to the more intrusive, such as using a walker to help us move around independently will require more of our attention. We may encounter physical illnesses with all the many side effects involved. Eventually, these forces may cause us to move to new locations offering the care and assistance we need. As we move through late adulthood we will need to cope with these changes, making the best of our situation as we go.

The challenges of aging often push us to reach deep within ourselves for inner strength, creative problem solving, and wisdom. As we work through the many demands that come with young and middle adulthood we learn about our own coping styles, the types of situations we can handle well, and the circumstances that push us to our limits. As we age we will call upon those same coping strategies and develop new ones as we adjust to a shrinking pool of resources. Some older adults will embrace and adapt readily to technologies that can improve their quality of life while others will avoid them. Some will excel in building social support

COMMON SENSE
Myth or Reality?

Mark each of the following items with either an M, if you think it is a myth, or an R, if you think the statement reflects reality. By paying close attention you can find all the answers in this chapter. If needed, the answers are also given at the end of the chapter.

1. _____ Developmental psychologists believe that each phase of life has both gains and losses, including late adulthood.
2. _____ Levels of emotional intensity are the same for young and older adults.
3. _____ The ability to control one's emotional responses, moving them toward a positive outlook, increases with age into late adulthood.
4. _____ Older drivers cause the greatest number of accidents when the weather is bad.
5. _____ There is a great difference in the number of computer users when comparing those between the ages of 50 and 64 and those ages 65 and older.
6. _____ High amounts of unsolicited support for an older adult are associated with negative well-being.
7. _____ On average, a care recipient receiving informal care from a spouse or adult child is in his or her mid-60s.
8. _____ The average informal caregiver provides over 40 hours of care per week for over 4 years.
9. _____ Almost all religions have rites of passage and celebrations that mark middle age and late adulthood.
10. _____ Higher levels of religiosity are associated with better physical and mental health among older adults.
11. _____ Church attendance tends to decrease with age.

and creative problem solving, whereas others may feel awkward, less willing to be socially assertive. Some will readily accept help from those who offer, while others will not. This chapter emphasizes the need to take personal initiative to make changes in our environment, reach out to others, and turn to our inner strength to cope.

Before We Get Started . . .

Before we move into a discussion of the ways older adults might cope with their changing bodies and environment, take a few moments to consider the ways you cope with the stressors in your life. First of all, what are your primary stressors?

- Name three minor hassles you cope with almost all of the time.
- Name three people or relationships that frequently cause you stress, worry, or anxiety.
- Name three of the most significant stressors you've had to deal with recently.

Thinking about these different types of stressors, how well do you handle them? Certainly, distinct categories of stressors will have different qualities that prompt specialized ways of coping. In some cases the best approach may be problem solving aimed at tackling a specific issue. For example, if one of your daily hassles is that you are routinely late to appointments, then perhaps setting an alarm on your watch or cell phone would resolve the problem. On the other hand, some stressors are very emotional. If, for example, the source of stress is a love relationship that has broken up, the best strategy may to engage in stress-reducing activities, keep a journal for exploring your emotions, and make an effort to socialize with trusted friends and family.

This chapter explores the use of problem-solving strategies, technology, social support, and inner strength and personal spirituality. Do you engage in any of those areas when you are stressed? For each of the sources of stress you listed above, ask yourself:

- Are there changes I can make in my home or neighborhood environment that would ease my stress?
- Are there technologies I can utilize that might help me with my stressors or my emotions?

- Are there people I can reach out to, either face-to-face or through the use of technology?
- Whether it is meditation, reading, journaling, praying, or something similar, is there anything I can do to help me feel psychologically stronger?

One of the most important reasons to think about your personal coping style is that the way you cope with challenges at this point in your life is a good indicator of the way you will cope with stressors in late adulthood. Along with maintaining a healthy, active lifestyle and engaging in financial planning, learning to engage in productive, healthy coping skills now will likely improve your quality of life in late adulthood.

Coping Strategies and Aging

Each phase of adulthood has unique challenges, including late adulthood. Older adults must adjust to the expected and yet frustrating physiological and cognitive changes that accompany old age. It is likely they will face ageism, lifestyle and housing transitions, unanticipated disease and illness, and spend more time in bereavement and pondering their own life and death (Settersten, 2006). Social scientists find it particularly difficult to make general statements about older adults because they are more diverse than adults at younger ages. When compared to young and middle adulthood there are greater variations among older individuals in terms of cognitive and physical abilities, health status, and housing and financial situations (Consedine, Magai, & Conway, 2004; Settersten, 2006). There are also dramatic differences within late adulthood when comparing the *young-old, old-old,* and *oldest-old,* distinctions that are often made because of the increasing numbers of years we spend in this stage of life.

Your Thoughts?

What might lead to greater diversity among older adults, or conversely more similarity among young adults?

In spite of their diversity and personal challenges, studies find that older adults are generally *more* satisfied with their lives than young adults or those in middle age (George, 2006). One contributing factor to this finding may be the use of mature, adaptive coping strategies that offer a sense of control and influence. In this section we consider some of the many ways to conceptualize or model coping strategies and then focus on the three strategies most associated with lifespan developmental psychology.

Nondevelopmental Models of Coping

There are many frameworks around which to conceptualize coping methods. One popular and long-standing way of describing cognitive coping strategies is through the use of coping mechanisms. These mechanisms can range from the more deliberately used and adaptive, such as humor, to the more involuntary, immature, and maladaptive, such as extreme denial of a source of stress (Vaillant, 2000). Another framework for conceptualizing coping strategies is to divide strategies by focus, particularly into problem-focused and emotion-focused categories. Problem-focused strategies are aimed at searching for workable solutions or resolutions to the issues creating the stress. Emotion-focused coping is generally used when the target or source of the stress cannot be changed or eliminated. When a stressor is not likely to fade or disappear soon, our only option may be to adjust our own emotional reactions and responses (Sasaki & Yamasaki, 2007). Studies show that problem-focused coping tends to decrease with age while the results are mixed on the use of emotion-focused coping in late adulthood (Lachapelle & Hadjistavropoulos, 2005; Osowiecki & Compas, 1998). Both of these frameworks, originating in clinical and counseling psychology, have been useful in developmental psychology, offering ways to describe the methods adults use when coping with age-related changes.

Your Thoughts?

Do you think the ratio of problem-focused to emotion-focused coping changes across adulthood? Why or why not?

ON THE LEADING EDGE
Mindfulness Training

Although mindfulness-based stress reduction (MBSR) was developed over two decades ago, the therapy aimed at sustained stress reduction is now finding application in the field of nursing. MBSR training teaches nurses to observe their thoughts and emotions but to let them fade. The individual practicing MBSR will not focus on emotions, particularly negative emotions, but let those pass and remain focused on the immediate moment. During MBSR training participants are taught to scan their bodies for tension and instructed in meditation techniques. As high stress and burnout are common among healthcare providers, organizations are finding MBSR a valuable tool (Praissman, 2008).

The nursing profession has a long history as a high-stress and high-burnout occupation. Among the frequently cited issues are the long hours and often physically exhausting work, compounded by the feelings of helplessness in light of the physician-controlled environment. No matter what may be happening in their own personal lives or with other patients, while at work nurses are expected to give continual emotional support to each patient. For the nurses whose patients are the most critically ill, they are expected to cope with the intensity of observing patients and their families deal with pain, suffering, and death on a daily basis. In recent years the nursing field had experienced shortages, which has increased the emotional and physical workload placed on those who remain. As many as 15–30% of all nurses do not continue in the profession, and one reason for that is likely to be the great amounts of stress and resulting burnout. The nurses who do experience burnout and choose to remain in the profession often experience physical and psychological problems (Cohen-Katz, Wiley, Capuano, Baker, & Shapiro, 2004, 2005).

Sharon Praissman, a nurse practitioner with the Community Psychiatric Program at Johns Hopkins Bayview Medical Center in Baltimore, Maryland, surveyed the research on mindfulness in the primary psychological and health-related databases published between 2000 and 2006. Not only did she find MBSR to be successful in reducing stress, she also noted no negative outcomes from the use of MBSR (Praissman, 2008). One example of the kinds of programs Praissman surveyed is that reported by researchers from the Lehigh Valley Hospital and Health Network in Allentown, Pennsylvania, who have developed and implemented an MBSR program for nurses.

Joanne Cohen-Katz, Ph.D., from the Department of Family Medicine, and her colleagues Susan Wiley, M.D., Terry Capuano, M.S.N., Debra Baker, M.A., and Shauna Shapiro, Ph.D., conducted both a quantitative and qualitative study of MBSR. In the testing phase, an 8-week program was offered to all nurses affiliated with the health network. Those who were interested were placed in either the MBSR program (the treatment group) or told the workshops were full and that they needed to wait until the next program started (the wait-list control or comparison group).

When comparing data gathered from those who participated and those who did not (the wait-list control group), the researchers found that completing the MBSR program reduced emotional exhaustion and depersonalization. Nurses who learned to use the mindfulness techniques felt less strain on their emotions in general while experiencing more emotional investment in their patients. The MBSR workshop leaders and the researchers felt that the program was a great success. They encourage other institutions and educational programs to incorporate mindfulness in their human resources curriculum and to provide ongoing support and follow-up for their employees (Cohen-Katz, Wiley, Capuano, Baker, & Shapiro, 2004, 2005).

Developmental Regulation

One of the guiding principles in lifespan developmental psychology is the assumption that each stage or phase of life has the potential for both gains and losses. Late adulthood is distinct from young and middle adulthood in that there will be periods in old age when the losses are greater than the gains (Settersten, 2006). Gains can be made, such as making new friends or gaining lifelong insight and wisdom, but chances are there will be times when the losses and reduction in resources will dominate our perspective (Riediger & Freund, 2006). To achieve optimal or successful aging, a goal that also serves as a guiding principle in developmental psychology, individuals are encouraged to maximize gains as much as possible while adjusting to changes and losses as they come (Settersten, 2006).

The coping theory of ***developmental regulation*** offers a strategy for maintaining a sense of personal control over our situation, which is likely to contribute to successful aging. Using the processes of primary and secondary control, developmental regulation serves as a way to directly influence personal development and adjust to uncontrollable constraints. Primary control involves gaining functional control through actively changing our immediate physical and social surroundings (Heckhausen, 1997). An older adult who rearranges items in her kitchen so that she doesn't have to bend her knees or get on the floor to get frequently used items is exerting primary control. She may also exert primary control over her social environment by learning to send text messages with her phone or baking items for her neighbors as a way to stay in contact with them. Believing that we have the ability and power to exert influence over a situation, causing the desired response, will ease stress and increase confidence. That belief will also motivate us to not only react when challenges arise but also to engage in coping through proactive means in an attempt to prevent future stressors. The use of primary control generally increases in young adulthood, peaks in middle adulthood, and decreases at the end of life (Magai, 2001).

Whereas primary control generally involves outward or external actions, secondary control involves deliberately adjusting our internal sense of self, identity, and motivation to cope with external changes (Heckhausen, 1997). Also different from primary control, secondary control can increase throughout life. Secondary control relies to a greater extent on personal reflections for adaptation and goal setting (Magai, 2001). An older adult who realizes that his physical abilities are changing such that he has trouble maintaining his home may start imagining himself as a resident in an assisted living center. He may use secondary control to shift his identity by thinking of himself as among the youngest and most vibrant of those in the center, thus having some advantages the other residents do not have. He may focus on the notion that in an assisted-living center he will have more time for things that are fun, rather than worrying about cleaning and fixing items around his house.

Your Thoughts?

What parallels do you find between primary and secondary control and problem-focused and emotion-focused coping? What differences?

Socioemotional Selectivity Theory

The socioemotional selectivity theory (SST) emphasizes, as its name suggests, coping with stresses through the selection of social relationships that are most likely to foster positive emotions (Burnett-Wolle & Godbey, 2007; Carstensen, 1992; Carstensen, Mikels, & Mather, 2006). Most people maintain the size of their social support network until very late in life. Finding and maintaining productive, helpful social connections may prove to be a challenge with age, as generally those in their 80s and older will experience the shrinking of their social convoys. There are several theories as to why this occurs. ***Decremental theories*** emphasize the losses due to the deaths of friends and relatives along with the loss of energy and awareness that is associated with old age. ***Selectivity theories,*** on the other hand, emphasize the ability of older adults to better choose their friends based on years of experience. These theories acknowledge that older adults may not have as much energy for friendships as they did when they were younger, and because they have limited resources they choose to associate only with the most enjoyable of their friends and most reliable of their sources of social support. In contrast to the findings of smaller friendship groups with age, researchers have found instances in which friendship networks increase for older adults, usually occurring when there is a crisis or other special circumstances. No matter what age, by maintaining a reliable social support network we provide ourselves with a cushion or buffer through which to interact with the world. Adults who have developed a convoy have more resources and receive more practical help in difficult times than those without such networks. They also have better mental health and a greater sense of well-being (Antonucci, 2001; Siebert, Mutran, & Reitzes, 1999), all of which increases the potential of coping successfully with the challenges of late adulthood.

The SST is built on the assertion that emotional regulation and knowledge acquisition, the two primary reasons for social interaction, shift in importance with age (Riediger,

Li, & Lindenberger, 2006). In young adulthood we are focused on preparing for the long life ahead of us, thus the goal of knowledge acquisition is dominant in social relationships. The shift that takes place in middle adulthood and continues into late adulthood is not necessarily motivated by a sense of dread and doom, but rather may be a realistic awareness that no one is immune to death and everyone's years of high-quality life are limited. As this sense of a limited, shorter life intensifies, we shift our perspective on life from a focus on knowledge gathering to ***emotional regulation*** (Riediger et al., 2006), which is the ability to monitor and adjust emotional direction and intensity by managing the experience of positive and negative emotions (Carstensen, 1992; Carstensen et al., 2006; Consedine et al., 2004). For example, a recent meta-analysis of studies involving interviews on emotional topics found that with age the use of positive emotion words significantly increases (see Figure 12.1). When considering relationships, older adults are aware that they have limited time and energy, and as such are motivated to select and maintain only the social relationships that are the most meaningful, emotionally close, and positive in terms of emotional response (Magai, 2001; Pennebaker & Stone, 2003; Riediger & Freund, 2006). Older adults value close relationships that provide social support, companionship, and assistance, resulting in positive emotional responses, healthy adaptation to change, and successful aging (Magai, 2001).

Your Thoughts?

What might motivate younger adults to maintain social relationships that are not emotionally positive?

The SST emphasizes the role of emotions more than the other coping models based on developmental theory. Studies show that emotional responses grow more complex with age, maintaining the same intensity as in young adulthood but activated less often in older adults. There is a debate as to whether this decrease in activation is a blunting of emotions, consistent with decremental theories, or a sign that older adults are better at regulating or managing their emotions (Magai, 2001), consistent with selectivity theories. Carstensen, who developed the SST, believes that older adults are purposeful in adjusting their social networks in order to maximize gains made in emotionally positive or helpful relationships and avoid relationships that increase emotional risks. Referencing one of the primary principles in developmental theory that each stage has gains and losses, one of the gains made in late adulthood is increased emotional regulation, resulting in the experience of more positive emotions and greater sense of personal well-being (Carstensen, 1992; Carstensen et al., 2006; Consedine et al., 2004).

Your Thoughts?

How would you design a study to find out if or how young and middle-aged adults evaluate their friendships and end them if needed?

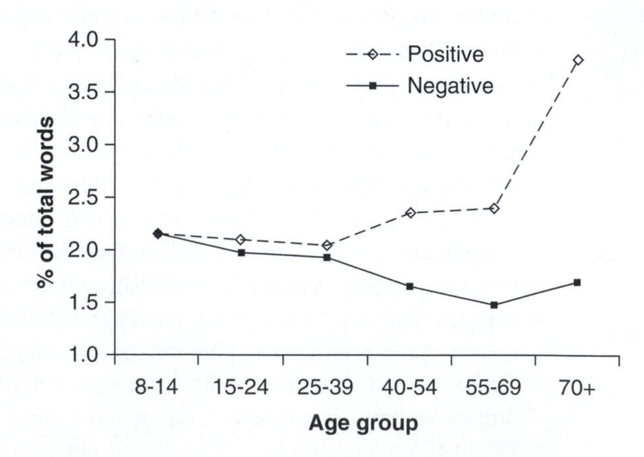

FIGURE 12.1 ***Pennebaker and Stone (2003) graphed the use of positive and negative emotion words across the life span, illustrating the dramatic difference in late adulthood.***

From Pennebaker & Stone (2003, p. 296). Copyright by the American Psychological Association. Reprinted with permission.

Selection, Optimization, and Compensation

The selection, optimization, and compensation (SOC) model, which was discussed in Chapter 1 as an overarching approach to adult development (Baltes, Staudinger, & Lindenberger, 1999; Riediger et al., 2006), is often effectively applied to circumstances requiring coping and support in late adulthood. A credit to the popularity, flexibility, and applicability of the SOC model, it has been applied to many areas including overall life management and the domains of health, relationships, and cognition in adult development (Burnett-Wolle & Godbey, 2007). The SOC model is one of several exploring coping, similar to the dual-process assimilation and accommodation model developed by Brandtstadter. This approach to coping highlights the interaction of *assimilation,* adjusting personal circumstances to cope with a situation judged to be negative or disappointing, and *accommodation,* the process of adjusting goals, often by lowering expectations to better cope with problematic and disappointing situations (Reidiger et al., 2006; Rothermund & Brandtstadter, 2003).

Your Thoughts?

How might identifying goals in the SOC model differ from creating a to-do list? How might the process or outcome differ from New Year's resolutions?

The selection aspect of the SOC involves surveying resources, including time and energy, determining priorities, and identifying goals (Burnett-Wolle & Godbey, 2007). In coping with a diagnosis of cancer, for example, imagine a hypothetical character named Jessica, a 72-year-old married woman, who engages the SOC process by reevaluating her priorities and goals in light of her new circumstances. It's likely that anyone who first receives a diagnosis of cancer will feel overwhelmed with emotions, information, and concern from others. Jessica can use selection aspect of the SOC to focus her attention on her most important needs, desires, and tasks, while ignoring things now determined to be distractions (Riediger & Freund, 2006). Soon after the initial shock Jessica will likely find new resources, such as local support groups for people with cancer, as well as groups her husband may join as a loved one of someone in cancer treatment. It is also likely that Jessica will lose some resources, such as the social interaction she had through her volunteer work at the local library, which she chose to stop. Even without such a difficult situation as Jessica's, it is expected that in the transition from middle age to late adulthood we will increasingly demonstrate motivational selectivity,

Following the SOC model, the adult with a cancer diagnosis who chooses to make becoming a cancer survivor a top priority will likely spend a great deal of time researching the disease and the latest treatments while letting other activities go.

much like emotional selectivity, restricting our focus to the most important areas of life and limiting the number of high-priority goals (Riediger & Freund, 2006).

The optimization aspect of the SOC model is demonstrated in the motivation to maximize performance on our selected goals. This may involve learning new information or skills, networking, or calling on others for help (Burnett-Wolle & Godbey, 2007). If Jessica selects the goal of becoming a cancer survivor as her top priority, then she may spend a great deal of time on the Internet, the phone, and with support groups to find out everything she can about the particular type of cancer she has and the best treatments. She and her husband may even choose to move to another location in order to be closer to a particular health care facility or medical specialist. In addition to selecting priorities and optimizing efforts and resources, the compensation piece of the SOC model involves adjusting to limitations, constraints, and losses (Burnett-Wolle & Godbey, 2007). In coping with limitations such as being unable to drive after treatments, Jessica may compensate by calling on relatives, friends, and neighbors to help when her husband cannot take her or pick her up. She may compensate for the loss in social interaction she experienced when volunteering by inviting people to her home and spending more time on the phone and using email. It's likely in a situation such as this hypothetical but realistic one that Jessica would apply the SOC coping strategy in many situations to manage both her immediate daily needs as well as the large-scale changes in her lifestyle and perspective.

Your Thoughts?

What parallels do you see between the SOC model and problem-focused and emotion-focused coping? What differences?

Section Summary

- Late adulthood presents new challenges as adults enter their elderly years.
- Coping mechanisms, problem-focused and emotion-focused coping strategies are among the most popular nondevelopmental models of coping.
- Developmental regulation highlights differences between primary control, which peaks in middle adulthood, and secondary control, which increases in strength and effectiveness throughout adulthood.
- The SST emphasizes the role of emotional regulation in coping by encouraging older adults to surround themselves with only the closest, most positive and supportive relationships.
- The SOC model encourages older adults to survey their resources and select reasonable goals and priorities, optimize their resources with a focus on achieving those goals, and to use their resources to compensate for losses.
- While considered a meta-theory and applied to many areas of life, the SOC model is well suited as a coping strategy for older adults who are adjusting to limited resources and abilities.

Coping and Adaptive Technology

In the broadest sense of the term, assistive technologies are abundant in the lives of many adults of all ages. Work-at-home adults can use the Internet to earn an income while remaining at home to care for children or elderly parents. Many adults use PDAs (personal data assistants) and smart phones to keep track of email, tasks, reminders, and a host of other items. Many Americans rely on Internet connections to keep up with personal finances, health information, social relationships, and entertainment. It makes sense that experts are developing items that will extend the use of personal technologies to assist older adults as well. The technology exists to do so many things that would help older adults remain independent, as seen in the promising field of robotics and the development of "smart houses" full of monitoring devices (Cutler, 2006). So why aren't those technologies a part of older adults' lives now? The development of such products requires more than simply the ability to do so. The products must be profitable to those who create, manufacture, and sell the items while also available, affordable, and embraced by older adults, the medical community, and the health care industry.

Environmental Gerontology

The study of the use of adaptive or assistive technologies as coping tools for older adults is part of a larger field of study known as ***environmental gerontology***, which is the study of the ways adults and their environments function and interact as both are changing with age. When considering coping strategies, particularly those aimed at functioning well and aging successfully, it's also important that we notice how our homes, neighborhoods, and larger communities are changing over time. Just like younger adults who may find that their once adequate apartment may be too small when starting a family, older adults may find their environment is not meeting their current needs and desires. Circumstances that were once nonissues, such as managing a house with stairs or driving on a busy highway, may become difficult and anxiety provoking with advanced age. Even a task that was a pleasure years earlier, such as caring for a large yard, may come to feel like an unnecessary chore and burden (Scheidt & Windley, 2006).

> **Your Thoughts?**
>
> How might socioeconomic status influence these circumstances? How might financial resources influence an older adult's responses to these challenges?

Much of the research in environmental gerontology has focused on home environments, though it has extended out into neighborhoods and larger areas as well (Wahl, 2001). As the focus of this chapter shifts to the use of adaptive technologies, it's important to remember that older adults adapt by changing their behaviors as well as their environment. When trying to remain independent in our homes as long as possible, we must find workable coping strategies for handling everyday, routine situations that have grown more challenging with age. For example, in a study comparing the adjustments made by younger and older adults as they carried groceries up a set of stairs, Kemper, Herman, and Nartowicz (2005) found that younger adults engaged in multitasking by talking in shorter, less complex sentences while climbing the stairs. The older adults chose to divide the tasks by alternating talking and climbing the stairs. It is common for older adults to prioritize sensory functions and safe motor movement over cognitive functioning when the domains are in conflict (Riediger & Lindenberger, 2006), and that in itself is a coping-related decision. Whether it is considering concerns in the home, such as loose rugs and poor lighting (Wahl, 2001), or outdoor concerns such as uneven sidewalks and availability of elderly-friendly public transportation, the goal of those who work in environmental gerontology is to create the best person–environment fit. Optimal aging may require changes in our thoughts and behaviors as well as changes in our living environment (Scheidt & Windley, 2006).

> **Your Thoughts?**
>
> What environmental changes are needed to make your local neighborhood or university campus more welcoming and comfortable for older adults?

Adaptive Technology and Older Adults

At all ages we are likely to gain valuable tips from our peers and older adults are no exception. Whether it is chatting at the park, grocery, medical clinic, or over a card game, older adults are likely to discuss everything from what helps them sleep at night to how they get their lawn work done to which restaurants have the largest-print menus and the best lighting. It's also likely that older adults will be encouraged by health care providers, loved ones, and others in their social network to try various technologies and modifications as ways to cope with their changing bodies and minds. A recent study of older adults living independently in their own homes found that approximately half have made some modifications to the structure, such as adding handrails in the bathroom, to accommodate their changing needs (Joint Center for Housing Studies, 2001). Changes that help older adults feel safer and more functional will reduce some of the worry and anxiety experienced by loved ones and may reduce the time or number of tasks needed from a caregiver. In some cases the cost of the technology may be less

> **Your Thoughts?**
>
> What generational or cohort differences would you predict might influence the preference for either a technological solution or a trained caregiver?

than the cost involved in hiring a person to take care of the same task (Cutler, 2006). For example, purchasing and programming a watch to sound an alarm when an older adult should take medicines would be much less expensive than hiring someone to stop by that individual's home to make sure the medicine was taken.

Whether applying the principles of primary control as part of developmental regulation, or any part of the SOC model, these coping strategies involve taking control and making decisions. Often when technologies are involved there are several ways to accomplish the same goal, and it's important that adult children and others in their social network allow older adults to exercise choice. For example, in some cases adaptive technology can be applied to either the environment or the individual (Scialfa & Fernie, 2006). An individual who is having trouble hearing the sound from the television may choose an adaptation to the environment, an amplifier added to the television, or may choose a personal adaptation, a hearing aid. The ability to exercise personal control by choosing their preferred strategy will increase an older adult's sense of well-being (George, 2006).

Adaptive technology can be applied to many personal needs, from the most basic to the most sophisticated. Among the most basic and yet most important skills for remaining independent is functioning in the bathroom. The most common physical problems in the bathroom are associated with the lack of space around the toilet and shower, particularly if a wheelchair is involved, and the ease of transitioning from any adaptive device (i.e., wheelchair, walker, cane) to the toilet or a bench in the shower. If an older adult is trying to cope with cognitive problems related to functioning in the bathroom, a different strategy is needed. The simple solution may be to have someone accompany the older adult or check on them when finished in the bathroom, but that takes time and patience, and may even be costly if it involves hiring a home care provider. Computer vision systems and artificial intelligence software have the potential to monitor movement in the bathroom and give verbal prompts when needed to those with dementia or other cognitive impairments (Scialfa & Fernie, 2006).

Your Thoughts?

If user-friendly and affordable, what might be some other applications for this technology around the house? For hospitals? For community centers and businesses?

Although the term *technology* may bring to mind visions of cutting-edge high-tech gadgets, adaptive technologies vary in levels of complexity. When older adults have difficulty moving around they may choose to use a cane, one of the oldest and simplest adaptations, or a walker, a metal frame that may or may not have wheels and a fold down seat for resting. On the other hand, depending on their level of disability, older adults may choose a wheelchair or a scooter. Wheelchairs vary in terms of ability to get into tight spaces, center of gravity and risk of tipping, radius for turning, and various types of sophisticated computer adaptations for powered movement. Scooters, which generally work better for outdoor movement, have many of the same characteristics along with swiveling chairs (Cutler, 2006; Scialfa & Fernie, 2006). From simple walking sticks to computerized scooters with GPS (global positioning systems) and built-in smart phones, technologies vary in complexity and cost.

The concept of person–environment fit is critical when considering the complexities of particular technologies. While younger adults are probably very familiar with computers and software-related technologies, there are likely to be some older adults who find anything like that uncomfortable and intimidating (Cutler, 2006; Scialfa & Fernie, 2006). Some older adults may shy away from a complicated watch, PDA, or smart phone with calendar reminders, opting for a standard, simple wall calendar instead. (It may also be that the watch, PDA, or smart phone has displays that are too small to read, buttons that are too small and hard to push, and alarms that are not loud enough.) On the other hand, there are many older adults who are embracing new technologies. I have many friends in their late 70s and early 80s who are quite savvy at getting around on the Internet, using their digital cameras and emailing pictures, and have mastered specialized software. One particular friend, the woman to whom this book is dedicated, is amazing at converting digital images into embroidery patterns for her computerized sewing machine while another does a high-quality job with desktop publishing for his

Your Thoughts?

Would you find it adaptive or insulting to give a child's television remote or a child's clock to an older adult because it is more user-friendly?

While there are many useful technologies available to those who can afford them, it is important that an older adult feel comfortable with an assistive device.

religious community. The concept of person–environment fit reminds us that there is no "one solution fits all" in most cases. A device cannot be adaptive or assistive if the person who could benefit from it chooses not to use it.

Technology and Older Drivers

Certainly automobiles, particularly the latest models with computerized technology, are among the most sophisticated mobility devices to which most people have access. Although vehicles are generally not thought of as assistive technologies, they do represent a form of person–environment interaction that helps older adults meet their needs in their own community. Having the independence, freedom, and decision-making power of being able to choose when and where to drive enhances most adults' quality of life. Personal transportation allows older adults to take control of their time, choose when and where to purchase and gather resources, and maintain social interactions as desired. On the other hand, it is clear that this technology has the potential to cause great harm to an older adult driver and others on the road. Except for very young adults, older adults are involved in more accidents than adults of younger ages. The automotive industry has responded with some changes, such as adding antiglare glass, variable-speed windshield wipers, and daytime running lights. Many roads now have reflective paints and rumble strips to assist drivers as well (Scialfa & Fernie, 2006).

Your Thoughts?

Should more money be spent on increasing public transportation or improving personal vehicles for elderly drivers? Give reasons to support your opinion.

Often older adults realize they are not as competent to drive as they once were, and they will voluntarily make adjustments. They will choose their routes carefully, avoid congested areas, drive when the traffic is light, and avoid driving at night or in bad weather. These adaptations are evident in the findings that, although older drivers do have many accidents, they are much less likely to be involved in accidents when the weather is bad or at night (Sommer, Falkmer, Bekiaris, & Panou, 2004). Older drivers will also combine errands in order to drive fewer miles and drive at slower speeds (Bauer, Adler, Kuskowski, & Rottunda, 2003). Studies have found that older adults are willing to incorporate new technologies for driving because their autonomy and freedom of choice is so very precious to them (Scialfa & Fernie, 2006). My older friends, for example, have embraced GPS navigation systems in their cars that give verbal directions. They use their devices even in familiar surroundings just so they don't miss a turn.

Generally, though, older drivers will continue to drive well beyond the point at which they are safe. In a recent study involving 645 drivers age 55 years and older, incorporating many measures of cognitive and physical abilities along with driving habits, researchers found that self-regulation was not enough to reduce the high rate of at-fault car crashes (Ross et al., 2009). As the number of older drivers with reduced physical and cognitive skills increases, the burden of taking away driving privileges is falling on family members and loved ones, state governments via fitness-to-drive evaluations and other laws, and personal physicians (Carr, Duchek, Meuser, & Morris, 2006). I've heard many stories from family members, friends, and acquaintances, usually in their 50s, who had to take a car away from an elderly parent who wasn't safe to drive. Most of them waited until Mom or Dad had an accident before taking action, and thankfully most of the accidents were minor. I've found in these many anecdotal accounts that not only do these adult children understand the personal and social consequences resulting from this blow to their parents' independence, but they realize that their turn will likely come in a decade or so. These conversations often start with "My mother . . ." and end with "I told my children that when I get that old . . ."

Your Thoughts?

Will fitness-to-drive evaluations make a difference in keeping older drivers safe? Why, why not, or under what circumstances?

Computer Literacy and Older Adults

While the use of assistive technology in general increases with age, for current generations of older adults the use of computer software and the Internet decreases in very late adulthood, along with the use of cell phones and ATMs. It is difficult to determine how much of this disuse, and perhaps discomfort, is related to aging alone and how much is attributed to cohort and generational differences (Cutler, 2006). On the one hand, studies find that many websites are not elderly-friendly in terms of their visual and auditory presentation. With their decreasing sensory and motor abilities older adults may find website navigation difficult. Sites with many pop-up windows and moving items can distract older adults and create frustration (Scialfa & Fernie, 2006). On the other hand, some studies do find generational differences. For example, in a recent study of 2,000 adults conducted by the Kaiser Family Foundation (2005), it was found that 70% of those between the ages of 50 and 64 had been online while only 31% of those ages 65 and older had done so. Studies show that with appropriate training, older adults can learn to use computer technology and find they enjoy it (Cutler, 2006).

Your Thoughts?

How would you design a study to compare these 2006 results to current websites older adults might want to visit?

For the older adults who are able and take advantage of it, technologies exist in smart phones and computers that provide many ways for them to find information and engage in social interaction (Scialfa & Fernie, 2006). Exchanging email and locating health-related information are the two most popular uses for the Internet among older adults. Older adults also frequently access community and political information (Cutler, 2006). For some older adults the final nudge to use the Internet may come from adult children and grandchildren who want to share email, pictures, and videos. In some cases, the Internet might even provide some income for older adults who are able to work from home. Particularly for those who are not driving anymore and feel somewhat confined to their homes, being able to shop online, find needed information, and interact socially with loved ones and in supportive online communities can provide needed resources, cognitive stimulation, and social support (Scialfa & Fernie, 2006).

Your Thoughts?

What might be the first steps in introducing older adults to computer use, both in terms of skills and reducing anxiety?

ON THE LEADING EDGE
Person–Computer Fit for Older Adults

Researchers Neil Charness and Walter Boot of the Department of Psychology at Florida State University set out to learn more about the barriers to computer use for older adults. While one might expect generational differences in computer acceptance, and taking into account that individuals in school and those employed may have computer access at those locations, the differences in Internet and computer usage drops dramatically across adulthood. A national survey conducted in 2007 found that 85% of the young adults and 67% of the middle-aged adults surveyed said they had used the Internet in the past year, while only 39% of those 65-74 and 24% of those 75-84 said they had used the Internet in the past year. The same survey asked about using the computer in the last year and the results were similar with less than 40% of those 65 years and older saying they had used a computer in the last 12 months.

After reviewing the literature Charness and Boot (2009) found several barriers that hinder older adults' acceptance of computers and similar technologies, such as smart phones or DVD players. Some of the computer-related anxiety and disinterest may stem from the findings that many computer interfaces are not designed well for older adults. Screens with low contrast items, small print, and lots of distracting movement make it difficult for older adults to get the information they need. Also, whether it is a computer mouse, keyboard, smart phone, or remote control, the buttons need to be well marked, usually large, and easy to push or manipulate.

Another factor is that older adults tend to view a computer as a tool more than a source of entertainment. This is consistent with an earlier study of 12 computer users between the ages of 55 and 84 years old published in 2004 by researchers Michael Hilt and Jeremy Lipschultz from the Department of Communication at the University of Nebraska. The participants used their computers for emailing friends and family and the Internet as a replacement for a library. They tended to avoid browsing, preferring to go straight to the special interest information they were seeking. Even though these participants were good at finding items through the Internet, they still preferred to receive general information through the newspaper, radio, and television (Hilt & Lipschultz, 2004). Charness and Boot (2009) recommend capitalizing on this tendency by developing computer programs that in some way help older adults remain physically and mentally active and independent in their homes as long as possible. One area of promise is computer games and "brain fitness software" programs that challenge older adults to practice the information processing skills that tend to slow with age. Another promising area involves monitoring devices that can communicate with a computer or smart phone to let older adults know that a stove burner is on or that someone is at the door.

Found that rather than viewing the Internet as a place to browse for pleasure, the older adults viewed the Internet as a replacement for a library. They tended to avoid browsing, preferring to go straight to the special interest information they were seeking. Even though these participants were good at finding items through the Internet, they still preferred to receive general information through the newspaper, radio, and television. Based on their research, Hilt and Lipschultz encourage local organizations, such as television stations, radio stations, hospitals, and community groups, to develop an Internet presence that encourages the involvement of older adults and directs them to important, useful information.

The motivation to find health-related information on the Internet is of particular interest to those working with older adults. On any given day more people go to the Internet for medical advice than will actually see a health care professional in person (Scialfa & Fernie, 2006). The Kaiser Family Foundation (2005) survey found that 53% of those ages 50–64 and 21% of those ages 65 and older had searched for health information online. Although experts find that most of the health information online is reliable, much of it is written with too much jargon and high-level vocabulary, and in general is written at a reading level inaccessible to many older adults. Even with the obstacles presented by health literacy, navigation difficulties (Scialfa & Fernie, 2006), and concern that older adults will fall prey to Internet scams and false information (Cutler, 2006), the general consensus is that acquiring access and comfort with the Internet has the potential to greatly enhance the quality of life of older adults.

Your Thoughts?

How might access to Internet-based health information help the relationships between older adults and health care professionals? What problems might it cause?

Section Summary

- The recently developed field of environmental gerontology explores the ways both older adults and their environments change with age.
- The use of various types of adaptive technologies as coping tools in order to remain as independent and functional as possible is of great interest to researchers in environmental gerontology.
- Adaptive or assistive technologies can be applied to basic or complex tasks, and may be simple, like using a cane, or more complex, as can be found in sophisticated motorized, computer-controlled wheelchairs.
- It is important that older adults choose comfortable technologies that will actually be used.
- Generally, older adults voluntarily make adaptations in their driving styles in order to maintain their driving privileges, and consequently a primary part of their personal independence and freedom.
- Exchanging email and locating health-related information are the two most popular uses for the Internet among older adults.

Coping by Accepting Social Support

Whether it is ceasing to drive their car or transitioning to live with an adult child, older adults generally do not want to give up their independence. In the same way, it may feel to some in late adulthood as though they are acknowledging weakness or lack of ability by accepting help from others, particularly if they believe they cannot return the favors and give back in an equal way. Older adults who can exchange a freshly baked pie for lawn care or a trip to the medical clinic will likely feel better about accepting help than older adults who need help with basic activities of daily living and don't have the resources to give much in the way of material items in return. While it may be frustrating, social support can make a dramatic difference in an older adult's quality of life and sense of well-being. This section explores both the influence a social support network may have on an older adult's quality of life, and the resulting effects of helping an older adult on the caregiver. Most often spouses and adult children (Pinquart & Sorensen, 2003), caregivers who provide many hours of assistance to older adults, often have to cope themselves with the stresses of restricting their own needs in order to meet the needs of their loved ones.

Your Thoughts?

What generational or societal factors might contribute to the reluctance some Americans feel to accepting help from other people?

Social Relationships and Support

As demonstrated by several theories of coping, particularly the socioemotional selectivity theory, older adults are wise to surround themselves with people who can help them cope and adapt to the challenges of aging. Social support can be conceptualized as one type of social relationship in an older adult's life, along with companionship, friendships, acquaintance-type relationships, and negative interactions (Krause, 2006b). A social support network is generally defined as a group of people who informally help or are willing to be called on to help a central individual (Greenglass, Fiksenbaum, & Eaton, 2006). The assistance provided to an older adult coping with reduced abilities and resources may include instrumental or physical help, needed information, or emotional support and comfort (Moren-Cross & Lin, 2006).

Your Thoughts?

What might be some of the conflicting feelings an adult might have over the need for an older parent to move into his or her home?

For older adults the primary source of support when available is that person's spouse or partner. If that person is unavailable or unable to help, older adults will often turn to their children, friends, and siblings for support. While adult children may have more resources, older adults are likely to have a better relationship with their friends and siblings who are of a

Spouses are the primary source of support for older adults who need assistance.

similar age and have similar backgrounds. An older adult's relationship with grown children brings with it the relationship's history, no matter whether they've had a good relationship or a bad one over the years, and a generational divide in terms of lifestyle, preferences, and values (Antonucci, 2001).

While it is true that social networks often grow smaller as adults age (Riediger et al., 2006), they will grow in size as an older adult increases in disability (Moren-Cross & Lin, 2006) and in times of crisis or special circumstances (Antonucci, 2001). Comparing the sizes of older adults' closest circles of support, most have five members in their inner circle, though those with lower SES tend to have smaller networks. African Americans also tend to report smaller networks (Antonucci, 2001). Generally, people with larger networks get more help with illness-related needs (Antonucci, 2001), however, that isn't always the case (Moren-Cross & Lin, 2006). One factor in the amount of help received is the length of time help may be needed. Whereas a specific crisis or stressful event is short in duration and requires quick but limited responses from the social network, a chronic condition may last for several months or years. Those offering help with a chronic condition may at some point feel that they are running out of resources and need to back away from the situation if they can (Krause, 2006b).

Your Thoughts?

Who might an older adult turn to if family members are not available or unwilling to offer assistance?

A network of supportive, high-quality relationships has been associated with better general functioning, more proactive coping, and less depression (Antonucci, 2001; Greenglass et al., 2006). Interestingly, *perceived* social support is associated with a sense of well-being; however, a high amount of *actual* support received, especially regarding housing and health issues, is associated with negative well-being (George, 2006). While older adults feel better when they know they have a social safety net if needed, receiving unsolicited support may cause them to feel that they cannot take care of themselves. Most people want to reciprocate and prefer to give more than they receive. It creates a feeling of indebtedness when older adults feel they have received too much without reciprocity. One method of coping is to come up with different ways of reciprocating (Antonucci, 2001) using whatever resources they have. They may offer baked goods, flowers or vegetables from their garden, or even a listening ear or a prayer. Another method of coping is to compensate by developing a way to think about the situation that makes it acceptable, such as by considering times they have helped others, usually earlier in life, and then consider the current unequal relationship to be their reward or payment.

Unfortunately, there are cases of poor social interactions that cannot accurately be called social *support.* Interactions that are conflictual would fall in this category, as well as those contributing to a feeling of overwhelming or unforgiving indebtedness. Negative interactions, such as behaviors or comments that make an older adult feel like a burden or a source of unnecessary stress, are associated with detrimental changes in physical health. While most social interactions are positive and helpful, those exchanges that are negative are more upsetting and seem to draw more mental attention than similar positive interactions (Krause, 2006b). This is an important point for caregivers and adult children to note because it may help explain some misunderstandings. For example, an adult who has a stressful day at work may arrive at her mother's house for a visit looking tired, yawning, and complaining about being too busy. Her mother may interpret this as a negative evaluation ("I feel bad that I'm causing you such problems"), when in reality her daughter's stress has little to do with her.

Your Thoughts?

What subtle behaviors from a caregiver might make an individual feel like a burden or source of stress?

Relationships that encourage or enable destructive behaviors are also examples of poor social influence. Any interactions that make it easy for older adults to get away from healthy eating, exercise, or other medical advice and fall into bad habits such as smoking or drinking too much are ultimately destructive (Antonucci, 2001). It may be fun in the moment to see someone's face light up when you bring them those forbidden items, but in the long run such behaviors may cause significant problems.

A Closer Look at Caregivers

In the 1980s researchers, social workers, and medical professionals started to take interest in the unique and challenging stresses placed on those members of social support networks who spent the most hours in caregiving. The focus of caregiving research is primarily spouses who provide the greatest amount of support, but also includes adult children (Pearlin, Pioli, & McLaughlin, 2001) and even grandchildren and adolescents in the family who participate in caregiving (Dellmann-Jenkins, Blankemeyer, & Pinkard, 2001; Ng, Loong, Liu, & Weatherall, 2000). There are positive feelings that stem from caregiving, such as knowing that a loved one is being cared for appropriately and that other related items, such as financial or housing issues, are under control. There may also be some secondary reinforcement in realizing the amount of money being saved by caring for a loved one informally. That said, the focus of much of the research has been on the stresses of caregiving, and there are many. Often caregiving takes a great deal of time, energy, and attention, requiring major adjustments to prior routines. For a spouse or a caregiver who lives with an older adult, the care can be an around-the-clock responsibility. Caregivers may find themselves in what feels like a lose–lose situation. A cycle of guilt can develop from the mental debate over feeling guilty about letting tasks and responsibilities go in order to provide care; however, if one stops caregiving to address those responsibilities then there is guilt over neglecting the older adult and not providing care (Pearlin et al., 2001).

Your Thoughts?

What factors might contribute to the finding that most caregivers are female? What factors might contribute to the fewer number of male caregivers?

Pinquart and Sorensen have conducted a series of meta-analyses exploring the characteristics of caregivers. In their 2003 analysis of 84 studies they found that most caregivers are female, in their early 60s, and either the spouse or the adult child of the care recipient. Taking an average across the studies, caregivers provide just over 40 hours of care per week for 4½ years. Those receiving care are usually in their 70s and equally as likely to be male or female. An important finding was that in comparing caregivers and noncaregivers with otherwise similar characteristics, Pinquart and Sorensen (2003) found that there were no differences in physical health but significant differences in psychological health. Caregivers have more depression, personal stress, and report a poorer sense of well-being. In a later meta-analysis of 116 studies, Pinquart and Sorensen (2005) found small but significant differences when comparing ethnic groups. Ethnic minority caregivers were more likely than white caregivers to be younger, come from a lower socioeconomic status background, provide more care, feel more responsibility toward caregiving, and were less likely to be a spouse. Again finding more depression among caregivers, Pinquart and Sorensen found that Hispanic and Asian Americans demonstrated the greatest depression, African Americans presented the least, and white caregivers showed a midrange level of depression.

Your Thoughts?

What practical things can family and friends do to ease the stress and depression experienced by the primary caregiver?

It is important for caregivers to realize that there may be help available for themselves and for the person in their care. Many government programs have been established to assist older adults and their caregivers, such as those associated with the Older Americans Act (Administration on Aging, 2010). For example, caregivers can often find support groups in their area. Acknowledging that it may be difficult for caregivers to leave for an extended time, involvement in a support group can provide useful information as well as social interaction with a group sympathetic to their situation. A quick search on the Internet will reveal many organizations, online support groups, and helpful websites. The National Cancer Institute (2007), for example, provides a printed and online booklet titled *Caring for the Caregiver* that offers instrumental help as well as emotional comfort for caregivers, reminding them to be realistic about their abilities, to acknowledge their own emotions, to ask for help, and to make time to take care of themselves. There are also resources available for family members who are not in the same geographic location as their loved one, often called *long-distance caregiving.*

Your Thoughts?

In what ways might an Internet support group ease the stress and depression experienced by the primary caregiver? Could such a group cause any problems?

Section Summary

- A helpful way to cope with the challenges of aging is to turn to trustworthy family members, friends, and neighbors.
- Social networks generally get smaller with age, but they will increase as an older adult experiences more disability and when a crisis occurs.
- Older adults who have a highly supportive social network are likely to demonstrate better overall functioning, more proactive coping, and less depression.
- On average, those providing the most care are female, in their 60s, and either the spouse or the adult child of the care recipient.
- Caregivers often experience a restricted personal life and higher levels of stress and depression.

Religiosity, Coping, and Aging

As demonstrated by the growing numbers of research articles and the number of chapters and references in the recent *Handbook of Psychology and Aging* and *Handbook of Aging and the Social Sciences,* the social sciences are interested and active in exploring the role of religiosity and spirituality in aging (Idler, 2006). The interest in ***religiosity***, the behaviors and activities related to a religious community, and ***spirituality***, one's sense of inner harmony, faith, and personal beliefs, as they relate to health and coping has played a key role in this growing interest

Your Thoughts?

Do you find the distinction between religiosity and spirituality helpful or confusing? Give reasons for your response.

among researchers, medical professionals, therapists, and counselors (Idler, 2006; Krause, 2006a). In our quest to understand adult development and aging we need to acknowledge what role religious beliefs, practices, and culture play in the lives of those adults who are committed and invested in a particular tradition. Whether you consider yourself religious or not, it is hard to ignore the influence of the predominant religion(s) on the cultural norms and traditions of a society. Whether it is determining calendar holidays and traditional observances, laying a foundation for moral attitudes and behaviors, or giving guidelines for the way people mark special events such as births, weddings, and funerals—all have historical roots in religious practices. In this section we step back from our focus on coping to consider some views of aging from some of the major world religions and consider a lifespan developmental approach to religion before exploring the interplay of coping and religion.

Religious Views of Aging

Few modern religions emphasize or celebrate late adulthood and aging, and generally the ones that do are Eastern rather than Western religions. While Judaism, Christianity, and Islam offer texts encouraging adherents to respect parents and elders, age is not emphasized as it is in Hinduism and Confucianism. Hindu literature describes a set of four distinct periods of life that involve stages of study, marriage/family, retirement, and renunciation. The student stage begins in puberty, leading to the stage of settling in marriage, having a family, and investing in work. The retirement stage begins with the birth of grandchildren. The stage of renunciation is expected to give an individual time to prepare for death so that the final transition comes without anxiety. These last two stages in life involve turning attention away from earthly and natural pleasures and toward spiritual practices and pursuits. Rather than stages, Confucianism emphasizes five relationships, three of which directly involve age differences: parent–child, older sibling–younger sibling, and older friend–younger friend. The other two relationships are husband–wife and ruler–subject.

In most religions, the rites of passage and celebrations are youth-focused, including some version of baptism, circumcision, confirmation, coming-of-age rituals, and recognition of marriages and births. Hinduism has a ceremony that marks the transition in the last stage of renunciation, and in the Jewish Seder the eldest male has a distinct place of honor and a special role in the ceremony. There are very few rituals designed to mark a transition to middle adulthood or to late adulthood. Although almost all religions have end-of-life rituals, they are not specifically aimed at older adults, as those practices would take place regardless of the age of the dying individual. Certainly, the major religions welcome older adherents, and often religious communities work diligently to take care of their older members. In terms of doctrine, theology, or ritual celebrations, however, middle age and late adulthood are largely ignored. Researchers have found that rituals can be psychologically powerful (Idler, 2006). Middle-aged and older adults might benefit from rituals that are designed to celebrate their milestones and accomplishments.

Your Thoughts?

What milestone or turning point could be celebrated as a rite of passage for entering middle adulthood? For entering late adulthood?

Adult Religious Development

Much of the activity in the field of psychology of religion has focused on measuring or determining which characteristics are more common among religious people, and how they are similar or different from nonreligious people. Unfortunately, little work has been focused on understanding religiosity itself and how it develops across adulthood (McFadden, 1999; Spilka, Hood, Hunsberger, & Gorsuch, 2003). Fowler's theory of ***faith development*** is one of the few models of religiosity across the lifespan, offering insight into adult religious development. Fowler extended work in the areas of cognitive development and moral development,

Your Thoughts?

How might the religious needs of a young adult differ from those of an older adult?

RESEARCH IN-DEPTH
Using Large Databanks

The 1998 General Social Survey (GSS), produced by the National Opinion Research Center (NORC) at the University of Chicago, provides a perfect example of a large database made available to all researchers for analysis. Staff at the NORC were able to survey thousands of Americans on a wide variety of topics. Once the data was stored in a useable format, any researcher could access pieces of the data for analysis. Shahabi and her colleagues (2002), representing several universities and institutions, chose to use the data from the 1998 GSS to explore spirituality. In order to do this, however, the researchers had to manipulate the survey data before any specific analyses could occur. They began with information from 1,422 adults who responded to the religion portion of the survey. The first action the researchers took was to calculate the descriptive statistics for their whole sample. They found that the average age was 45 years old, and that most of the adults were between 28 and 62 years old. They found that 55% were female, 79% were white, 47% were married, and 35% lived in urban areas.

Many different religion-related questions were asked, thus the researchers needed to decide which items to use to determine which participants were "spiritual," which were "religious," which were both, and which were neither. After considering the possibilities, Shahabi and her colleagues decided to sort the participants in four groups based on the questions, "To what extent do you consider yourself a spiritual person?" and "To what extent do you consider yourself a religious person?" For each question there were four response options ranging from 1 (very spiritual or religious) to 4 (not at all spiritual or religious). The researchers then used these self-rankings to conduct statistical analyses with other variables in order to find significant associations or relationships. Individuals who chose 1 or 2 for the spiritual question were labeled "spiritual" and those who chose 3 or 4 were labeled "not spiritual." The same was done for religion. Now, with these designations, the researchers can place each participant into one of four groups: Spiritual/Religious, Spiritual Only, Religion Only, and Neither. The researchers were most interested in spirituality and religiosity, so they excluded the Neither group from the rest of the analyses. The next step was to compare each of the remaining three groups to each other on a wide variety of items from the original survey.

The researchers chose to work with a wide variety of variables, such as social and demographic items (i.e., age, sex, ethnicity), religious denomination, religious or spiritual activities, religious beliefs, items reflecting psychological well-being, and levels of intolerance. They found that participants who were more likely to rate themselves high in spirituality were also more likely to be female, younger, have higher educational achievement, and indicate no religious preference. They were also less likely to have a Catholic background. In contrast, those who rated themselves high in religiousness tended to be older, a member of an ethnic minority group, less educated, and live in the southern United States.

Shahabi and her colleagues found that the members of the Spiritual/Religious group engaged in more spiritual or religious activities, such as meditation and Bible reading, than the other groups. They tended to be politically conservative, and along with the Religious Only group, were higher in intolerance than the Spiritual Only group. The members of the Spiritual/Religious group were stronger in the belief that life has a purpose. In contrast, the members of the Spiritual Only group tended to be politically liberal and tended to claim "no religion." They were more likely to engage in some activities, such as meditation, but less likely to engage in others, such as attendance at a worship service or other religious/ritual event. They were more tolerant and they were more likely to indicate that life has no special purpose. The third group studied, members of the Religious Only group, indicated higher levels of distress and cynical mistrust of others.

As is true of any research design there are advantages and disadvantages to using large databanks. In this case the researchers were able to gather data from a large, representative group of Americans, and do it fairly quickly. On the other hand, particularly with such complex issues as religiosity and spirituality, the questions are "forced choice," meaning that the participants must choose the best option of the ones available. Chances are that some participants in the GSS did not find suitable responses to the religion questions and simply skipped them or chose an answer that was the closest available but not truly descriptive of their views. Also, the researchers were limited to the particular questions and responses available in the GSS, and could not contact the participants for follow-up questions. While the limitations and shortcoming of any research should be considered when interpreting the results, there remains much to be learned from the GSS and other large collections of data.

Church attendance is associated with better health and longer life in older adults.

particularly Kohlberg's stages of moral reasoning, to the domain of religious development. Fowler's model, developed primarily with data from American Christian and Jewish samples, is best suited to Western religions.

The first two stages in Fowler's theory of faith development are generally considered childhood and adolescent stages. The first stage, *intuitive–projective faith,* is generally a childhood stage in which the ability to imagine or pretend allows the child to enter into dramatic religious feelings and emotions (Fowler, 1980, 1981, 2001). Often the child in this stage has faith in a Higher Power who has many of the characteristics of a superhero. *Mythic–literal faith,* stage 2, is the point in which one takes on the stories, beliefs, and observances that symbolize belonging to a community. The focus is on literal interpretations of rules and attitudes. This is typically the stage of early and middle childhood; however, as Fowler's data revealed, adults may be found operating in this stage. Here the individual tends to view religion in a concrete way. For example, a child may come to the conclusion that in order to be called an "angel" something must have wings or that in order to be "God" one must be an old man dressed in white.

Through data collection and observation Fowler concluded that the primary stages displayed by most adults in most American churches and synagogues are stage 3, synthetic–conventional faith, and stage 4, individuative–reflective faith. Stage 3, *synthetic–conventional faith,* typically begins in adolescence and continues into young adulthood. In this stage religion becomes personal, developing into a part of our identity. We begin to appreciate personal relationships and our religious heritage. This sense of connection may show itself as a desire to be a full participant in religious activities, as well as through simple means, such as wearing t-shirts, hats, and other displays of our group membership. In terms of coping with the challenges of aging, this stage would pull us toward our religious community, perhaps making it easier to receive their help but also intensifying our desire to participate and reciprocate.

While in this third stage we strive to synthesize values, religious doctrine, and personal identity. Often in this stage, similar to Kohlberg's third stage, *mutual interpersonal relationships,* beliefs and values are accepted from respected authorities without question. Stage 3 is often characterized as a period of conformity due to the high value placed on the expectations and judgments of significant others, including peers and religious leaders.

Stage 4, *individuative–reflective faith,* is commonly found in middle and late adulthood. This stage involves the critical analysis of the tensions or disagreement between evolving personal commitments, beliefs, and attitudes, and those defined by group membership. Whereas religious teachings were accepted in stage 3 as already proven information we should know, the onset of stage 4 brings questions, doubts, and concerns about those once-accepted teachings. In terms of coping with the challenges of aging, stage 4 may accelerate our need to find a way of approaching the gaps in our faith and understanding, perhaps by accepting the unknowns or seeking new or different interpretations. We may find that our doubts prohibit us from finding much comfort in our previous beliefs. It is also in stage 4 that we understand the ever-present conflict between personal needs and community needs. The adult in this stage experiences the tension between the drive for self-fulfillment and self-actualization and the drive to share services and resources with others. For example, when given a bonus at work, we may struggle between the personal need for a new computer and the needs of the religious community to purchase supplies for children's education or food for families in need.

Your Thoughts?

How might people in rural, suburban, and urban communities view community needs differently?

Similar to findings assessing Kohlberg's stages of moral development, these last two stages of faith are not as common among adults as stages 3 and 4. *Conjunctive faith,* Stage 5, can be conceptualized as a resolution to the personal analysis of stage 4. Conjunctive faith involves the reworking of our past beliefs and ideology to integrate our clarified sense of self (the positive and negative aspects) with our honest sense of faith, including the paradoxes and unanswered questions. Fowler sees this stage as one that "generates and maintains vulnerability to the strange truths of those who are 'other'" (1981, p. 198). The breakthrough of stage 5, as Fowler describes it, is the recognition of meaning in traditions, symbols, and rituals, while simultaneously recognizing the limitations and distortions of those very resources. In conjunctive faith we begin to understand the influences of social class, religious tradition, ethnic group, geographic location in the world, and cultural myths on our personal formulations of faith and belief. This understanding allows for greater appreciation of other religious traditions.

Your Thoughts?

Has American society become more tolerant of major world religions over the last 10 years? Give reasons to support your opinion.

The final faith stage is called *universalizing faith.* It is a rare and abstract stage that is, by its very nature, difficult to describe. Stage 6 is embodied in those rare people who have dedicated their lives to their highest religious principles. These individuals have lost their need to preserve their own sense of self or personal desires and have taken on an attitude of reckless abandon in living out their religious purpose (Fowler, 1980, 1981, 2001).

One of the criticisms often leveled at Fowler's theory is that it is too closely aligned with cognitive and moral development. Another criticism is aimed at its linearity, progressing through the six orderly stages, with no provisions for skipping a step or regressing. Clore and Fitzgerald (2002) explored the notion of linear faith development and religiosity with 509 Christians (Catholic) ranging in age from 18 to 84 years old. They found that rather than following a linear sequence, faith development involves revisiting and reworking similar issues. Their analysis did not support the stage model of development. Streib (2001) also acknowledges the benefits of Fowler's theory but argues that Fowler's model is too optimistic and does not explain the concrete, absolute, literal views of some adults.

Slee (2000) found Fowler's theory helpful but not adequate to describe the faith journey of women she interviewed. Slee felt she needed more than Fowler's theory to describe the process women went through. She proposed the addition of six strategies her participants used to work through their stages of faith, specifically:

- Conversational faith: Discussions that clarify thoughts and feelings
- Metaphoric faith: Using analogies that offer new insights
- Narrative faith: Making sense of their spiritual journey by telling their story
- Personalized faith: Gaining insights by engaging with role models
- Conceptual faith: Studying psychological and theological works
- Apophatic faith: Gaining insights by determining what faith is not

Fowler has continued to defend his faith development theory, holding to the belief that the stages offer a structure for understanding the ways people make sense of the religious and spiritual aspects of their lives (Fowler, 2001). His theory, while criticized, remains the most popular view of faith development.

Coping and Religiosity

Your Thoughts?

What lifestyle factors generally associated with the dominant religious groups in your area might lead to better physical and mental health?

Your Thoughts?

Is it immoral for an older adult to get involved in a local religious community for the social support network rather than the belief system?

The general consensus is that religiosity is associated with better overall physical health, mental health (George, 2006; Idler, 2006; Krause, 2006a), longer life, and better treatment outcomes when dealing with serious illness (Idler, 2006), although it is also the consensus that the research is difficult to summarize (George, 2006; Idler, 2006; Krause, 2006a). For example, the most frequently studied religious behavior, church attendance in the Christian tradition, is associated with better health and reduced mortality. What that finding does not provide is insight into why this occurs. One hypothesis is that church attendance increases the likelihood of developing a stronger social support network (Krause, 2006a). Generally, people get more involved with a religious community as they move from young to late adulthood, though the aspects of religious life with which they are involved vary. Some may be seeking personal spiritual development or religious education for their children or grandchildren while others may be seeking a social support network. Religious communities are unique in that they provide a location where it is expected that people of all ages will come together and be supported, a feature that is most appealing to those with a mindset similar to Fowler's third stage. For those in late adulthood many religious communities provide rides, make large-print programs, offer assisted hearing devices, and other assistance to older attendees. In these settings older people can reciprocate as they are able, such as bringing homemade food items for receptions, teaching religious education classes, participating in the choir, or other activities (Idler, 2006).

Research on church attendance also indicates that the behavior decreases with the oldest-old. This could be interpreted as older adults determining that the effort needed to get prepared and get to church is not worth it. It could also be the case that older adults need assistance that is unavailable on Sunday morning. Another option is that older adults may find it more appealing to listen to services on the radio or watch services on television where they can turn up the sound and remain comfortable in their home. Measuring religious behaviors and interpreting them can be very complex and imprecise (Krause, 2006a).

By analyzing archival data from the Institute of Human Development at the University of California, Berkeley, Wink and Dillon (2003) were able to assess the role of religiosity in the lives of 181 adults through records of extensive interviews given when the participants were in their 30s, 50s, 60s, and 70s. They found that both religiosity and spirituality played a beneficial role in adulthood but in distinctly different ways. Greater levels of religiosity were

Your Thoughts?

What might be happening in middle adulthood that would encourage adults to become interested in spiritual development?

related to social involvement in community activities, which provide the basis for meaningful interpersonal relationships. Greater levels of inner spirituality were related to more complex ways of thinking, interest in creative and knowledge-building activities, and wisdom. Wink and Dillon also found that levels of involvement in religious activities tended to remain stable across adulthood while interest and cultivation of spirituality did not become important until middle adulthood.

Section Summary

- There is a growing interest among researchers to understand the interactions between religiosity, health, coping, and aging.
- There is very little in Judaism, Christianity, or Islam that addresses aging, whereas Hinduism and Confucianism have doctrines that draw attention to adult age-related differences and aging.
- Most religious rites of passage are focused on childhood, adolescence, and young adulthood.
- Fowler's stages of faith, incorporating cognitive and moral development, describe a series of six stages moving from a very concrete view of God to an abstract, symbolic perspective.
- Generally, higher levels of religiosity have been associated with better physical and mental health, though the research conclusions are mixed and difficult to summarize.
- Many studies are correlational, thus one cannot tell what aspects or facets of religion actually contribute to better health.

Chapter Summary

Mature, productive coping mechanisms and strategies can play an essential role in successful aging. While useful at any point in adulthood, coping strategies are especially helpful in late adulthood when the losses and reduction of resources can overwhelm the potential gains. Many older adults have access to resources that can help them adjust and adapt to the challenges, such as coping strategies, low-level and sophisticated technologies, social support, and inner strength and resolve. Exerting control and taking advantage of these resources will increase the likelihood of successful aging. Here are some of the main points of the chapter:

- Among the popular but nondevelopmental ways of conceptualizing coping strategies is in terms of types of coping mechanisms and problem-focused or emotion-focused coping strategies.
- The coping strategy of developmental regulation emphasizes the reduction of the deliberate use of primary control in late adulthood and the purposeful increase in use of secondary control.
- The socioemotional selectivity theory (SST) encourages older adults to cope by regulating their emotional responses, primarily by limiting their social interactions to those that are positive and supportive.
- Selection, optimization, and compensation (SOC) encourages older adults to cope with changes by selecting reasonable goals after surveying resources, optimizing their

strengths and resources in achieving those goals, and using their resources to compensate for the inevitable losses.

- Environmental gerontology is the study of the development and interactions of older individuals and their environments over time.
- Adaptive technologies may be simple or complex, and may be applied to very basic or highly sophisticated tasks.
- The issue of driving a car is critical for many older adults who want to remain as independent as possible and retain a great deal of choice over how to spend their time.
- Studies show that in spite of the many accommodations older adults make to preserve their driving privileges, they have many accidents and often drive well beyond the point at which they are safe.
- Among older adults who are willing and able to use the Internet, the most popular uses are to interact with family and friends and to seek information on health, community, and political concerns.
- Social support networks may provide instrumental or physical help, needed information, or emotional support to an older adult, increasing that adult's sense of well-being and overall functioning.
- Social support networks often consist of a spouse or partner, siblings, adult children, close family members and friends, and may include neighbors and community members.
- Those providing informal care for older adults are likely to be females in their 60s who are spouses or adult children.
- Caregivers often provide over 40 hours of care per week for years, resulting for them in a restricted lifestyle with increased depression and stress.
- Eastern religions are more likely to directly address and incorporate aging in their doctrine, while very few religions celebrate any rites of passage that occur in midlife or late adulthood.
- Fowler's stages, which move from a concrete to an abstract stage embracing paradox and diversity in religion, have served as the primary psychological model of adult faith development.
- Higher levels of religiosity and greater religious involvement have been found to be correlated with better physical and mental health, although the research conclusions have been mixed and are difficult to interpret.

Key Terms

Developmental regulation **(312)**
Decremental theories **(313)**
Selectivity theories **(313)**
Emotional regulation **(314)**
Environmental gerontology **(317)**
Religiosity **(325)**
Spirituality **(325)**
Faith development **(326)**

Comprehension Questions

1. What are the three categories of coping mechanisms?
2. What is the primary difference in the target or source of stress when comparing problem-focused and emotion-focused coping strategies?
3. In developmental regulation, how is primary and secondary control similar to problem-focused and emotion-focused coping strategies?
4. How does the SST explain the smaller social circles of older adults?

5. Create an original example of a typical situation in which an older adult could apply the SOC model as a coping strategy, and explain how each piece might work.
6. What is the focus of environmental gerontology?
7. Why is the principle of achieving a good person–environment fit important in choosing adaptive technologies?
8. What types of voluntary adjustments do older drivers make once they realize they are not as competent to drive as they once were?
9. What are the most popular Internet activities for older adults?
10. What are some of the obstacles, challenges, or concerns for older adults on the Internet?
11. What is a social support network and how can it help improve an older adult's quality of life?
12. What kinds of interactions would be considered negative social influences?
13. What are the characteristics of a typical caregiver in the amount of care given?
14. How are ethnic minority caregivers likely to differ from white caregivers?
15. What are the four distinct periods in Hindu religion?
16. How does Confucianism address age differences?
17. Name and describe the key points with each of Fowler's stages of faith.

Answers for Common Sense: Myth or Reality?

1. Reality: Developmental psychologists believe that each phase of life has both gains and losses, including late adulthood. (See Developmental Regulation, page 312.)
2. Reality: Levels of emotional intensity are the same for young and older adults. (See Socioemotional Selectivity Theory, page 314.)
3. Reality: The ability to control one's emotional responses, moving them toward a positive outlook, increases with age into late adulthood. (See Socioemotional Selectivity Theory, page 314.)
4. Myth: Older drivers cause the greatest number of accidents when the weather is bad. (See Technology and Older Drivers, page 320.)
5. Reality: There is a great difference in the number of computer users when comparing those between the ages of 50 and 64 and those ages 65 and older. (See Computer Literacy and Older Adults, page 320.)
6. Reality: High amounts of unsolicited support for an older adult are associated with negative well-being. (See Social Relationships and Support, page 323.)
7. Myth: On average, a care recipient receiving informal care from a spouse or adult child is in his or her mid-60s. (See A Closer Look at Caregivers, page 325.)
8. Reality: The average informal caregiver provides over 40 hours of care per week for 4 years. (See A Closer Look at Caregivers, page 325.)
9. Myth: Almost all religions have rites of passage and celebrations that mark middle age and late adulthood. (See Religious Views of Aging, page 326.)
10. Reality: Higher levels of religiosity are associated with better physical and mental health among older adults. (See Coping and Religiosity, page 330.)
11. Reality: Church attendance tends to decrease with age. (See Coping and Religiosity, page 330.)

Suggested Readings

Psychological Explanations of Emotion, 1884

James, W. (1884). What is an emotion? *Mind, 9,* 188–205. Accessed at *Classics in the History of Psychology* (http://psychclassics.yorku.ca/topic.htm).

Prayer and Spirituality in Health: Ancient Practices, Modern Science

Published by the National Center for Complementary and Alternative Medicine in 2005, available at http://nccam.nih.gov/news/newsletter/2005_winter/prayer.htm.

Coping with Chronic Illness

A Patient Information Publication from the National Institutes of Health, available at http://www.cc.nih.gov/ccc/patient_education/pepubs/copechron.pdf.

Helping Behaviors Across Cultures

Levine, R. V. (2003). Measuring helping behavior across cultures. In W. J. Lonner, D. L. Dinnel, S. A. Hayes, & D. N. Sattler (Eds.), *Online readings in psychology and culture* (Unit 15, Chapter 9), (http://www.wwu.edu/~culture), Center for Cross-Cultural Research, Western Washington University, Bellingham, WA. Available at http://www.ac.wwu.edu/~culture/levine.htm.

Suggested Websites

Caregivers' Resources

A great place to start for those caring for loved ones who need assistance is Medline Plus, sponsored by the U.S. National Library of Medicine at http://www.nlm.nih.gov/medlineplus/caregivers.html.

Falls and Older Adults

From the National Institutes of Senior Health. Published in 2006, available at http://nihseniorhealth.gov/falls/toc.html.

National Center for Assisted Living

Part of the American Health Care Association, this website provides resources for those searching to understand the system and find an assisted-living center. Available at http://www.ncal.org/resource/index.cfm.

Beliefnet Community Support Groups

This is one example of many religiously based community areas for those seeking an online support group. Available at http://community.beliefnet.com/index.php?page_id=1000&site_page_id=1.

CHAPTER

13 Dying, Death, and Bereavement

Developmental psychology examines change over time, focusing on normal or typical developmental stages and transitions. Few things have been typical for all people across all of history other than basic functions such as eating, sleeping, reproducing, and dying. Although death is common to all people, we in American society seem to ignore the topic. We often avoid visiting and talking with older individuals who appear to be close to death. We tend not to say directly "she died," but rather she "passed away" or "expired." Often when a loved one dies we expect people to take only a few days out of their routine to grieve before returning to normal functioning. Also many adults, and particularly younger adults, tend to avoid thinking of their own death. It would seem that the topics of dying and death trigger something significant psychologically when considering that so many people avoid one of the few, inevitable experiences we will all have at some point.

This chapter explores dying and death primarily as a late adult event resulting from a disease process. Certainly individuals can die at any age and from many different causes. Acknowledging that many different sets of circumstances can lead to death, this chapter focuses on end-of-life issues and bereavement as part of the developmental life cycle. Specifically, the chapter explores the research challenges involved with these topics, end-of-life decisions, palliative care, the dying process, and death. Marking the end of the life of a loved one and the bereavement process are also explored. Research on death anxiety would suggest that many readers will find these topics uncomfortable. While that may be the reality, avoiding or ignoring such topics will not make the challenges go away. Adults who plan well, make difficult choices before an emergency arises, and share the appropriate documents with family, friends, and care providers will most likely ease their own stress level and make the tasks of loved ones less difficult. Adults who avoid planning for the end of life may find themselves and their loved ones in challenging financial, social, and medical situations with few options.

COMMON SENSE
Myth or Reality?

Mark each of the following items with either an M, if you think it is a myth, or an R, if you think the statement reflects reality. By paying close attention you can find all the answers in this chapter. If needed, the answers are also given at the end of the chapter.

1. _____ Death anxiety rises with age across adulthood.
2. _____ Women report higher levels of death anxiety than men.
3. _____ A living will designates what should be done with an individual's finances and property should that person be unconscious.
4. _____ It is not uncommon for families to refuse to allow a deceased loved one's organs to be donated even when that person had indicated "organ donor" on his or her driver's license.
5. _____ In order to be accepted for hospice care a patient's physician must believe that the individual has 6 months or less to live.
6. _____ A greater percentage of African American than white Americans take advantage of hospice services.
7. _____ Physician-assisted suicide is illegal in the United States.
8. _____ It is common for a physical body to continue to move even after the individual has died.
9. _____ It is important for loved ones to move away and stay away from a body once a person has died.
10. _____ The average funeral cost is over $10,000.

Before We Get Started . . .

Do you have death anxiety? Consider your comfort level when responding to the following questions:

- Would you take a college or community education class on dying and death?
- Would you be able to work in a hospital or nursing home in units where patients frequently died?
- Will you visit friends or loved ones who are near death?
- Do you attend funerals or memorial services for those you know who have died?
- Would you touch a body that has been embalmed?
- Would you be comfortable making a will now?
- Would you be comfortable outlining your wishes for lifesaving medical care?
- Do you worry about dying at a young age?
- Does it bother you to think about your body being buried or cremated?

Not only is death an event that all of us will experience at some point, with an aging population it is an event that will become more frequent in the coming years. At one time sexuality was a taboo subject, and although it is still to some degree, many schools have sex education courses. How would you feel about death education courses? What does your response tell you about your own level of death anxiety?

If you think you do have some death anxiety you are not alone. Many people are uncomfortable while thinking about death and related issues. Starting with something as simple as reading this chapter, gaining some familiarity with death and related issues, you may be able to reduce some of your anxiety so that you can think clearly about these important issues in relation to yourself and your family.

Death Anxiety

Death anxiety is considered a multidimensional construct involving fears of many death-related factors, including the dying process, moment of death, situation of our body and our spirit after death, and simply the unknown beyond this life, both for ourselves and for others.

Death anxiety also can include a fear of personal obliteration, meaning that one is forgotten and without any lasting impact on others or the environment (Fry, 2003). One of the most stable and consistent findings regarding death anxiety is that older adults, those most likely to be closer to their death, do *not* report higher levels of death anxiety than younger adults (Furer & Walker, 2008; Jackson, 2008). In fact, fear of death often peaks in young adulthood (Russac, Gatliff, Reece, & Spottswood, 2007) and declines through middle age and late adulthood (Fry, 2003). Some of the contributing factors to these findings may be that young adults are just starting their families, thus thoughts of permanent separation from their young children are particularly anxiety provoking. Another possible factor is that older adults may have a diminished quality of life, signaling their final years and prompting them to think about their own death. Also, it is likely that older adults have experienced the loss of several friends and loved ones, also prompting mental preparation for their own death (Russac et al., 2007). While their death anxiety levels are reduced, older adults do report some anxiety, especially regarding the fear of a prolonged dying process. Older adults report anxiety surrounding concerns that their dying process may be painful and that they may be abandoned when they are dying (Fry, 2003).

Your Thoughts?

What factors might contribute to the reduction in death anxiety starting in middle adulthood?

Another consistent finding is that women report higher levels of death anxiety than men (Furer & Walker, 2008; Harding, Flannelly, Weaver, & Costa, 2005; Jackson, 2008). Some have speculated that men are less willing to admit to death anxiety whereas women are more in touch with their emotions (Russac et al., 2007). Women are often primary caretakers for their household, children, and older parents and relatives, thus the thought of not being available may also increase death anxiety. In a survey of over 400 adults between 18 and 87 years old Russac et al. (2007) found, as expected, that death anxiety reached its highest levels in young adulthood and was stronger in women. They also found something unexpected, that women reported a second period of high death anxiety in their 50s. Judging by the age range, Russac and his colleagues speculated that this spike in anxiety may be associated with changes leading to menopause. In light of the findings that caregivers are more likely to be female and generally in this age range, it may be that women are more likely to be reminded of their own aging process as they care for aging spouses and elderly relatives. Watching a loved one deal with a painful dying process or express fear of dying alone, for example, may increase the caregiver's anxiety about her own circumstances when she is dying.

Your Thoughts?

What additional factors might cause women to experience more death anxiety?

Death anxiety, which can be triggered by cultural symbols of death, tends to peak in young adulthood.

Gender differences also appear when exploring self-efficacy, the view that we can be effective in influencing our situation, and levels of death anxiety. In a survey involving 288 individuals between the ages of 65 and 87, Fry (2003) found that men and women found comfort in different areas of self-efficacy. Among the women who participated, those who felt competent and confident in their ability to manage interpersonal relationships, generate social support, and stay calm under stress were less fearful of the unknown and dying. Looking to different strengths, men evaluated their competence in terms of their ability to take care of themselves, their home environment, and manage financial and business affairs. Men who displayed more confidence in those areas also expressed less fear of the unknown and dying (Fry, 2003).

One factor that is often speculated to make a difference in death anxiety is religiosity and spirituality. The findings in this area are mixed and controversial. In some cases personal religiosity has been found to provide comfort and decrease death anxiety, whereas in other cases increased religiosity is associated with increased anxiety (Fry, 2003). In their review Furer and Walker (2008) determined that religious beliefs were not related to levels of death anxiety; however, others have found certain theological beliefs (Harding et al., 2005) and one's inner faith and strength (Fry, 2003) were associated with reduced death anxiety and fear.

Section Summary

- Death anxiety in the general public is common, peaking in young adulthood and declining afterward.
- Women report higher levels of death anxiety than men.
- The research is mixed regarding the role religiosity plays in decreasing or increasing death anxiety.

End-of-Life Decisions

When coping with a terminal illness, no matter what age, adults and their loved ones should gather as much information as they can in order to direct their care as much as possible. The difficult news that we have a potentially life-ending illness is likely to be overwhelming. One method of coping is to direct and, as much as we can, take some control over our situation. Some of the best resources can be found through Internet searches, including up-to-date websites offering medical information and opportunities to correspond with other patients who have similar situations. Local support groups, if available, can also provide a wealth of helpful information as well as social support. It's important to gather information as quickly as possible regarding the expected progression of the disease, treatments, insurance-related issues, and care options (Merck, 2007). Prior to any emergencies it may be beneficial to discuss the types of issues covered in advance directives, such as the types of lifesaving measures desired. Most health care professionals agree that it is better for all involved if the patient makes his or her desires known verbally and through legal documents as early in the process as possible. This section explores some of those difficult topics and options.

Your Thoughts?

Do you know if your older family members have advance directives? If not, will you ask? Why, why not, or under what circumstances?

Advance Directives

The term ***advance directives*** refers to various types of legal documents detailing wishes of individuals regarding end-of-life concerns. These documents, prepared in advance of a crisis, are consulted when we are incapacitated or for any reason unable to speak for ourselves. Advance directives developed after medical advances, starting in the 1960s, allowed patients who would have died a chance to survive through emergency life-support technology (Perkins, 2007). In 1990 the Patient Self-Determination Act brought the efforts to empower patients even farther. It required Medicare and Medicaid providers to inform patients of their rights to direct their own health care, accept or refuse treatment, prepare advance directives documents, and to provide information regarding any health care facility's policies regarding these issues (Teno, Gruneir, Schwartz, Anada, & Wetle, 2007). More recently, the use of ***psychiatric advance directives,*** a similar practice in the mental health field, has gained respect and popularity. These are legal documents that allow individuals who are in a mentally competent state to choose the types of mental health treatments they desire, or to designate someone as a health care agent to make decisions, should an incapacitating psychiatric crisis arise (Elbogen et al., 2007).

Your Thoughts?

How might a hospital institute a policy to ensure that those who submit advance directives have enough understanding (health literacy) to make specific decisions?

One type of advance directive, a ***living will,*** specifies instructions which will be used to direct medical care intended to sustain or prolong life (National Cancer Institute [NCI], 2000). For example, a living will may detail an individual's wishes to use or withhold life-sustaining equipment, artificial hydration and nutrition, palliative care, and organ and tissue donation. Advance directives may also specify what types of care are to be given or withheld in specific circumstances, such as if the patient is thought to be permanently unconscious or if treatment is deemed "futile" (Kressel, Chapman, & Leventhal, 2007).

It's important that family members and others in a patient's social support system as well as appropriate medical professionals know about the documents and have copies of them. Obviously, the directives cannot be followed if they are not in the hands of the health care providers at the time decisions are being made. Patients might also keep a card in their wallet or purse informing the reader that they have a living will and where it can be found (NCI, 2000). One of the best places to keep a copy of the documents is with other permanent medical records files associated with appropriate health care providers (Perkins, 2007).

Preparing a document and making sure everyone who might need to know about such plans is informed is only part of the task. It's also important to revisit the documents periodically. Our choices for end-of-life decisions may change over time as we gather more information and observe the consequences of the choices our friends and loved ones made. Also, techniques, procedures, pharmaceutical treatments, and technologies will change over time, and our documents need to reflect that (NCI, 2000). With many health care providers offering websites with personal pages it may be that an individual can file and revise all types of advance directives via the Internet.

Your Thoughts?

Should anyone be allowed to serve as a health care proxy? Should there be some qualifications or requirements if the person is not a family member or intimate partner?

Another type of an advance directive is to legally appoint someone to make important decisions for you if and when needed. Rather than trying to record all your wishes ahead of time in a living will, this alternative allows you to designate someone as a ***health care proxy*** in a document called a ***durable power of attorney for health care.*** Your health care proxy can make decisions in the moment, perhaps involving a procedure or detail not covered in your living will (NCI, 2000). A ***durable power of attorney for finances*** may also be designated (NCI, 2000).

Although the use of advance directives is widely encouraged, analysis of the practice has resulted in a fair amount of criticism. In spite of the many educational programs and legal mandates, relatively few patients take advantage of the opportunity for advance directives. A recent nationwide study in the United States found that persons receiving hospice care or in a nursing home were more likely to have advance directives than those in hospitals (Teno et al., 2007). The same study also found that fewer blacks and Hispanics had advance directives, results consistent with previous research (Bullock, 2006). In addition to lack of use, another problem with advance directives is that without trusted counseling and advice patients may create a poorly written document that cannot be followed or designate a health proxy who may not want to play that role when the time comes. Often advance directives omit instructions regarding how the documents may be revoked or revised (Perkins, 2007).

Your Thoughts?

What may be some reasons why individuals choose not to take advantage of advance directives?

ON THE LEADING EDGE
Improving Communication About Advance Directives

It appears that there are numerous obstacles challenging the medical community's desire to increase the use of advance directives. One potential concern recently addressed by members of several divisions of the Mayo Clinic in Rochester, Minnesota (Mueller, et al., 2010) was that physicians are not trained in the details of advanced directives to a level that they feel comfortable discussing these documents with their patients. The researchers tested the effectiveness of adding an educational component on advance directives to the fourth year medical school curriculum. One hundred and eleven medical students were required to attend sessions on advance directives as well as complete Internet-based modules and exercises. After the educational training, which included an exercise leading the students through the development of their own advance directives, the students reported a greater understanding of both the technical aspects of the documentation and the psychological resistance expressed by some patients. They reported feelings of resistance to thinking about their own death, difficulty actually writing down their wishes, and trouble discussing the exercise with their loved ones. Some medical students found the exercise to be psychologically moving and in some cases a spiritual experience.

Physician–patient interactions are only one of several potential obstacles to the use of advance directives. Lindner, Davoren, Vollmer, Williams, and Landefeld (2007), affiliated with the San Francisco VA Medical Center and the University of California at San Francisco, recognized that too often when patients do have preferences about end-of-life choices those desires are not documented in a way that can be easily accessed by medical professionals when needed. In some cases the documents are not drawn up at all or are worded poorly. Only a few states in the United States have registries for advance directives, thus it falls on the patient, family member or friend to bring the documents to the attention of medical staff (Hughes, 2009). Rather than continue with these gaps in patient–physician communication, Lindner and his research team initiated a system in which medical professionals could engage in an "advance directives discussion" with patients and document those discussions with notes on patients' electronic medical records.

Lindner and his colleagues initiated several changes at a Veterans Administration nursing home in San Francisco beginning in 2004. One change made required the person filling out admissions forms to indicate the patient's wishes in the event of cardiopulmonary arrest, choosing from the same four options given on the California advance directives forms. Another change was to adapt the admissions software to include a drop-down box with a menu of items from the print version of the Physician Orders for Life-Sustaining Treatment form.

In addition to the admissions documentation, 24 hours after admission the primary medical professional for the particular patient would be alerted to discuss the choices made by the patient and to complete the full advance directives form. Alerts would be given every time the patient's medical record was accessed until the form was complete. This reminded physicians and others to discuss goals of care and emergency measures. These electronic forms also provided areas for health care proxies to be named and for the revision or revocation of previously written documents.

While the medical personnel at the nursing home knew changes were being made in the software, they did not know data was being collected on advance directives and resulting outcomes. Lindner and his colleagues found that prior to the changes advance directives discussion notes were completed for 4% of the admissions, whereas 3 months after the changes it rose to 63%. Of the patients who chose do-not-resuscitate status, prior to the changes such orders were actually written 86% of the time, whereas after the changes the percentage rose to 98%. Similar increases were seen with other directives as well. The research team believes these simple changes improved communication between patients and medical personnel and dramatically increased the chances that patients' choices will be honored (Lindner, Davoren, Vollmer, Williams, & Landefeld (2007). Changes such as these made to admissions procedures and forms, along with continued training and alerts provided to physicians and other health care professionals, are likely to increase the use of advance directives.

The health care community is often given the burden of trying to decide how to proceed when advance directives are not clear or conflict occurs. Imagine for a moment that an older widow is in a life-threatening situation and has officially designated her closest friend and neighbor her health care proxy. As decisions are being made a distant cousin of the woman calls the hospital to request that everything possible to done to save her loved one's life, which is different from what the designated health proxy is choosing. The cousin informs that physician in charge that she and her family are on their way to the hospital as they speak. What should the medical staff do? Now consider the commonly occurring example regarding organ donation. While nearly three-quarters of adults in the United States are willing to be organ donors, it is not uncommon for the families to refuse when a loved one has just died. Of those situations in which the person who died had indicated on their driver's license they would like to donate organs, approximately half of the time the family refuses. This puts medical authorities in a very difficult position. Do you honor the wishes of the person who died or the grieving family (May, Aulisio, & DeVita, 2000)? While most people agree that the intent of advance directives is ethical and valuable, many health care professionals are searching for ways to implement advance directives that will address some of these current concerns.

Palliative Care and Hospice Programs

Your Thoughts?

What might be the advantages of allowing a loved one to die at home? What might be some of the challenges or difficulties?

Another important end-of-life issue to consider is the use of ***palliative care***, and if so, when to start the program. Unlike treatments aimed at curing a disease, palliative care is focused on treating symptoms and keeping an individual comfortable (American Cancer Society, 2008; NCI, 2000). Palliative care can begin at any point after diagnosis (Stevens, 2006), and may involve antibiotics, nutrition, pain medication, and other interventions (NCI, 2000). A well-known type of palliative care, called ***hospice care***, is given in the last few months of life (Stevens, 2006).

Hospice care for terminally ill patients formally began in 1967 with two key events. In England St. Christopher's Hospice opened its doors and in the United States the home health care portion of the Hospice of New Haven, in Connecticut, started seeing clients (Marwit, 1997). The purpose of hospice care is to manage symptoms of a terminal illness so that patients can remain alert and as symptom-free as possible in their last days. Palliative care often requires that decisions be made regarding numerous concerns, such as pain management, shortness of breath, digestive problems, incontinence, skin breakdown, and fatigue. Decisions must also be made regarding psychological concerns, such as depression, anxiety, and confusion (Merck, 2007). Most hospice care takes place in patients' homes, although it does occur in hospitals, nursing homes, and private hospice facilities. In an ideal situation a patient can maintain dignity and quality of life surrounded by loved ones in a home-like setting for as long as possible (American Cancer Society, 2008).

Your Thoughts?

What factors might support the perspective that entering hospice is reflective of coping well? Reflective of giving up?

The decision to begin hospice care is a difficult one. One of the first requirements is a medical professional's prognosis that a patient has 6 months or less to live (Merck, 2007). Hospice care may be postponed, partly due to the hesitancy of medical professionals who are not comfortable predicting the amount of time a patient has to live (NCI, 2000). These medical professionals may also hesitate to discuss the seriousness of an illness with the patient and family (Friedman, Harwood, & Shields, 2002; Marwit, 1997) until they are confident in their assessment that, provided the disease follows the expected progression, the patient is within 6 months of death (Marwit, 1997). Referring a patient to hospice care may feel to the physician as if he or she has failed (Friedman et al., 2002). Entering hospice care may feel to the family like they are giving up or that the patient is surrendering rather than taking a positive "I'm going to beat this" attitude (American Cancer Society, 2008). It is inaccurate to assume that referral to hospice care means that any improvement is ignored. If a patient's disease goes into remission or the patient begins to recover then aggressive treatment can resume (American Cancer Society, 2008).

Your Thoughts?

If you were hiring professionals to work in hospice care, what characteristics would you look for beyond their technical abilities?

Consistent with its philosophy from the beginning, hospice care goes beyond minimal palliative care to consider the psychological and spiritual health of the patient and the family (Marwit, 1997). Often there is a team of professionals assisting the medical personnel, including social workers, counselors, clergy, psychological therapists, and trained volunteers. In order to meet the needs of the dying individual the hospice team spends a great deal of time

RESEARCH IN-DEPTH
Qualitative Analysis

Many fields in the social sciences, such as psychology and sociology, embrace both quantitative and qualitative research methods. ***Quantitative research methods***, which focus on precise measurements (quantities), originated in the natural sciences. The early founders of psychology built the new science of human mental and behavioral events on these quantitative methods. Many researchers still rely heavily on surveys, questionnaires, precise observations, and laboratory experiments to quantify, measure, and attempt to further understand human nature. While such measurements or instruments are useful, they are also restrictive. Individuals often want to say or do more than what they are allowed to in a quantitative study. For example, suppose a researcher asked an adult to rate the health care provided to his father by home health nurses. His choices may be 1 = Poor, 2 = Adequate, 3 = Outstanding. The participant may want to elaborate to say that it depended on the particular nurse or that the quality of the care changed over time. Perhaps the participant would like to express that the actual care was fine, however, the best part of the care was the compassion the nurses showed to his mother. Such additional information cannot be expressed with a limited set of responses.

Qualitative research methods were developed in response to the need to gather more in-depth information and to allow research participants to fully express themselves. Rather than focus on precise measurement (quantity), these more recent research methods focus on the qualities of the situation and participant. Often qualitative researchers use case studies, recording narratives and personal stories, interviews, and observations, sometimes even participating in the very activity being studied. One type of interview method, ***phenomenological interviews***, offers the opportunity to collect data in an unstructured way, much like a conversation between the researcher and participant. In the example above involving an assessment of his father's care, phenomenological interview questions would allow the participant to offer any information about any aspect of his father's care in as much detail as he would like. The greatest challenge in using this method comes when the researcher must create ways of summarizing the findings in order to report them to the greater scientific community. This can be difficult when participants take the conversation in many different directions.

Some researchers have looked for ways to give the participants the greatest opportunities to express themselves, as highlighted in qualitative research, while maintaining enough structure to be able to make brief and efficient summaries of the findings, as is emphasized in quantitative research. Hamilton and McDowell (2004) found a way to utilize the strengths of both methods by conducting ***structured interviews***. The researchers were interested in learning more about community nurses' roles when giving palliative care to patients who were being cared for at home or in smaller community hospitals. Hamilton and McDowell began by reviewing all the articles related to these topics published between 1996 and 2001. Based on that literature review the researchers put together a set of nine interview questions, including "What do you consider are the key aspects of the nurse's role?" and "What hinders the provision of palliative care within the community hospital setting?" The researchers recruited four registered nurses and two general practitioner physicians as participants. Following individual interviews the responses were transcribed and analyzed for recurring themes. Using this method the participants were able to comment without the restriction of using a rating scale or multiple-choice responses, while at the same time the researchers were able to focus on the specific topics identified in each question.

Hamilton and McDowell found six themes that occurred frequently in the response to health care providers' issues surrounding the medical care of those with life-limiting progressive illnesses: communication, teamwork and relationships, professional roles, holistic care, resources, and culture. The sense of teamwork, good working relationships, open communication, and engaging in professionalism were important for the health care providers themselves but also for the interactions between the professionals, the family members, and the patient. The focus on holistic care and resources reflected the nurses' need for physical and educational resources to support the many facets of their work. Hamilton and McDowell noticed that the participants repeatedly discussed the culture of helping, sharing, and getting to know each other that can occur in a small, community hospital setting. Using a qualitative research methodology allowed the participants to express their thoughts freely, leading to the identification of these important factors.

---

working with the patient, family, and friends to provide around-the-clock care (American Cancer Society, 2008). If needed, psychological therapists will help all involved cope with stress, depression, and the anticipated bereavement (Marwit, 1997). In some cases the primary caregiver, usually a spouse or family member, may need ***respite care*** involving some time off and away from the situation. In those cases the patient is cared for by someone else or is temporarily placed in a facility (American Cancer Society, 2008).

Hospice care usually costs less than traditional care. Generally, family members and friends provide most of the care, and there are far fewer costly tests or technologies involved. By relying on some combination of Medicare, Medicaid, Veterans Affairs benefits, and insurance plans, most people can afford hospice care. Often local hospice organizations have private money from donations and other financial gifts for those who can't afford the cost (American Cancer Society, 2008). One of the growing concerns regarding hospice care is not the cost but the lack of use by older members of ethnic minority groups. For example, in an analysis of data from the National Mortality Followback Study involving nearly 23,000 individuals, Greiner, Perera, and Ahluwalia (2003) found that African Americans have a 40% lower hospice usage rate than whites. The difference was not explained by education, socioeconomic situation, or differing access to health care (Greiner et al., 2003). Johnson and her colleagues (2005) found similar trends when pulling data from over 100,000 records of deceased individuals from 26 hospice programs across eight states.

Your Thoughts?

How would you design a study to learn more about why African Americans have been less likely to use hospice care?

Euthanasia and Physician-Assisted Death

Among the most difficult dilemmas some severely ill patients or their families may encounter is the question of initiating or continuing life-sustaining procedures once such efforts seem futile. In some cases patients will have already documented advance directives and their wishes regarding such decisions are known. Without those directives, patients who are unable to coherently communicate their wishes will rely on family members and medical professionals to make these difficult decisions. There are times when medical professionals will knowingly withhold lifesaving procedures, such as when the patient is thought to be likely to die in a matter of hours or days regardless of such measures. Without clear knowledge of their loved one's wishes it may be difficult for a spouse or other family members to agree to withhold any treatment, and even harder to stop treatments or life-support systems that are already being used. Such actions are considered to be ***passive euthanasia*,** which is allowing "nature to take its course" and allowing someone to succumb to the disease process or a related life-ending complication. Although many people feel that stopping a treatment once started is more severe than never starting the treatment, legally there is no difference (American Geriatric Society [AGS], 2005).

Your Thoughts?

Considering both courses of action will result in death, why is it harder to stop life support once started, even when determined to be futile, than to have never started it?

***Active euthanasia*,** which involves taking direct action to shorten a patient's life, is illegal. For example, a physician who deliberately gives a patient a lethal dose of something with the intention of shortening life, sometimes referred to as *mercy killing,* is violating the law. Closely related to this concept, however, is ***physician-assisted suicide*,** which is legal in the state of Oregon and in other parts of the world. In this case a physician in some way aids a patient in ending his or her own life. This could be simply responding to a patient's questions and explaining the dosage requirements or combinations of drugs that would cause death, or could involve the physician actually writing the prescription for such drugs (AGS, 2005).

Among the many controversies surrounding physician-assisted suicide is the question of whether individuals with terminal diseases are capable of clear, rational thought when considering such decisions for themselves. According to the National Institute of Mental Health (2008), over 90% of the people who commit suicide had a diagnosable mental disorder, with the most common being depression or substance abuse. While those considering physician-assisted suicide may be in a different situation than those in the general population who commit suicide, the possibility of a diagnosable mental disorder along with the complicating factors caused by a serious disease and treatment effects would seem to decrease the chances of rational reasoning even more. That said, there are likely to be those rare cases in which a patient is suffering terribly and is able to make a clear-headed decision regarding physician-assisted suicide.

Your Thoughts?

Would you vote in favor of allowing physician-assisted suicide in your state? Why, why not, or with what conditions?

Challenges to the assertion that physician-assisted suicide is wrong in all cases have made their way through the American court system. When taken to the U.S. Supreme Court it ruled that physician-assisted suicide is not necessarily unconstitutional, resulting in each state being given the responsibility of determining the legality of such actions (AGS, 2005). Currently, the only state to allow physician-assisted suicide is Oregon, passing the Death with Dignity Act in 1997. Data from the first 9 years of the Oregon program show that physician-assisted deaths account for one in every 1,000 deaths (or 0.01%) (Quill, 2007). Across the first 9 years 456 lethal prescriptions were written, and of those 292 individuals chose to follow through and end their lives (Hiscox, 2007). An important and welcome result of the Death with Dignity Act is that patients are more likely to discuss end-of-life issues and options with their physician. Although Oregon is the only state to pass such a law, there are similar movements in other states. On the world stage The Netherlands has been a leader in this effort, allowing euthanasia and physician-assisted suicide for nearly two decades and officially legalizing it in 2002 (Quill, 2007).

Your Thoughts?

What might be some of the reasons why those who sought prescriptions did not end their lives?

Section Summary

- It is important for all adults, and especially those who are diagnosed with a serious illness, to gather as much information as possible and put advance directives in place where desired.
- Advance directives documents, including a living will and durable power of attorney for health care, need to be written appropriately, distributed to all who need to be informed, and revised as needed.
- When the end of life is near, another key decision is if and/or when to start palliative care.
- Hospice care, the most well-known type of palliative care, involves keeping patients alert and symptom-free as possible during the last few months of life while also addressing the psychological and spiritual needs of the patient and the family.
- Passive euthanasia involves ceasing or not initiating life-sustaining measures and letting the disease process progress as it will.
- Although active euthanasia is illegal, physician-assisted suicide is legal in Oregon and in some parts of the world.

Close to Death

No matter how well we try to live our lives to the fullest, death will come to all of us at some point. This section explores the psychological and physiological changes that signal death is near and how we might interact with someone who is dying. There are so many possible circumstances and influences that it is difficult to predict what an individual who is near death is likely to think about. Death anxiety and the awkwardness of not having a script to follow or a familiar set of expectations can make sitting with a dying person difficult. One way to cope with these barriers is to learn more about the process, know what to expect, and have a simple plan of what to say and do when in the presence of someone who is dying.

End-of-Life Research Issues

One of the most informative ways for researchers to learn about the psychology of the dying process is to communicate with those who are experiencing it. This raises several difficult issues, most of which come from the desire of researchers to honor and respect individuals who are in their last few weeks or days of life. Numerous safeguards are put in place to ensure that only the studies of the highest quality requiring the least intrusion are allowed to be carried out.

Your Thoughts?

Would you be comfortable interviewing patients with terminal illnesses about dying? Why, why not, or under what circumstances?

Once a study is designed one or more Institutional Review Boards (IRBs) will review the plan. They must be satisfied that what could be learned from a particular study is worth the potential risk of emotional distress or upset caused by raising topics related to dying and death with individuals who have only a short time to live. IRBs must also be satisfied that controls are in place so that participants can give true informed consent. In some cases, if there is cognitive impairment, depression, or any other potentially interfering factor, the participants' guardians and possibly even their health care providers may be required to give consent (Williams, 2007).

Once the research is approved at all levels, the challenge of finding willing participants begins. Similar to the issues surrounding identifying patients who are candidates for hospice care, medical professionals are hesitant to make predictions of how long someone might live (NCI, 2000). The gravity of such situations is enormous. If health care professionals underestimate the time left it could lead a patient and family to prepare mentally for an event that doesn't come as expected, possibly stealing quality of life and creating a sense of "just waiting." On the other hand, if health care professionals overestimate the time left then the patient and family may have a sense of false hope and feel cheated when death comes earlier than expected.

Your Thoughts?

Considering how sensitive these issues are, would you ever approve of end-of-life research? Why, why not, or under what circumstances?

Once actual persons are identified as potential participants for an end-of-life study researchers may find that their families, social support networks, and health care professionals are protective of an individual's mental state (Williams, 2007). By agreeing to participate in an end-of-life study patients and all those in their support system are forced to acknowledge the current situation. Even when participants are recruited and the research is underway, there is the likelihood that some participants will leave the study prior to their death.

Psychological Changes

For many years those in the social and health sciences perceived the psychological adjustment to dying to be a stage-like process. Starting with her book *On Death and Dying,* published in 1969, Elisabeth Kubler-Ross was viewed for many years as the expert on the psychological stages of dying. Her work remained popular for many years (Telford, Kralik, & Koch, 2006) and set the standard as the primary theory of dying taught in nursing and medical schools into the 1990s (Downe-Wamboldt & Tamlyn, 1997). Based on data from hundreds of interviews with dying patients, her analysis resulted in the development of a five-stage model (Goffnett, 1979). During the first stage, *denial,* individuals may believe that there is a mistake in their diagnosis or perhaps they will be cured and the entire situation will fade or prove to be a false alarm. Once denial is no longer possible, sometimes due to deteriorating conditions, individuals often demonstrate *anger.* In this second stage people may be angry at God, loved ones, medical professionals, or even themselves. The anger may concentrate on nagging questions such as "Why me?" or "Why now?" The third stage, *bargaining,* focuses on postponing death. The individual may pray or meditate on an exchange such as, "If you'll just let me live until . . . then it will be okay" or "I promise if you let me live I will . . . ." Once those efforts seem to have no effect individuals often fall into *depression,* facing the reality that they are going to die soon. The final stage, *acceptance,* signals a move from depression to full acknowledgment of one's realistic situation and the need for internal mental preparation (Goffnett, 1979).

Your Thoughts?

What factors might push someone to move from the anger stage to the bargaining stage?

In recent years Kubler-Ross's work has lost stature and support, partly due to a great deal of criticism of her research and partly due to the availability of more research on the psychological process of dying. The primary criticisms of the model are aimed at the impression that all individuals move through this linear progression of stages, whereas further research shows that patients who are dying may move around in the stages or even skip stages (Abeles, Victor, & Delano-Wood, 2004). Individuals who are near death often withdraw and show less interest

Although Kubler-Ross's stages have fallen into disfavor, researchers do find that individuals who are near death withdraw and show less interest in socializing.

in socializing (NCI, 2000); however, the psychological roots of those behaviors probably vary more than Kubler-Ross's model allows. There is also a growing concern that by expecting people to function in a particular stage, health care professionals and loved ones may not truly listen to the particular needs and desires of the one who is dying (Telford et al., 2006). With a greater amount of research data to work with it is becoming clear that there are many individual differences influencing the experience of dying. Kubler-Ross's stages of dying can be helpful when viewed not as five strict, linear categories, but rather as potential perspectives we may encounter when spending time with someone who is dying.

Interacting with Those Who Are Dying

Your Thoughts?

Would the benefits outweigh the costs for hospitals to have classes on how to talk to loved ones who are dying? Why, why not, or under what circumstances?

Although people are unique in their response to the realization that they have only a short time to live, many people worry about being abandoned or becoming a burden. The first and most important thing you can do in terms of interacting with someone who is dying is actually be present to communicate. I use the term *present* to convey two key points. First, it is best to physically be present with someone who is dying, if nothing else to ease their fears of dying alone. Second, I use the term in the Buddhist and mindfulness sense of being attentive and psychologically being present in the moment. One way to do this is to notice and respond to the signals you get from the individual. Engage in conversation when he or she wishes to talk, and remain close and respectful if the person desires some privacy (Merck, 2007; NCI, 2002).

If there is conversation, it can be difficult to come up with things to talk about, particularly if one or both of us is nervous or uncomfortable. In typical situations many people move about their day with a future orientation, always thinking of next weekend or next summer or next year. Such a future orientation may feel inappropriate and awkward when talking with someone whose time is short. When not discussing the future many people fill their conversation with mundane talk about the weather, a sports team, or a film or video clip they saw. In light of the gravity of the situation we may feel odd talking about relatively trivial matters, and yet discussing matters of life and death may feel inappropriate as well. The result may be that we feel so uncomfortable and confused that we find some reason to quickly leave the situation.

I experienced all of these feelings when I sat with my mother while she was dying of cancer. She had chosen to spend her final days at home with hospice care. I was a student in the middle of an academic semester when it became clear that she probably wouldn't make it until my break. I left school and spent her last 3 days with her. Once we got beyond "How was your plane flight?" and "Are you hungry?" I found myself anxiously trying to think of something to talk about. I thought of asking if she planned to put out a garden next year . . . but the answer to that was obvious. I thought of commenting on how old the curtains were . . . but that was trivial in light of her condition. I decided to reminisce, "Mom, just the other day I saw a cat that reminded me of Smokey." That worked well to get us beyond the initial discomfort and to bring positive emotions to our conversation. Eventually, I asked her how she was feeling and what was on her mind, and that opened the door to one of the most powerful conversations I've ever had. We both cried. It was far from a smooth script, occasionally bumping into awkward topics, but when I reflect back on it I must say it is one of my fondest memories.

Although it may feel uncomfortable, it is much better to communicate about important matters rather than ignore the fact that one is dying. Approaching our own death is one of the most powerful events we can prepare for, and yet when we are facing that most important moment it may feel as if no one wants to talk to us about it or help us adjust (other than clergy or chaplains who are trained and experienced in these matters). It is hard to imagine how it might feel if we've never experienced that sense of dying, so consider this analogy: Imagine talking with a woman who is obviously nearing the end of a pregnancy and trying your hardest to ignore anything related to pregnancy or babies. Imagine saying to others, "If she brings it up try to change the subject." Imagine if the woman said, "I'm nervous" or "I'm scared"—and the people around her simply dismissed her concerns with phrases like "Everything will be fine" and changed the subject. Just as pregnancy is a life-altering situation and one of the most important experiences a person can have, so too is dying. Ignoring the fact that someone is obviously dying is just as insulting and hurtful as ignoring and downplaying the days before giving birth. Unless the dying person is in severe denial he or she is clearly aware of what is happening and that person may welcome a chance to talk about it.

Your Thoughts?

Is this analogy reasonable? What are the parallels? What are the differences?

An open question such as "What are you thinking?" may open the door to a much-needed conversation. Of course, once that opportunity is given the listener should be prepared to possibly be asked some hard questions, hear some difficult words, or receive uncomfortable emotions. Most people (much like the pregnant woman in the example) want to know about their condition. They want to be fully informed and make their desires and concerns known even if the conversation is a difficult one (Merck, 2007; NCI, 2002). For example, in those final conversations I had with my mother she asked me many questions about what her doctor had said to me, comparing what he had told her and analyzing her condition. She also passed along things that she wanted me to share with other members of the family.

Thankfully, those most serious conversations will likely be interspersed with reminiscing, health care chores, and perhaps even singing or listening to favorite songs. Based on interviews with hospice patients and relatives of loved ones who had died in hospice care, Masson (2002) found that it was important to place the life of the person who is dying in context as much as possible, both figuratively in conversation and literally in terms of location, atmosphere, family, friends, pets, and objects. As much as you can surround the individual with personal items that bring to mind fond memories.

Your Thoughts?

What factors in American history and culture contribute to the general discomfort we often feel being around someone who is dying?

Physiological Changes

Friends and loved ones who do spend a significant amount of time with someone who is dying will notice changes as death approaches. Often persons who are dying will display drowsiness and confusion. They may have less interest in food and water, reducing their intake. Caregivers may also notice a loss of bladder and bowel control. When very close to death, a person's limbs and skin may become cool to the touch. The individual may start to breath noisily, making gurgling sounds as throat muscles relax. This sound is sometimes referred to as a *death rattle.* In addition to changes in breathing there may be changes in heart rate as well. At the time of death there may be muscle contractions, chest movements, and other involuntary movements. The heart may beat for a short time after breathing stops and a brief seizure may occur (Merck, 2007; NCI, 2000). If a loved one is dying in a care facility the health care professionals will offer comfort and direction, as will hospice professionals when a person is dying at home.

Your Thoughts?

Do you think this would comfort the person who is dying? Would you be able to do this for a loved one? Why or why not?

As stated earlier, one of the primary concerns of those who are dying is that they will be left alone and abandoned. Unless the person who is dying has an infectious disease it is acceptable and maybe very comforting to hold hands, stroke his or her hair, or put an arm around the person's shoulders. After a person dies there is usually no need for emergency action. It may be helpful to the bereaved to stay with the body to talk, pray, or grieve together (Bern-Klug, 2004; Merck, 2007; NCI, 2000).

Section Summary

- Before an end-of-life research study can begin an IRB must agree that what can be learned from the study is worth the potential for discomfort.
- For many years the social and health sciences looked to Kubler-Ross's five stages of dying (denial, anger, bargaining, depression, and acceptance) as the standard portrayal of the dying experience.
- Rather than looking for an individual to follow a stage pattern, loved ones and health care professionals are encouraged to be present, listen, and be willing to engage in the difficult and emotional conversations.
- As an individual approaches death there are expected physiological signs, such as a decrease in appetite and bladder and bowel control, cool limbs, noisy breathing, muscle contractions, and an irregular heartbeat.

Transitions

Adjusting to the emptiness left when someone dies takes time. Often one of the first public steps in the adjustment process is a funeral or memorial service of some type during which people can gather to grieve, remember, and celebrate the life of the person who died. The closer and more integrated the deceased person's life was with your own, the longer the bereavement process may take. Even though most adults only take a few days off work or away from their typical routine to grieve, the actual process usually takes much longer. With time comes healing and new experiences that will help the bereaved in developing different routines, a new sense of what is normal, and be able to think of the good times they had with the deceased more so than the pain of the loss. Personally, having lost both of my parents when I was relatively young, my experience wasn't that I ever "got over it" but rather I learned to live with the reality of it, much like one learns to live with a scar.

Your Thoughts?

Would you consider writing the ceremony or choosing music for your own funeral or memorial service now, knowing you can update it later? Why or why not?

Your Thoughts?

Would you support a school district who offered death education, similar to health education and personal finance?

Your Thoughts?

What might be strong influences on our personal choice for burial or cremation? How would you design a study to learn more about those factors?

Marking the End of Life

When someone dies the people who knew that individual usually want to mark the event in some way beyond an obituary. The way the life of someone who just died is mourned or celebrated can vary dramatically, often influenced by culture, religious traditions, and personal and family preferences. Although difficult and emotional, a funeral or memorial service can facilitate closure on the past and mark the beginning of a new chapter in life. It allows loved ones a chance to talk about that special person, connect with a larger group of people, and perhaps bolster their own social support network.

In some cases an individual or the family may choose a *traditional funeral* involving preparation of the body, viewing and visitation, a service at a funeral home and at the grave site, and burial, entombment, or cremation. This usually involves the greatest cost and the most formal ceremony. Others may opt to have a memorial service without the body present, although the body must still be dealt with appropriately. Some may choose a *direct burial* involving no body preparation or embalming, a simple container, and a quick burial while others may choose *direct cremation.* Cemetery arrangements are needed for burial and possibly for cremation (Federal Trade Commission, 2000). When the body is dealt with separately the loved ones have many options in terms of timing, location, and level of formality in planning a memorial service.

Especially for those who desire a traditional funeral, the Federal Trade Commission (FTC) encourages adults to plan their funeral long before they are ill. It's important to know what is required and what is optional in terms of handling the body, the funeral, and the cemetery. Prices can vary, thus it is wise to make price comparisons and let loved ones know of your choices. Individuals can enter into contracts, actually purchase items ahead of time, or purchase insurance to cover costs—though the FTC and others warn that consumers should fully research the benefits and risks before entering into such arrangements (Bern-Klug, 2004; FTC, 2009).

For unprepared families the many funeral-related decisions and costs may seem overwhelming. Consumers spend approximately $6,000 on the primary items legally required for a

Some people prefer a traditional funeral while others opt for simple ceremonies or memorial services weeks or months later.

Your Thoughts?

Do you have any ethical objections to funeral planners, similar to wedding planners, hired to design a funeral and related activities?

funeral, and when adding to that cost flowers, limousines, and other items, the average funeral cost is over $10,000. The FTC and other consumer groups have been concerned that families may feel pressured or become so overwhelmed by their emotions that they make poor choices (FTC, 2009). Is it disrespectful to choose the least expensive casket? What memorial merchandise should we purchase (flowers, announcement cards, etc.)? What type of grave marker can we afford? These critical decisions may need to be made quickly and under conditions of emotional duress and exhaustion. Later, when the grieving has subsided and loved ones can think clearly they may regret some of their decisions (Bern-Klug, 2004). Careful discussions and planning ahead of time may ease the stress of these last minute decisions.

Bereavement

Your Thoughts?

In what ways might the bereavement process be different if the one who died was an infant? An adolescent? A soldier? An older adult?

Early models of grief, including Kubler-Ross's stages of dying, tended to be rigid and time-focused. Much like employers who designate a certain amount of time away for bereavement leave, early models emphasized the amount of time individuals might spend in particular stages of recovery. As research continued those models gave way to a focus on individual differences and the many variations in the experience of bereavement (Abeles et al., 2004). It is important to note that there is no correct way to cope with grief. The way an individual adjusts may be influenced by age, personality, the way the loved one died, religious and cultural background, and level of social support (NCI, 2006).

Professionals and researchers often make distinctions between bereavement, grief, and mourning. ***Bereavement*** refers to time between the experience of the loss and full adjustment to new routines and return to everyday living. To be bereaved is to be very mindful of the fact that something precious is missing or has been taken away. ***Grief*** refers to an individual's emotional reaction to the loss. Grief-related emotions may lead to crying, screaming, social withdrawal, insomnia, and changes in eating patterns. ***Mourning*** refers to the behaviors expected by one's cultural and/or religious tradition, such as wearing black clothing to a formal funeral service (NCI, 2006). Often in popular literature these terms are used interchangeably, though that may lead to some erroneous assumptions. While all human beings react when something precious is lost (bereavement) and most all of us respond with distressing emotions (grief), our expression of those emotions and our social expectations (mourning) may be quite different if one is following Jewish, Catholic, or Baptist customs (Hardy-Bougere, 2008).

Bereavement is often described as having four phases, with the first being *shock and numbness,* similar to Kubler-Ross's first stage of dying. Even when a death is anticipated there is often a surprising amount of shock and disbelief. The second phase involves an intense sense of *separation anxiety.* During this time loved ones may bring out pictures and personal mementos, sometimes creating a shrine for the deceased. It is important during this time for the bereaved to repeat the story of how the loved one died and tell of how they felt when they witnessed it or heard about it. This longing to be close to the memory of the deceased will eventually give way to the third phase, *disorganization and despair.* During this time individuals may find it hard to concentrate and maintain attention. They may also feel physically exhausted. For the bereaved who spent months or years in caregiving, staying with their loved one through their death, they may now feel the effects of years of physical and emotional exhaustion. The final phase is reorganization and the slow adjustment to *new routines* (NCI, 2006).

Your Thoughts?

Would you support a law that in the case of the death of a spouse an employee would automatically have one month off as bereavement leave?

It will take time to work through the bereavement period, particularly for those closely influenced by the one who died. Signs that healing is occurring are less crying, less sensitivity to other's comments, and less fatigue. As healing continues individuals will be able to comfortably spend time alone, concentrate on a book or video, and hear that person's favorite music without crying. Eventually those who were so distraught at one point will be able to

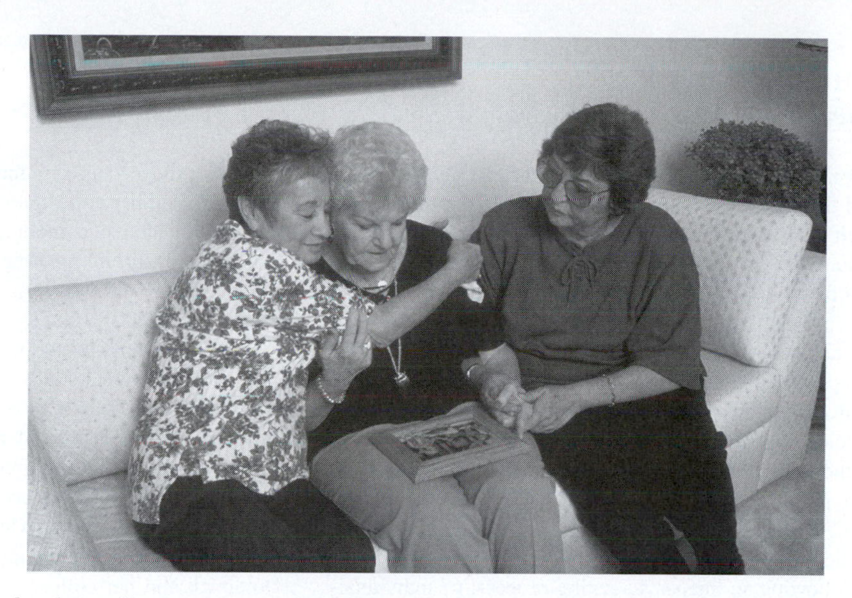

During the phase of bereavement in which separation anxiety is strong, widows may have difficulty putting away or letting go of items that remind them of their husbands.

look forward to holidays and new experiences, find things to be thankful for, and recall pleasant memories of the one who died (Fitzgerald, 2002).

Complicated Grief

Those who have an exceptionally difficult time adjusting, experiencing intense and long-lasting grief, bitterness, emptiness, and a bleak outlook on the future, may have developed ***complicated grief*** (Tomarken et al., 2008). For most people the symptoms of grief start to ease within 6 months. That doesn't mean that individuals have fully recovered, but that their grief is becoming manageable. Those with complicated grief may not experience any easing of their grief symptoms for many months or even years. Whereas under normal circumstances those who are grieving will have a bad day now and again, those with complicated grief may find it difficult to maintain employment, social relationships, or normal functioning (Mayo Clinic, 2007).

While the potential for complicated grief can exist in any number of situations, among those at high risk are individuals who have recently become widows or widowers. Adjusting to widowhood may involve issues of renegotiating one's place in the family, changes in residence, financial changes, and changes in personal relationships (Ott, 2003). Spouses who were primary caregivers for the deceased through a long illness are at particularly high risk for complicated grief as well as depression, emotional distress, insomnia, and if frail or ill, at a higher risk of death (Holtslander, 2008). A recent meta-analysis examining mental diagnoses among recently widowed individuals, involving approximately 8,000 adults, found that during the first year of bereavement nearly one out of every five widows was diagnosed with major depressive disorder. Slightly more than 1 out of every 10 met the criteria for posttraumatic stress disorder, and there were higher levels of panic disorder and generalized anxiety disorder (Onrust & Cuijpers, 2006). It will be important in the understanding and treatment of complicated grief to determine precisely how it is distinct from depression and posttraumatic stress disorder. It may be useful to isolate complicated grief as a diagnosis in the next edition of the

Your Thoughts?

How would you design a study to compare complicated grief, depression, and posttraumatic stress disorder?

ON THE LEADING EDGE
Internet-Based Therapy for Grieving Individuals

Sally Dominick and her associates from the Oregon Center for Applied Science teamed up with colleagues from the Oregon Research Institute, Yale University, College of New Rochelle, and Columbia University to explore the usefulness of Internet-based software designed to help individuals working through the grieving process. Among those whose grief experience is typical, rather than those whose experience is so intense they develop psychiatric symptoms, many report an increase in the use of alcohol or other drugs, greater absenteeism from work, more accidents, and increased visits to healthcare professionals during their recovery (Dominick, et al., 2010). A user-friendly software program that could be accessed at any time has the potential to help grieving individuals cope productively by finding help when they need it most.

Following an intense screening process, 67 individuals were selected to participate, with 33 receiving access to the software (treatment) and 34 serving as the control group. Most of the participants were female, middle-aged, employed, had attained college degrees, and grieving the loss of a parent. Dominick and her colleagues used an Internet-based software program divided into modules that included self-help questionnaires to explore grieving styles, surveys to assess coping skills, educational articles, and video testimonials. Participants were able to work through the modules in any order and to return to completed modules.

Results indicated that the software program was a great success, offering help to those who participants while creating no problems or detrimental side-effects. Those who used the Internet-based program progressed in their adjustment, improved in self-efficacy, and reduced their anxiety. Participants felt learning about different styles of grieving and hearing about processes others had gone through were particularly valuable. Dominick and her colleagues (2010) were able to show that even with something as personal as the process of grieving the use of Internet-based self-help programs could be effective in promoting healing and healthy coping skills.

DSM (Ott, 2003). Those who have developed complicated grief are encouraged to join a support group or seek psychotherapy rather than try to work through the symptoms on their own (Abeles et al., 2004; NCI, 2006; Wagner, Knaevelsrud, & Maercker, 2006).

Section Summary

- One of the first public signs of mourning following a death is often a funeral or memorial service.
- There are many decisions to be made whether the wishes of the deceased were to be buried or cremated, particularly if the family desires a traditional funeral.
- During the bereavement process individuals must learn to cope with the gap in their lives left by the deceased.
- For most people the symptoms of bereavement start to ease and significant healing takes place in the first 6 months.
- Some individuals experience depression, anxiety, and prolonged and intense grieving called *complicated grief.*
- Complicated grief can present symptoms similar to depression and posttraumatic stress disorder.

Chapter Summary

Having a conversation about dying and death can be difficult for many people. For the individual who is anticipating death there are decisions that can be made before emergencies arise, such as the types of advance directives desired. Once an individual is deemed to be at the end of life there are other issues that may be considered, such as palliative care. The individual moving through the dying process is often accompanied by friends and loved ones who will eventually mark the passing of that individual, cope with the bereavement process, and later begin to develop new routines. Here are some of the main points of the chapter:

- Death anxiety is common in the general public, usually higher in women, and peaks in intensity in young adulthood.
- Advance directives, such as living wills and durable power of attorney for health care, are designed to make the wishes of an individual known when that individual is incapacitated or cannot communicate.
- Hospice care, a type of palliative care, is an approach encompassing the physical, psychological, and spiritual needs of individuals in the last few months of life, helping terminally ill patients remain alert and symptom-free as much as possible.
- As a last resort and final measure some families or patients may choose passive euthanasia by ceasing or not initiating life-sustaining measures, allowing the disease to progress as it will.
- Although active euthanasia is illegal, physician-assisted suicide is legal in Oregon and in some parts of the world.
- End-of-life research projects face numerous challenges, including convincing an IRB that the study is worth the potential discomfort and locating qualified and willing participants.
- Once the standard theory of psychological stages of dying, Kubler-Ross's theory has fallen out of favor with those in the social and health sciences.
- When interacting with someone who is dying it is important to allow honest conversation about important matters, even if it is very emotional or in some other way uncomfortable.
- As an individual approaches death there are expected physiological signs, such as less social interaction, decrease in appetite and bladder and bowel control, cool limbs, noisy breathing, muscle contractions, and an irregular heartbeat.
- Following death decisions need to be made regarding burial or cremation and, if desired, the type of funeral, memorial service, or public recognition of the deceased.
- Generally, individuals in bereavement pass through phases of shock, avoiding separation, disorganization and despair, and reorganization and recovery, although there are many individual differences and circumstances that may influence one's thoughts, behaviors, and coping skills.
- Complicated grief occurs when an individual experiences intense grief for months or years that seems to block healing and interferes with their routine functioning.

Key Terms

Death anxiety **(336)**
Advance directives **(338)**
Psychiatric advance directives **(339)**
Living will **(339)**
Health care proxy **(339)**
Durable power of attorney for health care **(339)**
Durable power of attorney for finances **(339)**
Palliative care **(341)**
Hospice care **(341)**
Quantitative research methods **(342)**
Qualitative research methods **(342)**
Phenomenological interview **(342)**
Structured interview **(342)**
Respite care **(342)**
Passive euthanasia **(343)**
Active euthanasia **(343)**
Physician-assisted suicide **(343)**
Bereavement **(350)**
Grief **(350)**
Mourning **(350)**
Complicated grief **(351)**

Comprehension Questions

1. How does death anxiety differ with age and gender?
2. What is the relationship between death anxiety and religiosity?
3. What is the difference between a living will and durable power of attorney for health care?
4. Describe three criticisms or problems with advance directives as they are currently developed and used.
5. What is palliative care and hospice care, and how are they different?
6. What is the difference between passive euthanasia, active euthanasia, and physician-assisted suicide?
7. What would an IRB look for in a research proposal to study the dying process in participants with only a short time to live?
8. Name and describe Kubler-Ross's stages of dying.
9. What are the most important things a loved one can do when sitting with someone who is dying?
10. What are the physiological indicators that death is close?
11. What is the difference between a traditional funeral, direct burial, and direct cremation?
12. Why is the Federal Trade Commission concerned about the purchase of funeral-related services and merchandise?
13. What is the difference between the terms *bereavement, grief,* and *mourning?*
14. What are the four phases of bereavement?
15. What is complicated grief?

Answers for Common Sense: Myth or Reality?

1. Myth: Death anxiety rises with age across adulthood. (See Death Anxiety, page 337.)
2. Reality: Women report higher levels of death anxiety than men. (See Death Anxiety, page 337.)
3. Myth: A living will designates what should be done with an individual's finances and property should that person be unconscious. (See Advance Directives, page 339).
4. Reality: It is not uncommon for families to refuse to allow a deceased loved one's organs to be donated even when that person had indicated "organ donor" on his or her driver's license. (See Advance Directives, page 339).
5. Reality: In order to be accepted for hospice care a patient's physician must believe that the individual has 6 months or less to live. (See Palliative Care and Hospice Programs, page 341).
6. Myth: A greater percentage of African American than white Americans take advantage of hospice services. (See Palliative Care and Hospice Programs, page 343).
7. Myth: Physician-assisted suicide is illegal in the United States. (See Euthanasia and Physician-Assisted Death, page 343).
8. Reality: It is common for a physical body to continue to move even after the individual has died. (See Physiological Changes, page 348).
9. Myth: It is important for loved ones to move away and stay away from a body once a person has died. (See Physiological Changes, page 348).
10. Reality: The average funeral cost is over $10,000. (See Marking the End of Life, page 350).

Suggested Readings

Cultural Influences on Conceptions of Death and Dying

Gire, J. T. (2002). How death imitates life: Cultural influences on conceptions of death and dying. In W. J. Lonner, D. L. Dinnel, S. A. Hayes, & D. N. Sattler (Eds.), *Online readings in psychology and culture* (Unit 14, Chapter 2), (http://www.wwu.edu/~culture), Center for Cross-Cultural Research, Western Washington University, Bellingham, WA. Available at http://www.ac.wwu.edu/~culture/gire.htm.

Anticipating Death and Bereavement

National Cancer Institute. (2010, May). Facing forward: When someone you love has completed cancer treatment. This booklet can be found at http://www.cancer.gov/cancertopics/Facing-Forward-When-Someone-You-Love-Has-Completed-Cancer-Treatment/PDF.

End-of-Life Issues in American Culture

Kolsky, K. (2008, January). End of life: Helping with comfort and care (NIH Publication No. 08-6036). Bethesda, MD: National Institute on Aging. This publication is available at http://www.nia.nih.gov/HealthInformation/Publications/endoflife/.

Dying and Death in Nigerian Culture

Eyetsemitan, F. (2002). Cultural interpretation of dying and death in a non-Western society: The case of Nigeria. In W. J. Lonner, D. L. Dinnel, S. A. Hayes, & D. N. Sattler (Eds.), *Online readings in psychology and culture* (Unit 14, Chapter 1), (http://www.wwu.edu/~culture), Center for Cross-Cultural Research, Western Washington University, Bellingham, WA. Available at http://www.ac.wwu.edu/~culture/Eyetsemitan2.htm.

Suggested Websites

Hospice Care

Medline Plus, sponsored by the U.S. National Library of Medicine and the National Institutes of Health, provides links to information, organizations, laws and related policies, and financial information on hospice care at http://www.nlm.nih.gov/medlineplus/bereavement.html.

Euthanasia and End-of-Life Decisions

See this website, supported by the University of San Diego, which provides links to readings, videos, statistical data, legal information, and medical issues surrounding euthanasia at http://ethics.sandiego.edu/Applied/Euthanasia/.

Facts about the Costs of Funerals

The Federal Trade Commission has supplied a detailed description of the "funeral rule" as part of their program "Protecting American's Consumers" at http://www.ftc.gov/bcp/conline/pubs/buspubs/funeral.shtm.

Bereavement

Medline Plus, sponsored by the U.S. National Library of Medicine and the National Institutes of Health, provides links to resources and information on coping and working through the pain of losing a loved one at http://www.nlm.nih.gov/medlineplus/bereavement.html.

CHAPTER

14 Life Satisfaction

Consistent with a focus on successful aging, this book ends not with the expected topics of dying and death, but rather with an overall perspective on adult development. When considering optimal development and life satisfaction it is important to ask how we perceive our *self,* and how that changes with age and experience. As demonstrated by practically all the topics in this text, development is highly influenced by individual differences. The way we view ourselves shapes the way we present ourselves to our social environment, and in turn will influence the ways people in our social environment respond to us. One's sense of self-esteem, self-worth, and identity are likely to influence our perspective on personal life satisfaction.

Whereas our sense of self may be viewed as foundational development, the wisdom that comes from experience may be conceptualized as meaningful development. This chapter explores the notion of successful aging as "the good life"—not defined in ideal, philosophical, or theological terms, but rather in terms of the wisdom human beings gain across their lives, learning from experience what really matters in life and how best to achieve happiness and contentment. Of course, some of those experiential lessons are learned from tragedy, difficult times, and the sting of living with regrets.

If psychologists had beyond-human powers the most appropriate research study for this chapter would be to interview those who have completed their lives, asking them for their lessons learned. Imagine asking, "Now that you have experienced all of life, what do you think are the most important things people should know, value, or do? Overall, what things brought you the most happiness? What things do you regret?" Clearly, such a study is not an option, so we are left to gather the lessons we learn across adulthood. This chapter brings this book to a close by briefly revisiting some of the most important points from previous chapters, particularly those items that may influence life satisfaction and successful aging.

COMMON SENSE
Myth or Reality?

Mark each of the following items with either an M, if you think it is a myth, or an R, if you think the statement reflects reality. By paying close attention you can find all the answers in this chapter. If needed, the answers are also given at the end of the chapter.

1. _____ Most researchers see "self" as a unified concept and approach it that way.
2. _____ Researchers find that people that are continually reinventing and adjusting their identity and sense of self have the highest life satisfaction.
3. _____ Morals or values tend to be separate from self-esteem.
4. _____ People with low self-esteem tend to create negative meaning from neutral events.
5. _____ Researchers find that by watching others we develop a sense of our own chances of succeeding at a particular task.
6. _____ Researchers have found that having a strong belief that one can succeed in an area is not related to one's performance in that area.
7. _____ Researchers find that individuals' image of their ideal selves change throughout adulthood.
8. _____ The goal of wisdom is to develop a sophisticated way of thinking such that there are no contradictions, paradoxes, or gaps in understanding.
9. _____ Differences in subjective (personally determined) well-being are large when comparing various racial/ethnic groups.
10. _____ Life satisfaction is higher among people who are married.
11. _____ Life satisfaction is strongly associated with personality characteristics.
12. _____ People have more regrets related to their education than they do regarding their career or romantic life.
13. _____ People have more intense regret over actions taken that turned out to be poor choices than they do over opportunities they didn't take.

Before We Get Started . . .

Although it appears from ancient writing humankind has sought wisdom for centuries, psychologists still find it difficult to define or capture. Much like creativity, people can recognize wisdom in words and actions, and yet it is difficult to quantify or teach. Later in this chapter we will find two different psychological approaches to measuring wisdom. In order to better understand these approaches, take a few minutes to write your response to the following two questions:

1. A 40-year-old man wants to quit his job and go to college. What would you say to him? What should he consider and/or do? Write down as many responses as you can.
2. What are the characteristics of a wise person? Write down as many characteristics, traits, or descriptions as you can think of for a wise person.

Item 1, Wise Words and Actions: Wisdom may reveal itself in the advice someone gives to another person, much like what you might say to a hypothetical middle-aged man who wants to go to college. Some psychologists look for wisdom in folk sayings, proverbs, parables, and fables. Later in this chapter we revisit the hypothetical character in item one and you can get an idea of how well you might have done on that wisdom question.

Item 2, Wise People: When you think of a wise person did you think of a generic, hypothetical figure, a real person, or a character from media, literature, or history? Now that you've given it some thought, do you think a wise person is practically a perfect person? Do you think a wise person has to be intelligent? Successful? Nice? Religious? Do you think that only older adults can be wise? Did you think of men and women when thinking of someone wise? Did you think of people of different ethnic groups than yours?

You can compare your views on what wisdom is with the various theorists as you read through this chapter. Some psychologists believe that wisdom is found in advice or good counsel, whereas others believe wisdom is a characteristic or trait a person has, leading that person to do and say wise things.

Self: The Core of Development

Most, if not all, of the personal topics discussed in this book are filtered through our ever-evolving sense of self. While there is no universally accepted definition of self-concept (Byrne, 1996), the term generally refers to everything an individual thinks about him- or herself. Our self-concept is our personal, *subjective* perception, no matter how accurate or removed from reality others may judge that perception to be. Most of us have a complex set of private assumptions that make up our ***self-concept.*** Have you ever felt like a certain style of clothing, a haircut, or even a particular type of music just *fit* you? Or, perhaps you had the opposite experience, such as looking at yourself after a haircut and thinking, "That just doesn't fit me at all." In those cases you are trying to match an external image with your concept of your inner self.

> **Your Thoughts?**
>
> How would you describe or explain self-concept without using the words *self* or *concept?*

The recent trend in self-concept research has been to move away from the idea that self is a unified or global construct toward a view of self as a collection of many different features (Labouvie-Vief, Chiodo, Goguen, Diehl, & Orwoll, 1995). Generally, the models of self that do include a generalized self-concept envision it as being made up of many different yet overlapping components, such as social self-concept, physical self-concept, and intellectual or academic self-concept, as illustrated in Figure 14.1. Often those are broken down as well into different social roles, types of physical activity and appearance, and various academic disciplines and talents (Byrne, 1996; Seeshing Yeung et al., 2000). Another indication that research on

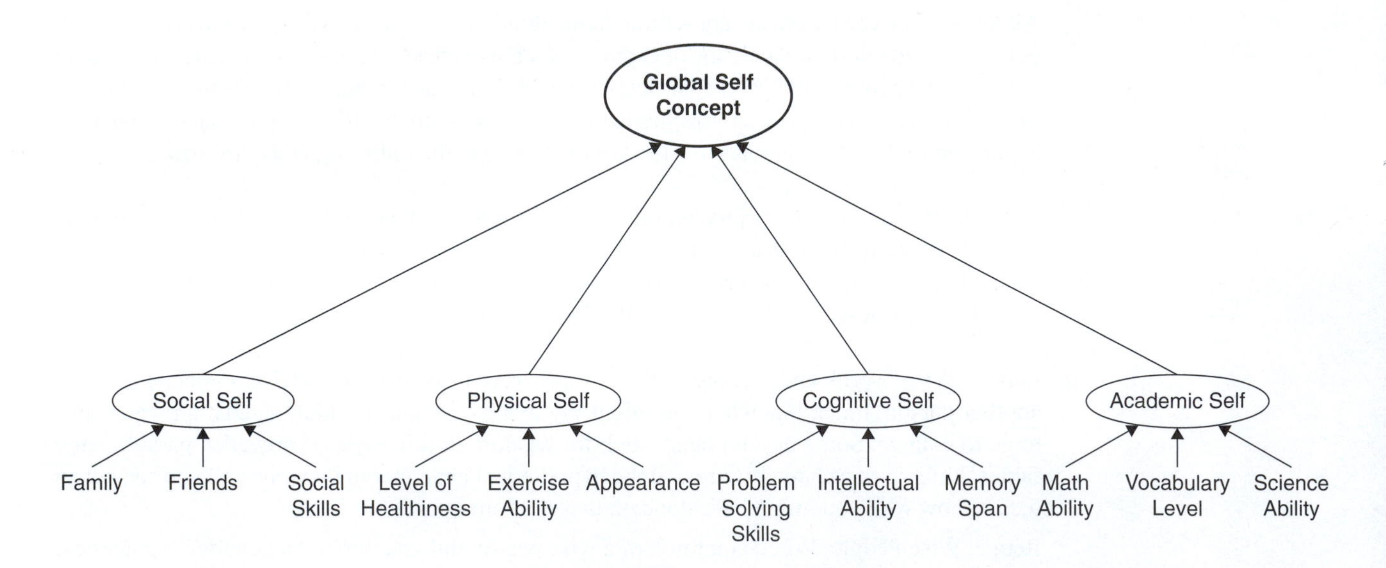

FIGURE 14.1 ***Common Model of Generalized Self-Concept***

Seeshing Yeung, Chui, Lau, McInerney, Rossell-Bowie, & Suliman (2000). Copyright by the American Psychological Association. Reprinted with permission.

Your Thoughts?

In which of these aspects of self would you predict the most changes across adulthood? Which would be the most stable?

self-concept has focused on specific domains is the growing number of research terms that begin with "self," such as:

self-acceptance
self-actualization
self-appraisal
self-assurance
self-awareness
self-concept
self-confidence
self-consciousness
self-control
self-criticism
self-definition
self-determination
self-discipline
self-efficacy
self-enhancement
self-esteem
self-evaluation
self-image
self-management
self-perception
self-regard
self-regulation
self-representation
self-respect
self-worth

This section considers several important aspects of the self, but by no means will it cover all the possible areas. True to an emphasis on adult development, this section on self is primarily focused on change and stability with age.

Self-Schemas and Identity Process Theory

Some psychologists find it useful to view self-concept as a specialized type of ***schema.*** Cognitive-developmental psychologist Jean Piaget used the term *schemas* to refer to the networks individuals use to organize the information stored in their memories. Piaget viewed cognitive development as the continued adjusting of our schemas using assimilation and accommodation. ***Assimilation*** involves interpreting new information based on current schemas, whereas ***accommodation*** involves creating new schemas and refining established ones. For example, when my nephew was in preschool he received a puppy for his birthday. When I asked him if the puppy was a boy or a girl he looked at me in a confused way and said, "Dogs are boys and cats are girls." He was in the process of building his schemas of boy-things and girl-things. In this case he was *assimilating* because he took this new item, his puppy, and placed it in his pre-existing boy-things schema. At some point after our conversation he was forced to *accommodate* and realize that dogs can be girls too, thus changing his schema accordingly. While Piaget's work is primarily associated with child development, adults may employ assimilation and accommodation as well.

Self-schemas refer to the structure or framework people use to cluster or network together complex information about themselves (Markus, 1977). Susan Krauss Whitbourne and her colleagues have combined the processes of building self-schemas, assimilation, accommodation, and Erikson's work on identity to create ***identity process theory*** (Whitbourne, Sneed, & Skultety, 2002). Young adults have, presumably, worked through their identity crisis and have incorporated their identity into their self-schema. That self-schema is not fixed but will continue to evolve as those young adults become employees, spouses/partners, parents, homeowners, and members of the community. Whitbourne's view is that young adults reconcile these new roles with their self-schemas through the use of ***identity assimilation*** and ***identity accommodation.*** When using identity assimilation individuals can maintain consistency by interpreting any new information in light of their existing self-schema. For example, consider a middle-aged man who has been a well-respected high school teacher for over 20 years. His self-schema includes the characteristics of "outstanding" and "experienced" teacher. When a student gets upset at this man after receiving a bad grade, telling the teacher "You're the worst teacher in the school," this man can easily use identity assimilation to dismiss the comment. He knows better, and this assertiont does not fit his self-schema. When identity accommodation occurs individuals must modify their existing self-schema and perhaps create new aspects or understandings of self. Suppose our experienced male teacher is also a faithful husband who finds out that his wife is having an affair, and after confronting her with the information, she states that she wants a divorce. Consider how his self-schema may change in the midst of this traumatic experience. He is forced by the situation to accommodate by eliminating those characteristics that do not fit anymore, such as "happily married" and perhaps even "trusting." He must begin to incorporate some new characteristics into his self-schema, such as "divorced" and, at least for a while, "suspicious of others."

Your Thoughts?

What additional examples of an event, positive or negative, might equally jolt a person's self-schema?

Identity process theory can be applied to late adulthood and aging as well. One can choose to maintain a sense of self as younger, using identity assimilation, or use identity accommodation to modify and create a new sense of "me" as older. Is it healthy for a woman in her 70s, for example, to color her hair, wear makeup, and dress in a younger fashion so that she can assimilate her appearance into her younger self-schema? Is it better for such a woman not to hide her gray hair or try to make her face look younger, and incorporate *old, wise,* and perhaps *grandmotherly* into her self-schema? Based on data collected from 94 adults ranging in age from 21 to 64, Sneed and Whitbourne (2001) found that those who rely mostly on identity accommodation felt less satisfied with their self-concept. They were not comfortable with a continually changing and less stable self-schema. Those who used identity assimilation displayed moderately high satisfaction with their self-concept. Based on these findings one might conclude that identity assimilation is preferable; however, there are other issues to be considered. Whitbourne suggests that older adults who rely on identity assimilation, insisting that they are young when they are not, may ignore important warning signs of illness or hurt themselves in their effort to ignore the aging process (Whitbourne et al., 2002).

Your Thoughts?

What personality traits might influence a person's preference or willingness to engage in identity assimilation and accommodation?

Sneed and Whitbourne (2001) found that the participants who employed ***identity balance,*** that is, the use of both identity assimilation and accommodation, demonstrated the highest levels of satisfaction and self-esteem across adulthood. They successfully adjusted to the aging process by flexibly adapting to age-related changes through accommodation and yet used assimilation to maintain a self-schema that was stable (Whitbourne et al., 2002). In late adulthood individuals may have to accommodate to include such changes as returning to single life when a spouse or partner dies, walking with a cane, or downsizing to a manageable living space. At the same time, however, those who maintain identity balance will use assimilation to maintain the core characteristics of their self-schema, such as "loving, competent, and good" (Sneed & Whitbourne, 2001).

Self-Esteem

Your Thoughts?

Would you support an employer who determined whether to hire applicants partly on their self-esteem? Why, why not, or under what circumstances?

The question, "How satisfied am I with the person I've become?" is one of personal evaluation and judgment, reflected in our ***self-esteem.*** People with high self-esteem feel good about themselves and that confidence often translates into success in many areas of their lives. In fact, many psychologists have considered self-esteem to be a primary indicator of well-being and overall psychological health (Tsai, Ying, & Lee, 2001). People who do not feel confident or happy with themselves have low self-esteem. Self-esteem is subjective in that, while it may be somewhat influenced by outside information, the final evaluation is determined by each individual.

After many years of research Coopersmith (1967) concluded that most people determine their self-esteem based on four areas of life: power, significance, competence, and virtue. Table 14.1 provides a summary of these four criteria. A sense of *power* comes from gaining reasonable control and decision-making power over one's own life and environment. Whether

TABLE 14.1 ***Coopersmith's Criteria for Self-Esteem***

Criteria	*Description*	*Characteristics*
Power	Range of ability to influence and control one's self and others	Self-discipline and self-control, respect, social poise, leadership, independence
Significance	Receiving acceptance, attention, and affection from others	Love, concern, interest, and appreciation shared and expressed by others and level of popularity
Competence	Ability to perform successfully and achieve	Success or mastery in age-appropriate tasks, such as those found in academics, athletics, and occupational challenges
Virtue	Adherence to moral and ethical standards	Following or practicing one's chosen principles, such as obeying laws, being truthful, and respecting others

Based on Coopersmith (1967).

it is gaining control over a disorganized schedule or personal finances, the ability to make our own choices regarding important factors will raise our self-esteem. The second area, *significance,* stems from our ties to friends, family, coworkers, community members, and others in the social environment. Those who feel socially accepted and have a social support network will have higher self-esteem. When we believe we have mastered an important task or knowledge base we gain in our evaluation of personal *competence.* For example, a young adult may feel competent because she has mastered the latest computer software while her grandfather may feel competent because at his advanced age he can still drive his car and maintain his own residence. In both cases the feeling of competence will lead to higher self-esteem. The final area, *virtue,* refers to the inner sense of being a "good person" based on our personal moral, ethical, and/or religious code. If, for example, we feel very strongly that communities should take care of older adults, then we will likely feel virtuous when volunteering at a local care facility, boosting our self-esteem. Coopersmith found that individuals do not need to believe that they are doing well in all four categories to achieve high self-esteem. Excelling in even one category alone can bring high self-esteem, as long as it is a category valued by the individual (Noller & Shugm, 1988; Reiter & Costanzo, 1986).

Your Thoughts?

How might Coopersmith's model be used by an employer to boost the morale of employees?

Researchers have found that individuals with high and low self-esteem are quite distinct. For example, Trzesniewski, Donnellan, and Robins (2003), in their meta-analysis of 50 research studies involving over 70,000 adults, found evidence that high self-esteem is related to numerous positive outcomes, such as occupational success, healthy social relationships, and a sense of well-being. In another review of previous studies, Rosenberg and Owens (2001) found that high self-esteem adults were motivated to continue to grow and develop even though they were basically content and happy with their self-concept. High self-esteem adults described personal challenges as gratifying and rewarding, whether they were ultimately successful at the challenges or not. On the other hand, low self-esteem adults, while not satisfied with themselves, are often not motivated to challenge themselves or pursue their dreams. Rosenberg and Owens found that these adults are hypersensitive to events or experiences that can be interpreted as a threat to their self-concept, such as personal criticism. Previous research has shown that these individuals will often create negative

Your Thoughts?

Would you support a health insurance company that required clients with low self-esteem to seek therapy before anxiety or depression had developed? Why or why not?

meaning from neutral events and they tend to exaggerate any negative experiences. Low self-esteem individuals view the avoidance of even the threat of failure or criticism as a higher priority than challenging themselves. Those with low self-esteem often display poor self-confidence, greater social anxiety, and depression and their general outlook is often quite cynical and pessimistic.

Researchers have found various factors to influence self-esteem. For example, Robins, Trzesniewski, Tracy, Gosling, and Potter (2002) found in a sample of 300,000 participants ranging in age from 9 to 90 years old that as a whole group, most of the participants displayed high self-esteem. When comparing by age groups, children displayed the highest levels of self-esteem whereas adolescents and participants 80 years old reflected the lowest self-esteem. Self-esteem was low in college-age participants, and then generally increased to a peak for those in their 50s. In terms of stability, researchers have found that self-esteem is less stable during middle and late adulthood (Trzesniewski et al., 2003). Just as self-schemas are evolving throughout adulthood as identity characteristics are assimilated and accommodated, self-esteem is apparently adjusting to the changing self-schemas as well.

Your Thoughts?

What factors might lead adults in their 50s to feel the best about their sense of self?

While there have been numerous studies of self-esteem, the construct is not without controversy. One area of concern is in defining terms with precision so that there are clear distinctions between such terms as *self-esteem, self-criticism,* and *self-worth.* Another related area of concern is determining which of the many questionnaires and interview techniques are the most accurate at measuring self-esteem (Robins et al., 2002). Even with such debate, the notion of self-esteem remains powerful.

Self-Efficacy

The first constructs presented in this section, self-concept, self-schemas, and self-esteem, have emphasized the way individuals currently view themselves. The aspect of self presented here, self-efficacy, and the notion of possible selves presented in the next section, emphasize the projections individuals make about their sense of self in the future. In terms of evaluating my current level of life satisfaction it could be that I believe I'm currently in a less desirable circumstance, with low satisfaction; however, I may believe that I am competent in particular areas or domains (self-efficacy) and with those competences in the future I will create a general self I am more satisfied with (possible ideal self).

Self-efficacy, introduced by well-known psychologist Albert Bandura, refers to our beliefs about our abilities, and thus our expectations regarding success at a task or effectiveness in an area of life. Researchers have found that self-efficacy varies according to situations and contexts. Regarding problem solving, for example, Artistico, Cervone, and Pezzuti (2003) found that younger and older adults demonstrate greater self-efficacy in areas that are common to their lifestyles. Younger adult participants expressed more confidence with problems relating to exams and computer use, while the older adults expressed higher self-efficacy regarding problems such as wanting relatives to visit more often and dealing with requests for babysitting. Studies have also demonstrated that raising the level of self-efficacy regarding memory in late adulthood participants can increase improvement in memory training sessions (West, Bagwell, & Dark-Freudeman, 2008).

Your Thoughts?

In addition to familiarity, what factors would contribute to younger adults having more confidence in these areas?

According to Bandura (1989, 1993), there are four primary influences on self-efficacy:

- Level of success in past experiences
- Observing others' experiences
- Advice from others
- Emotions related to the behaviors

To further explore Bandura's four foundations for self-efficacy, consider a hypothetical character, Juanita, who is wondering how she will be as a first-time mother. Bandura found that we often appraise our chances of success with a particular challenge based on similar kinds of experiences we have had in the past. Juanita will likely think of interactions she has had with infants and children, perhaps as a babysitter or at family gatherings. We also look to other people who are similar to us and consider how they performed in similar situations. This may lead Juanita to think of how her sister and her close friends were as first-time mothers. Juanita may be thinking, "If she can do a good job I know I can too." We are also likely to pay attention to words of encouragement from others. Juanita will probably ask the important people in her life, "Do you think I'm ready for parenting?" and she will pay close attention to their responses. Words of encouragement or caution will likely sway Juanita's attitude. The last of the four primary influences is the emotional response felt after imagining the expected behaviors or after experiencing something similar to the expected behaviors. Juanita may think of the great satisfaction she feels when she helps her nephew with his homework or how envious she is when she watches her friend interacting with his infant daughter. Bandura would predict that Juanita would consider all these influences in creating her sense of self-efficacy regarding parenting. He would also predict that her final appraisal of self-efficacy will then influence her cognitions and emotions regarding parenting, influencing her motivation and level of satisfaction after she actually becomes a parent.

Your Thoughts?

If your grandmother is sure she could not use a computer, how might you use the four influences to change her mind?

One area of recent research with older adults has been to assess the influence of self-efficacy on issues of health and aging. In a study of 216 older adults with arthritis, Gyurcsik, Estabrooks, and Frahm-Templar (2003) found that those with higher exercise-related self-efficacy were more likely to regularly attend exercise sessions. These results are consistent with earlier studies, which found that not only will self-efficacy increase participation in exercise routines, but also that involvement in regular exercise increases exercise-related self-efficacy, thus creating a cycle of confidence and exercise adherence. Li, McAuley, Harmer, Duncan, and Chaumeton (2001) found a similar healthy cycle of self-efficacy and persistence when observing older adults involved in low-impact tai chi, a Chinese form of exercise. Those who believed they could be successful with tai chi participated more, and the more they participated the stronger their self-efficacy became. Even in end-of-life issues, levels of self-efficacy are important for older adults. Working with 288 adults ranging in age from 65 to 87 years old, Fry (2003) found that women who believed they could succeed in areas of interpersonal, social, and emotional matters, and thus displayed stronger self-efficacy in these areas, also demonstrated less fear of the unknown, dying, and death. Fry found that the men in the study, those who had stronger self-efficacy in instrumental or active areas, organizational skills, and in physical domains, also demonstrated less fear of the unknown, dying, and death. High self-efficacy in key areas can be quite an asset for older adults, and a predictor of overall sense of life satisfaction.

Your Thoughts?

For all adults, but particularly young adults, what other domains might be influenced by high self-efficacy in academic classroom tasks?

Possible Selves

Your Thoughts?

In addition to personal influences, what societal or cultural factors might influence the characteristics of our ideal and feared selves?

Whereas self-efficacy is focused on one's prediction of success or failure in particular areas of life, ***possible selves*** reflect a general image of what we believe we could potentially become in the future. What do you hope your life will be like in 5 or 10 years? What are you hoping for in terms of your lifestyle, career, family life, and physical characteristics? Your responses to those questions reflect your ***ideal self***, which is your realistically possible best future self. Your ***feared self***, on the other hand, reflects your worst possible self. Do you worry that you might fail in some areas of life or experience deteriorating health? Your feared self contains all those things you are afraid you may become in the future. Possible selves are viewed as a link between self-concept and motivation regarding the future (Oyserman & Markus, 1990) and as

Becoming homeless and without income may be, for some people, their feared self.

a powerful influence in performance in particular domains (Cross & Markus, 1994; Ruvolo & Markus, 1992). One way of gauging life satisfaction is to ask how close we are to becoming either our ideal selves or our feared selves.

Generally, self-growth involves continual modification and enhancement of our ideal selves, inspiring us toward something greater and greater from childhood, through adolescence, and into young adulthood. For example, the ideal self for a college student may include a "perfect" body, greater than average wealth, a high-status job, and a fast-paced, exciting lifestyle. There are many possible reasons for this elaborate vision, including the improved cognitive abilities of adolescents and young adults and the influence of their peers and culture. In some cases it is likely that a young adult's actual circumstance is very far from this elaborate ideal self. It is debated as to whether a large gap between one's real and ideal self is productive or destructive. Carl Rogers, a noted personality theorist, believed that a great distance between these two parts of the self was depressing, nonmotivating, and indicated psychopathology. Bybee and Wells's (2003) review of the literature found some indications that grand ideal selves can provide inspiration and motivation. The motivated individual may then begin making decisions, setting goals, and working in earnest toward that ideal self.

Your Thoughts?

What factors might lead someone to refuse to modify the younger version of their ideal self? What might be the consequences of resisting change?

As we move beyond young adulthood we restructure our ideal selves into more realistic yet still inspiring images. For example, the dream of having a "perfect" body may change to the goal of maintaining a body in good physical shape. The dream of having a particular job may change once we realize the amount of work and stress involved in that occupational role. The ideal self may shift to the goal of being happy with whatever job one has. The achievement of cognitive stability and full socialization into the culture are often suggested as reasons for these changes in the ideal self (Bybee & Wells, 2003).

Consistent with what Bybee and Wells (2003) found in their literature review, Cross and Markus (1991) also found that ideal and feared selves change with age. In their study of 173 adults the researchers found that with age participants gave progressively fewer characteristics for their ideal and feared selves. Those under age 25 tended to give extremely positive and unrealistic ideal selves, and their feared selves tended to be negations of their ideal selves. For example, an ideal self characteristic might be to have great wealth while the feared self characteristic includes having no job or income. They also tended to be concerned with the major transitions in their lives, particularly regarding marriage, family, and career matters. The participants, ranging in age from 25 to 39 years old, gave less extreme, more realistic, and more concrete ideal selves. They mentioned more characteristics related to personal and leisure activities, and their feared selves were more focused on social status and role expectations. For these adults their ideal self might include exercising every day, while the feared self might include failing as a parent or spouse. The midlife participants, ages 40–59 years old, were more connected with their current selves. Their ideal selves tended to focus on enjoying what they had, while their feared selves reflected worries with aging. Many of their feared selves focused on losing their abilities, finances, and family support in late adulthood (Cross & Markus, 1991).

The oldest group in this study, those ages 60–86, tended to place issues of aging at the center of their ideal and feared selves. Their ideal selves involved images of maintaining physical activity as well as personal development and growth. Their feared selves reflected the detrimental effects of mental and physical aging (Cross & Markus, 1991), such as memory deficits (Dark-Freudeman, West, & Viverito, 2006). Frazier, Cotrell, and Hooker (2003) explored these patterns further by comparing a group of adults diagnosed with the early stages of Alzheimer's disease, a group diagnosed with Parkinson's disease, and a group of healthy adults ranging in age between 55 and 85 years old. They found that the three groups were balanced in terms of the selves they "hoped for" and those they feared, although among the feared selves the two groups with illness feared losing independence more than the healthy group. Frazier et al., believe these findings suggest that the use of possible selves in counseling with patients may help them move toward realist-to-achieve selves that are positive and motivating.

Your Thoughts?

How might the SOC model be applied to these shifts in self assessment?

Although the trend in self-related research studies is to explore distinct aspects of self, it appears that these concepts are integrated. As individuals make judgments (self-esteem) about themselves (self-concept) they also adjust their motivation (self-efficacy), dreams (ideal self), and worries (feared self), allowing all of that information to be filtered through their self-schemas (identity process theory). Ultimately, our sense of overall life satisfaction will be influenced by these shifts in self.

Self-Actualization

This section on the self as the core of development concludes with a theory that, while not a developmental model associated with aging, does offer a framework through which we can better understand our sense of self and life satisfaction. Abraham Maslow, a well-known humanistic psychologist, promoted the concept of ***self-actualization*** as a key motivator in human nature. Consistent with the movement toward positive psychology, Maslow wanted to expand the focus of psychology in the 1960s from not only understanding pathology but also life satisfaction. He was intrigued by those who were happiest and most satisfied with their lives. Ultimately, he created his theory around four basic principles:

Your Thoughts?

Do you agree that people are responsible for what they become? Why, why not, or under what circumstances?

- Our sense of self is important
- Our self can change and grow
- We should take responsibility for what we become
- We have the ability to influence social development (Pearson, 1999)

Maslow (1968/1999, 1970, 1971) believed that all people are born with an internal motivation to be their best, which would be to reach self-actualization. To be self-actualized does not mean that we have become perfect or achieved our ideal possible self, but rather we have achieved our realistic potential. Maslow believed that such a focus on personal growth and life satisfaction can be achieved only after certain needs in our lives have been met. He prioritized in value from the most basic survival needs to more abstract psychological needs

TABLE 14.2 ***Maslow's Hierarchy of Needs***

Needs	*Examples*	*Types of Needs*
Self-actualization	Need to develop individual differences, potential, talent, self-fulfillment	Growth
Esteem needs	Social status, respect, recognition, self-worth, self-confidence, mastery	Deficiency
Belongingness and love needs	Close friends, intimacy, family, group membership	Deficiency
Safety needs	Shelter, security, protection, order and structure	Deficiency
Physiological needs	Food, water, air, sleep, pain avoidance, sex and reproduction	Deficiency

Based on Maslow (1970).

(see Table 14.2). No matter what age, if adults do not have enough food or water their sense of life satisfaction depends on getting those survival needs met. When those basic needs are not in question, attention and energy is turned toward safety. If we do not feel safe from harm in our home, such as the experience of victims of domestic violence or elder abuse, we will be afraid and anxious. The need to feel safe must be addressed before we can move up to the next level, the need for affiliation, friends, family, love, and affection. As those needs are adequately met we move to the next level, which is focused on self-esteem needs. At this level we are seeking respect and recognition from family, friends, and the greater community. Finally, when all the lower needs are met, we can move into the experience of self-actualization.

It is important to note that these are not once-filled-and-forever-filled steps or stages, and that we may be moving through the hierarchy at any age. For example, a successful high school student may be focused on self-actualization until moving away from home to college. On campus that student may become focused on basic needs, spending time and energy getting used to a new living space, perhaps eating more than usual, and trying to find like-minded people to make friends. It will take some time to move up to esteem needs and self-actualization again. A similar experience may be found with older adults as they transition to living with adult children or moving to an assisted-living center. Movement in the hierarchy of needs may occur due to a tragedy, such as the diagnosis of an illness or the death of a spouse. Although not directly tied to age, the structure of the hierarchy and the quest for self-actualization can provide further understanding of our ultimate goal of achieving and maintaining high life satisfaction.

Your Thoughts?

How might posttraumatic stress syndrome or disorder be related to Maslow's hierarchy of needs?

Section Summary

- The study of *self,* as it evolves with age and experience, is usually divided into various facets or components, such as self-concept, self-schemas, and self-esteem.
- Identity process theory proposes that individuals continually evaluate environmental information using assimilation and accommodation to maintain or modify their self-schemas.
- The evaluation of whether one is satisfied with his or her sense of self, one's self-esteem, is often shaped by a sense of power, significance, competence, and virtue.
- Whereas self-concept, self-schemas, and self-esteem focus on current perspectives, self-efficacy extends that to predicting future success in particular areas.

- Possible selves include the best we can dream of realistically becoming (ideal self) and the worst we can imagine of ourselves (feared self).
- Maslow's hierarchy of needs provides a pathway that leads from deficiencies (physiological, security, affiliation, and esteem needs) to self-growth and self-actualization.

Wisdom: Meaningful Development

Wisdom involves integrating the lessons learned from life experiences into an expertise that can be applied to difficult problems and challenges. Although not a guaranteed outcome of life experience, those who reflect on the lessons learned are likely to adjust their sense of self, grow in wisdom, make better choices, and gain in life satisfaction. The quest to understand wisdom as the ultimate stage in adult development has presented numerous research challenges. How might wisdom be defined and measured? Erikson and other personality theorists have used terms such as *integrated, advanced,* and *mature* in defining wisdom (Kramer, 2003; Shedlock & Cornelius, 2003), all of which are still rather vague and difficult to define terms. Baltes and Staudinger, who established one of the most well-known wisdom research programs in the world, wrote, "Wisdom may be beyond what psychological methods and concepts can achieve" (2000, p. 123). Sternberg, whose research has explored love and intelligence as well as wisdom, reminds all of us that "To understand wisdom fully and correctly probably requires more wisdom than any of us have" (1990a, p. 3). Nonetheless, theorists and researchers continue to investigate wisdom in its forms as advanced cognition, actions, and expertise in difficult life situations.

Your Thoughts?

Is it reasonable to spend research money and time on wisdom or should those resources be put into other efforts? Give reasons to support your response.

Wisdom as Advanced Cognition

Several theories of wisdom came from the desire to extend Piaget's theory of cognitive development further into adulthood. In his four-stage model, Piaget proposed that infants begin learning through their five senses and through moving around, thus his first stage was called the *sensorimotor* stage. That was followed by a basic understanding of concepts and labeling, which he called *preoperations. Concrete operations* follows in the elementary school years, during which children learn to categorize concepts and use simple forms of logic. The "concreteness" of concrete operations keeps these individuals focused on literal meanings and physical observations. The final stage of cognitive development in Piaget's theory is *formal operations.* Adolescents in this advanced stage are now capable of sophisticated logical and abstract reasoning. In Piagetian theory, this mathematical, logical, scientific reasoning is the most advanced. When the field of lifespan developmental psychology began to thrive, and with it the study of young, middle, and late adulthood, the area of ***postformal operations*** was developed. Rather than creating a new stage of more complex logical reasoning, postformal operations are generally described as a series of stages that emphasize the integration of emotions, social context, paradoxes, intuition, and subjectivity with logical and abstract processing, as well as highlighting the many uncertainties and unknowns that are often a part of major life situations.

Your Thoughts?

What type of everyday problem might not be solved by a scientific, logical line of reasoning but rather by wisdom?

One example, the theory of *postformal levels,* developed by Labouvie-Vief (1990), highlights the integration and growing complexity of advanced reasoning. The first level, the *intrasystemic reasoning level,* involves the ability to use one particular way of thinking, such as using logic to lead to truths, the right answer, or the only solution. The next level, the *intersystemic reasoning level,* advances cognition so that separate, multiple ways of thinking or systems are recognized. In this level we often experience conflict and tension because the different ways of thinking seem incompatible and irreconcilable. For example, operating in this level we may realize that the way our religion has taught us to respond to a situation (one system) may be quite different from cultural expectations (a second system). The final stage, the *integrated reasoning level,* brings an appreciation of many perspectives and paradoxes. We gain a better understanding of how all of us are shaped by our environmental and historical context. This new awareness helps us put our self-chosen principles in perspective when searching for the most appropriate response to a situation (Labouvie-Vief, 1990; Sebby & Papini, 1994). Commons and Richards (2003) extended the levels of integration proposed by Labouvie-Vief by creating the *postformal orders of hierarchical complexity* in which systems and overarching paradigms are compared, contrasted, and combined.

Your Thoughts?

What examples can you think of in which a well-known religious teaching is generally contradictory to societal expectations?

Another example of advanced cognition, Sinnott's *postformal complex thought,* emphasizes the role of uncertainties. She believes that a primary characteristic of postformal operations is "the realization that knowledge and truth are not absolute but must be chosen from possible truths by the knower" (1994, p. 107). When conducting research interviews measuring postformal thought Sinnott analyzes participants' responses for several characteristics, which are summarized in Table 14.3. Postformal complex thought involves the recognition that there are many ways to view, consider, and respond to any situation or piece of information. It also includes the ability to consider the ideal, hypothetical, concrete, and practical aspects of the current situation and to appreciate contradictions, paradoxes, missing pieces, and unknowable items in knowledge bases (Sinnott, 2003). It allows adults to hold several different ways of thinking in balance, such as a scientific way of thinking and an emotional or spiritual way of thinking. Balance is a way of acknowledging that all knowledge has some subjectivity within it, and that different ways of knowing or understanding can be equally valid (Sinnott, 1994, 1998, 2003). In a somewhat similar perspective, Meacham (1990) viewed wisdom not as the product of knowledge gained or developed personality characteristics, but rather as the appropriate use of doubt. Wise people realize what they do not know, and they

Your Thoughts?

Do you think Sinnott's or Meachm's perspectives are anti-religious? Why, why not, or under what circumstances?

ON THE LEADING EDGE
Social Conflicts and Wisdom

Igor Grossmann, Jinkyung Na, Michael Varnum, Shinobu Kitayama, and Richard Nisbett of the Department of Psychology at the University of Michigan along with Denise Park of the Center for Vital Longevity at the University of Texas at Dallas explored the commonly-held notion that wisdom, particularly good judgment about social conflicts, improves as people age.

When recruiting participants the researchers deliberately included individuals from a wide range of social classes and income levels. The 247 participants were approximately equal in gender and age ranges. They were divided into age groups of 25-40 years, 41-59 years, and 60 years old and older.

Grossmann and his colleagues developed stories to measure wisdom that involved conflicts between social groups and individuals. In one phase they asked participants to read a story written like a newspaper article about conflicts between two groups of people. Participants were then asked to explain what they thought would happen next and why, and then offered a chance to comment on anything else. In another phase they ask the participants to read stories in the form of a letter seeking advice from a third party. Again the participants were asked what they think happened after the letter was written and why, and what they believed should be done in the situation. In a final stage the researchers involved "experts" in wisdom from the Wisdom Research Network database in order to validate their scoring system.

Once data was collected the researchers could then begin assessing the participant's comments on six dimensions of wisdom that included flexibility in thinking, taking other's perspectives, observations on conflict and compromise, and ability to work with unknown or hard-to-predict facets of the dilemma. The results indicated that even though the younger adults scored higher on measures of traditional intelligence involving processing speed, the older adults did score higher on the measures of wisdom. Based on these findings Grossman and his colleagues (2010) suggest that older adults may be able to play key roles in intergroup negotiations and interpersonal conflicts.

TABLE 14.3 ***Sinnott's Postformal Complex Thought***

Examples of Postformal Characteristic	*Description*
Parameter setting	Realizing that a problem can be viewed in many different contexts and from many different angles, such that seemingly unrelated aspects may be related in some way
Problem definition	Considering many ways a problem can be interpreted or described, reflecting various priorities, motivations, and points of view
Process–product shift	Ability to move between choosing a process that works for problems of a particular type and choosing a specific product or outcome for a particular problem
Meta-theory shift	Ability to move between the ideal or theoretical and the practical
Pragmatism	Ability to order possible solutions from better to worse, choose a logical or rationale for the better solutions, and stick with that rationale
Multiple solutions	Generating multiple appropriate solutions to a problem that stem from using different rationales or approaches to the problem
Paradox	Ability to see contradictory outcomes or the ironic parts of problems and solutions, stemming from the multiple contexts of the problem
Self-referential thought	Realizing that one is using a complex thought process to consider the multiple facets of a problem, and realizing that ultimately one must choose a rationale and stick with it

Based on Sinnott (2003).

realize that even what they *think* they know may be filled with error or totally wrong. In his view, wise people are good at balancing confidence in their own knowledge and skills with useful doubt and skepticism.

Wisdom as Balancing Cognition and Action

While most psychologists would agree that advanced cognition is certainly a primary component of wisdom, Sternberg (1998, 2000a; Sternberg & Lubart, 2001) designed the *balance theory of wisdom* to highlight the interaction of internal wisdom and external behaviors or actions. Based on his years of research, Sternberg believes that wisdom requires a special type of knowledge called ***tacit knowledge.*** This type of knowledge is used in personally interesting, messy dilemmas that involve uncertain or unknowable factors, problems different from those usually found on standard intelligence tests. To better understand tacit knowledge consider a hypothetical scenario involving Clara, a college student who is sitting in her psychology class taking a traditional examination. She knows that there should be only one correct answer for each question, and that she must work quickly, individually, and quietly. She will use a different set of problem-solving skills for her psychology exam than she will when she returns to her

Your Thoughts?

Can a person display wise actions without thinking wise thoughts, or have wise thoughts without showing wise behaviors?

apartment to find her two roommates engrossed in a major disagreement. Her roommates' problems are probably more interesting on a personal level than the exam questions. On the exam the questions and answer choices were clear, whereas with the roommates Clara is not exactly sure what the primary conflict is or what can be done about it. There are other uncertainties and unknowns that influence the roommates' issues, such as discrepancies between each roommate's recollections of important events. Clara is pondering many possible solutions, such as one or the other moving out, both seeing a conflict mediator, or getting professors or counselors involved, but each possible solution has unpredictable aspects and each has its advantages and disadvantages. The roommate problem is a type of problem that requires tacit knowledge.

Your Thoughts?

What would you advise Clara to do?

Sternberg described tacit knowledge as the action-oriented knowledge we gain informally in life that guides us toward our personally valued goals. According to Sternberg, tacit knowledge has three main features. It is (1) comprised of procedures, (2) relevant to personally valued goals, and (3) usually acquired informally, with very little help from others. Tacit knowledge involves a very practical type of understanding of the environment and how to get things done in particular settings or situations. Someone who is high in tacit knowledge realizes that wise actions are context-specific, such that what is helpful in one situation may not be helpful in another. Returning to the roommate example, Clara is using tacit knowledge when she realizes that the language, tone, and mannerisms she uses with her roommates when they are arguing should not be used when she is talking to one of her professors.

Your Thoughts?

How is this view of wisdom similar to common sense? Different? Can you give examples to illustrate your points?

Sternberg calls his theory the *balance* theory because he believes that wisdom involves balancing three sets of interests, specifically:

- Intrapersonal (self interests)
- Interpersonal (the interests of others)
- Extrapersonal (the larger context)

The balance theory of wisdom challenges individuals to find the strategy or solution that allows them to achieve personal goals and desires while also finding the best good for others and the larger context, which may include an employer, city, society, or the environment. In Sternberg's view an individual who seeks only personal gain and/or harm to others or the environment is not wise, even if that person is academically intelligent. For example, Clara may determine that her priority is to have a calm atmosphere for relaxation and study in her apartment, an intrapersonal interest. Even though she may be able to accomplish that temporarily by lying about her roommates in order to get them evicted, Sternberg would not accept her intention to harm her roommates as a wise choice. In order for Clara to appropriately use the balance theory of wisdom, she must use tacit knowledge to determine the most productive intrapersonal, interpersonal, and extrapersonal responses.

Your Thoughts?

Can you think of someone who is/was successful but not wise? Someone who is/was wise and not successful?

In some cases the individual may use personal *adaptation,* which is changing oneself to adapt to the environment; *shaping,* which involves changing the environment to something more compatible with oneself; or *selection,* which is to move to a different environment completely (Berg & Sternberg, 2003; Sternberg & Lubart, 2001). Returning to Clara's roommate situation, she may try to adapt by learning about conflict resolution in order to help her roommates. She may also try to shape the environment, by helping one of the feuding roommates find another place to live; or she may decide the best choice for her is to change environments completely and find herself a new place to live. Once Clara takes action she will have utilized all aspects of the balance theory by applying tacit knowledge and her choice of behaviors in order to move closer to her own goals while working to the benefit of the environment.

By meeting the needs of a college class (self-interests) this student is also helping others (interpersonal) and the larger community (extrapersonal).

Wisdom as Expertise in Life

Along with postformal operations and the balance theory, another popular theory of wisdom is the *expertise in life theory of wisdom* developed by Baltes and his colleagues. They believe that wisdom includes several key elements, specifically good insights into the issue or dilemma requiring a wise response, factual and procedural knowledge, and knowledge of the context, values, and uncertainties of life (Smith & Baltes, 1990). The one general and five specific criteria used are listed in Table 14.4 (Baltes, Staudinger, Maercker, & Smith, 1995), along with some responses to the question posed in the Before We Get Started section of the chapter regarding the 40-year-old male who wants to quit his job to go to college. These are the criteria Baltes and his colleagues use to score responses to interview questions, which are similar to this 40-year-old's dilemma.

> **Your Thoughts?**
>
> Based on these criteria can a child be wise? Why, why not, or under what circumstances?

Typically, a participant in one of Baltes's studies would be asked to "think aloud" about a given dilemma. The dilemmas are presented with a very limited amount of information in order to observe the participant's assumptions and shifts in assumptions (Smith & Baltes, 1990). For example, did you assume that the 40-year-old male is an American or living in a Western culture? Did you assume he had a family and that his salary was the primary or only income? Did you assume that he was going to college to get a better job rather than going for self-fulfillment or a sense of accomplishment? Would it make a difference if you knew he had a terminal illness? Or that his employer was highly likely to go out of business? Or that he was recently divorced?

> **Your Thoughts?**
>
> Do you think wisdom is truly that rare? If so, why? If not, what might be flawed in their approach to studying wisdom?

Baltes and his colleagues have noted several consistent trends in wisdom research. Regarding age, the folk wisdom that as you get older you get wiser does not hold true in the data. For example, Smith and Baltes (1990) gave the wisdom interview test to German adults who ranged in age from 25 to 81 years old. The researchers did not expect wisdom to be very common in any age group, and the results indicated that only 5% of the 240 responses qualified as wise. Those responses were evenly distributed between the young, middle, and late adulthood groups. They did find, however, that participants gave wiser responses to dilemmas

TABLE 14.4 ***Baltes's Criteria for Wise Responses***

Wisdom Criteria	*Description*	*Example: A 40-Year-Old Man Asks, "Should I Quit My Job to Go to College?"*
General Criteria: Insight	Good advice, judgment, and commentary	This doesn't have to be an "all-or-nothing" situation. Perhaps you could take a course or two without quitting your job to see how you like it.
Basic Criteria: Factual Knowledge	Both general and specific knowledge about life that are related to the main character and the dilemma	Are you supporting other people with your income? Do you have a job you like that pays well? Is there a college near you with the major you want, or do you need to move to another location? What do you hope to gain in college?
Basic Criteria: Procedural Knowledge	Strategies or ways to approach the dilemma	Have you talked to a college advisor or a career counselor about this? Have you talked to other nontraditional-aged college students to find out how they handled the transition and to get their general advice? Have you tried listing all the positives and all the negatives about going to college?
Meta-level Criteria: Lifespan Contextual Knowledge	Aspects of past, current, and future life contexts and circumstances	What do your close family members and friends think of this idea? How will society treat you as an adult male starting college at 40? How are you going to feel starting a new career in your mid-40s?
Meta-level Criteria: Relativism	Values, goals, and priorities involved in the dilemma	How will the financial impact of this affect your lifestyle? What do you want to accomplish in your life? How much do you value having a college education?
Meta-level Criteria: Uncertainty	Knowledge of ways to manage the unknowns and the unpredictable aspects of life	What will you do if you start college and decide you don't like it? Will you have some kind of health insurance in case something happens? How will you feel if the job market is not as favorable in 4 years?

Based on Baltes, Staudinger, Maercker, & Smith (1995).

that were aimed at people their own age. Although similar studies have found the same results (Baltes et al., 1995; Smith, Staudinger, & Baltes, 1994; Staudinger, Smith, & Baltes, 1992), it is important to keep in mind that these findings are specific to the way Baltes and his colleagues are defining and measuring wisdom.

Wisdom as the Ultimate Stage of Development

One of the more confusing aspects of wisdom is its indescribable qualities. Perhaps because it is so hard to articulate, many people prefer to avoid direct language and instead use parables, songs, poetry, proverbs, sayings, fables, and stories to convey wisdom. Another complicating factor is that, assuming wisdom is rare, most of us are trying to understand something we haven't achieved. Inquiry into the highest stages of adult development, especially when considering cognitive and emotional models, will reveal the same difficulties in understanding and expressing the abstract, complex traits of those advanced stages. Perhaps the best description of wisdom, according to developmental psychologists, is that wisdom is the integration of the highest stages of development, including identity development, self development, moral reasoning, faith development, postformal operations, and balance and expertise in life management.

Your Thoughts?

Based on this description is it fair to say that a wise person is a perfect person? Why or why not?

While acknowledging the many difficulties in the study of wisdom, many researchers believe it is of critical importance. Baltes and Staudinger (2000) view wisdom as the hope for the future. They view the cultural knowledge and wisdom passed down from generation to generation as one of the most unique and powerful traits of humankind. Labouvie-Vief (1990) acknowledges the fact that wisdom is an ideal concept, but she maintains it is one worth studying, even though it is rare and sometimes difficult to articulate. She compares it to models of optimal health, which very few people actually achieve and maintain. The value in studying wisdom, just as with optimal health, is to learn more about the concept and to try to determine where people get off track in their efforts to achieve these ideals. In addition, Sinnott (2003) reminds us that wisdom is a process. There is no destination or point at which we have acquired total wisdom or at which we are totally developed. Finally, Sternberg emphasizes the need to view wisdom as more than individual development, but also as a much-needed resource in the world. He points out that while psychologists have been focused on increasing IQs and increasing cognitive acuity with age, the conflict and destruction in the world at large continues to escalate. He believes that the development of wisdom, beginning with children's education, may be part of the solution to major world conflicts (Sternberg & Lubart, 2001).

Your Thoughts?

Would you support a school district that eliminated some of their current curriculum to make room for classes in wisdom? Why or why not?

Section Summary

- The study of wisdom is complicated by many factors, including the difficulty in defining, locating, and measuring it.
- Theories of postformal operations, such as postformal levels, postformal orders of hierarchical complexity, and postformal complex thought, present wisdom as advanced cognition that can manage conflicting systems, paradoxes, and uncertainties.
- Combining wise thoughts with behaviors, Sternberg's balance theory of wisdom uses tacit knowledge to find a balance between internal, interpersonal, cultural, and societal needs when trying to solve a messy problem with many unknown pieces.
- Baltes's view of wisdom highlights a different angle, the expertise in resolving major life dilemmas, using insight, factual and strategic knowledge, and sensitivity to context, relativism and personal values, and uncertainties.
- Wisdom may be viewed as the ultimate developmental stage, and though rare, critically important.

Subjective Well-Being

For many years philosophers and theologians have considered the components of *the good life.* As far back as the Classic Greeks of the 6th century B.C., the concept of *eudaemonia* or *living well* was viewed as a topic worth exploring and writing about (Steel, Schmidt, & Shultz, 2008). In psychological terminology the phrase ***subjective well-being*** has evolved to cover many of the terms we casually associate with living well, such as happiness, positive and pleasant moods, and life satisfaction. In a more technical sense, allowing for someone to be high or low in subjective well-being, the term is often defined as the combined influence of life satisfaction, positive and negative emotions, and mood (called *affect*) (Heller, Watson, & Ilies, 2004; Mroczek & Spiro, 2005; Steel et al., 2008). Trends in the research show that subjective well-being is high for most adults. Among the differentiating factors, higher subjective well-being is found among those who are married and have more social roles and relationships. Income is a stronger predictor of subjective well-being among younger adults whereas health is a better predictor for older adults. Race/ethnicity is generally not a predictor of level of subjective well-being (George, 2006).

Your Thoughts?

Why might those who are more socially connected have higher subjective well-being?

Life Satisfaction

Life satisfaction, one of the key components in overall subjective well-being, refers to the cognitive evaluation of one's life (Heller et al., 2004; Schimmack & Oishi, 2005). Researchers have found evidence that adults in late life report higher life satisfaction than young adults, reflecting the general trend that life satisfaction increases into late adulthood (George, 2006). In a study involving nearly 2,000 men across a 22-year span, Mroczek and Spiro (2005) found that life satisfaction continued to increase for most participants until around 65 to 70 years old and then declined. As we move into late adulthood it is important to be realistic in our expectations,

Life satisfaction generally increases with age.

Your Thoughts?

Would you predict the same results as Cheng et al. if the participants were in their 20s? How would you design a study to test your hypothesis?

which has been found to directly influence our sense of well-being. In a study of 200 adults age 60 years and older, Cheng, Fung, and Chan (2009) found that individuals who underestimated their future selves by imagining typical age-related deficits reported a greater sense of well-being than those who overestimated the future functioning.

Using a meta-analysis to summarize over 70 studies, Heller et al. (2004) found that the domains of employment, marital status, health status, and social networks were related to global life satisfaction. Based on their analysis Heller and his colleagues believe that it is not simply the status, such as whether one is employed or married, but rather the quality of each of those domains that actually influences life satisfaction. Even though these areas may change, such as moving to a different job or divorce and remarriage, generally life satisfaction scores across long periods of time are stable (Schimmack & Oishi, 2005).

RESEARCH IN-DEPTH
Predictive Models

The Research In-Depth sections have covered basic statistical procedures, questionnaire design, descriptive and experimental studies, and qualitative research. This last section is focused on the sophisticated technique of predictive modeling. Going beyond descriptive statistics to create a visual model of collected data allows researchers to gauge the flow of influence between variables and then use that equation to predict future outcomes.

Schimmack, Radhakrishnan, Oishi, Dzokoto, and Ahadi (2002) sought to learn more about the flow and intensity of influence between emotional satisfaction (hedonic balance), cognitive satisfaction (life satisfaction), personality, cultural factors, and subjective well-being. In order to make certain cultures differ, the researchers included participants from Germany, Ghana, Japan, Mexico, and the United States, with Germany and the United States representing individualistic cultures, and Japan, Mexico, and Ghana representing collectivistic cultures. Across the five regions over 650 people completed questionnaires. To assess personality Schimmack and his colleagues used items measuring extraversion and neuroticism from the five-factor personality model.

Once the data were collected the researchers applied several statistical procedures, including structural equation modeling. Using indicators based on correlations and other statistical comparisons, the researchers were able to try various models to see how well particular equations would predict the actual data. They concluded with three primary findings.

The best model and confirming statistical tests showed that (1) extraversion and neuroticism (personality) influenced emotional balance equally in either type of culture. The effect of personality on the emotional aspects of subjective well-being was similar across cultures. More specifically, they found:

- Higher Extraversion and Lower Neuroticism find More Pleasant Emotional Balance

(2) Emotional balance was found to be a stronger predictor of cognitive assessment of life satisfaction in individualistic cultures. The influence of personality on the cognitive component of subjective well-being is influenced by culture.

- More Pleasant Emotional Balance More Life Satisfaction in Collectivistic Cultures
- More Pleasant Emotional Balance More Life Satisfaction in Individualistic Cultures

(3) Extraversion and neuroticism (personality) worked with emotional balance to create an effect on cognitive assessment of life satisfaction.

- Personality *influences* Emotional Balance, and Emotional Balance then *influences* Life Satisfaction

These findings are portrayed as a model in Figure 14.2 on page 376.

Schimmack and his colleagues believe that their model raises many interesting questions for further research. Personality traits are thought to have strong genetic influence, thus this model suggests that perhaps this biological component of personality could influence emotional balance and ultimately life satisfaction. At the same time, cultural interpretations and expectations may also have significant influence. For example, to what extent might an individual in a collectivist culture feel emotionally unpleasant (unhappy) and still feel life satisfaction in terms of working for the good of the group? By building a model Schimmack and his colleagues have established a foundation for additional models, hypotheses, and research investigations, leading to a complex foundation of equations predicting human thoughts and behaviors.

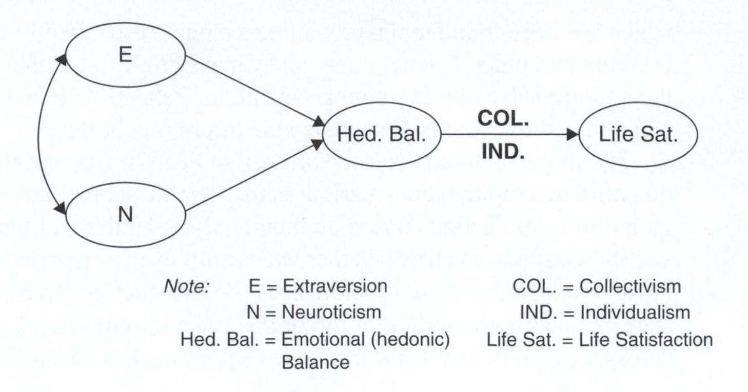

FIGURE 14.2 ***Model of Personality, Emotions, and Life Satisfaction***
Based on Schimmack, Radhakrishnan, Oishi, Dzokoto, & Ahadi (2002, p. 589).

Positive and Negative Affect

> **Your Thoughts?**
>
> Would you support an employer who determined whether to hire applicants partly on their predominant mood? Why, why not, or under what circumstances?

Subjective well-being is not only comprised of a cognitive or reasoned assessment of life satisfaction but also involves an emotional response to that assessment. When you reflect on your current or recent life circumstances, is your emotional response one of pleasant feelings and emotions (positive affect) or uncomfortable feelings and emotions (negative affect)? Much of the research on subjective well-being has focused on the influence of positive and negative affect (Mroczek & Spiro, 2005). Often positive affect is associated with the personality trait of extraversion, and negative affect with neuroticism, whereas both are associated with life satisfaction and overall subjective well-being (Heller et al., 2004; Steel et al., 2008). Consistent with research on life satisfaction, positive and negative affect are fairly stable from adolescence through adulthood, showing a slight increase in positive affect with age (Magai, 2001).

The psychological study of positive affect has frequently been linked to the study of happiness. Both positive mood and long-term happiness have been related to positive perceptions of self and others, sociability and activity, likeability and cooperation, helping behaviors, physical well-being and coping, problem solving, and creativity (Lyubomirsky, King, & Diener, 2005). In fact, the parallels are so strong that some scholars have gone so far as to propose that happiness and subjective well-being are essentially the same concept (Mroczek & Kolarz, 1998). Happy people report the feeling of mild positive emotions most of the time. Although researchers often consider the source of happiness in terms of genetic factors, personality traits, or domains of life, many people attribute happiness to the things society values, such as a loving relationship, comfortable income, and long life (Lyubomirsky et al., 2005). Happy people tend to be successful, demonstrating that they are better able to approach challenges and achieve their goals (Lyubomirsky et al., 2005).

Section Summary

- Subjective well-being, a psychological term for happiness, pleasant feelings, and generally living well, is usually measured in terms of life satisfaction (cognitive component) and positive and negative affect (emotional component).
- Generally, subjective well-being is high for most adults.
- Life satisfaction usually increases with age and is strongly associated with higher levels of extraversion and lower levels of neuroticism.

ON THE LEADING EDGE
Material and Psychosocial Prosperity

Ed Diener of the University of Illnois at Urbana-Champaign, Weiting Ng of the Singapore Institute of Management, and James Harter and Raksha Arora of The Gallup Organization analyzed data from "the first representative sample of planet Earth," the Gallup World Poll, to explore the factors that contribute to positive well-being. The poll involved 125 thousand surveys collected across 132 countries (Diener, Ng, Harter, & Arora, 2010).

Diener and his colleagues found that a participant's level of income had a stronger association with life evaluations than with the personal experience of positive or negative emotions. Life evaluation is a type of well-being, measured in this case by asking participants to rate their lives on a scale of 0 (worst possible life) to 10 (best possible life). Income had a much stronger connection to this type of rating, although higher incomes were associated with more positive emotions and fewer negative emotions. Emotions were measured by asking participants if they had experienced particular feelings in the previous 24 hours, such as enjoyment, smiling, laughing, worry, sadness, and anger.

Feelings were more strongly associated with social psychological prosperity than with material income. Social prosperity was measured by asking participants to rate whether they had been treated with respect in the last 24 hours and if they had a friend and family member they could count on in an emergency. Psychological prosperity was measured by asking if participants had learned something new, performed at their best, and had the luxury of choosing how to spend some of their time in the last 24 hours. They were also asked how many hours they had worked the previous day. The characteristics that defined high levels of social and psychological prosperity demonstrated a much stronger association with experiencing positive emotions than did income. Conversely, those who felt they were lacking in social and psychological prosperity also reported experiencing more negative emotions, and that relationship was stronger than that between negative emotions and lower income.

Diener and his colleagues offer a way to consider the age-old question: Can money buy happiness? The data here show that, while income is a factor, if happiness is viewed as positive emotions then social and psychological prosperity is a stronger factor than material prosperity.

- Positive and negative affect are generally stable across adulthood, with a slight increase in positive affect with age.
- People who are happy tend to have a fairly consistent, mild sense of pleasant emotion and mood.
- Happy people tend to have success in achieving their goals and function better personally and socially.

Regrets

Your Thoughts?

Would you predict that individuals who scored high in wisdom on Baltes's measure would have fewer, equal, or more regrets than those without wisdom?

Much of this chapter, in the spirit of positive psychology, has been devoted to positive growth and development. While self-growth and increased wisdom will hopefully lead us to a high level of subjective well-being, it is important that some thought is given to what may be learned from decisions that seem later to have been mistakes. We often use the term ***regret*** for those mistakes. Regrets are lingering, negative emotions including self-blame and disappointment over thoughts, actions, or inaction, in a situation that, later in hindsight, we wish we had handled differently (Roese & Summerville, 2005; Wrosch & Heckhausen, 2002). Regrets are often framed as "I should have . . ." or "It would have been better if I had . . .".

An important facet of the feeling of regret is the sense that we *could have* taken a different course or offered a different response. Perceived opportunities and choices must have been present in order for self-blame to occur. In other words, you can't blame yourself if you had no choice in a matter. As demonstrated in a meta-analysis of studies asking participants to list regrets and rank them in importance, Roese and Summerville (2005) found that the regrets that bother people the most are in areas that participants felt they had the best chances for growth and change. The five most frequently cited areas of regret were, in order: education, career, romance, parenting/family, and self-improvement. For example, regarding education, participants offered regrets such as "I wish I had stayed in school" or "I should have worked harder when I was in school." Consistent with these findings, in a study involving 176 participants ranging in age from 19 to 82, Jokisaari (2004) found that regrets concerning education and work were associated with less overall life satisfaction.

Not only are regrets found in areas of multiple opportunities, but also in areas involving inactivity (Roese & Summerville, 2005). When a poor choice is made the primary correction is "I shouldn't have done that." When one doesn't take action, such as not following advice to try a different college major or not pursuing a job opportunity, then there are many possible options and imaginable outcomes, resulting in many "what if?" ruminations. Regrets of inaction tend to persist longer than those involving a wrong choice. Also regrets that cannot be readdressed in some way are often more difficult emotionally (Wrosch & Heckhausen, 2002). For example, if an individual regrets not finishing a college degree, although he or she may regret the time lost in the interim, that person may be able to finish the degree years later. If readdressing the regret involves people who are no longer available or a situation that cannot be altered, such as, "I wish I had spent more time with my kids when they were little," then the individual must find a way to cope with the memories and the emotions.

Your Thoughts?

What personality characteristics might lead someone to inactivity in key situations?

Section Summary

- Regrets are lingering, negative emotions including self-blame and disappointment over thoughts, actions, or inaction, in a situation that, later in hindsight, we wish we had handled differently.
- Generally, people regret poor decisions in the areas of education, career, romance, parenting/family, and self-improvement.
- Regrets over missed opportunities and inaction are more intense than regrets over poor decisions.
- Regrets that cannot be readdressed in some way are often more difficult emotionally.

Closing Reflections

As we come to the close of this survey of adult development it is time to reflect on what we have learned, consider how we might use that information, and make some predictions about the future of the field. As a college professor I find that when the last day of class comes it is important, much like a graduation speaker, to be quick and to the point. I'll stick to that piece of wisdom here as well.

Personal Lessons Learned

What are some lessons that perhaps you can take away from your observations of adult development? Here are some suggestions:

Your Thoughts?

Which of these do you need to focus on the most at this point in your life?

You're Exceptional (Individual and Intraindividual Differences). Personal, social, and cultural differences seem to magnify in adulthood, making generalizations very difficult. Along with that, personality, identity, and self-development are important growth domains in adulthood, adding to the view that adulthood is dynamic, flowing, and continually changing. Adulthood is anything but static, and just as you are still growing and changing so are all the other adults around you, including the ones older than you. Be careful making assumptions about "typical" adults!

Now that we have explored the full cycle of adult development, what are the most important things you've learned?

Take Care of Your Health. Achieving and maintaining good physical health is foundational to many other aspects of adult life. Eating and exercising appropriately, while getting enough sleep, stopping smoking, and being careful with alcohol, seem to be keys to a healthier and happier lifestyle in the short run and the long term. Are you concerned about aging? A healthy body will make the journey much better.

Use it or Lose it. Another piece of wisdom that seems to surface often, in both the physical and cognitive realms, is that if you want to keep a skill, talent, or function active into old age you need to use it. Although younger adults may not lose abilities as quickly as older adults, many of us have lost some physical stamina and flexibility as well as cognitive processing speed, skills, and knowledge because of nonuse. Research shows that just about all of us, no matter how old or out of shape, can improve physically and cognitively with practice and exercise. What are you doing to keep your cognitive and physical skills sharp?

Value Other People. As we've surveyed many topics related to adulthood we also see the importance of friends, family, and helpful social support and social networks. Whether it is developing friendships, creating a family, or seeking advice or help with problem solving, our social support networks can play a critical role in life satisfaction. Are you choosing your friends wisely? Are you giving as much socially as you are receiving?

Find Meaningful Work or Activities. Many of us will move through several jobs and careers during our working life. Even when retired most people want to use their talents and skills for as long as possible. Do you have work, hobbies, or community endeavors that you find meaningful? Can you practice the balance theory of wisdom by finding ways to meet your own needs for income and meaningful work while also building relationships and contributing to the greater good?

Practice Good Coping Skills. Whether it is cycling through the phases of work, family, physical aging, or disease processes, it seems that the life of an adult is seldom stable. One of the hallmarks in successful aging is the ability to adapt and adjust as needs and situations change. How well do you cope with stressors? How are you with creative problem solving?

Aging Happens, Ready or Not. You can pretend it won't happen. You can even ignore the signs. Eventually, however, you will have to acknowledge that you too are getting old! Think of how long it seemed to be from birthday to birthday when you were a child, and how long it seems now. Time just moves faster and faster, and the result is that we get older. The more you can plan ahead, thinking not only of the next few weeks or months, but also the next few decades, the more you increase your chances of high life satisfaction in all phases of adulthood. Can you make even one minor plan or change now that will likely enhance your life decades from now?

Future Directions

The field of adult development seems to be expanding as quickly as the size of the aging population. Even within the chaos of a rapidly changing and evolving field of study there are some trends that stand out. One shift that will continue to have beneficial outcomes for the field is the move away from categorizing adults by age-related, linear stage progressions, and moving toward a better understanding of individual and intraindividual differences and the dynamic nature of modern adulthood. Perhaps at one time in American society it appeared that a linear move-through-the-stages view of career development or marital/family development was achievable, but that doesn't seem to be the case anymore. Fewer and fewer of those major institutions are *traditional* (and as such, predictable) anymore. Rather than age as the organizing characteristic it will become one of many descriptive characteristics found when exploring life domains and situations (Settersten, 2006).

It is also likely that the search to understand the physiological foundations of psychological constructs, fueled by rapidly improving technologies and sophisticated computer modeling, will continue. The National Institute on Aging (2007c) reflects this direction in their strategic directions for future research:

- Improve understanding of healthy aging, disease, and disability
- Improve understanding and interventions to prevent and treat dementias
- Improve understanding of aging society
- Work on policy decisions, reduce health disparities, and eliminate health inequities
- Develop and disseminate information

It is likely that great strides will be made in the prevention and treatment of numerous conditions in the coming years. Consider not only the biological, medical, and pharmaceutical research we are now capable of, but also the many ways the use of personal computers and affordable technologies can assist individuals in maintaining independence, cognitive stimulation, and social connection. Like science fiction writers, we can only imagine the types of technology that will assist today's children when they are grandparents.

Finally, it is also likely that, from a practical point of view, a great deal of effort in the field of adult development will continue to be placed on finding ways to safely and economically care for older adults. It is to almost everyone's liking and best interest to keep the aging population as physically and mentally healthy and independent as long as possible. This trend can be seen in the movement toward health and wellness programs in the workplace and the promotion of interactive health-related websites, such as the American government's MyPyramid nutritional program. This can also be seen in the rise in popularity and research efforts in the cognitive areas of practical intelligence, wisdom, and models emphasizing problem solving and coping, such as the selection, optimization, and compensation model. For those who are not capable of living totally independent lives efforts will continue to find the safest and most economical ways of adapting environments to best serve aging adults with disabilities. This multidisciplinary effort will involve building facilities, equipping living spaces, enhancing social networks and communication, and encouraging personal physical and cognitive exercise to maintain as much function as possible. Aging is unique in that young and middle-aged adults, no matter their view or attitude toward "old people," will eventually become a member of this studied and often stereotyped group. As professionals, citizens, and loved ones, all of us benefit from learning more about adult development and aging.

Chapter Summary

Following the themes of Erikson's work in adult development and the movement toward positive psychology, this book is ending with a focus on life satisfaction. No matter what twists and turns our life story may take, it will always be seen and interpreted from our own vantage point. Our own self-concept, with its many facets and components, will form the core of our sense of our own development. Wisdom, expertise in life, and good reasoning often comes as we reflect on our life experiences, eventually detaching ourselves to be able to see our strengths, weaknesses, and lessons learned. Ultimately, the good life, from a psychological point of view, can be captured in happiness, life satisfaction, positive subjective well-being, and successful aging. Here are some of the main points of the chapter:

- The trend in the study of self-concept is to consider particular areas of self, such as academic self-concept and social self-concept, as well as to consider different facets contributing to an overall self-concept, such as self-schemas and self-esteem.
- Research in identity process theory, building self-schemas through identity assimilation and identity accommodation, indicates that a balance between the two creates the greatest life satisfaction.
- Coopersmith found that self-esteem, one's evaluation or judgment of self-concept, is primarily based on one's sense of power, significance, competence, and virtue.
- Self-efficacy, one's personal belief about how successful or effective one can be in a particular area of life, often influences achievement motivation and life satisfaction.
- Young adults often display the grandest, most unrealistic ideal selves (hoped-for possible self), while older adults often focus both their ideal and feared selves (worst possible self) on physical characteristics.
- Maslow's hierarchy of needs provides a pathway that leads from deficiencies (physiological, security, affiliation, and esteem needs) to self-growth and self-actualization.
- The psychological study of wisdom is a new area full of basic challenges, such as how to define and measure the rare construct.
- The postformal levels theory developed by Labouvie-Vief and Commons and Richards's theory, postformal orders of hierarchical complexity, emphasize the ability to understand several systems of thought as well as merge those systems to create new understandings, while Sinnots's model, postformal complex thought, is designed to highlight ways of dealing with uncertainties and unknowns.

- Sternberg's balance theory balances wise thoughts and actions by incorporating tacit knowledge as the way to balance levels of internal, interpersonal, cultural, and societal needs.
- Baltes's model of wisdom, as expertise in life, has been captured in an interview technique that emphasizes insight, factual and strategic knowledge, and sensitivity to context, values, and uncertainties.
- Baltes and his colleagues have found that wisdom is not age related among adults.
- Wisdom can be viewed as the ultimate stage in human development, synthesizing the most mature level of development in the areas of identity, self, moral reasoning, faith, postformal operations, tacit knowledge, and life expertise.
- Subjective well-being is generally viewed as the combined influences of life satisfaction and positive and negative affect.
- Life satisfaction, the cognitive element of subjective well-being, is related to the quality of various domains, such as marital and health status, and to personality traits, such as higher extraversion and lower neuroticism.
- Positive and negative affect, the emotional components of subjective well-being, reflect many of the same patterns as life satisfaction regarding age and personality.
- Both positive mood and long-term happiness have been related to many positive outcomes, such as sociability, likeability and cooperation, physical well-being and coping, problem solving, creativity, and general overall success.
- Regret is a lingering emotion involving self-blame over action or inaction that later, in hindsight, probably should have been handled differently.

Key Terms

Self-concept **(358)**
Schema **(359)**
Assimilation **(359)**
Accommodation **(359)**
Self-schemas **(359)**
Identity process theory **(359)**
Identity assimilation **(359)**
Identity accommodation **(359)**
Identity balance **(360)**
Self-esteem **(360)**
Self-efficacy **(362)**
Possible selves **(363)**
Ideal self **(363)**
Feared self **(363)**
Self-actualization **(365)**
Postformal operations **(367)**
Tacit knowledge **(369)**
Subjective well-being **(374)**
Life satisfaction **(374)**
Regret **(377)**

Comprehension Questions

1. Give examples of some of the subareas or facets of self-concept.
2. Explain the process of identity assimilation and identity accommodation in identity process theory.
3. In the context of identity process theory, what is meant by identity balance?
4. What is the difference between self-concept and self-esteem?
5. Name and describe the four areas identified by Coopersmith as important criteria for healthy self-esteem.
6. What are the four primary influences on self-efficacy described by Bandura?
7. Explain the terms *possible self, ideal self,* and *feared self.*
8. What have researchers found regarding the development and modifications of the ideal self in young, middle, and late adulthood?
9. Describe Maslow's hierarchy of needs as it relates to growth and deficiency needs.

10. How did the term *postformal* operations develop and how does it relate to wisdom?
11. How is the theory of postformal levels (Labouvie-Vief) different from the theory of postformal complex thought (Sinnott)?
12. Explain the three primary elements involved in tacit knowledge.
13. Explain Sternberg's balance theory of wisdom, particularly in terms of what elements are being balanced.
14. What are the criteria Baltes and his colleagues use to judge a wise response to an interview question?
15. Summarize the reasons given as to why studying wisdom is important.
16. What is subjective well-being?
17. What does the term *affect* refer to?
18. What research trends do life satisfaction and positive and negative affect have in common?
19. What is the relationship between positive mood and happiness?
20. What is the relationship between regret and choice or opportunity?
21. What are the primary areas in which Americans have regrets?

Answers for Common Sense: Myth or Reality?

1. Myth: Most researchers see "self" as a unified concept and approach it that way. (See Self: The Core of Development, page 358.)
2. Myth: Researchers find that people that are continually reinventing and adjusting their identity and sense of self have the highest life satisfaction. (See Self-Schemas and Identity Process Theory, page 360.)
3. Myth: Morals or values tend to be separate from self-esteem. (See Self-Esteem, page 361.)
4. Reality: People with low self-esteem tend to create negative meaning from neutral events. (See Self-Esteem, page 362).
5. Reality: Researchers find that by watching others we develop a sense of our own chances of succeeding at a particular task. (See Self-Efficacy, page 362.)
6. Myth: Researchers have found that having a strong belief that one can succeed in an area is not related to one's performance in that area. (See Self-Efficacy, page 363.)
7. Reality: Researchers find that individuals' image of their ideal selves change throughout adulthood. (See Possible Selves, page 364.)
8. Myth: The goal of wisdom is to develop a sophisticated way of thinking such that there are no contradictions, paradoxes, or gaps in understanding. (See Wisdom as Advanced Cognition, page 367.)
9. Myth: Differences in subjective (personally determined) well-being are large when comparing various racial/ethnic groups. (See Subjective Well-Being, page 374.)
10. Reality: Life satisfaction is higher among people who are married. (See Life Satisfaction, page 375.)
11. Reality: Life satisfaction is strongly associated with personality characteristics. (See Positive and Negative Affect, page 376.)
12. Reality: People have more regrets related to their education than they do regarding their career or romantic life. (See Regrets, page 378.)
13. Myth: People have more intense regret over actions taken that turned out to be poor choices than they do over opportunities they didn't take. (See Regrets, page 378.)

Suggested Readings

About Human Motivation, from Maslow Himself

Maslow, A. H. (1943). A theory of human motivation. *Psychological Review, 50,* 370–396. Accessed at *Classics in the History of Psychology* (http://psychclassics.yorku.ca/topic.htm).

The Psychological View of "Self," 1915

Calkins, M. W. (1915). The self in scientific psychology. *American Journal of Psychology, 26,* 495–524. Accessed at *Classics in the History of Psychology* (http://psychclassics.yorku.ca/topic.htm).

Subjective Well-Being Across Cultures

Suh, E. M., & Oishi, S. (2002). Subjective well-being across cultures. In W. J. Lonner, D. L. Dinnel, S. A. Hayes, & D. N. Sattler (Eds.), *Online readings in psychology and culture* (Unit 7, Chapter 1), (http://www.wwu.edu/~culture), Center for Cross-Cultural Research, Western Washington University, Bellingham, WA. Available at http://www.ac.wwu.edu/~culture/Suh_Oishi.htm.

Internationalism in Psychology: Why We Need It Now

Cole, M. (2006). Internationalism in psychology: We need it now more than ever. *American Psychologist, 61*(8), 904–917.

Suggested Websites

Health-Related Quality of Life

The National Center for Chronic Disease Prevention and Health Promotion, part of the Centers for Disease Control and Prevention, gives an overview of the recent Quality of Life study at http://www.cdc.gov/hrqol/.

Successful Aging

The Center on Aging Studies Without Walls, sponsored by the University of Missouri at Kansas City and the University of Missouri Outreach and Extension program, provides a website with many interesting findings and links at http://cas.umkc.edu/casww/.

Healthy Living

MedlinePlus, sponsored by the U.S. National Library of Medicine and the National Institutes of Health, provides links to resources and information on healthy lifestyles and successful aging at http://www.nlm.nih.gov/medlineplus/healthyliving.html.

Quality of Life and Positive Psychology

The website for the Quality of Life Research Center at Claremont Graduate University has interesting information and many links to similar sites. You can find it at http://qlrc.cgu.edu/about.htm.

APPENDIX

Research Appendix

The *Research In-Depth* sections found in each chapter are designed to complement the information provided in this appendix. While research designs and statistical analyses can be the objects of study in their own right, as might happen in the fields of statistics, experimental psychology, or psychometrics, the focus here is on the ways various techniques may be applied. Most people who want to learn more about a psychological study beyond what might be highlighted in the media will need to turn to scientific journals. This research appendix is organized in the same basic order or structure as one would find in a standard psychology research-based journal article: literature review and hypotheses; research designs; measurements, methods, and procedures; analyses and results; discussion and conclusions. The *Research In-Depth* sections in each chapter expand the information given here by explaining the topics listed below and using real research examples as demonstrations:

Chapter 1, Cross-Sectional and Longitudinal Studies
Chapter 2, Cross-Cultural and Multicultural Research
Chapter 3, Descriptive Analysis and Comparing Means
Chapter 4, Correlational Analysis
Chapter 5, Reliability
Chapter 6, Assessment Validity and Naturalistic Observation
Chapter 7, Self-Report Diary Entries
Chapter 8, Deception
Chapter 9, True Experiments
Chapter 10, Physiological Measures
Chapter 11, Quasi-Experiments
Chapter 12, Using Large Databanks
Chapter 13, Qualitative Analysis
Chapter 14, Predictive Models

When I was an undergraduate student I found it difficult to study an entire chapter on research design and analysis if it was presented without any application or particular topic as an example. The *Research In-Depth* sections are designed to provide that application and context as well as to spread the discussion of design and analysis throughout the book rather than condense it in one chapter. Together this research appendix and the *Research In-Depth* sections provide a good foundation for understanding psychological research.

Literature Review and Hypotheses

Most research articles begin by providing definitions and background material for the primary items being studied. The items being investigated, which are thought to vary, either by person, situation, or both, are simply called ***variables.*** The literature review will summarize related research studies and theories that apply to the key variables, often starting with broad overviews of an area before narrowing the discussion to the exact focus and scope of the study. For the author of the article, this part of the writing process is often a natural extension of the research process. When planning a study the first step is to read published articles and consult other resources to determine what research has been done, how it was done, and how the work in the area may be extended. Those who narrow the scope of their program of ongoing research to particular areas will have the advantage of familiarity with the previous studies, allowing more time to focus on current and future studies. Often the student who is familiar with journal searches can trace the work in an area by following the publications of key researchers who continually extend their studies with new variables.

It is equally important for the literature review to provide wide-ranging background information needed to understand the larger research context while also setting the boundaries for what is being studied and what is not. For example, a study of those who serve as caregivers for individuals with Alzheimer's disease may begin with a broad overview of the psychological and physiological impact of the disease on individuals, and then discuss how caregivers must adapt to changes in the ones they are caring for. As the literature review progresses it may become clear to the reader that this particular study focuses on something rather specific, such as the success of Internet-based support groups in reducing depression among female spouses serving as the primary caregivers for their husbands who are in the early stages of Alzheimer's disease. Much like building a persuasive argument, the literature review often leads the reader directly to the ***hypotheses,*** the primary research questions guiding the study. As researchers narrow the focus of the literature review to the key variables it should be clear to the reader why those variables were chosen and how they may be related. Using this hypothetical example, by the time the reader finished the literature review it would be clear that the researchers are predicting that the treatment (Internet-based support groups) will reduce depression for women in this situation and why they believe this treatment would be successful.

Research Design and Methodology

Following the literature review and description of the hypotheses, researchers shift to describing the actual procedures and methodology. The exact order of these items may vary, but almost all studies will describe the participants or the source of the data and the way the variables were measured. The design and methodology section will also describe exactly how the data were collected. These design decisions—basically *who, what, when, where,* and *how*—are critical to the integrity of the study.

Cross-Sectional, Longitudinal, and Sequential Designs

Developmental psychologists must determine the best way to measure change over time based on the hypotheses for their study. The *Research In-Depth* section in Chapter 1 explains and gives examples of the two basic designs for managing time: cross-sectional and longitudinal. To briefly summarize, ***cross-sectional designs*** involve assessing people of different ages at basically the same point in calendar time. This comparison often saves time and resources, but rests on the assumption that the younger participants will be like the older participants when they reach the same age. Associating data across ages overlooks ***cohort*** or generational effects. For example, a cross-sectional study of depression among wives caring for husbands with Alzheimer's disease might survey women in this situation who are ages 60, 63, 66, and 69 with the assumption that the current 60-year-olds would respond in the same way as the 69-year-olds if they were that age. ***Longitudinal designs*** involve assessing and reassessing the same participants across time. These designs are often plagued by low enrollment, signaling a hesitation to commit to long-term research involvement, and high dropout or attrition rates as participants decide to end their association with the study. In some cases the participants cannot be located for follow-up. Another complicating factor with longitudinal designs is attempting to estimate the influence of individual and environmental factors on the data. Returning to the example of caregiving and Internet-based support groups, the authors would need to consider participants' access to and comfort level with available online information, resources, and cyber-based support groups. These environmental or historical factors represent the dilemma often referred to as ***time of measurement*** effects.

Another option is to combine the two designs, resulting in a group of research methodologies called ***sequential designs.*** These designs start with a cross-sectional study, and then follow those participants over time while also adding new participants with each round of data collection. For example, expanding the hypothetical study of depression in wives caring for husbands with Alzheimer's disease to focus on the long-term changes in the wives, considering how levels of depression change with personal age and as their spouses' Alzheimer's disease worsens, death occurs, and the they recover, researchers may start with four groups of participants consisting of:

- 10 women who are 60 years old
- 10 women who are 63 years old
- 10 women who are 66 years old
- 10 women who are 69 years old

To add the longitudinal quality to this cross-sectional study, those 40 women would be reassessed for depression every third year. In a sequential design researchers would add a new group of 60-year-old women 3 years later with the next round of data collection. The point of data collection would include (ideally, without attrition):

- 10 women who are 60 years old and new to the study
- 10 women who are now 63 years old (60 in the last round)
- 10 women who are now 66 years old (63 in the last round)
- 10 women who are now 69 years old (66 in the last round)
- 10 women who are now 72 years old (69 in the last round)

Imagine that every 3 years another new group of 60-year-olds is added, and the older groups continue to participate as long as they are alive. Now there are several options for analysis. A *time-lag design* would, for example, analyze only one age group from each 3-year assessment. This would indicate how generations of women may be changing in terms of levels of depression as historical and environmental variables change. Most sequential designs are aimed at examining changes with age while also sorting out a primary issue with cross-sectional designs, cohort effects, and a problem with longitudinal designs, that of time measurement effects. For example, a *cohort-sequential design* is focused on age and cohort effects, a *time-sequential design* is aimed at isolating age and time of measurement effects, and a *cross-sequential design,* the most complex of the three, is focused on cohort and time of measurement effects. The choice of design is influenced not only by what the researchers believe is the best way to study particular variables, but also what will work realistically within the constraints of professional time, budgets, other resources, and the availability of participants. Authors of research articles usually explain their choice of design, particularly if it is complex.

Quantitative and Qualitative Design

Another basic decision point for researchers that is usually made clear in the methodology is the use of quantitative, qualitative, or both types of methodologies. Generally speaking, a ***quantitative*** methodology involves data collection methods that are precise measurements lending themselves to traditional statistical analysis. Often quantitative assessments are in the form of surveys or questionnaires yielding many scores and in the form of measurements taken with laboratory equipment. A ***qualitative*** methodology is less focused on capturing precise data and more concerned with the qualities of the situation and participant. Often qualitative researchers use case studies, recorded narratives and personal stories, interviews, and observations, often made at the location of the people or events being studied (called *ethnography*). In some situations researchers are actually *participant observers* who join in the group or activity under study. The *Research In-Depth* section in Chapter 13 discusses interviews as a type of qualitative assessment.

Data Sources and Considerations

Another portion of the methodology should be devoted to explaining the choices made in terms of where and how to collect data for analysis. In psychological research the potential sources of data are numerous, including human participants, animals, artificial intelligence programs, large databanks, and even previous studies. The field of adult development and aging draws from all of these areas. For example, those studying Alzheimer's disease may involve animals in treatment-related studies, artificial intelligence to model the progression of the disease and various treatments, databanks of surveys or other data collected on individuals with Alzheimer's disease, reanalysis of data collected from many previous studies (called a ***meta-analysis***), or studies of individuals who are currently living with Alzheimer's disease. While it is generally not stated in most research articles, it is expected that all research has received the approval of all appropriate ethics boards, which may include the ***Institutional Animal Care and Use Committee*** or the ***Institutional Review Board*** for one or more institutions (see Chapter 1 for more details).

The most likely participants in any developmental study are human beings. The methodology section will usually provide the number of participants, the gender ratio, average age or age ranges, and other information pertinent to the study, such as average income or educational attainment. In some cases the selection of participants may have been influenced by the desire to reduce ***confounding variables*** that may interfere with the interpretation of the results. In the hypothetical study of depression in wives who are caregivers to husbands with Alzheimer's disease, it might be important to exclude any wife who had been diagnosed with a mental disorder prior to caregiving or who takes medication that may cause depression as a side effect. If participants were not screened for these confounding variables there would be much more room for error in associating caregiving or a treatment with easing or increasing depression.

Another common practice is to match participants on important variables in order to make fairer comparisons. For example, in a study comparing groups of wives as caregivers, such as those caring for husbands with Alzheimer's disease versus those whose husbands have cancer, it may be important to match each group on age, income, and educational attainment. Income level, for example, may influence the quality of health care the husband is receiving as well as the ability to hire occasional assistance in caregiving. To achieve a fairer comparison it is often best to have equal or close to equal numbers of participants from various income levels or to choose participants from only one income level. Another example of matching can be found in the *Research In-Depth* section in Chapter 9.

Quasi-Experimental and True Experimental Methodologies

While both true experimental research (see *Research In-Depth* in Chapter 9) and quasi-experimental research (see *Research In-Depth* in Chapter 11) offer valuable insight to the field of psychology, the distinction between these techniques is important to the way results are interpreted. True experiments are designed and carried out in precise and strict ways in order to allow researchers to conclude with confidence that a particular variable or set of variables *caused* a particular response. Variables in a true experiment are clearly distinguished as either independent or dependent variables. ***Independent variables*** are controlled by the researchers, and might include selected medications or specific questionnaires. The ***dependent variables*** are the outcomes that are dependent on the selected variables, such as the effects of specific medications or the scores on a particular questionnaire.

In true experiments participants are well matched, all significant confounding variables are controlled, and participants are randomly assigned to various groups. To clarify, random assignment guarantees that each participant had an equal chance of being placed in any group. The groups may be experimental groups that receive some type of treatment or intervention or a control group receiving no manipulation. The control groups serve as a baseline and point for comparison for the experimental groups. The researcher may choose a *between-subjects design* that involves assessing different participants, such as when randomly assigning individuals to different groups. When researchers measure a variable twice from the same participants they are using a *within-subjects* design.

Quasi-experimental designs, ones in which the participants are not randomly assigned, are much more common in developmental psychology than true experiments. In true experiments each participant has an equal chance of being placed in any of the experimental groups or the control group. In quasi-experimental designs the members of the groups are not controlled by the researcher. Returning to the caregiving example, suppose a researcher wanted to compare levels of depression among women whose husbands are healthy, women whose husbands have cancer, and women whose husbands have Alzheimer's disease. The placement of women into groups cannot be truly random because the women enrolled in the study with specific situations. A woman whose husband has Alzheimer's disease cannot be placed in the group for women with healthy husbands. It is extremely difficult in most situations involving humans to reduce the influence of all potential confounding variables, successfully match all participants on all characteristics, and fully reduce environmental intrusions, in order to make causal statements with confidence, thus quasi-experimental designs are much more common in the study of adult development.

Description and Quality of Assessments

A section of the methodology in a research article will likely be devoted to a description of the instruments used to measure the variables in the study. This could involve descriptions of laboratory equipment, software, questionnaires, or questions used in interviews. This could also involve explaining a sequence of events or the order in which participants may be given particular questionnaires or tasks. Often in the description of instruments researchers will provide data on the reliability and validity of the assessment tools. For the reader who has some background in statistics and psychometrics, these are very important pieces of information. If the article involves the development of a questionnaire or new technique, it is likely that a good amount of the discussion of methodology and results will focus on the establishment of reliability and validity. In some cases instructions or instruments need to be translated into another language or culture, which will require further consideration of reliability and validity. (Translation issues are discussed in the *Research In-Depth* section in Chapter 2.)

The *Research In-Depth* sections in Chapters 5 and 6 are focused on the ways researchers build questionnaires, with a particular emphasis on reliability and validity. Although these concepts are often associated with questionnaires, they can be applied to any technique used to measure or assess thoughts or behaviors. The process of standardizing a questionnaire includes a literature review, finding similar questionnaires, drafting the new questionnaire, establishing reliability and validity, testing and establishing norms, and finally publishing the results. The concept of reliability is important in the process of designing a questionnaire because, before the researcher can determine if the questionnaire is measuring the correct concept (validity) it needs to be clear that the questionnaire is measuring *something* consistently. Consider the dilemma of stepping on scales at the gym to see how much you weigh, and your first attempt shows you weighing much more than you thought. You get off the scales, let them return to 0, and then step back on. This time the scales show you weighing much less than you thought. Suppose you get on and off the scales several times over a couple of minutes, and each time the weight is different. You would probably assume the scales are broken and walk away, having no idea how much you weigh. With a questionnaire, just as with the scales, if the scores change dramatically and unpredictably, like your reported weight changed, then you know nothing about the concept but you do know that your questionnaire is unreliable. The type of reliability discussed in the *Research In-Depth* section in Chapter 5 is a commonly used technique, test–retest reliability. There are other ways to establish reliability, such as interitem reliability, comparing the responses to items on the same questionnaire that are designed to measure the same thing, and interrater reliability, which is desirable when comparing scores from an interview or a procedure that requires several researchers to make personal judgments based on scoring criteria. No matter which test of reliability is used it is important that any measure demonstrate adequate reliability, as determined through statistical procedures. If a test is not reliable then the research cannot progress until the measure is revised and retested until the reliability is sound.

To continue with the example, suppose the gym installs new scales. You step on and find your weight to be 10 pounds more than you would have expected. You step off the scales, let them return to 0, step back on, and you find the same results. Upset that you might have gained 10 pounds, you step on and off several times, but the scales are reliable and consistently give you the same weight. With reliability established, now you are seeking validity. *Are these scales measuring my weight accurately?* That is the validity question. How can you find out? One strategy is to weigh yourself at several other locations to compare what other scales record in relation to the scales at the gym. This type of validity, convergent validity, is one of several types discussed in the *Research In-Depth* section in Chapter 6. As with reliability, a measure must show adequate validity. When a measure has inadequate validity then the researchers are not sure what is being measured, thus the measure is meaningless.

When studying adult development and aging there is an added concern with the concepts of reliability and validity. If a questionnaire was found to be reliable for young adults, can it be assumed that it would be reliable for older adults as well? The same question can be asked of validity. While it would increase the burden of test development even more to ask researchers to establish reliability and validity for young adults, middle-aged, and older adults without extending the preliminary work on a new measure, the question of reliability and validity across ages will remain.

Methods of Data Collection

After the research design, measures, and participants have been described, authors usually move to a discussion of the methods used to measure each variable. In some cases little more is needed of the researcher than to look around and record bits of data in a notebook. Using a technique called ***naturalistic observation*** researchers may position themselves in a public setting and write down the number of times particular behaviors are seen. The *Research In-Depth* section in Chapter 6 offers an example of naturalistic observation.

In other cases, such as physiological data collected from human or animal participants, authors will describe the apparatus needed to measure the particular variable. For example, if in our hypothetical study of wives caring for husbands with Alzheimer's disease a researcher wants to see if relaxation therapy will decrease levels of depression, it might be helpful to design a *laboratory or structured observation.* In this case wives would be invited to a clinic or laboratory setting to have their blood pressure or heart rate monitored during relaxation training to find out if the women are truly learning how to relax. (The *Research In-Depth* section in Chapter 10 discusses physiological measures.) While this type of measurement is desired because it is clearly accurate, the connection between physiological and psychological outcomes must be inferred. Although levels of relaxation may be directly inferred from physiological measurements, some other, more abstract variables, such as self-esteem or intelligence, would be more difficult to measure physiologically.

For those concepts that are difficult to infer from physiological data, researchers in adult development may rely on participants to offer accurate "self-reports" of their thoughts, feelings, and behaviors. Whether asking for opinions on a questionnaire or in a face-to-face interview, there is a constant concern that participants will not give truthful responses but rather give the proper or socially desirable responses. Even when participants are assured of confidentiality and anonymity they may be hesitant to admit to embarrassing or shameful thoughts and behaviors. For example, in our hypothetical study, suppose we asked wives who are the primary caregivers for husbands with Alzheimer's disease if within the last year they have desired or engaged in an extramarital affair for comfort. Do you think those who had such thoughts or actual affairs would admit to it? Some researchers will move away from self-report data by asking relatives, friends, coworkers, or others who know the participant to comment on their observations of the participant. Rather than self-report, researchers would ask people who knew the wives whether those women had engaged in an extramarital affair. Again, the question of honesty still lingers. In some cases the desired information may be so sensitive that researchers will use deceptive techniques in their study. The *Research In-Depth* section in Chapter 8 is focused on deception and debriefing.

In some cases the need for accuracy and in-depth, detailed information may be such that interview techniques are the most appropriate method of data collection. There are different types of interviews, including completely open-ended, conversational style ***phenomenological interviews,*** probing and directed ***clinical interviews,*** and ***structured interviews*** in which all participants are asked the exact same questions (no matter what their responses are). These types of interviews are explored in the *Research In-Depth* section in Chapter 13. These one-to-one interviews range from a one-time session that may go for several hours to a ***case study*** in which a participant is interviewed many times over many weeks, months, or years. While it may be that asking participants to fully explain their thoughts through interview questions provides the most accurate information, from a practical standpoint interviews require a great deal of time and effort on the part of the researchers as well as the participants. One compromise is to work with ***focus groups*** rather than individuals. Rather than interview only one person at a time, with a focus group researchers may interview several people at once. Again, researchers need to consider what is practical and appropriate for their specific hypotheses and variables. If the variables are not likely to be controversial then a focus group might work well because participants would not be as concerned about confidentiality and anonymity. If the variables are sensitive topics, a focus group setting may not work because participants would not want to share their true thoughts, behaviors, or experiences.

If researchers decide that they cannot take the time and/or do not have the resources for many interviews, they may choose to use some form of questionnaire. The items may range from answering open-ended questions, filling in sentences, rating their choices on a scale, or choosing between true and false statements or multiple-choice items. These questions might be answered face-to-face, over the phone, over the Internet, or perhaps completed on a computer or with pencil and paper. In contrast to the interview techniques, by using questionnaires researchers can survey a large number of people very quickly. Depending on the ways the responses are recorded, such as through a computer software program or with response sheets that can be run through a scanner, the data may be recorded quickly as well. Every research technique has its advantages and disadvantages, and questionnaires are no different. The difficulty with questionnaires comes in creating questions and responses that allow participants to express their thoughts in the most accurate way. Returning to our hypothetical study, suppose we asked wives who are caring for husbands with Alzheimer's disease the following yes/no question: "Do you believe your adult children should be more involved in their father's care?" Some participants might have preferred to express how much more involvement would be desired on a scale rather than simply responding "yes" or "no." This question does not give any indication of how involved the children are to begin with, and some participants may actually desire less involvement from their children. In some cases the participants may desire more help from some of their adult children and less or no help from others. Finally, this question does not address those participants who do not have adult children.

Regardless of the many measurement issues, questionnaire data remain very popular among researchers in developmental psychology. In some cases researchers will use archival records or data that has already been collected by large, well-planned, census-like gathering techniques for their analyses. The sources of such databanks might be educational institutions, health-related industries, governmental agencies, or private/commercial entities. When using an already established databank the researchers are forced to trust the accuracy of data and to work with whatever data is available. The use of large databanks or archival records is discussed in the *Research In-Depth* section in Chapter 12.

Results

For the reader without a background in statistics the results section will likely prove to be the most challenging to decipher. Keep in mind that there are many helpful resources on the Internet that can offer explanations of key terms when needed. Entering terms such as "correlation" or "*t*-test" in a search engine will bring many helpful resources forward.

Often the first items reported in the results section of a journal article are descriptive statistics. As the name implies, they are summary statistics that describe the sample of participants and may be presented in graph form as well as number form. In addition to giving the *frequencies* of appropriate variables, measures of central tendency are often among the first results reported. The most well-known measure, the *mean* or the average, can give useful but limited information. This is illustrated, along with statistical significance and *t*-tests, in the *Research In-Depth* section in Chapter 3. The mean is often reported with the *standard deviation,* a number reflecting the extent to which numbers differed or deviated from the mean. In some cases it is useful to know the *mode* of a distribution (the most frequently appearing number or score) or the *median* (the middle when numbers are placed in order). The *range,* the difference between the highest and lowest number or score, can also be helpful when given with other descriptive statistics.

Comparing the Means

Once the researchers move beyond simply describing the data they often report *inferential statistics.* These procedures allow researchers to make generalizations about the entire population beyond just a description of the sample of people who participated, while also allowing for a calculation of the confidence placed in those generalizations. One of the most basic inferential statistical analyses, a *t-test,* is often used to determine whether the differences in two groups of data are due to experimental error and chance, or if the differences are statistically significant. A *t*-test considers the mean of each set of scores as well as the variation around the mean. Returning to our example of wives caring for husbands with Alzheimer's disease (group 1) and wives caring for husbands with cancer (group 2), if we wanted to know if the two groups demonstrated the same levels of depression or if one showed more depression than the other we could compare the scores each group had on a depression questionnaire using a *t*-test. Distinctions are usually made between an *independent t,* applied to scores or measurements taken from different participants or sources, and *dependent t* or *paired-sample t-tests,* applied when data in the two groups can be matched to the same participants, such as when comparing a pre- and post-treatment measure. (The use of *t*-tests is explored in the *Research In-Depth* section in Chapter 3.) When comparing the means from three or more groups researchers often conduct an *analysis of variance* or *ANOVA.*

Correlational Analysis

Correlational techniques are described in the *Research In-Depth* section in Chapter 4. Correlations give more information than descriptive studies because they tell researchers about relationships between variables. On the other hand, they cannot show cause-and-effect, which is the exclusive domain of the true experiment. To summarize the information given in Chapter 4, statistical correlations range in numerical value from –1.00 to +1.00, with numbers approaching either end reflecting a stronger relationship. Correlations are usually reported in research articles as r values, such as $r = 0.75$ or $r = -0.82$, with the most common calculation of r being the *Pearson product moment correlation coefficient.* Distinctions are also made between positive and negative correlations. Positive correlations, those with r values above 0.00, indicate that the scores move in the same direction. Thus, participants who have a high number for variable A also had a high number for variable B, and the opposite. In our hypothetical example, researchers might find that the amount of time wives spend online with their cyber-support group is correlated with the amount of time their husbands spend sleeping. Wives whose husbands sleep more often during the day (high snooze rate) spend more time with the group (high cyber-chat). Also, wives whose husbands sleep less often during the day (low snooze rate) spend less time with the group (less cyber-chat). Negative correlations, those with r values below 0.00, indicate that the scores move in opposite directions. Thus, participants who have a high number for variable A displayed a low number for variable B, and the opposite. Continuing with the example, researchers may find that women who spend more time with their cyber-groups (high cyber-chat) report less depression (low depression scores) whereas those women who spend less time online with their support group (less cyber-chat) report more depression (high depression scores).

Additional Common Statistical Procedures

Taking correlational analysis to more complex levels, various types of *multiple regression* can show, statistically, whether several variables are working together to influence other variables. For example, considering the mental health of wives caring for a husband with Alzheimer's disease, regression analysis can show how age, education level, financial support, social support, and severity of her husband's illness as variables may combine or "team up" to influence the mental health of the caregiver. Although regression analyses cannot establish cause-and-effect they can give researchers a better sense of how variables are combining (or not) to influence other variables.

Another design that builds on the basic foundation of correlational analysis is *factor analysis.* The typical way to utilize factor analysis is to give questionnaire items to many participants and then analyze the results for trends or clusters of items called factors. For example, researchers might develop a lengthy questionnaire for caregivers, which includes many questions about mood, emotions, coping, and self-concept. Factor analysis might show that women who ranked the item "I am concerned that a situation will arise and I won't know what to do" as one they strongly agree with also ranked high agreement with the item "Every night I lay awake wondering if I can handle whatever might happen during the night." A cluster of items such as these would indicate that feeling unprepared or worrying about the unknown are key factors for these wives. One of the best examples of factor analysis is described in Chapter 4 regarding the development of the five-factor personality model.

Much of the work with more sophisticated statistics in the social sciences have moved toward developing models of the ways variables are related (statistically) and then using those models to make predictions. These sophisticated models not only reveal relationships but also the strength of associations between variables and the direction of the influence. The *Research In-Depth* section in Chapter 14 discusses one of the modeling techniques, structural equation modeling.

Analyzing Qualitative Data

When working with narratives it is a more complex process to code data and count items to generate the numbers or scores that can be used with the standard statistical procedures discussed here. The goal in analyzing qualitative data is less about generating many precise scores and more about the desire to document and summarize the trends, repeated phrases, tone, emotion, and overall essence of the data. When working with qualitative data the researchers will most likely have to comb through the material several times to determine what the commonalities might be between the various narratives, and then scan the data even more closely to document the frequency of particular themes or variables. For example, the wives caring for husbands with Alzheimer's disease may be asked to keep a journal. Rather than asking them to answer predesigned questions, the researcher may simply ask them to write whatever is on their mind. Through those narratives researchers may discover something unexpected, such as those wives who talk about their pets express less depression. It might not have occurred to researchers writing a questionnaire to ask about pets; however, in journal entries the wives have the opportunity to share what is important to them and by doing so pet companions may attract attention. There are software packages that can assist in combing through and coding data. Often qualitative data will bring to light new concepts and ideas that may translate into questions that can become quantitative instruments.

Discussion and Conclusions

Perhaps the most important part of a research article is the discussion. Here the reader will find a useful summary of the results in a narrative rather than in statistical notation. Researchers will often tie their findings back to their original literature review, explaining which findings were consistent with their hypotheses and previous research as well as which findings were inconsistent with their hypotheses and previous research. As discussed in light of true experiments, it is important to remember that in psychology researchers seldom use the powerful term "prove" because it is so difficult to control all the confounding variables. Even with that said, anyone reading a psychological study should be careful with the temptation to overgeneralize the results. For example, if the study of the effects of a cyber-community on depression in women who are caring for husbands with Alzheimer's disease shows that the depression decreased for those in a cyber-community, readers should be careful not to overgeneralize by assuming cyber-communities can help ease depression in anyone, regardless of circumstances. It is also important to be careful not to inflate the importance of only one study. In any piece of research there is a possibility of participant error, such as not understanding the instructions to reporting in a way to put oneself in the best light (self-report bias). There is also the possibility of researcher bias in the way the research was designed or interpreted.

Most articles will include a discussion of the limitations of the study and suggestions for changes in future research. Such limitations are often the result of finite time and resources. For example, a researcher may dream of interviewing several hundred wives across the United States who are caring for husbands in various stages of Alzheimer's disease, but it would take a great deal of time, money, and resources to collect the data and analyze it. A researcher may want to send questionnaires to 1,000 people, but the costs may be prohibitive. Often researchers must use the wisdom of previous research and some creative problem solving to find the most efficient way to conduct the most comprehensive study possible with the resources available.

GLOSSARY

Accommodation: A term attributed to Piaget and used to describe the process of modifying existing schemas when information is not consistent, and creating new schemas when needed.

Acculturation: Term used to describe the level of adaptation to a new culture, with low acculturation referring to retaining one's native culture and high acculturation referring to largely adopting the characteristics of the host culture.

Acronym: A type of mnemonic that involves making a word from the first letters of items to be remembered.

Acrostic: A type of mnemonic that involves making a sentence using words that start with the same letters as the to-be-remembered words in the same order as the to-be-remembered words.

Active euthanasia: Intentionally engaging in direct action(s) to shorten a patient's life.

Adult development and aging: An area of developmental psychology that is focused on the ways mental and behavioral processes change with age across adulthood.

Adult students: College students who do not fit the traditional profile, and may be older, employed full time, caring for dependents, or even taking courses in retirement.

Advance directives: Documents detailing the wishes of individuals regarding end-of-life concerns that should be consulted if individuals are unable to speak for themselves.

Affective work commitment: Experienced by employees who take pride in their organization and find their identity in the affiliation with their employer.

Ageism: Prejudicial or discriminatory actions reflecting negative stereotypes based on age.

Aging in place: A lifestyle desired by many older adults who want to choose where to live, usually a traditional community, and have needed assistance and services delivered there.

Agreeableness: One of the factors that make up the five-factor model of personality, which refers to the tendency to be helpful, caring, cooperative, and trustworthy.

Allocative discrimination: Refers to the unfair trends indicating that some groups of people tend to be hired primarily for lower level positions at lower pay scales.

Alopecia: The medical term for hair loss from the scalp or baldness.

Alzheimer's disease: The most common cause of dementia, this progressive disease involves the accumulation of lesions on the brain and brain shrinkage affecting cognition processing, memory, language, balance, and coordination.

Androgenetic alopecia: The medical term for the commonly seen male pattern baldness.

Androgynous: A personality style that emphasizes developing one's best feminine and masculine qualities to be the best person, regardless of one's sex.

Andropause: For most men between the ages of 35 and 65 years old, the reduction in hormones and related symptoms.

Aneurysm: A weak or thin spot on an artery wall that can leak blood or rupture.

Anxiety disorders: A DSM-IV category including panic disorder, social anxiety disorder, generalized anxiety disorder, posttraumatic stress disorder, and obsessive–compulsive disorder.

Anxious-ambivalent attachment style: Learned from their early infant–caregiver bonding experience, adults with this style believe that their partners are worthy of love, however, they themselves are not. This style is also called the preoccupied attachment style.

Assimilation: A term attributed to Piaget and used to describe the process of interpreting new information in terms of preexisting schemas or networks of knowledge.

Assisted living: Services offered to older adults to help with the activities of daily living, such as preparing meals, housekeeping, transportation, social and recreational activities, health care, and security.

Atherosclerosis: Term for the buildup of plaque in the arteries that supply blood to the heart muscle, causing the arteries to harden and narrow.

Attachment styles: Generally, refers to the quality of the emotional bond between an infant and caregiver; however, when applied to adulthood refers to the parallel between infant–caregiver bonds and types of bonds adults create with their lovers.

Autobiographical memory bump: Refers to the shape of the graph when charting the frequency by age of individuals' most important memories, which usually produces a "bump" reflecting significantly more memories from late adolescence and early adulthood than from other times across life.

Avoidant attachment style: Learned from their early infant–caregiver bonding experience, adults with this style believe they are worthy of love and seek love, however, they have difficulties trusting their partner.

Avoidant-dismissing attachment style: Learned from their early infant–caregiver bonding experience, adults with this style believe that they are valuable and worthy of love, however, they do not trust their lover to return that love.

Avoidant-fearful attachment style: Learned from their early infant–caregiver bonding experience, adults with this style believe that they believe that they are worthy of love, however, others cannot be trusted and it is better to simply avoid love relationships entirely.

Behaviorism: One of the major branches of psychology in which the primary focus is specifically definable, observable, measurable behaviors, with practically no consideration of mental processes of the mind.

Bereavement: Refers to time between the death of someone close to you and full adjustment to new routines and return to everyday living.

Bioecological theory: Developed by Bronfenbrenner, it conceptualizes individual development as occurring with influential interactions from personal relationships and other social factors, which are categorized into microsystems, mesosystems, exosystems, macrosystems, and chronosystems.

Biological age: Refers to an adult's physical health, particularly of vital organ systems, as compared to others of the same chronological age.

Biomarker: Refers to a measure of biological age, such as lung capacity or heart functioning.

Body mass index: A calculation based on weight and height that determines if an individual is underweight (score of less than 18.5), in a healthy weight range (18.5–24.9), overweight (25–29.9), or obese (30 or more).

Bogus pipeline: A research method in which participants are led to believe that they are being monitored by a lie detector of some sort, when in reality they are being deceived.

Brain atrophy: Refers to the decrease in the amount of brain tissue in older adults.

Bridge employment: Work that serves as the transition from full-time employment to retirement and total withdrawal from the workforce.

Burnout: Refers to the emotional exhaustion, depersonalization, cynicism, and lack of productivity resulting from sustained high levels of stress in the work environment.

Cancer: Refers to a broad category of diseases that begin with abnormal cell growth that destroys healthy tissue around it and may metastasize to other parts of the body.

Carcinogens: Cancer-causing substances, such as those found in tobacco, asbestos, or asphalt fumes.

Cardiovascular disease: Also called heart disease, refers to a broad category of diseases and conditions that affect the functioning of the heart, such as high blood pressure, coronary artery disease, and heart attack.

Caregiving trajectory theory: The path that many adult children take through concern, urging, and action, as they observe their parents move from independence to dependence on others.

Cataracts: Clouded eye lens often safely corrected with surgery.

Causal theory: A theory explaining the cohabitation effect which states that cohabiting causes changes in the individuals which lead to divorce.

Centenarians: Refers to individuals who are 100 years or older.

Central executive processes: Part of the working memory in information processing theory that coordinates the information from short-term/primary and long-term memory.

Cerebrovascular disease: Refers to a broad category of diseases and conditions that affect blood flow to the brain resulting in brain damage and dysfunction.

Cerebrum: The largest and most developed area of the brain that is composed of the left and right hemispheres.

Childfree: Refers to the position of an individual who is choosing, voluntarily, not to be a parent.

Childless: Refers to the position of an infertile individual who would like to be a biological parent but cannot, and thus parenting is not a part of his or her life.

Chronological age: Time since birth, usually given in years for adults.

Cognitive mechanics: Refers to the biological processes involved in thinking, similar to fluid intelligence.

Cognitive perspective on intelligence: View of intelligence that focuses on information processing and areas of fluid and crystallized intelligence.

Cognitive pragmatics: Refers to the influence of cultural and social information on thinking, similar to crystallized intelligence.

Cognitive revolution: A movement in the 1960s that moved American psychology away from a science of behaviorism to one that includes both the study of cognitive (mental) processes and behaviors.

Cognitive-self models: Models that emphasize the way an individual views him- or herself and the factors that influence and alter that self-perception.

Cohabitation: The term for individuals who are living together in a romantic relationship as a non-married couple.

Cohabitation effect: The research finding that couples who cohabit prior to marriage are more likely to divorce.

Cohort: A group of people shaped by the same powerful normative history-graded experiences.

Collectivism: The worldview, in contrast to individualism, that elevates the interdependence and mutual responsibility of all members of society as the primary source of meaning.

Comparable worth: Refers to the principle that individuals who are engaged in different jobs that are substantially equal in terms of skills, effort, responsibility, and working conditions in the same organization should be given equal wages.

Compensation model: A model of family role transitions that emphasizes the ways adults compensate for losses by engaging in something new or increasing other activities.

Complicated grief: A mental disorder involving prolonged, intense grief, similar to depression and posttraumatic stress disorder, which interferes with routine functioning.

Compression of functional morbidity: Refers to maintaining a healthy lifestyle in order to reduce the amount of time spent at the end of life with disease or disability.

Computerized tomography (CT) scans: Body imaging technology that utilized x-rays to highlight bones, soft tissue, and fluids, which can be used to study brain structures.

Connectionist approaches to development: Prominent in cognitive psychology and neuroscience modeling, the emphasis is on associating units of information, based on weights, to form networks of related information.

Conscientiousness: One of the factors that make up the five-factor model of personality, which refers to the tendency to be organized, achievement-oriented, and responsible.

Contextual metatheory: A philosophy of human development that emphasizes the bidirectional interaction and simultaneous influences of internal forces, such as genetically predetermined patterns, and external forces, such as culture, experience, and other environmental factors.

Contextual perspective on intelligence: View of intelligence that focuses on the role of the environment or context in solving everyday problems intelligently.

Continuance work commitment: Experienced by employees who feel stuck in an employment situation they are not happy with because there are no other reasonable alternatives.

Continuing care retirement communities: Retirement villages that provide a campus of structures allowing for levels of care from total independence to full nursing home care.

Continuing education units (CEUs): Credits needed by members of some professional organizations to receive or maintain an active license or certification.

Continuous development: A philosophy or view that individuals tend to grow or develop in smooth, steady ways, such that when graphed the result is closer to a flowing line rather than jagged steps.

Control group: A group of participants in a research study who do not experience the independent variable(s) and serve as a comparison group to other participants who did experience the independent variable(s).

Convoy model of friendship: Conceptualizes friendships in inner, middle, and outer circles reflecting layers of closeness and support through which friends and family members move in and out.

Correlation: A statistical term referring to the relationship, either positive or negative, between two variables in a research study.

Cortex: The surface of the cerebrum that contains most of the cognitive processing in the brain; also called gray matter.

Creativity: Defined in many different ways, it generally reflects characteristics of flexibility, originality, and unusualness.

Cross-cultural: Comparing or involving different cultures.

Cross-sectional design: A research design that involves testing distinct groups of people of varying ages at the same point in time for comparison.

Crystallized intelligence: Refers to the knowledge gained throughout life, particularly through educational and cultural experiences, similar to cognitive pragmatics.

Culture: A broad term including a groups' sense of art, science and technology, moral and governance systems, symbols and beliefs, social customs, language and education system, and health care practices.

Cumulative disadvantage model: A model of family role transitions that emphasizes the ways that early life disadvantages may accumulate to significantly influence role transitions later in life.

Death anxiety: A multidimensional construct involving many death-related fears, including fear of the dying process, moment of death, situation of the body and the spirit after death, and the unknown, both for one's self and for others.

Debriefing: The action of informing participants in an IRB-approved study of the true nature of research that involved deception.

Deception in research: With IRB approval, researchers may omit some aspects of the study in the informed consent document and/or provide false or misleading information in order to collect more accurate data.

Decremental theories: Theories of aging that emphasize the losses due to the deaths of friends and relatives along with the loss of energy and awareness.

Dementia: A group of symptoms, primarily the deterioration of memory, reasoning ability, judgment, and communicative skills, which can be caused by different diseases or conditions.

Dependent variable: An outcome variable in a research study that reflects the change that occurred from exposure to the independent variable.

Developmental psychology: An area of psychology focused on normal or typical changes in mental and behavioral processes across the lifespan.

Developmental regulation: Coping through the use of primary and secondary control to directly influence personal development and to adjust to uncontrollable constraints.

Diabetes: Refers to three primary conditions in which the pancreas produces no or very little insulin, or the cells that need insulin do not use it well, resulting in high levels of glucose in the blood.

***Diagnostic and Statistical Manual of Mental Disorders* (DSM):** Provides the standard naming and criteria system for all mental disorders and associated issues by categorizing concerns on five axes describing the primary conditions, long-term influences, medical conditions, psychosocial concerns, and global functioning.

Discontinuous development: A philosophy or view that individuals tend to grow or develop in stages, with each succeeding stage qualitatively distinct from the previous.

Disease: Physiological characteristics, symptoms, and changes that are diagnosed and used to determine the primary pathology.

Disorder: The preferred term of the American Psychiatric Association when referring to psychopathology or mental illness.

Diversity: Refers to distinctions among individuals' cultures.

Divided attention: The ability to maintain attention and focus on more than one stimulus.

Double jeopardy: When used in reference to individual and multicultural differences the term is used to describe individuals who are in more than one minority or stereotypically negative group.

Durable power of attorney for finances: A document specifying someone who is authorized by an individual to make financial decisions and transactions for that individual if the person is unable to speak for him- or herself.

Durable power of attorney for health care: A document specifying someone as a health care proxy authorized by an individual to make health care decisions for that individual if the person is unable to speak for him- or herself.

Ego integrity versus despair: Erikson's late adulthood stage in which individuals are challenged to develop wisdom and a cohesive identity, rather than dwell on fear and regrets.

Elderspeak: Slow, exaggerated, and simplified speech, similar to that used with infants and pets, used with older adults based on the assumption that they are hearing and cognitively impaired.

Embolism: The formation of a blood clot within a blood vessel somewhere in the body that moves to the brain, possibly causing an ischemic stroke.

Emotion-focused strategies: Refers to coping methods for high-stress situations that involve taking actions to better manage one's personal anxiety level and reactions to stressors.

Emotional regulation: The ability to monitor and control the experience of positive and negative emotions.

Encoding: Part of the information processing theory that refers to the process of translating sensory signals into brain signals.

Environmental gerontology: The study of the ways the changing needs of aging adults can best be addressed by changes in their environment.

Episodic memories: Memories for personal experiences, often organized by time and context.

Equifinality: The view that the same neurological function may be achieved in different ways, recognizing the potential for individual differences in brain activity.

Equipotentiality: The view that brain cells may develop to take on new or different functions, recognizing the potential for individual differences in brain activity.

Error theories of biological aging: A group of theories that explains aging by emphasizing the accumulated influences of external, environmental, or accidental assaults across the lifespan.

Ethnicity: The cultural group an individual identifies with, accepting the norms of the group.

Experimental research designs: Research designs in which participants are randomly assigned to experience independent variable(s), producing changes in dependent variable(s), thus establishing cause-and-effect.

Extraversion: One of the factors that make up the five-factor model of personality, which refers to the tendency to be social, energetic, spontaneous, and cheerful.

Factor analysis: A statistical procedure that produces factors or themes based on trends or groupings in the data, such as the five-factor model of personality.

Faith development: Refers to Fowler's stage theory, which describes the ways individuals make sense of the notion of a higher power and find meaning in life.

False memories: The phenomenon in which individuals believe they remember something that, in reality, did not occur.

Feared self: Individuals' views of their realistically worst possible future selves.

Federal Interagency Forum on Aging-Related Statistics: A group of 14 agencies, headed by the National Institute on Aging, the National Center for Health Statistics, and the Census Bureau, who pool their data and provide public reports on key areas of aging.

Feminism: Although there are many forms of feminism, varying in intensity and focus, at its base it is the belief that women should be valued and treated like human beings.

Flashbulb memories: Stable and long-lasting memories of one's personal circumstances and reactions to events that are generally unexpected, emotional, and high in consequentiality.

Fluid intelligence: Skills needed to actively process and transform information, similar to cognitive mechanics.

Foreclosure: One of Marcia's adolescent identity statuses, which involves an unwillingness to explore options because commitments are made very early in adolescence.

Four-component model of moral behavior: Refers to the model developed by Narvaez and Rest, which states that the production of moral behavior requires moral sensitivity, reasoning, motivation, and character.

Friendship: An intimate, stimulating companionship that is a source of help, a reliable alliance, self-validation, and emotional security.

Frontal lobes: The front section of each hemisphere of the cerebrum, which is associated with reasoning, planning, memory processes, problem solving, and other cognitive functions.

Functional age: Refers to an adult's age in terms of biological, psychological, and social age.

Functional magnetic resonance imaging (fMRI): A type of functional scan that creates an image of tissue and fluid movement by monitoring the ratio of oxygenated to deoxygenated blood, which can be used to study the functioning of brain structures.

Functional scans: Brain imaging scans that highlight the ways brain structures function by monitoring the movement of various substances.

Gender: A psychological sense of femininity or masculinity and corresponding social attitudes and behaviors.

Gender-graded influences: Influences on development experience due to one's gender.

Gender identity: The aspect of one's self-concept that reflects a personal sense of femininity or masculinity.

Gender roles: Individuals' behaviors that stem directly from personal and social expectations of someone of that gender.

Gender role stereotypes: Narrowly defined, oversimplified perceptions of male or female thoughts and behaviors.

Generativity versus stagnation: Erikson's middle adulthood stage in which individuals are challenged to mentor, provide resources, and guide the next generation, rather than grow self-absorbed and stagnant.

Gerotranscendence: Found in late adulthood, a shift in perspectives from a physical, rational, and practical approach to one that is more spiritual, universal, and transcendent in nature.

Glaucoma: A group of diseases that cause high pressure inside the eyeball and damage to the optic nerve.

Gray matter: The cortex, which is the surface of the cerebrum, containing most of the cognitive processing in the brain.

Grief: Refers to an individual's emotional reaction to another person's death.

Health care proxy: A person designated a durable power of attorney for health care who is authorized by an individual to make health care decisions for that individual if the person is unable to speak for him- or herself.

Heterosexism: The attitude that heterosexual practices are the only healthy and appropriate practices, thus anything different should be seen as deviant and rejected.

Hippocampus: A small structure in the inner brain that directs the storage and retrieval of memories.

Hospice care: A special type of palliative care that is focused on keeping patients as alert, engaged, and comfortable as possible during the last few months of life.

Hostile environment sexual harassment: Refers to harassment that stems from a work environment that is so stressful, due to behavior of a sexual nature, that one cannot perform his or her job adequately.

Ideal self: Individuals' views of their realistically best possible future selves.

Identity: In Erikson's theory it refers to the roles one takes on as well as that individual's personal sense of values, attitudes, beliefs, occupation, and goals.

Identity accommodation: Associated with Whitbourne's identity process theory, it involves the ability to change one's self-schema and create new facets to one's self-schema based on new information.

Identity achievement: One of Marcia's adolescent identity statuses, which is the healthiest, involving full exploration of options and the ability to make commitments.

Identity assimilation: Associated with Whitbourne's identity process theory, it involves the ability to maintain one's identity even when conflicting information is presented by rationalizing the new information to fit existing self-schemas.

Identity balance: Associated with Whitbourne's identity process theory, it involves responding to new information about one's self with a balance of identity accommodation and identity assimilation.

Identity cohesion versus role confusion: Erikson's adolescent psychosocial stage that emphasizes the need to explore and select one's goals, occupation, values, morals, attitudes, and beliefs.

Identity crisis: Erikson's term for an individual's struggle to develop a personal identity that includes personal attitudes, values, beliefs, ethics, and goals.

Identity diffusion: One of Marcia's adolescent identity statuses, which is the least healthy, involving little interest or avoidance in considering options and inability and unwillingness to make commitments.

Identity process theory: Usually refers to Whitbourne's work involving assimilation and accommodation in evolving identity development.

Identity statuses: Usually refers to Marcia's research into the identity state or status of individuals at different points along Erikson's adolescent and adult stages of development.

Ill-defined problems: Problems in which the starting point, ending point, and possible ways to get from one point to the other are not clear, making the strategies for problem solving hinged on the best predictions for a reasonable solution.

Illiteracy: The inability to read and understand written information at a level that is functional and productive.

Illness: The general physical, psychological, and social side effects caused by or associated with a disease.

Independent variable: A variable in a research study that is under the control of the experimenter and applied to the participants.

Infertility: A medical disease affecting males and females that results in the inability of a couple to conceive a child through male–female intercourse.

Information processing theory: A theory of memory that follows information through the sensory registers to the short-term memory and then to long-term memory.

Informed consent: Prior to participation in any research endeavors, human subjects should be informed of all aspects of the study, usually in a written document, and agree to participate.

Inner brain: The part of the brain located beneath the hemispheres of the cerebrum.

Institutional Animal Care and Use Committee (IACUC): A committee of peers at any institution that conducts research with animals who reviews every animal study proposed for compliance with current federal regulations.

Institutional Review Board (IRB): A committee of peers at any institution that conducts research with human participants who reviews every human study proposed for compliance with current federal regulations.

Intelligence quotient (IQ): Refers to the comparison of an individual's mental age, as measured by a test of cognitive skills, to the expected skills level for someone of that individual's chronological age.

Interfaith marriage: A marriage in which the spouses have different religious preferences.

Intimacy versus isolation: Erikson's young adulthood stage in which individuals are challenged to develop trust and love, rather than a fear of vulnerability.

Intraindividual variation: Changes in the measurement of one or more variables within one individual that are not known to be related to developmental gains or losses.

Introversion: Refers to the personality trait of low extraversion, which includes the characteristics of quiet, passive, shy, reserved, and withdrawn.

Life-course model: A model of family role transitions that emphasizes the life cycle as anticipated stages, gains, losses, and opportunities for growth and development.

Life expectancy: Refers to an individual's predicted lifespan based on genetic, environmental, and behavioral factors.

Life satisfaction: One component, along with positive and negative affect, that contributes to overall subjective well-being.

Lifelong learning: The movement encouraging individuals to continue their education throughout their lives in order to remain competitive in employment and to improve their quality of life.

Life-wide learning: A term given to formal and informal educational programs that focus on areas of life other than work or financial gain, such as parenting or fitness education.

Living will: An advance directive document that specifies an individual's wishes regarding the use of specific end-of-life procedures intended to sustain or prolong life.

Longevity: Refers to actual lifespan or the actual number of years a person lives.

Long-term memory: Part of the information processing theory that is the permanent storage of information that has come through the sensory registers and the short-term memory.

Longitudinal design: A research design that involves testing and retesting the same group of people over a long period of time to chart their developmental patterns.

Love styles: Lee's theory that love can be experienced as eros (physical), ludus (a game), storge (friendship), pragma (practical), mania (possessiveness), or agape (selflessness).

Macrostressors: Sources of stress that are major life events.

Macular degeneration: A disease that causes deterioration of part of the retina responsible for central vision.

Magnetic resonance imaging (MRI) scans: Body imaging technology that utilizes magnetic and radio waves to differentiate types of soft tissue, which can be used to study brain structures.

Marital aggrandizement: The inability or lack of willingness to acknowledge any interpersonal negative experiences with one's spouse.

Measurement theory: A theory explaining the cohabitation effect that states that researchers should consider the entire amount of time couples have lived together, both as cohabiting and married, when gauging the success of a relationship.

Mechanistic metatheory: A philosophy of human development that views individuals as machine-like, with a focus on the functioning of particular parts.

Menopause: For most women in their late 40s or early 50s, the state of ceasing menstruation defined by one full calendar year without a menstrual cycle.

Meta-analysis: A research methodology that analyzes the findings of many individual research studies in order to reveal common findings and generalized trends.

Method-of-loci: A mnemonic that uses the strategy of associating the to-be-remembered items with various familiar locations.

Microstressors: Sources of stress that are minor, often referred to as daily hassles.

Mid-life Transition: Part of Levinson's Middle Adulthood stage, which occurs from ages 40 to 45 and consists of finding balance between the polarities of young/old, destruction/creation, masculine/feminine, and attachment/separateness.

Mnemonics: Techniques designed to enhance memory processing and retrieval by adding or enhancing the meaning of the information, such as with the use of acronyms, acrostics, rhymes, and songs.

Mood disorders: A DSM-IV category including major depressive disorder, dysthymic disorder, and bipolar disorder.

Moral development: Refers to the study of the ways individuals resolve moral dilemmas, often discussed in terms of Kohlberg's stages of moral reasoning.

Moral reasoning: Refers to Kohlberg's six stages of reasoning emphasizing the movement from self-centered problem solving to thinking that is others-centered and eventually to reasoning that is values and principles-centered.

Moratorium: One of Marcia's adolescent identity statuses, which involves the exploration of options but the unwillingness or inability to make commitments.

Mourning: Refers to the displaying of behaviors expected by one's cultural and/or religious tradition following the death of another person.

Multiculturalism: A perspective supporting the notion that societies should allow for distinct cultures to exist with equal status.

Multiple intelligences: Gardner's theory that there are separate, unique intelligences, primarily logical-mathematical, linguistic, spatial, musical, bodily-kinesthetic, interpersonal, intrapersonal, and naturalistic intelligence.

Negative correlation: A statistical term referring to the opposite relationship between two variables in a study, such that as one variable increases the negatively correlated variable decreases.

Neo-Piagetian perspective on intelligence: View of intelligence that explores adult development beyond Piaget's final formal operations stage, particularly post-formal operations and wisdom.

Neuropsychology: The area within the field of psychology that studies the interaction between biological systems and psychological variables; also called biopsychology and behavioral neuroscience.

Neuroticism: One of the factors that make up the five-factor model of personality, which refers to the tendency to be nervous, anxious, moody, and experiencing a great deal of worry and guilt.

Non-normative influences: Events or influences that are unique to an individual, often unexpected, personal events that shape our lives.

Normative age-graded influences: Typical events or influences that show a strong relationship with age, thus occurring for most people at about the same age.

Normative-crisis models: Normal or typical challenges, events, or obstacles encountered by most people around the same age.

Normative history-graded influences: Events or influences experienced by a culture or society at a particular point in history affecting the personal development of a large group of individuals.

Novice Phase: Part of Levinson's Early Adulthood stage, which includes the Early Adult Transition (ages 17–22), Entering the Adult World (ages 22–28), and the Age Thirty Transition (ages 28–33).

Obesity: The health condition in which an individual has a body mass index (BMI) of 30 or more, or by a different measure, a woman with a waist measurement greater than 35 inches or a man with a waist measurement greater than 40 inches.

Occipital lobes: The back section of each hemisphere of the cerebrum, which is associated with visual processing.

Open adoption: Refers to a legal arrangement allowing the birth mother or biological family to have contact with the adopted child.

Openness to Experience: One of the factors that make up the five-factor model of personality, which refers to the tendency to be curious, daring, imaginative, and open to new ideas.

Optimal aging: Also called successful aging, this facet of the study of aging emphasizes healthy lifestyles, prevention where possible, and the ability to adjust and cope well with changes that do occur with age.

Organismic metatheory: A philosophy of human development that emphasizes an individual's genetically predetermined patterns or stages of development that become evident through maturation and stimulation provided by the environment.

Palliative care: Medical care and treatment aimed not at curing a disease but at treating symptoms and keeping patients comfortable.

Papillary miosis: An eye condition, common with age, in which the average diameter of the pupil decreases.

Parallel distributed processing theory (PDP): A theory of memory stating that units of information are connected by bonds, and that retrieval of information involves directing energy down many paths of the mental networks at one time.

Parietal lobes: The section of each hemisphere of the cerebrum located behind the frontal lobes, which is associated with sensory processing, reading, and arithmetic.

Passive euthanasia: Allowing a disease process and related complications to proceed, either as a result of withholding treatments or ceasing those that have already been in place, resulting in a patient's death.

Peg-word mnemonic: A two-step mnemonic process that involves associating words that rhyme with numbers, and then visualizing items in order with each particular rhyming word.

Perimenopause: The process of physiological changes, and the corresponding symptoms, women experience leading up to the achievement of menopause, which occurs 1 year after their last menstrual cycle.

Personal authority in the family system: Refers to the adult developmental stage in which adults make the transition from being seen as their parents' child to an individual with authority within the family.

Personality: The collection traits that characterize the way individuals show their sense of self and the ways they interact with others.

Phenomenological interview: A type of data collection method that approaches an interview in a way similar to a conversation, allowing the participants to direct the flow of topics discussed.

Photoaging: The term used by dermatologists to categorize skin-related aging conditions caused by exposure to the sun.

Physician-assisted suicide: Refers to the circumstance in which a physician in some way, usually through a prescription for a lethal drug, aids a patient in ending his or her own life.

Pictorial mnemonic: A type of mnemonic that involves linking information to pictures or mental images.

Plasticity: Refers to the brain's potential to reorganize and structure itself due to environmental stimulation and demands, resulting in improved functioning.

Positive correlation: A statistical term referring to the parallel relationship between two variables in a study, such that as one variable increases or decreases the positively correlated variable increases or decreases in a similar way.

Positive psychology: A strengths-based approach permeating all areas of psychology, emphasizing individuals' strengths and resilient qualities that allow for productive coping and for personal growth.

Positron emission tomography (PET) scans: A type of functional scan that creates an image of tissue and fluid movement by following a radioactive isotope as an indication of blood flow, which can be used to study the functioning of brain structures.

Possible selves: Individuals' sense of their potential, both as their best possible selves, their ideal selves, but also as their feared or dreaded selves.

Postformal operations: Advanced cognition that is complex, integrating the uncertainty of knowledge, emotions, values, reasoning, and situational or cultural circumstances in a way that produces wisdom.

Preoccupied attachment style: Learned from their early infant–caregiver bonding experience, adults with this style believe that their partners are worthy of love, however, they themselves are not. This style is also called the anxious-ambivalent attachment style.

Presbycusis: Hearing loss, particularly for high-frequency sounds, which is a normal part of the aging process.

Presbyopia: The inability to focus on objects close to the face, often occurring in middle and late adulthood and easily corrected with reading glasses.

Primary aging: Physical change over time that is normal and nonpathological.

Primary memory: The temporary storage area of the working memory, also known as short-term memory.

Problem-focused strategies: Refers to coping methods for high-stress situations that involve problem solving aimed directly at the stressor(s).

Procedural memories: Memories for routine and often repeated information or behaviors.

Programmed theories of biological aging: A group of theories that explains aging by proposing that aging is controlled by a biologically determined mechanism and timetable.

Proprioception: A sensory skill used in balance and movement, it is the ability to sense the location of body segments or parts based not on vision but on signals from joints and muscles.

Psychiatric advance directives: Legal documents that allow individuals who are in a competent state to choose the types of mental health treatments they desire should an incapacitating psychiatric crisis arise or to designate someone as a health care agent to make decisions.

Psychological age: Refers to an adult's ability to cope with and adjust to changes in the environment, as compared to others of the same chronological age.

Psychology: One of the social sciences, specifically engaging in the scientific study of mental and behavioral processes.

Psychometric perspective on intelligence: View of intelligence that involves the traditional measuring of IQ points, often through the assessment of verbal reasoning and problem-solving skills.

Psychometrics: The area of psychology focused on developing precise instruments, some of which are questionnaires, to measure human traits, such as intelligence, parts of personality, and levels of mental disorder.

Psychosocial theory: Usually refers to Erikson's theory of human development, which emphasizes the social interactions involved in psychological development.

Ptosis: An eye condition, common with age, in which eyelids sag and cover part of the pupil, decreasing the light and information coming into the eye.

Qualitative design: A research philosophy or method that emphasizes the detection of periods of transition and periods of stability, called stages, which have a more complex quality than the previous stage.

Qualitative research methods: Research design that emphasizes the participants' expression of psychological variables, often through narratives, and the summarizing of data into themes.

Quantitative design: A research philosophy or method that emphasizes the study of variables that can be observed and objectively measured.

Quantitative research methods: Research design that emphasizes the researchers' precise measurement of psychological variables and the statistical analysis of those measurements.

Quasi-experimental design: A research design with most of the characteristics of a true experiment except that the participants are not randomly assigned to groups.

Quid pro quo sexual harassment: Refers to harassment that is based on a request or demand for sexual activity as a condition for something in the workplace.

Race: The group an individual is place in based on physical characteristics, either due to genetic traits or social categorization.

Regret: A negative emotion involving self-blame and disappointment over a situation that, in hindsight, we wish we had handled differently.

Reliability: A step in the process of developing a psychological test that demonstrates a test is stable in terms of giving a consistent measurement.

Religiosity: Refers to commitment to and active involvement in religious institutions or traditions. The level to which one is involved in a religious organization or incorporates the behaviors encouraged or expected by one's religious community.

Remarriage: The term for a marriage in which one or both spouses are not in a first marriage.

Respite care: Refers to the vacation time away needed by primary caregivers who are caring for an ill loved one on a full-time basis.

Role conflict theory: Refers to tension created when the expectations associated with success in various roles compete or are incompatible, as when family roles and employment demands conflict.

Role-taking opportunities: Refers to the opportunities individuals have to experience a different perspective on a situation by mentally or physically placing themselves in another person's position.

Schema: A term attributed to Piaget and used to describe the framework, based on themes or topics, that individuals use to cognitively organize information.

Search: Refers to the use of attention processes to scan an area in search of a specific stimulus.

Secondary aging: Physical change over time that is directly caused by or influenced by disease, detrimental lifestyle choices, or environmental factors.

Secure attachment style: Learned from their early infant–caregiver bonding experience, adults with this style believe that they and their lovers are valuable and worthy of love.

Selection theory: A theory explaining the cohabitation effect that states that those who cohabit have certain characteristics that lead to cohabiting and later to divorce.

Selection, optimization, and compensation theory: Describes management of the gains and losses accompanying each phase of life as the interaction of selecting the best option from realistic choices, optimizing strengths and resources, and compensating for losses by adjusting strategies or goals.

Selective attention: Occurs when there are two or more stimuli competing for attention and the individual must select one stimulus to attend to and ignore the other(s).

Selectivity theories: Theories of aging that emphasize the ability of older adults to better choose how to spend their limited energy and resources.

Self-actualization: A concept made popular by Maslow, which refers to reaching one's full potential.

Self-concept: The collection of everything a person thinks and believes about him- or herself.

Self-efficacy: Refers to individuals' beliefs about their ability to succeed in certain areas of life or to master certain types of tasks.

Self-esteem: The evaluation or judgment individuals make about themselves, determining how satisfied they are with themselves.

Self-schemas: Refer to the framework people use to organize the complex pieces of information and characteristics they have grouped together about themselves.

Semantic memories: Memories for factual and knowledge-based information, often organized by concepts or themes.

Sensory registers: Part of information processing theory that takes in external information through the five senses.

Serial monogamy: Occurs when an individual moves through a series of primary sexual relationships, maintaining fidelity to each partner while in that particular relationship.

Settling Down Period: Part of Levinson's Early Adulthood stage, which occurs from ages 33–40.

Sexual harassment: Defined by the Equal Employment Opportunity Commission (EEOC) as "unwelcome sexual advances, requests for sexual favors, and other verbal or physical conduct of a sexual nature" that occur in the workplace, and "when submission to or rejection of this conduct explicitly or implicitly affects an individual's employment, unreasonably interferes with an individual's work performance, or creates an intimidating, hostile or offensive work environment."

Short-term memory: Part of information processing theory that is the temporary or transitory memory between the sensory registers and the long-term memory.

Social age: Refers to the way one functions in relation to social roles and expectations of someone of the same chronological age.

Social cohesion: As applied to neighborhoods, refers to the belief that others are trustworthy, helpful, and similar in values and attitudes.

Sociocultural theories of development: Theories of human development that give more attention to the societal, social, cultural, and environmental influences on personal development.

Socioeconomic status: A commonly used research variable reflecting individuals' educational attainment, income level, and occupational status.

Spirituality: Refers to the internal, private state that reflects one's faith, beliefs, and sense of inner harmony. One's sense of inner harmony, personal faith, personal beliefs, or commitment to one's personal spiritual journey.

Stage models: Models that emphasize the general development of most people through the progression of qualitatively different stages.

Stenosis: The severe narrowing of an artery located in or leading to the brain, possibly causing an ischemic stroke.

Stereotype: The assumption or belief that a target group of people share, almost without exception, an exaggerated and oversimplified set of characteristics.

Stress reactivity: An individual's level of intensity and emotional sensitivity in response to stressors.

Structural scans: Brain imaging scans that identify parts or structures in the brain, such as computerized tomography (CT) and magnetic resonance imaging (MRI) scans.

Structured interview: A type of data collection method in which all participants are asked the same set of open-ended questions.

Subjective well-being: The general term for happiness and living well, often defined as combined influence of life satisfaction, positive and negative emotions, and mood.

Supercentenarians: Refers to individuals who are 110 years or older.

Surrogate parents: The label for grandparents who are the primary caregivers, acting as the custodial parents, for their grandchildren.

Swan song phenomenon: The name given to the desire of many artists to push themselves to produce a "master work" at the end of their lives.

Tacit knowledge: Action-oriented knowledge or procedures aimed at one's goals, priorities, or values, which is usually acquired informally.

Temporal lobes: The section of each hemisphere of the cerebrum located underneath the frontal, parietal, and occipital lobes, which is associated with forming and retrieving memories, particularly those for sounds and music.

Tertiary aging: Rapid loss in cognitive and physical functioning just before death.

Thrombosis: The formation of a blood clot within a blood vessel in the brain or neck that may lead to an ischemic stroke.

Timing-of-events models: Models that emphasize the interaction between an individual's characteristics, personal situation, and historical context.

Tinnitus: The common, and generally harmless, condition of ringing in the ears or head noise.

Traditional college students: Students who enter full-time college directly from high school, live on-campus, and have no or very little employment, and complete their degree in 4–5 years.

Trait models: Models that emphasize lifelong patterns or characteristics that are consistent over time and across situations.

Transculturation: Blending or merging once separate cultures.

Triangular theory of love: Sternberg's theory that love is comprised of varying and changing levels of intimacy, passion, and commitment or decision to love.

Triarchic theory of intelligence: Developed by Sternberg, this approach views intelligence as being comprised of analytic, creative, and practical elements.

Validity: The step in the process of developing a standardized test that determines that the test is measuring the intended concept or behavior.

Valuative discrimination: Refers to the unfair trends indicating that some occupations are valued less primarily because they are dominated by certain groups of people, such as women and/or members of racial minorities.

Variable: Any item or factor being studied in a research investigation that may vary, either by person, situation, or both.

Vigilance: A type of attention that involves sustained attention or concentration over time.

Well-defined problems: Problems in which the starting point, ending point, and procedure(s) required to get from one to the other are clear and exact, making the challenge of problem solving focused on the discovery or retrieval of key information.

Within-job wage discrimination: Refers to inequality in pay in situations where some individuals are receiving lower wages than others when working in the same position for the same establishment.

Working memory: Part of the information processing theory that contains and manipulates information from the short-term/primary memory and long-term memory through the use of the central executive processes.

REFERENCES

AARP Andrus Foundation & International Longevity Center-USA. (2002). *Is there an anti-aging medicine?* New York: International Longevity Center-USA.

AARP Foundation & International Longevity Center-USA. (2003). *Getting your zzzzzzz's: How sleep affects health and aging*. New York: International Longevity Center-USA.

AARP. (2004). Housing choices. Washington, DC: Author. Retrieved November 6, 2004, from http://www.aarp.org/life/housingchoices/.

Abel, M. H. (2002). Humor, stress, and coping strategies. *Humor: International Journal of Humor Research, 15*(4), 365–376.

Abeles, N., Victor, T. L., & Delano-Wood, L. (2004). The impact of an older adult's death on the family. *Professional Psychology: Research and Practice, 35*(3), 234–239.

Ackerman, P. L., & Rolfhus, E. L. (1999). The locus of adult intelligence: Knowledge, abilities, and non-ability traits. *Psychology and Aging, 14*(2), 314–330.

Adams, M. S., Oye, J., & Parker, T. S. (2003). Sexuality of older adults and the Internet: From sex education to cybersex. *Sexual and Relationship Therapy, 18*(3), 405–415.

Adams-Price, C., & Steinman, B. (2007). Crafts and generative expression: A qualitative study of the meaning of creativity in women who make jewelry in midlife. *International Journal of Aging and Human Development, 65*(4), 315–333.

Adherents.com. (2005). Largest religious groups in the United States of America. Retrieved August 8, 2007, from http://adherents.com/rel_USA.html.

Administration on Aging. (2010, April 19). Older Americans act and aging network. Retrieved July 18, 2010 from http://www.aoa.gov/AoARoot/AoA_Programs/OAA/Introduction.aspx.

Ahrons, C. (1980). Divorce: A crisis of family transition and change. *Family Relations, 29*(4), 533–540.

Akiyama, H., Antonucci, T., Takahashi, K., & Langfahl, E. (2003). Negative interactions in close relationships across the life span. *Journals of Gerontology: Series B: Psychological sciences and social sciences. 58B*(2), 70–79.

Albert, M. S., & Killiany, R. J. (2001). Age-related cognitive change and brain-behavior relationships. In J. E. Birren & K. W. Schaie (Eds.), *Handbook of the psychology of aging* (5th ed., pp. 161–185). San Diego, CA: Academic Press.

Aldwin, C. M., & Gilmer, D. F. (2004). *Health, illness, and optimal aging*. Thousand Oaks, CA: Sage.

Aldwin, C. M., Spiro, A., & Park, C. L. (2006). Health, behavior, and optimal aging: A life span developmental perspective. In J. E. Birren & K. W. Schaie (Eds.), *Handbook of the psychology of aging* (6th ed., pp. 85–104). San Diego, CA: Academic Press.

Alexander, M. G., & Fisher, T. D. (2003). Truth and consequences: Using the bogus pipeline to examine sex differences in self-reported sexuality. *Journal of Sex Research, 40*(1), 2–35.

Alford, S. M. (2000). A qualitative study of the college social adjustment of black students from lower socioeconomic communities. *Journal of Multicultural Counseling and Development, 28*(1), 2–15.

Allaire, J. C., & Marsiske, M. (2002). Well- and ill-defined measures of everyday cognition: Relationship to older adults' intellectual ability and functional status. *Psychology and Aging, 17*(1), 101–115.

Allen, E. S., Baucom, D. H., Burnett, C. K., Epstein, N., & Rankin-Esquer, L. A. (2001). Decision-making power, autonomy, and communication in remarried spouses compared with first-married spouses. *Family Relations, 50*(4), 326–334.

Allik, J., & McCrae, R. R. (2004). Toward a geography of personality traits: Patterns of profiles across 36 cultures. *Journal of Cross-Cultural Psychology, 35*(1), 14–28.

Alternatives to Marriage Project. (2009). Statistics. Brooklyn, NY: Author. Retrieved November 27, 2009, from http://www.unmarried.org/statistics.html#households.

Amato, P. R., & Previti, D. (2003). People's reasons for divorcing: Gender, social class, the life course, and adjustment. *Journal of Family Issues, 24*(5), 602–626.

Ambler, M. (2004). Distance education comes home. *Tribal College, 15*(4), 8–9.

American Academy of Dermatology. (2008a). Causes of aging skin. Retrieved May 16, 2008, from http://www.skincarephysicians.com/agingskinnet/basicfacts.html.

American Academy of Dermatology. (2008b). Frequently asked questions about aging skin. Retrieved May 16, 2008, from http://www.skincarephysicians.com/agingskinnet/FAQs.html.

American Academy of Family Physicians. (2000). Memory loss with aging: What's normal, what's not. Leawood, KS: Author. Retrieved August 2, 2004, from http://familydoctor.org/124.xml.

American Academy of Pediatrics. (2002, February). Coparent or second-parent adoption by same-sex parents. Elk Grove Village, IL: Author. Retrieved October 22, 2004, from http://aappolicy.aappublications.org/cgi/content/full/pediatrics%3b109/2/339.

American Academy of Physicians. (2002, March). Hair loss and its causes. Retrieved January 11, 2005, from http://familydoctor.org/081.xml.

American Anthropological Association. (2004, February 25). Statement on marriage and the family from the American Anthropological Association. Arlington, VA: Author. Retrieved October 19, 2004, from http://www.aaanet.org/press/ma_stmt_marriage.htm.

American Art Therapy Association. (2010). Art Therapy. Alexandria, VA: Author. Retrieved July 17, 2010 from http://www.arttherapy.org/aata-aboutus.html.

American Cancer Society. (2008, April 4). What is hospice care? Retrieved July 20, 2008, from http://www.cancer.org/docroot/eto/content/eto_2_5x_what_is_hospice_care.asp?sitearea=mlt.

American Council on Education. (2003, August). ACE Issue Brief: Student success: Understanding graduation and persistence rates. Washington, DC: Author. Retrieved August 13, 2004, from http://www.acenet.edu/resources/higheredfacts/issue-briefs/2003student_success.pdf.

American Geriatric Society Foundation for Health and Aging. (2005, February 25). Ethical and legal issues. Retrieved July 20, 2008, from http://www.healthinaging.org/agingintheknow/chapters_ch_trial.asp?ch=4.

American Heart Association. (2008). Facts about women and cardiovascular diseases. Retrieved July 7, 2008, from http://www.americanheart.org/presenter.jhtml?identifier=2876.

American Osteopathic Association. (2008). Shatter the myths of male pattern baldness. Retrieved May 16, 2008, from http://www.osteopathic.org/index.cfm?PageID=you_baldness.

American Psychiatric Association. (1994). Diagnostic and statistical manual of mental disorders (4th ed.). Washington, DC: Author.

American Psychological Association. (2002). *Guidelines on multicultural education, training, research, practice, and organization for psychologists*. Washington, DC; Author.

American Psychological Association. (2003, June 1). *Ethical principles of psychologists and code of conduct*. Washington, DC: Author. Retrieved June 6, 2007, from http://www.apa.org/ethics/code2002.html.

American Psychological Association. (2004a). APA supports legalization of same-sex civil marriages and opposes discrimination against lesbian and gay parents. Washington, DC: Author. Retrieved April 30, 2005, from http://www.apa.org/releases/gaymarriage.html.

American Psychological Association (2004b). Guidelines for psychological practice with older adults. *American Psychologist, 59*(4), 236–260.

American Society of Reproductive Medicine. (2004). Frequently asked questions about infertility. Retrieved October 19, 2004, from http://www.asrm.org/Patients/faqs.html.

Anderson-Butcher, D. (2004). Transforming schools into 21st century community learning centers. *Children and Schools, 26*(4), 248–252.

Angel, R. J., & Angel, J. L. (2006). Diversity and aging in the United States. In R. H. Binstock & L. K. George (Eds.), *Handbook of aging and the social sciences* (6th ed., pp. 94–110). San Diego, CA: Academic Press.

Anstey, K. J. (2004). Within-person variability as a dynamic measure of late-life development: New methodologies and future directions. *Gerontology, 50*(4), 255–258.

Anstey, K. J., Dain, S., Andrews, S., & Drobny, J. (2002). Visual abilities in older adults explain age-differences in Stroop and fluid intelligence but not face recognition: Implications for the vision-cognition connection. *Aging, Neuropsychology and Cognition, 9*(4), 253–265.

Antoncic, B. (2009). The entrepreneur's general personality traits and technological developments. *Proceedings of World Academy of Science, Engineering and Technology, 41*, 2070–3740.

Antonucci, T. C. (2001). Social relations: An examination of social networks, social support, and sense of control. In J. E. Birren & K. W. Schaie (Eds.) *Handbook of the psychology of aging* (5th ed., pp. 425–453). San Diego, CA: Academic Press.

Antonucci, T. C., Lansford, J. E., & Akiyama, H. (2001). Impact of positive and negative aspects of marital relationships and friendships on well-being of older adults. *Applied Developmental Science, 5*(2), 68–75.

Anxiety Disorders Association of America. (2010a). Facts and statistics. Silver Spring, MD: Author. Retrieved July 14, 2010, from http://www.adaa.org/about-adaa/press-room/facts-statistics.

Anxiety Disorders Association of America. (2010b). Older adults. Silver Spring, MD: Author. Retrieved July 14, 2010, from http://www.adaa.org/living-with-anxiety/older-adults.

Anxiety Disorders Association of America. (2010c). Understanding anxiety. Silver Spring, MD: Author. Retrieved July 14, 2008, from http://www.adaa.org/understanding-anxiety.

Araujo, A., Mohr, B., & McKinlay, J. (2004). Changes in sexual function in middle-aged and older men: Longitudinal data from the Massachusetts Male Aging study. *Journal of the American Geriatrics Society, 52*(9), 1502–1509.

Aron, A., & Westbay, L. (1996). Dimensions of the prototype of love. *Journal of Personality and Social Psychology, 70*(3), 535–551.

Artistico, D., Cervone, D., & Pezzuti, L. (2003). Perceived self-efficacy and everyday problem solving among young and older adults. *Psychology and Aging, 18*(1), 68–79.

Atkins, D. C., Baucom, D. H., & Jacobson, N. S. (2001). Understanding infidelity: Correlates in a national random sample. *Journal of Family Psychology, 15*(4), 735–749.

Austrom, M., Perkins, A. J., Damush, A. J., & Hendrie, H. C. (2003). Predictors of life satisfaction in retired physicians and spouses. *Social Psychiatry and Psychiatric Epidemiology, 38*(3), 134–141.

Azar, S. T. (2003). Adult development and parenthood. In J. Demick & C. Andreoletti (Eds.), *Handbook of adult development* (pp. 391–415). New York: Kluwer Academic/Plenum Press.

Backman, L., & Nilsson, L. (1996). Semantic memory functioning across the adult life span. *European Psychologist, 1*(1), 27–33.

Backman, L., Small, B. J., & Wahlin, A. (2001). Aging and memory: Cognitive and biological perspectives. In J. E. Birren & K. W. Schaie (Eds.), *Handbook of the psychology of aging* (5th ed., pp. 347–377). San Diego, CA: Academic Press.

Backman, L., Wahlin, A., Small, B. J., Herlitz, A., Winblad, B., & Fratiglioni, L. (2004). Cognitive functioning in aging and dementia: The Kungsholmen project. *Aging, Neuropsychology and Cognition, 11*(2–3), 212–244.

Baddeley, A. D. (2002). Is working memory still working? *European Psychologist, 7*(2), 85–97.

Baddeley, A. D., & Hitch, G. J. (1994). Developments in the concept for working memory. *Neuropsychology, 8*(4), 485–493.

Ballard, S. M., & Morris, M. L. (2003). The family life education needs of midlife and older adults. *Family Relations: Interdisciplinary Journal of Applied Family Studies, 52*(2), 129–136.

Baltes, B. B., & Heydens-Gahir, H. A. (2003). Reduction of work–family conflict through the use of selection, optimization, and compensation behaviors. *Journal of Applied Psychology, 88*(6), 1005–1018.

Baltes, P. B. (1982). Life span developmental psychology: Some converging observations on history and theory. In K. W. Schaie & J. Geiwitz (Ed.), *Readings in adult development and aging* (pp. 12–25). Boston: Little, Brown.

Baltes, P. B. (1987). Theoretical propositions of life-span developmental psychology: On the dynamics between growth and decline. *Developmental Psychology, 23*(5) 611–626.

Baltes, P. B., & Baltes M. M. (1990). Psychological perspectives on successful aging: The model of selective optimization with compensation. In P. B. Baltes & M. M. Baltes (Eds.), *Successful aging: Perspectives from the behavioral sciences* (pp. 1–34). New York: Cambridge University Press.

Baltes, P. B., & Staudinger, U. M. (1993). The search for a psychology of wisdom. *Current Directions in Psychological Science*, 2(3), 75–80.

Baltes, P. B., & Staudinger, U. M. (2000). Wisdom: A metaheuristic (pragmatic) to orchestrate mind and virtue toward excellence. *American Psychologist,* 55(1), 122–136.

Baltes, P. B., Staudinger, U. M., & Lindenberger, U. (1999). Lifespan psychology: Theory and application to intellectual functioning. *Annual Reviews in Psychology, 50,* 471–507.

Baltes, P. B., Staudinger, U. M., Maercker, A., & Smith, J. (1995). People nominated as wise: A comparative study of wisdom-related knowledge. *Psychology and Aging,* 10(2), 155–166.

Bandura, A. (1989). Human agency in social cognitive theory. *American Psychologist, 44,* 1175–1184.

Bandura, A. (1993). Perceived self-efficacy in cognitive development and functioning. *Educational Psychologist, 28,* 117–148.

Barbara, A. M., & Dion, K. L. (2000). Breaking up is hard to do, especially for strongly "preoccupied" lovers. *Journal of Personal & Interpersonal Loss, 5*(4), 315–342.

Barnes, S. L. (2003). Determinants of individual neighborhood ties and social resources in poor urban neighborhoods. *Sociological Spectrum, 23*, 463–497.

Batalova, J. A., & Cohen, P. N. (2002). Premarital cohabitation and housework: Couples in cross-national perspectives. *Journal of Marriage & Family, 64*(3), 743–755.

Bauer, M. J., Adler, G., Kuskowski, M. A., & Rottunda, S. The influence of age and gender on driving patterns of older adults. *Journal of Women and Aging, 15*(4), 3–16.

Baumeister, R. F. (1988). Should we stop studying sex differences altogether? *American Psychologist, 43*(12), 1092–1095.

Bekker, M. H., Nijssen, A., & Hens, G. (2001). Stress prevention training: Sex differences in types of stressors, coping, and training effects. *Stress & Health: Journal of the International Society for the Investigation of Stress, 17*(4), 207–218.

Berardi, A., Parasuraman, R., & Haxby, J. V. (2001). Overall vigilance and sustained attention decrements in healthy aging. *Experimental Aging Research, 27*, 19–39.

Berg, C. (2000). Intellectual development in adulthood. In R. J. Sternberg (Ed.), *Handbook of Intelligence* (pp. 117–137). New York: Cambridge University Press.

Berg, C. A., & Sternberg, R. J. (1992). Adult's conceptions of intelligence across the adult life span. *Psychology and Aging*, 7(2), 221–231.

Berg, C. A., & Sternberg, R. J. (2003). Multiple perspectives on the development of adult intelligence. In J. Demick & C. Andreoletti (Eds.), *Handbook of adult development* (pp. 103–119). New York: Kluwer Academic/Plenum Press.

Berkman, L. F. (1988). The changing and heterogeneous nature of aging and longevity: A social and biomedical perspective. *Annual Review of Gerontology and Geriatrics, 8*, 37–88.

Bernal, G., Trimble, J., Burlew, A., & Leong, F. (2003). Introduction: The psychological study of racial and ethnic minority psychology. In G. Bernal, J. Trimble, A. Burlew, & F. Leong (Eds.) *Handbook of racial and ethnic minority psychology* (pp. 1–12). Thousand Oaks, CA: Sage.

Bern-Klug, M. (2004). The decision labyrinth: Helping families find their way through funeral options. *Generations, 28*(2), 31–36.

Bernsten, D., & Rubin, D. C. (2002). Emotionally charged autobiographical memories across the life span: The recall of happy, sad, traumatic, and involuntary memories. *Psychology and Aging, 17*(4), 636–652.

Bertakis, K. D., Azari, R., Helms, L. J., Callahan, E. J., & Robbins, J. A. (2000). Gender differences in the utilization of health care services. *Journal of Family Practice, 49*(2), 147–152.

Binstock, R. H., Fishman, J. R., & Johnson, T. E. (2006). Anti-aging medicine and science: Social implications. In R. H. Binstock & L. K. George (Eds.), *Handbook of aging and the social sciences* (6th ed., pp. 436–455). San Diego, CA: Academic Press.

Binstock, R. H., & Quadagno, J. (2001). Aging and politics. In R. H. Binstock & L. K. George (Eds.), *Handbook of aging and the social sciences* (5th ed., pp. 333–351). San Diego, CA: Academic Press.

Birditt, K., Miller, L., Fingerman, K., & Lefkowitz, E. (2009). Tensions in the parent and adult child relationship: Links to solidarity and ambivalence. *Psychology and Aging, 24*(2), 287–295.

Birren, J. E., & Schroots, J. J. F. (2006). Autobiographical memory and the narrative self over the life span. In J. E. Birren & K. W. Schaie (Eds.), *Handbook of the psychology of aging* (6th ed., pp. 477–498). San Diego, CA: Academic Press.

Birren, J. E., & Schroots, J. J. F. (2001). History of Geropsychology. In J. E. Birren & K. W. Schaie (Eds.), *Handbook of the psychology of aging* (5th ed., pp. 3–28). San Diego, CA: Academic Press.

Bishop, S., & Cain, A. C. (2003). Widowed young parents: Changing perspectives on remarriage and cohabitation rates and their determinants. *Omega: Journal of Death and Dying, 47*(4), 299–312.

Blasi, A. (1980). Bridging moral cognition and moral action: A critical review of the literature. *Psychological Bulletin, 88*, 1–45.

Bliwise, D. L., & Bergmann, B. M. (1987). Individual differences in stages 3 and 4 sleep. *Psychophysiology, 24*(1), 35–40.

Boen, F., Vanbeselaere, N., Pandelaere, M., Dewitte, S., Duriez, B., Snauwaert, B., et al. (2002). Politics and basking-in-reflected-glory: A field study in Flanders. *Basic and Applied Social Psychology, 24*(3), 205–214.

Bogg, T., & Roberts, B. W. (2004). Conscientiousness and health-related behaviors: A meta-analysis of the leading behavioral contributors to mortality. *Psychological Bulletin, 130*(6), 887–919.

Bood, S., Archer, T., & Norlander, T. (2004). Affective personality in relationship to general personality, self-reported stress, coping and optimism. *Individual Differences Research, 2*(1), 26–37.

Bornstein, M. H. (2002). Toward a multiculture, multiage, multimethod science. *Human Development, 45*(4), 257–263.

Boston University School of Medicine. (2004, October 16). New England Centenarian Study. Boston: Author. Retrieved January 5, 2005, from http://www.bumc.bu.edu/Dept/Home.aspx?DepartmentID=361.

Boston University School of Medicine. (2004, September 7). New England Centenarian Study: A look at centenarians. Boston: Author. Retrieved July 1, 2008, from http://www.bumc.bu.edu/Dept/Content.aspx?PageID=5890&DepartmentID=361.

Boston University School of Medicine. (2007, March 2). New England Centenarian Study. Boston: Author. Retrieved July 10, 1007, from http://www.bumc.bu.edu/Dept/Home.aspx?DepartmentID=361.

Boston University School of Medicine. (2007, March 20). New England Supercententarian Study. Boston: Author. Retrieved August 24, 2007, from http://www.bumc.bu.edu/Dept/Home.aspx?DepartmentID=505.

Boulter, L. T. (2002). Self-concept as a predictor of college freshman academic adjustment. *College Student Journal, 36*(2), 234–246.

Bowden, S. C., Weiss, L. G., Holdnack, J. A., & Lloyd, D. (2006). Age-related invariance of abilities measured with the Wechsler Adult Intelligence Scale–III. *Psychological Assessment, 18*(3), 334–339.

Bowling, A. (2007). Aspirations for older age in the 21st century: What is successful aging? *International Journal of Aging & Human Development, 64*(3), 263–297.

Bradley, C. L., & Marcia, J. E. (1998). Generativity-stagnation: A five category model. *Journal of Personality, 66*, 39–64.

Brennan, P., Nichol, A., & Moos, R. (2003). Older and younger patients with substance use disorders: Outpatient mental health service use and functioning over a 12-month interval. *Psychology of Addictive Behaviors, 17*(1), 42–48.

Bronfenbrenner, U. (1977). Toward an experimental ecology of human development. *American Psychologist, 32*(7), 513–531.

Bronfenbrenner, U. (1986). Ecology of the family as a context for human development: Research perspectives. *Developmental Psychology, 22*(6), 723–742.

Bronfenbrenner, U., & Ceci, S. J. (1994). Nature-nurture reconceptualized in developmental perspective: A bioecological model. *Psychological Review, 101*(4), 568–586.

Brook, J., Brook, D., Zhang, C., & Cohen, P. (2004). Tobacco use and health in young adulthood. *Journal of Genetic Psychology, 165*(3), 310–323.

Brown, S. L., Snyder, A. R. (2006). Rural differences in cohabitor's union transitions. *Rural Sociology, 71*(2), 311–334.

Browne, C., & Broderick, A. (1994). Asian and Pacific Island elders: Issues for social work practice and education. *Social Work, 39*(3), 252–259.

Bucholz, K. (1992). Alcohol abuse and dependence from a psychiatric epidemiologic perspective. *Alcohol Health and Research World, 16*(3), 197–208.

Buckworth, J., & Nigg, C. (2004). Physical activity, exercise, and sedentary behavior in college students. *Journal of American College Health, 53*(1), 28–34.

Bullock, K. (2005). Grandfathers and the impact of raising grandchildren. *Journal of Sociology and Social Welfare, 32*(1), 43–59.

Bullock, K. (2006). Promoting advance directives among African Americans: A faith-based model. *Journal of Palliative Medicine, 9*(1), 183–195.

Burke, G. L., Arnold, A. M., Bild, D. E., Cushman, M., Fried, L. P., Newman, A., et al. (2001). Factors associated with healthy aging: The cardiovascular health study. *Journal of the American Geriatrics Society, 49*(3), 254–262.

Burnett-Wolle, S., & Godbey, G. (2007). Refining research on older adults' leisure: Implications of selection, optimization, and compensation and socioemotional selectivity theories. *Journal of Leisure Research, 39*(3), 498–513.

Bushfield, S. (2004). Fathers in prison: Impact of parenting education. *Journal of Correctional Education, 55*(2), 104–116.

Butler, C. M. (2003). Generativity in midlife baby-boomer women without children: A psychological study. *Dissertation Abstracts International, 64*(4-B), 1932.

Butler, K. (2010, April). Double duty: Schools as community centers. *District Administration*, 50–58.

Bybee, J. A., & Wells, Y. V. (2003). The development of possible selves during adulthood. In J. Demick & C. Andreoletti (Eds.), *Handbook of adult development* (pp. 257–270). New York: Kluwer Academic/Plenum Press.

Byrne, B. M. (1996). *Measuring self-concept across the life span.* Washington, DC: American Psychological Association.

Cafri, G., Thompson, J. K., Roehrig, M., van den Berg, P., Jacobsen, P. B., & Start, S. (2006). An investigation of appearance motives for tanning: The development and evaluation of the Physical Appearance Reasons for Tanning Scale (PARTS) and its relation to sunbathing and indoor tanning intentions. *Body Image, 3*(3), 199–209.

Cain, V. S., Johannes, C. B., Avis, N. E., Mohr, B., Schocken, M., Skurnick, J., et al. (2003). Sexual functioning and practices in a multi-ethnic study of midlife women: Baseline results from SWAN. *The Journal of Sex Research, 40*(3), 266–276.

Calasanti, T. (2007). Bodacious berry, potency wood and the aging monster: Gender and aging relations in anti-aging ads. *Social Forces, 86*(1), 335–355.

Callahan, C. M. (2000). Intelligence and giftedness. In R. J. Sternberg (Ed.), *Handbook of intelligence* (pp. 151–175). New York: Cambridge University Press.

Campbell, T., & Whiteley, C. (2006). Working clinically with gay men with sexual performance problems. *Sexual and relationship therapy, 21*(4), 419–428.

Carr, D. B., Duchek, J. M., Meuser, T. M., & Morris, J. C. (2006). Older adult drivers with cognitive impairment. *American Family Physician, 73*(6), 1029–1034.

Carr, D. B., & Ott, B. R. (2010). The older driver with cognitive impairment. *JAMA, 303*(16), 1632–1641.

Carroll, B., & Alexandris, K. (1997). Perception of constraints and strength of motivation: Their relationship to recreational sport participation in Greece. *Journal of Leisure Research, 29*(3), 279–299.

Carstensen, L. L. (1992). Social and emotional patterns in adulthood: Support for socioemotional selectivity theory. *Psychology and Aging, 7*(3), 331–338.

Carstensen, L. L., Mikels, J. A., & Mather, M. (2006). Aging and the intersection of cognition, motivation, and emotion. In J. E. Birren & K. W. Schaie (Eds.), *Handbook of the psychology of aging* (6th ed., pp. 343–362). San Diego, CA: Academic Press.

Carter, M. A., & Cook, K. (1995). Adaptation to retirement: Role changes and psychological resources. *Career Development Quarterly, 44*(1), 67–82.

Cassidy, T. (2000). Stress, healthiness and health behaviours: An exploration of the role of life events, daily hassles, cognitive appraisal and the coping process. *Counselling Psychology Quarterly, 13*(3), 293–311.

Centers for Disease Control and Prevention. (2004, February 6). Prevalence of no leisure-time physical activity—35 states and the District of Columbia, 1988–2002. *Morbidity and Mortality Weekly Report, 53*(4), 82–86. Retrieved August 20, 2004, from http://www.cdc.gov/mmwr/preview/mmwrhtml/mm5304a4.htm.

Centers for Disease Control and Prevention. (2005a, June 30). *Press release: Smoking deaths cost nation $92 billion in lost productivity annually*. Atlanta, GA: Author. Retrieved June 27, 2010, from http://www.cdc.gov/media/pressrel/r050630.htm.

Centers for Disease Control and Prevention. (2005b, May 26). *Press release: The percentage of U.S. adults who smoke continues to decline.* Atlanta, GA: Author. Retrieved June 27, 2010, from http://www.searo.who.int/LinkFiles/GHPS_Report_PressRel.pdf.

Centers for Disease Control and Prevention. (2007a, May). Trends in health and aging. Atlanta, GA: Author. Retrieved June 9, 2007, from http://www.cdc.gov/nchs/agingact.htm.

Centers for Disease Control and Prevention. (2007b, December 4). Obesity among adults in the United States—no statistically significant change since 2003–2004. Atlanta, GA: Author. Retrieved July 30, 2010, from http://www.cdc.gov/nchs/data/databriefs/db01.pdf.

Centers for Disease Control and Prevention. (2008a, March 26). *Overcoming barriers to physical activity*. Atlanta, GA: Author. Retrieved May 28, 2008, from http://www.cdc.gov/nccdphp/dnpa/physical/everyone/get_active/overcome.htm.

Centers for Disease Control and Prevention. (2008b, August 6). *Quick stats: General information on alcohol use and health*. Atlanta, GA: Author. Retrieved June 27, 2010, from http://www.cdc.gov/alcohol/quickstats/general_info.htm.

Centers for Disease Control and Prevention. (2009a, December 17). *Chronic disease prevention and health promotion*. Atlanta, GA: Author. Retrieved June 27, 2010, from http://www.cdc.gov/nccdphp/publications/aag/dnpa.htm.

Centers for Disease Control and Prevention. (2009b, April 21). *FastStats: Exercise or physical activity*. Atlanta, GA: Author. Retrieved June 27, 2010, from http://www.cdc.gov/nchs/fastats/exercise.htm.

Centers for Disease Control and Prevention. (2009c, December 1). *Health effects of cigarette smoking*. Atlanta, GA: Author. Retrieved June 27, 2010, from http://www.cdc.gov/tobacco/data_statistics/fact_sheets/health_effects/effects_cig_smoking/.

Centers for Disease Control and Prevention. (2009d, May 4). *NIOSH safety and health topic: Occupational cancer*. Bethesda, MD: Author. Retrieved July 15, 2010, from http://www.cdc.gov/niosh/topics/cancer/.

Centers for Disease Control and Prevention. (2009e, September 14). *Nutrition for everyone*. Atlanta, GA: Author. Retrieved June 27, 2010, from http://www.cdc.gov/nccdphp/dnpa/nutrition/nutrition_for_everyone/index.htm.

Centers for Disease Control and Prevention. (2010a, June 28). *FastStats: Deaths and mortality*. Atlanta, GA: Author. Retrieved July 14, 2010 from http://www.cdc.gov/nchs/fastats/deaths.htm.

Centers for Disease Control and Prevention. (2010b, May 25). *Heart disease*. Atlanta, GA: Author. Retrieved July 14, 2010, from http://www.cdc.gov/HeartDisease/index.htm.

Centers for Disease Control and Prevention. (2010c, June 21). *How much physical activity do you need?* Atlanta, GA: Author. Retrieved June 27, 2010, from http://www.cdc.gov/physicalactivity/everyone/guidelines/index.html.

Centers for Disease Control and Prevention. (2010d, March 12). 2007 National diabetes fact sheet. Atlanta, GA: Author. Retrieved July 15, 2010, from http://www.cdc.gov/Diabetes/pubs/general07.htm.

Centers for Disease Control and Prevention. (2010e, June 21). *Overweight and obesity*. Atlanta, GA: Author. Retrieved June 27, 2010, from http://www.cdc.gov/nccdphp/dnpa/obesity/defining.htm.

Centers for Disease Control and Prevention. (2010f, May 10). *Physical activity and health: The benefits of physical activity*. Atlanta, GA: Author. Retrieved June 29, 2010, from http://www.cdc.gov/physicalactivity/everyone/health/index.html.

Centers for Disease Control and Prevention. (2010g, April 23). *Press release: New CDC report says increase efforts, high-impact strategies needed to reduce smoking and save lives*. Atlanta, GA: Author. Retrieved June 27, 2010, from http://www.cdc.gov/media/pressrel/2010/r100423.htm.

Centers for Disease Control and Prevention. (2010h). *United States cancer statistics: 1999–2006 incidence and mortality web-based report*. Retrieved July 15, 2010, from http://www.cdc.gov/uscs.

Chambers, S. M., Hardy, J. C., Smith, B. J., & Sienty, S. F. (2003). Personality indicators and emergency permit teachers' willingness to embrace technology. *Journal of Instructional Technology, 30*(3), 185–188.

Charnes, N., & Boot, W., (2009). Aging and information technology use: Potential and barriers. *Current Directions in Psychological Science, 18*(5), 253–258.

Chemers, M. M., Hu, L., & Garcia, B. F. (2001). Academic self-efficacy and first-year college student performance and adjustment. *Journal of Educational Psychology, 93*(1), 55–64.

Cheng, S., Fung, H., & Chan, A., (2009). Self-perception and psychological well-being: The benefits of foreseeing a worse future. *Psychology and Aging, 24*(3), 623–633.

Cheng, S., & Strough, J. (2004). A comparison of collaborative and individual everyday problem solving in younger and older adults. *International Journal of Aging and Human Development, 58*(2), 167–195.

Cherry, B. J., Adamson, M., Duclos, A., & Hellige, J. B. (2005). Aging and individual variation in interhemispheric collaboration and hemispheric asymmetry. *Aging, Neuropsychology, and Cognition, 12*(4), 316–339.

Chinitz, J. G., & Brown, R. A. (2001). Religious homogamy, marital conflict, and stability in same-faith and interfaith Jewish marriages. *Journal for the Scientific Study of Religion, 40*(4), 723–733.

Chodzko-Zajko, W. (2000). Successful aging in the new millennium: The role of regular physical activity. *Quest (Human Kinetics), 52*(4), 333–343.

Cicirelli, V. G. (2000). An examination of the trajectory of the adult child's caregiving for an elderly parent. *Family Relations, 49*(2), 169–175.

Clements, M. L., Stanley, S. M., & Markman, H. J. (2004). Before they said "I do": Discriminating among marital outcomes over 13 years. *Journal of Marriage and Family, 66*(3), 613–627.

Clements, R., & Swensen, C. H. (2000). Commitment to one's spouse as a predictor of marital quality among older couples. *Current Psychology, 19*(2), 110–119.

Clore, V., & Fitzgerald, J. (2002). Intentional faith: An alternative view of faith development. *Journal of Adult Development, 9*(2), 97–107.

Cohan, C. L., & Kleinbaum, S. (2002). Toward a greater understanding of the cohabitation effect: Premarital cohabitation and marital communication. *Journal of Marriage and Family, 64*(1), 180–193.

Cohen, D., & Gunz, A. (2002) As seen by the other: Perspectives on the self in the memories and emotional perceptions of Easterners and Westerners. *Psychological Science, 13*(1), 55–59.

Cohen, G., Kiss, G., & LeVoi, M. (1993). *Memory: Current issues* (2nd ed.). Philadelphia: Open University Press.

Cohen, O., & Savaya, R. (2003). Adjustment to divorce: A preliminary study among Muslim Arab citizens of Israel. *Family Process, 42*(2), 269–290.

Cohen-Katz, J., Wiley, S. D., Capuano, T., Baker, D. M., & Shapiro, S. (2004). The effects of mindfulness-based stress reduction on nurse stress and burnout. *Holistic Nursing Practice, 18*(6), 302–308.

Cohen-Katz, J., Wiley, S. D., Capuano, T., Baker, D. M., & Shapiro, S. (2005). The effects of mindfulness-based stress reduction on nurse stress and burnout, part II. *Holistic Nursing Practice, 19*(1), 26–35.

Colbert, A. E., Mount, M. K., Harter, J. K., Witt, L. A., & Barrick, M. R. (2004). Interactive effects of personality and perceptions of the work situation on workplace deviance. *Journal of Applied Psychology, 89*(4), 599–609.

Coleman, M., Ganong, L., & Fine, M. (2000). Reinvestigating remarriage: Another decade of progress. *Journal of Marriage & Family, 62*(4), 1288–1307.

Coleman, R., & Wilkins, L. (2002). Searching for the ethical journalist: An exploratory study of the moral development of news workers. *Journal of Mass Media Ethics, 17*(3), 209–225.

Collins, N. L. & Feeney, B. C. (2004). An attachment theory perspective on closeness and intimacy. In D. J. Mashek & A. Aron (Eds.), *Handbook of closeness and intimacy* (pp. 163–187). Mahwah, NJ: Erlbaum.

Commons, M. L. (2002). Introduction: Attaining a new stage. *Journal of Adult Development, 9*(3), 155–157.

Commons, M. L., & Richards, F. A. (2003). Four postformal stages. In J. Demick & C. Andreoletti (Eds.), *Handbook of adult development* (pp. 199–219). New York: Kluwer Academic/Plenum Press.

Compton, D. M., Avet-Compton, T. L., Bachman, L. D., & Brand, D. (2003). Working memory and perceptual speed mediation of age-associated changes in cognition within a sample of highly-educated adults. *North American Journal of Psychology, 5*(3), 451–478.

Connidis, I., & Campbell, L. (1995). Closeness, confiding, and contact among siblings in middle and late adulthood. *Journal of Family Issues, 16*(6), 722–745.

Consedine, N. S., Magai, C., & Conway, F. (2004). Predicting ethnic variation in adaptation to later life: Styles of socioemotional functioning and constrained heterotopy. *Journal of Cross-Cultural Gerontology, 19*(2), 97–131.

Converse, P. D., Oswald, F. L., Gillespie, M. A., Field, K. A., & Bizot, E. B. (2004). Matching individuals to occupations using abilities and the O*NET. *Personnel Psychology, 57*(2), 451–487.

Conway, M. (2003). Autobiographical memory. In J. Byrne (Editor-in-Chief), *Learning and memory* (2nd ed., pp 51–54). New York: Thompson Gale.

Conway, M. A., & Holmes, A. (2004). Psychosocial stages and the accessibility of autobiographical memories across the life cycle. *Journal of Personality, 72*(3), 461–480.

Coopersmith, S. (1967). *The antecedents of self-esteem.* San Francisco: W. H. Freeman.

Costa, P. T., & McCrae, R. R. (1997). Stability and change in personality assessment: The revised NEO personality inventory in the year 2000. *Journal of Personality Assessment, 68*(1), 86–94.

Costa, P. T., Terracciano, A., & McCrae, R. R. (2001). Gender differences in personality traits across cultures: Robust and surprising findings. *Journal of Personality and Social Psychology, 81*(2), 322–331.

Costigan, C., Cox, M., & Cauce, A. (2003). Work-parenting linkages among dual-earner couples at the transition to parenthood. *Journal of Family Psychology, 17*(3), 397–408.

Courtenay, B. C. (1994). Are psychological models of adult development still important for the practice of adult education? *Adult Education Quarterly, 44*(3), 145–153.

Craft, C. (2004). Adoption: Gay and lesbian adoptions. Retrieved October 19, 2004, from http://adoption.about.com/od/gaylesbian/a/gayadopt.htm.

Craik, F. (2003). Aging and memory in humans. In J. Byrne (Editor-in-Chief), *Learning and memory* (2nd ed., pp 10–14). New York: Thompson Gale.

Crews, J. E. (2003). The role of public health in addressing aging and sensory loss. *Generations, 27*(1), 83–90.

Cropley, A. J. (2000). Defining and measuring creativity: Are creativity tests worth using? *Roeper Review, 23*(2), 72–79.

Cross, S. E., & Markus, H. R. (1991). Possible selves across the life span. *Human Development 34*(4), 230–255.

Cross, S. E., & Markus, H. R. (1994). Self-schemas: Possible selves, and competent performance. *Journal of Educational Psychology, 86*(3), 423–438.

Culpepper, R. A., Gamble, J. E., & Blubaugh, M. G. (2004). Employee stock ownership plans and three-component commitment. *Journal of Occupational and Organizational Psychology, 77*(2), 155–170.

Cutler, S. J. (2006). Technological change and aging. In R. H. Binstock & L. K. George (Eds.), *Handbook of aging and the social sciences* (6th ed., pp. 257–276). San Diego, CA: Academic Press.

Czaja, S. (2001). Technological change and the older worker. In J. E. Birren & K. W. Schaie (Eds.), *Handbook of the psychology of aging* (5th ed., pp. 547–568). San Diego, CA: Academic Press.

Dannefer, D. (1984). Adult development and social theory: A paradigmatic reappraisal. *American Sociological Review, 49*, 100–116.

Dark-Freudeman, A., West, R., & Viverito, K. (2006). Future selves and aging: Older adults' memory fears. *Educational Gerontology, 32*(2), 85–109.

Davidson, J. E., & Downing, C. L. (2000). Contemporary models of intelligence. In R. J. Sternberg (Ed.), *Handbook of intelligence* (pp. 34–49). New York: Cambridge University Press.

Dawis, R. V. (1992). The individual differences tradition in counseling psychology. *Journal of Counseling Psychology, 3*(91), 7–19.

Dawson, T. L. (2002). New tools, new insights: Kohlberg's moral judgment stages revisited. *International Journal of Behavioral Development, 26*(2), 154–166.

Dawson-Tunik, T. L., Commons, M., Wilson, M., & Fischer, K. W. (2005). The shape of development. *European Journal of Developmental Psychology, 2*(2), 163–195.

Degges-White, S. (2005). Understanding gerotranscendence in older adults: A new perspective for counselors. *Adultspan: Theory Research & Practice, 4*(1), 36–48.

Dehon, H., & Bredart, S. (2004). False memories: Young and older adults think of semantic associates at the same rate, but young adults are more successful at source monitoring. *Psychology and Aging, 19*(1), 191–197.

DeLamater, J., and Friedrich, W. N. (2002). Human sexual development. *Journal of Sex Research, 39*(1), 10–14.

Dellmann-Jenkins, M., Blankemeyer, M., & Olesh, M. (2002). Adults in expanded grandparent roles: Considerations for practice, policy, and research. *Educational Gerontology, 28*(3), 219–235.

Dellmann-Jenkins, M., Blankemeyer, M., & Pinkard, O. (2001). Incorporating the elder caregiving role into the developmental tasks of young adulthood. *International Journal of Aging and Human Development, 52*(1), 1–18.

Dempsey, K., & deVaus, D. (2004). Who cohabits in 2001?: The significance of age, gender, religion and ethnicity. *Journal of Sociology, 40*(2), 155–178.

DeNavas-Walt, C., Proctor, B. D., & Smith, J. (2007, August). *U.S. Census Bureau, Current Population Reports, P60–233, Income, poverty, and health insurance coverage in the United States: 2006.* Washington, DC: U.S. Government Printing Office.

Department of Labor, Bureau of Labor Statistics. (2000). Working in the 21st century. Retrieved September 1, 2004, from http://www.bls.gov/opub/working/home.htm.

Department of Labor, Bureau of Labor Statistics. (2004, February 11). BLS releases 2000–2010 employment projections. Retrieved September 1, 2004, from http://stats.bls.gov/news.release/ecopro.nr0.htm.

De Rekeneire, N., Visser, M., Peila, R., Nevitt, M. C., Cauley, J. A., Tylawsky, F. A., et al. (2003). Is a fall just a fall?: Correlated of falling in healthy older persons. *Journal of the American Geriatrics Society, 51*(6), 841–846.

Derwinger, A., Neely, A. S., MacDonald, S., & Backman, L. (2005). Forgetting numbers in old age: Strategy and learning speed matter. *Gerontology, 51*(4), 277–284.

DeVaus, D., Qu, L., & Weston, R. (2003). Premarital cohabitation and subsequent marital stability. *Family Matters, 65*, 34–39.

Diaz, E. (2009). Congress speaks out on pay discrimination claims. *Woman Advocate, 15*(1), 6–7.

DiChristina, M. (2004). The challenges of longevity. *Scientific American Special Edition, 14*(3), 3.

Diener, E., Ng, W., Harter, J., & Arora, R. (2010). Wealth and happiness across the world: Material prosperity predicts life evaluation, whereas psychosocial prosperity predicts positive feeling. *Journal of Personality and Social Psychology, 99*(1), 52–61.

Dobbs, D. (2004). The adjustment to a new home. *Journal of Housing for the Elderly, 18*(1), 51–71.

Dollinger, S. J., Dollinger, S. M. C., & Centeno, L. (2005). Identity and creativity. *Identity: An International Journal of Theory and Research, 5*(4), 315–339.

Dominick, S. A., et al. (2010). An Internet tool to normalize grief. *Omega, 60*(1), 71–87.

Donaldson, J. F. (1999). A model of college outcomes for adults. *Adult Education Quarterly, 50*(1), 24–40.

Downe-Wamboldt, B., & Tamlyn, D. (1997). An international survey of death education trends in faculties of nursing and medicine. *Death Studies, 21*(2), 177–188.

Doyle, K. O. (1992). The symbolic meaning of house and home: An exploration in the psychology of goods. *American Behavioral Scientist, 35*(6), 790–802.

Dretzke, B. J. (1993). Effects of pictorial mnemonic strategy usage on prose recall of young, middle-aged, and older adults. *Educational Gerontology, 19*(6), 487–502.

Dupre, M. E. (2007). Educational differences in age-related patterns of disease: Reconsidering the cumulative disadvantage and age-as-leveler hypotheses. *Journal of Health & Social Behavior, 48*(1), 1–15.

Durant, L. E., Carey, M. P., & Schroder, K. E. (2002). Effects of anonymity, gender, and erotophilia on the quality of data obtained from self-reports of socially sensitive behaviors. *Journal of Behavioral Medicine, 25*(5), 439–467.

Dush, C. M. K., Cohan, C. L., & Amato, P. R. (2003). The relationship between cohabitation and marital quality and stability: Change across cohorts? *Journal of Marriage & Family, 65*(3), 539–549.

Eagly, A. J. (1995). The science and politics of comparing women and men. *American Psychologist, 50*(3), 145–158.

Eamon, M. K. (2001). The effects of poverty on children's socioemotional development: An ecological systems analysis. *Social Work, 46*(3), 256–266.

Ecklund, E. H., & Park, J. Z. (2007). Religious diversity and community volunteerism among Asian Americans. *Journal for the Scientific Study of Religion, 46*(2), 233–244.

Eisenberg, N. (2000). Emotion, regulation, and moral development. *Annual Review of Psychology, 51*, 665–697.

Elbogen, E. B., Swanson, J. W., Swartz, M. S., Van Dorn, R., Ferron, J., Wagner, H. R., et al. (2007). Effectively implementing psychiatric advance directives to promote self-determination of treatment among people with mental illness. *Psychology, Public Policy, and Law, 13*(4), 273–288.

Equal Employment Opportunity Commission. (2002, June). Facts about sexual harassment. Retrieved on August 26, 2004, from http://www.eeoc.gov/facts/fs-sex.html.

Equal Employment Opportunity Commission. (2004, March). Sexual harassment charges EEOC & FEPAs combined: FY 1992–FY 2003. Retrieved August 26, 2004, from http://www.eeoc.gov/stats/harass.html.

Equal Employment Opportunity Commission. (2005, March 2). Equal pay and compensation discrimination. Retrieved May 4, 2005, from http://www.eeoc.gov/types/epa.html.

Equal Employment Opportunity Commission. (n.d.). Sexual harassment charges EEOC & FEPAs combined: FY 1997–FY 2009. Retrieved July 3, 2010, from http://www.eeoc.gov/eeoc/statistics/enforcement/sexual_harassment.cfm.

Erickson, M. J. (1998). Re-visioning the family life cycle theory and paradigm in marriage and family therapy. *American Journal of Family Therapy, 26*, 341–356.

Erikson, E. H. (1950). *Childhood and society*. New York: Norton.

Erikson, E. H. (1968). *Identity youth and crisis*. New York: Norton.

Erikson, E. H., Erikson, J. M., & Kivnick, H. Q. (1986). *Vital involvement in old age*. New York: Norton.

Erlen, J. A. (2004). Functional health illiteracy. *Orthopaedic Nursing, 23*(2), 150–153.

Espmark, A. K., Rosenhall, U., Erlandsson, S., & Steen, B. (2002). The two faces of presbycusis: hearing impairment and psychosocial consequences. *International Journal of Audiology, 41*(2), 125–135.

Fabiani, M., Friedman, D., & Cheng, J. C. (1998). Individual differences in P3 scalp distribution in older adults, and their relationship to frontal lobe function. *Psychophysiology, 35*(6), 698–708.

Fairchild, A. L., & Bayer, R. (1999). Uses and abuses of Tuskegee. *Science, 284*, 919–921.

Falconi, A., & Mullet, E. (2003). Cognitive algebra of love through the adult life. *International Journal of Aging and Human Development, 57*(3), 275–290.

Farmer, S. M., & Fedor, D. B. (2001). Changing the focus on volunteering: An investigation of volunteers' multiple contributions to a charitable organization. *Journal of Management, 27*, 191–211.

Farrell, S. J., Aubry, T., & Coulombe, D. (2004). Neighborhoods and neighbors: Do they contribute to personal well-being? *Journal of Community Psychology, 32*(1), 9–25.

Federal Interagency Forum on Aging-Related Statistics. (2006, May). *Older Americans update 2006: Key indicators of well-being*. Washington, DC: U.S. Government Printing Office. Retrieved June 6, 2007, from http://agingstats.gov/agingstatsdotnet/Main_Site/Data/2006_Documents/OA_2006.pdf.

Federal Interagency Forum on Aging-Related Statistics. (2008, December). *Older Americans 2008: Key Indicators of Well-Being*. Washington, DC: U.S. Government Printing Office. Retrieved July 3, 2010, from http://www.aoa.gov/agingstatsdotnet/Main_Site/Data/2008_Documents/Population.aspx.

Federal Trade Commission. (2009). Funerals: A consumer guide. Retrieved July 19, 2010, from http://www.ftc.gov/bcp/edu/pubs/consumer/products/pro19.shtm.

Fehr, B. (2004). A prototype model of intimacy interactions in same-sex friendships. In D. Mashek & A. Aron (Eds.), *Handbook of closeness and intimacy* (pp. 9–26). Mahwah, NJ: Erlbaum.

Feist, G., & Barron, F. (2003). Predicting creativity from early to late in adulthood: Intellect, potential, and personality. *Journal of Research in Personality, 37*(2), 62–88.

Felsten, G. (2002). Minor stressors and depressed mood: Reactivity is more strongly correlated than total stress. *Stress and Health: Journal of the International Society for the Investigation of Stress, 18*(2), 75–81.

Ferraro, K. F. (2001). Aging and role transitions. In R. H. Birrenstock & L. K. George (Eds.), *Handbook of aging and the social sciences* (5th ed., pp. 313–330). San Diego, CA: Academic Press.

Ferraro, K. F. (2006). Health and aging. In R. H. Binstock & L. K. George (Eds.), *Handbook of aging and the social sciences* (6th ed., pp. 238–256). San Diego, CA: Academic Press.

Fiese, B. H., & Tomcho, T. J. (2001). Finding meaning in religious practices: The relation between religious holiday rituals and marital satisfaction. *Journal of Family Psychology, 15*(4), 595–609.

Fine, M. A., & Kurdek, L. A. (1995). Relation between marital quality and (step)parent–child relationship quality for parents and stepparents in stepfamilies. *Journal of Family Psychology, 9*(2), 216–223.

Fischer, L. C., & McWhirter, J. J. (2001). The deaf identity development scale: A revision and validation. *Journal of Counseling Psychology, 48*(3), 355–358.

Fisher, K. J., Li, F., Michael, Y., & Cleveland, M. (2004). Neighborhood-level influences on physical activity among older adults: A multilevel analysis. *Journal of Aging and Physical Activity, 12*(1), 45–63.

Fitzgerald, H. (2002). You know you are getting better when. Washington, DC: American Hospice Foundation. Retrieved July 23, 2008, from http://www.americanhospice.org/index.php?option=com_content&task=view&id=97&Itemid=8.

Foley, R. M., & Gao, J. (2004). Correctional education: Characteristics of academic programs serving incarcerated adults. *Journal of Correctional Education, 55*(1), 6–21.

Foos, P. W., Clark, M. C., & Terrell, D. F. (2006). Adult age, gender, and race group differences in images of aging. *Journal of Genetic Psychology, 167*(3), 309–325.

Fowler, J. W. (1980). Moral stages and the development of faith. In B. Munsey (Ed.), *Moral Development, Moral Education, and Kohlberg* (pp. 130–160). Birmingham, AL: Religious Education Press.

Fowler, J. W. (1981). *Stages of faith: The psychology of human development and the quest for meaning.* San Francisco: Harper & Row.

Fowler, J. W. (2001). Faith development theory and the postmodern challenges. *International Journal for the Psychology of Religion, 11*(3), 159–172.

Fozard, J. L., & Gordon-Salant, S. (2001). Changes in vision and hearing with aging. In J. E. Birren & K. W. Schaie (Eds.), *Handbook of the psychology of aging* (5th ed., pp. 241–266). San Diego, CA: Academic Press.

Frazier, L., Cotrell, V., & Hooker, K. (2003). Possible selves and illness: A comparison of individuals with Parkinson's disease, early-stage Alzheimer's disease, and healthy older adults. *International Journal of Behavioral Development, 27*(1), 1–11.

Friedman, B. T., Harwood, M. K., & Shields, M. (2002). Barriers and enablers to hospice referrals: An expert overview. *Journal of Palliative Medicine, 5*(1), 73–84.

Fry, P. S. (2003). Perceived self-efficacy domains as predictors of fear of the unknown and fear of dying among older adults. *Psychology and Aging, 18*(3), 474–486.

Furer, P., & Walker, J. R. (2008). Death anxiety: A cognitive-behavioral approach. *Journal of Cognitive Psychotherapy, 22*(2), 167–182.

Furnham, A. (2001). Vocational preference and the P–O fit: Reflections on Holland's theory of vocational choice. *Applied Psychology: An International Review, 50*(1), 5–29.

Gallo, L. C., Smith, T. W., & Ruiz, J. M. (2003). An interpersonal analysis of adult attachment style. *Journal of Personality, 71*(2), 141–181.

Gardner, H. (1993). *Frames of mind: The theory of multiple intelligences* (10th anniversary ed.). New York: Basic Books.

Gardner, H. (1998). A multiplicity of intelligences. *Scientific American Presents, 279*(3), 18–23.

Gatz, M., & Smyer, M. A. (2001). Mental health and aging at the outset of the twenty-first century. In J. E. Birren & K. W. Schaie (Eds.), *Handbook of psychology and aging* (5th ed., pp. 523–544). San Diego, CA: Academic Press.

Generations United. (2004, June 29). Kinship care. Washington, DC: Author. Retrieved October 24, 2004, from http://www.gu.org/projg&ointro.htm.

George, L. (1990). Gender, age, and psychiatric disorders. *Generations: Journal of the American Society on Aging, 14*(3), 22–27.

George, L. (2001). The social psychology of health. In R. H. Binstock & L. K. George (Eds.), *Handbook of aging and the social sciences* (5th ed., pp. 217–237). San Diego, CA: Academic Press.

George, L. K. (2006). Perceived quality of life. In R. H. Binstock & L. K. George (Eds.), *Handbook of aging and the social sciences* (6th ed., pp. 320–336). San Diego, CA: Academic Press.

Gerardi, R. J. (2003). Retirement continues to elude me. *Educational Research Quarterly, 27*(1), 3–4.

Gheytanchi, A., Joseph, L., Geirlach, E., Kimpara, S., Housley, J., Franco, Z., et al. (2007). The dirty dozen: Twelve failures of the Hurricane Katrina response and how psychology can help. *American Psychologist, 62*(2), 118–130.

Giambra, L. M., Arenberg, D., Zonderman, A. B., Kawas, C., & Costa, P. T. (1995). Adult life span changes in immediate visual memory and verbal intelligence. *Psychology and Aging, 10*(1), 123–139.

Gibbs, J. C. (1995). The cognitive developmental perspective. In W. M. Kurtines & J. L. Gewirtz (Eds.), *Moral development: An introduction* (pp. 27–48). Boston: Allyn & Bacon.

Gilligan, C. (1982). *In a different voice: Psychological theory and women's development.* Cambridge, MA: Harvard University Press.

Glass, J. C., & Huneycutt, T. L. (2002). Grandparents parenting grandchildren: Extent of situation, issues involved, and educational implications. *Educational Gerontology, 28*, 139–161.

Glastra, F. J., Hake, B. J., & Schedler, P. E. (2004). Lifelong learning as transitional learning. *Adult Education Quarterly, 54*(4), 291–307.

Glock, C. Y. (1962). On the study of religious commitment. *Religious Education, 57*, 98–110.

Glover, R. J. (2001). Discriminators of moral orientation: Gender role or personality? *Journal of Adult Development, 8*(1), 1–7.

Gluttman, C. (2004). Botulinum toxin long-term safety study finds "no news is good news." *Dermatology Times, 25*(9), 94–95.

Goffnett, C. (1979). Your patient's dying; now what? *Nursing, 9*(11), 27–33.

Goldberg, A. E., & Perry-Jenkins, M. (2004). Division of labor and working-class women's well-being across the transition to parenthood. *Journal of Family Psychology, 18*(1), 225–236.

Goldberg, P. D., Peterson, B. D., Rosen, K. H., & Sara, M. L. (2008). Cybersex: The impact of a contemporary problem on the practices of marriage and family therapists. *Journal of Marital and Family Therapy, 34*(4), 469–480.

Goldscheider, F., Goldscheider, C., St. Clair, P., & Hodges, J. (1999). Changes in returning home in the United States, 1925–1985. *Social Forces, 78*(2), 695–728.

Goodnow, J. J. (2002). Adding culture to studies of development: Toward changes in procedure and theory. *Human Development, 45*(4), 237–245.

Gottlieb, G. (2001). The relevance of developmental-psychobiological metatheory to developmental neuropsychology. *Developmental Neuropsychology, 19*(1), 1–9.

Gottman, J. M., & Levenson, R. W. (2000). The timing of divorce: Predicting when a couple will divorce over a 14-year period. *Journal of Marriage and Family, 62*(3), 735–745.

Gottman, J. M., Levenson, R. W., Gross, J., Frederickson, B. L., McCoy, K., Rosenthal, L., et al. (2003). Correlates of gay and lesbian couples' relationship satisfaction and relationship dissolution. *Journal of Homosexuality, 45*(1), 23–43.

Graham, S., & Donaldson, J. F. (1999). Adult students' academic and intellectual development in college. *Adult Education Quarterly, 49*(3), 147–161.

Gray, M., Mission, S., & Hayes, A. (2005). Young children and their grandparents. *Family Matters, 72*, 10–17.

Greenglass, E., Fiksenbaum, L., & Eaton, J. (2006). The relationship between coping, social support, functional disability and depression in the elderly. *Anxiety, Stress and Coping, 19*(1), 15–31.

Greiner, K. A., Perera, S., & Ahluwalia, J. S. (2003). Hospice usage by minorities in the last year of life: Results from the National Mortality Followback Survey. *Journal of the American Geriatrics Society, 51*(7), 970–978.

Groger, L. (1995). A nursing home can be a home. *Journal of Aging Studies, 9*(2), 137–153.

Grossmann, I., Na, J., Varnum, M., Park, D., Kitayama, S., & Nisbett, R. (2010). Reasoning about social conflicts improves into old age. *Proceedings of the National Academy of Sciences, 107*(16), 7246–7250.

Gurucharri, C., & Selman, R. L. (1982). The development of interpersonal understanding during childhood, preadolescence, and adolescence: A longitudinal follow-up study. *Child Development, 53*(4), 924–927.

Gyurcsik, N. C., Estabrooks, P. A., & Frahm-Templar, M. J. (2003). Exercise-related goals and self-efficacy as correlates of aquatic exercise in individuals with arthritis. *Arthritis and Rheumatism, 49*(3), 306–313.

Haber, D. (2005). Cultural diversity among older adults: Addressing health education. *Educational Gerontology 31*(9), 683–697.

Hall, C. S., & Lindzey, G. (1978). *Theories of personality* (3rd ed.). New York: Wiley.

Hall, P. A., & Fong, G. T. (2003). The effects of a brief time perspective intervention for increasing physical activity among young adults. *Psychology and Health, 18*(6), 685–706.

Halliwell, E., & Dittmar, H. (2003). A qualitative investigation of women's and men's body image concerns and their attitudes toward aging. *Sex Roles, 49*(11/12), 675–684.

Hamachek, D. (1990). Evaluating self-concept and ego status in Erikson's last three psychosocial stages. *Journal of Counseling & Development, 68*(6), 677–683.

Hamarat, E., Thompson, D., Zarbrucky, K. M., Steele, D., Matheny, K. B., & Aysan, F. (2001). Perceived stress and coping resource availability as predictors of life satisfaction in young, middle-aged, and older adults. *Experimental Aging Research, 27*(2), 181–196.

Hamilton, F., & McDowell, J. (2004). Identifying the palliative care role of the nurse working in community hospitals: An exploratory study. *International Journal of Palliative Nursing, 19*(9), 426–434.

Hannigan, B., Edwards, D., & Burnard, P. (2004). Stress and stress management in clinical psychology: Findings from a systematic review. *Journal of Mental Health, 13*(3), 235–245.

Hanson, M., & Gutheil, I. (2004). Motivational strategies with alcohol-involved older adults: Implications for social work practice. *Social Work, 49*(3), 364–372.

Harding, S. R., Flannelly, K. J., Weaver, A. J., & Costa, K. G. (2005). The influence of religion on death anxiety and death acceptance. *Mental Health, Religion and Culture, 8*(4), 253–261.

Hardy, M. (2006). Older workers. In R. H. Binstock & L. K. George (Eds.), *Handbook of aging and the social sciences* (6th ed., pp. 201–218). San Diego, CA: Academic Press.

Hardy-Bougere, M. (2008). Cultural manifestations of grief and bereavement: A clinical perspective. *Journal of Cultural Diversity, 15*(2), 66–69.

Harvard School of Public Health. (2010a). *The nutrition source: Getting to your healthy weight*. Cambridge, MA: Author. Retrieved June 27, 2010, from http://www.hsph.harvard.edu/nutritionsource/weight.html.

Harvard School of Public Health. (2010b). *The nutrition source: Healthy eating pyramid*. Cambridge, MA: Author. Retrieved June 27, 2010 from http://www.hsph.harvard.edu/nutritionsource/pyramids.html.

Harwood, H., Mark, T., McKusick, D., Coffey, R., King, E., & Genuardi, J. (2003). National spending on mental health and substance abuse treatment by age of clients, 1997. *Journal of Behavioral Health Services and Research, 30*(4), 433–443.

Hastings, E. C., & West, R. L. (2009). The relative success of a self-help and a group-based memory training program for older adults. *Psychology and Aging, 24*(3), 586–594.

Hastings, S., & O'Neill, T. (2009). Predicting workplace deviance using broad versus narrow personality variables. *Personality & Individual Differences, 47*(4), 289–293.

Haught, P. A., Hill, L. A., Nardi, A. H., & Walls, R. T. (2000). Perceived ability and level of education as predictors of traditional and practical adult problem solving. *Experimental Aging Research, 26*, 810–101.

Hayslip, B., Henderson, C. E., & Shore, R. J. (2003). The structure of grandparental role meaning. *Journal of Adult Development, 10*(1), 1–11.

Hearn, S. (1993). *Integrity, despair, and in between: Toward construct validation of Erikson's eighth stage.* Unpublished doctoral dissertation, Simon Fraser University, Burnaby, BC, Canada.

Heckhausen, J. (1997). Developmental regulation across adulthood: Primary and secondary control of age-related challenges. *Developmental Psychology, 33*(1), 176–187.

Heiman, T. (2004). Examination of the salutogenic model, support resources, coping style, and stressors among Israeli university students. *Journal of Psychology, 138*(6), 505–520.

Heller, D., Watson, D., & Ilies, R. (2004). The role of person versus situation in life satisfaction: A critical examination. *Psychological Bulletin, 130*(4), 574–600.

Helson, R., & Mitchell, V. (1990). Women's prime of life. *Psychology of Women Quarterly*, 14, 451–470.

Helson, R., & Moane, G. (1987). Personality change in women from college to midlife. *Journal of Personality and Social Psychology, 53*(1), 176–186.

Helson, R., & Wink, P. (1992). Personality change in women from the early 40s to the early 50s. *Psychology and Aging, 7*(1), 46–55.

Henderson, S. (2004). Driver and traffic safety in older adults. *Topics in Geriatric Rehabilitation, 20*(3), 173–184.

Hendricks, J., & Hatch, L. R. (2006). Lifestyle and aging. In R. H. Binstock & L. K. George (Eds.), *Handbook of aging and the social sciences* (6th ed., pp. 301–319). San Diego, CA: Academic Press.

Henretta, J. C. (2001). Work and retirement. In R. H. Birrenstock & L. K. George (Eds.), *Handbook of aging and the social sciences* (5th ed., pp. 255–271). San Diego, CA: Academic Press.

Hertzog, C., Dixon, R. A., Hultsch, D. F., & MacDonald, S. W. S. (2003). Latent change models of adult cognition: Are changes in processing speed and working memory associated with changes in episodic memory? *Psychology and Aging, 18*(4), 755–769.

Hertzog, C., & Schaie, K. W. (1986). Stability and change in adult intelligence: 1. Analysis of longitudinal covariance structures. *Psychology and Aging, 1*(2), 159–171.

Hertzog, C., & Schaie, K. W. (1988). Stability and change in adult intelligence: 2. Simultaneous analysis of longitudinal means and covariance structures. *Psychology and Aging, 3*(2), 122–130.

Hess, T. M. (2006). Attitudes toward aging and their effect on behavior. In J. E. Birren & K. W. Schaie (Eds.), *Handbook of the psychology of aging* (6th ed., pp. 377–406). San Diego, CA: Academic Press.

Hicks, T. V., & Leitenberg, H. (2001). Sexual fantasies about one's partner versus someone else: Gender differences in incidence and frequency. *Journal of Sex Research, 38*(1), 43–50.

Hietanen, A., Era, P., Sorri, M., & Heikkinen, E. (2004). Changes in hearing in 80-year-old people: A 10-year follow-up study. *International Journal of Audiology, 43*(3), 126–135.

Higgins, A. (1995). Educating for justice and community: Lawrence Kohlberg's vision of moral education. In W. M. Kurtines & J. L. Gewirtz (Eds.), *Moral development: An introduction* (pp. 49–79). Boston: Allyn & Bacon.

Hilt, M. L., & Lipschultz, J. H. (2004). Elderly Americans and the Internet: E-mail, TV news, information and entertainment websites. *Educational Gerontology, 30,* 57–72.

Hinrichsen, G. A. (2006). Why multicultural issues matter for practitioners working with older adults. *Professional Psychology: Research and Practice, 37*(1), 29–35.

Hiscox, W. E. (2007). Physician-assisted suicide in Oregon: The "Death With Dignity" data. *Medical Law International, 8*(3), 197–220.

Hofer, S. M., & Sliwinski, M. J. (2001). Understanding ageing. *Gerontology, 47*, 341–352.

Hofer, S. M., & Sliwinski, M. J.. (2006). Design and analysis of longitudinal studies on aging. In J. E. Birren & K. W. Schaie (Eds.), *Handbook of the psychology of aging* (6th ed., pp. 15–37). San Diego, CA: Academic Press.

Hojat, M., Nasca, T., Erdmann, J. B., Frisby, A. J., Veloski, J. J., & Gonnella, J. S. (2003). An operational measure of physician lifelong learning: Its development, components and preliminary psychometric data. *Medical Teacher, 25*(4), 433–437.

Holahan, C. J., Valentiner, D. P., & Moos, R. H. (1994). Parental support and psychological adjustment during the transition to young adulthood in a college sample. *Journal of Family Psychology, 8*(2), 215–223.

Holden, K., & Hatcher, C. (2006). Economic status of the aged. In R. H. Binstock & L. K. George (Eds.), *Handbook of aging and the social sciences* (6th ed., pp. 219–237). San Diego, CA: Academic Press.

Holtslander, L. F. (2008). Caring for bereaved family caregivers: Analyzing the context of care. *Clinical Journal of Oncology Nursing, 12*(3), 501–516.

Horowitz, A. (2004). The prevalence and consequences of vision impairment in later life. *Topics in Geriatric Rehabilitation, 20*(3), 185–195.

Horwitz, A. V., White, H. R., & Howell-White, S. (1996). Becoming married and mental health: A longitudinal study of a cohort of young adults. *Journal of Marriage and the Family, 58*, 895–907.

Houran, J., & Lange, R. (2004). Expectations of finding a "soul mate" with online dating. *North American Journal of Psychology, 6*(2), 295–308.

Hoyer, W. J., & Verhaeghen, P. (2006). Memory aging. In J. E. Birren & K. W. Schaie (Eds.), *Handbook of the psychology of aging* (6th ed., pp. 209–232). San Diego, CA: Academic Press.

Huang, T., Harris, K. J., Lee, R. E., Nazir, N., Born, W., & Kaur, H. (2003). Assessing overweight, obesity, diet, and physical activity in college students. *Journal of American College Health, 52*(2), 83–87.

Huffman, M. L., & Cohen, P. N. (2004). Racial wage inequality: Job segregation and devaluation across U.S. labor markets. *American Journal of Sociology, 109*(4), 902–936.

Hughes, A., (2009). State advance directive registries: A survey and assessment. *Bifocal, 31*(2), 23–50.

Hummert, M. L., Garstak, R. A., Shaner, J. L., & Strahm, S. (1994). Stereotypes of the elderly held by young, middle-aged, and elderly adults. *Journal of Gerontology, 49*(5), 240–250.

Hunter, S. K., & Thompson, M. W. (2001). Reaction time, strength, and physical activity in women aged 20–89 years. *Journal of Aging and Physical Activity, 9*(1), 32–42.

Huston, S. L., Evenson, K. R., Bors, P., & Gizlice, Z. (2003). Neighborhood environment, access to places for activity, and leisure-time physical activity in a diverse North Carolina population. *American Journal of Health Promotion, 18*(1), 58–69.

Huston, T. L., Caughlin, J. P., Houts, R. M., Smith, S. E., & George, L. J. (2001). The connubial crucible: Newlywed years as predictors of marital delight, distress, and divorce. *Journal of Personality and Social Psychology, 80*(2), 235–252.

Idler, E. (2006). Religion and aging. In R. H. Binstock & L. K. George (Eds.), *Handbook of aging and the social sciences* (6th ed., pp. 277–300). San Diego, CA: Academic Press.

Ikkink, K. K., van Tilburg, T., & Knipscheer, K. (1999). Perceived instrumental support exchanges in relationships between elderly parents and their adult children: Normative and structural explanations. *Journal of Marriage and Family, 61*(4), 831–844.

Impett, E. A., Beals, K. P., & Peplau, L. A. (2001). Testing the investment model of relationship commitment and stability in a longitudinal study of married couples. *Current Psychology, 20*(4), 312–326.

International Longevity Center-USA. (2003). *Sleep, health, and aging*. New York: Author.

International Longevity Center-USA. (n.d.). *Longevity genes: From primitive organisms to humans*. New York. Author.

Ishii-Kuntz, M., & Ihinger-Tallman, M. (1991). The subjective well-being of parents. *Journal of Family Issues, 12*(1), 58–68.

Jackson, B. R. (2008). How gender and self-esteem impact death anxiety across adulthood. *Psi Chi Journal of Undergraduate Research, 13*(2), 96–101.

Jaffee, S., & Hyde, J. S. (2000). Gender differences in moral orientation: A meta-analysis. *Psychological Bulletin, 126*(5), 703–726.

Jamieson, L., Anderson, M., McCrone, D., Bechhofer, F., Stewart, R., & Li, Y. (2002). Cohabitation and commitment: Partnership plans of young men and women. *Sociological Review, 50*(3), 356–377.

Janke, M., Davey, A., & Kleiber, D. (2006). Modeling change in older adults' leisure activities. *Leisure Sciences, 28*(3), 285–303.

Jansari, Z., & Parkin, A. (1996). Things that go bump in your life: Explaining the reminiscence bump in autobiographical memory. *Psychology and Aging, 11*(1), 85–91.

Jendrek, M. (1993). Grandparents who parent their grandchildren: Effects on lifestyle. *Journal of Marriage and the Family, 55*(3), 609–621.

Jennings, J. M., & Darwin, A. L. (2003). Efficacy beliefs, everyday behavior, and memory performance among older elderly adults. *Educational Gerontologist, 29*, 71–91.

Jessberger, S., & Gage, F. H. (2008). Stem-cell-associated structural and functional plasticity in the aging hippocampus. *Psychology and Aging, 23*(4), 692–701.

Johanyak, D. (2004, January 19). Learning for Life. *Community College Week 16*(12), 4–5.

Johnson, K. S., Kuchibhatala, M., Sloane, R. J., Tanis, D., Galanos, A. N., & Tulsky, J. A. (2005). Ethnic differences in the place of death of elderly hospice enrollees. *Journal of the American Geriatrics Society, 53*(12), 2209–2215.

Johnson, M. A. (2001). Variables associated with friendship in an adult population. *Journal of Social Psychology, 129*(3), 379–390.

Johnson, W., & Drueger, R. F. (2005). Higher perceived life control decreases genetic variance in physical health: Evidence from a national twin study. *Journal of Personality and Social Psychology, 88*(1), 165–173.

Joint Center for Housing Studies of Harvard University Neighborhood Reinvestment Corporation. (2001). Aging in place: Coordinating housing and health care provision for America's growing elderly population. Cambridge, MA: Author. Retrieved June 10, 2008, from http://www.jchs.harvard.edu/publications/seniors/lawler_w01-13.pdf.

Jokisaari, M. (2004). Regrets and subjective well-being: A life course approach. *Journal of Adult Development, 11*(4), 281–288.

Jones, W. P. (1995). Holland vocational personality codes and people with visual disabilities: A need for caution. *Re:View, 95*(27), 53–63.

Josselson, R. (1987). *Finding herself: Pathways to identity development in women*. San Francisco: Jossey-Bass.

Josselson, R. (1996). *Revising herself: The story of women's identity from college to midlife*. London: Oxford University Press.

Judge, S. (2003). Determinants of parents stress in families adopting children from Eastern Europe. *Family Relations, 52*(3), 241–248.

Judge, T. A., & Colquitt, J. A. (2004). Organizational justice and stress: The mediating role of work-family conflict. *Journal of Applied Psychology, 89*(3), 395–404.

Julien, D., Chartrand, E., Simard, M., Bouthillier, D., & Begin, J. (2003). Conflict, social support, and relationship quality: An observational study of heterosexual, gay male, and lesbian couples' communication. *Journal of Family Psychology, 17*(3), 419–428.

Kaiser Family Foundation (2005, January). e-Health and the elderly: How seniors use the Internet for health-survey. Menlo Park, CA: Author. Retrieved June 6, 2008, from http://www.kff.org/entmedia/entmedia011205pkg.cfm.

Kaplan, R. M. (2007). Should Medicare reimburse providers for weight loss interventions? *American Psychologist, 62*(3), 217–219.

Kasen, S., Chen, H., Sneed, J., Crawford, T., & Cohen, P. (2006). Social role and birth cohort influences on gender-linked personality traits in women: A 20-year longitudinal analysis. *Journal of Personality and Social Psychology, 91*(5), 944–958.

Kaufman, A. (2000). Tests of intelligence. In R. J. Sternberg (Ed.), *Handbook of intelligence* (pp. 445–476). New York: Cambridge University Press.

Kemeny, A. (2002). Driven to excel: A portrait of Canada's workaholics. *Canadian Social Trends, 64*, 2–7.

Kemper, S., Herman, R. E., & Nartowicz, J. (2005). Different effects of dual task demands on the speech of young and older adults. *Aging, Neuropsychology, and Cognition, 12,* 340–358.

Kemper, S., & Mitzner, T. L. (2001). Language production and comprehension. In J. E. Birren & K. W. Schaie (Eds.), *Handbook of the psychology of aging* (5th ed., pp. 378–398). San Diego, CA: Academic Press.

Kennet, J., McGuire, L., Willis, S. L., & Schaie, K. W. (2000). Memorability functions in verbal memory: A longitudinal approach. *Experimental Aging Research, 26*, 121–137.

Kennon, S., Mackintosh, V., & Myers, B. (2009). Parenting education for incarcerated mothers. *The Journal of Correctional Education, 60*(1), 10–30.

Kenny, M. E., & Barton, C. E. (2003). Attachment theory and research. In J. Demick & C. Andreoletti (Eds.), *Handbook of adult development* (pp. 371–390). New York: Kluwer Academic/Plenum Press.

Kensinger, E., & Corkin, S. (2003). Neural changes in aging. In L. Nadel (Editor-in-Chief), *Encyclopedia of cognitive science* (Vol. 1, pp. 70–78). London: Nature Publishing Group.

Ketcham, C. J., & Stelmach, G. E. (2001). Age-related declines in motor control. In J. E. Birren & K. W. Schaie (Eds.), *Handbook of the psychology of aging* (5th ed., pp. 313–348). San Diego, CA: Academic Press.

Kim, A., & Merriam, S. B. (2004). Motivations for learning among older adults in a learning in retirement institute. *Educational Gerontology, 30*(6), 441–455.

Kim, S., & Feldman, D. C. (2000). Working in retirement: The antecedents of bridge employment and its consequences for quality of life in retirement. *Academy of Management Journal, 43*(6), 1195–1210.

Kingsberg, S. A. (2000). The psychological impact of aging on sexuality and relationships. *Journal of Women's Health and Gender-Based Medicine, 9*(1), 33–38.

Kirby, P. G., Biever, J. L., Martinez, I. G., & Gomez, J. P. (2004). Adults returning to school: The impact on family and work. *Journal of Psychology, 138*(1), 65–76.

Kirk, J., Weisbrod, J., & Ericson, K. (2002). *Psychosocial and behavioral aspects of medicine*. Philadelphia: Lippincott Williams & Wilkins.

Kitayama, S., Markus, H. R., Matsumoto, H., & Norasakkunkit, V., (1997). Individual and collective processes in the construction of the self: Self-enhancement in the United States and self-criticism in Japan. *Journal of Personality and Social Psychology, 72*(6), 1245–1267.

Kite, M. E., Stockdale, G. D., Whitley, B. E., & Johnson, B. T. (2005). Attitudes toward younger and older adults: An updated meta-analytic review. *Journal of Social Issues, 61*(2), 241–266.

Kittrell, D. (1998). A comparison of the evolution of men's and women's dreams in Daniel Levinson's theory of adult development. *Journal of Adult Development, 5*(2), 105–115.

Kline, G. H., Stanley, S. M., Markman, H. J., Olmos-Gallo, P. A., St. Peters, M., Whitton, S. W., et al. (2004). Timing is everything: Pre-engagement cohabitation and increased risk for poor marital outcomes. *Journal of Family Psychology, 18*(2), 311–318.

Klitzing, S. W. (2004). Women living in a homeless shelter: Stress, coping and leisure. *Journal of Leisure Research, 36*(4), 483–512.

Knight, B. G., Kaskie, B., Shurgot, G. R., & Davis, J. (2006). Improving the mental health of older adults. In J. E. Birren & K. W. Schaie (Eds.), *Handbook of the psychology of aging* (6th ed., pp. 407–424). San Diego, CA: Academic Press.

Knudsen, H. K., Roman, P. M., & Johnson, J. A. (2004). The management of workplace deviance: Organizational responses to employee drug use. *Journal of Drug Issues, 34*(1), 121–143.

Kohlberg, L. (1976). Moral stages and moralization: The cognitive-developmental approach. In T. Lickona (Ed.), *Moral development and behavior: Theory, research, and social issues* (pp. 31–53). New York: Holt, Rinehart & Winston.

Kohlberg, L. (1984). *The psychology of moral development: Essays on moral development* (Vol. 2). San Francisco: Harper & Row.

Kohn, C., Henderson, C. S., & Walton-Brooks, D. (2003, May 26). Health illiteracy adds billions to healthcare costs. *Managed Care Weekly Digest,* pp. 44–45.

Koltko-Rivera, M. E. (2004). The psychology of worldviews. *Review of General Psychology, 8*(1), 3–58.

Kramer, A. F., Fabiani, M., & Colcombe, S. J. (2006). Contributions of cognitive neuroscience to the understanding of behavior and aging. In J. E. Birren & K. W. Schaie (Eds.), *Handbook of the psychology of aging* (6th ed., pp. 57–83). San Diego, CA: Academic Press.

Kramer, D. (2003). The ontogeny of wisdom in its variations. In J. Demick & C. Andreoletti (Eds.), *Handbook of adult development* (pp. 131–151). New York: Kluwer Academic/Plenum Press.

Krause, N. (2001). Social support. In R. H. Birrenstock & L. K. George (Eds.), *Handbook of aging and the social sciences* (5th ed., pp. 272–294). San Diego, CA: Academic Press.

Krause, N. (2006a). Religion and health in late life. In J. E. Birren & K. W. Schaie (Eds.), *Handbook of the psychology of aging* (6th ed., pp. 499–518). San Diego, CA: Academic Press.

Krause, N. (2006b). Social relationships in late life. In R. H. Binstock & L. K. George (Eds.), *Handbook of aging and the social sciences* (6th ed., pp. 181–200). San Diego, CA: Academic Press.

Krebs-Smith, S. M., & Kris-Etherton, P. (2007). How does MyPyramid compare to other population-based recommendations for controlling chronic disease? *Journal of the American Dietetic Association, 107*(5), 830–837.

Kressel, L. M., Chapman, G. B., & Leventhal, E. (2007). The influence of default options on the expression of end-of-life treatment preferences in advance directives. *Journal of General Internal Medicine, 22*(7), 1007–1010.

Kristiansen, C. M., & Hotte, A. M. (1996). Morality and the self: Implications for the when and how of value-attitude-behavior relations. In C. Seligman, J. M. Olson, and M. P. Zanna (Eds.), *The psychology of values: The Ontario Symposium, Volume 8* (pp. 77–105). Mahwah, NJ: Erlbaum.

Kroger, J. (2000). Ego identity status research in the new millennium. *International Journal of Behavioral Development, 24*, 145–148.

Kroger, J. (2002a). Identity processes and contents through the years of late adulthood. *Identity: An International Journal of Theory and Research, 2*(1), 81–99.

Kroger, J. (2002b). Introduction: Identity development through adulthood. *Identity: An International Journal of Theory and Research, 2*(1), 1–5.

Kryger, M., Monjan, A., Bliwise, D., & Ancoli-Israel, S. (2004). *Sleep, health, and aging, 59*(1), 24–28.

Kumashiro, M., Finkel, E. J., & Rusbult, C. E. (2002). Self-respect and pro-relationship behavior in marital relationships. *Journal of Personality, 70*(6), 1009–1049.

Kung, W. W., Hung, S., & Chan, C. L. (2004). How the socio-cultural context shapes women's divorce experience in Hong Kong. *Journal of Comparative Family Studies, 35*(1), 33–50.

Kurdek, L. A. (1994). Areas of conflict for gay, lesbian, and heterosexual couples: What couples argue about influences relationship satisfaction. *Journal of Marriage and the Family, 56*(4), 923–934.

Kurdek, L. A. (1998). Relationship outcomes and their predictors: Longitudinal evidence from heterosexual married, gay cohabiting, and lesbian cohabiting couples. *Journal of Marriage and the Family, 60,* 553–568.

Kurdek, L. A. (2002). Predicting the timing of separation and marital satisfaction: An eight-year prospective longitudinal study. *Journal of Marriage and Family, 64*(1), 163–179.

Kurdek, L. A. (2004). Are gay and lesbian cohabiting couples really different from heterosexual married couples? *Journal of Marriage and Family, 66*(4), 880–900.

Laanan, F. S. (2003). Older adults in community colleges: Choices, attitudes, and goals. *Educational Gerontology, 29*(9), 757–776.

Labouvie-Vief, G. (1990). Wisdom as integrated thought: Historical and developmental perspectives. In R. J. Sternberg (Ed.), *Wisdom: Its nature, origins, and development* (pp. 52–83). New York: Cambridge University Press.

Labouvie-Vief, G., Chiodo, L. M., Goguen, L. A., Diehl, M., & Orwoll, L. (1995). Representations of self across the life span. *Psychology and Aging, 10*(3), 404–415.

Lachapelle, D. L., & Hadjistavropoulos, T. (2005). Age-related differences among adults coping with pain: Evaluation of a development life-contextual model. *Canadian Journal of Behavioural Science, 37*(2), 123–137.

Lande, R., Tarpley, V., Francis, J., & Boucher, R. (2010). Combat trauma art therapy scale. *The Arts in Psychotherapy, 37*(2), 42–45.

Langer, E. J., & Moldoveanu, M. (2000). Mindfulness research and the future. *Journal of Social Issues, 56*(1), 129–139.

Larrison, C. R., Velez-Ortiz, D., Hernandez, P. M., Piedra, L. M., & Goldberg, A. (2010). Brokering language and culture: Can ad hoc interpreters fill the language service gap at community health centers? *Social Work in Public Health, 25*, 387–410.

Lawson, D. M., & Brossart, D. F. (2004). The developmental course of personal authority in the family system. *Family Process, 43*(3), 391–409.

LeBourdais, C., & Lapierre-Adamcyk, E. (2004). Changes in conjugal life in Canada: Is cohabitation progressively replacing marriage? *Journal of Marriage and Family, 66*(4), 929–942.

Lee, D. H., & Schaninger, C. M. (2003). Attitudinal and consumption differences among traditional and nontraditional "childless" couple households. *Journal of Consumer Behaviour, 2*(3), 248–268.

Lee, T. R., Mancini, J. A., & Maxwell, J. W. (1990). Sibling relationships in adulthood: Contact patterns and motivations. *Journal of Marriage & the Family, 52*, 431–440.

Lees, F. D., Clark, P. G., Nigg, C. R., & Newman, P. (2005). Barriers to exercise behavior among older adults: A focus-group study. *Journal of Aging and Physical Activity, 13*(1), 23–34.

LeJune, J., Steinman, B., & Mascia, J. (2003). Enhancing socialization of older people experiencing loss of both vision and hearing. *Generations, 27*(1), 95–97.

LeMastro, B. (2001). Childless by choice?: Attributions and attitudes concerning family size. *Social Behavior and Personality: An International Journal, 29*(3), 231–243.

Lentillon-Kaestner, V., & Carstairs, C. (2010). Doping use among young elite cyclists: A qualitative psychosociological approach. *Scandinavian Journal of Medicine &Science in Sports, 20*, 336–345.

Lerner, R. M., & Tubman, J. G. (1989). Conceptual issues in studying continuity and discontinuity in personal development across life. *Journal of Personality, 57*(2), 343–373.

Letherby, G. (2002). Childless and bereft?: Stereotypes and realities in relation to "voluntary" and involuntary childlessness and womanhood. *Sociological Inquiry, 72*(1), 5–20.

Leventhal, H., Rabin, C., Leventhal, E. A., & Burns, E. (2001). Health risk behaviors and aging. In J. E. Birren & K. W. Schaie (Eds.), *Handbook of the psychology of aging* (5th ed., pp. 186–214). San Diego, CA: Academic Press.

Levine, B., Svoboda, E., Hay, J., Winocur, G., & Moscovitch, M. (2002). Aging and autobiographical memory: Dissociating episodic from semantic retrieval. *Psychology & Aging, 17*(4), 677–689.

Levinson, D. (1978). *The seasons of a man's life*. New York: Ballantine Books.

Levitt, M. J., Weber, R. A., & Guacci, N. (1993). Convoys of social support: An intergenerational analysis. *Psychology and Aging, 8*(3), 323–326.

Lewis, H. (1990). *Questions of values*. San Francisco: HarperCollins.

Lewis, R. J., Derlega, V. J., Griffin, J. L., & Krowinski, A. C. (2003). Stressors for gay men and lesbians: Life stress, gay-related stress, stigma consciousness, and depressive symptoms. *Journal of Social & Clinical Psychology, 22*(6), 716–729.

Leyden, K. M. (2003). Social capital and the built environment: The importance of walkable neighborhoods. *American Journal of Public Health, 93*(9), 1546–1551.

Li, F., McAuley, E., Harmer, P., Duncan, T. E., & Chaumeton, N. R. (2001). Tai chi enhances self-efficacy and exercise behavior in older adults. *Journal of Aging and Physical Activity, 9*, 161–171.

Li., S., Aggen, S. H., Nesselroade, J. R., & Baltes, P. B. (2001). Short-term fluctuations in elderly people's sensorimotor functioning predict text and spatial memory performance: The Mac Arthur Successful Aging Studies. *Gerontology, 47*(2), 100–116.

Li, S., Schmiedek, F., Huxhold, O., Rocke, C., Smith, J., & Lindenberger, U. (2008). Working memory plasticity in old age: Practice gain, transfer, and maintenance. *Psychology and Aging, 23*(4), 692–701.

Li, Y., & Ferraro, K. F. (2006). Volunteering in middle and later life: Is health a benefit, barrier or both? *Social Forces, 85*(1), 497–519.

Lichtenstein, M. J., Pruski, L. A., Marshall, C. E., Blalock, C. L., Shuko, L., & Plaetke, R. (2003). Sentence completion to assess children's views about aging. *Gerontologist, 43*(6), 839–848.

Lindfield, K. C., & Wingfield, A. (1999). An experimental and computational analysis of age differences in the recognition of fragmented pictures: Inhibitory connections versus speed of processing. *Experimental Aging Research, 25*, 223–242.

Lindner, S. A., Davoren, J. B., Vollmer, A., Williams, B., & Landefeld, C. S. (2007). An electronic medical record intervention increased nursing home advance directive orders and documentation. *Journal of the American Geriatrics Society, 55*(7), 1001–1006.

Lippert, L. (1997). Women at midlife: Implications for theories of women's adult development. *Journal of Counseling and Development, 76*, 16–22.

Lips, H. M. (2003). The gender pay gap: Concrete indicator of women's progress toward equality. *Analyses of Social Issues & Public Policy, 3*(1), 87–109.

Litwak, E., & Longino, C.F. (1987). Migration patterns among the elderly: A developmental perspective. *Gerontologist, 27*(3), 266–272.

Liu, J. H., Ng, S. H., Loong, C., Gee, S., & Weatherall, A. (2003). Cultural stereotypes and social representations of elders from Chinese and European perspectives. *Journal of Cross-Cultural Gerontology, 18*(2), 149–168.

Lo, R., & Brown, R. (1999). Stress and adaptation: Preparation for successful retirement. *Australian and New Zealand Journal of Mental Health Nursing, 8*, 30–38.

Longino, C. F. (1990). Geographical mobility and family caregiving in nonmetropolitan America: Three-decade evidence from the U.S. census. *Family Relations, 39*(1), 38–43.

Longino, C. F. (2001). Geographical distribution and migration. In R. H. Binstock & L. George (Eds.), *Handbook of aging and the social sciences* (5th ed., pp. 103–124). San Diego, CA: Academic Press.

Longino, C. F., & Bradley, D. E. (2006). Internal and international migration. In R. H. Binstock & L. K. George (Eds.), *Handbook of aging and the social sciences* (6th ed., pp. 76–93). San Diego, CA: Academic Press.

Lorensen, M., Wilson, M. E., & White, M. A. (2004). Norwegian families: Transition to parenthood. *Health Care for Women International, 25*(4), 334–348.

Lundberg, C. A. (2003). The influence of time-limitations, faculty, and peer relationships on adult student learning: A causal model. *Journal of Higher Education, 74*(6), 665–688.

Lussier, G., Deater-Deckard, K., Dunn, J., & Davies, L. (2002). Support across two generations: Children's closeness to grandparents following parental divorce and remarriage. *Journal of Family Psychology, 16*(3), 363–376.

Lyddy, F., Barnes-Holmes, D., & Hampson, P. J. (2001). A transfer of sequence function via equivalence in a connectionist network. *Psychological Record, 51*, 409–428.

Lyubomirsky, S., King, L., & Diener, E. (2005). The benefits of frequent positive affect: Does happiness lead to success? *Psychological Bulletin, 131*(6), 803–855.

MacDonald, S. W., Hultsch, D. F., & Dixon, R. A. (2003). Performance variability is related to change in cognition: Evidence from the Victoria longitudinal study. *Psychology and Aging, 18*(3), 510–523.

Mack, M. G., & Shaddox, L. A. (2004). Changes in short-term attitudes toward physical activity and exercise of university personal wellness students. *College Student Journal, 38*(4), 587–593.

Magai, C. (2001). Emotions over the life span. In J. E. Birren & K. W. Schaie (Eds.), *Handbook of the psychology of aging* (5th ed., pp. 399–426). San Diego, CA: Academic Press.

Marcia, J. E. (2001). A comment on Seth Schwartz's review of identity theory and research. *Identity: An International Journal of Theory and Research 1*(1), 59–65.

Marcia, J. E. (2002a). Adolescence, identity, and the Bernardone family. *Identity: An International Journal of Theory and Research, 2*, 199–209.

Marcia, J. E. (2002b). Identity and psychosocial development in adulthood. *Identity: An International Journal of Theory and Research, (2)*, 7–28.

Markus, H. R. (1977). Self-schemata and processing information about the self. *Journal of Personality and Social Psychology, 35*, 63–78.

Marsiske, M., & Margrett, J. A. (2006). Everyday problem solving and decision making. In J. E. Birren & K. W. Schaie (Eds.), *Handbook of the psychology of aging* (6th ed., pp. 315–342). San Diego, CA: Academic Press.

Martin, M., & Hofer, S. M. (2004). Intraindividual variability, change, and aging: conceptual and analytical issues. *Gerontology, 50*(1), 7–11.

Martin, R. G. (2005). Serving American Indian students in tribal colleges: Lessons for mainstream colleges. *New Directions for Student Services, 109*, 79–86.

Martinson, M. (2006). Opportunities or obligations?: Civic engagement and older adults. *Generations, 30*(4), 59–65.

Marwit, S. J. (1997). Professional psychology's role in hospice care. *Professional Psychology: Research and Practice, 28*(5), 457–463.

Maslow, A. H. (1970). *Motivation and personality* (2nd ed.). New York: Harper & Row.

Maslow, A. H. (1971). *The farther reaches of human nature.* New York: Penguin.

Maslow, A. H. (1999). *Toward a psychology of being* (3rd ed.). New York: Wiley. (Original work published 1968)

Mason, M. G. (2004). *Taking sides: Clashing views on controversial issues in cognitive science.* Guildford, CT: McGraw-Hill/Dushkin.

Masson, J. D. (2002). Non-professional perceptions of "good death": A study of the views of hospice care patients and relatives of deceased hospice care patients. *Mortality, 7*(2), 191–209.

Mastekaasa, A. (1995). Age variations in the suicide rates and self-reported subjective well-being of married and never married persons. *Journal of Community and Applied Social Psychology, 5*, 21–39.

Masunaga, H., & Horn, J. (2001). Expertise and age-related changes in components of intelligence. *Psychology and Aging, 16*(2), 293–311.

May, T., Aulisio, M. P., & DeVita, M. A. (2000). Patients, families, and organ donation: Who should decide? *Milbank Quarterly, 78*(2), 323–336.

Mayo Clinic. (2004). Keeping health in mind: 10 steps to keep your memory sharp. Retrieved July 31, 2004, from http://www.mayoclinic.com/invoke.cfm?id=HA00001.

Mayo Clinic. (2007, September 28). Complicated grief. Retrieved July 24, 2008, from http://www.mayoclinic.com/print/complicated-grief/DS01023/DSECTION=all&METHOD=print.

Mayo Clinic. (2008a, August 9). Aging: What to expect as you get older. Retrieved July 8, 2010, from http://www.mayoclinic.com/health/aging/HA00040.

Mayo Clinic. (2008b, August 26). Dry macular degeneration. Retrieved July 8, 2010, from http://www.mayoclinic.com/health/macular-degeneration/DS00284/LOCID==.

Mayo Clinic. (2008c, July 17). Glaucoma. Retrieved July 8, 2010, from http://www.mayoclinic.com/health/glaucoma/DS00283/LOCID==.

Mayo Clinic. (2008d, September 16). Perimenopause. Retrieved July 9, 2010, http://www.mayoclinic.com/health/perimenopause/DS00554.

Mayo Clinic. (2008e, August 1). Tinnitus. Retrieved July 8, 2010, from http://www.mayoclinic.com/health/tinnitus/DS00365/LOCID==.

Mayo Clinic. (2009a, April 17). Dementia. Retrieved July 15, 2010, from http://www.mayoclinic.com/health/dementia/DS01131/METHOD=print.

Mayo Clinic. (2009b, April 7). Dry mouth. Retrieved July 8, 2010, from http://www.mayoclinic.com/health/dry-mouth/HA00034.

Mayo Clinic. (2009c, August). Hearing loss. Retrieved July 8, 2010, from http://www.mayoclinic.com/health/hearing-loss/DS00172.

Mayo Clinic. (2009d, January 28) Heart disease. Retrieved July 15, 2010, from http://www.mayoclinic.com/health/heart-disease/DS01120/METHOD=print.

Mayo Clinic. (2009e, August 7). High blood pressure (hypertension). Retrieved July 8, 2010, from http://www.mayoclinic.com/health/high-blood-pressure/DS00100/LOCID==.

Mayo Clinic. (2009f, May 8). Presbyopia. Retrieved July 8, 2010, from http://www.mayoclinic.com/health/presbyopia/DS00589=.

Mayo Clinic. (2009g, September 19). Sexual health and aging: Keep the passion alive. Retrieved July 8, 2010, from http://www.mayoclinic.com/health/sexual-health/HA00035.

Mayo Clinic. (2010a, May 20). Cataracts. Retrieved July 8, 2010, from http://www.mayoclinic.com/health/cataracts/DS00050/LOCID==.

Mayo Clinic. (2010b, June 12). Dry eyes. Retrieved July 8, 2010, from http://www.mayoclinic.com/health/dry-eyes/DS00463.

Mayo Clinic. (2010c, April 24). Female sexual dysfunction. Retrieved July 8, 2010, from http://www.mayoclinic.com/print/female-sexual-dysfunction/DS00701/METHOD=print&DSECTION=all.

Mayo Clinic. (2010d, February 2). Hair loss. Retrieved July 8, 2010, from http://www.mayoclinic.com/health/hair-loss/DS00278.

Mayo Clinic. (2010e, February 19). Hormone therapy: Is it right for you? Retrieved July 8, 2010, from http://www.mayoclinic.com/health/hormone-therapy/WO00046/LOCID==.

Mazur, A., Mueller, U., Krause, W., & Booth, A. (2002). Causes of sexual decline in aging married men: Germany and America. *International Journal of Impotence Research, 14*, 101–106.

McAdams, D. P., & St. Aubin, E. (Eds.). (1998). *Generativity and adult development: How and why we care for the next generation*. Washington, DC: American Psychological Association.

McCool, A. C., Huls, A., Peppones, M., & Schlenker, E. (2001). Nutrition of older persons: A key to healthy aging. *Topics in Clinical Nutrition, 17*(1), 52–71.

McCrae, R. R. (2001). Trait psychology and culture: Exploring intercultural comparisons. *Journal of Personality, 69*(6), 819–846.

McCrae, R. R. (2004). Human nature and culture: A trait perspective. *Journal of Research in Personality, 38*(1), 4–14.

McCrae, R. R., & Costa, P. T. (1987). Validation of the five-factor model of personality across instruments and observers. *Journal of Personality and Social Psychology, 52*(1), 81–90.

McCrae, R. R., Costa, P. T., Terracciano, A., Parker, W. D., Mills, C. J., De Fruyt, F., et al. (2002). Personality trait development from age 12 to 18: Longitudinal, cross-sectional, and cross-cultural analyses. *Journal of Personality and Social Psychology, 83*(6), 1456–1468.

McCrae, R. R., & John, O. P. (1992). An introduction to the five-factor model and its applications. *Journal of Personality, 60*(2), 175–215.

McFadden S. H. (1999). Religion, personality, and aging: A life span perspective. *Journal of Personality, 67*(6), 1081–1104.

McFadden, S. H., & Gerl, R. R. (1990). Approaches to understanding spirituality in the second half of life. *Generations: Journal of the American Society on Aging, 14*(4), 35–38.

McManus, I. C., Winder, B. C., & Gordon, D. (2002). The causal links between stress and burnout in a longitudinal study of UK doctors. *Lancet, 359*, 2089–2090.

Meacham, J. A. (1990). The loss of wisdom. In R. J. Sternberg (Ed.), *Wisdom: Its nature, origins, and development* (pp. 181–211). New York: Cambridge University Press.

Meegan, S. P., & Berg, C. A. (2002). Contexts, functions, forms, and processes of collaborative everyday problem solving in older adulthood. *International Journal of Behavioral Development, 26*(1), 6–15.

Mehrotra, C. M. (2003). In defense of offering educational programs for older adults. *Educational Gerontology, 29*(8), 645–655.

Mejia, S., Pineda, D., Alvarez, L. M., & Ardila, A. (1998). Individual differences in memory and executive function abilities during normal aging. *International Journal of Neuroscience, 95*(3/4), 271–284.

Mendelson, M. J., & Aboud, F. E. (1999). Measuring friendship quality in late adolescents and young adults: McGill friendship questionnaires. *Canadian Journal of Behavioural Science, 31*(2), 130–132.

Merck Manuals Online Medical Library. (2007, October). Death and dying. Retrieved July 16, 2008, from http://www.merck.com/mmhe/sec01/ch008/ch008a.html.

Miinino, A. M., Xu, J., Kochanek, K. D., & Tejada-Verz, B. (2009, December). Death in the United States, 2007. National Center for Health Statistics Data Brief. Retrieved July 14, 2010, from http://www.cdc.gov/nchs/data/databriefs/db26.pdf

Minter, L. E., & Samuels, C. A. (1998). The impact of "the dream" on women's experience of the midlife transition. *Journal of Adult Development, 5*(1), 31–43.

Miranda, A., Frevert, V. S., & Kern, R. M. (1998). Lifestyle differences between bicultural and low- and high-acculturation-level Latino adults. *Journal of Individual Psychology, 54*(1), 119–134.

Mitchell, D. B., Brown, A. S., & Murphy, D. R. (1990). Dissociations between procedural and episodic memory: Effects of time and aging. *Psychology and Aging, 5*(2), 264–276.

Miville, J. L., Koonce, D., Darlington, P., & Whitlock, B. (2000). Exploring the relationship between racial/cultural identity and ego identity among African Americans and Mexican Americans. *Journal of Multicultural Counseling and Development, 28*(4), 208–224.

Moen, P., & Spencer, D. (2006). Converging divergences in age, gender, health, and well-being: Strategic selection in the third age. In R. H. Binstock & L. K. George (Eds.), *Handbook of aging and the social sciences* (6th ed., pp. 127–144). San Diego, CA: Academic Press.

Montano, J. J. (2003). Emerging technologies for hearing loss: An ecological approach. *Generations, 27*(1), 71–77.

Montgomery, M. J., & Sorell, G. T. (1997). Differences in love attitudes across family life stages. *Family Relations: Interdisciplinary Journal of Applied Family Studies, 46*(1), 55–61.

Moon, M. (2006). Organization and financing of health care. In R. H. Binstock & L. K. George (Eds.), *Handbook of aging and the social sciences* (6th ed., pp. 380–396). San Diego, CA: Academic Press.

Moren-Cross, J. L., & Lin, N. (2006). Social networks and health. In R. H. Binstock & L. K. George (Eds.), *Handbook of aging and the social sciences* (6th ed., pp. 111–126). San Diego, CA: Academic Press.

Moyer, M. (1992). Sibling relationships among older adults. *Generations: Journal of the American Society on Aging, 17*(3), 55–58.

Mroczek, D. K., & Kolarz, C. M. (1998). The effect of age on positive and negative affect: A developmental perspective on happiness. *Journal of Personality and Social Psychology, 75*(5), 1333–1349.

Mroczek, D. K., & Spiro, A. (2005). Change in life satisfaction during adulthood: Findings from the Veterans Affairs Normative Aging Study. *Journal of Personality and Social Psychology, 88*(1), 189–202.

Mueller, M., Wilhelm, B., & Elder, G. (2002). Variations in grandparenting. *Research on Aging, 24*(3), 360–388.

Mueller, P., Litin, S., Hook, C., Creagan, E., Cha, S., & Beckman, T. (2010). A novel advance directives course provides a transformative learning experience for medical students. *Teaching and Learning in Medicine, 22*(2), 137–141.

Munakata, Y., & McClelland, J. L. (2003). Connectionist models of development. *Developmental Science, 6*(4), 413–429.

Murphy, H., & Roopchand, N. (2003). Intrinsic motivation and self-esteem in traditional and mature students at a post-1992 university in the north-east of England. *Educational Studies, 29*(2/3), 243–259.

Mutchler, J. E., Burr, J. A., & Caro, F. G. (2003). From paid worker to volunteer: Leaving the paid workforce and volunteering in later life. *Social Forces, 81*(4), 1267–1293.

Myers, D. G. (2005). Scientific pursuit of happiness. *Innovation, 5*(3), 32–33.

Myers, S., & Bryant, L. (2008). The use of behavioral indicators of sibling commitment among emerging adults. *Journal of Family Communication, 8*(2), 101–125.

Nanda, U., Gaydos, H., Hathorn, K., & Watkins, N. (2010). Art and posttraumatic stress: A review of the empirical literature on the therapeutic implications of artwork for war veterans with posttraumatic stress disorder. Environment and Behavior, 42(3), 376–390.

Narvaez, D., & Rest, J. (1995). The four components of acting morally. In W. M. Kurtines & J. L. Gewirtz (Eds.), *Moral development: An introduction* (pp. 27–48). Boston: Allyn & Bacon.

National Adoption Information Clearinghouse. (2003). Adoption: Where do I start? Retrieved October 19, 2004, from http://naic.acf.hhs.gov/pubs/f_start.cfm.

National Adoption Information Clearinghouse. (2004). Parties to an adoption. Retrieved October 19, 2004, from http://naic.acf.hhs.gov/general/legal/statutes/parties.cfm.

National Assessments of Adult Literacy, National Center for Education Statistics, Institute of Education Sciences, U.S. Department of Education. (n.d.). Defining Literacy and Sample Items. Retrieved August 20, 2004, from http://nces.ed.gov/naal/defining/defining.asp.

National Association of Social Workers. (2004, August 16). Social workers come out in support of marriage for same-sex couples. Washington, DC: Author. Retrieved October 19, 2004, from http://www.socialworkers.org/pressroom/2004/081704.asp.

National Cancer Institute. (2000, March 7). Advance directives. Bethesda, MD: Author. Retrieved July 15, 2000, from http://www.cancer.gov/cancertopics/factsheet/support/advance-directives.

National Cancer Institute. (2002, October 30). End-of-life care: Questions and answers. Bethesda, MD: Author. Retrieved July 15, 2008, from http://www.cancer.gov/cancertopics/factsheet/support/end-of-life-care.

National Cancer Institute. (2004, September 1). Metastatic cancer: Questions and answers. Bethesda, MD: Author. Retrieved July 15, 2010, from http://www.cancer.gov/cancertopics/factsheet/Sites-Types/metastatic.

National Cancer Institute. (2005, June, 6). Cancer: Questions and answers. Bethesda, MD: Author. Retrieved July 15, 2010, from http://www.cancer.gov/cancertopics/factsheet/Sites-Types/general.

National Cancer Institute. (2006, June 19). Loss, grief, and bereavement. Bethesda, MD: Author. Retrieved July 20, 2008, from http://www.cancer.gov/cancertopics/pdq/supportivecare/bereavement/Patient/page1.

National Cancer Institute. (2007, June 29). Caring for the caregiver. Bethesda, MD: Author. Retrieved June 20, 2008, from http://www.cancer.gov/cancertopics/caring-for-the-caregiver/page1.

National Cancer Institute. (2009, October 29). Introduction to the prostate. Retrieved July 8, 2010 from http://www.cancer.gov/cancertopics/understanding-prostate-changes.

National Center for Educational Statistics. (2002, August). Special Analysis 2002: Nontraditional undergraduates. Retrieved August 12, 2004, from http://nces.ed.gov/programs/coe/2002/analyses/nontraditional/index.asp.

National Center on Birth Defects and Developmental Disabilities. (2004, September 1). Birth defects. Atlanta, GA: Centers for Disease Control and Prevention. Retrieved October 19, 2004, from http://www.cdc.gov/ncbddd/bd/abc.htm.

National Center on Physical Activity and Disability. (2009, March 10). Exercise/Fitness. Chicago, IL: University of Illinois at Chicago. Retrieved June 29, 2010 from http://www.ncpad.org/exercise/fact_sheet.php?sheet=378&view=all#3.

National Clearing House for Long-Term Care Information. (2008, May 16). What does long-term care cost? Retrieved June 14, 2008, from http://www.longtermcare.gov/LTC/Main_Site/Paying_LTC/Costs_Of_Care/Costs_Of_Care.aspx.

National Diabetes Information Clearinghouse. (2008, November). Diabetes overview. Bethesda, MD: Author. Retrieved July 15, 2010, from http://diabetes.niddk.nih.gov/dm/pubs/overview/.

National Eye Institute, National Institutes of Health. (December, 2006). Diagram of the eye. Retrieved May 16, 2008, from http://www.nei.nih.gov/health/eyediagram/eyeimages1.asp.

National Heart Lung and Blood Institute, (2009, February), What is coronary artery disease? Bethesda, MD: Author. Retrieved July 15, 2010, from http://www.nhlbi.nih.gov/health/dci/Diseases/Cad/CAD_WhatIs.html.

National Infertility Association. (2010). *What is infertility?* McLean, VA: Author. Retrieved July 2, 2010, from http://www.resolve.org/infertility-overview/what-is-infertility/.

National Institute for Literacy. (n.d.). Literacy fact sheets overview. Retrieved August 20, 2004, from http://www.nifl.gov/nifl/facts/facts_overview.html.

National Institute of Arthritis and Musculoskeletal and Skin Diseases. (2009, May). Bone health overview. Retrieved July 8, 2010, from http://www.niams.nih.gov/Health_Info/Bone/Bone_Health/default.asp.

National Institute of Mental Health. (2008, June 26). The numbers count: Mental disorders in America. Bethesda, MD: Author. Retrieved July 6, 2008, from http://www.nimh.nih.gov/health/publications/the-numbers-count-mental-disorders-in-america.shtml.

National Institute of Mental Health. (2009, September 23). Depression. Bethesda, MD: Author. Retrieved July 15, 2010, from http://www.nimh.nih.gov/health/publications/depression/index.shtml.

National Institute of Mental Health. (2010a, March 18). Anxiety disorders. Bethesda, MD: Author. Retrieved July 15, 2010, from http://www.nimh.nih.gov/health/publications/anxiety-disorders/complete-index.shtml.

National Institute of Mental Health. (2010b, July 9). The numbers count: Mental disorders in America. Bethesda, MD: Author. Retrieved July 15, 2010, from http://www.nimh.nih.gov/health/publications/the-numbers-count-mental-disorders-in-america.shtml.

National Institute of Neurological Disorders and Stroke. (2003, March). Know stroke. Bethesda, MD: Author. Retrieved July 2, 2008, from http://stroke.ninds.nih.gov/documents/ninds_ks_english_4x9_brochure.pdf.

National Institute of Neurological Disorders and Stroke. (2007, May 1). Brain basics: Know your brain. Bethesda, MD: Author. Retrieved May 20, 2008, from http://www.ninds.nih.gov/disorders/brain_basics/know_your_brain.htm.

National Institute of Neurological Disorders and Stroke. (2010a, June 17). NIH senior health: Stroke. Bethesda, MD: Author. Retrieved July 15, 2010, from http://nihseniorhealth.gov/stroke/toc.html.

National Institute of Neurological Disorders and Stroke. (2010b, July 15). NINDS Alzheimer's disease information page. Bethesda, MD: Author. Retrieved July 15, 2010, from http://www.ninds.nih.gov/disorders/alzheimersdisease/alzheimersdisease.htm.

National Institute on Aging. (2001). *Exercise: A Guide from the National Institute on Aging*. Bethesda, MD: Author. Retrieved December 22, 2004 from http://www.nia.nih.gov/NR/rdonlyres/25C76114-D120-4960-946A-3F576B528BBD/0/ExerciseGuide_2008.pdf.

National Institute on Aging. (2003, December). Alzheimer's disease: Unraveling the mystery. Retrieved July 7, 2008, from http://www.nia.nih.gov/NR/rdonlyres/A294D332-71A2-4866-BDD7-A0DF216DAAA4/0/Alzheimers_Disease_Unraveling_the_Mystery.pdf.

National Institute on Aging. (2007a, May 16). *Aging under the microscope*. Bethesda, MD: Author Retrieved June 26, 2007, from http://www.nia.nih.gov/HealthInformation/Publications/AgingUndertheMicroscope/.

National Institute on Aging. (2007b). Growing older in America: The health and retirement study. Retrieved June 2, 2008, from http://www.nia.nih.gov/ResearchInformation/ExtramuralPrograms/BehavioralAndSocialResearch/HRS.htm.

National Institute on Aging. (2007c, November). Live long and well in the 21st century: Strategic direction for research on aging (NIH Publication No. 07-6252). Retrieved May 25, 2008, from http://www.nia.nih.gov/AboutNIA/StrategicDirections.

National Institute on Aging. (2008a, April). *Age page: Dietary supplements*. Bethesda, MD: Author. Retrieved June 27, 2010, from http://www.nia.nih.gov/healthinformation/publications/supplements.htm.

National Institute on Aging. (2008b, March 27). Americans living longer, enjoying greater health and prosperity, but important disparities remain, says federal report. Retrieved June 10, 2008 from http://|www.nia.nih.gov/NewsAndEvents/PressReleases/PR20080327OlderAmericans.htm.

National Institute on Aging. (2009a, August 6). *Age page:Skin care and aging*. Retrieved July 8, 2010, from http://www.nia.nih.gov/HealthInformation/Publications/skin.htm.

National Institute on Aging. (2009b, August 13). *Age page: Urinary incontinence*. Retrieved July 8, 2010, from http://www.nia.nih.gov/healthinformation/publications/urinary.htm.

National Institute on Aging. (2009c, January). *Exercise & physical activity: Your everyday guide from the National Institute on Aging*. Bethesda, MD: Author. Retrieved June 27, 2010, from http://www.nia.nih.gov/HealthInformation/Publications/ExerciseGuide/.

National Institute on Aging. (2010a, April 20). *Age page: Cancer facts for people over 50*. Retrieved July 15, 2010, from http://www.nia.nih.gov/HealthInformation/Publications/cancer.htm.

National Institute on Aging. (2010b, April 20). *Age page: Menopause*. Retrieved July 8, 2010, from http://www.nia.nih.gov/HealthInformation/Publications/menopause.htm.

National Institute on Aging. (2010c, April 20). *Age page: Sexuality in later life*. Retrieved July 8, 2010, from http://www.nia.nih.gov/HealthInformation/Publications/sexuality.htm.

National Institute on Aging (2010d, February 19). Alzheimer's disease fact sheet. Retrieved July 15, 2010, from http://www.nia.nih.gov/Alzheimers/Publications/adfact.htm.

National Institute on Aging (2010e, May 12). Alzheimer's information: General information. Retrieved July 15, 2010, from http://www.nia.nih.gov/Alzheimers/AlzheimersInformation/GeneralInfo/.

National Institute on Aging. (2010f, May 28). *Exercise and physical activity: Getting fit for life*. Bethesda, MD: Author. Retrieved from http://www.niapublications.org/agepages/exercise.asp.

National Institute on Alcohol Abuse and Alcoholism. (2007, February). *FAQ for the General Public*. Retrieved June 27, 2010, from http://www.niaaa.nih.gov/FAQs/General-English/.

National Institute on Deafness and Other Communication Disorders. (2010a, June 7). Hearing loss and older adults. Retrieved July 8, 2010, from http://www.nidcd.nih.gov/health/hearing/older.asp.

National Institute on Deafness and Other Communication Disorders. (2010b, June 7). Presbycusis. Retrieved July 8, 2010, from missing retrieval info http://www.nidcd.nih.gov/health/hearing/presbycusis.html

National Institute on Deafness and Other Communication Disorders. (2010c, June 16). Quick statistics. Retrieved July 9, 2010, from http://www.nidcd.nih.gov/health/statistics/quick.htm.

National Institute on Drug Abuse. (2005, June 17). *Faces of addiction*. Bethesda, MD: Author. Retrieved August 6, 2005, from http://www.nida.nih.gov/about/welcome/aboutdrugabuse/faces/.

National Institute on Drug Abuse (2009, July). NIDA infofacts: Steroids (anabolic-androgenic). Retrieved July 20, 2010 from http://www.nida.nih.gov/infofacts/steroids.html.

National Intelligence Council. (2000, December). *Global Trends 2015*. Washington, D.C.: Central Intelligence Agency. Retrieved June 9, 2007, from http://nanotech.sc.mahidol.ac.th/doc/global-2015.pdf.

National Kidney and Urologic Diseases Information Clearing House. (2006, June). Prostate enlargement: Benign prostatic hyperplasia. Retrieved July 9, 2010, from http://kidney.niddk.nih.gov/kudiseases/pubs/prostateenlargement/#common.

National Library of Medicine Medline Plus. (2008a, October 27). Aging changes in hair and nails. Retrieved July 8, 2010, from http://www.nlm.nih.gov/medlineplus/ency/article/004005.htm.

National Library of Medicine Medline Plus. (2008b, August 10). Aging changes in the bones–muscles–joints. Retrieved July 8, 2010, from http://www.nlm.nih.gov/medlineplus/ency/article/004015.htm.

National Library of Medicine Medline Plus. (2010a, March 22). Digestive diseases. Retrieved July 9, 2010, from http://www.nlm.nih.gov/medlineplus/digestivediseases.html.

National Library of Medicine Medline Plus. (2010b, March 27). Hair problems. Retrieved July 9, 2010, from http://www.nlm.nih.gov/medlineplus/hairdiseasesandhairloss.html.

National Library of Medicine Medline Plus. (2010c, June 29). Heart diseases—Prevention. Retrieved July 9, 2010, from http://www.nlm.nih.gov/medlineplus/heartdiseasesprevention.html.

National Library of Medicine Medline Plus (2010d, June 18). Skin aging. Retrieved July 9, 2010, from http://www.nlm.nih.gov/medlineplus/skinaging.html#cat1.

National Statistics Office. (2004, October 28). Gender pay gap: Narrows slightly to record low. Retrieved May 5, 2005, from http://www.statistics.gov.uk/cci/nugget.asp?id=167.

National Women's Health Information Center. (2009a). Heart disease: Frequently asked questions. Retrieved July 15, 2010, from http://womenshealth.gov/faq/heart-disease.cfm#k.

National Women's Health Information Center. (2009b, June 1). Men's health: Aging male syndrome. Retrieved July 9, 2010, from http://womenshealth.gov/mens/sexual/ams.cfm.

Nesselroade, J. R. (2004). Intraindividual variability and short-term change. *Gerontology, 50*(1), 44–47.

Neugarten, B. L., & Datan, N. (1973). Sociological perspectives on the life cycle. In P. Baltes & K. W. Schaie (Eds.), *Life-span developmental psychology: Personality and socialization* (pp. 54–69). New York: Academic Press.

Neugarten, B., & Weinstein, K. (1964). The changing American grandparent. *Journal of Marriage and the Family, 26*(2), 199–206.

Neveh-Benjamin, M., Craik, F., Guez, J., & Kreuger, S. (2005). Divided attention in younger and older adults: Effects of strategy and relatedness on memory performance and secondary task costs. *Journal of Experimental Psychology: Learning, Memory, and Cognition, 31*(3), 520–537.

Newell, K. M., Vaillancourt, D. E., & Sosnoff, J. J. (2006). Aging, complexity, and motor movement. In J. E. Birren & K. W. Schaie (Eds.), *Handbook of the psychology of aging* (6th ed., pp. 163–182). San Diego, CA: Academic Press.

Newton, R. A. (2003). Balance and falls among older people. *Generations, 27*(1), 27–31.

Nezu, A. M., Nezu, C. M., Felgoise, S. H., McClure, K. S., & Houts, P. S. (2003). Project genesis: Assessing the efficacy of problem-solving therapy for distressed adult cancer patients. *Journal of Consulting and Clinical Psychology, 71*(6), 1036–1048.

Ng, S. H., Loong, C. S. F., Liu, J. H., & Weatherall, A. (2000). Will the young support the old?: An individual- and family-level study of filial obligations in two New Zealand cultures. *Asian Journal of Social Psychology, 3*(2), 163–182.

Nisbett, R., & Norenzayan, A. (2002). Culture and cognition. In H. Pashler (Series Ed.) & D. Medin (Vol. Ed.), *Steven's handbook of experimental psychology: Vol. 2. Memory and cognitive processes* (3rd ed., pp. 561–597). New York: Wiley.

Nobre, P. J., Wiegel, M., Bach, A. K., Weisberg, R. B., Brown, T. A., Wincze, J. P., et al. (2004). Determinants of sexual arousal and the accuracy of its self-estimation in sexually functional males. *The Journal of Sex Research, 41*(4), 363–371.

Noller, P., & Shugm, D. (1988). The Coopersmith self-esteem inventory in an adult sample. *Psychological Test Bulletin, 1*(1), 3–7.

Nomaguchi, K. M., & Milkie, M. A. (2003). Costs and rewards of children: The effects of becoming a parent on adults' lives. *Journal of Marriage and Family, 65*(2), 356–374.

Noor, N. M. (2004). Work-family conflict, work- and family-role salience, and women's well-being. *Journal of Social Psychology, 144*(4), 389–405.

Nordin, S., Razani, L. J., Markison, S., & Murphy, C. (2003). Age-associated increases in intensity discrimination for taste. *Experimental Aging Research, 29*(3), 371–381.

O'Connor, D. B., & Shimizu, M. (2002). Sense of personal control, stress and coping style: a cross-cultural study. *Stress and Health: Journal of the International Society for the Investigation of Stress, 18*(4), 173–183.

O'Connor, M. G., & Kaplan, E. F. (2003). Age-related changes in memory. In J. Demick and C. Andreoletti (Eds.), *Handbook of adult development* (pp. 121–130). New York: Kluwer Academic/Plenum Press.

O'Connor, M. L., Edwards, J. D., Wadley, V. G., & Crowe, M., (2010). Changes in mobility among older adults with psychometrically defined mild cognitive impairment. *Psychological Sciences, 65B*(3), 306–316.

Oesterle, S., Johnson, M. K., & Mortimer, J. T. (2004). Volunteerism during the transition to adulthood: A life course perspective. *Social Forces, 82*(3), 1123–1149.

Office for Human Research Protections, U.S. Department of Health and Human Services. (n.d.). IRB Guidebook. Washington, DC: Author. Retrieved July 10, 2007 from http://www.hhs.gov/ohrp/irb/irb_guidebook.htm.

Office of Human Subjects Research, National Institutes of Health (2005). Regulations and ethical guidelines. Bethesda, MD: Author. Retrieved July 10, 2007, from http://ohsr.od.nih.gov/guidelines/45cfr46.html#46.116.

Ohno, Y., Aoki, R., Tamakoshi, A., Kawamura, T., Wakai, K., Hashimoto, S., et al. (2000). Successful aging and social activity in older Japanese adults. *Journal of Aging and Physical Activity, 8*(2), 129–139.

Onrust, S. A., & Cuijpers, P. (2006). Mood and anxiety disorders in widowhood: A systematic review. *Aging and Mental Health, 10*(4), 327–334.

Orlofsky, J. S. (1993). The intimacy statuses. In J. E. Marcia, A. S. Waterman, D. R. Matteson, S. A. Archer, & J. S. Orlofsky (Eds.), *Ego identity: A handbook for psychosocial research* (pp. 111–133). New York: Springer-Verlag.

Orlofsky, J. S., Marcia, J. E., & Lesser, I. M. (1973). Ego identity status and the intimacy versus isolation crisis of young adulthood. *Journal of Personality and Social Psychology, 27*(2), 211–219.

O'Rourke, N., & Cappeliez, P. (2002). Development and validation of a couples measure of biased responding: The Marital Aggrandizement Scale. *Journal of Personality Assessment, 78*(2), 301–320.

Osowiecki, D., & Compas, B. E. (1998). Psychological adjustment to cancer: Control beliefs and coping in adult cancer patients. *Cognitive Therapy and Research, 22*(5), 483–499.

Ott, C. H. (2003). The impact of complicated grief on mental and physical health at various points in the bereavement process. *Death Studies, 27*(3), 249–272.

Oyserman, D., & Markus, H. R. (1990). Possible selves and delinquency. *Journal of Personality and Social Psychology, 59*(1), 112–125.

Panagakos, A. (2003). Downloading new identities: Ethnicity, technology, and media in the global Greek village. *Global Studies in Culture and Power, 10*, 201–219.

Park, C. L., & Fenster, J. R. (2004). Stress-related growth: Predictors of occurrence and correlates with psychological adjustment. *Journal of Social and Clinical Psychology, 23*(2), 195–215.

Park, D. C., Lautenschlager, G., Hedden, T., Davidson, N. S., Smith, A .D., & Smith, P. K. (2002). Models of visuospatial and verbal memory across the adult life span. *Psychology and Aging, 17*(2), 299–320.

Parker, H., & Williams, L. (2003). Intoxicated weekends: Young adults' work hard–play hard lifestyles, public health and public disorder. *Drugs: Education, Prevention and Policy, 10*(4), 345–362.

Parsons, T. D., Rizzo, A. R., Van Der Zaag, C., McGee, J., & Buckwalter, J. G. (2005). Gender differences and cognition among older adults. *Aging, Neuropsychology and Cognition, 12*(1), 78–88.

Patrick, J., & Strough, J. (2004). Everyday problem solving: Experience, strategies, and behavioral intentions. *Journal of Adult Development, 11*(1), 9–18.

Paul, E. L., & Brier, S. (2001). Friendsickness in the transition to college: Precollege predictors and college adjustment correlates. *Journal of Counseling and Development, 79*(1), 77–89.

Pearlin, L. I., Pioli, M. F., & McLaughlin, A. E. (2001). Caregiving by adult children: Involvement, role disruption, and health. In R. H. Binstock & L. K. George (Eds.), *Handbook of aging and the social sciences* (5th ed., pp. 238–254). San Diego, CA: Academic Press.

Pearson, E. M. (1999). Humanism and individualism: Maslow and his critics. *Adult Education Quarterly, 50*(1), 41–55.

Pellegrini, P., & Gibson, K. (1998). *Patterns of residential mobility in Franklin County, OH.* Paper presented at the annual meeting of the Association of American Geographers, Boston.

Pennebaker, J. W., & Stone, L. D. (2003). Words of wisdom: Language use over the life span. *Journal of Personality and Social Psychology, 85*(2), 291–301.

Percil, S. E., & Torres-Gil, F. M. (1991). Diversity and beyond: A commentary. *Generations, 15*(4), 5–6.

Perkins, H. S. (2007). Controlling death: The false promise of advance directives. *Annals of Internal Medicine, 147*(1), 51–57.

Perls, T., & Terry, D. (2003). Understanding the determinants of exceptional longevity. *Annals of Internal Medicine, Part 2, 139*(5), 445–449.

Perry, R. P., Hladkyj, S., Pekrun, R. H., & Pelletier, S. T. (2001). Academic control and action control in the achievement of college students: A longitudinal field study. *Journal of Educational Psychology, 93*(4), 776–789.

Petersen, T., & Sporta, I. (2004). The opportunity structure for discrimination. *American Journal of Sociology, 109*(4), 852–901.

Peterson, B. E. (2002). Longitudinal analysis of midlife generativity, intergenerational roles and care giving. *Psychology and Aging, 17*(1), 161–168.

Peterson, C. (1999). Grandfathers' and grandmothers' satisfaction with the grandparenting role. *International Journal of Aging & Human Development, 49*(1), 61–78.

Petroczi, A., & Aidman, E. (2008). Psychological drivers in doping: The life-cycle model of performance enhancement. *Substance Abuse Treatment, Prevention, and Policy, 3*(7), 1–12.

Pezdek, K. (2003). Event memory and autobiographical memory for the events of September 11, 2001. *Applied Cognitive Psychology, 17*, 1033–1045.

Phelan, E. A., & Larson, E. B. (2002). Successful aging—Where next? *Journal of the American Geriatrics Society, 50*(7), 1306–1308.

Phillips, F. (2003). Nutrition for healthy ageing. *British Nutrition Foundation Bulletin, 28,* 253–263.

Pierce, J. L., O'Driscoll, M. P., & Coghlan, A. (2004). Work environment structure and psychological ownership: The mediating effects of control. *Journal of Social Psychology, 144*(5), 507–534.

Pinquart, M., & Sorensen, S. (2003). Differences between caregivers and noncaregivers in psychological health and physical health: A meta-analysis. *Psychology and Aging, 18*(2), 250–267.

Pinquart, M., & Sorensen, S. (2005). Ethnic differences in stressors, resources, and psychological outcomes of family caregiving: A meta-analysis. *Gerontologist, 45*(1), 90–106.

Plaza, D. (2009). Transnational identity maintenance via the Internet. *Human Architecture: Journal of the Sociology of Self-Knowledge, 7*(4), 37–52.

Pointon, C. (2004). When is the right time to retire? *Counselling and Psychotherapy Journal, 15*(4), 18–21.

Porter, S., Spencer, L., & Birt, A. R. (2003). Blinded by emotion?: Effect of emotionality of a scene on susceptibility to false memories. *Canadian Journal of Behavioural Science, 35*(2), 165–175.

Posig, M., & Kickul, J. (2003). Extending our understanding of burnout: Test of an integrated model in nonservice occupations. *Journal of Occupational Health Psychology, 8*(1), 3–19.

Powell, L. H., & Calvin, J. E. (2007). Effective obesity treatments. *American Psychologist, 62*(3), 234–246.

Praissman, S. (2008). Mindfulness-based stress reduction: A literature review and clinicians guide. *Journal of the American Academy of Nurse Practitioners, 20,* 212–216.

Pratt, M. W., Diessner, R., Hunsberger, B., Pancer, S. M., & Savoy, K. (1991). Four pathways in the analysis of adult development and aging: Comparing analyses of reasoning about personal-life dilemmas. *Psychology and Aging, 6*(4) 666–675.

Prediger, D., Swaney, K., & Mau, W. (1993). Extending Holland's hexagon: Procedures, counseling applications, and research. *Journal of Counseling and Development, 71*(4), 422–428.

President's Council on Physical Fitness and Sports. (2010a, June 27). *A Report of the Surgeon General: Physical activity and health*. Retrieved June 27, 2010, from http://www.fitness.gov/adults.htm.

President's Council on Physical Fitness and Sports. (2010b, June 27). *Exercise and weight control*. Retrieved June 27, 2010, from http://www.fitness.gov/exerciseweight.htm.

President's Council on Physical Fitness and Sports. (2010c, June 27). *Pep up your life: A fitness book for mid-life and older persons*. Retrieved June 27, 2010, from http://www.fitness.gov/pepup.htm.

Prezza, M., Amici, M., Roberti, T., & Tedeschi, G. (2001). Sense of community referred to the whole town: Its relations with neighboring, loneliness, life satisfaction, and area of residence. *Journal of Community Psychology, 29*(1), 29–52.

Prezza, M., & Constantini, S. (1998). Sense of community and life satisfaction: Investigation in three different territorial contexts. *Journal of Community and Applied Social Psychology, 8*(3), 181–194.

Price, C. A. (2000). Women and retirement: Relinquishing professional identity. *Journal of Aging Studies, 14*(1), 81–101.

Quill, T. E. (2007). Legal regulation of physician-assisted death: The latest report cards. *New England Journal of Medicine, 356*(19), 1911–1913.

Rabbitt, P. (2002). Aging and cognition. In H. Pashler (Series Ed.) & J. Wixted (Vol. Ed.), *Steven's handbook of experimental psychology: Vol. 4. Methodology in experimental psychology* (3rd ed., pp. 793–860). New York: Wiley.

Ram, N., Rabbitt, P., Stollery, B., & Nesselroade, J. R. (2005). Cognitive performance inconsistency: Intraindividual change and variability. *Psychology and Aging, 20*(4), 623–633.

Randolph, D. S. (2005). Predicting the effect of extrinsic and intrinsic job satisfaction on recruitment and retention of rehabilitation professionals, *Journal of Healthcare Management, 50*(1), 49–60.

Rasmusson, D. X., Rebok, G. W., Bylsma, F. W., & Brandt, J. (1999). Effects of three types of memory training in normal elderly. *Aging, Neuropsychology, and Cognition, 6*(1), 56–66.

Ratanasiripong, P., Sverduk, K., Hayashino, D., & Prince, J. (2010). Setting up the next generations biofeedback program for stress and anxiety management for college students: A simple and cost-effective approach. *College Student Journal, 44*(1), 97–100.

Reed, I. C. (2005). Creativity: Self-perceptions over time. *International Journal of Aging & Human Development, 60*(1), 1–18.

Reeker, G. T. (2001). Prospective predictors of successful aging in community-resident and institutionalized Canadian elderly. *Ageing International, 27*(1), 42–64.

Reese, C. M., & Cherry, K. E. (2004). Practical memory concerns in adulthood. *International Journal of Aging & Human Development, 59*(3), 235–253.

Reese, S. (2004, January). Career and technical education at tribal colleges. *Techniques: Connecting Education and Careers, 79*(1), 18–23.

Reiter, H. H., & Costanzo, D. (1986). Relation between personality variables and the Coopersmith self-esteem inventory. *Mankind Quarterly, 27*(2), 161–165.

Rest, J., & Narvaez, D. (1991). The college experience and moral development. In W. M. Kurtines & J. L. Gewirtz (Eds.), *Handbook of moral behavior and development: Vol. 2. Research* (pp. 229–245). Hillsdale, NJ: Erlbaum.

Rest, J., & Narvaez, D. (Eds.). (1994). *Moral development in the professions: Psychology and applied ethics*. Mahwah, NJ: Erlbaum.

Reynolds, C. F., Buysse, D. J., Nofzinger, E. A., Hall, M., Dew, M. A., & Monk, T. H. (2001). Age wise: Aging well by sleeping well. *Journal of the American Geriatrics Society, 49*(4), 491.

Reynolds, G. P., Wright, J. V., & Beale, B. (2003). The roles of grandparents in educating today's children. *Journal of Instructional Psychology, 30*(4), 316–325.

Rice, D. P., & Fineman, N. (2004). Economic implications of increased longevity in the United States. *Annual Review of Public Health, 25*(1), 457–473.

Riediger, M., & Freund, A. M. (2006). Focusing and restricting: Two aspects of motivational selectivity in adulthood. *Psychology and Aging, 21*(1) 173–185.

Riediger, M., Li, S., & Lindenberger, U. (2006). Selection, optimization, and compensation as developmental mechanisms of adaptive resource allocation: Review and preview. In J. E. Birren & K. W. Schaie (Eds.), *Handbook of the psychology of aging* (6th ed., pp. 289–313). San Diego, CA: Academic Press.

Roberts, B. W., Robins, R. W., Caspi, A., & Trzesniewski, K. H. (2003). Personality trait development in adulthood. In J. L. Mortimer, & M. Shanahan (Eds.), *Handbook of the life course* (pp. 579–596). New York: Kluwer Academic.

Roberts, N. A., & Levenson, R. W. (2001). The remains of the workday: Impact of job stress and exhaustion on marital interaction in police couples. *Journal of Marriage and the Family, 63*(4), 1052–1067.

Roberts, P., & Newton, P. M. (1987). Levinsonian studies of women's adult development. *Psychology and Aging, 2*(2), 154–163.

Robinaugh, D. J., & McNally, R. J. (2010). Autobiographical memory for shame or guilt provoking events: Association with psychological symptoms. *Behavior Research and Therapy, 48*, 646–652.

Robins, R. W., Trzesniewski, K. H., Tracy, J. L., Gosling, S. D., & Potter, J. (2002). Global self-esteem across the life span. *Psychology and Aging, 17*(3), 423–434.

Robinson-Rowe, M. A. (2002). Meaning and satisfaction in the lives of midlife, never-married heterosexual women. (Doctoral dissertation, Alliant International University, 2002). *Dissertation Abstracts International, 63*(2-A), 789.

Rockwood, K., Davis, H. S., Merry, H. R., MacKnight, C., & McDowell, I. (2001). Sleep disturbances and mortality: Results from the Canadian study of health and aging. *Journal of the American Geriatrics Society, 49*(5), 639–641.

Rodriguez, M. M., Donovick, M. R., & Crowley, S. L. (2009). Parenting styles in a cultural context: Observations of "protective parenting" in first-generation Latinos. *Family Process, 48*(2), 195–210.

Roese, N. J., & Summerville, A. (2005). What we regret most, and why. *Personality and Social Psychology Bulletin, 31*(9), 1273–1285.

Rogers, H., & Matthews, J. (2004). The parenting sense of competence scale: Investigation of the factor structure, reliability, and validity for an Australian sample. *Australian Psychologist, 39*(1), 88–96.

Rogers, S. J., & May, D. C. (2003). Spillover between marital quality and job satisfaction: Long-term patterns and gender differences. *Journal of Marriage and Family, 65*(2), 482–495.

Rogers, S. J., & White, L. K. (1998). Satisfaction with parenting: The role of marital happiness, family structure, and parents' gender. *Journal of Marriage and the Family, 60*(2), 293–308.

Rogers, W. A., & Fisk, A. D. (2001). Understanding the role of attention in cognitive aging research. In J. E. Birren & K. W. Schaie (Eds.), *Handbook of the psychology of aging* (5th ed., pp. 267–287). San Diego, CA: Academic Press.

Rokeach, M. (1973). *The nature of human values*. New York: Free Press.

Roman, S. P. (2004). Illiteracy and older adults: Individual and societal implications. *Educational Gerontology, 30*, 79–93.

Ronnlund, R., Nyberg, L., Backman, L., & Nilsson, L. (2005). Stability, growth, and decline in adult life span development of declarative memory: cross-sectional and longitudinal data from a population-based study. *Psychology of Aging, 20*(1), 3–18.

Rose, D. E., et al. (2010). Use of interpreters by physicians treatment limited English proficient women with breast cancer: Results from the provider survey of the Los Angeles women's health study. *Health Services Research, 45*(1), 172–194.

Rosenberg, M., & Owens, T. J. (2001). Low self-esteem people. In T. J. Owens, S. Stryker, & N. Goodman (Eds.), *Extending self-esteem theory and research* (pp. 400–436). New York: Cambridge University Press.

Rosen-Grandon, J. R., Myers, J. E., & Hattie, J. A. (2004). The relationship between marital characteristics, marital interaction processes, and marital satisfaction. *Journal of Counseling and Development, 82*(1), 58–68.

Rosenkoetter, M. M., & Garris, J. M. (2001). Retirement planning, use of time, and psychosocial adjustment. *Issues in Mental Health Nursing, 22*, 703–722.

Ross, L. A., Clay, O. J., Edwards, J. D., Ball, K. K., Wadley, V. G., Vance, D. E., et al. (2009). Do older drivers at-risk for crashes modify their driving over time? *Journal of Gerontology: Psychological Science, 64B*(2), 163–170.

Rosser, S. V., & Miller, P. H. (2003). Viewing developmental psychology through the lenses of feminist theories. *Anuario de Psicologla, 34*(2), 291–303.

Rothermund, K., & Brandtstadter. J. (2003). Coping with deficits and losses in later life: From compensatory action to accommodation. *Psychology and Aging, 18*(4), 896–905.

Rotolo, T., & Wilson, J. (2004). What happened to the "long civic generation"? Explaining cohort differences in volunteerism. *Social Forces, 82*(3), 1091–1121.

Rotundo, M., & Sackett, P. R. (2004). Specific versus general skills and abilities: A job level examination of relationships with wage. *Journal of Occupational and Organizational Psychology, 77*(2), 127–148.

Rubin, D. C., Feldman, M., & Beckham, J. C. (2004). Reliving, emotions, and fragmentation in the autobiographical memories of veterans diagnosed with PTSD. *Applied Cognitive Psychology, 18*, 17–35.

Russac, R. J., Gatliff, C., Reece, M., & Spottswood, D., (2007). Death anxiety across the adult years: An examination of age and gender effects. *Death Studies, 31*(6), 549–561.

Ruvolo, A. P., & Markus, H. R. (1992). Possible selves and performance: The power of self-relevant imagery. *Social Cognition, 10*(1), 95–124.

Ryan, E. B., Anas, A. P., Beamer, M., & Bajorek, S. (2003). Coping with age-related vision loss in everyday reading activities. *Educational Gerontology, 29*, 37–54.

Ryff, C. D., Kwan, C. M., & Singer, B. H. (2001). Personality and aging: Flourishing agendas and future challenges. In J. E. Birren & K. W. Schaie (Eds.), *Handbook of the psychology of aging* (5th ed., pp. 477–499). San Diego, CA: Academic Press.

Sagiv, M., Vogelaere, P. P., Soudry, M., & Ehrsam, R. (2000). Role of physical activity training in attenuation of height loss through aging. *Gerontology, 46*(5), 266–270.

Salgado, J. F., Anderson, N., Moscoso, S., Bertua, C., de Fruyt, F., & Rolland, J. P. (2003). A meta-analytic study of general mental ability validity for different occupations in the European community. *Journal of Applied Psychology, 88*(6), 1068–1081.

Salthouse, T. A. (2006a). Mental exercise and mental aging. *Perspectives on Psychological Science, 1*(1), 68–87.

Salthouse, T. A. (2006b). Theoretical issues in the psychology of aging. In J. E. Birren & K. W. Schaie (Eds.), *Handbook of the psychology of aging* (6th ed., pp. 3–13). San Diego, CA: Academic Press.

Salthouse, T. A. (2007). Reply to Schooler: Consistent is not conclusive. *Perspectives on Psychological Science, 2*(1), 30–32.

Sasaki, M., & Yamasaki, K. (2007). Stress coping and the adjustment process among university freshmen. *Counselling Psychology Quarterly, 20*(1), 51–67.

Sassler, S. (2004). The process of entering into cohabiting unions. *Journal of Marriage and Family, 66*(2), 491–505.

Saucier, M. G. (2004). Midlife and beyond: Issues for aging women. *Journal of Counseling and Development, 82*(4), 420–425.

Sawyer, R. K. (2003). Emergence in creativity and development. In R. K. Sawyer, V. John-Steiner, S. Moran, R. J. Sternberg, D. H. Feldman, J. Nakamura, et al. (Eds.), *Creativity and development* (pp. 12–60). New York: Oxford University Press.

Schacter, D. L. (1999). The seven sins of memory: Insights from psychology and cognitive neuroscience. *American Psychologist, 54(3)*, 182–203.

Schaie, K. W. (1993). The Seattle longitudinal studies of adult intelligence. *Current Directions in Psychological Science, 2*(6), 171–175.

Schaie, K. W. (2000). The impact of longitudinal studies on understanding development from young adulthood to old age. *International Journal of Behavioral Development, 24*(3), 257–266.

Schaie, K. W., & Willis, S. L. (1993). Age difference patterns of psychometric intelligence in adulthood: Generalizability within and across ability domains. *Psychology and Aging, 8*(1), 44–55.

Scheidt, R. J., & Windley, P. G. (2006). Environmental gerontology: Progress in the post-Lawton era. In J. E. Birren & K. W. Schaie (Eds.), *Handbook of the psychology of aging* (6th ed., pp. 105–125). San Diego, CA: Academic Press.

Schieber, F. (2006). Vision and aging. In J. E. Birren & K. W. Schaie (Eds.), *Handbook of the psychology of aging* (6th ed., pp. 129–161). San Diego, CA: Academic Press.

Schiller, R. A. (1998). The relationship of developmental tasks to life satisfaction, moral reasoning, and occupational attainment at age 28. *Journal of Adult Development, 5*(4), 239–254.

Schimmack, U., & Oishi, S. (2005). The influence of chronically and temporarily accessible information on life satisfaction judgments. *Journal of Personality and Social Psychology, 89*(3), 395–406.

Schimmack, U., Radhakrishnan, P., Oishi, S., Dzokoto, V., & Ahadi, S. (2002). Culture, personality, and subjective well-being: Integrating process models of life satisfaction. *Journal of Personality and Social Psychology, 82*(4), 582–593.

Schneider, E. L. (1992). Biological theories of aging. *Generations, 16*(4), 7–10.

Schneider, W. (2000). Research on memory development: Historical trends and current themes. *International Journal of Behavioral Development, 24*(4), 407–420.

Schnittker, J. (2007). Working more and feeling better: Women's health, employment, and family life, 1974–2004. *American Sociological Review, 72*(2), 221–238.

Scholly, K., Katz, A. R., Gascoigne, J., & Holck, P. S. (2005). Using social norms theory to explain perceptions and sexual health behaviors of undergraduate college students: An exploratory study. *Journal of American College Health, 53*(4), 159–166.

Schooler, C. (2007). Use it—and keep it, longer, probably: A reply to Salthouse (2006). *Perspectives on Psychological Science, 2*(1), 24–29.

Schulz, J. H., & Borowski, A. (2006). Economic security in retirement: Reshaping the public-private pension mix. In R. H. Binstock & L. K. George (Eds.), *Handbook of aging and the social sciences* (6th ed., pp. 360–379). San Diego, CA: Academic Press.

Schwartz, S. (1996). Value priorities and behavior: Applying a theory of integrated value systems. In C. Seligman, J. M. Olson, & M. P. Zanna (Eds.), *The psychology of values: The Ontario Symposium, Volume 8* (pp. 1–24). Mahwah, NJ: Erlbaum.

Scialfa, C., & Fernie, G. R. (2006). Adaptive technology. In J. E. Birren & K. W. Schaie (Eds.), *Handbook of the psychology of aging* (6th ed., pp. 425–441). San Diego, CA: Academic Press.

Sebby, R. A., & Papini, D. R. (1994). Postformal reasoning during adolescence and young adulthood: The influence of problem relevancy. *Adolescence, 29*(114), 389–400.

Seeshing Yeung, A., Chui, H., Lau, I., McInerney, D., Rossell-Bowie, D., & Suliman, R. (2000). Where is the hierarchy of academic self-concept? *Journal of Educational Psychology, 92*(3), 556–567.

Segall, M. H., Lonner, W. J., & Berry, J. W. (1998). Cross-cultural psychology as a scholarly discipline: On the flowering of culture in behavioral research. *American Psychologist, 53*(10), 1101–1110.

Seligman, C., & Katz, A. N. (1996). The dynamics of value systems. In C. Seligman, J. M. Olson, & M. P., Zanna (Eds.), *The psychology of values: The Ontario Symposium, Volume 8* (pp. 53–75). Mahwah, NJ: Erlbaum.

Seligman, M. E. P., & Csikszentmihalyi, M. (2000). Positive psychology: An introduction. *American Psychologist, 55*(1), 5–14.

Seligman, M. E., Rashid, T., & Parks, A. (2006). Positive psychotherapy. *American Psychologist, 61*(8), 774–788.

Settersten, R. A. (2006). Aging and the life course. In R. H. Binstock & L. K. George (Eds.), *Handbook of aging and the social sciences* (6th ed., pp. 3–19). San Diego, CA: Academic Press.

Shahabi, L., Powell, L. H., Musick, M. A., Pargament, K. I., Thoresen, C. E., Williams, D., et al. (2002). Correlates of self-perceptions of spirituality in American adults. *Annals of Behavioral Medicine, 24*(1), 59–68.

Shedlock, D. J., & Cornelius, S. W. (2003). Psychological approaches to wisdom and its development. In J. Demick & C. Andreoletti (Eds.), *Handbook of adult development* (pp. 153–167). New York: Kluwer Academic/Plenum Press.

Shinew, K. J., Glover, T. D., & Parry, D. C. (2004). Leisure spaces as potential sites for interracial interaction: Community gardens in urban areas. *Journal of Leisure Research, 36*(3), 336–355.

Shmotkin, D., Blumstein, T., & Modan, B. (2003). Beyond keeping active: Concomitants of being a volunteer in old-old age. *Psychology and Aging, 18*(3), 602–607.

Shu-Chen, L., Aggen, S. H., Nesselroade, J. R., Baltes, P. B. (2001). Short-term fluctuations in elderly people's sensorimotor functioning predict text and spatial memory performance: The Mac Arthur Successful Aging Studies. *Gerontology, 47*(2), 100–116.

Siebert, D. C., Mutran, E. J., & Reitzes, D. C. (1999). Friendship and social support: The importance of role identity to aging adults. *Social Work, 44*(6), 522–533.

Siegel, D. (2003). Open adoption of infants: Adoptive parents' feelings seven years later. *Social Work, 48*(3), 409–419.

Simon, H. B. (2004). Longevity: The ultimate gender gap. *Scientific American Special Edition, 14*(3), 18–23.

Simonton, D. (1989). The swan-song phenomenon: Last-works effects for 172 classical composers. *Psychology and Aging, 4*(1), 42–47.

Sinnott, J. D. (1994). Postformal thought and learning. In J. D. Sinnott (Ed.), *Interdisciplinary handbook of adult lifespan learning* (pp. 105–119). Westport, CT: Greenwood Press.

Sinnott, J. D. (1998). *The development of logic in adulthood: Postformal thought and its applications.* New York: Plenum Press.

Sinnott, J. D. (2003). Postformal thought and adult development. In J. Demick & C. Andreoletti (Eds.), *Handbook of adult development* (pp. 221–238). New York: Kluwer Academic/Plenum Press.

Sinnott, J. D., & Shifren, K. (2001). Gender and aging: Gender differences and gender roles. In J. E. Birren & K. W. Schaie (Eds.), *Handbook of the psychology of aging* (5th ed., pp. 427–476). San Diego, CA: Academic Press.

Skaldeman, P., & Montgomery, H. (1999). Interpretational incongruence of value-profiles: Perception of own and partner's values in married and divorced couples. *Journal of Social Behavior & Personality, 14*(3), 345–365.

Skoe, E. E. A., & von der Lippe, A. L. (2002). Ego development and the ethics of care and justice: The relations among them revisited. *Journal of Personality, 70*(4), 485–508.

Skorupa, Kenn (2002, December). Adult learners as consumers. *The Academic Advising News, 25*(3). Retrieved from the NACADA Clearinghouse of Academic Advising Resources website: http://www.nacada.ksu.edu/Clearinghouse/AdvisingIssues/adultlearners.htm.

Skowron, E. A., Wester, S. R., & Azen, R. (2004). Differentiation of self mediates college stress and adjustment. *Journal of Counseling & Development, 82*(1), 69–78.

Skutch, L. P. (2001). Childless-by-choice women and mothers-by-choice: A comparative study of attitudes and behaviors on quality of life and feminist perspectives. *Dissertation Abstracts International, 62*(2-B), 1145.

Slater, C. L. (2003). Generativity versus stagnation: An elaboration of Erikson's adult stage of human development. *Journal of Adult Development, 10*(1), 54–65.

Slee, N. (2000). Some patterns and processes of women's faith development. *Journal of Beliefs and Values: Studies in Religion and Education, 21*(1), 5–16.

Smith, J., & Baltes, P. B. (1990). Wisdom-related knowledge: Age/cohort differences in response to life-planning problems. *Developmental Psychology,* 26(3), 494–505.

Smith, J., Staudinger, U. M., & Baltes, P. B. (1994). Occupational settings facilitating wisdom-related knowledge: The sample case of clinical psychologists. *Journal of Consulting and Clinical Psychology, 62*(5), 989–999.

Smith, M. B. (1991). *Values, self and society: Toward a humanistic social psychology*. New Brunswick, NJ: Transaction Press.

Smith, M. C., & Pourchot, T. (1998). What does educational psychology know about adult learning and development? In M. C. Smith and T. Pourchot (Eds.), *Adult learning and development: Perspectives from educational psychology* (pp. 3–11). Mahwah, NJ: Erlbaum.

Smith, M. C., Bibi, R., & Sheard, D. E. (2003). Evidence for the differential impact of time and emotion on personal and event memories for September 11, 2001. *Applied Cognitive Psychology, 17*, 1047–1055.

Sneed, J. R., & Whitbourne, S. K. (2001). Identity processing styles and the need for self-esteem in middle-aged and older adults. *International Journal of Aging and Human Development, 52*(4), 311–321.

Snow, L., & Pan, C. (2004). How do physicians think about successful aging? *Annals of Internal Medicine, 140*(10), 852.

Snowden, L. R., Masland, M., & Guerrero, R. (2007). Federal civil rights policy and mental health treatment access for persons with limited English. *American Psychologist, 62*(2), 109–117.

Social Security Administration. (2008, May). Understanding the benefits. Retrieved June 10, 2008, from http://www.ssa.gov/pubs/10024.html.

Sofianidis, G., Hatzitaki, V., Douka, S., & Grouios, G. (2009). Effect of a 10-week traditional dance program on static and dynamic balance control in elderly adults. *Journal of Aging and Physical Activity, 17*, 167–180.

Solomon, S. E., Rothblum, E. D., & Balsam, K. F. (2004). Pioneers in partnership: Lesbian and gay male couples in civil unions compared with those not in civil unions and married heterosexual siblings. *Journal of Family Psychology, 18*(2), 275–286.

Sommer, S. M., Falkmer, T., Bekiaris, E., & Panou, M. (2004). Toward a client-centered approach to fitness-to-drive assessment of elderly drivers. *Scandinavian Journal of Occupational Therapy, 11*(2), 62–69.

Sontag, J. C. (1996). Toward a comprehensive theoretical framework for disability research: Bronfenbrenner revisited. *Journal of Special Education, 30*(3), 319–344.

Sorrell, G. T., & Montgomery, M. J. (2001). Feminist perspectives on Erikson's theory: Their relevance for contemporary identity development research. *Identity: An International Journal of Theory and Research, 1*(2), 97–128.

Souchay, C., Isingrini, M., & Espagnet, L. (2000). Aging, episodic memory, feeling-of-knowing, and frontal functioning. *Neuropsychology, 14*(2), 297–309.

Spanier, G. B., & Margolis, R. L. (1983). Marital separation and extramarital sexual behavior. *Journal of Sex Research, 19*(1), 23–48.

Spilka, B., Hood, R. W., Hunsberger, B., & Gorsuch, R. (2003). *The psychology of religion: An empirical approach.* New York: Guilford Press.

Sprafkin, J., Gadow, K. D., Salisbury, H., Schneider, J., & Loney, J. (2002). Further evidence of reliability and validity of the Child Symptom Inventory-4: Parent checklist in clinically referred boys. *Journal of Clinical Child & Adolescent Psychology, 31*(4), 513–525.

Srivastava, S., John, O. P., Gosling, S. D., & Potter, J. (2003). Development of personality in early and middle adulthood: Set like plaster or persistent change? *Journal of Personality and Social Psychology 84*(5), 1041–1053.

Staats, S., & Pierfelice, L. (2003). Travel: A long-range goal of retired women. *Journal of Psychology, 137*(5), 483–494.

Stack, S., & Eshleman, J. R. (1998). Marital status and happiness: A 15-nation study. *Journal of Marriage and the Family, 60*(2), 525–536.

Stanley, S. (2005). What really is the divorce rate? Retrieved April 9, 2005, from http://divorcesupport.about.com/cs/divorcestep1/a/aa061699_2.htm.

Staudinger, U. M., Smith, J., & Baltes, P. B. (1992). Wisdom-related knowledge in a life review task: Age differences and the role of professional specialization. *Psychology and Aging, 7*(2), 271–281.

Steel, P., Schmidt, J., & Shultz, J. (2008). Refining the relationship between personality and subjective well-being. *Psychological Bulletin, 134*(1), 138–161.

Sternberg, R. J. (1986). A triangular theory of love. *Psychological Review, 93*(2), 119–135.

Sternberg, R. J. (1990a). Understanding wisdom. In R. J. Sternberg (Ed.), *Wisdom: Its nature, origins, and development* (pp. 3–9). New York: Cambridge University Press.

Sternberg, R. J. (1994). Intelligence. In R. J. Sternberg (Ed.), *Thinking and problem solving* (pp. 263–288). San Diego, CA: Academic Press.

Sternberg, R. J. (1997a). Construct validation of a triangular love scale. *European Journal of Social Psychology, 27*(3), 313–334.

Sternberg, R. J. (1997b). Managerial intelligence: Why IQ isn't enough. *Journal of Management, 23*(3), 475–493.

Sternberg, R. J. (1998). A balance theory of wisdom. *Review of General Psychology,* 2(4), 347–365.

Sternberg, R. J. (2000a). Intelligence and wisdom. In R. J. Sternberg (Ed.), *Handbook of intelligence* (pp. 631–649). New York: Cambridge University Press.

Sternberg, R. J. (2000b). Patterns of giftedness: A triarchic analysis. *Roeper Review, 22*(4), 231–235.

Sternberg, R. J., & Lubart, T. I. (2001). Wisdom and creativity. In J. E. Birren & K. W. Schaie (Eds.), *Handbook of the psychology of aging* (5th ed., pp. 500–522). San Diego, CA: Academic Press.

Sternberg, R. J., Castejon, J. L., Prieto, M. D., Hautamaki, J., & Grigorenko, E. L. (2001). Confirmatory factor analysis of the Sternberg Triarchic Abilities Test in three international samples: An empirical test of the triarchic theory of intelligence. *European Journal of Psychological Assessment, 17*(1), 1–16.

Stevens, L. M. (2006). JAMA Patient Page: Palliative care. *Journal of American Medical Association, 296*(11), 1428. Retrieved July 20, 2008, from http://jama.ama-assn.org/cgi/reprint/296/11/1428.pdf.

Stober, J. (2003). Self-pity: Exploring the links to personality, control beliefs, and anger. *Journal of Personality, 71*(2), 184–220.

Stobert, S., & Kemeny, A. (2003). Childfree by choice. *Canadian Social Trends, 69*, 5–10.

Stone, R. (2006). Emerging issues in long-term care. In R. H. Binstock & L. K. George (Eds.), *Handbook of aging and the social sciences* (6th ed., pp. 397–418). San Diego, CA: Academic Press.

Strage, A. (2000). Predictors of college adjustment and success: Similarities and differences among Southeast Asian-American, Hispanic and white students. *Education, 120*(4), 731–740.

Strage, A., & Brandt, T. S. (1999). Authoritative parenting and college students' academic adjustment and success. *Journal of Educational Psychology, 91*(1), 146–156.

Street, W. R. (1994). Today in the history of psychology. Retrieved July 20, 2007, from http://www.cwu.edu/~warren/today.html.

Streib, H. (2001). Faith development theory revisited: The religious styles perspective. *International Journal for the Psychology of Religion, 11*(3), 143–158.

Strom, R., Carter, T., & Schmidt, K. (2004). African-Americans in senior settings: On the need for educating grandparents. *Educational Gerontology, 30*(4), 285–303.

Strough, J., Patrick, J., Swenson, L., Cheng, S., & Barnes, K. (2003). Collaborative everyday problem solving: Interpersonal relationships and problem dimensions. *International Journal of Aging & Human Development, 56*(1), 43–66.

Substance Abuse and Mental Health Services Administration. (2005, July 27). Highlights of recent reports on substance abuse and mental health. Retrieved August 6, 2005, from http://www.oas.samhsa.gov/highlights.htm#2k5Pubs.

Suinn, R. M. (1999). Progress in ethnic minority psychology: An overview and challenge, or "when you wish upon a star." *Cultural Diversity and Ethnic Minority Psychology, 5*(1), 37–42.

Sullivan, S. E. (1999). The changing nature of careers: A review and research agenda. *Journal of Management, 25*(3), 457–484.

Super, D. E., Osborne, W. L., Walsh, D. J., Brown, S. D., & Niles, S. G. (1992). Developmental career assessment and counseling: The C-DAC model. *Journal of Counseling & Development, 71*, 74–80.

Takahashi, M., & Overton, W. F. (2002). Wisdom: A culturally inclusive developmental perspective. *International Journal of Behavioral Development, 26*(3), 269–277.

Tamashiro, R. T. (1978). Development stages in the conceptualization of marriage. *Family Coordinator, 27*(3), 235–244.

Taris, T. W., & Feij, J. (2004). Learning and strain among newcomers: A three-wave study on the effects of job demands and job control. *Journal of Psychology, 138*(6), 543–563.

Taylor, K. (1996). Why psychological models of adult development are important for the practice of adult education: A response to Courtenay. *Adult Education Quarterly, 47*(1), 54–62.

Taylor, M. A., & Shore, L. M. (1995). Predictors of planned retirement age: An application of Beehr's model. *Psychology and Aging, 10*(1), 76–83.

Tekcan, A. I., Ece, B., Gulgoz, S., & Er, N. (2003). Autobiographical and event memory for 9/11: Changes across one year. *Applied Cognitive Psychology, 17*, 1057–1066.

Telford, K., Kralik, D., & Koch, T. (2006). Acceptance and denial: Implications for people adapting to chronic illness. *Journal of Advanced Nursing, 55*(4), 457–464.

Teno, J. M., Gruneir, A., Schwartz, Z., Anada, A., & Wetle, T. (2007). Association between advance directives and quality of end-of-life care: A national study. *Journal of the American Geriatrics Society, 55*(2), 189–194.

Thelen, E., & Bates, E. (2003). Connectionism and dynamic systems: Are they really different? *Developmental Sciences, 6*(4), 378–391.

Thomas, M. L., & Kuh, G. D. (1982). Understanding development during the early adult years: A composite framework. *Personnel & Guidance Journal, 61*(1), 14–17.

Thornton, R., & Light, L. L. (2006). Language comprehension and production in normal aging. In J. E. Birren & K. W. Schaie (Eds.), *Handbook of the psychology of aging* (6th ed., pp. 261–287). San Diego, CA: Academic Press.

Thornton, W., & Dumke, H. (2005). Age differences in everyday problem-solving and decision-making effectiveness: A meta-analytic review. *Psychology and Aging, 20*(1), 85–99.

Toma, C. L., & Hancock, J. T. (2010). Looks and lies: The role of physical attractiveness in online dating self-presentation and deception. *Communication Research, 37*(3), 335–351.

Tomarken, A., Holland, J., Schachter, S., Vanderwerker, L., Zuckerman, E., Nelson, C., et al. (2008). Factors of complicated grief pre-death in caregivers of cancer patients. *Psycho-Oncology, 17*(2), 105–111.

Tomiyama, A. J., Westling, E., Lew, A., Samuels, B., & Chatman, J. (2007). Medicare's search for effective obesity treatments: Diets are not the answer. *American Psychologist, 62*(3), 220–233.

Tornstam, L. (1997). Gerotranscendence: The contemplative dimension of aging. *Journal of Aging Studies, 11*(2), 143–154.

Toth, J. F., Brown, R. B., & Xu, X. (2002). Separate family and community realities?: An urban–rural comparison of the association between family life satisfaction and community satisfaction. *Community, Work & Family, 5*(2), 181–202.

Traeen, B., Stigum, H., & Sorensen, D. (2002). Sexual diversity in urban Norwegians. *Journal of Sex Research, 39*(4), 249–258.

Travis, L. A., Boerner, K., Reinhardt, J. P., & Horowitz, A. (2004). Exploring functional disability in older adults with low vision. *Journal of Visual Impairment and Blindness, 98*(9), 534–545.

Treboux, D., Crowell, J. A., & Waters, E. (2004). When "new" meets "old": Configurations of adult attachment representations and their implications for marital functioning. *Developmental Psychology, 40*(2), 295–314.

Trzesniewski, K. H., Donnellan, M. B., & Robins, R. W. (2003). Stability of self-esteem across the life span. *Journal of Personality and Social Psychology, 84*, 205–220.

Tsai, J. L., Ying, Y., & Lee, P. L. (2001) Cultural predictors of self-esteem: A study of Chinese American male and male young adults. *Cultural Diversity and Ethnic Minority Psychology, 7*(3), 284–297.

Tuijman, A. (2003). Measuring lifelong learning for the new economy. *Compare: A Journal of Comparative Education, 33*(4), 471–482.

Tully, A. (2004). Stress, sources of stress and ways of coping among psychiatric nursing students. *Journal of Psychiatric and Mental Health Nursing, 11*(1), 43–47.

Tulving, E. (1985). How many memory systems are there? *American Psychologist, 40*, 385–398.

Twenge, J. M., & Campbell, W. K. (2002). Self-esteem and socioeconomic statuses: A meta-analytic review. *Personality and Social Psychology Review, 6*(1), 59–71.

Twenge, J. M., Campbell, W. K., & Foster, C. A. (2003). Parenthood and marital satisfaction: A meta-analytic review. *Journal of Marriage and Family, 64*, 574–583.

U.S. Census Bureau. (2006a, August). American Housing Survey for the United States: 2005. Retrieved June 6, 2008, from http://www.census.gov/prod/2006pubs/h150-05.pdf.

U.S. Census Bureau. (2006b, December). *The 2007 Statistical Abstract*. Retrieved June 9, 2007, from http://www.census.gov/compendia/statab/.

U.S. Census Bureau (2007). Population profile of the United States: Dynamic version. Retrieved July 7, 2007, from http://www.census.gov/population/pop-profile/dynamic/OLDER.pdf.

U.S. Census Bureau. (2008a, May 22). Age data of the United States, the older population in the United States: 2006. Retrieved May 28, 2008, from http://www.census.gov/population/www/socdemo/age/age_2006.html.

U.S. Census Bureau. (2008b, March). 2008 Statistical Abstract. Table 537. U.S. Households Owning IRAs: 2002 to 2005. Retrieved June 8, 2008, from http://www.census.gov/compendia/statab/cats/social_insurance_human_services/social_security_retirement_plans.html.

U.S. Department of Agriculture. (n.d.) *Dietary guidelines*. Retrieved July 10, 2007, from http://www.mypyramid.gov/guidelines/index.html.

U.S. Department of Education. (2009, September 22). White house initiative on tribal colleges and universities: Tribal colleges and universities address list. Washington, DC: Author. Retrieved July 1, 2010, from http://www2.ed.gov/about/inits/list/whtc/edlite-tclist.html.

U.S. Department of Health and Human Services. (2000). *Healthy People 2010. Understanding and Improving Health.* 2nd ed. Retrieved June 26, 2010, from http://www.healthypeople.gov/document/pdf/uih/1020uih.pdf.

U.S. Department of Health and Human Services. (2004, October 10). Healthy Marriage Initiative: Helping form and sustain healthy marriages. Washington, DC: Author. Retrieved October 10, 2004, from http://www.acf.dhhs.gov/healthymarriage/index.html.

U.S. Department of Health and Human Services. (2006, October 16). *Dietary guidelines for Americans*. Retrieved July 18, 2007, from http://www.health.gov/dietaryguidelines/.

Ulrich, M. (2008). Introduction to the special section of cognitive plasticity in the aging mind. *Psychology and Aging, 23*(4), 681–683.

University of Maryland Medical Center. (2009, February 19). Aging changes in the senses. Retrieved July 9, 2010, from http://www.umm.edu/ency/article/004013.htm.

Uttl, B., & Van Alstine, C. (2003). Rising verbal intelligence scores: Implications for research and clinical practice. *Psychology and Aging, 18*(3), 616–621.

Vaillant, G. (2000). Adaptive mental mechanisms: Their role in a positive psychology. *American Psychologist, 55*(1), 89–98.

Vaillant, G. E. (1977). *Adaptation to life*. Boston: Little, Brown.

Van Buren, A., & Cooley, E. L. (2002). Attachment styles, view of self and negative affect. *North American Journal of Psychology, 4*(3), 415–430.

Van Laningham, J., Johnson, D. R., & Amato, P. (2001). Marital happiness, marital duration, and the u-shaped curve: Evidence from a five-wave panel study. *Social Forces, 79*(4), 1313–1341.

Van Willigen, M. (2000). Differential benefits of volunteering across the life course. *Journals of Gerontology: Series B: Psychological Science and Social Sciences, 55B*(5), S308–S318.

Veach, T. L., Rahe, R. H., Tolles, R. L., & Newhall, L. M. (2003). Effectiveness of an intensive stress intervention workshop for senior managers. *Stress and Health: Journal of the International Society for the Investigation of Stress, 19*(5), 257–264.

Veiel, L., & Storandt, M. (2003). Processing costs of semantic and episodic retrieval in younger and older adults. *Aging Neuropsychology and Cognition, 19*(1), 61–73.

Verhaeghen, P., Marcoen, A., & Goossens, L. (1992). Improving memory performance in the aged through mnemonic training: A meta-analytic study. *Psychology and Aging, 7*, 242–251.

Vinters, H. V. (2001). Aging and the human nervous system. In J. E. Birren & K. W. Schaie (Eds.), *Handbook of the psychology of aging* (5th ed. pp. 135–160). San Diego, CA: Academic Press.

Vogler, G. P. (2006). Behavior genetics and aging. In J. E. Birren & K. W. Schaie (Eds.), *Handbook of the psychology of aging* (6th ed., pp. 41–55). San Diego, CA: Academic Press.

Volling, B. L., Notaro, P. C., & Larsen, J. J. (1998). Adult attachment styles: Relations with emotional well-being, marriage, and parenting. *Family Relations, 47*(4), 355–367.

Volunteer.gov. (2004). Frequently asked questions about volunteering with partner agencies of Volunteer.Gov/Gov. Retrieved November 16, 2004, from http://www.volunteer.gov/gov/FAQ.cfm.

Vukman, K. B. (2005). Developmental differences in metacognition and their connections with cognitive development in adulthood. *Journal of Adult Development, 12*(4), 211–221.

Wadensten, B. (2005). Introducing older people to the theory of gerotranscendence. *Journal of Advanced Nursing, 52*(4), 381–388.

Wagner, R. K. (2000). Practical intelligence. In R. J. Sternberg (Ed.), *Handbook of intelligence* (pp. 380–395). New York: Cambridge University Press.

Wahl, H. (2001). Environmental influences on aging and behavior. In J. E. Birren & K. W. Schaie (Eds.), *Handbook of the psychology of aging* (5th ed., pp. 215–237). San Diego, CA: Academic Press.

Wahl, H., Becker, S., Burmedi, D., & Schilling, O. (2004). The role of primary and secondary control in adaptation to age-related vision loss: A study of older adults with macular degeneration. *Psychology and Aging, 19*(1), 235–239.

Wahlqvist, M. L., & Savige, G. S. (2000). Interventions aimed at dietary and lifestyle changes to promote healthy aging. *European Journal of Clinical Nutrition, 54*(6), 148–156.

Waldron-Hennessey, R., & Sabatelli, R. M. (1997). The parental comparison levels index: A measure for assessing parental rewards and costs relative to expectations. *Journal of Marriage and the Family, 59*(4), 824–833.

Walker, A. (2006). Aging and politics: An international perspective. In R. H. Binstock & L. K. George (Eds.), *Handbook of aging and the social sciences* (6th ed., pp. 339–359). San Diego, CA: Academic Press.

Walker, L. J. (1991). Sex differences in moral reasoning. In W. M. Kurtines & J. L. Gewirtz (Eds.), *Handbook of moral behavior and development: Vol. 2. Research* (pp. 333–364). Hillsdale, NJ: Erlbaum.

Walker, L. J. (1995). Sexism in Kohlberg's moral psychology? In W. M. Kurtines & J. L. Gewirtz (Eds.), *Moral development: An introduction* (pp. 83–107). Boston: Allyn & Bacon.

Walker, L. J. (2002). The model and the measure: An appraisal of the Minnesota approach to moral development. *Journal of Moral Education, 31*(3), 353–367.

Walker, L. J., Frimer, J. A., & Dunlop W. L. (2010). Varieties of moral personality: Beyond the banality of heroism. *Journal of Personality, 78*(3), 907–942.

Walker, L. J., & Hennig, K. H. (2004). Differing conceptions of moral exemplarity: Just, brave, and caring. *Journal of Personality and Social Psychology, 86*(4), 629–647.

Wang, H., & Amato, P. R. (2000). Predictors of divorce adjustment: Stressors, resources, and definitions. *Journal of Marriage & Family, 62*(3), 655–668.

Ward, R., Spitze, G., & Deane, G. (2009). The more the merrier?: Multiple parent–adult child relations. *Journal of Marriage and Family, 71*(1), 161–173.

Warde, C. M., Moonesignhe, K., Allen, W., & Gelberg, L. (1999). Marital and parental satisfaction of married physicians with children. *Journal of General Internal Medicine, 14*(3), 155–165.

Webster, J. D. (1999). World views and narrative gerontology: Situating reminiscence behavior within a lifespan perspective. *Journal of Aging Studies, 13*(1), 29–42.

Wentura, D., & Brandtstadter, J. (2003). Age stereotypes in younger and older women: Analysis of accommodative shifts with a sentence-priming task. *Experimental Psychology 50*(1), 16–26.

West, R. L., Bagwell, D. K., & Dark-Freudeman, A. (2008). Self-efficacy and memory aging: The impact of a memory intervention based on self-efficacy. *Aging, Neuropsychology and Cognition, 15*(3), 302–329.

Whitbourne, S. K. (2005). *Adult development and aging: Biopsychosocial perspectives* (2nd ed.). Hoboken, NJ: Wiley.

Whitbourne, S. K., Sneed, J. R., & Skultety, K. M. (2002). Identity processes in adulthood: Theoretical and methodological challenges. *Identity, 2*(1), 29–45.

White, L. K., & Riedmann, A. (1992). Ties among adult siblings. *Social Forces, 71*(1), 85–102.

Whitfield, K. E., & Wiggins, S. (2003). The influence of social support and health on everyday problem solving in adult African Americans. *Experimental Aging Research, 29*(1), 1–12.

Whiting, W. L. (2003). Adult age differences in divided attention: Effects of elaboration during memory encoding. *Aging, Neuropsychology, and Cognition, 10*(2), 141–157.

Whitty, M., & Quigley, L. (2008). Emotional and sexual infidelity offline and in cyberspace. *Journal of Marital and Family Therapy, 34*(4), 461–468.

Willert, A., & Semans, M. (2000). Knowledge and attitudes about later life sexuality: What clinicians need to know about helping the elderly. *Contemporary Family Therapy, 22*(4), 415–435.

Williams, A. (2007). Recruitment challenges for end-of-life research. *Journal of Hospice and Palliative Nursing, 9*(2), 79–85.

Wink, P., & Dillon, M. (2002). Spiritual development across the adult life course: Findings from a longitudinal study. *Journal of Adult Development, 9*(1), 79–94.

Wink, P., & Dillon, M. (2003). Religiousness, spirituality, and psychosocial functioning in late adulthood: Findings from a longitudinal study. *Psychology and Aging, 18*(4), 916–924.

Woolverton, M., Scogin, F., Schakelford, J., Black, S., & Duke, L. (2001). Problem-targeted memory training for older adults. *Aging, Neuropsychology and Cognition, 8*(4), 241–255.

Woosley, S. A. (2003). How important are the first few weeks of college?: The long term effects of initial college experiences. *College Student Journal, 37*(2), 201–207.

Wortley, D. B., & Amatea, E. S. (1982). Mapping adult life changes: A conceptual framework for organizing adult developmental theory. *Personnel and Guidance Journal, 60*(8), 476–482.

Wrosch, C., & Heckhausen, J. (2002). Perceived control of life regrets: Good for young and bad for old adults. *Psychology and Aging, 17*(2), 340–350.

Wulff, D. M. (1996). The psychology of religion: An overview. In E. P. Shafranske (Ed.), *Religion and theclinical practice of psychology* (pp. 43–70). Washington, DC: American Psychological Association.

Wulff, D. M. (1997). *Psychology of religion: Classic and contemporary* (2nd ed.). New York: Wiley.

Wyatt, G., Sikorskii, A., Siddiqi, A., & Given, C. W. (2007). Feasibility of a reflexology and guided imagery intervention during chemotherapy: Results of a quasi-experimental study. *Oncology Nursing Forum, 34*(3), 635–642.

Yang, Y. (2007). Is old age depressing?: Growth trajectories and cohort variations in late-life depression. *Journal of Health and Social Behavior, 48*(1), 16–32.

Yuen, H. (2010). Exploring critical family issues in cross-border marriages: Four women from Tin Shui Wai. *Journal of Youth Studies, 13*(1), 54–67.

Zajicek, A. M., & Koski, P. R. (2003). Strategies of resistance to stigmatization among white middle-class singles. *Sociological Spectrum, 23*, 375–403.

Zhang, T., Kaber, D., Zhu, B., Swangneir, M., Mosaly, P., & Hodge, L. (2010). Service robot feature design effects on user perceptions and emotional responses, *Intel Serv Robotics, 3*, 73–88.

Zhiwei, Z., & Snizek, W. E. (2003). Occupation, job characteristics, and the use of alcohol and other drugs. *Social Behavior and Personality: An International Journal. 31*(4), 395–412.

Zimprich, D., Hofer, S. M., & Aartsen, M. J. (2004). Short-term versus long-term longitudinal changes in processing speed. *Gerontology, 50*(1), 17–21.

Zimprich, D., & Martin, M. (2002). Can longitudinal changes in processing speed explain longitudinal changes in fluid intelligence? *Psychology and Aging, 17*(4), 690–695.

Zucker, A. N., Ostrove, J. M., & Stewart, A. J. (2002). College-educated women's personality development in adulthood: Perceptions and age differences. *Psychology and Aging, 17*(2), 236–244.

NAME INDEX

SUBJECT INDEX

Note: Page numbers with "f" indicate figures: those with "t" indicate tables.